Abbreviations

n.	Noun
v.	Verb
adj.	Adjective
adv.	Adverb
prep.	Preposition
pron.	Pronoun
conj.	Conjunction
interj.	Interjection
det.	Determiner

ഇംഗ്ലീഷ് - മലയാളം

ENGLISH – MALAYALAM

Rapidex® Dictionary of Spoken Words

പ്രയോഗവാക്യങ്ങൾ സഹിതം

Malayalam Version
Gopan Nair

PUSTAK MAHAL®
Delhi • Mumbai • Patna • Hyderabad • Bangalore

Pustak Mahal®, Delhi

J-3/16 , Daryaganj, New Delhi-110002
☎ 23276539, 23272783, 23272784 • *Fax:* 011-23260518
E-mail: info@pustakmahal.com • *Website:* www.pustakmahal.com

Sales Centre
10-B, Netaji Subhash Marg, Daryaganj, New Delhi-110002
☎ 23268292, 23268293, 23279900 • *Fax:* 011-23280567
E-mail: rapidexdelhi@indiatimes.com

Branch Offices
Bangalore: ☎ 22234025 • *Telefax:* 22240209
E-mail: pmblr@sancharnet.in • pustak@sancharnet.in
Mumbai: ☎ 22010941
E-mail: rapidex@bom5.vsnl.net.in
Patna: ☎ 3294193 • *Telefax:* 0612-2302719
E-mail: rapidexptn@rediffmail.com
Hyderabad: *Telefax:* 040-24737290
E-mail: pustakmahalhyd@yahoo.co.in

ISBN 978-81-223-1059-7

Edition : 2009

Printed at: *Unique Color Carton, New Delhi-110064*

A

A എ - ഇംഗ്ലീഷ് അക്ഷരമാലയിലെ ആദ്യക്ഷരം, ഏറ്റവും ഉയർന്ന, ഏറ്റവും നല്ല

He is an *A* class artist.

I got an *A* grade in my English test.

A/An ആ/ആൻ - ഒരു, ഓരോ

1. Do you have *a* book of short stories?

I drink milk twice *a* day.

He drove eighty miles in *an* hour.

2. *(Indefinite articles) A* & *An* as indefinite articles are used before a single countable noun. *A* is used before a consonant sound and *An* before a vowel sound:

Seema is *a* teacher.

Rahul is *an* engineer.

Abandon *(v.)* അബാൻഡൻ - ഉപേക്ഷിക്കുക, ത്യജിക്കുക, വിട്ടുകളയുക

Why did you *abandon* your studies?

Abbreviation *(n.)* അബ്രിവിയേഷൻ - സംക്ഷേപം, സംക്ഷിപ്ത രൂപം

U.N.O. is the *abbreviation* of United Nations Organisation.

Abide *(v.)* അബൈഡ് - പാലിക്കുക

We should *abide* by the laws of the country.

Ablaze *(adj.)* അബ്ലേസ് - കത്തുന്ന, ജ്വലിക്കുന്ന

Fireman rushed to the house, which was *ablaze*.

Able *(adj.)* ഏബിൾ - കഴിവുറ്റ, സമർത്ഥ

Anil was not *able* to play football as he had broken his leg in an accident.

Abnormal *(adj.)* അബ്നോർമൽ - അസാധാരണ

It is quite *abnormal* to have rain along with the sunshine.

Aboard *(adj.)* എബോർഡ് - കപ്പൽ, വിമാനം അല്ലെങ്കിൽ ട്രെയിനിൽ സഞ്ചരിക്കുക

We had great fun *aboard* the plane on our way to the U.S.A.

Abolish *(v.)* അബോളിഷ് - അവസാനിപ്പിക്കുക, റദ്ദാക്കുക

Some people think we should *abolish* the death sentence.

About *(prep.)* എബൗട്ട് - 1. സംബന്ധിച്ച

I am reading a book *about* birds.

2. നാല് ചുറ്റും, അവിടവിടെ

The children walked *about* the zoo.

3. അടുത്ത്, സമീപം

He came here at *about* ten o'clock.

4. ഏതാ് അത്ര തന്നെ

Sudha is *about* as tall as Meena.

Above *(prep.)* മേലെ, മുകളിൽ

The plane flies *above* the clouds.

Abreast *(adj.)* അബ്രെസ്റ്റ് - ഒരേ നിരയിൽ, അണിയായി

The soldiers marched forward *abreast*.

Abridge *(v.)* അബ്രിജ് - ചുരുക്കുക, സംഗ്രഹിക്കുക

(v.) We cannot *abridge* this book; it is copyrighted.

(adj.) This is the *abridged* version of Jane Austen's Pride and Prejudice.

Abroad *(adj.)* എബ്റോഡ് - വിദേശത്ത്

I spent four years *abroad*.

Abrupt *(adj.)* അബ്രപ്റ്റ് - പൊടുന്നനേ, ആകസ്മികമായി

The music competition came to an *abrupt* end when the lights went out.

Abscess *(n.)* അബ്സെസ്സ് - വ്രണം, ശരീര ഭാഗത്തിലെ പഴുപ്പ്

The doctor removed the *abscess* from Dinesh's foot.

Absent *(adj.)* ആബ്സെന്റ് - ഹാജരല്ല

Four boys were *absent* from school today.

(n.) അസാന്നിദ്ധ്യം

My *absence* from office was due to my illness.

Absent-minded *(adj.)* ആബ്സന്റ് - മൈൻഡഡ് - മറവിയുള്ള

(adj.) He is always *absent-minded* in the class.

(adv.) The student replied to the teacher *absent-mindedly*.

Absolutely *(adv.)* അബ്സല്യൂട്ട്ലി - തികച്ചും, തീർച്ചയായും

Your hands must be *absolutely* clean before you have your meal.

Absorb *(v.)* അബ്സോർബ് - വലിച്ചെടുക്കുക, ആഗിരണം ചെയ്യുക

Blotting paper *absorbs* ink.

(To be) absorbed in ലയിച്ചിരിക്കുക

The children *were* so *absorbed* in the story that they did not hear the bell ring.

Absurd *(adj.)* അബ്സേർഡ് - അസംബന്ധമായ, അർത്ഥശൂന്യമായ, പൊള്ളയായ

Ramesh's *absurd* talk showed his foolishness.

Abundant *(adj.)* അ ബ ൻ്റ് - ധാരാളം, സമൃദ്ധമായ

This library has an *abundant* stock of books.

Rice is *abundant* in Kerala.

(n.) സുലഭം

The fruits are in *abundance* in Himachal Pradesh.

Abuse *(v.)* അബ്യൂസ് - 1. ചീത്ത വിളിക്കുക, പുലഭ്യം പറയുക

Children should be taught never to *abuse* anybody.

2. ദുരുപയോഗം ചെയ്യുക

Kundan was clever but he *abused* his cleverness when he cheated the poor man.

(n.) 3. അനുചിതമായ ഉപയോഗം

Overstaying in the host's house will be an *abuse* of his hospitality.

Academy *(n.)* അക്കാഡമി - 1. പാഠശാല - വിദ്യാഭ്യാസ സ്ഥാപനം

He teaches singing in an *academy* of music.

2. വിദ്യാപീഠം

The Sahitya *Academy* published books on literature.

Accent *(n.)* ആക്സെൻ്റ് - ഉച്ചാരണ ശൈലി

Raman speaks English with a South Indian *accent.*

Accept *(v.)* അക്സെപ്ട് - 1. സ്വീകരിക്കുക

The beggar *accepted* alms from the rich man.

2. സമ്മതിച്ച് തരുക

I am sorry I cannot *accept* what you say.

Access അക്സെസ് - ഏതെങ്കിലും സാധനം ഉപയോഗിക്കാനുള്ള സൗകര്യം

(n.) I do not have *access* to Internet.

(v.) You need to contact your service provider if you cannot *access* the Internet.

Accident *(n.)* ആക്സിഡൻ്റ് - 1. അപകടം, അത്യാഹിതം

Gopal met with a car *accident* yesterday.

Acclaim അക്ലെയിം - പ്രശംസ

(n.) In spite of an average business, the movie won critical *acclaim.*

(v.) The Shadow Lines was *acclaimed* by the readers.

Accommodation *(n.)* അക്കാമഡേഷൻ - താമസസ്ഥലം അല്ലെങ്കിൽ സൗകര്യം

She is looking for *accommodation* these days.

Accompany *(v.)* അക്കമ്പനി - 1. അനുഗമിക്കുക

Sudhir was *accompanied* by his wife to the musical concert.

2. ചേർന്ന് പാടുക അല്ലെങ്കിൽ വാദ്യം വായിക്കുക

The musician played the Sitar and his young son *accompanied* him on the Tabla.

Accomplish *(v.)* അക്കംപ്ലിഷ് - പൂർത്തിയാക്കുക, നേടുക

Congratulations on *accomplishing* such a difficult task!

According to *(prep.)* അക്കോർഡിംഗ് ടു - പ്രകാരം, അനുസരിച്ച്

(prep.) We must act *according to* our strategy.

(adv.) Whenever you are in trouble, follow your mind and act *accordingly.*

Account *(n.)* അക്കൗ - 1. വിവരണം

His *account* of the event was very interesting.

2. കണക്ക് സൂക്ഷിക്കൽ

I do not know how to keep *accounts.*

(v.) 3. കാരണം ബോധിപ്പിക്കുക

How did Kamal *account* for being late today?

Accountable *(adj.)* അക്കൗ ബിൾ - ഉത്തരവാദി

I am not *accountable* for what happened yesterday.

Accumulate *(v.)* അക്യൂമുലേറ്റ് - ശേഖരിക്കുക, അടിഞ്ഞുകൂടുക

Dust will *accumulate* in the room if you do not clean it daily.

Accurate *(adj.)* അക്യുറേറ്റ് - കൃത്യമായ, ശരിയായ

My wrist-watch always shows the *accurate* time.

Accuse *(v.)* അക്യൂസ് - ആരോപിക്കുക, കുറ്റം ചാർത്തുക

The servant was *accused* of stealing a golden ring.

Accustom *(v.)* അകസ്റ്റം - ശീലമാക്കുക, പരിചയപ്പെടുക.

We are not *accustomed* to very cold weather.

We should *accustom* ourselves to the idea of space travel.

Ache ഏക്, വേദന, കഴപ്പ്

(n.) If you have a tooth-*ache*, you should go to a dentist.

കഴപ്പ് തോന്നുക

(v.) My leg is *aching.*

Achieve *(v.)* അച്ചീവ് - പൂർത്തിയാക്കുക, അവസാനിപ്പിക്കുക, നേടുക

Congratulations on *achieving* success in the I.A.S. examination!

Acknowledge *(v.)* അക്നോളജ് - 1. സമ്മതിക്കുക, അംഗീകരിക്കുക

They all *acknowledged* that Deepak was the best player in the team.

2. കൈപ്പറ്റുക

I *acknowledged* the receipt of his letter.

Acquaintance *(n.)* അക്വിൻടെൻസ് പരിചയക്കാർ, പരിചിതർ

Harish has many *acquaintances* but very few friends.

Acquire *(v.)* അക്വയർ - സമ്പാദിക്കുക, നേടുക

The businessman *acquired* a lot of money by hard work.

Across എക്രോസ് - അക്കരെ, കുറുക്കെ

(prep.) There are many bridges *across* the Yamuna in Delhi.

(adv.) I came *across* an old school friend in the market today.

Act *(n.)* ആക്ട് - 1. പ്രവൃത്തി, പെരുമാറ്റം

A boy-scout does an *act* of kindness every day.

2. നിയമം

There are many *acts* in the Indian Penal Code.

3. നാടകത്തിന്റെ രംഗം

The last *act* of the play is about to begin.

(v.) 4. പ്രവർത്തിക്കുക, ചെയ്യുക

One should never *act* in haste.

Active *(adj.)* ആക്ടീവ് - സജീവം

(adj.) A balanced diet makes you more *active*.

(adv.) He climbed up the stairs *actively.*

Activist *(n.)* ആക്ടിവിസ്റ്റ് - പ്രവർത്തകൻ

His father is a social *activist*.

Actual *(adj.)* ആക്ച്വൽ - യഥാർത്ഥ, ശരിക്കുള്ള

This is an expensive ring, but I do not know the *actual* price.

Acute *(adj.)* അക്യൂട്ട് - 1.കടുത്ത, രൂക്ഷമായ

She complained of an *acute* pain in her stomach last night.

2. രോഗത്തിന്റെ ഗുരുതരാവസ്ഥ

He is a patient of *acute* bronchitis.

3. തീവ്രമായ

Animals have an *acute* sense of hearing.

Adapt *(v.)* അഡാപ്റ്റ് - ഇണങ്ങിച്ചേരുക

We should try to *adapt* ourselves to changing circumstances.

Add *(v.)* ആഡ് - കൂട്ടുക

You have made a mistake in *adding* these figures.

(n.) ചേർക്കുക

We are going to do some of the *additions* today.

Addict *(n.)* അഡിക്റ്റ് - ശീലമാക്കിയയാൾ

(n.) I encountered a drug *addict* in the subway.

(adj.) He is *addicted* to smoking.

(n.) I have an *addiction* for chocolates.

Address *(v.)* അഡ്രസ്സ് - 1. വിലാസം, മുഖപ്രസംഗം, വ്യാഖ്യാനം
He wrote down my *address* in his notebook.
2. വ്യാഖ്യാനം നൽകുക, അഭിസംബോധന ചെയ്യുക
(v.) The headmaster *addressed* the students.

Adept *(adj.)* അഡെപ്റ്റ് - സമർത്ഥൻ
He is *adept* at public speaking.

Adequate *(n.)* ആഡിക്വേറ്റ് - തികവ്, അനുയോജ്യം
The amount of money I have is not *adequate* for buying a car.

Adhere *(v.)* അഡ്ഹിയർ - ഉറച്ചിരിക്കുക
Make sure the paper is *adhered* to the cardboard properly.
2. പാലിക്കുക
It is better you *adhere* to the company rules.

Adjacent *(adj.)* അഡ്ജസെന്റ് - തൊട്ടടുത്ത്
My house is *adjacent* to the school.

Adjoin *(v.)* അഡ്ജോയിൻ - ചേർന്നുള്ള, ഒന്നായ
The officer's residence *adjoins* his office.

Adjoining *(adj.)* അഡ്ജോയിനിംഗ് - അടുത്തടുത്തുള്ള
Rama and Uma live in *adjoining* houses.

Adjourn *(v.)* അഡ്ജോൺ - പിരിച്ച് വിടുക
The meeting was *adjourned* till the next day.

Adjust *(v.)* അഡ്ജസ്റ്റ് - ശരിപ്പെടുത്തുക, ക്രമീകരിക്കുക
He *adjusted* the lamp so that he could read better.

Administer *(v.)* അഡ്മിനിസ്റ്റർ - ഭരിക്കുക, മേൽനോട്ടം വഹിക്കുക
The headmaster *administers* the school.
(n.) മേൽനോട്ടം, ഭരണം
The *administration* of a city is the work of its municipal corporation.

Admire *(v.)* അഡ്മയർ - പ്രശംസിക്കുക, സ്തുതിക്കുക
(v.) All the friends of Smita *admired* her beautiful sari.
(adj.) പ്രശംസനീയ
Courage is an *admirable* quality.
(n.) പ്രശംസ
We all felt *admiration* for his great strength.

Admit *(v.)* അഡ്മിറ്റ് - 1 സമ്മതിക്കുക, ഏൽക്കുക
The boy *admitted* that he broke the windowpane.
2. പ്രവേശിപ്പിക്കുക
The headmaster *admitted* the new boy to his school.

Adolescent *(n.)* ആഡോളസെന്റ് - കൗമാര ദശക്കാർ
(n.) *Adolescents* often find the advice of their parents rubbish.
(v.) *Adolescence* is the age of emotional changes in the children.

Adopt *(v.)* അഡോപ്റ്റ് - സ്വീകരിക്കുക, അംഗീകരിക്കുക
The Lok Sabha *adopted* the annual budget for discussion.
2. ഏറ്റെടുക്കുക, ദത്തെടുക്കുക
The childless couple *adopted* a boy.

Adore *(v.)* അഡോർ - വളരെ സ്നേഹിക്കുക, വളരെ ഇഷ്ടപ്പെടുക
Every mother *adores* her child.

Adrift *(adv.)* അഡ്രിഫ്റ്റ് - അങ്ങിങ്ങ് ഒഴുകി നടക്കുക
The small boat was *adrift* on the high seas for four days.

Adult *(n.)* അഡൽറ്റ് - പ്രായപൂർത്തിയായ ആൾ
Adults have the right to marry as per their will.

Advance *(v.)* അഡ്വാൻസ് - മുന്നേറുക, ഉയർച്ച നേടുക
The army *advanced* towards the enemy's fort.
(n.) മുൻകൂർ
Ramesh requested his employer to pay him an *advance of* Rs. 2000.

Advantage *(n.)* അഡ്വാൻടേജ് - ലാഭം, നേട്ടം
Knowledge of English is a great *advantage*.

Adventure *(n.)* അഡ്വഞ്ചർ - സാഹസിക
I like to read the stories of *adventure.*

Adverse *(adj.)* അഡ്‌വേർസ് - പ്രതികൂല
(adj.) Deserts offer *adverse* living conditions.
(n.) Sweet are the uses of *adversity*.

Advertise *(v.)* അഡ്വർടൈസ് - പരസ്യപ്പെടുത്തുക, പ്രചാരം നൽകുക
This book is widely *advertised.*

Advertisement *(v.)* അഡ്വർടൈസ്മെന്റ് - പരസ്യം
If you want to sell your product, give its *advertisements* in the newspapers.

Advice *(n.)* അഡ്വൈസ് - ഉപദേശം

You must follow the doctor's *advice* to take rest for a week.

(v.) ഉപദേശം നൽകുക

He *adviced* me to consult a doctor.

Advocate അഡ്വക്കേറ്റ് - അഭിഭാഷകൻ, വാദിക്കുക

(n.) His father is an *advocate* in the Supreme Court.

(v.) I *advocated* the plan suggested by him.

Affair *(n.)* അഫയർ - 1. പ്രവർത്തനം, ജോലി

Cooking is largely considered a woman's *affair*.

2. സംഭവം

After the *affair* was over, everyone went home.

Affect *(v.)* അഫെക്റ്റ് - ബാധിക്കുക

His chest was *affected* by constant smoking.

Affection *(n.)* അഫെക്ഷൻ - സ്നേഹം, അനുരാഗം

There was great *affection* between Ram and Laxman.

(adj.) സ്നേഹസമ്പന്നൻ

My brother is a very *affectionate* person.

Affinity *(n.)* അഫിനിറ്റി - അടുപ്പം, താല്പര്യം

I have an *affinity* for dogs.

Afflict *(v.)* അഫ്ലിക്റ്റ് - ദുഃഖിപ്പിക്കുക

The poor are always *afflicted* with troubles.

Affluent *(adj.)* അഫ്ലുവെന്റ് - സമ്പന്നമായ

(adj.) She belongs to an *affluent* family of businessmen.

(n.) She often boasts of her *affluence*.

Afford *(v.)* അഫോർഡ് - നേരിടാവുന്ന, താങ്ങാവുന്ന

The poor rickshaw-puller could not *afford* to send his children to school.

Afraid *(adj.)* അഫ്രെയ്ഡ് - 1. ഭയന്ന, പേടിച്ച

Little children are *afraid* of dogs.

2. സവിനയം ക്ഷമ ചോദിക്കുക

I am *afraid* I cannot accept your invitation.

After *(prep.)* ആഫ്ടർ - 1. ശേഷം

The boys played cricket *after* the school was over.

2. പിന്നാലെ

The horses galloped one *after* another.

Again *(adv.)* എഗെയ്ൻ - വീണ്ടും, ഒരിക്കൽകൂടി

Please sing that song once *again*.

Against *(prep.)* എഗൻസ്റ്റ് - 1. എതിരെ, എതിരായി

He fought bravely *against* the enemy.

2. ചേർത്ത്, ചാരി

Keep you bicycle *against* the wall.

Age *(n.)* ഏജ് - 1. പ്രായം, വയസ്സ്, ദശ

What is your *age*?

2. യുഗം, കാലം

The period of Chandragupta Maurya is known as the Golden *Age* of India.

Aged *(adj.)* ഏജഡ് - പ്രായമായ, വയസ്സുചെന്ന

It is difficult to change the habits of *aged* people.

Agency *(n.)* ഏജൻസി - പ്രത്യേക സേവനം നൽകുന്ന സ്ഥാപനം

We contacted an advertising *agency* to promote our brand.

Agenda *(n.)* അജ - കാര്യപരിപാടി

Eradicating unemployment is the first thing in the government *agenda*.

Aggravate *(v.)* അഗ്രവേറ്റ് - മൂർച്ഛിപ്പിക്കുക, ഗുരുതരമാക്കുക

Going out into the cold will *aggravate* your illness.

Aggregate *(n.)* അഗ്രഗേറ്റ് - മൊത്തത്തിലുള്ള, ആകെ

In the India-Pakistan match, the *aggregate* score of both the teams crossed 500.

Aggressive *(adj.)* അഗ്രസ്സീവ് - ആക്രമണ സ്വഭാവം

(adj.) He had never expected such an *aggressive* behaviour from the teacher.

(n.) Growing *aggression* in children is a matter of concern for the parents.

Agile *(adj.)* എജൈൽ - ചുറുചുറുക്ക്, ഗതിവേഗം

(adj.) A rabbit is an *agile* animal.

(n.) Running between the wickets requires a lot of *agility* from both the batsmen.

Agitate *(v.)* അജിറ്റേറ്റ് - പ്രക്ഷോഭണം നടത്തുക

(v.) The workers *agitated* when forced to stay late in the office.

(*adj.*) The *agitated* students boycotted the exams.
(*n.*) The policy of reservation led to *agitation* among the doctors.

Ago (*adv.*) എഗോ - മുമ്പ്, ആദ്യം
He left this city four years *ago.*

Agony (*n.*) ആഗണി - അസഹ്യമായ വേദന
I was in great *agony* when I broke my arm.

Agree (*v.*) എഗ്രീ - സമ്മതിക്കുക, അംഗീകരിക്കുക
He did not *agree* to my proposal.
(*n.*) ധാരണ, ഒത്തുതീർപ്പ്
The partners signed an *agreement* before starting their business.
(*adj.*) ആരും ഇഷ്ടപ്പെടുന്ന
Lata has an *agreeable* (pleasant) personality.

Agriculture (*n.*) അഗ്രികൾച്ചർ - കൃഷി
Most people in India depend upon *agriculture* for their livelihood.

Ahead (*adv.*) എഹഡ് - മുമ്പേ
Please go *ahead;* I will follow you.

Aid (*n.*) എയ്ഡ് - സഹായം
When the tiger attacked me, the hunter came to my *aid.*
(*v.*) സഹായിക്കുക
I *aided* my mother in cooking the food.

Ailment (*n.*) എയ്ൽമെന്റ് - അസുഖം, നിസ്സാര രോഗം
She will soon recover from her *ailment*.

Aim (*v.*) എയിം - 1. ലക്ഷ്യമിടുക, ഉന്നം പിടിക്കുക
The hunter *aimed* his gun at the tiger.
(*n.*) 2. ലക്ഷ്യം, ഉദ്ദേശ്യം
My *aim* is to become an engineer.

Air (*n.*) എയർ - വായു, കാറ്റ്
Without *air,* we would not be able to live.

Aisle (*n.*) എയ്ൽ - ഇടനാഴി
It was difficult to find the way through the *aisles*.

Alarm (*n.*) അലാം ഭീതി, ഭയം
When the plane began to dive, the passengers were filled with *alarm.*
2. അപകട സൂചന, അലാറം
The silence of the night was suddenly broken by a fire *alarm.*
(*v.*) പേടിപ്പിക്കുക
You really *alarmed* me by screaming so loudly.

Alas (*Interj.*) അലാസ് - കഷ്ടം! ഹായ്!
We wanted to go for a walk, but *alas,* it rained.

Album (*n.*) ആൽബം - ആൽബം
He has pasted the stamps of many countries in his *album.*

Alcohol (*n.*) ആൽക്കഹാൾ - മദ്യം
Don't drive after consuming *alcohol.*

Alert (*adj.*) അലെർട്ട് - ജാഗ്രത, ശ്രദ്ധ
The *alert* engine driver averted a major accident of his train.

Alien ഏലിയൻ - അന്യമായ, വിദേശീയ
(*n.*) The movie showed the hero fighting against a group of *aliens* from the other planet.
(*adj.*) I am completely *alien* to baseball.

Alight (*v.*) എലൈറ്റ് - 1. ഇറങ്ങുക
The driver opened the door and his master *alighted* from the car.
(*adj.*) 2. ജ്വലിപ്പിക്കുക
He struck the match and it was *alighted.*

Alike എലൈക് - ഒരേപോലുള്ള, സാദൃശ്യമുള്ള
(*adv.*) The twin brothers look *alike.*
(*adj.*) The mother and the daughter are *alike* in their looks.

Alive (*adj.*) എലൈവ് - ജീവനുള്ള
Some people were still *alive* under the debris of a collapsed building.

All ആൾ - എല്ലാം, എല്ലാവരും
(*n.*) Very few people come forward to sacrifice their *all* for the country.
(*adj.*) I have read *all* the books on this subject.

Allege (*v.*) അലേജ് - ആരോപണം ഉന്നയിക്കുക
(*v.*) The lady *alleged* that he had attacked her.
(*n.*) The lady put the *allegation* of an attack on him.

(adv.) The lady was *allegedly* attacked by him.

Allergy *(n.)* അലർജി - അലർജി
(n.) I have an *allergy* to pollen grains.
(adj.) I am *allergic* to pollen grains.

Alliance *(n.)* അലയൻസ് - സഖ്യം
The two groups formed an *alliance* to oppose the government.

Allot *(v.)* അലോട്ട്- അനുവദിക്കുക, നീക്കിവയ്ക്കുക
We entered the room *allotted* to us.

Allow *(v.)* അലൗവ്- അനുവാദം നൽകുക, അനുമതി നൽകുക
Please *allow* me to help you.

Allowance *(n.)* അലവൻസ്- ബത്ത
I give my son a monthly *allowance* for sundry expenses.

All-round *(adj.)* ആൾറൗ് - സകലകലാവല്ലഭൻ
Yuvraj Singh is an *all-round* cricket player.

All-time *(adj.)* ആൾ - ടൈം - എന്നന്നേക്കും, സദാസമയവും
This is my *all-time* favourite movie.

Allure അല്യൂർ - പ്രലോഭനം, ആകർഷണം
(n.) The *allure* of working in a foreign country can never fade.
(v.) Big cities always *allure* people of small towns.

Ally *(n.)* അലൈ - സഖ്യ, സഹായക, സുഹൃദ്
England and America were *allies* in the Second World War.

Almighty *(n.)* ആൾമൈറ്റി - സർവ്വശക്തൻ
Have faith in *Almighty* and do your best.

Almost *(adv.)* ആൾമോസ്റ്റ് - ഏറെക്കുറെ, ഏതാ്
The little boy walked *almost* four miles to reach home.

Alms *(n.)* ആംസ് - ഭിക്ഷ
The rich lady distributed *alms* among the beggars.

Alone എലോൺ - തനിയെ, ഒറ്റയ്ക്ക്, ഏകൻ, മാത്രം
(adv.) She was afraid to go out *alone* in the dark.
(adj.) The general *alone* could give the order to attack.

Along *(prep.)* എലോംഗ് - അരികിലൂടെ
He followed the path *along* the river.

Aloud *(adv.)* എലൗഡ് - ഉച്ചത്തിൽ, ശബ്ദമുയർത്തി
He spoke *aloud* so that I could hear him.

Already *(adv.)* ആൾറെഡി - ആദ്യമേ, നേരത്തേ
Our guests have *already* arrived.

Also ആൾസോ - ഒപ്പം, കൂട്ടത്തിൽ
(adv.) When Anil came, Anita *also* came.
(conj.) She not only plays piano, but *also* writes songs.

Alter *(v.)* ആൾട്ടർ - മാറ്റുക, പുതുക്കുക
The tailor *altered* David's old coat to fit him.

Alternate *(adj.)* ആൾട്ടർനേറ്റ് - ഒന്നിടവിട്ട്
We have our classes on *alternate* days.

Alternative ആൾട്ടർനേറ്റിവ് - ബദൽ, പകരം
(n.) Is there any *alternative* to this plan?
(adj.) These days, people have little faith on *alternative* medicine.

Although *(conj.)* ആൾദോ - എങ്കിലും, എന്നാലും
He ran fast *although* his leg was injured.

Altogether *(adv.)* ആൾടുഗദർ - എല്ലാംകൂടി, എല്ലാം ചേർത്ത്
Altogether, at home and in the bank, I have five thousand rupees.

Always *(adv.)* ആൾവേയ്സ് - എപ്പോഴും, സദാ
He is *always* busy.

A.M. എ.എം. - രാവിലെ, ഉച്ചയ്ക്ക് പന്ത്രണ്ട് മണിക്ക് മുമ്പ്
My office starts at 10.00 *A.M.*

Amateur *(n.)* അമച്വർ - അമച്വർ, അവിദഗ്ദ്ധ
The *amateur* athletes surprisingly put up a good show in comparison to the professional ones.

Amaze *(v.)* അമേസ് - അത്ഭുതപ്പെടുത്തുക
The child wrestler's great strength *amazed* everybody.

Ambassador *(n.)* അംബാസഡർ - സ്ഥാനപതി
Ambassadors' role is quite significant in projecting their country's good image to the outside world.

Ambience *(n.)* ആംബിയെൻസ് - അന്തരീക്ഷം
Dim lights and soft music were providing a romantic *ambience.*

Ambiguity *(n.)* ആംബിഗ്വുറ്റി - അവ്യക്തത
(n.) There was an *ambiguity* in his expression.
(adj.) His writings are often *ambiguous*.

Ambition *(n.)* ആംബിഷൻ - മോഹം, ഉൽക്കർഷേച്ഛ
My son's *ambition* is to be a doctor.
(adj.) ഉൽക്കർഷേച്ഛയുള്ള
Success knocks at the doors of *ambitious* and hard-working people.

Amble *(v.)* ആംബിൾ - മന്ദഗമനം ചെയ്യുക
The weary traveller *ambled* along the street.

Ambulance *(n.)* ആംബുലൻസ് - ആംബുലൻസ്
The wounded man was taken to the hospital in an *ambulance*.

Amend *(v.)* അമെൻഡ് - ഭേദഗതി ചെയ്യുക
(v.) Our Constitution has been *amended* many times.
(n.) Certain clauses in this agreement need *amendment*.

Amenity *(n.)* അമെനിറ്റി - സൗകര്യങ്ങൾ
Big cities offer good civic *amenities*.

Amiable *(adj.)* അമിയെബിൾ - രമ്യസ്വഭാവമുള്ള
My mother is an *amiable* lady.

Amid *(prep.)* എമിഡ് - ഇടയ്ക്ക്
In India, we often see honesty *amid* poverty.

Amiss *(adv.)* എമിഡ് - അനുചിതമായി
I did not mean to hurt his feelings, but he took it *amiss*.
(adj.) തെറ്റായ, അനുചിതമായ
There is nothing *amiss* in this plan.

Among(st) *(prep.)* എമംഗ്(സ്റ്റ്) ഇടയ്ക്ക്, കൂട്ടത്തിൽ
She distributed the sweets *among* her children.

Amount *(n.)* എമൗ് - 1. തുക
It is risky to carry a large *amount* in cash.
2. അളവ്
What is the *amount* of flour needed to prepare a small cake?

Ample *(adj.)* ആംപിൾ - വേത്ര, ധാരാളം
The little boy has an *ample* stock of story books.

Amuse *(v.)* അമ്യൂസ് - ഉല്ലസിപ്പിക്കുക, രസിപ്പിക്കുക
The clown in the circus *amused* the children with his antics.

Analyse *(v.)* അനലൈസ് - വിശകലനം ചെയ്യുക
(v.) Let us *analyse* the situation well and come up with an appropriate solution.
(n.) The situation needs an in-depth *analysis*.

Anarchy *(n.)* അനാർക്കി - അരാജകത്വം
The death of the Chief Minister led to *anarchy* in the city.

Ancestor *(n.)* ആൻസെസ്റ്റർ - പൂർവ്വികൻ
According to Darwin, monkeys were the *ancestors* of human beings.

Anchor *(n.)* ആങ്കർ - നങ്കൂരം
A large ship was at *anchor* in the harbour.
(v.) നങ്കൂരമടിക്കുക
The ship was *anchored* when it arrived at the port.

Ancient *(adj.)* ഏൻഷ്യന്റ് - പ്രാചീന, പുരാതന, പുരാണ
(adj.) Ancient India was a land of glory.

Angel *(n.)* ഏഞ്ചൽ - മാലാഖ, ദൈവദൂതൻ
It is said that when a saint dies, *angels* come to take his soul to heaven.

Anger *(n.)* ആംഗർ - കോപം, ദേഷ്യം
Good people do not get filled with *anger* for others' lapses.
(adj.) ദേഷ്യപ്പെടുക
My brother will be *angry* with me if I lose his pen.

Angle *(n.)* ആംഗിൾ - കോൺ
A triangle has three *angles*.

Anguish *(n.)* ആംഗ്വിഷ് - വേദന, വ്യഥ
Three consecutive defeats caused *anguish* to the captain.

Animal *(n.)* ആനിമൽ - മൃഗം
The zoo in New Delhi has some rare wild *animals*.

Ankle *(n.)* ആങ്കിൾ - കണങ്കാൽ
I sprained my *ankle* this morning.

Annihilate *(v.)* അനിഹിലേറ്റ് - നശിപ്പിക്കുക
(v.) The fire *annihilated* the whole forest.
(n.) The sages guided the path from *annihilation* to resurrection.

Annotate *(v.)* അനൊടേറ്റ് - ടിപ്പണി നൽകുക

(v.) The translator *annotated* the poem to make it easy to understand.

(n.) *Annotations* to the regional words are provided at the end of the book.

Announce *(v.)* അനൗൺസ് - പ്രഖ്യാപിക്കുക, അറിയിക്കുക, വെളിപ്പെടുത്തുക

The Principal *announced* that the school would be closed for winter vacation.

(n.) അനൗൺസർ

The *announcer* read out the news on the radio.

(n.) പ്രഖ്യാപനം, അറിയിപ്പ്

The chief guest made an *announcement* of the names of the prize winners.

Annoy *(v.)* അനോയ് - ചൊടിപ്പിക്കുക, വിഷമിപ്പിക്കുക

(v.) The student's carelessness *annoyed* the teacher.

(adj.) It is *annoying* to miss a bus when you are in a hurry.

(n.) A loud radio is often an *annoyance.*

Annual *(adj.)* ആന്വൽ - 1. വാർഷിക, പ്രതിവർഷ

The *annual* gathering of our club will be held next month.

(n.) 2. വിശേഷാൽ പതിപ്പ്

Generally, the *annual* of a monthly magazine is bigger than its regular issue.

Anonymous *(adj.)* അനോണിമസ് - അജ്ഞാത, പേരുവയ്ക്കാത്ത

The story was submitted by an *anonymous* writer.

Another അനദർ - മറ്റൊരു, ഒന്നുകൂടി

(adj.) May I have *another* cup of tea?

(pron.) One man was walking; *another* was running.

Answer *(v.)* ആൻസർ - 1. ഉത്തരം, മറുപടി പറയുക

He could not *answer* my question.

(n.) 2. പരിഹാരം

The bright boy quickly found out the *answer* of the sum.

Ant *(n.)* ആന്റ് - ഉറുമ്പ്

I saw a long line of *ants* carrying granules of sugar.

Anthem *(n.)* ആൻഥം - വിശേഷ ഗാനം, സ്തുതി ഗീതം

We sing our national *anthem* at all national festivals.

Anthology *(n.)* ആൻഥോളജി - സഞ്ചയം

The book is an *anthology* of stories written by famous writers.

Antibiotic *(n.)* ആന്റിബയോട്ടിക് - പ്രത്യേക ഔഷധം

An *antibiotic* might cure your headache.

Antique *(adj.)* ആന്റീക് - പ്രാചീനമായതിനാൽ അപൂർവവും വിലപിടിച്ചതും

My mother is fond of collecting *antique* pieces of art.

Antisocial *(adj.)* ആന്റിസോഷ്യൽ - സാമൂഹ്യ വിരുദ്ധ

Dealing with *antisocial* elements is really a headache for the government.

Antithesis *(n.)* ആന്റിതീസിസ് - നേർ വിപരീതം

The aged wrestler now looks an *antithesis* of what he was earlier.

Anvil *(n.)* ആൻവിൽ - അടകല്ല്, കൂടകല്ല്

The blacksmith was shaping a hot piece of iron on his *anvil.*

Anxious *(adj.)* ആങ്ഷിയസ് - 1. ആകാംക്ഷ

He was *anxious* to see her.

2. വേവലാതിയുള്ള, ചിന്താഗ്രസ്ത

Students were *anxious* about their examination result.

(n.) 3. വേവലാതി, ഉത്കണ്ഠ

The baby's mother was full of *anxiety* about her infant's health.

Any *(adj.)* എനി - 1. വല്ലതും, ഏതാനും

Have you *any* stamps?

2. ആരെങ്കിലും, ഏതെങ്കിലും

You can buy pastries from *any* bakery.

Apart *(adv.)* എപാർട്ട് - 1. അല്ലാതെ

Apart from movies, Ramesh was also fond of good food.

2. വേറിട്ട്, വെവ്വേറെ

The child tore the book apart.

Apartment *(n.)* അപ്പാർട്ട്മെന്റ് - മുറി, ഫ്ളാറ്റ്

Apartments on the main road are very costly.

Ape *(n.)* ഏപ്പ്-1. വാനരം, കുരങ്ങൻ
I saw an *ape* in the zoo.
(v.) 2. അനുസരിക്കുക
We should not *ape* the western manners.

Apologise *(v.)* അപോളജൈസ്-മാപ്പ് ചോദിക്കുക, ക്ഷമായാചനം ചെയ്യുക
(v.) The minister *apologised* for arriving late.
(n.) മാപ്പ്, ക്ഷമാപണം
Rakesh sent an *apology* for not being able to attend my sister's wedding.

Apostle *(n.)* അപ്പോസൽ - ദൂതൻ, ദൈവ ദൂതൻ
Gandhiji is known as an *apostle* of non-violence.

Appal *(v.)* അപ്പാൽ-ഭയചകിതരാക്കുക
(v.) The news of a likely bomb blast *appalled* the whole city.
(adj.) The news of the bomb blast was *appalling*.
(adj.) The city was *appalled* at the news of a likely bomb blast.

Apparent *(adj.)* അപ്പാരന്റ്-പ്രകടം, സ്പഷ്ടം, പ്രത്യക്ഷം
It was *apparent* from Arun's face that he didn't like Amit's rude manners.
(adv.) The traveller was *apparently* lost, for he was not sure which way to proceed.

Appeal *(v. & n.)* അപ്പീൽ-അഭ്യർത്ഥന (നടത്തുക)
(v.) The politician *appealed* to the people to vote for his party.
(n.) The labourers made an *appeal* to the contractor for an increase in their salaries.

Appear *(v.)* അപ്പിയർ-1. പ്രത്യക്ഷപ്പെടുക
The passengers were happy to see the long delayed train *appear* on the platform.
2. തോന്നുക, പ്രതീതി ഉാവുക
It *appears* that he wants to avoid me.
3. പ്രവേശിക്കുക
Geeta has *appeared* for I.A.S. examination this year.

Appetite *(n.)* ആപ്പടൈറ്റ്-വിശപ്പ്
During illness, patients often lose their *appetite*.

Applaud *(v.)* അപ്ലാഡ്-പ്രശംസിക്കുക, കയ്യടിച്ച് അഭിനന്ദിക്കുക
The entire gathering *applauded* the little boy's fine acting.
(n.) Our principal was greeted with *applause* when he rose to speak at the annual function.

Appliance *(n.)* അപ്ലൈയൻസ്-ഉപകരണം, യന്ത്രം
The modern housewife has many domestic *appliances* at her disposal.

Apply *(v.)* അപ്ലൈ - 1. അപേക്ഷ നൽകുക
Shikha and Juhi *applied* for a job in the same firm.
2. അടിക്കുക
It will take a week to *apply* paint to our house.
3. ബാധകമാകുക (ആക്കുക)
Laws of the land *apply* to everyone.
(n.) അപേക്ഷ
Rama's job *application* was rejected.

Appoint *(v.)* അപ്പോയിന്റ്-1. നിയമിക്കുക, ജോലിക്കെടുക്കുക
My brother has been *appointed* as the manager in a good company.
(n.) 2. സമയം കിട്ടുക
Today my father has got an *appointment* with the dentist.

Appreciate *(v.)* അപ്രീഷിയേറ്റ് - ആസ്വദിക്കുക
He *appreciates* classical music.
(n.) പ്രശംസ, അഭിനന്ദനം
The audience showed their *appreciation* for the singer by clapping.

Apprehend *(v.)* അപ്രഹെൻഡ് - പിടി കൂടുക, ബന്ധിക്കുക
The servant was *apprehended* for the theft in the house.

Apprentice *(n.)* അപ്രന്റീസ് - അപ്രന്റീസ് പ്രാഥമിക വിദ്യാർത്ഥി
He is working as an *apprentice* with a carpenter.

Approach *(v.)* അപ്രോച്ച്-സമീപിക്കുക, അടുത്തെത്തുക
The thief *approached* the locker silently.

Appropriate *(adj.)* അപ്രോപ്രിയേറ്റ് - 1. ഉചിതമായ, അനുയോജ്യമായ
The guest of honour made a brief speech *appropriate* to the occasion.

(v.) 2. എന്തിനെങ്കിലും വേറി നീക്കിവയ്ക്കുക
My mother *appropriated* some money to buy our school uniform.
3. തിരിമറി നടത്തുക
The union leader was accused of *appropriating* the employees' welfare fund for his personal gains.

Approve *(v.)* അപ്രൂവ് - അംഗീകരിക്കുക, ഇഷ്ടപ്പെടുക, നല്ലതായി കരുതുക
No one can *approve* of such misbehaviour.
(n.) അംഗീകാരം
His proposal could not get anybody's *approval.*

Approximate *(adj.)* അപ്രോക്സിമേറ്റ് - സുമാർ, ഉദ്ദേശം
What is the *approximate* number of students in your school?
(adv.) The distance between Delhi and Agra is *approximately* a hundred and twenty miles.

Apt *(adj.)* ആപ്റ്റ് - യോഗ്യം, പ്രസക്തം, സാദ്ധ്യത
The accomplished speaker made an *apt* speech.
I am *apt* to doze if I sit in an easy chair.

Aptitude *(n.)* ആപ്റ്റിട്യൂഡ് - അഭിരുചി
She has an *aptitude* for literature.

Arbitrary *(adj.)* സ്വേച്ഛാപരം, അനുചിതം
Their decision of shifting to Dwarka turned out to be *arbitrary.*

Arch *(n.)* ആർച്ച് - കമാനം, തോരണം
Many *arches* were erected on the roads to welcome the visiting leader.

Architect *(n.)* ആർക്കിടെക്റ്റ് - വാസ്തുശില്പി, നിർമ്മാതാവ്
Your beautiful house is obviously designed by an able *architect.*

Ardent *(adj.)* ആർഡെന്റ് - തീഷ്ണമായ, തികഞ്ഞ
The kids are *ardent* admirers of Harry Potter.

Area *(n.)* ഏരിയാ - പ്രദേശം, മേഖല
The Chambal ravines are known as an *area* of dacoits.

Argue *(v.)* ആർഗ്യൂ - തർക്കിക്കുക, സ്ഥാപിക്കുക, വാദിക്കുക
The critics *argued* a lot about the good and bad points of the celebrated painting.
(n.) വാദം
Today, the *argument* that all politicians are after power seems true.

Arise *(v.)* എറൈസ് - ഉയർത്തെഴുന്നേല്ക്കുക
Arise, awake, and stop not till the goal is reached.
2. ഉദയം ചെയ്യുക
Because of the limited seats, a quarrel *arose* among the passengers.

Aristocrat *(n.)* അരിസ്റ്റോക്രാറ്റ് - കുലീനവർഗ്ഗം
His forefathers belonged to the class of *aristocrats* in pre-independence India.

Arm *(n.)* ആർമ് - കൈ, ബാഹു, കരം
I have hurt my *arm.*

Armed *(adj.)* ആർമ്ഡ് - സായുധരായ
Four *armed* men broke into the house and committed the robbery.

Armour *(n.)* ആർമർ - കവചം
(n.) The shell of a tortoise protects it like the *armour* protects a warrior.

Arms *(n.)* ആംസ് - ആയുധം
There seems to be a race to possess more *arms* among the countries of the world.

Army *(n.)* ആർമി - 1. സൈന്യം
The Indian *Army* fights bravely at the times of wars.
2. കൂട്ടം, സംഘം
There was a huge *army* of ants in the garden.

Aroma *(n.)* അരോമ - സുഗന്ധം
An *aroma* of various delicacies was surrounding the kitchen.

Around *(adv.)* എറൗ് - ചുറ്റും
People gathered *around* the famous film star.

Arouse *(v.)* എറൗസ് - ഉണർത്തുക, ഉത്തേജിപ്പിക്കുക
She *aroused* her sleeping son.

Arrange *(v.)* അറേഞ്ച് - അലങ്കരിക്കുക, അടുക്കുക, ക്രമീകരിക്കുക
She *arranged* the furniture in her sitting room.

2. തിട്ടമാക്കുക
Rupa *arranged* to meet Shikha.
(n.) 3. വിധാനം, സജ്ജീകരണം
It's a beautiful flower *arrangement.*

Arrest *(v.)* അറസ്റ്റ് - ബന്ധിക്കുക, പിടികൂടുക
The policeman *arrested* the thief.
(n.) അറസ്റ്റ്, തടവിലാക്കൽ
The *arrest* of the notorious smuggler caused a great sensation.

Arrive *(v.)* അറൈവ് - എത്തുക, വന്നുചേരുക
The Rajdhani Express *arrives* in the morning.
(n.) ആഗമനം
Delay in the *arrival* of the train is not unusual.

Arrogant *(n.)* അറൊഗന്റ് - ധിക്കാരം
Being the only son of a rich industrialist, he is very *arrogant.*

Arrow *(n.)* ആരോ - അസ്ത്രം, അമ്പ്, ശരം
The hunter shot an *arrow* at the deer.
2. സൂചന
Follow the *arrows* to reach the venue.

Art *(n.)* ആർട്ട്- കല, പാടവം, കൗശലം
Painting is a fine *art.*

Artful *(adj.)* ആർട്ട്ഫുൾ - അടവ്, തന്ത്രം
She escaped the teacher's anger through her *artful* behaviour.

Artist *(n.)* ആർട്ടിസ്റ്റ് - കലാകാരൻ
He is a well-known *artist.*

Article *(n.)*ആർട്ടിക്കിൾ -1. ലേഖനം, പ്രബന്ധം
The *articles* in India Today give a good coverage of current topics.
2. സാധനം, പദാർത്ഥം
She put all the *articles* in her shopping bag.

Artificial *(adj.)* ആർട്ടിഫിഷ്യൽ - കൃത്രിമ
Nowdays we can buy sweaters made of *artificial* wool.

Ascend അസെൻഡ് - കയറുക
The old man *ascended* the steep staircase with great difficulty.

Ascertain *(v.)* അസെർട്ടെൻ - വിലയിരുത്തുക, മനസ്സിലാക്കുക
We need to *ascertain* the practicality of this plan.

Ascetic *(n.)* അസെറ്റിക് - സന്യാസി
The *ascetic* did penance for several years.

Ash *(n.)* ആഷ് - ചാരം, ഭസ്മം
A major fire reduced the house to *ashes.*

Ashamed *(adj.)* അഷെയ്മ്ഡ്- നാണക്കേട്, ലജ്ജ
Are you not *ashamed* of being seen in the company of such vagabonds?

Ashore *(adv.)* അഷോർ - കരയ്ക്ക്, തീരത്ത്
When the ship anchored at the harbour, the sailors came *ashore.*

Aside *(adv.)* അസൈഡ് - ഒരു വശത്ത്, മാറി
He took me *aside* to tell something confidential.

Ask *(v.)* ആസ്ക് - 1. ചോദിക്കുക, പറയുക
"How are you?" he *asked* me.
2. ആവശ്യപ്പെടുക, പറയുക
The beggar *asked* him for money.
Please *ask* Anil to see me this evening.

Asleep *(adv.)* അസ്ലീപ് - ഉറങ്ങിപ്പോവുക
The tired man fell *asleep* immediately.

Aspect *(n.)* ആസ്പെക്റ്റ് - വശം
You should consider all the *aspects* of the matter before taking a decision.

Assault *(v.)* അസ്സാൾട്ട്-ആക്രമിക്കുക, പ്രഹരിക്കുക
He was arrested for *assaulting* his neighbour.
(n.) 2. കയറ്റം
The mountaineers launched an *assault* on the high peak.

Assemble *(v.)* അസംബിൾ - സമ്മേളിക്കുക, കൂട്ടംചേരുക
The headmaster asked the students to *assemble* in the courtyard of the school.
(n.) സഭ
The *assembly* passed the resolution unanimously.

Assert *(v.)* അസെർട്ട് - തറപ്പിച്ച് പറയുക, വാദിക്കുക
He kept *asserting* that he was not wrong.

Assess *(v.)* അസെസ് - വിലയിരുത്തുക
(v.) The causes of failure of this strategy must be *assessed* soon.
(n.) It is important to make an

assessment of the expenditure involved.

Assign *(v.)* അസൈൻ - ചുമതലപ്പെടുത്തുക
I was *assigned* the job of collecting funds.

Assist *(v.)* അസിസ്റ്റ്-സഹായിക്കുക, സഹകരിക്കുക
He *assisted* the blind man to cross the street.
(adj.) സഹായി
There are half a dozen *assistant* editors on the staff of that newspaper.
(n.) സഹായം
Can I be of any *assistance* to you?

Association *(n.)* അസോസിയേഷൻ - 1. സംഘടന, സമാജം, സ്ഥാപനം
They have formed an *association* called Friends of Freedom.
2. കൂട്ടുകെട്ട്, ചങ്ങാത്തം
He warned his son against *association* with bad boys.

Assume *(v.)* അസ്യൂം-1. ഊഹിക്കുക, സങ്കല്പിക്കുക
Why do you *assume* that you are never wrong?
2. സ്ഥാനാരോഹണം ചെയ്യുക, ഏറ്റെടുക്കുക
The prince *assumed* sovereign power on the death of the king.

Assure *(v.)* അഷ്വൂർ - ഉറപ്പു നൽകുക, വിശ്വസിപ്പിക്കുക
He *assured* me of his full co-operation.
(n.) ഉറപ്പ്
I give you my *assurance* that you will come to no harm.

Astonish *(v.)* അസ്റ്റോണിഷ് - അതിശയിക്കുകയോ, അതിശയിപ്പിക്കുകയോ ചെയ്യുക, അത്ഭുതപ്പെടുകയോ, അത്ഭുതപ്പെടുത്തുകയോ ചെയ്യുക
I was *astonished* to hear him say such a foolish thing.

Astrology *(n.)* അസ്ട്രോളജി-ജ്യോതിഷശാസ്ത്രം
Not everyone believes in *astrology.*

Astronomy *(n.)* അസ്ട്രോണമി-വാനശാസ്ത്രം
India is making huge progress in the field of *astronomy.*

Athlete *(n.)* അത്‌ലെറ്റ് - കായികതാരം
The college selected five *athletes* to participate in the race competition.

Atlas *(n.)* അറ്റ്ലസ് - ഭൂപടം
You cannot learn Geography without an *atlas.*

Atmosphere *(n.)* അറ്റ്മസ്ഫിയർ-അന്തരീക്ഷം
Pollution of the *atmosphere* becomes a serious problem in industrialised countries.

Atrocity *(n.)* അട്രോസിറ്റി - അതിക്രമം
The institute committed *atrocity* on the poor students by abolishing the scholarship.

Attach *(v.)* അറ്റാച്ച്-1. കോർക്കുക, ചേർക്കുക
Babu *attached* a nice new chain to his puppy's collar.
2. അടുപ്പമാകുക, സ്നേഹിക്കുക
Babu is very *attached* to his auntie.

Attack *(v.)* അറ്റാക്ക് - 1. ആക്രമിക്കുക, കയ്യേറ്റം നടത്തുക
The tiger *attacked* the deer.
2. അധിക്ഷേപിക്കുക
The newspapers *attacked* the new policy of the government.
(n.) ആക്രമണം
Attack is the best form of defence.
3. രോഗബാധ
He is recovering from an *attack* of 'flu'.

Attain *(v.)* അറ്റെയ്ൻ - നേടാൻ കഴിയുക
I *attained* success after strong efforts.

Attempt അറ്റെംറ്റ് - ശ്രമം (നടത്തുക), കൈവരിക്കുക
(n.) Deepak passed the tough examination at the first *attempt.*
(v.) Dilip *attempted* to climb the tall tree, but it was too steep.

Attend *(v.)* അറ്റെൻഡ് - 1. ഹാജരാകുക
Do you *attend* school regularly?
2. ശ്രദ്ധിക്കുക
Please *attend* to what I say.
3. പരിചരിക്കുക, സേവിക്കുക
This nurse has to *attend* to many patients.
(n.) സാന്നിദ്ധ്യം
Your teacher must certify your *attendance.*

Attendant *(n.)* അറ്റെൻഡന്റ് - ഭൃത്യൻ, പരിചാരകൻ

The *attendant* in the cinema hall showed me my seat.

Attention *(n.)* അറ്റൻഷൻ - 1. ശ്രദ്ധ, നിഷ്കർഷ

The huge gathering listened to the leader's speech with great *attention.*

2. അറ്റൻഷനായി നിൽക്കുക

The soldiers stood in *attention.*

(adv.) ശ്രദ്ധയോടെ

I listened *attentively* to what he had to say.

Attest *(v.)* അറ്റെസ്റ്റ് - സാക്ഷ്യപ്പെടുത്തുക

The copies of the documents need to be *attested* for admission.

Attire *(n.)* അറ്റയർ - വേഷവിധാനം

She looked beautiful in the bridal *attire.*

Attitude *(n.)* ആറ്റിറ്റ്യൂഡ് - സമീപനം, മനോഭാവം

The *attitude* of the society towards working women has changed a lot.

Attract *(v.)* അട്രാക്റ്റ് - ആകർഷിക്കുക, മോഹിപ്പിക്കുക

Nature *attracts* one and all.

(adj.) ആകർഷകമായ

She has *attractive* features.

(n.) ആകർഷണം

Movies have great *attraction* for the youth today.

Attribute *(v.)* ആറ്റ്റിബ്യൂട്ട് - ശ്രേയസ്സ് നൽകി

He *attributed* his success to hard work.

Auction ഓക്ഷൻ - ലേലം

(n.) The *auction* of the land is scheduled to take place next week.

(v.) The land was *auctioned* last week.

Audacity *(n.)* ആഡാസിറ്റി - ധിക്കാരം

He had the *audacity* to answer back to the teacher.

Audible *(adj.)* ആഡിബിൾ - കേൾക്കത്തക്ക

Her voice was hardly *audible.*

Audience *(n.)* ആഡിയൻസ് - സദസ്സ്

A good speaker always attracts a large *audience.*

Aunt *(n.)* ആൺട് - മാതുല, അമ്മായി, ചെറിയമ്മ, വല്യമ്മ

She has gone to stay with her *aunt* for a week.

Auspicious *(adj.)* ആസ്പിഷ്യസ് - സൗഭാഗ്യശാലി

Her birth was considered *auspicious* in the family.

Authentic *(adj.)* ഓഥെന്റിക് - ആധികാരികം, പ്രാമാണികം

This is an *authentic* M F Hussain painting.

Author *(n.)* ഓഥർ - ഗ്രന്ഥകർത്താവ്

A best-seller book makes its *author* famous.

Authority *(n.)* ഒഥോറിറ്റി - അധികാരം

In any company, the *authority* to sign cheques is normally given to trustworthy persons.

Automatic *(adj.)* ഓട്ടോമാറ്റിക് - സ്വയം പ്രവർത്തക

Automatic machines save us a lot of manual labour.

Available *(adj.)* അവെയ്‌ലബ്ൾ - ലഭ്യമായ, പ്രാപ്യമായ

For some days cooking oil was not *available* in the market.

Avalanche *(n.)* അവലാൻഷ് - ഹിമപ്രവാഹം

Mountaineers must always guard themselves against *avalanches.*

Avenue *(n.)* അവന്യൂ - നടപ്പാത, വഴി

New Delhi is full of tree-lined *avenues.*

Average ആവറേജ് - ശരാശരി, സാധാരണ, സാമാന്യ

(adj.) What is the *average* attendance in your class?

(n.) Your marks are below *average.*

Avoid *(v.)* അവോയ്ഡ് - 1. ഒഴിവാക്കുക, ഒഴിഞ്ഞുമാറുക

He tries to *avoid* me because he owes me some money.

2. രക്ഷപ്പെടുക

You should try to *avoid* catching a cold.

Await *(v.)* അവെയ്റ്റ് - പ്രതീക്ഷിക്കുക, കാത്തിരിക്കുക

The whole assembly *awaited* the chief guest's arrival.

Awake അവേക് - ഉണർന്നിരിക്കുക, ജാഗ്രത പാലിക്കുക

(adj.) Yesterday I was *awake* till midnight.

(v.) I was *awakened* by a loud noise.

Award അവാർഡ് - പുരസ്കാരം, സമ്മാനം (നൽകുക)

(*v.*) Rekha was *awarded* a stereo tape recorder for winning the first prize in music competition.

(*n.*) Our company has won an *award* for export promotion.

Aware (*adj.*) അവെയ്ർ - അറിവുാകുക

Satish was not *aware* that his sister would also accompany him to London.

Away (*adv.*) എവേ - പുറത്ത്, ദൂരെ, അകലെ

How long will he be *away?*

The child threw *away* the broken toy.

Awful (*adj.*) ഓവ്ഫുൾ - 1. ഭയാനകമായ

It was an *awful* sight to see the dead man lying in the middle of the road.

(*adv.*) 2. വളരെയേറെ

I am *awfully* sorry to have kept you waiting so long.

Awkward (*adj.*) ഓക്വർഡ് - ചമ്മൽ തോന്നുക

I feel *awkward* while facing a large audience.

(*adv.*) She got up *awkwardly* when caught cheating.

Axe (*n.*) ആക്സ് - കോടാലി, മഴു

The wood-cutter felled the tree with his *axe.*

Axle (*n.*) ആക്സിൽ - അച്ചുത്, കടയാണി

He met with an accident when the *axle* of his car suddenly broke down.

B

Baby (*n.*) ബേബി – കുഞ്ഞ്, ശിശു

She took her *baby* into the lap.

Bachelor (*n.*) ബാച്ചലർ – അവിവാഹിതൻ, കുമാരൻ

Bhishma Pitamah remained a *bachelor* all his life.

Back (*n.*) ബാക്ക്–1, മുതുക്, നടുവ്

There is a mole on my *back.*

2. പിൻവശം, പിന്നാമ്പുറം

The little boy had blotches of ink at the *back* of his hand.

He ran to the *back of the house.*

(*v.*) പിന്നോട്ടാവുക, പിന്നോട്ടെടുക്കുക

I *backed* my car before taking the turn.

(*adj.*) തിരികെ

The servant entered the house through the *back* door.

(*adv.*) 3. തിരികെ

Please come *back* quickly.

Backward (*adj.*) ബാക്ക്വർഡ്– പിന്നോക്കാവസ്ഥയിലുള്ള

Many of the Indian villages are still *backward* with no electricity.

Backwards (*adv.*) ബാക്ക്വർഡ് – പിന്നിലേക്ക്

On seeing the lion in the forest, everyone ran *backwards.*

Bad (*adj.*) ബാഡ് 1. ചീത്ത, മോശമായ

Do not keep company with *bad* boys.

2. കേട് വന്ന

We cannot eat this fish, as it has gone *bad.*

(*adv.*) 3. വളരെയേറെ, ഗുരുതരമായി

The driver was *badly* injured.

Badge (*n.*) ബാജ് – ബാഡ്ജ്, മുദ്ര

Every student is required to wear the school *badge.*

Baffle (*v.*) ബാഫ്ൾ–അത്ഭുതപ്പെടുത്തുക, അമ്പരപ്പിക്കുക

Students were *baffled* by the difficult question paper.

Bag (*n.*) ബാഗ് – 1. സഞ്ചി, ചാക്ക്, കെട്ട്

He put all the books in his school *bag.*

(*v.*) 2. നേടുക, കരസ്ഥമാക്കുക

Dinesh *bagged* the first prize in the essay competition.

Baggage (*n.*) ബാഗേജ്–ലഗേജ്, സാധനങ്ങൾ

I put all my *baggage* in the brake van.

Bail (*n.*) ബെയ്ൽ – ജാമ്യം

The accused was released on *bail.*

Bait (*n. & v.*) ബെയ്റ്റ്–പ്രലോഭിപ്പിക്കുക, ഇരയിടുക

(*n.*) He put a piece of cheese in the mouse-trap as a *bait.*

(*v.*) Rahul *baited* his hook to catch the fish.

Bake (*v.*) ബേക് - വേവിക്കുക, ബേക്ക് ചെയ്യുക

She *baked* bread for her family.

Balance (*v.*) ബാലൻസ്-1. സന്തുലനം പാലിക്കുക, ബാലൻസ് ചെയ്യുക

The acrobat *balanced* himself on the high rope.

2. ത്രാസ്, തുലാസ്

An honest shopkeeper keeps an accurate *balance.*

3. ബാക്കി തുക

I want to know the *balance* in my bank account.

Balcony (*n.*) ബാൽക്കണി - ബാൽക്കണി, മുൻവരാന്ത

We get a nice view of the sea from our *balcony.*

Bald (*adj.*) ബാൾഡ് - കഷണ്ടിയുള്ള, അനാവൃത അലങ്കാരരഹിത

Bald men have formed an organisation called Baldies International.

Bale (*n.*) ബെയ്ൽ - കെട്ട്, പിടി

Bales of cotton were lying in the compound of the textile mill.

Ball (*n.*) ബാൾ - 1. പന്ത്

The children were playing with a *ball.*

2. നൃത്തം

We were invited to a *ball.*

Balloon (*n.*) ബലൂൺ - ബലൂൺ

Children like to play with *balloons.*

Ballot (*n.& adj.*) ബാലറ്റ് - സമ്മതിദാനം, സമ്മതിപത്രം

(*adj.*) The election officer sealed the *ballot* papers after the voting was over.

(*n.*) The new chairman was chosen through a *ballot.*

Balm (*n.*) ബാം - ഔഷധം, ലേപനം

She applied *balm* on her forehead to get rid of headache.

Ban ബാൻ - നിരോധനം

(*n.*) The government put a *ban* on sale of liquor in the city.

(*v.*) The screening of the movie was *banned* in Gujarat.

Banana (*n.*) ബനാനാ - വാഴപ്പഴം

Eating *bananas* with milk is a nutritious breakfast.

Band (*n.*) ബാൻഡ്-1. ബാൻഡ്, വൃന്ദവാദ്യം

We had a big *band* at my sister's wedding.

2. സംഘം, സമൂഹം

A *band* of devoted workers helps in popularising a political party.

3. വളയം

The clerk put a rubber *band* round the file.

Bandage (*n.*) ബാൻഡേജ് - ബാൻഡേജ്, വച്ച്കെട്ട്

The doctor put a *bandage* round a wound on Deepak's foot.

Bandit (*n.*) ബാന്ഡിറ്റ് - കൊള്ളക്കാരൻ

Bandits live in forest.

Bang ബാംഗ്

1. ശക്തമായി അടിക്കുക

(*v.*) He angrily *banged* the table.

2. കോളിളക്കത്തോടെ

(*n.*) The Indian hockey team is back with a *bang.*

Bangle (*n.*) ബാംഗ്ൾ - വള

The bride was wearing *bangles* made of gold.

Banish (*n.*) ബാനിഷ് - നാട് കടത്തുക, പുറത്താക്കുക

The king *banished* his rebellious son from the kingdom.

Bank (*n.*) ബാങ്ക് - 1 ബാങ്ക്

It is safe to keep money in the *bank.*

2. തീരം, തടം, കര

I walked along the *bank* of the river.

(*n.*) 3. വിശ്വസിക്കുക

Can I *bank* upon your help?

Bankrupt ബാങ്ക്റപ്റ്റ് - പാപ്പരാവുക

(*n.*) His increasing losses and growing debts eventually made him *bankrupt.*

(*v.*) The increasing losses *bankrupted* him.

Banner (*n.*) ബാനർ-തോരണം, കൊടിക്കൂറ

During elections, *banners* of various political parties are seen everywhere.

Banquet *(n.)* ബാങ്ക്വറ്റ്–വിരുന്ന്, സല്ക്കാരം
The visiting head of state was given a grand *banquet.*

Bar *(n.)* ബാർ – 1. അഴി, കമ്പി
The wooden *bars* erected in a row divided the courtyard into two parts.
2. മദ്യശാല
Among the Indian middle class people, going to the *bar* daily is not considered good.
(v.) 3. തടയുക, നിരോധിക്കുക
The policeman *barred* the entry of traffic into the procession route.

Barbarous *(adj.)* ബാർബറസ് – ക്രൂരമായ, മൃഗീയമായ
In ancient times, *barbarous* customs like human sacrifice prevailed in our country.

Barber *(n.)* ബാർബർ–ക്ഷുരകൻ, ബാർബർ
I went to the *barber's* shop to have a haircut.

Bare *(adj.)* ബെയർ – നഗ്ന, അരക്ഷിത
The poor man walked bare foot in the hot sun.

Barely *(adv.)* ബെയർലി – പ്രയാസപ്പെട്ട്, ബുദ്ധിമുട്ടി
I could *barely* hear her voice from there.

Bargain ബാർഗെയ്ൻ – വിലപേശുക
(n.) For fifty rupees, this chair is a good *bargain.*
(v.) The customer *bargained* hard with the shopkeeper.

Barge ബാർജ്
1. പത്തേമാരി
(n.) We saw an ancient *barge* in the museum.
2. തള്ളിക്കയറുക
(v.) The thieves *barged* into the house at night.

Bark *(v.)* ബാർക് – 1 കുരയ്ക്കുക
My dog began to *bark* when it saw a stranger approaching our house.
(n.) 2. തോൽ, പട്ട
The *barks* of some trees have medicinal values.

Barn *(n.)* ബാൺ – കളപ്പുര, പത്തായപ്പുര
We have a huge *barn* in the village.

Baron *(n.)* ബാരൺ–പ്രഭു, മാടമ്പി, ശ്രീമാൻ
His father is a printing *baron.*

Barracks *(n.)* ബാരക്സ്–പാളയം, ബാരക്സ്
Soldiers live in *barracks.*

Barrel *(n.)* ബാരൽ – 1. കുഴൽ
The hunter pointed the *barrel* of his gun at the tiger.
2. വീപ്പ
He poured the oil into the *barrel.*

Barren *(adj.)* ബാരൻ–തരിശ്, പാഴ്, വന്ധ്യ
You cannot grow any crop in this *barren* land.
A *barren* woman cannot bear a child.

Barrier *(n.)* ബാരിയർ–പ്രതിബന്ധം, തടസ്സം, വേലി
The police put up a *barrier* to stop all cars.

Base *(n.)* ബേസ് – 1. അടിത്തട്ട്, അടിത്തറ
Some dirt was sticking to the *base* of the glass.
2. മോശമായ, ഹീനമായ
Even a good deed done with a *base* motive is not appreciable.

Basement *(n.)* ബേസ്മെന്റ് – അടിത്തളം
His house has a large *basement.*

Bash ബാഷ്
1. ശക്തമായി ഇടിക്കുക
(v.) He *bashed* his car in the tree.
2. ആഘോഷം
(n.) A huge birthday *bash* awaited me at home.

Basic *(adj.)* ബേസിക് – അടിസ്ഥാനം
I have gathered the *basic* information about the place.

Basics *(n.)* ബേസിക്–ബാലപാഠം, കാതൽ
For mastering any subject, it is important to understand the *basics* first.

Basin *(n.)* ബേസിൻ – താലം, ബേസിൻ
The doctor asked for hot water in the *basin.*

Basis ബേസിസ്

1. അടിസ്ഥാനം, ആധാരം

(n.) We improved the product on the *basis* of the feedback received from the customers.

2. നിഷ്ഠയായി

(n.) I play cricket on a regular *basis.*

Bask *(v.)* ബാസ്ക് - വെയിൽ കായുക

Basking in the winter sun is a soothing experience.

Basket *(n.)* ബാസ്കറ്റ് - കൂട, ബാസ്കറ്റ്

She put the flowers in a *basket.*

Bat *(n.)* ബാറ്റ് - 1. ബാറ്റ്

Rahul was presented a cricket *bat* by his father on his birthday.

2. വവ്വാൽ

Bats can fly at night.

Batch *(n.)* ബാച്ച് - സംഘം

A *batch* of doctors was sent to the area affected by the epidemic.

Bath *(n.)* ബാത്ത് - കുളി, സ്നാനം

I was taking a *bath* when he came to see me.

(v.) In summer, I *bathe* twice a day.

Baton *(n.)* ബാറ്റൺ - വടി, ലാത്തി

A policeman carrying a *baton* walked towards him.

Battalion *(n.)* ബറ്റാലിയൻ - സേനാദലം

The commander called another *battalion* for the war.

Batter *(n.)* ബാറ്റർ - അടിച്ച് തകർക്കുക, തല്ലിചതയ്ക്കുക

The angry crowd *battered* the hooligan with fists and kicks.

Battery *(n.)* ബാറ്ററി - 1. ബാറ്ററി

I put a new *battery* in my car.

2. പീരങ്കിപ്പട

They could not hold out before the enemy's *battery.*

Battle ബാറ്റിൽ - യുദ്ധം, പോര്

(n.) There was a fierce *battle* between the two armies.

(v.) Both the armies *battled* fiercely.

Be *(v.)* ബി - ആകുക

Don't *be* late for the meeting.

Beach *(n.)* ബീച്ച് - സമുദ്രതീരം, കടലോരം

Kerala has many lovely *beaches.*

Bead *(n.)* ബീഡ് - മണി

The girl wore a string of colourful *beads.*

Beak *(n.)* ബീക് - പക്ഷിയുടെ കൊക്ക്

The parrot has a curved *beak.*

Beam *(n.)* ബീം - 1. കിരണം, രശ്മി

The diamond sparkled in the *beams* of sunlight.

2. ഉത്തരം, തുലാത്ത്

The roof was supported by a thick *beam* in the centre.

Bean *(n.)* ബീൻ - തുവര, പയറ്

Among vegetables, i like French *beans* the most.

Bear *(n.)* ബെയർ - കരടി

There are white *bears* in Siberia.

(v.) 2. സഹിക്കുക

She could not *bear* the pain.

3. ജന്മം നൽകുക, വിളയിക്കുക

To *bear* children is a natural function of women.

Bearer *(n.)* ബെയറർ - സന്ദേശവാഹകൻ

Rehman received an urgent note from the *bearer* sent by his father.

2. വിളമ്പുകാരൻ, വെയിറ്റർ

Ramesh ordered the *bearer* to bring him a cup of coffee.

Beard *(n.)* ബിയർഡ് - താടി

Rabindranath Tagore had a flowing *beard.*

Beast *(n.)* ബീസ്റ്റ് - മൃഗം

Tiger is a ferocious *beast.*

Beat *(v.)* ബീറ്റ് - 1. അടിക്കുക, തല്ലുക

Some cruel masters *beat* their servants even on minor mistakes.

2. തോല്പിക്കുക

Our team was *beaten* in the match.

3. മിടിക്കുക

My heart was *beating* loudly before my result was announced.

Beautiful *(adj.)* ബ്യൂട്ടിഫുൾ-സുന്ദരം, മനോഹരം, കമനീയം

Beautiful girls mostly take modelling as a career.

Because ബികാസ്-കാരണം, എന്തെന്നാൽ

I did not go to work yesterday *because* I was not well.

Because of the rain, we could not go for a walk.

Beckon *(v.)* ബെക്കൺ–സൂചന നൽകുക, വിളിക്കുക

I *beckoned* the waiter to come to my table.

Become *(v.)* ബികം – 1. ആയിതീരുക

Mr. Rao *became* the headmaster last year.

2. ചമയുക, അലങ്കരിക്കുക

This sari *becomes* you.

Bed *(n.)* ബെഡ്–കിടക്ക, ശയ്യ

When did you go to *bed* last night?

Bee *(n.)* ബീ – തേനീച്ച

Bees gather nectar to produce honey.

Beef *(n.)* ബീഫ് – മാട്ടിറച്ചി

Hindus do not eat *beef.*

Beehive *(n.)* ബീഹൈവ്–തേനീച്ച കൂട്

The boy threw a stone at the *beehive.*

Beer *(n.)* ബീർ – ബിയർ

He ordered for a bottle of *beer.*

Beetle *(n.)* ബീറ്റിൽ – വ്

I saw many *beetles* in the garden.

Beetroot *(n.)* ബീറ്റ്റൂട്ട്, ബീറ്റ് കിഴങ്ങ്

We purchased some *beetroots* from the market.

Before *(adv.)* ബിഫോർ–1. മുമ്പ്, നേരത്തെ

Sunil reached office *before* time.

I have seen him *before,* but I cannot remember where.

2. എതിരെ, മുന്നിൽ

Ram stood *before* the house where he had lived twenty years ago.

Beg *(v.)* ബെഗ്–യാചിക്കുക

The hungry man *begged* for food.

2. അപേക്ഷിക്കുക

Uma *begged* her husband not to consume liquor.

3. അറിയാതെ തൊടുകയോ പറഞ്ഞത് കേൾക്കാതിരിക്കുകയോ ചെയ്യുമ്പോൾ

I *beg* your pardon.

Beggar *(n.)* ബെഗ്ഗർ – യാചകൻ

(n.) I met an old *beggar* at the stairs of the temple.

(n.) Beggary is a curse on humanity.

Begin *(v.)* ബിഗിൻ – തുടങ്ങുക

The meeting *began* half an hour late.

Behave *(v.)* ബിഹേവ് – പെരുമാറുക

Every mother teaches her children to *behave* properly.

(n.) Everyone praised Amit's courteous *behaviour.*

Behind *(adv.)* ബിഹൈൻഡ്–1. പുറകിൽ, പിന്നിൽ

The ball fell *behind* the wall.

2. വൈകി

The train was running *behind time.*

Being *(n.)* ബീയിംഗ് – പ്രാണി, ജീവി

We are all human *beings.*

Belief *(n.)* ബിലീഫ് – വിശ്വാസം

He is ready to sacrifice everything for the sake of his *beliefs.*

Believe *(v.)* ബിലീവ് – വിശ്വസിക്കുക

I strongly *believe* in the existence of God.

Belittle *(v.)* ബിലിറ്റിൽ–കൊച്ചാക്കുക, നിസ്സാരമാക്കുക, വിലയിടിക്കുക

By comparing to his own achievements, the father *belittled* the small success of his son.

Bell *(n.)* ബെൽ – മണി

There are many *bells* in the temple.

Bellow *(v.)* ബെല്ലോ – മുക്കറയിടുക, അലറുക

The bull *bellowed* because it was tied up.

Belly *(n.)* ബെല്ലി – വയറ്

These days she is exercising to get her *belly* in shape.

Belong *(v.)* ബിലോംഗ് – സ്വന്തമാക്കുക, അംഗമാകുക

This book *belongs* to me.

We *bolong* to the same club.

(n.) He put all his *belongings* in the room.

Beloved ബിലവഡ് – പ്രിയപ്പെട്ട, കാമുകി

(adj.) At last, I reached my *beloved* grandmother's place.

(n.) He introduced her as his *beloved.*

Below *(prep.)* ബിലോ – താഴെ

The boy hid the novel *below* the desk.

Some rich men think it is *below* their dignity to talk with the poor people.

Belt *(n.)* ബെൽറ്റ്–ബെൽറ്റ്, അരപ്പട്ട
Broad *belts* are in fashion among the young people.

Bench *(n.)* ബെഞ്ച് – ബെഞ്ച്, ഇരിപ്പടം
Many patients sat on the *bench* outside the doctor's cabin.

Bend ബെൻഡ് – കുനിയുക, വളയുക, വളയ്ക്കുക, തിരിവ്, വളവ്
(v.) It is not easy to *bend* a steel rod.
(n.) His house is round the *bend* on the main road.

Beneath ബിനീത്ത് – താഴെ, ചുവട്ടിൽ
(adv.) The mountaineer looked *beneath* from the top of the hill.
(prep.) The tired shepherd sat down to take rest *beneath* the tree.

Benefit ബെനിഫിറ്റ്–ലാഭം, നേട്ടം, പ്രയോജനപ്പെടുക, പ്രയോജനപ്പെടുത്തുക
(n.) His wise advice was of great *benefit* to me.
(v.) I *benefited* greatly from his advice.

Benevolent *(adj.)* ബെനവലന്റ് – ദയാലു, ധർമ്മിഷ്ഠൻ
God is believed to be very *benevolent.*

Berserk *(adj.)* ബെർസെർക്–ക്രോധോന്മത്തനാകുക
When the team did not win the match, the coach went *berserk.*

Berth*(n.)* ബെർത്ത് – 1. ബെർത്ത്
I reserved a *berth* on the night train.
2. നങ്കുരമടിക്കുക
The huge ship by the *berth* was an oil tanker.

Beside *(prep.)* ബിസൈഡ്–അടുത്ത്, അരികെ
He stood *beside* his brother.

Besides *(prep.)* ബിസൈഡ്സ് – ഇതല്ലാതെ, പുറമെ, കൂടാതെ
Besides your raincoat, you should also bring an umbrella.

Best *(adj.)* ബെസ്റ്റ്–സർവ്വോത്തമം, ഏറ്റവും മികച്ചത്
It is *best* to consider various aspects before starting a new venture.

Bestow *(v.)* ബെസ്റ്റോ–സമർപ്പിക്കുക, സമ്മാനിക്കുക
The title of Padma Shri is *bestowed* by the president.

Bestseller *(n.)* ബെസ്റ്റ്സെല്ലർ – ചുടപ്പം പോലെ വിറ്റഴിയുന്ന പുസ്തകം
All her novels have turned out to be *bestsellers.*

Bet ബെറ്റ് – വാതുവയ്ക്കുക
(v.) I *bet* you'll miss the flight.
(n.) My *bet* is that you'll miss the flight.

Better *(adj.)* ബെറ്റർ–താരതമ്യേന മികച്ചത്
His performance in the second match was *better* than that in the first match.

Betray *(v.)* ബിട്രേ–വഞ്ചിക്കുക, ചതിക്കുക
Jesus Christ was *betrayed* by one of his disciples.

Between *(prep.)* ബിട്വീൻ–ഇടയ്ക്ക്, മദ്ധ്യേ
She divided the sweets *between* her two sons.
(adv.) Please see me *between* two and three o'clock.

Beverage *(n.)* ബിവറേജ് – പാനീയം
We need to decide upon the food and *beverage* for the party.

Beware *(v.)* ബിവെയർ – സൂക്ഷിക്കുക, കരുതലോടെയിരിക്കുക.
Beware of pick-pockets.

Bewilder *(v.)* ബിവിൽഡെർ –അമ്പരക്കുക, അന്ധാളിക്കുക
He was *bewildered* to see the sudden change in her mood.

Bewitch *(v.)* ബിവിച്ച് – മോഹിപ്പിക്കുക
The beautiful interiors of the building *bewitched* us.

Beyond *(prep.)* ബിയോ് – അപ്പുറം
There was a temple *beyond* the mountains.

Bias ബയാസ് – പക്ഷപാതം
(n.) A *bias* against aged workers is visible in most of the companies.
(v.) His opinion about the best cricket player was *biased* towards Yuvraj Singh.

Bid *(v.)* ബിഡ്–ലേലത്തിൽ പിടിക്കുക
Our company is also *bidding* for the land to be auctioned.

Big *(adj.)* ബിഗ് – വലിയ, വലിപ്പമുള്ള
They bought a *big* cake for their son's birthday.

Bill *(n.)* ബിൽ – 1. ബിൽ
The shopkeeper gave me the *bill* and I paid the money.

2. കൊക്ക്
A stork has a long *bill.*

Billion *(number)* ബില്യൺ – നൂറ് കോടി
Hinduism has about one *billion* followers all over the world.

Billow *(n.)* ബില്ലോ – തിരമാല
As the force of the tempest grew, the ocean became a mass of roaring *billows.*

Bin *(n.)* ബിൻ – ചവറ്റുകൊട്ട, കൂട
I threw the scraps of paper into the dust *bin.*

Bind *(v.)* ബൈൻഡ് – കൂട്ടികെട്ടുക
After the thief was caught, the policemen *bound* him with a rope.

Binoculars *(n.)* ബൈനോക്കുലേർസ് – ഭൂതക്കണ്ണാടി
The sailor looked through his *binoculars* to find the seashore.

Biography *(n)* ബയോഗ്രഫി–ജീവിത ചരിത്രം
I enjoyed reading the *biography* of Kishore Kumar.

Bird *(n.)* ബേർഡ് – പക്ഷി, കിളി
Birds lay eggs in the nests.

Birth *(n.)* ബെർത്ത് – ജനനം
Mrs. Kapur gave *birth* to a son this morning.

Bit *(n.)* ബിറ്റ് – തു്, കഷണം
The glass was broken into many *bits.*

Bitter *(adj.)* ബിറ്റർ – 1. കയ്പുള്ള
This medicine is very *bitter.*
2. ദുഃഖം തോന്നുക, വിഷമിക്കുക
The servant was *bitter* about the rude behaviour of his cruel master.

Black *(adj.)* ബ്ലാക്ക് – കറുത്ത
Please give me a bottle of *black* ink.

Blade *(n.)* ബ്ലേഡ് – 1. ബ്ലേഡ്
This knife has a sharp *blade.*
2. ഇല, ദലം
Not even a *blade* of grass grows in this field.

Blame ബ്ലെയിം – കുറ്റം (ചാർത്തുക) ദോഷം (ആരോപിക്കുക)
(v.) The bus driver was *blamed* for the accident.
(n.) Everybody put the *blame* on him.

Blank *(adj.)* ബ്ലാങ്ക്–ഒന്നും എഴുതാത്ത, കാലി
She took out a *blank* sheet of paper to write.

Blanket *(n.)* ബ്ലാങ്കറ്റ് – പുതപ്പ്, കമ്പിളി
As winter is nearing, I must buy a *blanket.*

Blare *(v.)* ബ്ലെയർ–ഗർജ്ജിക്കുക, മുഴക്കുക, ഒച്ചയിടുക
During the traffic jam, the car horns *blared* full blast.

Blast *(n.)* ബ്ലാസ്റ്റ്–1. സ്ഫോടനം, പൊട്ടിത്തെറി
The *blast* of the motorist's horn startled the pedestrian.
The *blast* of the explosion shook the whole building.
2. ആഞ്ഞ് വീശൽ
As Arun opened the door, he was thrown back by a *blast* of wind.
(v.) പൊട്ടിത്തെറിക്കുക
A bomb *blasted* in the market this morning.

Blaze *(n.)* ബ്ലേസ്–തിളക്കം, പ്രകാശം, ജ്വാല
The decorated hall was a *blaze* of light.
(v.) The bonfire *blazed* brightly in the dark winter night.

Blazer *(n.)* ബ്ലേസർ – ജായ്ക്കറ്റ്
All the members of the cricket team wore *blazers.*

Bleach *(v.)* ബ്ലീച്ച് – വെളുപ്പിക്കുക
Ladies with a dark complexion often *bleach* their skin to look fair.

Bleak *(adj.)* ബ്ലീക്ക് – തണുത്ത, വിളറിയ
A *bleak* wind blew over the mountain top.
Geeta's *bleak* face indicated that something was wrong with her.

Bleary *(adj.)* ബ്ലിയറി – തളർന്ന് ചുവന്ന കണ്ണുകളോടെ
He looked *bleary*-eyed after drinking.

Bleat *(v.)* ബ്ലീറ്റ്–ആടിനെപ്പോലെ കരയുക
The sheep *bleated* in the field.

Bleed *(v.)* ബ്ലീഡ് – രക്തം വാർന്ന
His wound was *bleeding.*

Blemish ബ്ലെമിഷ്–പാട്, കല
(n.) The pimple left a *blemish* on her face.

(v.) The politician's corrupt behaviour *blemished* the image of the party.

Blend ബ്ലെൻഡ്-മിശ്രണം, കലർപ്പ്, കലർത്തുക

(n.) In the evening, the sky appeared a beautiful *blend* of colours.

(v.) The painter *blended* the colours before starting to paint.

Bless *(v.)* ബ്ലെസ്സ്-അനുഗ്രഹിക്കുക, അനുഗ്രഹം

The temple priest *blessed* the devotees.

(n.) Adversity can prove a *blessing* in disguise.

Blind *(adj.)* ബ്ലൈൻഡ്-അന്ധ, ബുദ്ധിഹീന

She felt pity for the *blind* beggar.

(n.) തട്ടി

She pulled down the *blinds* to avoid the light.

Blink *(v.)* ബ്ലിങ്ക് - കണ്ണ് ചിമ്മുക

The strong light made him *blink.*

Blister *(n.)* ബ്ലിസ്റ്റർ - കുരു, പരു

The intense heat caused *blisters* on the baby's tender skin.

(v.) The boiling water fell on Amit's hand and *blistered* it.

Bloated *(adj.)* ബ്ലോറ്റഡ് - വീർക്കുക

He felt *bloated* after the heavy lunch.

Block *(n.)* ബ്ലോക്ക് - ഇഷ്ടിക, കട്ട

This house was built with the *blocks* of cement.

2. ഒരു വലിയ കെട്ടിടത്തിന്റെ ഭാഗം

I have rented a three-room *block.*

(v.) 3. തടുക്കുക, പ്രതിബന്ധം സൃഷ്ടിക്കുക

The demonstrators *blocked* the road.

Blonde *(n.)* ബ്ലോണ്ട് - ചാരനിറമുള്ള മുടിയും പിംഗല വർണ്ണവുമുള്ള

It is rare to come across a *blonde* in India.

Blood *(n.)* ബ്ലഡ് - രക്തം, ചോര

It is a misconception that healthy persons become weak after donating *blood.*

Bloom ബ്ലൂം - പുഷ്പിക്കുക, പൂക്കാലം

(v.) Many flowers *bloom* in my garden.

(n.) The *blooms* of this plant wilt in the evening.

Blossom ബ്ലോസം - മുകുളം, വിരിക്കുക

(n.) I saw a new *blossom* in the rose plant.

(v.) The rose plant is *blossoming.*

Blot *(n.)* ബ്ലോട്ട് - കറ, പാട്, കളങ്കം

There was a large *blot* of ink on the clean sheet of paper.

Ram's misconduct is a *blot* on the fair name of his family.

(v.) Ram's behaviour has *blotted* the good image of his parents.

Blotch *(n.)* ബ്ലോച്ച് - നേർത്ത പാട്

Sweat left *blotches* on his shirt.

Blouse *(n.)* ബ്ലൗസ് - ബ്ലൗസ്

She stitched a matching *blouse* for her new sari.

Blow *(n.)* ബ്ലോ - 1. പ്രഹരം, തല്ല്, അടി

They had a fight and exchanged *blows.*

(v.) 2. വീശുക, ഊതുക (ഊതി കൊടുത്തുക

Cool air was *blowing* gently.

Please *blow* out (extinguish) the candle.

Terrorists *blew* up (destroyed) the bridge with dynamite.

Blue *(adj.)* ബ്ലൂ - നീല

Blue is my favourite colour.

Blunder *(n.)* ബ്ലർ-അബദ്ധം, കടുത്ത തെറ്റ്

Your refusal to go with him was a *blunder* for yourself.

(v.) You have *blundered* by agreeing to lend him the money.

Blunt *(adj.)* ബ്ല് 1. മൂർച്ചയില്ലാത്ത

This knife is of no use, its edge is *blunt.*

2. കർക്കശമായ, പരുത്ത

Your *blunt* speech hurt his feelings.

Blur *(v.)* ബ്ലർ-മങ്ങൽ ഏൽപ്പിക്കുക

The dust storm *blurred* my vision.

Blurt *(v.)* ബ്ലർട്ട്-ആലോചിക്കാതെ പറയുക

She suddenly *blurted* out the secret she did not want to reveal.

Blush *(v.)* ബ്ലഷ്-നാണിക്കുക, ലജ്ജിക്കുക

She *blushed* at the sight of her lover.

Boar *(n.)* ബോർ – കാട്ടുപന്നി
The hunter killed a wild *boar.*

Board *(n.)* ബോർഡ് – പലക
That wooden house has walls made of *boards.*
(v.) 2. കയറുക, സവാരി ചെയ്യുക
The train started only a couple of minutes after he *boarded* it.
3. വില നൽകി വാങ്ങുന്ന ഭക്ഷണം
What does your hotel charge for bed and *board* ?

Boast ബോസ്റ്റ് – വീമ്പിളക്കുക, വമ്പ് പറയുക
(v.) One should never *boast* of one's accomplishments.
(n.) His *boast* that he could fight with a lion impressed nobody.

Boat *(n.)* ബോട്ട് – വഞ്ചി, നൗക
He went to England by *boat.*

Body ബോഡി – ശരീരം, ഉടൽ, വ്യക്തി
The police found the dead *body* of a man in the lake.
Somobody (some person) informed the police about the road accident.

Bog *(n.)* ബോഗ് – ചതുപ്പ് നിലം
The wild buffalo got stuck in the *bog.*

Bogus *(adj.)* ബോഗസ് – വ്യാജ, കപട
These papers are not original, but *bogus.*

Boil *(v.)* ബോയിൽ – 1. തിളപ്പിക്കുക, ക്ഷോഭിക്കുക
She *boiled* the milk.
(n.) 2. പരു, കുരു
He has a big *boil* on his arm.

Bold *(adj.)* ബോൾഡ് – നിർഭയ, ധീര
The *bold* man refused to tell a lie to save himself.
(adv.) The young man *boldly* faced the angry bull.

Bolster *(v.)* ബോൾസ്റ്റെർ–താങ്ങ് നൽകുക
He sweet smile *bolstered* his sagging spirits.

Bolt *(v.&n.)* ബോൾട്ട് – 1. സാക്ഷ (ഇടുക, ഓടാമ്പൽ
(v.) Did you *bolt* the door?
(n.) After closing the door, he slipped the *bolt* in the place.
2. അമ്പ് പോലെ പായുക
The horse *bolted* down the lane.

Bomb ബോംബ് – ബോംബ്, ബോംബിടുക
(n.) A *bomb* exploded and killed two persons on the spot.
(v.) The air force planes *bombed* the enemy's camps.

Bond ബോ – ബന്ധം, ചേർച്ച
(n.) They share an emotional *bond* between themselves.
(v.) I always *bonded* well with her.

Bone *(n.)* ബോൺ – എല്ല്, അസ്ഥി
The broken *bones* of his leg took a long time to heal.

Bonfire *(n.)* ബോൺഫയർ – ഉത്സവാഗ്നി
The children danced happily round the *bonfire* for a long time.

Bonnet *(n.)* ബോണറ്റ് – 1. മൂടി, ബോണറ്റ്
He opened the *bonnet* of his car.
2. തൊപ്പി
Western ladies wear *bonnets* to protect their head.

Bonus *(n.)* ബോണസ്–അധിക ലാഭാംശം, ബോണസ്
Our employers are good paymasters, and flexible working hours are an added *bonus.*

Bony *(adj.)* ബോണി – മെലിഞ്ഞ, എല്ലും തോലുമായ
The small *bony* child begged for food.

Book *(n.)* ബുക്ക് – 1. പുസ്തകം, ഗ്രന്ഥം
This is an interesting *book.*
(v.) 2. ടിക്കറ്റെടുക്കുക
I have *booked* a ticket for the evening show.
Have you *booked* your ticket for Mumbai?

Boom *(n.)* ബൂം – കുതിച്ചുകയറ്റം
Last month, there was a major *boom* in the stock market.

Boon *(n.)* ബൂൺ – വരം, വരദാനം
Working with like-minded and experienced people proved to be a *boon.*

Boot *(n.)* ബൂട്ട് – 1. ചെരുപ്പ്, ബൂട്ട്
Soldiers wear heavy *boots.*
2. ഡിക്കി, അറ
He put the bag in the *boot* of his car.

Booth *(n.)* ബൂത്ത് – കൊട്ടിൽ, ബൂത്ത്
Voters crowded the voting *booth.*

Booty *(n.)* ബൂട്ടി – കൊള്ള മുതൽ
The robbers shared the *booty* among themselves.

Border *(n.)* ബോർഡർ – 1. അതിർത്തി
The *border* between the two countries is heavily guarded.
2. തീരം, കര
She wore a yellow sari with a black *border.*

Bore *(v.)* ബോർ–1. തുളയിടുക, കുഴിക്കുക
It is necessary to *bore* deep holes in the earth to find petroleum.
(n.) 2. ബോറൻ, മുഷിപ്പൻ, വിരസൻ
Everybody avoids a *bore.*
3. തുള, ദ്വാരം
He drilled a deep *bore* in the ground.

Born ബോൺ – ജനിക്കുക അനുഗ്രഹീത
(v.) I was *born* in Delhi.
(adj.) He is a *born* athlete.

Borrow *(v.)* ബോറോ – കടമെടുക്കുക
May I *borrow* your pen for a few minutes?

Boss ബോസ്സ് – ഉടമ, മേലാൾ
(n.) Her *boss* was irritated when she could not complete the project on time.
(v.) No one likes to be *bossed* around.
(adj.) Stop behaving so *bossy.*

Both *(adj.)* ബോത്ത് – ഇരുവരും
Both my brothers are elder than me.
I put *both* the apples on the table.
(prep.) Both of us are going.

Bother *(v.)* ബോദർ – ശല്യം ചെയ്യുക, വിഷമിപ്പിക്കുക
Please do not *bother* me when I am working.
Please do not *bother* to come personally.

Bottle *(n.)* ബോട്ടിൽ – കുപ്പി
He poured the milk from the *bottle* into the pot.

Bottom *(v.)* ബോട്ടം – അടിത്തട്ട്
The ship sank to the *bottom* of the sea.

Bough *(n.)* ബൗ – ശാഖ, കൊമ്പ്
The *bough* of the tree was laden with fruits.

Boulder *(n.)* ബോൾഡർ – ഉരുളൻ പാറ
The seashore was strewn with *boulders.*

Bounce *(v.)* ബൗൺസ്–1. തട്ടിതിരിച്ച് വരുക, കുതിച്ച് പൊങ്ങുക.
The ball *bounced* back after hitting the wall.
2. (ചെക്ക്) തിരിച്ചുവരുക
The cheque *bounced* as there was not enough money in the account.

Bound *(v.)* ബൗ – 1. പിന്തുടർന്നോടുക
The dog *bounded* after the rabbit.
2. അതിർത്തി, പരിധി
This area is out of *bounds* for civilians.
(adj.) തീർച്ചയായും
He is *bound* to win the race.

Boundary *(n.)* ബൗറി – അതിർത്തി
The river is the *boundary* between the two countries.

Bouquet *(n.)* ബൊക്കെ – പൂച്ചെ്
He presented her with a lovely *bouquet.*

Bow *(n.)* ബോ – വില്ല്
Arjun attached an arrow to his *bow.*
2. റിബ്ബൺ കെട്ടുക
She tied the ribbon into a *bow.*
(v.) തലകുനിക്കുക, തൊഴുക
He *bowed* respectfully to the old man.
(n.) The servant welcomed his master with a *bow.*

Bowl *(v.)* ബൗൾ – 1. ഔട്ടാക്കുക
The batsman was *bowled* out.
(n.) 2. കിണ്ണം
She poured some milk in a *bowl* for her cat.

Box *(n.)* ബോക്സ് – 1. പെട്ടി
Tinku put his toys in a *box.*
2. മുഷ്ഠിയുദ്ധം, ഇടിക്കുക
(v.) He *boxed* his opponent.

Boy *(n.)* ബോയ് – കുട്ടി, ബാലൻ
How many *boys* are there in your class?

Boycott *(v.)* ബോയ്കോട്ട്-ബഹിഷ്കരിക്കുക
Opposition *boycotted* the proposal of the ruling party.

Brace ബ്രേസ്-പല്ല് കെട്ടുന്നതിനുള്ള കമ്പി
(n.) The use of *braces* shaped his teeth.
2. ഏത് അവസ്ഥയും നേരിടാൻ ഒരുങ്ങുക
(v.) Brace yourself for a termination.

Bracelet *(n.)* ബ്രേസ്‌ലെറ്റ് - വള, കങ്കണം
Anil presented a *bracelet* to Neera on her birthday.

Bracket *(n.)* ബ്രാക്കറ്റ് - 1. ആവരണ ചിഹ്നം, ബ്രാക്കറ്റ്
The meanings to the foreign words are given in the *brackets.*
2. വർഗ്ഗം
Editors too come in the *bracket* of journalists.
3. *(v.)* ഒരു വർഗ്ഗത്തിൽ വയ്ക്കുക
A number of problems are *bracketed* together with working in night shifts.

Brag *(v.)* ബ്രാഗ്-വമ്പ് പറയുക, വീമ്പിളക്കുക
Stop *bragging* about your high contacts.

Braid *(n.)* ബ്രെയിഡ് - പിന്നുക
She coiled her hair into a *braid.*

Brain *(n.)* ബ്രെയിൻ - തലച്ചോറ്, ബുദ്ധി
Arun used his *brains* to solve a complex Maths problem.

Brainchild *(n.)* ബ്രെയിൻചൈൽഡ് - സൃഷ്ടി, രചന
This book is a *brainchild* of a famous painter.

Brainstorm ബ്രെയിൻ സ്റ്റോം - തല പുണ്ണാക്കുക, ഗാഢമായി ചിന്തിക്കുക
(n.) We had a *brainstorm* for so long, but could not find a solution to the problem.
(v.) We *brainstormed* a lot, but could not find a solution.

Brainwash *(v.)* ബ്രെയിൻ വാഷ് - മനം മാറ്റുക
His friends *brainwashed* him into taking Science instead of Commerce.

Brake *(n.)* ബ്രേക്ക് - 1. ബ്രേക്ക്, നിർത്തുക
He applied the *brake* to stop the car when he saw a pit in the middle of the road.
2. തീവിയിൽ സാധനങ്ങൾ വയ്ക്കാനുള്ള അറ
I put all my luggage in the *brake* van.

Bramble *(n.)* ബ്രാമ്പ്ൾ - മുൾച്ചെടി
This area is full of *brambles.*

Branch *(n.)* ബ്രാഞ്ച് - ശാഖ, കൊമ്പ്
The nimble boy climbed a high *branch* of the tree.
The big banks have *branches* in all major cities and towns.

Brand ബ്രാൻഡ് - 1. വ്യാപാര മുദ്ര
(n.) Which *brand* of toothpaste do you use?
(adj.) 2. ഏറ്റവും പുതിയ, പുതുപുത്തൻ
Today he came to office in a *brand* new car.

Brass *(n.)* ബ്രാസ്സ് - പിത്തള
Indian housewives use utensils of *brass.*

Brave *(adj.)* ബ്രേവ് - ധീര, സാഹസിക
The *brave* man fought with the tiger without a weapon.

Brawl *(n.)* ബ്രാൾ-കലഹം, വഴക്ക്
Children had a *brawl* while playing.

Breach *(n.)* ബ്രീച്ച് - 1. ലംഘനം
The company fired him on the grounds of *breach* of confidence.
2. വിടവ്
Hunger for power created a *breach* between the politician brothers.
(v.) 3. നിയമം അല്ലെങ്കിൽ ഒത്തുതീർപ്പിന്റെ ലംഘനം
I do not intend to *breach* the contract in the middle.

Bread *(n.)* ബ്രെഡ്-റൊട്ടി, ഉപജീവന മാർഗ്ഗം
I eat *bread* and butter for breakfast.
Labourers toil whole day to earn their *bread.*

Breadth *(n.)* ബ്രെഡ്ത് - വീതി
Area is defined as length into *breadth.*

Break *(v.)* ബ്രേക്ക്-പൊട്ടിക്കുക, തകർക്കുക
The boy *broke* the window-pane with a stone. Fire *broke out* (suddenly started) in the kitchen of the house.
The thieves *broke into* (forcibly entered) the house at night.
Arun's car *broke down* (stopped working) when he was about to reach his office.

(n.) പഠിത്തം അല്ലെങ്കിൽ ജോലിക്കിടയ്ക്കുള്ള വിരാമം

School children came out to play during the *break.*

Breakfast *(n.)* ബ്രേക്ക്ഫാസ്റ്റ് – പ്രാതൽ

According to some dieticians, *breakfast* is the most important meal of the day.

Breakthrough *(n.)* ബ്രേക്ക്ത്രൂ – മുന്നേറ്റം

Introduction of colour was a major *breakthrough* in cinema.

Breath *(v.)* ബ്രീഥ് – ശ്വാസം

The swimmer took a deep *breath* and plunged into the water.

Breathe *(v.)* ബ്രീത്ത് – ശ്വാസമെടുക്കുക

He was finding it difficult to *breathe.*

Breed *(n.)* ബ്രീഡ് – 1. ജനുസ്സ്, ഇനം

Dobberman is a *breed* of dogs.

(v.) 2. പെറ്റ് പെരുകുക

Mosquitoes *breed* and multiply very fast.

(n.) 3. ജന്മം

He is a man of noble *breeding.*

Breeze *(n.)* ബ്രീസ് – ഇളം കാറ്റ്

He sat in the garden to enjoy the cool *breeze.*

Brevity *(n.)* ബ്രെവിറ്റി–സംഗ്രഹത, ക്ഷണികത്വം

Brevity is the soul of wit.

Bribe *(n. & v.)* ബ്രൈബ്–കൈക്കൂലി, കോഴ (നൽകുക)

(n.) Never give or take a *bribe.*

The clerk was arrested on a charge of *bribery.*

(v.) He *bribed* the clerk to get his work done.

Brick *(n.)* ബ്രിക് – ഇഷ്ടിക

Houses are built with *bricks.*

Bride *(n.)* ബ്രൈഡ് – വധു, മണവാട്ടി

The *bride* wore a gorgeous sari.

Bridge *(n. & v.)* ബ്രിഡ്ജ്–പാലം, അകലം (ഇല്ലാതാക്കുക)

(n.) There are many *bridges* across the Yamuna in Delhi.

(v.) It is difficult to *bridge* the gap between the rich and the poor.

Bridegroom *(n.)* ബ്രൈഡ്ഗ്രൂം – വരൻ

The bridegroom was dressed in a *sherwani* at the wedding.

Bridle *(n. & v.)* ബ്രൈഡ്ൽ – കടിഞ്ഞാൺ, ലഗാൻ

(n.) You cannot control a horse without a *bridle.*

(v.) He *bridled* his horse and started on his journey.

Brief *(adj.)* ബ്രീഫ്–സംക്ഷിപ്ത, ചുരുങ്ങിയ

He gave me a *brief* account of the accident.

Brigade *(n.)* ബ്രിഗേഡ് – ബ്രിഗേഡ്, സേനാ സമൂഹം

The fire *brigade* was called to put out the fire in the cinema hall.

Bright *(adj.)* ബ്രൈറ്റ് – തിളക്കമുള്ള, ജ്വലിക്കുന്ന, സമർത്ഥൻ

A *bright* light was shining in the room.

Children like toys of *bright* colours.

He is one of the *bright* boys in the class.

Brilliant *(adj.)* ബ്രില്ലിയന്റ്–പ്രകാശമുള്ള, പ്രാവീണ്യമുള്ള

We should wear goggles to protect our eyes from the *brilliant* sunlight.

Neeraj is a *brilliant* student.

Brim *(n.)* ബ്രിം – 1. അറ്റം, വക്ക്

The glass was full to the *brim* with tea.

2. തൊപ്പിയുടെ കീഴറ്റം

He pulled down the *brim* of his hat.

Bring *(v.)* ബ്രിംഗ് – കൊുവരിക

Please *bring* me a glass of water.

Brink *(n.)* ബ്രിങ്ക് – അരിക്, അറ്റം

The mountaineer went to the *brink* of the cliff and looked down.

Brisk *(adj.)* ബ്രിസ്ക് – ചുറുചുറുക്കുള്ള, തകൃതിയായി

Property business is *brisk* these days.

Bristle *(n.)* ബ്രിസ്റ്റ്ലെ – ഇഴനാര്

My toothbrush is made of plastic *bristles.*

Brittle *(adj.)* ബ്രിറ്റ്ൽ – എളുപ്പത്തിൽ പൊട്ടുന്ന

Glass is a *brittle* substance.

Broad *(adj.)* ബ്രോഡ്–വീതിയുള്ള വിസ്തൃതമായ

In Old Delhi, it is rare to find a *broad* avenue.

Broadcast *(n.)* ബ്രോഡ്കാസ്റ്റ്–പ്രക്ഷേപണം, റേഡിയോ പ്രോഗ്രാം

I heard the news in the morning *broadcast.*

(v.) AIR *broadcasts* a running commentary of the Rupublic Day Parade.

Broadly *(adv.)* ബ്രോഡ്‌ലി-വിശാലമായി, പൊതുവേ

I will explain you the situation *broadly.*

Broad-minded *(adj.)* ബ്രോഡ്-മൈൻഡഡ്- വിശാല മനസ്ഥിതി

Today parents do not mind their daughters travelling alone; they have become *broad-minded.*

Brochure *(n.)* ബ്രോഷർ - ലഘുലേഖ

Get me the *brochures* of the companies.

Broker *(n.)* ബ്രോക്കർ - ദല്ലാൾ

I called the *broker* to know about some good investment plans.

Brooch *(n.)* ബ്രോച്ച് - പതക്കം

She pinned a diamond *brooch* on her blouse.

Brood *(v.)* ബ്രൂഡ് - ആലോചിക്കുക, ചിന്തിക്കുക

Why are you *brooding* over the past?

(n.) 2. കുട്ടികൾ, സന്താനം

The mother goose waddled across the street with her *brood.*

Brook *(n.)* ബ്രൂത്ത്-1. ചെറു നദി, കൈവഴി

Some rivers are fed by many *brooks.*

(v.) 2. സഹിക്കുക, ക്ഷമിക്കുക

He *brooks* no interference in his work.

Broom *(n.)* ബ്രൂം - ചൂൽ, തുറപ്പ

The municipal sweepers were given new *brooms.*

Brother *(n.)* ബ്രദർ - സഹോദരൻ

How many *brothers* do you have?

Brow *(n.)* ബ്രോ - പുരികം

He has thick eye-*brows.*

Brown *(adj.)* ബ്രൗൺ - തവിട്ട്

Brown is my favourite colour.

Browse *(v.)* ബ്രൗസ്

1. കറങ്ങുക, സമയം, ചെലവിടുക

I *browsed* in the bookshop for half an hour.

2. ഓടിച്ചുനോക്കുക

I *browsed* the Internet for information on latest cars.

Bruise*(v.&n.)* ബ്രൂസ്-മുറിവ്, പരിക്ക്പറ്റുക

(v.) I *bruised* my leg when I fell down.

(n.) My *bruise* is not healing.

Brush ബ്രഷ് - ബ്രഷ്

(n.) I have lost my tooth-*brush.*

(v.) We should *brush* our teeth regularly.

Brute *(n.)* ബ്രൂട്ട് - മൃഗം

The big *brute* rushed towards us.

(adj.) He is notorious for his *brutal* behaviour.

Bubble *(n.&v.)* ബബ്ൾ-കുമിള, തുളുമ്പുക

(n.) Children are fond of blowing soap *bubbles.*

Bubbles rose on the boiling water.

(v.) The bride *bubbled* with happiness on the wedding day.

Bucket *(n.)* ബക്കറ്റ് - തൊട്ടി

Please bring me a *bucket* of hot water.

Buckle *(n.)* ബക്ക്ൾ-കൊളുത്ത്, ബക്ക്ൾ

(n.) He bought a fashionable new *buckle* for his belt.

(v.) He *buckled* his shoes and left for work.

Bud *(n.)* ബഡ് - മുകുളം, മൊട്ട്

These *buds* will bloom by tomorrow morning.

Budge *(v.)* ബജ്-അനങ്ങുക, തിരിയുക

She *budged* a little and slept again.

Budget ബജറ്റ് - ബഡ്ജറ്റ്, അടങ്കൽ

(n.) We might go over-*budget* in this project.

(v.) The government *budgeted* a huge amount for an amusement park.

Buffalo *(n.)* ബഫലോ - എരുമ

In India, we normally drink the milk of *buffalo.*

Buffet ബുഫേ-1. സ്വയം ആഹാരം എടുത്തു കഴിക്കുന്ന വിരുന്ന്

(n.) We will follow *buffet* system in the party.

2. ബഫിറ്റ് - ഇടിക്കുക

(v.) The car was *buffeted* by the truck.

Bug *(n.)* ബഗ് - മൂട്ട

I could not sleep last night because of *bugs.*

Bugle *(n.)* ബ്യൂഗ്ൾ - ബ്യൂഗ്ൾ, കാഹളം
At the call of the *bugle,* the soldiers hurried out of their barracks.

Build *(v.)* ബിൽഡ്-പണിയുക, നിർമ്മിക്കുക
When are you going to *build* your own house?

Bulb *(n.)* ബൾബ്-ബൾബ്, ഗോളം, കിഴങ്ങ്
There was just one electric *bulb* in the big room.

Bulge ബൾജ്-ഉന്തി നിൽക്കുക, വീർക്കുക, തള്ളിവരിക
(n.) The thick wallet in his pocket made a *bulge* in his coat.
(v.) His eyes *bulged* out as he tried to lift the heavy box.

Bulk *(n.)* ബൾക് - വൻതോതിൽ
We ordered the raw material in *bulk.*

Bull *(n.)* ബുൾ - കാള, മൂരി
An angry *bull* is a fearsome animal.

Bullet *(n.)* ബുള്ളറ്റ് - വെടിയു
A revolver contains six *bullets.*

Bulletin *(n.)* ബുള്ളറ്റിൻ - ബുള്ളറ്റിൻ, വൃത്താന്ത വിവരണം
I'll watch the news *bulletin* at 8.

Bullock *(n.)* ബുള്ളക് - കാള
The farmer yoked the *bullocks* to the plough.

Bully *(n.&v.)* ബുള്ളി-ധിക്കാരി, കലഹ പ്രിയൻ
(n.) Everyone dislikes a *bully.*
(v.) The robber *bullied* the bus passengers to surrender their valuables.

Bump *(n.)* ബമ്പ് - 1. മുഴ, തടിപ്പ്
There appeared a *bump* on Amit's head where the ball hit him.
(v.) 2. കൂട്ടിയിടിക്കുക, മുട്ടുക
While walking hurriedly, Arun *bumped* into a stranger.

Bun *(n.)* ബൺ - മുധര റൊട്ടി, മുടിക്കെട്ട്
I went to the bakery to buy a *bun.*
She coiled her hair into a *bun.*

Bunch *(n.)* ബഞ്ച് - പൂക്കുല
She put the *bunch* of fresh flowers in a flower-vase.

Bundle *(n.)* ബൽ - കെട്ട്, ഭാണ്ഡം
He gave the *bundle* of soiled clothes to the washerman.

Bungalow *(n.)* ബംഗ്ലാവ്, മന്ദിരം
There was a beautiful *bungalow* on the top of the hill.

Burden ബർഡൻ-ഭാരം, ചുമട്, ഭാരം കയറ്റുക
(n.) The old man was carrying a heavy *burden* on his frail shoulders.
(v.) Do not *burden* yourself with unnecessary work.

Burglar *(n.)* ബർഗ്ളർ - കള്ളൻ, മോഷ്ടാവ്
The *burglar* broke open the safe but was caught before he could escape with the valuables.

Burn ബേൺ-പൊള്ളൽ, കത്തുക, കത്തിക്കുക
(n.) Apply a soothing ointment on the *burn.*
(v.) The fire *burned* brightly.
She *burnt* all the letters her lover had written to her.

Burrow ബറോ - മാളം, മാളം കുഴിക്കുക
(n.) The rabbit jumped into its *burrow* when it saw a dog.
(v.) The rabbit *burrowed* a deep hole under a tree.

Burst *(v.)* ബർസ്റ്റ്-പൊട്ടുക, പൊട്ടിച്ചിരിക്കുക
The tyre of the car *burst* with a bang.
They *burst* out laughing at the funny story.

Bury *(v.)* ബറി - കുഴിച്ച് മൂടുക
Muslims and Christians *bury* their dead.

Bus *(n.)* ബസ് - ബസ്
My son goes to school by *bus.*

Bush *(n.)* ബുഷ് - കുറ്റിക്കാട്
There are no big trees here, only *bushes.*

Business *(n.)* ബിസിനസ്-ബിസിനസ്, വ്യവസായം
Ram joined his father's *business* after completing his education.

Bustle ബസ്ൽ-ഇരമ്പൽ, തിക്കും തിരക്കും
(n.) There was a lot of *bustle* in the market.
(v.) The market was *bustling* with people.

Busy *(adj.)* ബിസി - തിരക്ക്
Are you *busy* this evening?

Butcher *(n.)* ബുച്ചർ – അറവ്കാരൻ
I went to the *butcher's* shop to buy some meat.

Butter *(n.)* ബട്ടർ – വെണ്ണ
We always have bread and *butter* for breakfast.

Butterfly *(n.)* ബട്ടർഫ്ളൈ–പൂമ്പാറ്റ, ചിത്രശലഭം
Butterflies are beautiful to look at.

Buttermilk *(n.)* ബട്ടർമിൽക്ക് – മോര്
Buttermilk is a protein-rich drink.

Buy *(v.)* ബൈ – വാങ്ങുക
Generally, housewives *buy* the vegetables.

Buzz *(n. & v.)* ബസ് – മുരൾച്ച, മുരളുക, മന്ത്രിക്കുക
(n.) In the summer, the garden is full of the *buzz* of insects.
(v.) This bee is constantly *buzzing* and disturbing me.

By *(prep.)* ബൈ – അരികിലൂടെ, അടുത്ത്, സമീപം
I saw a couple walking *by* the river.
A policeman was standing *by* the police jeep.
The letter was delivered *by* hand (not by post.)
He has learnt the poem *by* heart. (He can recite it without looking at the book.)

Bygone *(adj.)* ബൈഗാൺ–പിന്നിട്ട, കഴിഞ്ഞുപോയ
Taj Mahal evokes the memories of a *bygone* era.

By-product *(n.)* ബൈ–പ്രോഡക്ട് – ഉപോല്പന്നം
Pollution is a *by-product* of growing number of vehicles in the city.

C

Cab *(n.)* കാബ്–വി, കുതിരവി, ടാക്സി
I hired a *cab* to go to the railway station.

Cabbage *(n.)* കാബേജ് – മുട്ടക്കോസ്
Cabbage is my favourite vegetable.

Cabin *(n.)* കാബിൻ – 1. മുറി, അറ
Which is the General Manager's *cabin?*
2. കുടിൽ
The poor family lived in a *cabin* on the edge of the town.

Cabinet *(n.)* കാബിനറ്റ് – 1. അലമാരി
Uma arranged the new crockery on the shelves of the *cabinet*.
2. മന്ത്രിസഭ
Mostly decisions are taken unanimously by the *Cabinet.*

Cable *(n.)* കേബ്ൾ – 1. കേബ്ൾ, കമ്പി
The workmen dug the ground to repair the telephone *cables.*
2. കമ്പി അടിയ്ക്കുക
My brother *cabled* from London that he was coming to India.

Cafe *(n.)* കഫേ – കാപ്പിഷാപ്പ്, ഹോട്ടൽ
A South Indian *cafe* usually serves a nice cup of filter coffee.

Cage കേജ് – കിളിക്കൂട്, കൂട്ടിലടയ്ക്കുക
(n.) The little girl brought a *cage* for her pet parrot.
(v.) Rahul *caged* his pet rabbits before going out.

Cajole *(v.)* കജോൾ–മിരട്ടുക, വശത്താക്കുക
We can't *cajole* him into being a part of our team.

Cake *(n.)* കേക്ക് – കേക്ക്, അപ്പം
My father bought a big *cake* for my birthday.

Calamity *(n.)* കലാമിറ്റി – ദുരന്തം
It is always difficult to deal with a natural *calamity*.

Calculate *(v.)* കാൽക്കുലേറ്റ്–കണക്ക് കൂട്ടുക
Harish knows well how to *calculate.*

Calendar *(n.)* കലർ–കലർ, പഞ്ചാംഗം
Companies use *calendars* for their publicity.

Calf *(n.)* കാഫ്–1. കന്നുകുട്ടി, പശുക്കുട്ടി
The *calf* walked behind the cow.
2. കാൽവണ്ണ
The doctor dressed the wound on the labourer's *calf.*

Calibre *(n.)* കാലിബർ–യോഗ്യത, സാമർത്ഥ്യം
She has the *calibre* of translating the book into German without any mistake.

Call *(v.)* കാൾ – 1. വിളിക്കുക
I *called* out loudly when I saw Ram.
2. പറയപ്പെടുക, അറിയപ്പെടുക
A heart specialist is *called* the cardiologist.
3. കാണാൻ പോവുക
The Prime Minister *called* on the President.
(n.) 4. ടെലഫോൺ കാൾ
I have a phone *call* to make.
(n.) 5. സന്ദർശകർ
Sunil had many *callers* yesterday.

Callous *(adj.)* കാലസ് – ക്രൂരത
The master was *callous* enough to make his ill servant work.

Calm *(adj.)* കാം – ശാന്തമായിരിക്കുക
One should always be *calm* and composed.

Camel *(n.)* കാമൽ – ഒട്ടകം
Camel is called the ship of the desert.

Camera *(n.)* ക്യാമറ – ക്യാമറ
A professional photographer requires a good *camera.*

Camp കാമ്പ്–ശിബിരം, തങ്ങുക, ക്യാമ്പടിക്കുക
(n.) The boy-scout's summer *camp* was a great success.
(v.) The soldiers *camped* by the side of the river.

Campaign *(n.)* കാമ്പെയ്ൻ–പ്രസ്ഥാനം, യജ്ഞം
The government launched a *campaign* against smugglers.
(v.) He spent his life *campaigning* for the rights of the poor.

Campus *(n.)* കാമ്പസ് – പരിസരം, വളപ്പ്
I've lost my purse in the school *campus* itself.

Can *(n.)* കാൻ – 1. പാത്രം, ഡബ്ബ
I bought a *can* of apple jam.
(v.) 2. കഴിയുക, സാമർത്ഥ്യമുാവുക
Can you drive a car?

Canal *(n.)* കനാൽ – തോട്, ഓട
Punjab is a land of *canals.*

Cancel *(n.)* ക്യാൻസൽ – റദ്ദാക്കുക, നീക്കംചെയ്യുക
He *cancelled* all his appointments as he was not feeling well.

Candid *(adj.)* കാൻഡിഡ് – വ്യക്തമായ
She gave a *candid* reply when asked why she was still single.

Candidate *(n.)* കാൻഡിഡേറ്റ് – സ്ഥാനാർത്ഥി, പരീക്ഷാർത്ഥി
My elder brother was a *candidate* in the last municipal election.

Candle *(n.)* കാൻഡിൽ – മെഴുകുതിരി
She bought a box of *candles* for Diwali.

Cane *(n.)* കെയ്ൻ – 1. കരിമ്പ്, മുള, ചൂരൽ
Sugar is made from *cane.*
(v.) 2. ചൂരൽവരിയുക, ചൂരൽ പ്രയോഗം
The unruly mob was *caned* by the police.

Cannibal *(n.)* കാനിബൽ – നരഭോജി
Power-hungry politicians have really turned into a race of *cannibals.*

Cannon കാനൺ – പീരങ്കി, പീരങ്കിയാക്രമണം നടത്തുക
(n.) The fort was protected by *cannons* mounted on its turrets.
(v.) The fort was *cannoned* by the enemy.

Cantonment *(n.)* കന്റോൺമെന്റ് – സൈനിക പാളയം
No outsiders were allowed in the *cantonment* area.

Canoe *(n.)* കാനോ – നൗക
The adventurous young man crossed the sea in a *canoe.*

Canvas *(n.)* കാൻവാസ് – കാൻവാസ്
Sportsmen wear shoes of *canvas.*

Cap *(v.)* കാപ് – തൊപ്പി
The *cap* provides protection from the sun.
(v.) 2. പിന്നിടുക, നേട്ടം ഉറപ്പിക്കുക
The batsman *capped* his brilliant century with a sixer.

Capable *(adj.)* കേപ്പബ്ൾ–1. കഴിവുറ്റ, പ്രതിഭാശാലി

A *capable* executive always rises in his organisation.

2. ശേഷിയുള്ള, സാമർത്ഥ്യമുള്ള

Are you *capable* of handling office correspondence independently?

Capacity *(n.)* കപ്പാസിറ്റി–1. ശേഷി, ക്ഷമത

The theatre was filled to its *capacity.*

2. സാമർത്ഥ്യം, കഴിവ്, യോഗ്യത

He has great *capacity* for work.

Capital *(n.)* കാപ്പിറ്റൽ–1. രാജധാനി, തലസ്ഥാനം

Delhi is the *capital* of India.

2. മൂലധനം

He invested his *capital* in business.

(adj.) 3. അതിപ്രധാനം, ഉത്തമം

Whether or not to start this venture would be a decision of *capital* importance.

(adj.) 4. വലിയ അക്ഷരം

Write the address in *capital* letters.

Capsicum *(n.)* ക്യാപ്സിക്കം–സിംലാ മുളക്

My mother prepared stuffed *capsicums* for lunch.

Capsize *(v.)* ക്യാപ്സൈസ്–വള്ളം മറിയുക

The sea storm *capsized* the boat.

Capsule *(n.)* ക്യാപ്സൂൾ – ഗുളിക

The doctor prescribed B-complex *capsules* to my mother to overcome her weakness.

Captain *(n.)* ക്യാപ്റ്റൻ – കപ്പിത്താൻ, ക്യാപ്റ്റൻ

Balraj is a *captain* in Army.

2. കളിക്കാരുടെ ടീമിന്റെ തലവൻ

Anil was selected as the *captain* of the football team of his school.

Caption *(n.)* ക്യാപ്ഷൻ – അടിക്കുറിപ്പ്, തലവാചകം

Please write an interesting *caption* for this picture.

Captive *(n.)* കാപ്റ്റീവ് – തടവ് പുള്ളി

The *captive* was put in a dark cell.

Capture *(v.)* കാപ്ചർ – പിടികൂടുക, തടവിലാക്കുക

The thief was *captured* by the policeman after a chase.

Caravan *(n.)* കാരവാൻ–സാർത്ഥവാഹകർ

The *caravan* slowly travelled across the desert.

Carcass *(n.)* കർകാസ്–ജന്തുക്കളുടെ ശവം

The *carcass* of a pig was found on the beach.

Card *(n.)* കാർഡ് – കാർഡ്, ചീട്ട്, കത്ത്

I am interested in playing *cards.*

Do you have your visiting *card?*

Please bring this invitation *card* with you.

He packed the books in a *cardboard* box.

Do not fail to drop me a post-*card.*

Cardamom *(n.)* കാർഡമം – ഏലയ്ക്ക

The porridge became tastier with the flavour of *cardamom.*

Cardiac *(adj.)* കാർഡിയാക് – ഹൃദയ സംബന്ധം

She died of a *cardiac* arrest.

Cardigan *(n.)* കാർഡിഗൻ–തുന്നിയ കമ്പിളി ജായ്ക്കറ്റ്

Uma wore a matching *cardigan* over her sari.

Care കെയർ – കരുതൽ, പരിചരണം, വകവയ്ക്കൽ, ശ്രദ്ധ

(n.) Take care when you cross the road.

(v.) There was no one to *care* for (look after) the child after its parents died.

I don't *care* (it does not matter to me) what you do.

Career *(n.)* കാരീർ – ഉപജീവന വൃത്തി

Journalism offers good *career* opportunities.

Caress *(v.)* കറെസ്–ലാളിക്കുക, തഴുകുക

The mother *caressed* the sleeping child.

Caretaker *(n.)* കെയർടേക്കർ – സൂക്ഷിപ്പുകാരൻ

The *caretaker* of the old bungalow opened the gate for us.

Cargo *(n.)* കാർഗോ – ചരക്ക്

A ship can carry a lot of *cargo.*

Caricature *(n.)* കാരിക്കേച്ചർ–ഹാസ്യ ചിത്രം, അതിവർണ്ണന

She raised objection against her *caricature* in the magazine.

Carnival *(n.)* കാർനിവൽ – ആഘോഷ മേള, കാർണിവൽ

Visiting Goa at the time of *carnival* was an exciting experience.

Carnivore *(n.)*
കാർണിവോർ–മാംസഭോജി
A lion is a *carnivore.*

Carpenter *(n.)* കാർപെന്റർ–തച്ചൻ, തടി ആശാരി
Some *carpenters* specialise in making artistic furniture.

Carpet *(n.)* കാർപെറ്റ്–പരവതാനി, കമ്പളം
The rich man bought an expensive *carpet* for his sitting room.

Carriage *(n.)* കാരിജ് – തീവി മുറി
They always travel by the first-class *carriage.*

Carrier *(n.)* കാരിയർ–1. ചരക്ക് വി
We need a *carrier* to transport our goods to the other city.
2. രോഗം പകർത്തുക
Insects are the *carriers* of germs.

Carrot *(n.)* കാരറ്റ് – കാരറ്റ്
It is good to eat *carrots* in winter.

Carry *(v.)* കാരി – ചുമക്കുക, വഹിക്കുക, പാലിക്കുക
The porter *carried* Ram's luggage.
The soldiers *carried* out (obeyed) the General's orders.
(n.) We travelled in the rear *carriage* of the train.

Cart *(n.)* കാർട്ട് – ഭാര വി
The farmer bought a pair of bullocks for his *cart.*

Carton *(n.)* കാർട്ടൺ–കാർഡ് ബോർഡ് പെട്ടി
Arun bought a *carton* of ice-cream for his son's birthday party.

Carve *(v.)* കാർവ് – മുറിക്കുക, ചെത്തി മിനുക്കുക
The sculptor *carved* a beautiful statue out of the rock.

Case *(n.)* കേസ് – 1. കൂട്, പെട്ടി
The carpenter made a *book-case* for me.
2. കോടതി വ്യവഹാരം
Ram filed a *case* against his employer.

Cash *(n.)* കാഷ് – രൊക്കം പണം
(n.) It is safe to make large payments through cheque instead of *cash*.
(v.) I have to go to the bank to *cash* a cheque.
(n.) 2. ഖജാൻജി
He received the payment from the *cashier.*

Casserole *(n.)* കാസറോൾ – ആഹാരം ചൂടോടെ സൂക്ഷിക്കാൻ മൂടിയുള്ള പാത്രം
Food stored in a *casserole* remains warm for a long time.

Cassette *(n.)* കസെറ്റ് – കാസെറ്റ്
Today CDs have replaced the *cassettes.*

Cast കാസ്റ്റ് 1. എറിയുക, വീശുക
(v.) The fisherman *cast* his net into the sea.
2. അഭിനേതാക്കളുടെ നിര
Some films flop despite their big star *cast.*

Castle *(n.)* കാസ്ൽ–ദുർഗ്ഗം, കോട്ട, മന്ദിരം, കൊട്ടാരം
Akbar built many *castles.*

Casual *(adj.)* കാഷ്വൽ–1. യാദൃശ്ചികം, മുൻകൂട്ടി ആലോചിക്കാത്ത
His question was only a *casual* inquiry.
2. അലക്ഷ്യമായി
Raju was *casually* dressed.

Casualty *(n.)* കാഷ്വാലിറ്റി–അപകടത്തിൽ പരിക്കേറ്റയാൾ
The *casualties* of the blast were admitted to the hospital.

Cat *(n.)* കാറ്റ്–പൂച്ച
My mother is very fond of *cats.*

Catalogue *(n.)* കാറ്റലോഗ് – നാമാവലി, പട്ടിക
At the book fair, one can collect *catalogues* of many publishers.

Catapult *(n.)* കാറ്റാപുൾട്ട് – 1. തെറ്റാലി
Boys used *catapults* to hit the birds with stones.
2. മേലേക്ക് ഉയർത്തുക
A single box-office success can *catapult* a new actor to fame.

Cataract *(n.)* കാറ്ററാക്റ്റ്–1. തിമിരം
He has *cataract* in the left eye.
2. വെള്ളച്ചാട്ടം, ജലപ്രവാഹം
The water fell down the hillside in a roaring *cataract.*

Catastrophe *(n.)* കറ്റാസ്ട്രഫി–ആകസ്മിക ദുരന്തം
(n.) Tsunami proved to be a major *catastrophe* and killed many people.

(adj.) Earthquake was *catastrophic* to the whole city.

Catch *(v.)* കാച്ച് – 1. പിടിക്കുക
He could not *catch* the ball.
2. ഒപ്പത്തിനൊപ്പമെത്തുക
He ran fast but I *caught* up with him.
3. പിടിപെടുക
The baby has *caught* (got) a cold.
(n.) 4. കൊളുത്ത്
There is no *catch* on this window.

Category *(n.)* കാറ്റഗറി – വിഭാഗം, ഇനം
The garments were divided into *categories* as per their texture.

Cater *(v.)* കാറ്റർ – ആവശ്യാനുസരണം സേവനം ലഭ്യമാക്കുക
We *cater* to the overseas markets only.

Caterpillar *(n.)* കാറ്റർപില്ലർ – കമ്പിളിപ്പുഴു
A *caterpillar* grows into a butterfly.

Cattle *(n.)* കാറ്റിൽ – കന്നുകാലി
The *cattle* grazed in the shade of the tree.

Cause കാസ്–കാരണം, കാരണമായിതീരുക
(n.) An inquiry is on to find out the *cause* of the rail accident.
(v.) The accident *caused* the traffic jam.

Causeway *(n.)* കാസ്‌വേ–നടപ്പാത, സേതുപഥം
Mumbai has many *causeways.*

Caution കാഷൻ – മുന്നറിയിപ്പ് നൽകുക, ശ്രദ്ധയോടെ, സാവധാനം
(n.) You must take due *caution* while crossing a busy street.
(v.) Ram *cautioned* the new employee against his boss's short temper.
(adv.) The salesman *cautiously* opened the crockery box.

Cavalry *(n.)* കാവൽറി – അശ്വരൂഢ സേന, കുതിരപ്പട്ടാളം
Shivaji was famous for his *cavalry.*

Cave, Cavern *(n.)* കേവ്, കാവേൺ–ഗുഹ, മട
The hermit lived in a *cave* high in the hills.
The wounded tiger hid in a *cavern.*

Caw *(v. & n.)* കാ – കാക്ക കരയുക
I was disturbed by the *cawing* of a crow.

Cease *(v.)* സീസ് – അവസാനിക്കുക, അവസാനിപ്പിക്കുക, തുടർച്ചയായി
(v.) The milkman has *ceased* supplying milk because of non-payment of previous bills.
(adv.) The rain came down *ceaselessly* (continuously).

Ceiling *(n.)* സീലിംഗ് – മേൽക്കൂര
This room has a high *ceiling.*

Celebrate *(v.)* സെലിബ്രേറ്റ്– ആഘോഷിക്കുക
We *celebrate* Diwali with great joy.
The young couple *celebrated* the first birthday of their child.

Celebrated *(adj.)* സെലിബ്രേറ്റഡ്– പ്രശസ്ത, പേരുകേട്ട
Kalidas was a *celebrated* poet.

Celebrity *(n.)* സെലിബ്രിറ്റി–പ്രസിദ്ധ വ്യക്തി
These days everyone wants to be a *celebrity.*

Cell *(n.)* സെൽ – 1. അറ
The prisoner was kept in a dark *cell.*
2. വിഭാഗം
The police department set up a separate *cell* to deal with car thieves.

Cellar *(n.)* സെല്ലർ – നിലവറ, ഉള്ളറ
Residential houses are usually without a *cellar.*

Cemetery *(n.)* സെമിറ്ററി – ശ്മശാനം, ചുടുകാട്, സെമിത്തേരി
There is a *cemetery* just outside the village.

Censure *(v.)* സെൻഷർ–കുറ്റപ്പെടുത്തുക
The revolutionary was *censured* for misleading the masses.

Centre *(n.)* സെന്റർ – 1. കേന്ദ്രം, മദ്ധ്യ
The office of the municipal corporation is in the *centre* of the city.
2. സ്ഥാപനം
India International *Centre* in New Delhi is famous as a meeting place of intellectuals.

Century *(n.)* സെഞ്ചുറി–1. നൂറ്റ്, ശതാബ്ദം
We are living in the twenty-first *century.*
2. സെഞ്ചറി
Scoring a *century* at the Lord's in London is a dream of every batsman.

Cereal *(n.)* സെറിയൽ - ധാന്യം, അന്നം
Rice and wheat are *cereals.*

Ceremony *(n.)* സെറിമണി-ചടങ്ങ്, കർമ്മാദികൾ
The marriage *ceremony* will begin after the Pandit arrives.

Certain *(adj.)* സെർട്ടൻ-1. സുനിശ്ചിത, ഉറപ്പായ
Prakash is *certain* to pass the I.I.T. exam.
2. ചില, ചിലർ
Certain people are very fond of bragging.

Certificate *(n.)* സെർട്ടിഫിക്കറ്റ് - പ്രമാണ പത്രം
If you want medical leave, you must produce a doctor's *certificate.*

Chain ചെയ്ൻ-ശൃംഖല, മാല, നിര, ബന്ധിക്കുക
(n.) Uma wore a beautiful golden *chain* round her neck.
The Himalayas is a *chain* of mountains.
(v.) We *chain* our door at night.

Chair *(n.)* ചെയർ-1. കസേര, ആസനം, പീഠം
Please sit in this *chair.*
He was elected *chairman* (head) of the company.
2. പദം, പദവി
(v.) The *chair* of Prime Minister is not a bed of roses.

Chalk *(n.)* ചാക്ക് - ചാക്ക്
The teacher wrote on the blackboard with a piece of *chalk.*

Challenge ചലഞ്ച്-വെല്ലുവിളി, ആഹ്വാനം
(n.) He looked upon the difficult task as a *challenge* to his capability.
(v.) Mike Tyson *challenged* Evander Holyfield for a world heavyweight boxing match.

Chamber *(n.)* ചേമ്പർ - 1. മുറി, അറ
After the verdict was given, the judge retired to his *chamber.*
2. വാണിജ്യ മണ്ഡലം
The Maratha *Chamber* of Commerce has its headquarters in Pune.

Chameleon *(n.)* കമീല്യൻ - ഓന്ത്
I saw a *chameleon* in the garden.

Champion *(n.)* ചാമ്പ്യൻ - 1. വിജയി, സർവ്വശ്രേഷ്ഠൻ
He was declared the *champion* batsman of the year.
2. രക്ഷകൻ
Gandhiji was a *champion* of the downtrodden.

Chance *(n.)* ചാൻസ് - 1. അവസരം
In the quiz contest, Arun was given three *chances* to give the right answer.
2. യാദൃശ്ചികമായി
We met at a common friend's place by *chance.*
(v.) If you *chance* to meet Vishal, please tell him I am waiting for him here.

Change *(v.)* ചെയ്ഞ്ച് - 1. മാറുക, മാറ്റുക
The boss *changed* his travelling plan at the last moment.
2. ചില്ലറ
Do you have some *change?*
3. ഉടുപ്പ് മാറ്റുക
The guest wished to have a wash and a *change.*

Channel *(n.)* ചാനൽ - തോട്, ജലമാർഗ്ഗം, മാർഗ്ഗം, മാദ്ധ്യമം
The English *Channel* separates England from the continent of Europe.

Chant ചാന്റ്-കീർത്തനം, മന്ത്രോച്ചാരണം
(n.) A holy *chant* was echoing the temple.
(v.) The priests were *chanting* hymns in the temple.

Chaos *(n.)* കാഓസ്-അലങ്കോലം, താറുമാറ്
Heavy rains caused a *chaos* on the roads.

Chapter *(n.)* ചാപ്റ്റർ - അദ്ധ്യായം
The textbooks have many *chapters.*

Character *(n.)* കാരക്ടർ-1. ഗുണം, സ്വഭാവം, പ്രകൃതം
Good *character* is a man's most precious possession.
2. കഥാപാത്രം
How many *characters* are there in this play?

Characteristic കാരക്ടറിസ്റ്റിക് -1. പ്രത്യേക ലക്ഷണം
(n.) A round dome is a major *characteristic* of Muslim architecture.

2. സ്വതസിദ്ധമായ

(adj.) She laughed her *characteristic* sarcastic laugh.

Charcoal *(n.)* ചാർകോൾ – മരക്കരി

Charcoal is commonly used as a fuel in India.

Charge *(n.)* ചാർജ് – 1. ആരോപണം

The police arrested the servant on a *charge* of theft.

2. നിരക്ക്, കൂലി

What will be your *charge* for repairing my watch?

(v.) 3. മേൽനോട്ടം, ഉത്തരവാദിത്വം

I would like to see an honest person in *charge* of this office.

4. ആക്രമിക്കുക

The soldiers *charged* the enemy.

Chariot *(n.)* ചാരിയട്ട് – തേര്, രഥം

The king stopped his *chariot* outside the castle.

Charisma *(n.)* കരിസ്മ – ആകർഷണം

We were instantly charmed by her *charisma.*

Charity *(n.)* ചാരിറ്റി – ദീനദയ, ഉദാരത്വം, പരോപകാരം

The rich man gave away his wealth in *charity.*

(adj.) Homeopathy dispensaries are mostly *charitable* (free).

Ram has a *charitable* (kind) disposition.

Charm *(n.)* ചാം – 1. രക്ഷ, ഏലസ്

Arun wears a *charm* round his wrist.

2. ആകർഷണം, ശോഭ

Rekha is a lady with great *charm.*

(v.) വശീകരിക്കുക

Rakhi will *charm* you with her sunny smile.

Chart ചാർട്ട് – രേഖാചിത്രം

(n.) We prepared a *chart* on environmental problems.

2. ഏതെങ്കിലും സംഭവത്തിന്റെ വിശദവർണ്ണന

(v.) The book *charts* the growth and development of Indian cinema over the years.

Charter *(n.)* ചാർട്ടർ – 1. അവകാശവാദ പത്രം

The textile workers presented a *charter* of demands to the Government.

(v.) 2. വാടകയ്ക്കെടുക്കുക

The millionaire *chartered* a plane for his business tours.

Chase *(v.&n.)* ചേസ്–പിന്തുടരുക, പിന്നാലെ കൂടുക

(v.) The policeman *chased* the thief.

(n.) The policeman gave the thief a good *chase.*

Chat *(v.)* ചാറ്റ് – നേരമ്പോക്ക് പറയുക, സല്ലപിക്കുക

The two friends sat *chatting* for a long time.

(n.) The *chat* of two old friends was quite long.

Chatter *(v. & n.)* ചാറ്റർ – ചിലയ്ക്കുക, വായാടിത്തം പറയുക

The talkative little girl *chattered* continuously.

Chauffeur *(n.)* ഷാഫർ – ശമ്പളത്തിന് കാറോടിക്കുന്ന ഡ്രൈവർ

The *chauffeur* took us to the venue within an hour.

Cheap *(adj.)* ചീപ് – 1. വില കുറഞ്ഞ

Nothing is *cheap* these days.

2. അന്തസ്സില്ലാത്ത

Amit played a *cheap* trick on me.

3. തരം താണ

His taste in clothes is rather *cheap.*

Cheat *(v.)* ചീറ്റ് – വഞ്ചിക്കുക, ചതിക്കുക

A dishonest shopkeeper *cheats* his customers.

(n.) വഞ്ചകൻ

Beware! He is a *cheat.*

Check *(v.)* ചെക്ക് – 1. പരിശോധന, പരീക്ഷണം

Have you *checked* the air pressure in your car tyres?

2. തടയുക

The policemen at the gate of the Parliament House *checked* people from going in.

(n.) 3. കളമുള്ള

Shaloo wore a shirt with *checks.*

Cheek ചീക് – 1. കവിൾ, ചെകിട്

(n.) The teacher slapped him on his *cheek.*

2. ധിക്കാരം, ധാർഷ്ട്യം
(n.) She's got a *cheek,* coming late to the office every day!
(adj.) She is a *cheeky* little girl.

Cheer ചിയർ – 1. സന്തോഷപ്രകടനം, സന്തോഷിപ്പിക്കുക
(n.) *Cheers* for the holiday.
(v.) My visit *cheered* the sick man.
(adj.) He has a *cheerful* temperament.
2. അഭിനന്ദിക്കുക, കയ്യടിക്കുക
The school boys *cheered* when their team won the hockey match.

Cheese *(n.)* ചീസ് – പാൽക്കട്ടി
Rahul ordered for a plate of *cheese* pakoras.

Chemist *(n.)* കെമിസ്റ്റ് – ഔഷധവ്യാപാരി
At the *chemist's* shop, we can buy medicines.

Cheque *(n.)* ചെക്ക് – ചെക്ക്
It's safe to make payments by *cheque.*

Chess *(n.)* ചെസ്സ് – ചതുരംഗം
The game of *chess* originated in India.

Chest *(n.)* ചെസ്റ്റ് – 1. നെഞ്ച്, മാറിടം
A wrestler has a broad *chest.*
2. ഖജനാ, പെട്ടി
The jeweller locked his valuables in a strong *chest.*

Chew *(v.)* ച്യൂ–ചവയ്ക്കുക, അയവിറക്കുക
Young children should be taught to *chew* their food well.
Stop *chewing* over the past.

Chick(en) *(n.)* ചിക്ക്, ചിക്കൻ–1. കോഴിക്കുഞ്ഞ്
He bought a dozen *chicks* for his poultry farm.
2. വളർച്ചയെത്തിയ കോഴി
(n.) I had *chicken* for lunch.

Chickenpox *(n.)* ചിക്കൻപോക്സ് – മണ്ണൻ, പൊങ്ങൻപനി
The child was suffering from *chickenpox.*

Chief ചീഫ് – തലവൻ, മേധാവി
(n.) The Army head is called the *Chief* of Staff.
(adj.) Rarely, one rises from a clerk's post to become the *chief* executive.
(adv.) മുഖ്യമായും
We eat *chiefly* rice and wheat.

Child *(n.)* ചൈൽഡ് – 1. കുഞ്ഞ്, കുട്ടി
Mr. and Mrs. Sen brought their *child* with them to the party.
2. ബാല്യം
Where did you spend your *childhood?*

Chill *(n.)* ചിൽ – 1. ജലദോഷം
Infants quickly catch a *chill.*
(adj.) 2. തണുത്ത, ശീത
A *chilly* wind was blowing.

Chime *(n.)* ചൈം–മണിനാദം
The *chime* of the church bell could be heard from a distance.
(v.) The wall clock *chimes* every hour.

Chimney *(n.)* ചിമ്നി – ചിമ്മനി, പുകനാളി
The *chimney* smoke pollutes the atmosphere.

Chimpanzee *(n.)* ചിമ്പൻസി – മനുഷ്യക്കുരങ്ങ്
Human beings evolved from the *chimpanzees.*

Chin *(n.)* ചിൻ – കവിൾ
He nicked his *chin* while shaving.

China *(n.)* ചൈനാ – കളിമണ്ണ് (പാത്രം)
I went to the crockery store to buy *china.*

Chip *(n.)* ചിപ് – 1. കഷണം, തു്
Chips of wood catch fire quickly.
(adj.) This tea cup is old and *chipped.*

Chirp *(v.)* ചിർപ് – ചിലയ്ക്കുക, കീച്ചിടുക
Sparrows *chirp* together at the time of sunrise.

Chisel *(n.)* ചിസൽ – ഉളി
The sculptor worked on the block of stone with a *chisel.*

Chit *(n.)* ചിറ്റ് –തു് കടലാസ്
I left the note for him on a *chit.*

Chivalry *(n.)* ഷിവൽറി – സ്ത്രീകളോടുള്ള ആദരം
The days of *chivalry* are now gone.

Chocolate *(n.)* ചോക്ലേറ്റ് – ചോക്ലേറ്റ്
The child cried for a *chocolate.*

Choice *(n.)* ചോയിസ് – തിരഞ്ഞെടുക്കാനുള്ള അവകാശം
I had no *choice* but to shift to Mumbai.

Choir *(n.)* ക്വൊയർ – ഗായക സംഘം
She was a part of musical *choir* in the church.

Choke *(v.)* ചോക്ക് – 1. ശ്വാസം മുട്ടുക
In the Bhopal gas leakage tragedy, hundreds of people were *choked* to death.
2. അടഞ്ഞുപോവുക
The sewer gets *choked* with dirt.

Choose *(v.)* ചൂസ് – തിരഞ്ഞെടുക്കുക, ഇഷ്ടപ്പെടുക
Usha *chose* a black sari.

Chop *(v.)* ചോപ് – മുറിക്കുക, വെട്ടിവീഴ്ത്തുക
The woodcutter *chopped* down the tree with an axe.

Chore *(n.)* ചാർ – നിവർത്തിയില്ലാതെ ചെയ്യേിവരുന്ന ഇഷ്ടമില്ലാത്ത ജോലി
I always get bored of the household *chores.*

Choreograph *(v.)* കൊറിയാഗ്രാഫ് – നൃത്ത സംവിധാനം
(v.) Vaibhavi Merchant *choreographed* the song.
(n.) Choreography of Farah Khan is praiseworthy.
(n.) Saroj Khan is a veteran *choreographer.*

Chorus *(n.)* കോറസ് – 1. വൃന്ദഗാനം, ഗായക സംഘം
Some plays end with a *chorus.*
The agitators were shouting slogan in a *chorus.*
(v.) 2. ഒന്നിച്ച് വിളിച്ച് പറയുക
"We want to play cricket," the children *chorused.*

Chubby *(adj.)* ചബ്ബി – കൊഴുത്തുരു
I was very *chubby* in childhood.

Chuckle *(v.)* ചക്ക്ൾ – അടക്കിയ ചിരി
The old man *chuckled* at his own joke.

Chunk *(n.)* ചങ്ക് – വലിയ തു്
He took a large *chunk* of meat.

Church *(n.)* ചർച്ച് – കൃസ്ത്യൻ പള്ളി
The *church* was decorated beautifully on Christmas.

Churn *(v.)* ചേൺ–കടയുക, മഥനം ചെയ്യുക
The cyclone *churned* the sea completely.

Cinder(s) *(n.)* സിൻഡർ(സ്)–തീക്കനൽ, കരി
She tried to light a fire with the *cinders.*

Cinema *(n.)* സിനിമ – സിനിമ
1. സിനിമാകൊട്ടക
Let's watch a movie in a *cinema* hall.
2. ചലച്ചിത്ര വ്യവസായം
Indian *cinema* has progressed a lot in the past few years.

Cinnamon *(n.)* സിനമൺ – കറുകപ്പട്ട
Rice tasted better with the aroma of *cinnamon.*

Circle സർക്കിൾ–വൃത്തം, ചക്രം, വട്ടം ചുറ്റുക
(n.) The geometry teacher taught the students to draw a *circle.*
(v.) The dancers *circled* the tree as they danced.

Circular സർക്കുലർ –
1. വൃത്താകൃതിയിലുള്ള
(adj.) The Parliament House is a *circular* building.
(n.) 2. അറിയിപ്പ്, കുറിപ്പ്
The company sent a *circular* to all its clients about its new product.

Circuit *(n.)* സർക്ക്യൂട്ട് – വൈദ്യുത പ്രവാഹത്തിന്റെ പഥം
The factory caught fire because of the short *circuit.*

Circumstances *(n.)* സർക്കംസ്റ്റൻസെസ് – പരിതസ്ഥിതി, സാഹചര്യം
A man's courage and tolerance are put to test in adverse *circumstances.*

Circulate *(v.)* സർക്കുലേറ്റ് – വിതരണം ചെയ്യുക, പ്രചാരം
(v.) The pamphlets were *circulated* to all the houses in the area.
(n.) The Times of India claims to have the largest *circulation.*

Circus *(n.)* സർക്കസ് – സർക്കസ്
Children laughed at the clown in the *circus.*

Cite *(v.)* സൈറ്റ് – ഉദാഹരണ സഹിതം, കാര്യങ്ങൾ പറയുക
Can you *cite* an example to prove your point?

City *(n.)* സിറ്റി – നഗരം, പട്ടണം
Tokyo is the biggest *city* in the world.

Civil *(adj.)* സിവിൽ – പൗരൻ, സൈനികേതര, സർക്കാർ ജോലി
(adj.) Under *civil* rule, the Army has no role in the government functioning.

Subhash Chandra Bose was selected for the *civil* services (government service except service in the armed forces).

(n.) നാഗരീകത

In ancient times, many *civilisations* prospered on the river banks.

Civilian *(n.)*സിവിലിയൻ– സൈനികേതര, വിമുക്ത സൈനിക, സിവിലിയൻ

Rehman has retired from the Army, now he is a *civilian.*

Citizen *(n.)* സിറ്റിസൻ – പൗരൻ

We are responsible *citizens* of the country.

Civilisation *(n.)* സിവിലൈസേഷൻ – നാഗരീകത

Cleopatra was a powerful empress of the Roman *civilisation.*

Civilised *(adj.)* സിവിലൈസ്ഡ് – പരിഷ്കൃതം

His behaviour was highly *civilised* and sophisticated.

Claim *(v.&n.)* ക്ലെയിം–അവകാശം ഉന്നയിക്കുക

(v.) Daughters can also *claim* a share in their father's property.

(n.) A son's *claim* to his father's property is universally accepted.

Clan *(n.)* ക്ലാൻ – വംശം

Chanakya vowed to destroy the whole Nand *clan.*

Clap *(v.)* ക്ലാപ് – കയ്യടിക്കുക

Everyone *clapped* when the political leader rose to speak.

Clarification *(n.)* ക്ലാരിഫിക്കേഷൻ – വിശദീകരണം

(n.) I don't want any *clarification* for the mistakes you committed.

(v.) Let me *clarify* my point.

Clarity *(n.)* ക്ലാരിറ്റി – വ്യക്തത

Your essay lacks *clarity* of thought.

Clash *(n.)* ക്ലാഷ്–1. സംഘട്ടനം, ഏറ്റുമുട്ടൽ

Some people were injured during the *clash* between the two groups.

2. ഒച്ച

With a *clash* of cymbals, the band began to play.

(v.) 3. വഴക്കടിക്കുക

The two groups *clashed* and many people were injured.

Clasp *(v.)* ക്ലാസ്പ് – പിടിക്കുക, കവരുക, ആലിംഗനം ചെയ്യുക

He *clasped* my hand warmly.

(n.) 2. ബക്ക്ൾ

She bought a beautiful golden *clasp.*

Class *(n.)* ക്ലാസ്സ് – വർഗ്ഗം, തരം, ക്ലാസ്സ്

Under 10+2 system, the students study in school up to 12th *class.*

Rail journey in the first *class* is quite comfortable.

2. ഇനം, ജാതി

Cats and tigers belong to the same *class* of animals.

Classic *(adj.)* ക്ലാസിക് – ഉൽകൃഷ്ട, മഹദ്

Mrs. Dalloway is a *classic* novel.

Classify *(v.)* ക്ലാസിഫൈ–തരം തിരിക്കുക

(v.) The books were *classified* into various subjects.

(n.) The *classification* of books makes it easier for the reader to browse through.

Clatter *(n. & v.)* ക്ലാറ്റർ–കലപില ശബ്ദം (ഉാക്കുക)

The plate fell down from Usha's hand with a *clatter.*

(v.) Open doors and windows *clattered in the storm.*

Clause *(n.)* ക്ലാസ് – നിയമ വകുപ്പ്

She raised an objection against the *clause* of three-year bond.

Claw *(n.)* ക്ലാ – നഖം

The eagle flew away with the serpent in its *claws.*

Clay *(n.)* ക്ലേ – കളിമണ്ണ്

Crockery is made of *clay.*

Clean ക്ലീൻ – 1. വൃത്തിയാക്കുക, വൃത്തി

(v.) Did you *clean* your teeth today?

Sheela *cleaned* out the cupboard.

(adj.) We should wear *clean* clothes.

2. ശുദ്ധമായ

People with *clean* reputation get respect from all.

Clear *(adj.)* ക്ലിയർ – 1. തെളിഞ്ഞ, പ്രസന്ന

The sky was *clear* and cloudless.

2. വ്യക്തം

What you say is not quite *clear* to me.

(v.) 3. ഒതുക്കുക

I was busy *clearing* up my old papers.

Clench *(v.)* ക്ലെഞ്ച്–മുറുക്കുക, അമർത്തുക
He *clenched* his fists in anger.

Clerk *(n.)* ക്ലാർക്ക് – ക്ലാർക്ക്
It is not easy to get even a *clerk's* job.

Clever *(adj.)* ക്ലെവർ – 1.ബുദ്ധിമാൻ, സമർത്ഥൻ
Clever students generally score good marks.
2. നിപുണൻ, പ്രവീണൻ
Reena is *clever* at embroidery.

Cliché *(n.)* ക്ലിഷേ–പറഞ്ഞു പഴകിയ യുക്തി
You must avoid *clichés* in your writings.

Click ക്ലിക്ക് – 2. ഞൊടിക്കുക
(v.) She *clicked* her fingers to call the driver.
2. സ്റ്റാർട്ട് ബട്ടൺ അമർത്തുക
(v.) *Click* on Start button.
3. മൗസിന്റെ ബട്ടൺ അമർത്തുക
(n.) Sending e-mails is just a matter of a *click*.

Client *(n.)* ക്ലയന്റ് – കക്ഷി
The *clients* were impressed by the quality of work.

Cliff *(n.)* ക്ലിഫ് – കുത്തനെയുള്ള മല
As the ship approached the shore of England, we could see the white *cliffs* of Dover.

Climate *(n.)* ക്ലൈമറ്റ് – 1. കാലാവസ്ഥ
In summer, Delhi's *climate* is extremely hot.
2. അന്തരീക്ഷം
How is the political *climate* in the capital these days?

Climb *(v.)* ക്ലൈമ്പ് – കയറുക
You require special training to *climb a mountain.*
The old man *climbed* the staircase with great difficulty.
(n.) *Climb* to success is hard.

Cling *(v.)* ക്ലിങ്ങ് – കെട്ടിപ്പിടിക്കുക, ഒട്ടിനിൽക്കുക
Small children *cling* to their mother while sleeping.

Clip *(n.)* ക്ലിപ് – 1. ക്ലിപ്, കൊളുത്ത്
The loose sheets are put together with a paper *clip.*
(v.) 2. കത്രിക്കുക, മുറിക്കുക
Little boys like to *clip* pictures out of newspapers.

Cloak *(n.)* ക്ലോക്ക് – മേലങ്കി
The judge wore a long black *cloak.*

Clock *(n.)* ക്ലോക്ക് – ഘടികാരം
Some wall *clocks* chime every hour.

Clog *(v.)* ക്ലോഗ് – അടഞ്ഞുപോവുക
The sewer was *clogged* with dirt.

Close ക്ലോസ് – 1. അടയ്ക്കുക
(v.) Please *close* the door.
(adj.) 2. അടുത്ത്, അരികെ
The children sat *close* together.
(adj.) 3. തികഞ്ഞ
The audience paid *close* attention to the sermons of the Saint.

Clot ക്ലോട്ട് – 1. രക്തം കട്ടപിടിക്കുക
(n.) A blood *clot* formed inside his brain.
2. ഉറഞ്ഞു കട്ടപിടിക്കുക
(v.) The blood inside his brain began to *clot.*

Cloth *(n.)* ക്ലോത്ത് – തുണി, വസ്ത്രം
Nowadays shirts are made of synthetic *cloth.*

Clothes *(n.)* ക്ലോത്ത്സ് – ഉടയാട
Youngsters like fashionable *clothes.*

Cloudy *(adj.)* ക്ലൗഡി – മേഘാവൃതം
On a *cloudy* day, we cannot see the sun.

Clown *(n.)* ക്ലൗൺ – വിദൂഷകൻ, കോമാളി
The children laughed at the circus *clown's* antics.

Club *(n.)* ക്ലബ്ബ് – ക്ലബ്ബ്
Club is a place for recreation.
2. ഗദ, കനത്ത വടി, ലാത്തി
When the tiger attacked the farmer, he defended himself with his *club.*

Clue *(n.)* ക്ലൂ – തെളിവ്, സൂചന
The detectives looked for *clues* that could lead them to the murderer.

Clumsy *(adj.)* ക്ലംസി – വശമില്ലാത്ത, അശ്രദ്ധയോട് കൂടിയ
Radha is so *clumsy* that she is always breaking something or the other.

Cluster *(n. & v.)* ക്ലസ്റ്റർ–കൂട്ടം, പുരുഷാരം, ജനസമൂഹം, കൂട്ടം ചേരുക

(n.) The rabbit ran to the *cluster* of bushes to hide from the hound.

(v.) The children *clustered* round the ice cream vendor.

Clutch *(v.)* ക്ലച്ച് – മുറുകെ പിടിക്കുക

The frightened child *clutched* his mother's hand.

Clutter ക്ലറ്റർ–1. ഒച്ചപ്പാട്, കലകല ശബ്ദം

(n.) There was a lot of *clutter* on the table.

2. വാരി വലിച്ചിടുക

(v.) She *cluttered* the table with cosmetics.

(adj.) Her desk is always *cluttered.*

Coach *(n.)* കോച്ച് – കോച്ച്, യാത്രാമുറി

The Rajdhani Express has air-conditioned *coaches* only.

Coal *(n.)* കോൾ – കല്ക്കരി

Most industries in India run on *coal* energy.

Coalition *(n.)* കോഅലേഷൻ – മുന്നണി, കൂട്ടുകക്ഷി

A *coalition* government always faces problems.

Coarse *(adj.)* കോർസ് – 1. പരിക്കൻ

The poor woman wore a sari of *coarse* cloth.

2. മുരട്ട്, മര്യാദയില്ലാത്ത

Coarse manners are disliked by all.

Coast *(n.)* കോസ്റ്റ് – തീരം, കടൽക്കര

We could see the *coast* from the deck of the ship.

Coat *(n.)* കോട്ട് – 1. കോട്ട്, കുപ്പായം

The poor man had no *coat* to wear.

2. തേയ്പ്, ലേപം, പടലം

This door needs a fresh *coat* of paint.

3. പുരട്ടുക, പൊതിയുക

She *coated* the dough with fine flour before rolling it.

Coax *(v.)* കോക്സ്–മിരട്ടി സമ്മതിപ്പിക്കുക

Don't *coax* him to cook today.

Cobbler *(n.)* കോബ്ളർ – ചെരുപ്പുകുത്തി

The *cobbler* repairs and polishes the shoes.

Cobweb *(n.)* കോബ്‌വെബ് – ചിലന്തിവല

The unused room was dusty and full of *cobwebs.*

Cock *(n.)* കോക്ക് – കോഴി

The *cock* crows at the daybreak.

Cockroach *(n.)* കോക്രോച്ച് – പാറ്റ

Lizards eat the *cockroaches.*

Coconut *(n.)* കോക്കനട്ട്–നാളികേരം, തേങ്ങ

The *coconut* is considered a sacred fruit in India.

Code *(n.)* കോഡ്–1. സംഹിത, നിയമാവലി

There is a *code* of conduct for Government servants.

2. രഹസ്യ ചിഹ്നാവലി

The spy sent his secret message in *code.*

Coffin *(n.)* കോഫിൻ – ശവപ്പെട്ടി

The departed leader's *coffin* was ready for its last journey.

Coil *(v. & n.)* കോയ്ൽ – ചുരുൾ, ചുറ്റ്, ചുരുട്ടുക, ചുറ്റുക, പിന്നുക

The fan motor has a *coil* of wire.

(v.) Nisha got her hair *coiled* from a beauty parlour.

Coin *(n.)* കോയ്ൻ – നാണയം

Coins last longer than paper currency.

Coincidence *(n.)* കോഇൻസൈഡ്–സംയോഗം

I met him in the market by a sheer *coincidence.*

Cold *(adj.)* കോൾഡ് – 1. തണുത്ത, ശീതള

I like *cold* coffee.

2. തണുത്ത, ഉദാസീനമായ

Ram was upset by Gita's *cold* behaviour.

3. ജലദോഷം

Anil got wet in the rain and caught a *cold.*

Collaborate *(v.)* കൊളാബറേറ്റ് – സഹകരിക്കുക

(v.) She *collaborated* with a colleague to complete the project.

(n.) She has written this book in *collaboration* with a friend.

Collapse *(v.)* കൊളാപ്സ്-1. തകർന്നു വീഴുക.

The old house *collapsed* in the storm.

2. അടിപെടുക

In spite of expert medical treatment, the old man *collapsed* in a matter of hours.

Collar *(n.)* കോളർ - കോളർ

Shirts with short *collars* are no more in fashion.

Collect *(v.)* കളക്ട് - ശേഖരിക്കുക

Children love to *collect* coloured pebbles on the seashore.

College *(n.)* കോളേജ്-കോളേജ്, കലാലയം

Students face tough competition for getting admission in reputed *colleges* of Delhi.

Collide *(v.)* കൊളൈഡ്-കൂട്ടിമുട്ടുക, ഇടിക്കുക

When a taxi *collided* with a bus, all the traffic came to halt on the busy road.

2. കൂട്ടിമുട്ടൽ

The taxi was smashed in the *collision.*

Colloquial *(adj.)* കൊളോക്വിയൽ - സംസാര ഭാഷ

Avoid *colloquial* words in your essays.

Colony *(n.)* കോളനി - കോളനി, അധിവാസ സ്ഥലം

Deep in the woods, the traveller came across a *colony* of tribal people.

Colour *(v.)* കളർ - നിറം, വർണ്ണം

White *colour* is a combination of seven *colours.*

Column *(v.)* കോളം - 1. സ്തംഭം, തൂണ്

The old palace had huge *columns.*

2. പത്ര പംക്തി

The newspaper devoted a full *column* to the account of the rail accident.

3. നിര, അണി

The soldiers marched in a *column.*

Comb കോമ്പ് - 1. ചീപ്പ് (ചീകുക)

(v.) The mother *combed* her daughter's hair.

2. അരിക്കുക

The police *combed* the town for the thief.

(n.) I want to buy a new *comb.*

Combat കോമ്പാറ്റ് - യുദ്ധം

(n.) A *combat* took place between the police and the protestors.

(v.) Government is taking measures to *combat* poverty.

Combine *(v.)* കംബൈൻ-ചേർക്കുക, യോജിപ്പിക്കുക, വാണിജ്യ സംഘടന

The two companies *combined* to form one big corporation.

Come *(v.)* കം-വരിക, എത്തുക

Ram *came* to see me as I was ill.

Comfort കംഫർട്ട് - സുഖസൗകര്യം, സാന്ത്വനം, സുഖപ്രദം

(n.) Rich men live in great *comfort.*

(adj.) Five-star hotels are very *comfortable.*

(v.) I *comforted* the weeping child.

Command കമാ് - ആജ്ഞ, നിർദ്ദേശം, നയിക്കുക

(n.) The General gave the *command* to march.

A captain is in *command* of a company of soldiers.

(v.) The king *commanded* his army to attack.

Commence *(v.)* കമൻസ് - തുടങ്ങുക, ആരംഭിക്കുക

When does the show *commence?*

Commendable *(adj.)* ക മ ബ് ൾ - പ്രശംസനീയം, സ്തുത്യർഹം

She has really done a *commendable* job.

Comment കമന്റ് - ടിപ്പണി

(n.) She ignored the *comment* he made about her dress.

(v.) He *commented* on her dress.

Commerce *(n.)* കോമേർസ് - വാണിജ്യം, വ്യാപാരം

Mumbai is a big centre of *commerce.*

Commit *(v.)* കമ്മിറ്റ് - നടത്തുക, ചെയ്യുക

He *committed* many thefts before being caught.

Committee *(n.)* കമ്മിറ്റി - സമിതി, കമ്മിറ്റി

A *committee* was set up to go into the affairs of the company.

Commodity *(n.)* കമോഡിറ്റി - വില്പന വസ്തു, വ്യാപാര ചരക്ക്

Gold is a precious *commodity.*

Common *(adj.)* കോമൺ – 1. സാധാരണ
The crow is a *common* bird in India.
2. സാധാരണക്കാരൻ
A *common* man can't afford to buy a car.
3. സാമാന്യ ബുദ്ധി, സഹജ ബുദ്ധി
Fools have no *common* sense.

Community *(n.)* കമ്യൂണിറ്റി – സമുദായം, സമൂഹം
There is a large *community* of shoemakers in this locality.
The Parsi *community* is mainly concentrated in Mumbai.

Commute *(v.)* കമ്യൂട്ട്–നിത്യേന യാത്ര ചെയ്യുക
(n.) I *commute* from my home to office by bus.
(n.) The strike of buses created a problem for the *commuters.*

Companion *(n.)* കമ്പാനിയൻ–സുഹൃത്ത്, സഹയാത്രികൻ
Without a *companion,* one feels lonely on a long rail journey.
(adj.) 2. അനുബന്ധം
This is a *companion* volume to the previous publication.

Company *(n.)* കമ്പനി – 1. സ്ഥാപനം
At last, the *company* started making profits.
2. ദലം
A Captain commands a *company* of soldiers.
3. സുഹൃദ് വലയം
A man is known by the *company* he keeps.

Compare *(v.)* കോമ്പയർ–താരതമ്യപ്പെടുത്തുക, തുലനം ചെയ്യുക, സാമ്യം
One must *compare* the price and performance of different brands before buying a washing machine.
(n.) There is no *comparison* between the lifestyles of rich and poor.
(adj.) Of all the problems in the question paper, the last one was *comparatively* easy.

Compass *(n.)* കമ്പാസ്–1. ദിക്ക് കാട്ടിയന്ത്രം
A ship cannot be kept on its course without a *compass.*
2. വൃത്തം വരയ്ക്കാനുള്ള ഉപകരണം
The geometry teacher asked the students to buy a *compass* box.

Compassion *(n.)* കമ്പാഷൻ–സഹാനുഭൂതി
He has no *compassion* for the poor.

Compatible *(adj.)* കമ്പാറ്റിബ്ൾ – അനുകൂലം, അനുയോജ്യം
They were not *compatible* with the fast lifestyle abroad.

Compel *(v.)* കമ്പെൽ – നിർബന്ധിക്കുക
It's not good to *compel* a person to do something against his wish.

Compensate *(v.)* കാമ്പൻസേറ്റ് നഷ്ടപരിഹാരം നൽകുക
(v.) I had to *compensate* for the damage I caused to their car.
(n.) She did not ask for any *compensation* after she divorced her husband.

Competent *(adj.)* കാമ്പീറ്റന്റ് – കഴിവുറ്റ
She is one of the most *competent* workers of her company.

Competition *(n.)* കോമ്പറ്റിഷൻ – മത്സരം
Ramesh won the first prize in the painting *competition.*

Compile *(v.)* കമ്പൈൽ – സമാഹരിക്കുക
He *compiled* a book of short stories written by some great Indian writers.

Complacent *(adj.)* കംപ്ലേസ്മെന്റ് – അമിത വിശ്വാസം, അലംഭാവം
(adj.) He was *complacent* that he would win the elections; defeat came as a blow to him.
(n.) We lost that match because of *complacency.*

Complain *(v.)* കമ്പ്ളെൻ – പരാതിപ്പെടുക
The guests in the hotel *complained* about the bad food.
(n.) He lodged a *complaint* with the police about the theft in his house.

Complement കോംപ്ലിമെന്റ് –അനുയോജ്യം, അനുപൂരകം
(n.) This scarf is a perfect *complement* to that dress.
(v.) This scarf *complements* that dress very well.

Complete കംപ്ലീറ്റ് – 1. സമ്പൂർണ്ണം, പൂർണ്ണമാക്കുക

(adj.) My work here is not yet *complete.*

(v.) Complete your homework before you go to play.

(adj.) 2. പാടെ, പൂർണ്ണമായി

The building was *completely* destroyed in the fire.

Complex കോംപ്ലെക്സ്–1. സങ്കീർണ്ണമായ

(adj.) This is a *complex* problem, but we need to find a solution to it.

2. ഭവന ശൃംഖല

(n.) I shall see you in the shopping *complex.*

3. അപകർഷതാ ബോധം

(n.) She has developed a *complex* about her looks.

Complexion *(n.)* കോമ്പ്ളെക്ഷൻ – ചർമ്മത്തിന്റെ നിറം

She has a dusky *complexion,* but still looks good.

Complicated *(adj.)* കോപ്ലിക്കേറ്റഡ് – സങ്കീർണ്ണമായ, കുഴഞ്ഞു മറിഞ്ഞ

The Maths problem was too *complicated* to solve without the teacher's help.

Watch has a *complicated* machinery.

Compliment കോംപ്ലിമെന്റ്–അഭിനന്ദനം (നൽകുക)

(n.) I paid her a *compliment* for organising the party so well.

(v.) I *complimented* her for organising the party so well.

Component *(n.)* കോമ്പനെന്റ്–യന്ത്രഭാഗം

The *components* of this machine have rusted.

Composed *(adj.)* കമ്പോസ്ഡ്–ശാന്തചിത്തത

He looked *composed* at the funeral of his son.

Composition *(n.)* കോമ്പസിഷൻ–1. രചന

Arun's essay on Gandhiji was a fine piece of *composition.*

2. സംയോജനം, രൂപവല്ക്കരണം

The balanced *composition* of the new Cabinet was praised by the media.

Compound കാമ്പൗ ് –*(n.)* 1. പറമ്പ്, പുരയിടം

Her dead body was found in the *compound* of the building.

(v.) 2. സ്ഥിതി വഷളാക്കുക

The bad performance of the team along with the recent controversy *compounded* the problem further.

Comprehend *(v.)* കാമ്പ്രഹെൻഡ് – മനസ്സിലാക്കുക

(v.) I could not *comprehend* what he wanted to say.

(adj.) Illustrations and diagrams make the book more *comprehensible.*

(n.) Her excuses for arriving late every day are beyond my *comprehension.*

Comprehensive *(adj.)* കോമ്പ്രഹെൻസീവ് – സമഗ്രമായ

This dictionary is quite *comprehensive.*

Comprise *(v.)* കമ്പ്രൈസ് – അടങ്ങിയത്

Our family *comprises* four members in all.

Compromise കാമ്പ്രോമൈസ്–വിട്ടുവീഴ്ച, രാജിയാകൽ

(n.) Both the parties made a *compromise* to bring the situation under control.

(v.) With no other option left, we *compromised* with the situation.

Compulsory *(adj.)* കമ്പൽസറി–നിർബന്ധിതം

It is *compulsory* to wear a helmet while riding a bike.

Comrade *(n.)* കോംറേഡ് – സഖാവ്, സഹചാരി

He has been my *comrade* for many years.

Conceal *(v.)* കൺസീൽ– മറച്ചുവയ്ക്കുക, ഒളിപ്പിക്കുക

The stolen necklace was *concelaled* in the cupboard.

Concentrate *(v.)* കോൺസെൻട്രേറ്റ് – ഏകാഗ്രത പുലർത്തുക

(v.) You need to *concentrate* on your studies to pass the exams.

(n.) I lost my *concentration* and hit my bike against a car.

Concept *(n.)* കോൺസെപ്റ്റ്–ആധാര സിദ്ധാന്തം

Unless your *concepts* are clear, you won't understand trigonometry.

Concern *(v.)* കൺസേൺ – ബന്ധപ്പെട്ട, സംബന്ധിച്ച

This order *concerns* all government employees.

(prep.) Books *concerning* crime detection are very popular among the people.

(adj.) 2. ആശങ്ക

Amit is *concerned* about his health.

Concession *(n.)* കൺസെഷൻ – ഇളവ്

The poor students were granted half fee *concession* by the school.

Conclude *(v.)* കൺക്ലൂഡ് – 1. അവസാനിപ്പിക്കുക, അവസാനിക്കുക, തീരുക, നിഗമനത്തിലെത്തുക

The leader *concluded* his speech with an appeal for unity.

(n.) 2. നിഗമനം

On the basis of the evidence, the judge came to the *conclusion* that the accused was not guilty.

Concrete *(n.)* കോൺക്രീറ്റ്–1. കോൺക്രീറ്റ്

Lot of *concrete* is required to build a durable house.

(adj.) 2. സമഗ്രമായ, ഉറച്ച, വ്യക്തമായ

The employees gave some *concrete* proposals to the management to reduce the company losses.

Condemn *(v.)* കംെ – അപലപിക്കുക

Arya Samaj *condemned* idol worship.

Condense *(v.)* കൻെസ് – സംക്ഷിപ്തമാക്കുക, സംഗ്രഹിക്കുക

The long report of our school function was *condensed* into one paragraph by the newspapers.

Condition *(n.)* കിഷൻ–1. ദശ, അവസ്ഥ

This house is not in a good *condition.*

2. ഉപാധി, നിബന്ധന

What is your *condition* for joining us?

3. പരിതസ്ഥിതി

Under the stormy *conditions,* it is better to stay indoors.

Condolence *(n.)* കലൻസ്–അനുശോചനം

I offered my *condolences* to the father of my dead friend.

Conduct *(n.)* കോാക്ട് – 1. പെരുമാറ്റം, നടപ്പ്

A new recuit's *conduct* is always under watch.

(v.) 2. വഴി കാണിക്കുക

The doorkeeper *conducted* me to my seat in the cinema hall.

3. നടത്തിയെടുക്കുക

He presided over the conference and *conducted* it ably.

Conference *(n.)* കോൺഫെറൻസ് – സമ്മേളനം

A *conference* of religious leaders was held to discuss communal harmony.

Confess *(v.)* കൺഫെസ് – ഏറ്റുപറയുക, കുറ്റസമ്മതം

The boy *confessed* that he broke the window pane.

(n.) The thief made a full *confession* of his crimes before the judge.

Confide *(v.)* കൺഫൈഡ്–തുറന്നുപറയുക

I *confided* my feelings to my best friend.

Confidence *(n.)* വിശ്വാസം

The *confidence* on a friend is tested in a crisis.

(adj.) Ram was very *confident* of scoring good marks in the annual exams.

Confine *(v.)* കൺഫൈൻ–1. ഒതുക്കി നിർത്തുക

A fracture in the leg kept Ram *confined* to his home for a month.

(n.) 2. ബന്ധനസ്ഥൻ

The murderer was kept in a solitary *confinement.*

Confirm *(v.)* കൺഫേം–സ്ഥിരീകരിക്കുക

(v.) The India-Pakistan cricket tournament has been *confirmed.*

(n.) You need to send me a *confirmation* before coming for the meeting.

Conflict *(n.)* കോൺഫ്ളിക്റ്റ്–സംഘട്ടനം, യുദ്ധം

Pakistan and India have witnessed three *conflicts.*

(*adj.*) 2. പരസ്പര വിരുദ്ധ
Newspapers published *conflicting* (contradictory) reports about the plane hijack.
(*v.*) Sometimes, young generation's ideas *conflict* with those of their parents.

Confuse (*v.*) കൺഫ്യൂസ്–1. കുഴയ്ക്കുക, അമ്പരപ്പിക്കുക
The lawyer's question *confused* the witness.
2. ഒന്ന് മറ്റൊന്നായി തോന്നുക
Between the twins, it is usual to *confuse* one with the other.

Confusion (*n.*) കൺഫ്യൂഷൻ–ചിന്താക്കുഴപ്പം
A great *confusion* ensued on the overcrowded platform with the arrival of train.

Congested (*adj.*) കൺജെസ്റ്റഡ് – തിക്കും തിരക്കുമുള്ള
The roads in Old Delhi are very *congested.*

Congratulate (*v.*) കൺഗ്രാചുലേറ്റഡ് – അഭിനന്ദിക്കുക
Prakash *congratulated* Prabhat on his outstanding success in the examination.
(*n.*) Dinesh received a telegram of *congratulations* on his wedding day.

Connect (*v.*) കണക്ട് – കൂട്ടിചേർക്കുക, ബന്ധമുാവുക
He is well *connected* in Delhi's political circle.
This lane *connects* two busy streets.

Conquer (*v.*) കൺക്വർ – കീഴടക്കുക, പിടിച്ചടക്കുക
Hitler *conquered* a large part of Europe.
Tenzing *conquered* Mount Everest.

Conscience (*n.*) കോൺഷിയൻസ്–മനസാക്ഷി
Even a criminal's *conscience* warns him against committing crimes.

Conscious (*n.*) കാൺഷിയസ് –
1. സുബോധമുള്ള
The fatally injured accident victim was *conscious* enough to give his address to the policeman.
2. ബോധമുാവുക
Are you *conscious* of the serious consequences of you bad deeds?

Consecutive (*adj.*) കാൺസെക്യൂട്ടീവ് – തുടർച്ചയായ
She was absent for three *consecutive* days.

Consent (*v.*) കാൺസെന്റ്–സമ്മതിക്കുക
She *consented* to her daughter's marriage with a man of different caste.
(*n.*) 2. അനുമതി, സമ്മതം
Students were asked to have their parent's *consent* for a tour to Agra.

Consequence (*n.*) കാൺസിക്വൻസ് – അനന്തരഫലം, പരിണാമം, ഫലമായി
Often, thoughtless acts lead to serious *consequences.*
(*Conj.*) I missed the bus and *consequently* (as a result) was late for office.

Conservation (*n.*) കൺസർവേഷൻ – സംരക്ഷണം
We must take steps towards environmental *conservation.*

Consider (*v.*) കൺസിഡർ – 1. പരിഗണിക്കുക, ആലോചിക്കുക
Please *consider* this matter carefully.
2. സമ്മതിക്കുക, അംഗീകരിക്കുക
I do not *consider* it an important matter.

Considerable (*adj.*) കൺസിഡറബ്ൾ – ഗണ്യമായ, വളരെയേറെ
Dhanraj has a *considerable* amount of money in the bank.

Consist (*v.*) കാൺസിസ്റ്റ്– അടങ്ങിയിട്ടുള്ള
Our colony's welfare committee *consists* of five members and a chairman.

Console(*v.*) കൺസോൾ–സാന്ത്വനപ്പെടുത്തുക
She was hard to *console* when she came to know about her failure.

Conspire (*v.*) കൺസ്പയർ – ഗൂഢാലോചന (നടത്തുക)
(*v.*) The commander was held responsible for *conspiring* against his own country.
(*n.*) The commander was held responsible for hatching a *conspiracy.*

Constable (*n.*) കാൺസ്റ്റബിൾ – ശിപായി, കോൺസ്റ്റബിൾ
The traffic police *constable* signalled the speeding car to stop.

Constant *(adj.)* കോൺസ്റ്റന്റ് –1. സ്ഥിരമായ, ഒരേപോലെ

I drive my car at a *constant* speed.

(adv.) 2. നിരന്തരം, സദാ

She is *constantly* reading novels.

Constitution *(n.)* കോൺസ്റ്റിറ്റ്യൂഷൻ – ഭരണഘടന, നിയമാവലി

Students of law have to study the Indian *Constitution.*

2. ശരീര ഘടന

Meena has a delicate *constitution.*

Constraint *(n.)* കൺസ്ട്രെയിന്റ് –പരിമിതി

(n.) We left that project because of financial *constraints.*

(v.) Lack of funds *constrained* the expansion of our business.

Construct *(v.)* കൺസ്ട്രെക്റ്റ്–നിർമ്മിക്കുക

The company has *constructed* flats for its employees.

Consult *(v.)* കൺസൽറ്റ്–ഉപദേശം തേടുക

The rich lady *consulted* many specialists about her illness.

Consume *(v.)* കൺസ്യൂം – കഴിക്കുക, ഉപയോഗിക്കുക

He *consumed* several cups of tea.

Contact കോൺടാക്റ്റ് – സമ്പർക്കം

(n.) I don't have his *contact* details.

(v.) You can *contact* me at this number.

Contagious *(adj.)* കജേിയസ് – പകർച്ച, സാംക്രമിക

Tuberculosis is a *contagious* disease.

Contain *(v.)* കൺടെയ്ൻ – ഉൾപ്പെടുക, അടങ്ങിയിട്ടുള്ള

Textbooks *contain* many chapters.

Contemplate *(v.)* കൺടെംപ്ലേറ്റ് – ആലോചിക്കുക

I am *contemplating* taking a long leave.

Contempt *(n.)* കൺടെംപ്റ്റ്–നിന്ദ, വെറുപ്പ്

I was filled with *contempt* for the family who killed their daughter-in-law.

Contend *(v.)* കൺടെന്റ് –എതിരിടുക

I have my own problems to *contend* with.

2. മത്സരിക്കുക

Several companies were *contending* for the tender.

3. വാദിക്കുക

The servant *contended* that he did not commit the theft.

Content *(adj.)* കൺടെന്റ് –തൃപ്തിപ്പെടുക

The distinguished guest was *content* with the arrangements made for him.

Contents *(v.)* കൺടെന്റ്സ് – ഉള്ളടക്കം

It is better to go through the *contents* of the book before buying it.

Contest *(n.)* കാൺടെസ്റ്റ്–മത്സരം, വിവാദം

Rajendra bagged the first prize in the essay *contest.*

Continent *(n.)* കോിനെന്റ് – ഭൂഖണ്ഡം

India is in the *continent* of Asia.

Continue *(v.)* കിന്യൂ – തുടരുക

Many TV serials are *continued* even after a century of their episodes.

Contract *(n.)* കാൺട്രാക്റ്റ്–1. കരാർ, ഇടപാട്

The two friends entered into a *contract* to set up a company.

(n.) 2. കരാറുകാരൻ

Some firms prefer to give their various jobs to *contractors.*

(v.) 3. ചുരുങ്ങുക

Metals *contract* as they grow colder.

Contradict *(v.)* കോൺട്രഡിക്റ്റ് – നിഷേധിക്കുക

The minister *contradicted* the statement attributed to him by the press.

Contrary *(adj.)* കാൺട്രറി–വിപരീതം, വിരുദ്ധമായി

What Ram had done was *contrary* to the rules of his company.

Contrary to my expectations, Ramesh declined my invitation.

Contrast കോൺട്രാസ്റ്റ് – വ്യത്യാസം, പരസ്പര വിപരീതം

(n.) There is a remarkable *contrast* between the looks of the two brothers.

(v.) Bright lights *contrasted* beautifully with the dark night.

Contribute *(v.)* കോൺട്രിബ്യൂട്ട് – 1. സംഭാവന നൽകുക

People *contributed* generously to the flood relief fund.

2. ലേഖനം നൽകുക

I *contribute* articles to many journals.

Control കൺട്രോൾ – നിയന്ത്രണം, വരുതിയിലാക്കുക

(n.) The car suddenly got out of *control.*

The police brought the law and order situation in the riot-torn city under *control.*

(v.) The jockey *controlled* the untamed horse skilfully.

Convenient *(adj.)* കൺവീനിയന്റ് – സൗകര്യപ്രദം

When will it be *convenient* to you to come to my place?

Conventional *(adj.)* കൺവെൻഷണൽ – സാധാരണ, പതിവായ

I never liked the *conventional* 9 to 5 job.

Conversation *(n.)* കാൺവെർസേഷൻ – സംഭാഷണം

Geeta had a long *conversation* with her friend on the phone.

Convert കൺവെർട്ട് – 1. പരിവർത്തനം, മാറ്റം വരുത്തുക

(v.) Her very presence *converted* a dull party into a lively one.

2. വാഹനം

(n.) After reading so many books on Sikhism, I almost feel like a *convert* now.

Convey *(v.)* കൺവേ – അറിയിക്കുക, ധരിപ്പിക്കുക

Did you *convey* my message to Ram?

(n.) 2. വാഹനം

I go to office in my own *conveyance.*

Convict കൺവിക്ട് – അപരാധി

(n.) The *convict* was arrested soon.

(v.) He was *convicted* of a theft.

Conviction *(n.)* കൺവിക്ഷൻ–ഉറച്ച വിശ്വാസം

It was with great *conviction* that I contacted him.

Convince *(v.)* കൺവിൻസ്–ബോദ്ധ്യപ്പെടുത്തുക

The judge was *convinced* of the guilt of the accused.

Cook കുക്ക്–പാചകം ചെയ്യുക,പാചകക്കാരി

(v.) Sita's mother *cooks* very tasty food.

(n.) She is an excellent *cook.*

Cool *(adj.)* കൂൾ – തണുത്ത, ശീതള

The weather became quite *cool* after rain.

2. ശാന്തം, സംയമനമുള്ള

Arun's behaviour is always *cool* and composed.

Cooperate *(v.)* കോഓപ്പറേറ്റ് – സഹകരിക്കുക, ഒത്തുചേർന്ന് പണിയെടുക്കുക

All the villagers *cooperated* in building the village school.

Coordinate *(v.)* കോഓർഡിനേറ്റ് – ഏകോപിക്കുക

I'll have to *coordinate* with her to get this project completed.

Cope *(v.)* കോപ് – ബദ്ധപ്പെട്ട് നേരിടുക

It's difficult to *cope* with the ever-changing technology.

Copy കോപ്പി–പകർപ്പ്, പ്രതി, അനുകരിക്കുക

(n.) Usha asked for a *copy* of Sita's picture in the bridal make-up.

(v.) I *copied* down some booksellers' phone numbers from the directory.

Cord *(n.)* കോർഡ് – ചരട്, വള്ളി, കയറ്

He tied his bedding with a *cord.*

Core *(n.)* ഫോർ ഫാതൽ, സാരാംശം

One must first understand the *core* of a problem to solve it properly.

Cork *(n.)* കോർക്ക് – അടപ്പ്, കോർക്ക്

He closed the bottle with a *cork.*

Corn *(n.)* കോൺ – ധാന്യം

The farmers were busy harvesting the *corn.*

Corner *(n.)* കോർണർ – മൂല, വരമ്പ് പിടിക്കുക

The chemist's shop at the street *corner* had the entrance from two sides.

Old papers were stacked in a *corner* of the room.

(v.) The cat *cornered* the mouse and killed it.

Corpse *(n.)* കോർപ്പ്സ് – മൃതദേഹം, ശവം

The police took away the unclaimed *corpse* lying on the roadside.

Correct കറക്ട് – ശരി (ശരിയാക്കുക)

(v.) Please *correct* all these mistakes.

(adj.) Only Ramesh gave the *correct* answer.

Correspondence *(n.)* കറസ്പോൻസ് – എഴുത്തുകുത്ത്

Correpondence plays a significant role in business dealings.

Corridor *(n.)* കോറിഡോർ – ഇടനാഴി

The building had a long *corridor* leading to the servants quarter in the backyard.

Corrupt കറപ്റ്റ് – അഴിമതിക്കാർ

(adj.) A few *corrupt* officers have spoiled the reputation of the whole police department.

(v.) There are few who are not *corrupted* by money and power.

(n.) *Corruption* has spread like a disease in India.

Cost കോസ്റ്റ് – ചെലവ്, വില, എന്തു വില കൊടുത്തു

(v.) How much does this book *cost*?

(adj.) A necklace of diamonds is very *costly* (expensive).

(n.) For job interview, you must reach in time at all *costs* (in spite of difficulties).

Costume *(n.)* കോസ്ട്യൂം – വേഷവിധാനം

This *costume* suits your role well.

Cosy *(adj.)* കോസി – സുഖപ്രദം

Homeless people dreamed of a *cosy* home.

Cot *(n.)* കോട്ട് – കട്ടിൽ

The child was sleeping on the *cot.*

Cottage *(n.)* കോട്ടേജ് – കുടിൽ

The poor family lived in a *cottage* outside the town.

Cotton *(n.)* കോട്ടൺ – പരുത്തി, പഞ്ഞി, പരുത്തി വസ്ത്രം

Cotton clothes are the best in a hot country like India.

Cough കഫ് – ചുമ, ചുമയ്ക്കുക

(n.) He was suffering from cold and *cough.*

(v.) The patients *coughed* constantly.

Council *(n.)* കൗൺസിൽ – കൗൺസിൽ, സമിതി

Our association has a General *Council* and an Executive Committee.

Count *(n.)* കൗ് – എണ്ണുക, എണ്ണമെടുക്കുക

The little child was taught to *count.*

The teacher *counted* the students before distributing the papers.

2. എണ്ണമറ്റ

The Independence Day function was attended by *countless* people.

3. കുറ്റം, ആരോപണം

On what *count* was he charged?

Counter *(n.)* കൗണ്ടർ – കൗണ്ടർ

People queued up before the cashier's *counter.*

Country *(n.)* കൺട്രി – രാജ്യം, ദേശം

India is a very big *country.*

2. നാട്ടിൻപുറം, ഗ്രാമപ്രദേശം

Agriculture is the main occupation of the people in the *countryside.*

Couple *(n.)* കപ്പ്ൾ – ദമ്പതി, വധൂവരന്മാർ

The old man blessed the newly married *couple.*

2. ജോഡി

Please give me a *couple* of oranges.

Coupon *(n.)* കൂപ്പൺ – കൂപ്പൺ

The boys sold *coupons* for the school fete.

Courage *(n.)* കറേജ് – സാഹസം, ധൈര്യം

The soldier was awarded a medal for his extraordinary *courage.*

Courier *(n.)* കൊറിയർ – കൊറിയർ

I'll send you the documents by *courier.*

Course *(n.)* കോഴ്സ് – 1. പ്രസംഗ(ത്തിൽ), മദ്ധ്യേ

In the *course* of his lecture, the saint talked about the evils of drinking.

2. ഗതി, വഴി

The river changed its *course* during the flood.

3. പാഠ്യക്രമം, വിഷയം

Have you completed your *course* for the examination?

(adv.) *Of course* (certainly) I shall come.

Court *(n.)* കോർട്ട് – കോടതി

The culprit was produced in a *court* of law.

2. രാജ സദസ്സ്

The noblemen took their appointed places in the royal *court.*

(v.) 3. വരിക്കുക, പ്രേമിക്കുക

The Satyagrahis *courted* arrest.

Courtesy *(n.)* കർട്ട്സി – 1. വിനയം
Courtesy costs nothing.
(adj.) 2. മര്യാദ
Some people are very *courteous.*

Courtyard *(n.)* മുറ്റം, അങ്കണം
The children were playing in the *courtyard.*

Cousin *(n.)* കസിൻ – വകയിൽ സഹോദരൻ അല്ലെങ്കിൽ സഹോദരി
I visited my *cousin* in Mumbai last week.

Cover കവർ – 1. മൂടുക, അടയ്ക്കുക, പുതയ്ക്കുക
(v.) The mother *covered* her sleeping child with a blanket.
(n.) 2. മറവ്
The thief approached the house under the *cover* of darkness.

Cow *(n.)* കൗവ് – പശു
Cow's milk is good for babies.

Coward *(n.)* കൊവാർഡ് – ഭീരു
A *coward* cannot be a soldier.

Crack *(n.)* ക്രാക്ക് – പൊട്ടൽ, വെടിക്കൽ
Many *cracks* appeared in the building following the earthquake.
2. വെടി
The *crack* of a gun startled everybody in the market.
3. ദിനാരംഭം
A walk is good at the *crack* of dawn.
(adj.) 4. പൊട്ടിയ, വെടിച്ച
The *cracked* cup should be discarded.
(v.) 5. പൊട്ടി
The egg *cracked* and the chick came out.

Cradle *(n.)* ക്രാഡിൽ – 1. തൊട്ടിൽ
She put her baby in the *cradle.*
2. ഉത്ഭവസ്ഥാനം
India is the *cradle* of ancient civilisations.

Craft *(n.)* ക്രാഫ്റ്റ്–കരവിരുത്, ശില്പ ചാരുത
Wood carving is a *craft* of skill.
2. നൗക, വിമാനം
The *aircraft* took off on schedule.

Crafty *(adj.)* ക്രാഫ്റ്റി–ധൂർത്ത, കുടില, കപട
Never trust a *crafty* person.

Cram ക്രാം – 1. കുത്തി നിറയ്ക്കുക
(v.) She *crammed* all her cosmetics in a smali bag.
(adj.) The bus was *crammed* with passengers.
2. മനപാഠം ചെയ്യുക
(v.) I *crammed* the whole essay for the exams.

Cramp *(n.)* ക്രാംപ്-വലി, കഴപ്പ്, കൊളുത്ത്
I had terrible *cramps* in my stomach last night.

Cramped *(adj.)* ക്രാംപ്ഡ്–തിങ്ങി നിറഞ്ഞ
The room was too *cramped* to accommodate more people.

Crash *(n.)* ക്രാഷ് – 1. മഹാരവം
The building came down with a *crash.*
(v.) 2. കൂട്ടിമുട്ടുക
The motor-car *crashed* against a wall.
(adj.) 3. സത്വര, ത്വരിത
She joined a *crash* cooking course.

Crane -ക്രെയ്ൻ – 1. ഭാരിച്ച സാധനങ്ങൾ, ഉയർത്താനുള്ള യന്ത്രം
(n.) The car was picked up by a *crane.*
2. കൊക്ക്, കൊറ്റി
(n.) I saw two *cranes* near the lake.
3. കഴുത്ത് നീട്ടുക
(v.) She *craned* her neck out of the window to see what was happening outside.

Crawl *(v.)* ക്രാൾ – ഇഴയുക
The little baby *crawls* on its hands and feet.

Crazy *(adj.)* ക്രേസി – ഭ്രാന്ത് പിടിപ്പിക്കുക, മനോനില തെറ്റുക
The shock of her son's death drove the old mother *crazy.*

Cream *(n.)* ക്രീം – പാട, ക്രീം
I like coffee with *cream.*

Crave *(v.)* ക്രേവ് – കൊതിക്കുക
I was *craving* for a chocolate since morning.

Crease ക്രീസ് – ഉടവ്, ചുളിവ്, ഞൊറി

(n.) The sari was full of *creases.*

(v.) She *creased* the paper in the middle.

Create *(v.)* ക്രിയേറ്റ് – 1. സൃഷ്ടിക്കുക, നിർമ്മിക്കുക

God *created* the world.

(n.) 2. ജീവി, സൃഷ്ടി

We all are God's *creatures.*

Credible *(adj.)* ക്രെഡിബ്ൾ– വിശ്വസനീയം

It was hardly *credible* that India lost a match against Bangladesh.

Credit *(n.)* ക്രെഡിറ്റ് – 1. പ്രശസ്തമായി

He passed the examination with *credit.*

2. വായ്പ, കടം

Some shopkeepers give no *credit.*

3. വിശ്വാസം

Nobody placed *credit* in Rahul's story.

(v.) Only the brave are *credited* with success.

Creep *(v.)* ക്രീപ് – പതുങ്ങി കയറുക

The thief *crept* into the house without making a sound.

Creeper *(n.)* ക്രീപ്പർ – വള്ളി, ലത

The wall of the garden was covered with *creepers.*

Cremate *(v.)* ക്രിമേറ്റ്–അന്തിമ സംസ്കാരം നടത്തുക

My grandfather always wanted his dead body to be *cremated* in Haridwar.

Crescent *(n.)* ക്രെസന്റ് – അമ്പിളിക്കല, അർദ്ധചന്ദ്രാകൃതി

The *crescent* of the new moon could be seen in the clear sky.

Crest *(n.)* ക്രെസ്റ്റ് മകുടം, ശിഖ

During the storm, the ship was thrown up on the *crest* of a huge wave.

Some leaders win the elections on the *crest* of their wave of popularity.

Crew *(n.)* ക്രൂ – വിമാന ജോലിക്കാർ

The plane has a *crew* of six.

Cricket *(n.)* ക്രിക്കറ്റ് – ക്രിക്കറ്റ്, കളി

Indians love to watch *cricket.*

2. ചീവീട്

I saw *crickets* flying about in the garden.

Crime *(n.)* ക്രൈം – അപരാധം, കുറ്റം

It is a *crime* to steal.

The *criminal* was sent to jail.

Crimson ക്രിംസൺ – കടുംചുവപ്പ്, രക്തവർണ്ണം

At sunset, the clouds in the west become *crimson* in colour.

Crippled *(n.)* ക്രിപ്പിൾഡ് – വികലാംഗൻ, അശക്തമാക്കുക

The *crippled* hobbled down the street.

(v.) The spinner's absence *crippled* the team's bowling.

Crisis *(n.)* ക്രൈസിസ് – പ്രതിസന്ധി

She always supports me in the times of a *crisis.*

Crisp *(adj.)* ക്രിസ്പ് – 1. മൊരുമുരപ്പുള്ള

We enjoyed the *crisp* potato chips with tea.

2. ഉരുളയ്ക്കപ്പേരിയെന്നപോലെ

She gave a *crisp* reply to my question.

Criterion *(n.)* ക്രൈറ്റീരിയൻ – മാനദണ്ഡം

Score obtained in the entrance test is the sole *criterion* to get an admission in this course.

Critic *(n.)* ക്രിട്ടിക്ക് – വിമർശകൻ, നിരൂപകൻ, വിമർശനം

The art *critic* of the newspaper praised the exhibition of paintings.

The government's new education policy came in for a lot of *criticism.*

Critical *(adj.)* ക്രിട്ടിക്കൽ –

1. വിമർശനാത്മകമായി

Father was *critical* of his son's rude manners.

2. ഗുരുതര

The wounded man was taken to the hospital in a *critical* condition.

Criticise *(v.)* ക്രിട്ടിസൈസ്–വിമർശിക്കുക

The players were criticised for poor performance.

Croak *(v.)* ക്രൊാക്ക് – തവള കരയുക
Frogs are *croaking* in the pond.

Crocodile *(n.)* ക്രൊാക്കഡയൽ – ചീങ്കണ്ണി
There is a very big *crocodile* in the zoo.

Crook *(n.)* ക്രൂക്ക്–ചതിയൻ, വഞ്ചകൻ, കള്ളൻ
Crooks are quick to cheat the innocent.

Crooked *(adj.)* ക്രൂക്കഡ് – 1. വളഞ്ഞ, വക്ര
The boy drew a *crooked* line on his slate.
2. കപട ചിത്തരായ, നേര് കെട്ട
It is not good to keep company with *crooked* people.

Crop ക്രോപ് – 1. വിളവ്
(n.) Rain destroyed the whole *crop* of wheat.
2. വെട്ടി ചെറുതാക്കുക
(v.) He *cropped* his hair very short.
3. കലഹമുാക്കുക
(v.) A fight *cropped* up between the two neighbours.

Cross *(n.)* ക്രോസ് – 1. കുരിശ്
Jesus Christ died on the *cross.*
(v.) 2. കടക്കുക, മറിച്ച് കടക്കുക
We must use subways to *cross* the busy roads.
3. വെട്ടിക്കളയുക
The teacher *crossed* out the wrongly spelt words.
(adj.) 4. പിണങ്ങുക, കുപിത
Why do you look so *cross*?

Crouch ക്രൗച്ച് – പതുങ്ങിയിരിക്കുക
The cat *crouched* on the ground before jumping on the mouse.

Crow *(n.)* ക്രോവ്, – കാക്ക
The *crow* is a bird commonly found in India.
(v.) 2. കോഴി കൂവുക
Cock *crows* early in the morning.

Crowd ക്രൗഡ് – കൂട്ടം, ആൾക്കൂട്ടം, തിരക്കേറിയ, ചുറ്റും കൂടുക
(n.) A large *crowd* gathered at the airport to greet the leader.
(adj.) In Delhi, the buses are mostly *crowded.*
(v.) The journalists *crowded* around the chief minister.

Crown ക്രൗൺ–1. കിരീടം, കിരീട ധാരണം, സ്ഥാനാരോഹണം ചെയ്യുക
(n.) The king wore a glittering *crown.*
(v.) He was *crowned* as the king.
(n.) 2. മുടികെട്ട്, കേശാലങ്കാരം
Rekha has an attractive *crown.*

Crucial *(adj.)* ക്രൂഷ്യൽ – നിർണ്ണായക
Deciding between cutting costs and investing in a new project was a *crucial* choice to make.

Cruel *(adj.)* ക്രൂഅൽ – 1. ക്രൂര
Cruel Kans put Devaki and Vasudev into prison.
2. ക്രൂരത
Never show *cruelty* to dumb animals.

Cruise *(n.)* ക്രൂസ് – സമുദ്രയാത്ര
We went on a *cruise* during the holidays.

Crumb *(n.)* ക്രം – നുറുക്ക്, തു്
I threw a *crumb* of bread to the dog.

Crumble *(v.)* ക്രംബ്ൾ – ജീർണ്ണിക്കുക, പൊടിയുക
The old building is about to *crumble.*

Crush *(v.)* ക്രഷ് – ചതഞ്ഞരയുക
The unfortunate cyclist was *crushed* under the bus.

Crust *(n.)* ക്രസ്റ്റ് – മേൽപടലം
There was a thick *crust* on the surface of the old paint.

Crux *(n.)* ക്രക്സ്–ഏറ്റവും പ്രധാന ഭാഗം
The Kurukshetra war forms the *crux* of Mahabharata.

Cry ക്രൈ – 1. കരയുക, വിളിക്കുക
(v.) The little boy was *crying* for his mother.
2. ആക്രോശനം
Ram gave a *cry* of surprise when he saw Suresh after a long time.

Cub *(n.)* കബ് – മൃഗക്കുട്ടി
The lioness in the zoo gave birth to two *cubs.*

Culprit *(n.)* കൾപ്രിറ്റ്–കുറ്റവാളി, അപരാധി
The *culprit* was sent to the jail.

Cultivate *(v.)* കൾട്ടിവേറ്റ്–1. കൃഷി ചെയ്യുക, വിളവിറക്കുക
The farmer *cultivates* his land.
2. പരിചയം ഉറപ്പിക്കുക, അടുത്തു കൂടുക
Some people *cultivate* the influential people to get things done through them.

Culture *(n.)* കൾച്ചർ – സംസ്കാരം
Our scriptures reflect the richness of the Indian *culture*.

Cunning *(adj.)* കണ്ണിംഗ്–കൗശല, സൂത്രശാലി
The fox is a *cunning* animal.

Cup *(n.)* കപ് – ലോട്ട, കോപ്പ
Can I have a *cup* of tea?

Cure ക്യൂർ – ചികിത്സ, സുഖപ്പെടുത്തുക
(n.) There is no *cure* for the common cold.
(v.) The doctor *cured* the poor free of charge.

Curious *(adj.)* ക്യൂരിയസ് – 1. ജിജ്ഞാസ, കൗതുകം
Father was *curious* to see his little daughter's dance performance at the school function.
2. വിചിത്ര, അസാധാരണ
The archaeologists found some *curious* marks on the excavated articles.

Curl കേൾ – 1. ചുരുളുക, ചുരുറുകൂടുക
(v.) The cat *curled* up on the chair.
(n.) Sally's head is full of lovely *curls*.
2. ചുരുൾ മുടി
Sally has *curly* hair.

Current *(n.)* കറന്റ് –1. ധാര, പ്രവാഹം, ഒഴുക്ക്
The river flows with a swift *current*.
2. വൈദ്യുതി പ്രവാഹം
Turn off the *current* before you change the bulb.
(n.) 3. നടപ്പ്, നിലവിലുള്ള
Youngsters are quick to follow the *current* trends in dressing.

Curry *(n.)* കറി – കറി, വിഭവം
He is very fond of chicken *curry*.

Curse കഴ്സ്–ശപിക്കുക, പ്രാകുക, ശാപം
(v.) My ill-natured neighbour is always *cursing* the world.
(n.) Poverty is a *curse*.

Curtain *(n.)* കർട്ടൻ – തിരശ്ശീല
Curtains help in keeping out the summer heat.

Curve *(n.)* കർവ്–വളവ്, തിരിവ്, വക്രരേഖ
Rahul's home is round the *curve*.

Cushion *(n.)* കുഷൻ, ഇരിപ്പ് മെത്ത
I bought *cushions* for my sofa set.

Custody *(n.)* കസ്റ്റഡി – രക്ഷകർത്തൃത്വം
The *custody* of the child was granted to the mother.

Custom *(n.)* കസ്റ്റം – വഴക്കം, ആചാരം
Some Indian *customs* are quite old.

Customs *(n.)* കസ്റ്റംസ് – ചുങ്കം വകുപ്പ്
Dinesh is an officer in the *customs*.

Customer *(n.)* കസ്റ്റമർ–ക്രേതാവ്, പറ്റുകാരൻ
A good shopkeeper tries to please his *customers*.

Cut *(v.)* കട്ട് – 1. മുറിക്കുക
Uma *cut* her finger while slicing the apple.
(n.) 2. മുറിവ്
The doctor cleaned the *cut* on Uma's finger with an antiseptic lotion.
3. തു ് കഷണം
Please give me a *cut* of the meat.

Cute *(adj.)* ക്യൂട്ട് – ആകർഷകം
She looks *cute* with her dimpled cheeks.

Cycle സൈക്കിൾ–സൈക്കിൾ (ഓടിക്കുക) ചക്രം, കാലചക്രം
(n.) *Cycle* of seasons is an important phenomenon of Nature.
(v.) He *cycles* to office every day.

Cylinder *(n.)* സിലിർ – സിലിർ
The house caught fire when the gas *cylinder* burst.

Cynic *(n.)* സിനിക് – ദോഷൈകദൃക് പരുഷമായ
(n.) Stay away from him; he is a *cynic*.
(adj.) Don't be discouraged with his *cynical* remarks.

D

Dacoit *(n.)* ഡക്കോയറ്റ് - കൊള്ളക്കാരൻ
There used to be *dacoits* in the Chambal Valley many years ago.

Dagger *(n.)* ഡാഗർ - കഠാരി
A collection of *daggers* was on display in the museum.

Daily *(adv.)* ഡെയ്‌ലി–1. ദിവസേന, നിത്യവും
The doctor advised the heart patient to take a walk *daily* in the morning.
(n.) 2. ദിനപത്രം
Reena is employed as a reporter in a local *daily*.
(adj.) Exercise is an essential part of *daily* routine of a healthy person.

Dainty *(adj.)* ഡെയ്ൻടി - മനോഹരമായ, ആസ്വാദ്യമായ
We were all charmed by the dancer's *dainty* performance.

Dairy *(n.)* ഡെയ്റി - ഡെയ്റി, ക്ഷീരശാല
From which *dairy* do you get your milk supply?

Dam *(n.)* ഡാം - അണക്കെട്ട്
Have you seen the Bhakhra *Dam*?

Damage ഡാമേജ്–കേട്പാട്, നാശം വരുത്തുക
(v.) You will *damage* the apples if you let them fall on the ground.
(n.) The storm caused a lot of *damage* to the garden.

Damages *(n.)* ഡാമേജസ് - നഷ്ടപരിഹാരം
The principal asked the students to pay *damages* for the window panes they had broken while playing in the classroom.

Damp *(adv.)* ഡാംപ് - നനഞ്ഞ, ഈറൻ
We shall catch a cold if we wear *damp* clothes.

Dance *(n. & v.)* ഡാൻസ് - നൃത്തം, നൃത്തം ചെയ്യുക
(n.) Radha became famous after her first *dance* performance.
(v.) At the farewell party, the teachers and students *danced* together.

Danger *(n.)* ഡെയ്ഞ്ചർ - അപകടം
Roma was seriously ill last week, but now she is out of *danger*.

Dangle *(v.)* ഡാൻഗ്ൾ - ഞാന്നു കിടക്കുക, ഊഞ്ഞാലാടുക
The boy saw a kite *dangling* from the tree.

Dare *(v.)* ഡെയർ - 1. ധൈര്യപ്പെടുക
How *dare* he say such a nasty thing about you!
2. ഉറപ്പാക്കാനാവാതെ, തീർച്ചയില്ലാതെ
I *dare* say I shall be able to come.

Dark ഡാർക് - 1. ഇരുട്ട്, അന്ധകാരം
(adj.) Are you not afraid to go out in a *dark* night?
2. കടും
Some people dye their hair to make them *dark* black.
(n.) Don't go out in the *dark*.

Darling ഡാർലിംഗ് - ഓമന, പ്രിയ
(adj.) I want my *darling* daughter to be a famous singer.
(n.) A new prime minister is usually the *darling* of the media when he assumes charge.

Dart *(v.)* ഡാർട്ട് - ചാടുക, സത്വരം ഗമിക്ക
The squirrel was *darting* from branch to branch in the garden.

Dash *(v.)* ഡാഷ്–1.കുതിച്ചെത്തുക, പായുക
Suresh *dashed* into my room to give me the news of his selection in the school cricket team.
2. തകർന്നു പോകുക, നിരുത്സാഹപ്പെടുക
Rakesh's hopes of playing for the school were *dashed* when he was not selected in the hockey team.
(n.) 3. കുതിച്ചോടുക
The waiting passengers made a *dash* for the bus.

Data *(n.)* ഡേറ്റാ – സംഗ്രഹം
The *data* stored in the computer has corrupted.

Database *(n.)* ഡേറ്റാബേസ് – അടിസ്ഥാന സൂചിക
Prepare a *database* of all our customers.

Date *(n.)* ഡേറ്റ് – തീയതി
What will be the *date* next Monday?
(v.) തീയതി ഇടുക
Always *date* the official letters and job applications.

Daughter *(n.)* ഡാട്ടർ – മകൾ, പുത്രി
How old is your *daughter*?

Dawn *(n.)* ഡാൺ–പ്രഭാതം, പുലർച്ചെ, രാവിലെ
The villagers usually get up at *dawn.*

Day *(n.)* ഡേ – ദിവസം, ദിനം
I have to go to Mumbai for a couple of*days*.

Daze *(n.)* ഡേസ് – സ്തംഭിച്ച് പോവുക, അന്ധാളിക്കുക
I was so *dazed* by the accident that I did not know what to do.

Dazzle ഡാസ്ൽ–കണ്ണു മഞ്ഞളിപ്പിക്കുക, തിളക്കം
(v.) The sun will *dazzle* you if you look at it.
(n.) The *dazzle* of money attracts everybody.

Dead *(adj.)* ഡെഡ് – മരിച്ച, പരേത
The *dead* woman left her property to a distant poor relative.

Deadline *(n.)* ഡെഡ്‌ലൈൻ–സമയ പരിധി
The boss was very happy with our team when we met the unrealistic *deadline.*

Deadlock *(n.)* ഡെഡ്‌ലോക്ക് – പ്രതിബന്ധം, വഴിമുടക്കം
I tried to make them reconcile with each other, but their talks had reached a *deadlock.*

Deaf *(adj.)* ഡെഫ് – ബധിരം
The accident has made him *deaf* in one ear.

Deal *(v.)* ഡീൽ – 1. കൈകാര്യം ചെയ്യുക
Ram's job is to *deal* with routine correspondence in his office.
2. ഇടപാട് നടത്തുക, വ്യാപാരം ചെയ്യുക
We *deal* with M/s. Pustak Mahal and we have no complaint.
(n.) 3. അളവ്, വളരെ ഏറെ
Rats destroy a great *deal* of foodgrain.

Dean *(n.)* ഡീൻ–പ്രധാന അധികാരി, ഡീൻ
You need to take the permission from the *dean* for it.

Dear *(adj.)* ഡിയർ – പ്രിയപ്പെട്ട, പ്രിയ
Ramesh is a *dear* friend of mine.

Dearth *(n.)* ഡെർത്ത് – പഞ്ഞം, ക്ഷാമം
There is a *dearth* of talented professionals in this industry.

Death *(n.)* ഡെത്ത് – മരണം
Death of all living beings is certain.

Debate ഡിബേറ്റ് – ചർച്ച, വാദപ്രതിവാദം
(n.) I won the *debate* competition held in the school last week.
(v.) Rather than wasting time in *debating,* it's better we work on the solution to this problem.

Debit *(v.)* ഡെബിറ്റ് – ബാങ്ക് അക്കൗണ്ടിൽ നിന്ന് പണം പിൻവലിക്കുക
The instalment of the loan was *debited* directly from my bank account.

Debris *(n.)* ഡെബ്രി – അവശിഷ്ടങ്ങൾ
A lot many people are feared to be buried beneath the earthquake *debris.*

Debt *(n.)* ഡെറ്റ് – കടം, വായ്പ
Ram paid penalty to the bank because he could not clear his *debt* in time.

Decay *(v.)* ഡികേ – ജീർണ്ണിക്കുക, ചീയുക, ക്ഷയം സംഭവിക്കുക
Fruits *decay* fast if not kept in the refrigerator.
(n.) Eating cholocates causes tooth *decay.*

Decade *(n.)* ഡികെയ്ഡ് – ദശകം
Hindi cinema has undergone a dramatic change over the past one *decade.*

Deceive *(v.)* ഡിസീവ് – വഞ്ചിക്കുക, കളിപ്പിക്കുക
The cheat could not *deceive* the wise trader.

Decent *(adj.)* ഡീസെന്റ് – യോഗ്യതയുള്ള, മര്യാദയുള്ള
Your friend is a *decent* fellow.

Deception *(n.)* ഡിസെപ്ഷൻ – വഞ്ചന
(n.) This is a deliberate *deception* by the management to conceal the future plans.
(adj.) Looks are often *deceptive.*

Decide *(v.)* ഡിസൈഡ് – തീരുമാനിക്കുക
I couldn't *decide* whether to go to Shimla or Mumbai for my holidays.
The prime minister's *decision* to step down surprised both the politicians and the journalists.

Decipher *(v.)* ഡിസൈഫർ–വായിച്ചെടുക്കുക
Can you *decipher* which medicine the doctor has prescribed?

Decisive *(adj.)* ഡിസൈസീവ് – നിർണ്ണായക, ഉറപ്പായ
The First Battle of Panipat was a *decisive* battle that established the Mughal rule in India.

Declare *(v.)* ഡിക്ലയർ – 1. പ്രഖ്യാപിക്കുക, വെളിപ്പെടുത്തുക
Morality demands that all politicians must *declare* their assets.
(n.) The company's *declaration* of a special bonus was a pleasant surprise.
(v.) 2. ക്രിക്കറ്റിൽ ഇന്നിംഗ്സ് അവസാനിച്ചതായി പ്രഖ്യാപിക്കുക
The captain *declared* the innings when the total score reached 450.

Decline *(v.)* ഡിക്ലൈൻ –1. നിരസിക്കുക
Ramesh *declined* Rahul's invitation to dinner, as he had to go to Kolkata.
(n.) 2. ക്ഷയിച്ചു വരിക
Moral values are on a *decline* these days.

Decode *(v.)* ഡിക്കോഡ് – രഹസ്യ സന്ദേശത്തിന്റെ അർത്ഥം മനസ്സിലാക്കുക
This is a secret message; we need to *decode* it.

Decompose *(v.)* ഡീകംബോസ് – ജീർണ്ണിക്കുക, അഴുകുക
(v.) A *decomposed* body was found in the forest last week.

Décor *(n.)* ഡെകോർ – രംഗാലങ്കാരം
The interior *décor* of the building was praiseworthy.

Decorate *(v.)* ഡെക്കറേറ്റ് – അലങ്കരിക്കുക, മോടി പിടിപ്പിക്കുക, ബഹുമതി പട്ടം നൽകുക
Sita has *decorated* her drawing room very beautifully.

Decrease *(v.)* ഡിക്രീസ് – കുറയ്ക്കുക, വെട്ടിച്ചുരുക്കുക
The manager will *decrease* your pay if you work for fewer hours this week.

Decree ഡ്ക്രീ – വിളംബരം, കല്പന, വിധികല്പിതം
(n.) He was expelled from the services on the royal *decree.*
(v.) We thought we would win the competition, but fate *decreed* otherwise.

Dedicate *(v.)* ഡെഡിക്കേറ്റ് – സമർപ്പിക്കുക
(v.) Mother Teresa *dedicated* her whole life to serving the poor.
(adj.) She is completely dedicated to her career.
(n.) Her *dedication* to work is praiseworthy.

Deed *(n.)* ഡീഡ് – കർമ്മം, പ്രമാണം
Raju has done a good *deed* by saving a drowning child.
Two businessmen signed a *deed* of partnership.

Deduct *(v.)* ഡിഡക്ട്–അല്പം കുറയ്ക്കുക
The teacher *deducted* his marks for bad handwriting.

Deem *(v.)* ഡീം – നിരൂപിക്കുക, നിർണ്ണയിക്കുക
The airplane was *deemed* unsuitable for flying.

Deep *(adj.)* ഡീപ് – 1. ആഴമുള്ള, അഗാധമായ, കടുത്ത, എല്ലാ വശവും ചിന്തിക്കുക
Why have you dug such a *deep* hole in your garden?
Death of a dear son is a cause of *deep* sorrow for his parents.
My car is *deep* blue in colour.
(adj.) Have you thought *deeply* before deciding to resign from your present job?

Deer *(n.)* ഡിയർ – മാൻ മൃഗം
Let us take our children to the zoo to show them the golden *deer.*

Defeat ഡിഫീറ്റ് – തോൽവി, പരാജയം, തോല്പിക്കുക, വിഫലമാക്കുക

(n.) Losing his very first match was an upsetting *defeat* for the last year's champion.

(v.) How could a good player like you be *defeated* so easily?

Default *(n.)* ഡിഫോൾട്ട്–ആരുടെയെങ്കിലും അസാന്നിദ്ധ്യം കാരണം, കളിക്കാതെ തന്നെ

They won the championship by *default.*

Defend *(v.)* ഡിഫെൻഡ് – 1. സാധൂകരിക്കുക

Father did not *defend* his son's bad conduct in the school.

(n.) 2. രക്ഷ

What do you want to say in your *defence*?

Defect *(n.)* ഡിഫെക്ട് – ദോഷം

She has a slight *defect* in her eye.

Definite *(adj.)* ഡെഫിനിറ്റ്–സുനിശ്ചിതം

It is *definite* that she will not come.

Definitely *(adv.)* ഡെഫിനിറ്റ്ലി–തീർച്ചയായും

I shall *definitely* call you tonight.

Deficiency *(n.)* ഡെഫിഷ്യൻസി – കുറവ്, പോരായ്മ

(n.) Night blindness is caused by the *deficiency* in Vitamin A.

(adj.) Junk food is *deficient* in nutrients.

Deformity *(n.)* ഡിഫോമിറ്റി – വൈകല്യം

The doctor recorded no *deformity* in the child.

Defy *(v.)* ഡിഫൈ – അനുസരിക്കാതിരിക്കുക, എതിർക്കുക

An obedient son does not *defy* his parents.

Defuse *(v.)* ഡിഫ്യൂസ് – നിർവീര്യമാക്കുക

The bombs were defused successfully.

Degenerate *(v.)* ഡിജെനറേറ്റ് – കുറഞ്ഞു വരിക

Corruption has *degenerated* our society.

Degree *(n.)* ഡിഗ്രി – 1. ബിരുദം

Has your son taken the *degree* in Physics?

2. പരിധി, അളവ്

I agree with you to some *degree* (to some extent).

Degrade *(v.)* ഡിഗ്രേഡ് – തരം താഴ്ത്തുക, നഷ്ടപ്പെടുത്തുക

(v.) Growing urbanisation *degrades* the natural habitats of animals.

(n.) Pollution is the major cause of environmental *degradation.*

Deity *(n.)* ഡെയിറ്റി – ദൈവ വിഗ്രഹം

The devotee prostrated himself before the *deity.*

Delay ഡിലേ – കാലതാമസം (വരുത്തുക)

(v.) I was *delayed* by the traffic jam.

(n.) Do your homework without *delay.*

Dejected *(adj.)* ഡിജെക്റ്റഡ് – നിരാശ

He felt *dejected* with his marks.

Delegate ഡെലിഗേറ്റ് – പ്രതിനിധി, നിയോഗിക്കുക, ഏൽപ്പിക്കുക

(n.) We must impress the foreign *delegates* coming next week.

(v.) *Delegate* your work to your juniors.

(n.) *Delegation* of authority is an important principle of management.

Deliberately *(adv.)* ഡെലിബറേറ്റ്ലി – മനപൂർവ്വം, കരുതികൂട്ടി

Some mischievous students *deliberately* make their teacher angry.

Delicate *(adj.)* ഡെലിക്കേറ്റ് – ലോലമായ, മൃദുവായ, ദുർബലമായ

Let us not argue over this *delicate* point.

Your son's health is *delicate,* you should give him a good tonic.

Delicious *(adj.)* ഡിലിഷ്യസ് – സ്വാദിഷ്ടം

One tends to overeat if food is *delicious.*

Delight ഡിലൈറ്റ് – ആഹ്ലാദം കൊള്ളുക, സന്തോഷിക്കുക, ആനന്ദം

(v.) Shyam was *delighted* to receive the news of his son succeeding in the IAS exam.

(n.) Suresh was filled with *delight* to see his old friend.

Deliver *(v.)* ഡെലിവർ – 1. എത്തിക്കുക, ഏല്പിക്കുക

The postman *delivered* a parcel to Ramesh.

2. പ്രസംഗിക്കുക

You *delivered* your speech very well.

3. പ്രസവിക്കുക, ജന്മം നൽകുക

She *delivered* a healthy baby boy.

(n.) She had a normal *delivery.*

Demand *(v.)* ഡിമാന്റ് – 1. ആവശ്യപ്പെടുക
Have you *demanded* the compensation for your losses in the flood?
(n.) 2. ആവശ്യം, അവകാശവാദം
The *demand* for the new brand of soap is not good.

Delete *(v.)* ഡിലീറ്റ് – നീക്കം ചെയ്യുക
Delete this sentence; it is not required.

Demise *(n.)* ഡിമൈസ് – മരണം
The sudden *demise* of the president shocked the whole nation.

Democracy *(n.)* ഡെമോക്രസി– ജനാധിപത്യം
India is the largest *democracy* in the world.

Demolish *(v.)* ഡിമാളിഷ് – ഇടിച്ചു കളയുക
We decided to *demolish* the wall between our two houses.

Demon *(n.)* ഡീമൻ – രാക്ഷസൻ
Anger is a *demon* we must fight against.

Demonstrate *(v.)* ഡെമോൺസ്ട്രേറ്റ് – കാണിക്കുക, സ്ഥാപിക്കുക, വ്യക്തമാക്കുക
The housewife asked the salesman to *demonstrate* the right way of using the washing machine.

Den *(n.)* ഡെൻ – ഒളിസ്ഥലം, താവളം
The dacoits seem to be hiding in the *den*.

Denial *(n.)* ഡിനയൽ – നിഷേധം
(n.) How do we change his *denial* to affirmation?
(v.) Mother *denied* me permission to go out.

Dense *(adj.)* ഡെൻസ്–1. ഇടതൂർന്ന, കൊടും
In some *dense* forests, there is darkness even during the day time.
2. മന്ദബുദ്ധി
I am sure he is not as *dense* as he looks.

Dent *(n.)* ഡെന്റ് – ചതവ്, കുഴി
When did your car get this *dent* ?

Dentist *(n.)* ഡെന്റിസ്റ്റ് – ദന്തവൈദ്യൻ, ഡെന്റിസ്റ്റ്
The *dentist* looks after our teeth.

Deny *(v.)* ഡിനൈ–നിഷേധിക്കുക, നിരസിക്കുക
Politicians are often quick to *deny* statements attributed to them.
(n.) Politicians' *denial* of press reports does not convince the people.

Depart *(v.)* ഡിപാർട്ട് – പുറപ്പെടുക, യാത്ര തിരിക്കുക
The train *departed* on schedule.
(n.) What is the *departure* time of your train?

Department *(n.)* ഡിപ്പാർട്ട്മെന്റ് – വിഭാഗം
For a company's success, all its *departments* must work in coordination.

Depend *(v.)* ഡിപെൻഡ് – ആശ്രയിക്കുക, വിശ്വസിക്കുക
Villagers *depend* on agriculture for thier livelihood.

Dependent *(n.)* ഡിപെന്ഡന്റ് –ആശ്രിതൻ
How many *dependents* are there in your family?

Depict *(v.)* ഡെപിക്റ്റ് – ചിത്രീകരിക്കുക
The teacher asked us to make a chart *depicting* the effects of pollution.

Deplete *(v.)* ഡീപ്ലീറ്റ് – അളവ് കുറയ്ക്കുക
Harmful gases are depleting the ozone layer.

Deport *(v.)* ഡിപോർട്ട് – നാട് കടത്തുക
All the illegal immigrants were immediately *deported* from the country.

Deposit *(v. & n.)* ഡെപ്പോസിറ്റ് – 1. നിക്ഷേപിക്കുക, സുരക്ഷിതമാക്കുക
(v.) It is safe to *deposit* the valuables in bank locker.
(n.) 2. നിക്ഷേപം
Cooperative societies give loans against a compulsory *deposit* to their members.

Depot *(n.)* ഡിപ്പോ–ഡിപ്പോ, ഗുദാം ഭണ്ഡാരം
The ordnance *depot* supplies weapons to the armed forces.

Depress *(v.)* ഡിപ്രസ്സ് – വിഷമിക്കുക, ദുഃഖിപ്പിക്കുക
Poverty and human suffering *depress* me very much.
Wet weather always *depresses* me.

Depression *(n.)* ഡിപ്രഷൻ–മാന്ദ്യം, ഇടിവ്
Depression causes unemployment.
Failure causes *depression*.

Deprive *(v.)* ഡിപ്രൈവ് – നിഷേധിക്കുക, നഷ്ടപ്പെടുത്തുക
Depriving the dog of food would affect its health.

Depth *(n.)* ഡെപ്ത്ത് – ആഴം, അഗാധം
Before stepping into a lake, you must be aware of its *depth.*

Deputy ഡെപ്യൂട്ടി – ഡെപ്യൂട്ടി, ഉപ
My brother has been promoted to the post of *deputy* superintendent of police.

Derive *(v.)* ഡിറൈവ് – ഉദ്ഗമിക്കുക, ഉല്പത്തിയാകുക
The name of this place is *derived* from the famous temple of Shiva.

Descend *(v.)* ഡിസെൻഡ് – 1. ഇറങ്ങുക, താഴെ വരിക
The sick old man was unable to *descend* the steep staircase of his home.
2. വംശ പരമ്പര
Do you believe that man has *descended* from monkey?
(n.) Is it true that Harish's neighbours are *descendants* of a royal family?

Describe *(v.)* ഡിസ്ക്രൈബ്–വർണ്ണിക്കുക, വിവരിക്കുക
Arun *described* the accident in detail.
(n.) The woman gave the *description* of the man who tried to snatch her necklace.

Desert *(n.)* ഡെസർട്ട്–1. മരുഭൂമി, മണലാരണ്യം
Travelling in the *desert* is very difficult without having sufficient stock of water.
(v.) 2. വിട്ടുപോകുക, ഉപേക്ഷിക്കുക
We should not *desert* our friends just when they need us.

Deserve *(v.)* ഡിസർവ് – അർഹമായ
The school topper received the prize he *deserved* for his record marks.

Design ഡിസൈൻ–1. ആകൃതി, രൂപരേഖ
(n.) I appreciated the *design* of the building.
(v.) He *designed* the interiors well.
2. തന്ത്രം
(n.) We got to know about his evil *designs* on time.

Designate *(v.)* ഡെസിഗ്നേറ്റ്–പദവി നൽകുക
(v.) She was *designated* as the Marketing Executive.
(n.) She holds the *designation* of a Marketing Executive in the company.

Desire *(v.)* ഡിസയർ – ആഗ്രഹിക്കുക, ആശിക്കുക
Humans always *desire* to live a happy and peaceful life.
(n.) All the *desires* can't be fulfilled.
(adj.) An applicant for a job must have all the *desirable* qualifications.

Desk *(n.)* ഡെസ്ക് – ഡെസ്ക്, മേശ
I have to order some *desks* for my office.

Desktop *(n.)* ഡെസ്ക്ടോപ്–കമ്പ്യൂട്ടർ സ്ക്രീൻ
Suddenly, all the icons vanished from my computer *desktop.*

Desolate *(adj.)* ഡെസലേറ്റ് – 1. ശൂന്യം, വിജനം
Very few people prefer to live in a *desolate* place.
2. ഏകാന്തത, ഉദാസീനത
Why are you feeling so *desolate*?

Despair *(n.)* ഡിസ്പെയർ – നിരാശ, ഇച്ഛാഭംഗം
Never let *despair* overcome you.

Desperate *(adj.)* ഡെസ്പറിറ്റ് – നിരാശ, ആശയറ്റ
Don't get *desperate;* keep calm.

Despise *(v.)* ഡിസ്പൈസ് – നിന്ദിക്കുക, തിരസ്കരിക്കുക
We *despise* Ravana because he was an evil man.

Dessert *(n.)* ഡിസേർട്ട് – ഭക്ഷണാനന്തരം വിളമ്പുന്ന മധുരപദാർത്ഥം
The host served the *dessert* after the dinner was over.

Destination *(n.)* ഡെസ്റ്റിനേഷൻ – ലക്ഷ്യ സ്ഥാനം
Delhi is the *destination* of most of the trains starting from other states.

Destiny *(n.)* ഡെസ്റ്റിനി – വിധി
Don't curse the *destiny* for what happened.

Destroy *(v.)* ഡിസ്ട്രോയ് – 1. പൊട്ടിക്കുക, തകർക്കുക

The children often *destroy* their books by using them carelessly.

2. നശിപ്പിക്കുന്ന

Children should not do anything that would *destroy* their parents' confidence in them.

Destruction *(n.)* ഡിസ്ട്രക്ഷൻ – വിനാശം

Have you seen what *destruction* an earthquake can cause?

Detach *(v.)* ഡിറ്റാച്ച് – വേർപെടുത്തുക

He *detached* the hood from his coat and folded it.

Detail *(n.)* ഡീറ്റെയ്ൽ–വിശദമായി, വിവരിക്കുക

Please narrate the incident in *detail.*

(adj.) Give me a *detailed* account of the incident.

Detain *(n.)* ഡിറ്റെയ്ൻ – 1. തടയുക

Rahul could not reach college in time because he was *detained* in the traffic jam.

2. തടവിലാക്കുക

Many political prisoners were *detained* in the jails during freedom struggle.

Detect *(v.)* ഡിറ്റെക്ട് – കുപിടിക്കുക

The architect *detected* some faults in the building construction.

Deteriorate *(v.)* ഡിറ്റിറിയോറേറ്റ് – വഷളാക്കുക

His health has been *deteriorating* ever since he returned back from Jaipur.

Determine *(v.)* ഡിറ്റർമിൻ – നിർണ്ണയിക്കുക, നിശ്ചയിക്കുക

My son is *determinod* to become a writer.

(n.) Strong *determination* is needed to succeed in life.

Detest *(v.)* ഡിറ്റെസ്റ്റ് – വെറുക്കുക

I *detest* boastful talk.

Devastate ഡെവാസ്റ്റേറ്റ് – 1. സർവ്വനാശം വരുത്തുക

(v.) The nuclear bomb *devastated* Hiroshima completely.

(n.) The city faced a total *devastation* because of the earthquake.

2. *(adj.)* തകർന്നു പോകുക

He was *devastated* when he failed in exams.

Develop *(v.)* ഡെവലപ് – 1. വളർന്നു വലുതാകുക

Your son has *developed* into a healthy young man.

2. വികസിപ്പിക്കുക

Amit has *developed* a liking for coffee.

3. ഫോട്ടോയ്ക്കുവേി ക്യാമറാ ഫിലിം രാസപദാർത്ഥത്തിലിടുക

Rakesh didn't *develop* the film properly, so the photographs were spoilt.

(n.) All of us should contribute for the *development* of our country.

Device *(n.)* ഡിവൈസ് – ഉപായം, സാധനം

The scientist praised his students for the scientific *devices* made by them.

Devil *(n.)* ഡെവിൾ – ചെകുത്താൻ

This child is a naughty little *devil.*

Devoid *(adj.)* ഡിവോയിഡ് – വിഹീനം

She was *devoid* of words and did not know what to say.

Devote *(v.)* ഡിവോട്ട്–1. നൽകുക, മുഴുകുക.

During examination, sincere students *devote* more time to their studies.

2. ഭക്തി, കൂറ് പുലർത്തുക

The servant was *devoted* to his kind master.

(n.) The followers of the saint held him in great *devotion.*

Devour *(v.)* ഡിവൗർ – വാരി വിഴുങ്ങുക

Don't *devour* your food, chew it properly.

Devout *(adj.)* ഡിവൗട്ട് – ദൈവഭക്തിയുള്ള

My grandmother is a *devout* lady.

Dew *(n.)* ഡ്യൂ – മഞ്ഞുതുള്ളി

There were tiny drops of *dew* on the leaves in the morning.

Diabetes *(n.)* ഡയബറ്റീസ് – പ്രമേഹം

My grandfather was forbidden sweets as he was suffering from *diabetes.*

Diagnose *(n.)* ഡയഗ്നോസ്–രോഗ നിർണ്ണയം ചെയ്യുക.

He was *diagnosed* for typhoid.

Diagram *(n.)* ഡയഗ്രാം-രേഖാ ചിത്രം, രൂപം

The child drew a *diagram* of water cycle.

Dial *(n.)* ഡയൽ - 1. ഡയൽ, വാച്ചിലെ അക്കമെടയാളപ്പെടുത്തിയ തകിട്

The watch-maker changed the old *dial* of Uma's watch with a fancy one.

(v.) 2. നമ്പർ വിളിക്കുക

I *dialled* your number, but it was engaged.

Dialect *(n.)* ഡയലെക്ട് - ഭാഷാഭേദം, ഗ്രാമ്യ ഭാഷ

My wife understands our servant's *dialect.*

Dialogue *(n.)* ഡയലോഗ് - 1. സംഭാഷണം

She forgot her *dialogues* on the stage.

2. ചർച്ച

A *dialogue* between the board of directors would solve this problem.

Diamond *(n.)* ഡയമ് - വജ്രം

The *diamond* ring looked very pretty on the bride's finger.

Diary *(n.)* ഡയറി, ദിനകുറിപ്പ്

Ever since my school days, I am fond of writing a *dairy.*

Dice ഡൈസ് - 1. പകിട, പാശി

(n.) I threw the *dice* and moved my piece five spaces ahead.

2. കഷണങ്ങളായി മുറിക്കുക

(v.) Dice the potatoes in small pieces.

Dictate *(v.)* ഡിക്റ്റേറ്റ് - 1. എഴുതിക്കുക

The teacher *dictated* a poem, and the students wrote it down.

2. ആജ്ഞാപിക്കുക, അധികാരം കാണിക്കുക

You cannot befriend people if you *dictate* to them.

(n.) Take this *dictation* and type it fast.

Dictionary *(n.)* ഡിഷ്ണറി - നിഘണ്ടു

We should refer to a *dictionary* if we do not know the meaning of a word.

Die *(v.)* ഡൈ - മരിക്കുക, മരണമടയുക

Last evening, a man *died* in a car accident.

Diet *(n.)* ഡയറ്റ്-1. ആഹാരം, ആഹാരക്രമം

Wheat is the staple *diet* of North Indians.

2. ആരോഗ്യം മെച്ചപ്പെടുത്താൻ വിശിഷ്ടാഹാരങ്ങൾ പ്രത്യേക അളവിൽ കഴിക്കുക

Rekha was *dieting* to get slim.

Difference *(n.)* ഡിഫറൻസ് - വ്യത്യാസം

There should be no *difference* between what you say and what you mean.

Difficult *(adj.)* ഡിഫിക്കൽറ്റ് - വിഷമം പിടിച്ച

Many consider Maths a *difficult* subject.

(n.) Life these days is full of *difficulties.*

Dig *(v.)* ഡിഗ് - കുഴിക്കുക അന്വേഷിക്കുക

Why are you *digging* a hole in your own garden?

Digest *(v.)* ഡൈജസ്റ്റ് - 1. ദഹിക്കുക

I cannot *digest* spicy food.

(n.) 2. സാരം, സംഗ്രഹം

Please prepare a *digest* of this article.

Dignity *(n.)* ഡിഗ്നിറ്റി-മഹത്വം, പ്രാധാന്യം, അന്തസ്സ്, മാന്യത

We should accept the *dignity* of labour.

Always receive your guests with *dignity.*

(adj.) Be *dignified* in your behaviour always.

Digress *(v.)* ഡൈഗ്രെസ്- വ്യതിചരിക്കുക

Let's not *digress* from the main point of the discussion.

Dilemma *(n.)* ഡൈലെമാ-ചിന്താക്കുഴപ്പം

I was in a *dilemma* for a week as to which company to join.

Diligent *(adj.)* ഡിലിജന്റ് - പരിശ്രമി

(adj.) She is a *diligent* student and always stands first in the class.

(n.) He was appreciated for his *diligence* at work.

(adv.) She works *diligently* in the office.

Dilute *(v.)* ഡൈലൂട്ട് - നേർപ്പിക്കുക

He *diluted* the wine with a little water.

Dim *(adj.)* ഡിം – അര വെളിച്ചം, മങ്ങിയ
It was difficult to find our way in the *dim* light.

Dimension *(n.)* ഡൈമൻഷൻ – 1. അളവ് എടുക്കുക
Have you taken the *dimensions* of the room?
2. മാനം
The victim's mother's statement has given a new *dimension* to the case.

Diminish *(v.)* ഡിമിനിഷ്–മന്ദീഭവിപ്പിക്കുക
The rain *diminished* all the enthusiasm of the forthcoming match.

Dimple *(n.)* ഡിമ്പ്ൾ – നുണക്കുഴി
When she smiles, *dimples* form in her cheeks.

Din *(n.)* ഡിൻ – ഒച്ച, ശബ്ദകോലാഹലം
Sanjay made a great *din* with his drum.

Dinner *(n.)* ഡിന്നർ – അത്താഴം
Avoid taking *dinner* very late in the night.

Dip *(v.)* ഡിപ് – മുക്കുക
Don't *dip* your finger in the curry.

Direct *(v.)* ഡയറക്ട്–1. വഴി കാട്ടുക, അയക്കുക
Ram *directed* Arun to the nearest STD booth for making an urgent call.
2. സംവിധാനം ചെയ്യുക
Gulzar *directed* the award-winning film 'Maachis'.
3. നേരെയുള്ള
Which is the *direct* route to your house?
(n.) Which *direction* should I take to reach Janpath?

Directly *(adv.)* ഡയറക്ട്‌ലി–നേരെ, ശീഘ്രം
The speeding truck rammed *directly* into the stationary car.

Directory *(n.)* ഡയറക്ടറി–പേർ വിവരപ്പട്ടിക
The telephone *directory* is updated every year.

Dirty *(adj.)* ഡർട്ടി – അഴുക്കുള്ള, മലിന, നീച, കുത്സിത
Please wash your *dirty* hands before sitting down to eat.

Disabled ഡിസേബിൾഡ് – വികലാംഗർ
(n.) The college has a separate section for the *disabled.*
(v.) The accident *disabled* his arm.

Disadvantage *(n.)* ഡിസ്അഡ്വാൻടേജ് – ദോഷം, പോരായ്മ, കുറവ്
In the job market, being less educated is considered a major *disadvantage.*

Disagree *(v.)* ഡിസ്എഗ്രി–വിയോജിക്കുക
I *disagree* with you in this regard.

Disappear *(v.)* ഡിസ്അപ്പിയർ – കാണാതാവുക, മറയുക
I searched for him, but he *disappeared* in the crowd.

Disappoint *(v.)* ഡിസ്അപ്പോയിന്റ് – നിരാശപ്പെടുത്തുക, പ്രതീക്ഷ തകർക്കുക
Suresh was *disappointed* when he was not selected in the school cricket team.
(adj.) Your work is *disappointing.* I think you could do better.
(n.) The goalkeeper was filled with *disappointment* when he could not save the goal.

Disapprove *(v.)* ഡിസ്അപ്രൂപ് – ഇഷ്ടപ്പെടാതിരിക്കുക
I strongly *disapproved* of giving alms to beggars.

Disaster *(n.)* ഡിസാസ്റ്റർ–അപകടം, ദുരന്തം
Sixty persons were killed in the train *disaster.*

Disbelief *(n.)* ഡിസ്ബിലീഫ്–അവിശ്വാസം
She shook her head in *disbelief.*

Discharge *(v.)* ഡിസ്ചാർജ് – 1. നീക്കം ചെയ്യുക, പിരിച്ചുവിടുക
The clerk was *discharged* from his job when he was caught taking bribe.
2. (ആശുപത്രി, ജയിൽ, സൈന്യം) ഇവയിൽ നിന്ന് പുറത്തയക്കുക, മോചിപ്പിക്കുക
After recovery, Asha's mother was *discharged* from the hospital.
3. നിറവേറ്റുക, ജോലി ശരിയായി ചെയ്യുക
A sincere worker *discharges* his duty diligently.

Disciple *(n.)* ഡിസൈപ്പ്ൾ – ശിക്ഷ്യ
Ananda was the most loved *disciple* of Gautam Buddha.

Discipline *(n.)* ഡിസിപ്ലിൻ - അച്ചടക്കം
Don't you agree that *self-discipline* is the best form of *discipline*?

Disclose *(v.)* ഡിസ്ക്ലോസ്-വെളിപ്പെടുത്തുക
I tried hard, but she did not *disclose* the secret.

Discolour *(v.)* ഡിസ്കളർ - നിറം മാറ്റുക, നിറം മങ്ങിക്കുക
The season of autumn *discoloured* the leaves.

Discord *(n.)* ഡിസ്കോർഡ് - കലഹം
A *discord* took place between them.

Discourage *(v.)* ഡിസ്കറേജ്- നിരുത്സാഹപ്പെടുത്തുക
Her mother *discouraged* her from going for a movie.

Discover *(v.)* ഡിസ്കവർ-കു പിടിക്കുക, അന്വേഷിക്കുക
Columbus *discovered* America.
(n.) It was a great *discovery*.

Discriminate *(v.)* ഡിസ്ക്രിമിനേറ്റ് - വേർതിരിവ് കാണിക്കുക
In some Indian states, girls are still *discriminated* against boys.

Discuss *(v.)* ഡിസ്കസ് - ചർച്ച ചെയ്യുക
The Lok Sabha *discussed* the budget proposals.
(n.) A serious *discussion* on any subject helps us to reach a conclusion.

Disease *(n.)* ഡിസീസ് - രോഗം
Sometimes several tests are conducted to diagnose a patient's *disease*.

Disgrace *(v.)* ഡിസ്ഗ്രേസ്-കളങ്കം ചാർത്തുക
A society is *disgraced* by the criminal acts of its members.

Disguise *(n.)* ഡിസ്ഗൈസ്- മറപിടിക്കുക, മറവിൽ
Sometimes adversity turns out to be a blessing in *disguise*.
(v.) Pushpa tried to smile but she could not *disguise* her anger.

Disgusting *(adj.)* ഡിസ്ഗസ്റ്റിംഗ് - വിദ്വേഷജനകം, വെറുപ്പുളവാക്കുന്ന
Rahul's rude manners were *disgusting*.

Dish *(n.)* ഡിഷ്-1. പാത്രം
Usha wants to buy some *dishes*.
2. വിഭവം
For her guests, Sita prepared so many *dishes* in a very short time.

Disheartening *(adj.)* ഡിസ്ഹാർട്ടനിംഗ് - നിരാശാ ജനകം
It was *disheartening* to know that India lost the match against Kenya.

Dishonest *(adj.)* ഡിസ്ഓണസ്റ്റ് - സത്യസന്ധതയില്ലാത്ത
The *dishonest* servant was fired from the job.

Dislike *(v.)* ഡിസ്ലൈക്-ഇഷ്ടപ്പെടാതിരിക്കുക
I *dislike* reaching late to the office.

Dislocate *(v.)* ഡിസ്ലൊക്കേറ്റ്-അസ്ഥിക്ക് വ്യതിചലനം നേരിടുക
The accident *dislocated* his arm.

Dismal *(adj.)* ഡിസ്മൽ - മ്ലാനത
The cancer patient's face was very *dismal*.

Dismay ഡിസ്മേ-ഭയം, ധൈര്യം ചോർന്നു പോകുക
(n.) Amitabh was filled with *dismay* when he found he had to go alone in the dark.
(v.) Passengers were *dismayed* when they missed the train by just five minutes.

Dismiss *(v.)* ഡിസ്മിസ് - പിരിച്ചുവിടുക
The master *dismissed* his dishonest servant.

Disorder *(n.)* ഡിസ്ഓർഡർ- താറുമാറാകുക
The political state of the country is in a complete *disorder*.

Dispatch ഡിസ്പാച്ച്-അയക്കുക, വാർത്ത, റിപ്പോർട്ട്
(v.) Please *dispatch* this message immediately.
(n.) The reporter sent a quick *dispatch* on train accident to his newspaper office.

Dispensary *(n.)* ഡിസ്പെൻസറി-ഔഷധശാല
The wounded man was taken to the *dispensary*.

Dispense *(v.)* ഡിസ്പെൻസ്-1. വേണ്ടെന്ന് വയ്ക്കുക
One should *dispense* with the services of an inefficient secretary quickly.
2. മരുന്ന് തയ്യാറാക്കി നൽകുക
Does that chemist *dispense* good medicines?

Display ഡിസ്‌പ്ലേ – 1. പ്രദർശിപ്പിക്കുക, ഒരുക്കുക
(v.) New sarees are *displayed* in the shop window.
(n.) 2. പ്രദർശനം
Both girls and boys participated in the acrobatic *display*.

Dispose *(v.)* ഡിസ്‌പോസ് 1. വില്ക്കുക
I have *disposed* my old car.
2. ഒതുക്കുക, നീക്കുക
I have *disposed* of my work and now I am free.

Disposition *(n.)* ഡിസ്‌പൊസിഷൻ – മനോഗതി, പ്രകൃതം
Sheela has a very kind *disposition*.

Dispute ഡിസ്‌പ്യൂട്ട് – 1. തർക്കം, വിവാദം, വഴക്ക്, കലഹം
(n.) It is best to avoid taking your familial *disputes* to a court of law.
(v.) 2. എതിർക്കുക, ഖണ്ഡിക്കുക
The minister's statement on the improved law and order situation was *disputed* by the opposition members.

Disrupt *(v.)* ഡിസ്റപ്റ്റ് – അലങ്കോലപ്പെടുത്തുക, താറുമാറാക്കുക
Rain *disrupted* the match telecast.

Dissatisfaction *(n.)* ഡിസ്സാറ്റിസ്ഫാക്ഷൻ – അസംതൃപ്തി
(n.) The students expressed their *dissatisfaction* at the exam results.
(v.) The students were *dissatisfied* with the results.

Dissolve *(v.)* ഡിസ്സോൾവ് – 1. അലിയുക
A small piece of ice soon *dissolves* in water.
Sugar does not *dissolve* quickly in the chilled water.
2. പിരിച്ചുവിടുക, അവസാനിപ്പിക്കുക
When was the last Lok Sabha *dissolved*?

Distance *(n.)* ഡിസ്റ്റൻസ്–ദൂരം, അകലം, വിദൂര
What is the *distance* between your school and your home?
(adj.) Don't you like to read books on *distant* places?

Distinct *(adj.)* ഡിസ്റ്റിങ്ക്റ്റ് – വ്യത്യാസം, വിഭിന്നം, വ്യക്തമായി
I can easily read Minakshi's handwriting because it is so *distinct*.
Write your name *distinctly*.

Distinction *(n.)* ഡിസ്റ്റിങ്ക്ഷൻ – 1. ശ്രേഷ്ഠത, പ്രശസ്തി
Suresh's son passed the examination with *distinction*.
2. വ്യത്യാസം, അന്തരം
Is there any *distinction* between nylon and cotton?

Distinguish *(v.)* ഡിസ്റ്റിങ്ഗ്വിഷ്–1. തിരിച്ചറിയുക
I could not *distinguish* the approaching truck in the fog.
2. പ്രസിദ്ധി നേടുക
He *distinguished* himself as a doctor.
(adj.) He became a *distinguished* doctor.

Distress *(n.)* ദുഃഖം, വേദന, സങ്കടം
The poor old man was in great *distress*.
(v.) The bad news *distressed* us.

Distribute *(v.)* ഡിസ്ട്രിബ്യൂട്ട് – വിതരണം ചെയ്യുക
Rahul *distributed* sweets on the birth of his daughter.

District *(n.)* ഡിസ്ട്രിക്റ്റ് – ജില്ല
The case was passed on to the High Court from the *District* Court.

Disturb *(v.)* ഡിസ്ടർബ്– ശല്യപ്പെടുത്തുക, ശാന്തി ഭംഗപ്പെടുത്തുക
Do not *disturb* the people who are reading in the library.
(n.) Raju was feeling *disturbance* in his studies due to a marriage reception in the neighbourhood.

Ditch *(n.)* ഡിച്ച് – കുഴി, ഓട
The street leading to your house is full of *ditches*.

Dive *(v.)* ഡൈവ് – നീർക്കാങ്കുഴി ഇടുക, ഡൈവ് ചെയ്യുക
Can you *dive* into the swimming pool?

Divert *(v.)* ഡൈവർട്ട്–1. വഴി തിരിച്ചുവിടുക
The police *diverted* the traffic to give way to the religious procession.
2. ശ്രദ്ധ തിരിക്കുക
Don't let your attention get *diverted* while studying.

Diverse *(adj.)* ഡൈവേർസ് – വിവിധ, വൈവിദ്ധ്യമാർന്ന
India is the land of *diverse* cultures.

Divide *(v.)* ഡിവൈഡ് – പങ്കുവയ്ക്കുക, വിഭജിക്കുക
Let us *divide* this amount equally between us.

Division *(n.)* ഡിവിഷൻ–1. വിഭാഗം, വർഗ്ഗം
How many *divisions* does your company have?
2. ഹരിക്കൽ, വിഛേദനം
Is your child good at *division*?

Divine *(adj.)* ഡിവൈൻ–ദൈവീകം, ദിവ്യം
Don't you agree that there is something *divine* about Nature's beauty?

Dizzy *(adj.)* ഡിസി–തലചുറ്റൽ ഉാകുക, തലകറങ്ങുക
After riding the merry-go-round, I felt *dizzy*.

Do *(v.)* ഡൂ – 1. പൂർത്തിയാക്കുക
Do your homework before going to play.
2. ചെയ്യുക
What are you *doing* this evening?
3. ഗുണം ചെയ്യുക
This medicine will *do* you good.

Docile *(adj.)* ഡൊസൈൽ – ശാന്തമായ, വിധേയമായ
She is very *docile;* I don't think she'll raise any objection against the plan.

Doctor *(n.)* ഡോക്ടർ–1. ഡോക്ടർ, ഭിഷഗ്വരൻ
The *doctor* advised Shankar to take rest for a week.
2. അദ്ധ്യാപകൻ
Doctor Ram Lal Verma completed his Ph. D. at the young age of twenty-six.

Document *(n.)* ഡോക്കുമെന്റ്–രേഖ, പ്രമാണം
Send this *document* by courier.

Documentary *(n.)* ഡോക്കുമെന്ററി – ലഘുചിത്രം
Shah Rukh Khan first starred in a *documentary* named Anne.

Dodge *(v.)* ഡോഡ്ജ് – മാറിക്കളയുക, ഒഴിഞ്ഞുമാറുക
Ramu fell down while trying to *dodge* the cyclist.

Dog *(n.)* ഡോഗ് – നായ
Do you like a *dog* as a pet?

Doll *(n.)* ഡോൾ – പാവ
Rahul bought a *doll* for his little daughter.

Dome *(n.)* ഡോം–താഴികക്കുടം, ഗോപുരം
The *dome* of Golden Temple is plated with gold.

Domestic *(adj.)* ഡൊമസ്റ്റിക്–ഗാർഹിക, വീട്ട്
Modern men do not hesitate in helping their wives in the *domestic* work.

Dominate *(v.)* ഡോമിനേറ്റ് – ആധിപത്യം ഉറപ്പിക്കുക
The Indian cricket team *dominated* the 20-20 World Cup.

Donate *(v.)* ഡൊണേറ്റ് – ദാനം ചെയ്യുക
He *donated* blood on his 18th birthday.

Donkey *(n.)* ഡോങ്കി – കഴുത
The washerman's *donkey* carried the clothes to the river.

Door *(n.)* ഡോർ – വാതിൽ
It's safe to keep the main *door* closed.
Salesmen go *door to door* to sell their products.

Dormitory *(n.)* ഡാർമിറ്ററി – ശയന ശാല
The school had a big *dormitory* for its resident students.

Dose *(n.)* ഡോസ് – മാത്ര, ഡോസ്
The doctor asked the patient to take a *dose* of the medicine every four hours.

Dot *(n.)* ഡാട്ട് – ബിന്ദു
(n.) The teacher asked the children to circle the red *dot*.
(v.) You should *dot* the i's and cross the t's.

Dote *(v.)* ഡോട്ട്–അളവറ്റ് സ്നേഹിക്കുക
She *dotes* on her only child.

Double ഡബ്ൾ – ഇരട്ട, ഇരട്ടിയാക്കുക
(adj.) In the absence of his colleague, Ram had to do *double* work in the office.
(v.) Why have the vegetable prices *doubled* in such a short time?

Doubt ഡൗട്ട്–സംശയം, അവിശ്വസിക്കുക
(n.) This is without a *doubt* your handwriting.
(v.) I *doubt* whether you are telling me the truth.

Dough *(n.)* ഡൗ – കുഴച്ച മാവ്
If you knead the *dough* well, the bread would be soft.

2. ധനം
I am not a rich man, I do not have a lot of *dough.*

Dove *(n.)* ഡവ് – വെള്ളപ്രാവ്
The *dove* is considered a symbol of peace.

Down *(adj.)* ഡൗൺ – താഴെ, താഴേക്ക്
Please sit *down* here.
Are prices really coming *down*?
Write *down* your name and address.
Our air-conditioner has broken *down* (it does not work).

Download *(v.)* ഡൗൺലോഡ്–കമ്പ്യൂട്ടറിൽ നിന്ന് ഫയൽ ഇറക്കുക
I *downloaded* a few pictures from the Internet.

Downmarket *(adj.)* ഡൗൺമാർക്കറ്റ് – ഇടിവ്, മോശമായ
Arriving late in formal meetings is so *downmarket.*

Down-to-earth *(adj.)* ഡൗൺ–ടു–എർത്ത് – പച്ചയായ, സരള
Despite being very rich and affluent, she is very *down-to-earth.*

Dowry *(n.)* ഡൗറി – സ്ത്രീധനം
Dowry is a blot on humanity.

Doze *(v.)* ഡോസ് – മയങ്ങുക
I like to *doze* for some time after a heavy lunch.

Dozen *(n.)* ഡസൻ – ഡസൻ
I bought a *dozen* of bananas.

Draft ഡ്രാഫ്റ്റ് – കരടുാക്കുക
(v.) The workers' leader *drafted* the memorandum of demands to present to the management.
(n.) Several amendments were made in thc rough *draft* of the project.

Drag *(v.)* ഡ്രാഗ് – വലിച്ച് ഇഴയ്ക്കുക
If this load is too heavy for you to lift, you will have to *drag* it.

Dragon *(n.)* ഡ്രാഗൺ – ഡ്രാഗൺ
The child made a picture of a *dragon* breathing fire.

Drain ഡ്രെയ്ൻ – ഓട, ഒലിച്ചുപോവുക
(n.) All the *drains* in the colony were overflowing following a heavy downpour.
(v.) As I cleaned the outlet, the water *drained* out.

Drama *(n.)* ഡ്രാമ – നാടകം
The child artiste's performance in the *drama* was appreciated by all.

Drape *(v.)* ഡ്രേപ് – പൊതിയുക
Before leaving for vacations, they *draped* the furniture in plastic covers.

Draw *(v.)* ഡ്രാ – 1. ചിത്രം വരയ്ക്കുക
Can you *draw* good pictures?
2. വലിക്കുക
Two horses were *drawing* the carriage.
3. അടുത്തുവരിക
The spectators cheered loudly as the marathon winner *drew* closer to the finishing line.
4. ലോട്ടറി
Winners of the lucky *draw* looked very happy.

Drawback *(n.)* ഡ്രാബായ്ക്ക് – പോരായ്മ
A non-dancing partner proved to be a *drawback* for her in the dance competition.

Drawer *(n.)* ഡ്രായർ – വലിപ്പ്, മേശയറ
In which *drawer* have you put my pen?

Dread ഡ്രെഡ് – 1. പേടിക്കുക
(v.) A burnt child *dreads* the fire.
(adj.) 2. ഭയാനകമായ
Have you read the newspaper report of the *dreadful* accident?

Dream ഡ്രീം – സ്വപ്നം, കിനാവ് കാണുക
(n.) Do you sleep soundly or do you have *dreams*?
(v.) I always *dream* about being rich.

Drench *(v.)* ഡ്രെഞ്ച് – നനഞ്ഞ് കുളിക്കുക
I was *drenched* in the rain while coming to see you.

Dress *(n.)* ഡ്രെസ് – 1. വേഷം, കുപ്പായം
I'm not very particular about my *dress.*
(v.) 2. മുറിവ് വച്ചുകെട്ടുക
Do you know how to *dress* a wound?

Drift *(v.)* ഡ്രിഫ്റ്റ്–1. ഒഴുകിപ്പോകുക, കറങ്ങി നടക്കുക
Clouds were *drifting* in the wind.
2. ച്യുതി, വഴിതെറ്റുക, ഒഴുക്ക്
Never *drift* from the path of righreousness.

(*n.*) It is easy to swim with the *drift* of the stream.

Drill ഡ്രിൽ – വ്യായാമം

(*n.*) In our school, we have *drill* every day.

(*v.*) തുളയിടുക

Can you *drill* a hole in a very thick wall?

Drink ഡ്രിങ്ക് – 1. കുടിക്കുക, പാനീയം

(*v.*) *Drink* your tea before it gets cold.

2. മദ്യപാനം

Wayward youths are prone to start *drinking.*

(*n.*) He asked for a *drink,* but I refused.

Drip (*v.*) ഡ്രിപ് – ചോരുക

The tap in my bathroom has been *dripping* since yesterday.

Drive (*v.*) ഡ്രൈവ് – 1. ഓടിക്കുക

Can you *drive* a car?

(*n.*) 2. വിയിൽ സഞ്ചരിക്കുക

Let us go for a *drive* round the lake.

3. ചൊടി, കർമ്മശേഷി

A man with a strong *drive* is bound to succeed in his career.

Droop (*v.*) ഡ്രൂപ് – 1. കുനിയുക, വാടുക

The flowers in the garden were *drooping* due to intense heat.

2. നിരാശപ്പെടുക

Don't let your spirits *droop.*

Drop (*n.*) ഡ്രോപ് – 1. തുള്ളി

Sometimes even a *drop* of medicine does a lot of good to the patient.

(*v.*) 2. താഴെയിടുക, കൈവിട്ടുപോകുക

Be careful, don't *drop* that glass.

Drought (*n.*) ഡ്രൗട്ട് – വരൾച്ച, ഉണക്ക്

The crops were spoilt by the *drought.*

Drown (*v.*) ഡ്രൗൺ – മുങ്ങി മരിക്കുക

Thirty persons were *drowned* in the boat tragedy.

(*adj.*) Do you know how to rescue a *drowning* person?

Drowsy (*adj.*) ഡ്രൗസി – ഉറക്കം തൂങ്ങുക

After staying awake for the whole night, I was feeling *drowsy* in the morning.

Drug (*n.*) ഡ്രഗ് – 1. മരുന്ന്

Penicillin is a wonder *drug.*

2. മയക്ക് മരുന്ന്

Taking *drugs* is injurious to health.

Drum (*n.*) ഡ്രം – മദ്ദളം, മൃദംഗം

I want to buy a toy *drum* for my child.

Dry ഡ്രൈ–1. ഉണക്ക, ഉണങ്ങിയ, ഉണക്കുക

(*adj.*) Are your hands *dry* or wet?

(*v.*) I *dried* my clothes in the wind.

2. പരുഷ

You cannot make friends if you have a *dry* manner.

Dub (*v.*) ഡബ് – ഒരു ഭാഷയിൽ നിന്ന് മറ്റൊരു ഭാഷയിലാക്കുക

The movie Taare Zameen Par has been *dubbed* in other languages as well.

Due ഡ്യൂ–1. നൽകേ, കടപ്പെട്ടിരിക്കുന്ന

(*adj.*) Ram paid his insurance premium even before it became *due.*

2. നിശ്ചിത സമയത്ത് വരേ

The train is *due* in half an hour.

(*adj.*) 3. കാരണമായി, ഫലമായി, അർഹിക്കുന്നത്

I met with an accident *due* to my careless driving.

(*n.*) Give the devil his *due.*

Dull (*adj.*) ഡൾ – 1. മന്ദബുദ്ധി

Your son will pass, he is not *dull.*

2. വിരസമായ

A *dull* book mars the reputation of its author.

3. മേഘാവൃതമായ, മങ്ങലുള്ള

Today is a cloudy and *dull* day.

Dumb (*adj.*) ഡമ്പ് – ഊമ, മൂക

There is a school for the deaf and *dumb* near my house.

Dump ഡംപ് (*n.*) 1. ചവറിടുന്ന സ്ഥലം

Throw this letter in the waste paper*dump.*

(*v.*) 2. കൊ് തള്ളുക

She *dumped* the rubbish in the dustbin.

Dummy (*adj.*) ഡമ്മി – 1. വ്യാജ വസ്തു, അനുകരണ വസ്തു

I want to buy a *dummy* gun for my young son.

(n.) 2. ഡമ്മി രൂപം
This *dummy* of the dancer looks real.

During *(prep.)* ഡ്യൂറിംഗ് – ആ സമയത്ത്
You can always find me in my office *during* the working hours.

Duplicate ഡ്യൂപ്ലിക്കേറ്റ് – പ്രതിരൂപം
(n.) This key is a *duplicate* of the original one.
(adj.) Do you have a *duplicate* key of the car?
(v.) It is unethical to *duplicate* the original album.

Durable *(adj.)* ഡ്യൂറബിൾ – ഈടുറ്റ
This seems to be a *durable* plastic.

Duration *(n.)* ഡ്യൂറേഷൻ–സമയ ദൈർഘ്യം
The *duration* of the movie was more than 3 hours.

Dusk *(n.)* ഡസ്ക് – സന്ധ്യ, ഇരുട്ട്
I must return home before *dusk.*

Dusky *(adj.)* ഡസ്കി – ഇരു
She has a *dusky* complexion, but looks beautiful.

Dust *(n.)* ഡസ്റ്റ് – പൊടി
Wipe the *dust* off your desk daily.

Dusty *(adj.)* ഡസ്റ്റി – പൊടി നിറഞ്ഞ
I cannot work in such a *dusty* room.

Duty *(n.)* ഡ്യൂട്ടി – 1. കർത്തവ്യം, കടമ
Do your *duty* and have faith in God.
2. ജോലി
Shyam is always late for his *duty*.

Dwarf *(n.)* ഡ്വാർഫ് – കുനൻ
He is a *dwarf* by birth.

Dwell *(v.)* ഡ്വെൽ–താമസിക്കുക, പാർക്കുക
Don't *dwell* on your troubles.

Dwindle *(v.)* ഡ്വിൻഡിൽ–വല്ലാതെ കുറയുക
The food stock has been *dwindling* alarmingly over the past two years.

Dye ഡൈ–നിറം, വർണ്ണം, നിറം പിടിപ്പിക്കുക
(v.) Can you *dye* this saree deep blue?
(n.) What is the price of this hair-*dye*?

Dynamic *(adj.)* ഡൈനാമിക് – ചലനോജ്ജ്വല
It is time to bring some *dynamic* changes in our work culture.

Dynasty *(n.)* ഡൈനാസ്റ്റി – രാജവംശം
The Mughal *Dynasty* ended with Bahadur Shah Zafar deported to Rangoon.

E

Each *(adj.)* ഈച്ച് – ഓരോരോ, പരസ്പരം
The two neighbours were abusing *each* other.
The teacher checked *each* and every student's homework.

Eager *(adj.)* ഈഗർ–ഉൽസുക, ആഗ്രഹമുള്ള
You look *eager* to go home early.

Eagle *(n.)* ഈഗ്ൾ – കഴുകൻ
Can any other bird fly as high as the *eagle*?

Ear *(n.)* ഇയർ – 1. ചെവി
My father bought a hearing-aid for his left *ear.*
2. കതിര്
Look at those *ears* of corn heaped in the field.

Early ഏർലി–*(adv.)* 1. നേരത്തെ, പെട്ടെന്ന്
I went to the show *early* because I wanted a good seat.
(adj.) 2. രാവിലെ, പുലർച്ചയ്ക്ക്
I have my breakfast *early* in the day.

Earn *(v.)* ഏൺ – സമ്പാദിക്കുക
How much do you *earn* every month?

Earnest *(adj.)* ഏണസ്റ്റ് – ആത്മാർത്ഥത, ഉത്സാഹമുള്ള
If you want to succeed in life, you must be *earnest* about your work.

Earth *(n.)* എർത്ത് – 1. ഭൂമി

What is the shape of the *earth*?

2. മണ്ണ്, നിലം

Labourers were digging the *earth* to lay telephone cables.

Earthquake *(n.)* എർത്ത്ക്വേക്ക് – ഭൂകമ്പം

The *earthquake* destroyed the whole village.

Earthworm *(n.)* എർത്ത്വേം – മണ്ണിര

There were a number of *earthworms* in the garden.

East *(n.)* ഈസ്റ്റ് – കിഴക്ക്

In the morning, I pray facing the *east.*

Easy ഈസി – എളുപ്പം

(adj.) Some Maths problems are very *easy* to solve.

(v.) If you take an Aspro tablet, it will *ease* your headache.

Eat *(v.)* ഈറ്റ് – ആഹാരം കഴിക്കുക

Would you like something to *eat*?

Eccentric (adj.) എക്സെൻട്രിക് – മനോനില തെറ്റിയ

He is an *eccentric* old man.

Echo *(n.& v.)* എക്കോ–പ്രതിദ്ധ്വനി, മാറ്റൊലി

(n.) If you speak loudly in a big and empty hall, you can hear the *echo* of your voice.

(v.) His voice *echoed* in the empty hall.

Eclipse *(n.)* എക്ലിപ്സ് – 1. ഗ്രഹണം

Do you observe a fast during an *eclipse* of the sun or the moon?

(v.) 2. ഇരുട്ടിലാക്കുക

One defect in character can *eclipse* many good qualities.

Eco-friendly *(adj.)* ഇകോ–ഫ്രെ്ലി – പരിസ്ഥിതി സഹജം

Paper bags look good and are *eco-friendly.*

Ecstasy *(n.)* എക്സ്റ്റസി – അത്യാഹ്ലാദം

His *ecstasy* about the examination results knew no bounds.

(adj.) He was *ecstatic* about his examination results.

Edge *(n.)* എജ് – 1. വായ്ത്തല, മൂർച്ച

Be careful, that knife has a sharp *edge.*

2. അറ്റം, വിളിമ്പ്

Don't go near the *edge* of the cliff.

Edible *(adj.)* എഡിബ്ൾ – ഭക്ഷ്യയോഗ്യം

Which is the *edible* part of a potato?

Editor *(n.)* എഡിറ്റർ – പത്രാധിപർ

The *editor* of a newspaper is responsible for whatever it publishes.

Educate *(v.)* എഡ്യൂക്കേറ്റ് – പഠിപ്പിക്കുക വിദ്യാഭ്യാസം

Good art can *educate* as well as amuse us.

(n.) Education contributes a lot in building a person's career.

Effect *(n.)* ഇഫെക്റ്റ് – ഫലം, പ്രഭാവം

Doctor was not sure whether the rashes on the patient's body were the side-*effect* of the medicine he had taken.

Efficient *(adj.)* എഫിഷ്യന്റ് – കാര്യക്ഷമത

She is very *efficient* at communication.

Effort *(n.)* എഫർട്ട് – ശ്രമം, പ്രയത്നം

Did you make an *effort* to contact me over the phone?

Egg *(n.)* എഗ് – മുട്ട

I like boiled *eggs* for breakfast.

Ego *(n.)* ഈഗോ – അഹങ്കാരം

Self-pride is good, but *ego* is dangerous.

Either ഈദർ – 1. രിലൊന്ന്

(pron.) I have two pens, you can use *either* of them.

(conj.) Please have *either* an apple or an orange.

I will *either* write or read.

(adj.) 2. ഓരോ, രും

Put a flower pot on *either* side of the gate.

Elaborate *(v.)* ഇലാബറേറ്റ് – 1. വിശദമാക്കുക, സവിസ്തരം പ്രതിപാദിക്കുക

Will you please *elaborate* on this point?

(adj.) 2. സമ്പൂർണ്ണ, അലംകൃത

The bride wore an *elaborate* dress.

Elastic *(adj.)* ഇലാസ്റ്റിക് – അയവുള്ള

This rubber is not *elastic* enough.

Elbow എൽബോ–കൈമുട്ട്, തള്ളിക്കയറുക

(n.) Don't put your *elbows* on the table.

(v.) He *elbowed* his way through the crowd.

Elder *(adj.)* എൽഡർ – പ്രായത്തിൽ മൂത്തയാൾ

My *elder* sister is a journalist.

(n.) വയോധികർ

We should respect our *elders*.

Elect *(v.)* ഇലെക്റ്റ് – തിരഞ്ഞെടുക്കുക

The members of the company met to *elect* a new chairman.

(n.) Congratulations on your *election* as the chairman of the company.

When are the general *elections* going to be held?

Electricity *(n.)* ഇലക്ട്രിസിറ്റി – വൈദ്യുതി

Electricity is one of the greatest inventions of science.

(n.) Have you taken your diploma as an *electrician*?

I would like to buy an *electric* iron.

Elegant *(adj.)* എലിഗന്റ് – രമണീയ, അഴകോടെ

The young lady looked *elegant* in her new dress.

(adv.) Some people are always dressed very *elegantly*.

Elementary *(adj.)* എലിമെന്ററി–പ്രാഥമിക, പ്രാരംഭ

Do you have at least *elementary* knowledge of Chemistry?

Elephant *(n.)* എലിഫന്റ്– ആന

My younger son had an *elephant* ride in Jaipur.

Elevator *(n.)* എലിവേറ്റർ – ലിഫ്റ്റ്

He took the *elevator* to reach the third floor.

Eligible *(n.)* എലിജിബ്ൾ – അർഹതയുള്ള

Anyone passing the SSC examination is *eligible* to join a college.

Eliminate *(v.)* എലിമിനേറ്റ്– നിരാകരിക്കുക, നീക്കം ചെയ്യുക

Out of five teams, three will be *eliminated* and two will qualify for the finals.

Else എൽസ് – 1. മറ്റാരും, മറ്റാരുടെയോ

(adj.) No one *else* knows what I am going to tell you.

This isn't my book, it is someone *else's*.

(adv.) 2. അല്ലെങ്കിൽ, ഇല്ലെങ്കിൽ പിന്നെ

Walk carefully or *else* you may slip.

You must take a taxi, how *else* can you catch the train?

Elite *(n.)* എലീറ്റ് – ശ്രേഷ്ഠവർഗ്ഗം, പ്രമാണി വർഗ്ഗം

They consider themselves the intellectually *elite* people.

Email *(n.)* ഈമെയ്ൽ – ഈമെയ്ൽ

I sent him all the information by an *email*.

Embark *(v.)* എമ്പാർക്ക് – (വിമാനത്തിൽ) കയറുക, കയറ്റുക, തുടങ്ങുക

The announcer requested the passengers travelling to Mumbai to *embark* on the plane.

Emancipate *(v.)* ഇമാൻസിപേറ്റ് – സ്വാതന്ത്ര്യമുള്ള, ശാക്തീകൃതമായ

Today's women are *emancipated* enough to fend for themselves.

Embarrass *(v.)* എമ്പാരസ്–ലജ്ജ തോന്നുക

(v.) Tripping on the stage *embarrassed* me a lot.

(adj.) I was *embarrassed* at tripping on the stage.

Embassy *(n.)* എമ്പസി – സ്ഥാനപതി കാര്യാലയം

Her father works in a Russian *embassy*.

Embellish *(v.)* എമ്പലിഷ് – മോടി പിടിപ്പിക്കുക

The dress was *embellished* with stones and sequins.

Emblem *(n.)* എംബ്ലം – പ്രതീക ചിഹ്നം

We should respect our national *emblem* and flag.

Embrace *(v.)* ഇംബ്രേസ് – ആലിംഗനം ചെയ്യുക, സ്വീകരിക്കുക

My grandmother *embraced* me when I went to see her.

Embroidery *(n.)* എബ്രോയിഡറി – ചിത്ര തുന്നൽ

How good is your daughter at *embroidery*?

Emerald എമറാൾഡ് – പച്ചക്കല്ല്, മരതകം
(n.) Emerald is a precious stone.
(adj.) Emerald green is my favourite colour.

Emerge *(v.)* ഇമെർജ് – (പുറത്ത്/മുകളിൽ) കടക്കുക, പ്രത്യക്ഷപ്പെടുക
All were waiting for the doctor to *emerge from the operation* theatre.

Emergency *(n.)* എമർജെൻസി – ആപത്ത്, ആകസ്മിക ദുരന്തം
The doctors are trained well to deal wih the *emergencies.*

Emotion *(n.)* ഇമോഷൻ–വികാരം, മനോഭാവം
Even animals have *emotions.*
(adj.) Women are *emotional* by nature.

Emperor *(n.)* എമ്പറർ – ചക്രവർത്തി
Julius Caesar was a great Roman *emperor.*

Emphasis *(n.)* എംഫസിസ്–ഊന്നിപ്പറയുക
(n.) The teacher laid *emphasis* on studying in the morning, rather than staying awake all night.
(v.) The teacher *emphasised* on studying in the morning.

Employ *(v.)* ഇംപ്ലോയ്–1. ജോലിക്ക് വയ്ക്കുക
Ram was *employed* in a bank.
2. ഉപയോഗപ്പെടുത്തുക
How will you *employ* your time during the vacation?

Empty എംപ്റ്റി – ഒഴിഞ്ഞ, കാലിയാക്കുക
(adj.) Give me an *empty* glass.
(v.) Empty this glass and clean it.

Enable *(v.)* എനേബ്ൾ–പ്രാപ്തമാക്കുക, സൗകര്യം നൽകുക
My bonus *enabled* me to buy a TV set.

Enchanting *(adj.)* ഇൻചാന്റിംഗ് – മോഹിപ്പിക്കുക, രസിക്കുക
The song that she sang in the concert was really *enchanting.*

Enclose *(v.)* ഇൻക്ലോസ് 1. വളച്ച് കെട്ടുക, ഉള്ളിലാക്കുക
The garden was *enclosed* with a fence to keep the animals away.
2. ഒപ്പം ചേർക്കുക
She *enclosed* a form along with her letter.
(n.) The form was an *enclosure*.

Encounter ഇൻകൗണ്ടർ – 1. പ്രയാസം നേരിടുക
(v.) Aged people often *encounter* discrimination at work.
2. ആകസ്മിക കൂടിക്കാഴ്ച
(v.) I *encountered* a saint on my flight to Bangalore.
3. ഏറ്റുമുട്ടൽ
(n.) The criminal was killed in a police *encounter.*

Encourage *(v.)* എൻകറേജ് – പ്രോത്സാഹിപ്പിക്കുക, ധൈര്യം പകരുക
The students cheered loudly to *encourage* their school hockey team which was on victory path.
(n.) The teacher's kind words gave Arun *encouragement* to do better in exams.

End എൻഡ്–അവസാനം, അന്ത്യം, തീരുക
(n.) In the *end,* Arun agreed to accompany Suresh on his trip to Agra.
Do you like films with a sad *ending*?
(v.) Where does this road *end*?

Endangered *(adj.)* ഇൻഡെയ്ഞ്ചേർഡ് – വംശനാശം നേരിടുന്ന
We must protect the *endangered* species.

Endeavour *(n. & v.)* ഇൻഡവർ– ശ്രമിക്കുക, യത്നിക്കുക
Students *endeavour* to score good marks.
(v.) Rahul *endeavoured* to win the marathon race.

Endure *(v.)* ഇൻഡ്യൂർ – 1. സഹിക്കുക
Dr. B.R. Ambedkar *endured* many a hardship during his early education.
(n.) 2. സഹനശക്തി
Gandhiji was a man of *endurance.*

Enemy *(n.)* എനിമി – ശത്രു
Believe me, I'm your friend, not your *enemy*.

Energy *(n.)* എനർജി –1. പ്രവർത്തന ശക്തി, ഊക്ക്

Doctor advised the patient to take some tonic to increase his *energy*.

2. ഊർജം

Energy is essential for the working of both the human body and the machines.

Engage *(n.)* ഇൻഗേജ്–1. വിവാഹ നിശ്ചയം നടക്കുക

I am very happy to hear that you are *engaged*.

2. ജോലിക്ക് വയ്ക്കുക

How do you find the new servant you have *engaged*?

3. ജോലിത്തിരക്കുാകുക

In what work are you *engaged* at present?

(n.) Do you have any *engagement* this evening?

Engineer *(n.)* എൻജിനീയർ– എൻജീനീയർ

I called an *engineer* when my computer crashed.

Engrossed *(adj.)* ഇൻഗ്രോസ്ഡ് – മുഴുകിയിരിക്കുക

When I went to her place, she was *engrossed* in playing games on computer.

Enhance *(v.)* ഇൻഹാൻസ്–മികച്ചതാക്കുക

You can enhance this article by keeping the sentences short.

Enjoy *(v.)* ഇൻജോയ്–ആസ്വദിക്കുക, രസിക്കുക

Did you *enjoy* your trip to Simla?

I hope you *enjoyed* the dinner.

You will *enjoy* your visit to the zoo.

(n.) Some people find *enjoyment* in doing their work efficiently.

Enlarge *(v.)* ഇൻലാർജ് – വലുതാക്കുക, വിസ്തൃതമാക്കുക

There is a plan to *enlarge* our school by building new rooms.

Please get this photograph *enlarged.*

Enormous *(adj.)* ഇനാർമസ്–വളരെ വലിയ, വിപുലമായ

Former President of India Dr.S.D. Sharma gifted his *enormous* collection of books to the Bhopal library.

Enough ഇനഫ് – വേുവോളം, ധാരാളം

(adj.) You will find *enough* food in the fridge.

(adv.) Is the tea hot *enough*?

Enter *(v.)* എന്റർ–1. പ്രവേശിക്കുക, കടക്കുക

Ram stood in the queue to *enter* the theatre.

2. പങ്കെടുക്കുക, പേര് എഴുതുക, രേഖപ്പെടുത്തുക

The teacher *entered* the name of the new student in the attendance register.

Entertain *(v.)* എന്റർടെയ്ൻ–1. രസിക്കുക, വിനോദിപ്പിക്കുക

The elder brother *entertained* the children by telling them stories.

2. സല്ക്കരിക്കുക, സ്വീകരിക്കുക

The host *entertained* the guest lavishly.

Enthusiasm *(n.)* ഇൻതുസിയസം – ഉത്സാഹം, ആവേശം

(n.) He expressed great *enthusiasm* at the idea of a vacation in Ladakh.

(n.) He is a sports *enthusiast.*

(adj.) He is very *enthusiastic* about sports.

Entire *(adj.)* എന്റയർ – സമ്പൂർണ്ണ, സമഗ്ര

Have you brought the *entire* collection of your photographs?

(adv.) I *entirely* agree with you.

Envelope *(n.)* എൻവലപ്–ലക്കോട്ട്, കവചം

Put this letter in an *envelope* and post it.

Envious *(adj.)* എൻവിയസ് – അസൂയപ്പെടുക

Neighbours were *envious* of Rahul's new car.

Environment *(n.)* എൻവൈറൻമെന്റ് – 1. പരിസ്ഥിതി

We must protect our *environment* from pollution.

2. അന്തരീക്ഷം

Our office has a good work *environment.*

Episode *(n.)* എപ്പിസോഡ് – 1. സംഭവം

We should forget that humiliating *episode* and move on.

2. പരമ്പരയിലെ പതിപ്പ്

I missed the last *episode* of that serial.

Equal *(adj.)* ഈക്വൽ–സമാസമം, തുല്യം

The poor can never consider themselves *equal* to the rich.

Equip *(v.)* ഇക്വിപ് – സജ്ജമാക്കുക

Are you *equipped* to go on a hunting trip?

Dinesh wanted to *equip* his office with modern equipment.

(n.) He ordered some office *equipments.*

Era *(n.)* ഈറ – ചരിത്ര കാലഘട്ടം

The Qutub Minar was constructed long before the British *era.*

Eradicate *(v.)* ഇറാഡിക്കേറ്റ്–ഉന്മൂലമാക്കുക

The new Prime Minister promised to *eradicate* unemployment completely.

Erase *(v.)* ഇറേസ് – മാച്ചുകളയുക

She erased the previous answer and wrote a new one.

Erect *(adj.)* ഇറെക്റ്റ് – നിവർന്ന്

Stand *erect!*

(v.) 2. നിർത്തുക, സ്ഥാപിക്കുക

How much time does it take to *erect* a steel mill?

Err *(v.)* ഏർ – തെറ്റ് ചെയ്യുക, മറക്കുക

To *err* is human, to forgive divine.

Errand *(n.)* എറ് – ഏല്പിക്കുന്ന ജോലി

The servant was tired of doing many *errands* for his master.

Escape *(v.)* ഇസ്കേപ് – 1. ഓടിപ്പോവുക, തപ്പിച്ചോടുക

Prisoners' attempt to *escape* from the jail was foiled by alert guards.

2. രക്ഷപ്പെടുക

Amit *escaped* narrowly when his bike skidded.

(n.) He had a narrow *escape* when his bike skidded suddenly on the road.

Escort *(v.)* ഇസ്കോർട്ട് – അകമ്പടി സേവിക്കുക

I have to *escort* my daughter to school.

Especially *(adv.)* എസ്പെഷ്യലി – പ്രത്യേകിച്ച്, വിശിഷ്യ

Uma *especially* prepared delicious dishes for her daughter's birthday party.

Essay *(n.)* എസ്സേ – ഉപന്യാസം, പ്രബന്ധം

My son won the first prize in the *essay* writing competition.

Essential *(adj.)* എസൻഷ്യൽ – അനുപേക്ഷണീയം, പ്രധാന അടിസ്ഥാനം

Food, clothing and shelter are *essential* needs of a human being.

Establish *(v.)* എസ്റ്റാബ്ളിഷ്–സ്ഥാപിക്കുക, നടപ്പാക്കുക

How long ago was your business *established*?

Estate *(n.)* എസ്റ്റേറ്റ്–1. സമ്പത്ത്, ഭൂസ്വത്ത്

Rohit bought a large *estate* outside the town.

2. ഭൂവിഭാഗം

Rahul has a factory in the industrial *estate.*

Estimate *(n.)* എസ്റ്റിമേറ്റ് – അടങ്കൽ, കണക്കാക്കുക

The building contractor gave an *estimate* of the construction cost of Rahul's house.

Eternal *(adj.)* ഇറ്റേണൽ – ശാശ്വതം

Romeo and Juliet is an *eternal* love story.

Ethics *(n.)* എത്തിക്സ് – ധാർമ്മിക, സദാചാരപരം

We must not violate the code of *ethics* of our profession.

Ethnic *(adj.)* എത്നിക്–പ്രത്യേക ജാതിയെ പ്രതിനിധീകരിക്കുന്ന

She gave an *ethnic* look to her boutique.

Etiquette *(n.)* എറ്റിക്കെയ്റ്റ് – മര്യാദ, ശിഷ്ടാചാരം

He doesn't even have the *etiquette* to speak to a woman.

Evade *(v.)* ഇവേഡ് – ഒഴിവാക്കുക

Why are you trying to *evade* the question?

Evaluate *(v.)* ഇവാല്യുവേറ്റ്–വിലയിരുത്തുക

We must *evaluate* the market demands before launching a new product.

Evaporate *(v.)* ഇവാപൊറേറ്റ് – ബാഷ്പീകരിക്കുക

The water in the bowl *evaporated* when kept in the sun.

Eve *(n.)* ഈവ്–ഏതെങ്കിലും സംഭവത്തിന് തൊട്ട് മുമ്പ്
They met on the *eve* of Christmas.

Even ഈവൻ–1. ഒപ്പം, പോലും, ശേഷവും, പിന്നെയും
(adv.) Even if you have a good hand, you should get your letters typed.
(adj.) 2. സമതലം, ഒരേ പോലത്തെ
Your table does not have an *even* surface.

Evening *(n.)* ഈവനിംഗ് – വൈകുന്നേരം, സായാഹ്നം
By what time do you return from office in the *evening*?

Event *(n.)* ഇവന്റ് – സംഭവം, പരിണാമം
Sushil's selection for the IAS was an *event* suitable for celebration in his family.

Eventually *(adj.)* ഇവെൻചുലി അവസാനം, അന്തിമം
Eventually, Sheela realised her mistake.

Ever *(adv.)* എവർ–1. എപ്പോഴെങ്കിലും, എപ്പോഴും
Have you *ever* travelled by air?
2. മുതല്ക്ക്
I have known Anil ever since we were *children.*

Every *(adj.)* എവരി – ഓരോ, എല്ലാ
Students have to get up early *every* day.
Have you arranged *everything* properly?

Evidence *(n.)* എവിഡെൻസ് – തെളിവ്, പ്രമാണം, സാക്ഷ്യം
You cannot accuse your servant of theft without *evidence.*
Gopal's injured eye was an *evidence* that he had a fight.

Evil ഇവ്ൾ – ചീത്ത, അശുഭ, തിന്മ
(adj.) You will not escape the consequences of your *evil* acts.
(n.) Try to recognise *evil* and improve yourself.

Exact *(adj.)* എക്സാക്റ്റ് – കൃത്യമായ, സുനിശ്ചിത
Ram didn't know the *exact* location of his father's office.
(adv.) I left my office *exactly* at five o'clock.

Exaggerate *(v.)* എക്സാജറേറ്റ് – അതിശയോക്തി
He *exaggerated* his performance by comparing himself to Sachin Tenduikar.

Examine *(v.)* എക്സാമിൻ– പരീക്ഷിക്കുക, പരിശോധിക്കുക
The police *examined* the accident site.
(n.) പരീക്ഷ
After *examination,* results are eagerly awaited.

Example *(n.)* എക്സാമ്പ്ൾ–1. ഉദാഹരണം, ദൃഷ്ടാന്തം
Refer to the *example* if you cannot understand this question.
2. മാതൃക, ആദർശം
Your conduct should be an *example* to the others.

Exceed *(v.)* എക്സീഡ് – അധികമാകുക, അമിതമാകുക
Never *exceed* the permissible speed limit when you drive.

Excel *(v.)* എക്സെൽ – മികച്ചതാകുക, ശ്രേഷ്ഠമാകുക
In her dancing, Usha *excelled* all the other performers.
(adj.) The magazine cover had an *excellent* picture.

Except *(prep.)* എക്സെപ്പ്ട് – 1. ഒഴികെ, അല്ലാതെ
There is nothing in my pocket *except* a handkerchief.
(n.) 2. അപവാദങ്ങൾ
Exceptions are always there.

Excess *(n.)* അതിപ്രസരം, അമിതമായി
Excess of flowery phrases lessens the impact of a serlous article.
(adj.) He died of *excessive* drinking.

Exchange *(n. & v.)* എക്സ്ചേഞ്ച് – 1. വിനിമയം ചെയ്യുക, കൈമാറുക
(n.) I can give you my pen in *exchange* of your book.
(v.) The shopkeeper refused to *exchange* the shirt for any other item.
2. എക്സ്ചേഞ്ച്
Where is the telephone *exchange*?

Excite *(v.)* എക്സൈറ്റ് – ആവേശം കൊള്ളിക്കുക, ഇളക്കിമറിക്കുക

The union leader's speech *excited* the workers.

(adj.) Students were *excited* about their educational tour to Goa.

(n.) What is all this *excitement* about?

Exclaim *(v.)* എക്സ്ക്ലെയിം – അട്ടഹസിക്കുക, ഉച്ചത്തിൽ ശബ്ദമുാക്കുക

Ravi *exclaimed* in surprise when he saw his long lost friend.

Exclude *(v.)* എക്സ്ക്ലൂഡ് – വിട്ടുകളയുക

She was *excluded* from the volleyball team.

Excursion *(n.)* എക്സ്കർഷൻ – വിനോദയാത്ര

I took my family on an *excursion* to Suraj Kund.

Excuse *(v.)* എക്സ്ക്യൂസ് – 1. ക്ഷമാപണം ചെയ്യുക

Please *excuse* me for being late.

2. ഒഴിവാക്കുക

You will have to *excuse* me from coming to the meeting, as I am not well.

(n.) 3. ഒഴിവ്കഴിവ്

What is your *excuse* for being late?

Execute *(v.)* എക്സിക്യൂട്ട്–1. പൂർത്തിയാക്കുക, പാലിക്കുക

At the public rally, the VIP security plan was *executed* efficiently.

2. തൂക്കിലേറ്റുക

The murderer was *executed* early this morning.

Exercise എക്സർസൈസ് – 1. വ്യായാമം, കസർത്ത്

(n.) You must take *exercise* to keep fit.

(v.) We can *exercise* our brain as well as the body.

2. പരിശീലന പാഠം

Most students could not do the *exercise* given by the geometry teacher.

Exert *(v.)* എക്സർട്ട് – പരിശ്രമിക്കുക

You will have to *exert* yourself to pass the tough examination with good marks.

Exhaust എക്സാസ്റ്റ് – 1. പൂർണ്ണമായി അവസാനിക്കുക

(v.) The explorers had *exhausted* their food-supply before the rescue party arrived.

(adj.) 2. വല്ലാതെ തളരുക, ക്ഷീണിക്കുക

After a hard day's work, it's natural to feel *exhausted.*

Exhibit എക്സിബിറ്റ്–1. പ്രദർശിപ്പിക്കുക, പ്രദർശന വസ്തു

(v.) At which art gallery are you going to *exhibit* your paintings?

(n.) Among *exhibits* at the show was a rare antique piece.

2. പ്രദർശനം

Have you visited the *exhibition* of handloom fabrics?

Exist *(v.)* എക്സിസ്റ്റ് – നിലനില്ക്കുക, നിലവിലുള്ള

Man cannot *exist* without air and water.

(n.) Tell me, which is the largest animal in *existence*?

Exit എക്സിറ്റ് – പുറത്തേക്കുള്ള വഴി, പുറത്ത് പോകുക

(n.) As fire broke out in the cinema hall, we all rushed towards the *exit.*

(v.) We *exited* through the back door when the fire broke out.

Expand *(v.)* എക്സ്പാൻഡ് – വിപുലമാക്കുക, വ്യാപിപ്പിക്കുക

Ravi is planning to *expand* his business.

Expect *(v.)* എക്സ്പെക്റ്റ്– പ്രതീക്ഷിക്കുക, നോക്കിയിരിക്കുക

I did not *expect* you to return so soon.

Expel *(v.)* എക്സ്പെൽ – പുറത്താക്കുക, ബഹിഷ്ക്കരിക്കുക

The principal *expelled* the misbehaving students from the school.

Expend *(v.)* എക്സ്പെൻഡ് – ചെലവാക്കുക, വ്യയം ചെയ്യുക

Some youth *expend* most of their money and energy on entertainment.

(adj.) Your suit looks quite *expensive* (costly).

Experience *(n.)* എക്സ്പീരിയൻസ് – 1. അനുഭവം, പരിചയം

Do you have any *experience* of office work?

Tell me about your *experiences* abroad.

(v.) 2. അനുഭവിക്കുക, സഹിക്കുക
The mountaineers *experienced* many difficulties on their way to the Everest.

Experiment *(n. & v.)* എക്സ്പെരിമെന്റ് – പരീക്ഷണം നടത്തുക
(n.) Ram was very happy with the outcome of his *experiment* in Physics.
(v.) Scientists *experimented* with a model of the space shuttle to test its power supply system.

Expert *(adj.)* എക്സ്പെർട്ട് – വിദഗ്ദ്ധർ, സമർത്ഥൻ
The automobile mechanic was an *expert* at repairing all kinds of motor engines.

Expire *(v.)* എക്സ്പയർ–1. മരിക്കുക, ഉച്ഛ്വസിക്കുക
When did the old man *expire* ?
2. അവസാനിക്കുക, തീരുക
Our holidays *expire* next week.

Explain *(v.)* എക്സ്പ്ലെയ്ൻ–വിശദീകരിക്കുക, മനസ്സിലാക്കി കൊടുക്കുക
Please *explain* to me the working of this machine.

Explode *(v.)* എക്സ്പ്ലോഡ് – പൊട്ടിത്തെറിക്കുക, സ്ഫോടനമുാക്കുക
The boiler will *explode* unless you let some steam out of it.
(n.) We were all alarmed by the loud *explosion* in our neighbourhood.

Exploit *(v.)* എക്സ്പ്ലോയിറ്റ്–ചൂഷണം ചെയ്യുക
The child labourer was *exploited* by being made to work the whole day for a small amount.

Explore *(v.)* എക്സ്പ്ലോർ–അന്വേഷിക്കുക, പര്യവേക്ഷണം ചെയ്യുക
As soon as we arrived at the beach, we began to *explore* it.

Export എക്സ്പോർട്ട് – കയറ്റുമതി, കയറ്റി അയക്കുക
(n.) Are you in the *export* business?
(v.) We *export* mangoes to the Western countries.

Expose *(v.)* എക്സ്പോസ്–പുറത്തുകൊുവരിക, വെളിച്ചത്ത് കൊുവരിക
The inquiry committee *exposed* all dubious deals of the corrupt minister.

Exposure *(n.)* എക്സ്പോഷർ– പ്രദർശനം
Too much of media *exposure* succeeded in drawing the audience to the movie theatres.

Express എക്സ്പ്രസ്സ് – 1. വ്യക്തമാക്കുക, പ്രകടിപ്പിക്കുക
(v.) If you want to become a good speaker, you must learn to *express* yourself effectively.
(adj.) 2. വേഗമെത്തുന്ന
Is this an *express* train?

Expression *(n.)* എക്സ്പ്രഷൻ – മുഖഭാവം
Why do you have such a sad *expression* on your face?

Extend *(v.)* എക്സ്റ്റെൻഡ്–വിപുലമാക്കുക, വർദ്ധിപ്പിക്കുക, നൽകുക
You will have to *extend* your boundary wall to protect your garden.
Rahul thanked his friend for the warm hospitality *extended* to him.

Exterior *(n.)* എക്സ്റ്റീരിയർ – പുറം ഭാഗം
The *exterior* of the building was decorated with wooden carvings.

Extra *(adj.)* എക്സ്ട്രാ–അധികം, അതിരിക്ത
Do you have an *extra* pencil?

Extraordinary *(adj.)* എക്സ്ട്രാഓർഡിനറി –അനിതര സാധാരണമായ, അസാമാന്യമായ
Child artist's performance in the play was *extraordinary*.

Extravagant *(adj.)* എക്സ്ട്രാവഗന്റ് – ചെലവാളി
She is very *extravagant* and often buys things she does not require.

Extreme *(adj.)* എക്സ്ട്രീം–1. അത്യധികം, അളവറ്റ
Martyrs showed *extreme* courage by sacrificing their life for the country's freedom.
2. ഏറ്റവും, അവസാനത്തെ
I live at the *extreme* end of this street.
(adv.) I am *extremely* grateful to you for your assistance.

Extrovert *(n.)* എക്സ്ട്രാവെർട്ട്–ബഹിർമുഖൻ
He is an *extrovert,* while his brother is completely opposite.

Eye *(n.)* ഐ – 1. കണ്ണ്, നയനം
Shooters' *eyes* are quite sharp.
2. സൂചിക്കുഴ
Please put this thread through the *eye* of the needle.

F

Fable *(n.)* ഫാബ്ൾ – കഥ, കെട്ടുകഥ
Give your child Aesop's *Fables* to read.

Fabric *(n.)* ഫാബ്രിക് – തുണി, വസ്ത്രം
Cotton *fabric* is good for the skin.

Fabulous *(adj.)* ഫാബുലസ് – ഉത്കൃഷ്ടം
I had a fabulous dream in which I became a millionaire.

Face *(n.)* ഫേസ് – 1. മുഖം
Go and wash your *face*.
(v.) 2. നേരിടുക, ചെറുക്കുക
Rohit *faced* strong opposition from his parents in his inter-caste marriage.

Facet *(n.)* ഫാസിറ്റ് – വശങ്ങൾ
We must consider all the *facets* of this project before taking it up.

Facility *(n.)* ഫസിലിറ്റി – സൗകര്യം
The school provides excellent sports *facilities.*

Fact *(n.)* ഫാക്ട് – സത്യം, യാഥാർത്ഥ്യം
The police recorded all the *facts* of the murder case.

Factor *(n.)* ഫാക്ടർ – 1. ഘടകം, ഗുണാംശം
Find out the *factors* of this number.
2. കാരണം, നിമിത്തം
Corruption was the main *factor* behind the fall of the government.

Factory *(n.)* ഫാക്ടറി – തൊഴിൽശാല, ഫാക്ടറി
What articles do you manufacture in your *factory*?

Faculty *(n.)* ഫാക്കൽറ്റി – സർവ്വകലാശാല അല്ലെങ്കിൽ കോളേജിലെ അദ്ധ്യാപകഗണം
Contact the *faculty* members to get your doubts cleared.

Fade *(v.)* ഫേഡ് – മങ്ങുക
The colour of quality cloth doesn't *fade* easily.

Fail *(v.)* ഫെയ്ൽ – 1. പരാജയപ്പെടുക
Did he pass or *fail* in the examination?
2. പ്രവർത്തന രഹിതമാകുക
While we were having dinner, the power suddenly *failed.*

Faint ഫെയ്ന്റ് – 1. നേർത്ത, അവ്യക്ത
(adj.) I heard faint noises of someone crying.
2.*(v.)* ബോധം കെടുക
When you *faint,* you look as if you are in a deep sleep.

Fair *(adj.)* ഫെയ്ർ – 1. വെളുത്ത, സുന്ദരം, നിർമ്മല
Your daughter has a *fair* complexion.
2. ഉചിതം, നിക്ഷ്പക്ഷം, ന്യായമായ
I believe in *fair* play.
3. തരക്കേടില്ലാത്ത, സാധാരണ
Sheela's performance in the examination was just *fair*.
(n.) 4. മേള
People came in large numbers to see the trade *fair*.

Faith *(n.)* ഫെയ്ത്ത് – 1. വിശ്വാസം, ഉറപ്പ്
I have full *faith* in Indu, so I believe that she is not telling lies.
(adj.) 2. വിശ്വസ്തൻ, യഥാർത്ഥമായ
Our servant is very *faithful.*
Give me a *faithful* account of what you did.

Fake ഫേക്–വ്യാജ, കൃത്രിമം കാണിക്കുക
(n.) All these currency notes are a *fake.*
(adj.) These are *fake* currency notes.
(v.) He *faked* the documents.

Fall ഫാൾ – വീഴുക, വീഴ്ച, പതനം
(v.) Take care lest you *fall* down.
(n.) 'Pride hath a *fall*'.

False *(adj.)* ഫാൾസ്–1. തെറ്റായ, അസത്യ
We should never make a *false* statement.
2. കപട, നെറികെട്ട
Never be a *false* friend.
3. പുറംപൂച്ച്, കൃത്രിമ
Do you wear *false* teeth?

Fame *(n.)* ഫെയിം – പ്രശസ്തി
His fame increased by the success of his new book.

Familiar *(adj.)* ഫമിലിയർ – സുപരിചിത
Your face looks *familiar,* but I don't remember your name.
Ram was *familiar* with Rohit's entire family.
(n.) Too much *familiarity* breeds contempt.

Family *(n.)* ഫാമിലി–കുടുംബം, വീട്ടുകാർ
Have you sent away your *family* to Mumbai?

Famine *(n.)* ഫാമിൻ – ക്ഷാമം
The *famine* killed many people in Orissa.

Famous *(adj.)* ഫേമസ് – അതിപ്രശസ്തം
A Nobel prize winner becomes *famous* worldwide.

Fan *(n.)* ഫാൻ – പങ്ക
I would like to buy a table *fan.*

Fancy ഫാൻസി – 1. സങ്കല്പിക്കുക
(v.) I *fancy* I heard noises in the night.
2. ആഗ്രഹിക്കുക, ഇഷ്ടപ്പെടുക
I do not *fancy* gaudy clothes.
(adj.) 3. നിറപ്പകിട്ടുള്ള, വിചിത്ര
Youngsters like *fancy* clothes.
(n.) 4. വിചാരം, കല്പന
A *fancy* passed through my mind.

Fantastic *(adj.)* ഫന്റാസ്റ്റിക് – ഉൽകൃഷ്ടം
This is a *fantastic* book; you must read it.

Far ഫാർ – 1. ദൂരെ
(adj.) Ram's office was not too *far* from his home.
He went *far* and wide in search of his lost brother.
(adj.) 2. വളരെയേറെ
This nut is *far* harder to crack than I had imagined.

Fare *(n.)* ഫെയ്ർ – 1. യാത്രാക്കൂലി, നിരക്ക്
It's illegal to travel in the bus without paying the *fare.*
(v.) 2. ജയിക്കുകയോ തോൽക്കുകയോ ചെയ്യുക
Dolly *fared* well in the examination.

Farewell *(n.)* ഫെയർവെൽ–വിട, യാത്രയയപ്പ്
I gave a *farewell* party to my friend who was going abroad.

Farm *(n.)* ഫാം – കൃഷിയിടം
I have built a small cottage in my *farm.*

Fashion *(n.)* ഫാഷൻ – 1. ഫാഷൻ, വേഷാകൃതി
Narrow trousers are not in *fashion* these days.
(v.) 2. രൂപപ്പെടുത്തുക, നിർമ്മിക്കുക
He *fashioned* the sword and spear with great skill.

Fast ഫാസ്റ്റ് – 1. വേഗം
(adj.) Life in Delhi is very *fast.*
Walk *fast,* it is too late.
(adj.) 2. മുറകെ, ബലമായി
I held *fast* to my umbrella in the gale.
3. ഉപവാസം, നിരാഹാരം
(n.) My grandmother observes a *fast* every Monday.
(v.) My father *fasted* for three days.

Fasten *(v.)* ഫാസെൻ–കെട്ടുക, മുറുക്കുക
Fasten your seatbelts, the plane is about to take off.

Fat *(adj.)* ഫാറ്റ് – 1. കൊഴുത്ത, തടിച്ച
If you eat too much, you will become *fat.*
(n.) 2. കൊഴുപ്പ്
Do you cook in *fat* or oil?

Fatal *(adj.)* ഫേറ്റൽ – മാരകം
I heard your neighbour met with a *fatal* accident.

Fate *(n.)* ഫേറ്റ് – വിധി, ഭാഗ്യം
We can never know what our *fate* is.

Fatigue *(n.)* ഫറ്റീഗ് – ക്ഷീണം
She fainted of *fatigue.*

Fault *(n.)* ഫാൾട്ട് – 1. തെറ്റ്, മറവി
It was the employer's *fault* that the employees were not paid in time.
2. ദോഷം, പോരായ്മ, കുറവ്
The mechanic quickly repaired the *fault* in the car engine.

Favour *(v.)* ഫേവർ – 1. ദയ, അനുഗ്രഹം
Will you do me a *favour*?

(v.) 2. ഇഷ്ടപ്പെടുക, ആഗ്രഹിക്കുക
Between blue and red, which colour do you *favour*?
(adj.) Blue is my *favourite* colour.

Fear ഫിയർ–പേടി, പേടിക്കുക, ആശങ്കപ്പെടുക
(n.) *Fear* is a powerful enemy.
(v.) I *fear* I might miss the train.

Feast ഫീസ്റ്റ് – വിരുന്ന്, സദ്യ, സല്ക്കാരം
(n.) Ram invited all the neighbours on his daughter's birthday *feast*.
(v.) Our friends *feasted* and sang songs.

Feat (n.) ഫീറ്റ് – അഭ്യാസം, അസാമാന്യ ദൃശ്യം
Children were thrilled on seeing the *feats* of the acrobat.

Feather (n.) ഫെദർ – തൂവൽ
Collecting *feathers* of different birds is my hobby.

Feature (n.) ഫീച്ചർ–1. സ്വരൂപം, ആകാരം
Who is that young lady with sharp *features*?
2. സവിശേഷത, പ്രത്യേകത
Dusty winds are a *feature* of Delhi summers.
3. വിശേഷ ലേഖനം
The newspapers carry *features* on environment regularly.

Federation (n.) ഫെഡറേഷൻ – ഫെഡറേഷൻ, സംഘടന
The *Federation* is headed by a reputed industrialist.

Fee (n.) ഫീ – ഫീസ്
Have you paid your son's school *fees*?
We pay *fees* to doctors, tutors and lawyers.

Feeble (adj.) ഫീബ്ൾ–അശക്ത, ദുർബല
My long illness has made me *feeble*.
2. മങ്ങിയ, നേർത്ത
I was unable to read in the *feeble* candle light.

Feed (v.) ഫീഡ്–ഊട്ടുക, ഭക്ഷണം നൽകുക
To *feed* an infant with the mother's milk is good for his health.
(adj.) Where is the baby's *feeding* bottle?

Feedback (n.) ഫീഡ്ബാക്ക്– പ്രതികരണം
Let me have your *feedback*, so that I improve the article accordingly.

Feel (v.) ഫീൽ–1. സ്പർശിക്കുക, തൊടുക
The doctor *felt* the injured arm of Usha to see if there was a fracture.
2. തോന്നുക
We all *felt* happy at the good news.
(n.) 3. അനുഭവിക്കുക, അറിയാനുള്ള ക്ഷമത
The old woman had no *feeling* in her numb fingers.

Feign (v.) ഫെയ്ൻ – നടിക്കുക
The child *feigned* a headache to miss the school.

Fellow ഫെല്ലോ – 1. വിശിഷ്ടാംഗം
(n.) He is a *fellow* of the School of Planning and Architecture.
2. ഒരാൾ
(n.) Don't let that *fellow* enter my room.
3. സഹചാരി
(adj.) I share a good rapport with my *fellow* workers.

Female (adj. & n.) ഫീമെയ്ൽ–മഹിള, സ്ത്രീ
A *female* peacock is not beautiful.
(n.) The *female* of a deer is called doe.

Feminine (adj.) ഫെമിനിൻ സ്ത്രീ സംബന്ധ, സ്ത്രൈണ
The boy with *feminine* looks was given a female role in the play.

Fence ഫെൻസ്–വേലി, കയ്യാല, വേലി കെട്ടുക
(n.) Can you jump over this *fence*?
(v.) He *fenced* his garden to protect it from animals.

Ferocious (n.) ഫെറോഷ്യസ്–ഹിംസ്ര
Lion is a *ferocious* animal.

Ferry ഫെറി–കടത്തുവഞ്ചി, വള്ളം, അക്കരെ എത്തിക്കുക
(n.) We crossed to the Swarga Ashram in a *ferry*.
(v.) The pilgrims were *ferried* across the Ganges.

Fertile (adj.) ഫെർടൈൽ–വളക്കൂറുള്ള, ആശയ, സമൃദ്ധമായ
My farm is quite *fertile*.
You have a *fertile* brain.

Fervour (n.) ഫർവർ–അത്യുത്സാഹം
Diwali was celebrated with great *fervour* in the city.

Festival (n.) ഫെസ്റ്റിവൽ–ഉത്സവം
India is a land of *festivals*.

Fetch *(v.)* ഫെച്ച്–കൊുവരിക
Please *fetch* me a glass of water.

Feud *(n.)* ഫ്യൂഡ്–കുടിപ്പക
The issue of property resulted in a *feud* between the brothers.

Fever *(n.)* ഫീവർ–പനി
The doctor advised rest to Dinesh as he was having high *fever*.

Few *(adj.)* ഫ്യൂ–1. ഏതാനും, ചില
A *few* of my friends know that I can paint.
2. വളരെക്കുറച്ച്, ആർക്കുംതന്നെ
Few of my friends know that I can paint.

Fibre *(n.)* ഫൈബർ–നാരിഴ, തന്തു
Of what *fibre* is your shirt made?

Fickle *(adj.)* ഫിക്ൾ–ചപല
Don't believe him; he is very *fickle*-minded.

Fiction *(n.)* ഫിക്ഷൻ–കഥാസാഹിത്യം
I like to read *fiction*.

Fiddle *(v.)* ഫിഡ്ൽ–ആവശ്യമില്ലാതെ എന്തെങ്കിലും സാധനം കൈകാര്യം ചെയ്യുക
Why are you *fiddling* with my purse?

Fidelity *(n.)* ഫിഡെലിറ്റി–നിഷ്ഠ, വിശ്വസ്തത
He probably doubted her *fidelity*.

Fidget *(v.)* ഫിജിറ്റ്–ചാഞ്ചല്യം കാണിക്കുക, സ്വസ്ഥതയില്ലാതിരിക്കുക
You cannot concentrate on what you are reading if you keep *fidgeting*.

Field *(n.)* ഫീൽഡ്–1. വയൽ
What do you grow in your *field* ?
2. രംഗം
Do you have any experience in the *field* of social work?

Fierce *(adj.)* ഫിയേർസ്–ഉഗ്ര, രൗദ്ര
I assure you my dog is not a *fierce* animal.

Fight ഫൈറ്റ്–വഴക്ക് (കൂടുക).
(v.) The two neighbours were *fighting* over a petty issue.
(n.) It was a fierce *fight* among street dogs.

Figure *(n.)* ഫിഗർ–1. അംഗം, തുക, കണക്ക്
I am good at *figures*.
2. രൂപം, ആകാരം, ആകൃതി
In the dark, I could make out a *figure* moving about in the room.
(v.) ഊഹിക്കുക, കണക്കാക്കുക
Can you *figure* out how we can persuade the minister to preside over the function?

File ഫയൽ–1. ഫയൽ, ചേർത്തുവച്ച രേഖകൾ, ഫയൽ ചെയ്യുക
(n.) Where is the *file* of our correspondence with the government?
(v.) *File* these papers carefully.
2. നിര, അണി
Boys, march to your classrooms in a single *file*.
3. അരം
I bought a carpenter's *file* for some wood work in the house.

Fill *(v.)* ഫിൽ–നിറയ്ക്കുക, നിറയാൻ വിടുക, പൂരിപ്പിക്കുക
Please *fill* this glass with cold water.
Students were *filled* with joy at the declaration of vacations.

Film *(n.)* ഫിലിം–1. ചലച്ചിത്രം, സിനിമ
Are you fond of *films*?
2. ഫിലിം
Is there a *film* in your camera?
3. പടലം, പരപ്പ്
Don't drink this water, it has a *film* of oil on it.
There is a *film* of dust on the table.

Filter ഫിൽറ്റർ–അരിക്കുക, ഫിൽറ്റർ (ചെയ്യുക)
(v.) *Filter* this water before you drink it.
(n.) I have bought a water *filter*.

Filthy *(adj.)* ഫിൽത്തി–മലിന, അഴുക്ക് നിറഞ്ഞ, ചീത്ത
The house had been empty for years and was *filthy* inside.

Final *(adj.)* ഫൈനൽ–അവസാന, അന്തിമ
When is your *final* examination starting?
(adv.) Ram *finally* agreed to accompany Suresh to the trade fair.

Financial *(adj.)* ഫൈനാൻഷ്യൽ – സാമ്പത്തിക, ധനകാര്യ
The government offered *financial* aid to the farmers whose crops were destroyed in the floods.

Find *(v.)* ഫൈൻഡ്-കണ്ടെത്തുക, മനസ്സിലാക്കുക
Have you *found* the purse you had lost?
On reaching home, Rahul *found* his friend waiting for him.

Fine ഫൈൻ-1. മികച്ച, ശ്രേഷ്ഠമായ
(adj.) The acrobats presented a *fine* show.
2. സൂക്ഷ്മ, നേർത്ത
Sharpen your pencil and draw a *fine* line.
3. പിഴ
Ramesh had to pay a *fine* of five rupees for returning the library book late.

Finger *(n.)* ഫിംഗർ-വിരൽ
This ring looks beautiful on your little *finger*.

Finish *(v.)* ഫിനിഷ്-1. തീർക്കുക, പൂർണ്ണമാക്കുക
Have you *finished* your homework?
(n.) 2. തികവ്, നികവ്
Your dining table has a nice *finish*.

Finished *(adj.)* ഫിനിഷ്ഡ്-തയ്യാർ
Can you provide us the *finished* product if we provide you the raw material?

Fire *(n.)* ഫയർ-1. തീ, ജ്വാല
Last night, a *fire* broke out in our colony.
(v.) 2. വെടി വയ്ക്കുക
The police *fired* in the air to disperse a rioting mob.

Firm *(n.)* ഫേം-1. കമ്പനി, സ്ഥാപനം
I learn you have joined a big *firm*.
(adj.) 2. ഉറച്ച, ദൃഢ, നിശ്ചിത
It's my *firm* belief that God rewards hard work.
3. കട്ടിയുള്ള, ദൃഢമായ
I jumped from the boat on to the *firm* ground.

First *(adj.)* ഫസ്റ്റ്-1. ആദ്യത്തെ, പ്രഥമ
My son came *first* in the competition.
2. *First-aid* പ്രഥമ ചികിത്സ
Always keep a *first-aid* box in the house.
(adv.) 3. മുമ്പേ
Mother asked Usha to *first* take dinner and then watch TV programmes.

Fish *(n.)* ഫിഷ്-മത്സ്യം, മീൻ
Would you like fried *fish* for lunch?

Fist *(n.)* ഫിസ്റ്റ്-മുഷ്ടി
The children were imitating a fight sequence from the film by waving their *fists* in the air.

Fit *(v.)* ഫിറ്റ്-1. ചേർച്ചയുള്ള
This shirt *fits* me very well.
(adj.) 2. സുഖമാകുക, ആരോഗ്യം വീണ്ടെടുക്കുക
I was ill last month, but now I am *fit*.
3. അനുരൂപം, യോഗ്യതയുള്ള, ചേരുന്ന
The employer asked the job applicant whether he was *fit* enough to hold a supervisor's post.
(n.) 4. ചുഴലി
He slapped his son in a *fit* of anger.

Fix *(v.)* ഫിക്സ്-1. നിശ്ചയിക്കുക, തീർപ്പാക്കുക
What day shall we *fix* for the party?
2. ഉറപ്പിക്കുക
Who *fixed* this frame on the wall?

Flair *(n.)* ഫ്ളെയർ-സ്വതസിദ്ധമായ കഴിവ്
She has a *flair* for writing.

Flake ഫ്ളേക്ക്-പടലം
(n.) Huge *flakes* of snow covered the earth.
(v.) Plaster *flaked* off the wall.

Flag *(n.)* ഫ്ളാഗ്-പതാക, കൊടി
The Tricolour is our national *flag*.

Flame *(n.)* ഫ്ളെയിം-ജ്വാല, തീനാളം
Before sleeping, put out the *flames* in the fireplace.

Flap ഫ്ളാപ്-1. മൂടി, തൊങ്ങൽ
(n.) He sewed a *flap* on his pocket.
2. ചിറകടിക്കുക
(v.) The pigeon *flapped* its wings to fly.

Flare *(n.)* ഫ്ളെയർ-1. ജ്വലനം, തെളിച്ചം
In the *flare* of the match, I saw the lost ring on the floor.
(v.) 2. രോഷം കൊള്ളുക, പൊട്ടിത്തെറിക്കുക
You must give up your habit of *flaring* up without cause.

Flash ഫ്ളാഷ്–1. മിന്നൽ പിണർ, ദീപ്തി

(n.) There was a sudden *flash* of lightning in the clouded sky.

(v.) Why are your eyes *flashing* with anger?

2. അതിവേഗം കടന്നുപോവുക

The cars participating in the race *flashed* past us.

Flat *(n.)* ഫ്ളാറ്റ്–1. ഫ്ളാറ്റ്, പാർപ്പിടം

My *flat* has three rooms.

(adj.) 2. സമതലം, പരന്ന, നീ് നിവർന്ന

Lie *flat* on the bed to overcome tiredness.

Flatter *(v.)* ഫ്ളാറ്റർ–മുഖസ്തുതി, സ്തുതിക്കുക, പൊക്കിപറയുക

Everybody is *flattered* by a compliment.

(n.) The people who are adept at *flattery* are called *flatterers*.

Flavour ഫ്ളേവർ–സുഗന്ധം, ഫ്ളേവർ

(n.) Do you have the icecream in chocolate *flavour*?

(v.) Sheela's birthday cake was *flavoured* with vanilla essence.

Flaw *(n.)* ഫ്ളാ–ദോഷം, കുറ്റം

The advocates try to find a *flaw* in every law.

(adj.) In a TV programme, the famous beauty expert gave many tips to maintain a *flawless* complexion.

Flee *(v.)* ഫ്ളീ-ഓടിക്കളയുക, കടന്നു കളയുക

We all *fled* from the house on fire.

Fleet *(n.)* ഫ്ളീറ്റ്–വാഹന നിര

I dream of owning a huge *fleet* of cars.

Flesh *(n.)* ഫ്ളെഷ്–മാംസം, തടിവയ്ക്കുക

You have put on *flesh* during your foreign trip.

Flexible *(adj.)* ഫ്ളെക്സിബ്ൾ – അയവുള്ള, വളയുന്ന

Our arms and legs are *flexible*.

(n.) They have *flexibility*.

Flicker *(v.)* ഫ്ളിക്കർ–1. ചലിക്കുക, ആടുക

The candle flame *flickers* in the wind.

(adj.) Reading in the *flickering* flame of the candle is not good for one's eyes.

(n.) 2. കിരണം

The marooned flood victims had *flicker* of hope that they would be rescued.

Flimsy *(adj.)* ഫ്ളിംസി–നിസ്സാരമായ, കഴമ്പില്ലാത്ത

Stop making such *flimsy* excuses.

Fling *(v.)* ഫ്ളിംഗ്–എറിയുക, നിലത്തിടുക

Both the wrestlers were trying to *fling* each other on to the ground.

Don't *fling* baseless charges at me.

Flip *(v.)* ഫ്ളിപ്–പെട്ടെന്ന് മറിക്കുക

She *flipped* through the pages of the book to find the 10-rupee note inside it.

Float *(v.)* ഫ്ളോട്ട്–വെള്ളത്തിൽ പൊങ്ങി കിടക്കുക

I *float* for a while before I begin to swim.

People swim, wood *floats*, but a stone sinks.

Flock *(n.)* ഫ്ളോക്ക്–1. കൂട്ടം, പറ്റം

Look at that *flock* of birds in the sky.

(v.) 2. കൂട്ടം കൂടുക, ഒത്തുചേരുക

At the fair, the children *flocked* around the toy shops.

Flood *(n.)* ഫ്ളഡ്–1. വെള്ളപ്പൊക്കം, പ്രളയം, പേമാരി

I could not go to Patna last year because of the *floods* there.

2. ഒട്ടേറെ, ഒരുപിടി

On becoming an IAS officer, Sheela received a *flood* of greeting cards.

(v.) The rain water *flooded* our street.

Floor *(n.)* ഫ്ളോർ–1. തറ, നിലം

Don't throw the waste paper on the *floor*.

2. നില

How many *floors* does your school building have?

Flop ഫ്ളോപ്–പൊട്ടിയ, ചലച്ചിത്രം, പുസ്തകം

(n.) The film was a big *flop*.

(v.) The film *flopped* badly.

Flour *(n.)* ഫ്ളൗർ–മാവ്, നേർത്ത പൊടി

Give me some *flour* to make bread.

Flourish *(v.)* ഫ്ളറിഷ്–1. ഉയർച്ച നേടുക, വളർച്ച നേടുക

I hear your business is *flourishing*.

2. കുത്തിവരയ്ക്കുക, വിചിത്രമായി എഴുതുക

Don't *flourish* your pen in my face.

Flow ഫ്ളോ-പ്രവാഹം, ധാര, ഗതി, ഒഴുകുക
(*n.*) The *flow* of the river is swift in the hilly areas.
(*v.*) The river *flows* into the sea.

Flower (*n.*) ഫ്ളവർ-പൂവ്, പുഷ്പം
For whom are you making a garland of *flowers*?

Fluctuate (*v.*) ഫ്ളക്ചുവേറ്റ് - ഏറ്റകുറച്ചിലുവാവുക
The prices of shares keep on *fluctuating*.

Fluent (*adj.*) ഫ്ളുവന്റ് -ഒഴുക്കുള്ള, തടസ്സമില്ലാതെ
Sohan is *fluent* in French.
(*adv.*) Gurmeet can speak four languages *fluently*.

Fluid (*n.*) ഫ്ളൂയിഡ്-1. ദ്രാവകം
What is this golden-coloured *fluid* in the bottle?
(*adj.*) 2. തീർച്ചയില്ലാത്ത, അനിശ്ചിതം, മാറാവുന്നത്
The picnic programme is still *fluid*.

Flute (*n.*) ഫ്ളൂട്ട്-ഓടക്കുഴൽ
Krishna enchanted everyone by his *flute*.

Flutter (*v.*) ഫ്ളട്ടർ-ചിറകടിക്കുക, തത്തിപറക്കുക
I watched a sparrow *fluttering* its wings.

Fly (*v.*) ഫ്ളൈ-പറക്കുക, പറന്നുയരുക
At what speed does a jet plane *fly*?
2. ഓടിപോവുക
It is very late, I must *fly* home.
(*n.*) 3. ഈച്ച
Don't let *flies* sit on your food.

Foam (*n.*) ഫോം-പത, നുര
Does this soap give a lot of *foam*?

Focus (*v.*) ഫോക്കസ്-ശ്രദ്ധ നൽകുക
Focus on the work you are doing and you will always succeed.

Fodder (*n.*) ഫോഡർ-കാലിത്തീറ്റ
His father asked him to cut *fodder* for the cattle.

Foe ഫോ-ശത്രു, എതിരാളി
You should be able to distinguish between friends and *foes*.

Fog (*n.*) ഫോഗ്-മൂടൽ മഞ്ഞ്
Ships cannot sail safely in the *fog*.
(*adj.*) Don't drive in the *foggy* weather.

Foil (*n.*) ഫോയിൽ-പാളി
Mother wrapped the chapattis in aluminium *foil*.

Fold ഫോൾഡ്-മടക്കുക, മടക്ക്
(*v.*) *Fold* this letter and put it in an envelope.
(*n.*) The invitation card had three *folds*.

Folk (*n.*) ഫോക്-ജനം, കൂട്ടർ, സമൂഹം
The country *folk* were very kind to me.

Follow (*v.*) ഫോളോ-1. പിന്തുടരുക
Follow me into my room.
2. മനസ്സിലാക്കുക
Do you *follow* your professor's lectures?

Folly (*n.*) ഫോളി-വിഡ്ഢിത്തം, മൂഢത
It was a *folly* on Ashok's part to turn down a nice job offer.

Fond (*adj.*) ഫോ് -പ്രിയം, കമ്പം
My little son is *fond* of pastries.

Food (*n.*) ഫുഡ്-ഭക്ഷണം, ആഹാരം, അന്നം
Have you taken your *food*?

Fool ഫൂൾ-1. മടയൻ, മൻ
(*n.*) Don't be a *fool*.
(*v.*) 2. മനാക്കുക, കളിപ്പിക്കുക
Don't *fool* me.

Foot (*n.*) ഫുട്ട്-1. കാല്, പാദം
I hurt my left *foot* yesterday.
2. അടിഭാഗം, താഴെയറ്റം
Come up; don't stand at the *foot* of the staircase.
3. അടി (അളവ്)
How many inches are there in a *foot*?

Forbid (*v.*) ഫോർബിഡ്-വിലക്കുക, വിസമ്മതിക്കുക
I *forbid* you to go out in the rain.

Force (*n.*) ഫോഴ്സ്-1. ബലം, ശക്തി
Don't bang the door with great *force*.
2. സൈന്യം
Would you like to join the Air *Force*?
(*v.*) 3. നിർബന്ധിതനാക്കുക
Sustained questioning *forced* the robber to disclose his accomplices' names.

Forecast ഫോർകാസ്റ്റ്–പ്രവചനം
(n.) As per the weather *forecast,* it might rain today.
(n.) Astrologer forecast huge success in his career.

Forehead *(n.)* ഫോർഹെഡ്–നെറ്റി
She fell from the stairs and injured her *forehead.*

Foreign *(adj.)* ഫോറിൻ–വിദേശ, വിദേശി
Do you know any *foreign* language?
(n.) Would you like to meet a *foreigner*?

Forest *(n.)* ഫോറസ്റ്റ്–വനം, കാട്
My native place is a village on the edge of the *forest.*

Forever *(adv.)* ഫോറെവർ–എന്നന്നേക്കും, സദാ
I feel like leaving this place *forever.*

Forge *(v.)* ഫോർജ്–കൃത്രിമം കാണിക്കുക, കള്ളയൊപ്പിടുക
He *forged* his father's signature on the report card.

Forget *(v.)* ഫർഗെറ്റ്–മറക്കുക, വിസ്മരിപ്പിക്കുക
I *forgot* your telephone number.

Forgive *(v.)* ഫർഗീവ്–മാപ്പാക്കുക, ക്ഷമിക്കുക
Please *forgive* me for coming late.

Form *(n.&v.)* ഫോം–1. ഫാറം, പത്രം
Please fill up this admission *form.*
2. രൂപം, ആകൃതി
A cloud in the sky had taken the *form* of an elephant.
(v.) 3.സംഘടിപ്പിക്കുക, രൂപം നൽകുക
We have *formed* a literary association.

Formal *(adj.)* ഫോർമൽ–ഔപചാരിക, നിയമാനുസൃത
Some clubs allow entry to their members only in the *formal* dress.

Former *(adj.)* ഫോർമർ–മുമ്പത്തെ, പഴയ, ആദ്യത്തെ
My *former* tenant was a lawyer.

Formula *(n.)* ഫോർമുല–സിദ്ധാന്തം, സൂത്രം, വിധി
Do you know the chemical *formula* of water?

Forsake *(v.)* ഫർസേക്–ത്യജിക്കുക, വിട്ടുകളയുക
I cannot *forsake* my old friends.

Fort *(n.)* ഫോർട്ട്–കോട്ട, കൊത്തളം
On their trip to Rajasthan, students saw many historical *forts.*

Forth *(adv.)* ഫോർത്ത്–മുമ്പോട്ട് വയ്ക്കുക, ഉന്നയിക്കുക
The workers brought *forth* the problems they were facing at work.

Fortnight *(n.)* ഫോർട്ട്നൈറ്റ്–പക്ഷം, രാഴ്ച
The bank manager was on leave for a *fortnight.*

Fortune *(n.)* ഫോർച്യൂൺ–1. ഭാഗ്യം, യോഗം
Do you believe in *fortune*-telling?
2. സമ്പത്ത്, ലാഭം, ധനം
Satpal made a *fortune* in the export trade.

Fortunate *(adj.)* ഫോർച്ചുണേറ്റ് – ഭാഗ്യശാലി
I was *fortunate* enough to pass the pre-medical exam.

Forward ഫോർവേർഡ്–1. മുമ്പോട്ട്, അടുത്ത, നീങ്ങുന്ന
(adv.) Please move *forward.*
(v.) 2. അയക്കുക, മുമ്പോട്ടു വിടുക
Have you *forwarded* my application?

Foul *(adj.)* ഫൗൾ– കെട്ട, ചീഞ്ഞ, ബീഭത്സ
Foul smell emanated from the manhole.

Found *(v.)* ഫൗ് – 1. കെത്തി, കുകിട്ടി (Find-ന്റെ ഭൂതകാലം)
Have you *found* the book you had lost?
2. സ്ഥാപിക്കുക, അടിക്കല്ലിടുക
Who *founded* your school?
(n.) The *foundation* stone of Lok Nayak Setu in Delhi was laid by the then Prime Minister Chandra Shekhar.

Fountain *(n.)* ഫൗൻ–ജലധാര, നീരുറവ
In Delhi, many gardens have musical *fountains.*

Fowl *(n.)* ഫൗൾ–പൂവൻകോഴി, പിടകോഴി
I want to buy some *fowl* for my poultry farm.

Fox *(n.)* ഫോക്സ്–കുറുക്കൻ
Some persons are as cunning as a *fox.*

Fraction *(n.)* ഫ്രാക്ഷൻ–അംശം, ഭാഗം, തു
Rahul's father willed only a *fraction* of his huge property to him.

Fracture ഫ്രാക്ചർ–ഒടിവ്, പൊട്ടൽ
(n.) She had a *fracture* in her leg.
(v.) She fell while running and *fractured* her leg.

Fragile *(adj.)* ഫ്രാജെൽ-ലോലം, പെട്ടെന്ന്, ഉടയുന്ന
These glasses are very *fragile;* handle them with care.

Fragment *(n.)* ഫ്രാഗ്മെന്റ്-തുണ്ട്, ചില്ല്
Be careful while collecting the *fragments* of the broken glass.

Fragrance *(n.)* ഫ്രാഗ്റെൻസ്-സുഗന്ധം
The fragrance of the incense stick filled the whole room.

Frail *(adj.)* ഫ്രെയ്ൽ-ദുർബലം, മെലിഞ്ഞ
Behind the *frail* body of Mahatma Gandhi was a strong-willed man of principles.

Frame ഫ്രെയിം-1. ചട്ടക്കൂട്, കവചം
(n.) I want to buy a nice *frame* for this photograph.
2. മനോദശ, മനോഭാവം
You seem to be in an angry *frame* of mind today.
(v.) I want to *frame* this photograph.

Fraternity *(n.)* ഫ്രറ്റേണിറ്റി-ഒരേ സമൂഹം, സാഹോദര്യം
He is a known person in the architectural *fraternity.*

Fraud *(n.)* ഫ്രാഡ്-വഞ്ചന, കാപട്യം
An enquiry exposed the *fraud* played by the former bankmanager.

Freak ഫ്രീക്-1. ലോലമതി
(n.) She is a real fitness *freak.*
2. പ്രതികരിക്കുക
(v.) The mother *freaked* on seeing her child in dirty clothes.

Free ഫ്രീ-1. സ്വതന്ത്ര ആകുക
(v.) She opened the cage and *freed* the little bird.
(adj.) On what date did India become *free*?
2. ഒഴിവുാവുക, സാവകാശം ഉാവുക
Are you *free* this evening?
3. സൗജന്യം
I got a toothbrush *free* with a jar of face-cream.

Freeze *(v.)* ഫ്രീസ്-ഉറഞ്ഞു കട്ടിയാകുക, മരവിക്കുക, വിറങ്ങലിക്കുക
Dal Lake *freezes* in the winter.

Frequent *(adj.)* ഫ്രീക്വന്റ്-അടിക്കടി, തുടർച്ചയായി
I have made *frequent* trips to Mumbai.

Fresh *(adj.)* ഫ്രെഷ്-1. പുതിയ, പുത്തൻ
Seeing *fresh* flowers in the morning is quite refreshing.
2. ചൊടിയുാവുക, ഉന്മേഷം തോന്നുക
I feel *fresh* after I have a cup of tea.

Fret *(v.)* ഫ്രെറ്റ്-ക്ഷോഭിക്കുക, ചൊടിക്കുക
Why do you *fret* so much about domestic difficulties?

Friend *(n.)* ഫ്രെ-മിത്രം, സുഹൃത്ത്
I have a large circle of *friends.*

Fright *(n.)* ഫ്രൈറ്റ്-പേടി, ഭയം, ആശങ്ക
I had a *fright* when the dog rushed at me.

Fringe *(n.)* ഫ്രിഞ്ച്-അറ്റം
There was a hunting lodge on the *fringe* of the forest.

Frivolous *(adj.)* ഫ്രിവലസ്-നിസ്സാര, വൃഥാവിലുള്ള
Let's not get into a *frivolous* conversation now.

Front ഫ്ര-മുൻ, മുൻവശം
(adj.) Please open the *front* door.
(n.) The *front* of my house faces a park.

Frontier *(n.)* ഫ്രോിയർ-അതിർത്തി, സീമ
Our *frontier* with Pakistan has been fenced in Punjab.

Frost *(n.)* ഫ്രോസ്റ്റ്-നേർത്ത മഞ്ഞ്
The *frost* on the windscreen made it difficult to drive the car.

Froth *(n.)* ഫ്രോത്ത്-നുര, പത
The child licked at the *froth* on the shake.

Frown *(v. & n.)* ഫ്രൗൺ-മുഖം ചുളിക്കുക, ദേഷ്യം കാട്ടുക, കണ്ണുരുട്ടുക
Why are you *frowning* at me?
We could tell by her *frown* that she was angry.

Fruit *(n.)* ഫ്രൂട്ട്-1. പഴം
Which is your favourite *fruit*?
2. ഫലം, പരിണാമം
Good score is the *fruit* of regular study.

Frustrate *(v.)* ഫ്രസ്ട്രേറ്റ്–ഇച്ഛാഭംഗം തോന്നുക
She got *frustrated* when he arrived late.

Fry *(v.)* ഫ്രൈ–പൊരിക്കുക, വറക്കുക
I am *frying* fish.

Fuel *(n.)* ഫ്യൂഅൽ–ഇന്ധനം, ഫ്യൂഅൽ
We use petroleum gas for *fuel*.

Fugitive *(n.)* ഫ്യൂജിറ്റിവ്–പിടികിട്ടാ, ചാടിപ്പോയ
The newspapers published the picture of the *fugitive* prisoner.

Fulfil *(v.)* ഫുൾഫിൽ–പൂർത്തിയാക്കുക, നിറവേറ്റുക
I shall do my best to *fulfil* your expectations.

Full *(adj.)* ഫുൾ–പൂർണ്ണ, നിറഞ്ഞ, മുഴുവൻ, പൂർണ്ണമായി, നേരെ
My room is *full* of books.
Put a *full* stop at the end of each sentence.
The water tank is *full*.
(adv.) Only an honest person can look you *full* in the face.

Fumble *(v.)* ഫമ്പ്ൾ–വിക്കുക, തപ്പിതടയുക
She *fumbled* with the letter to find the name of the sender.

Fume *(v.)* ഫ്യൂം–ദേഷ്യപ്പെടുക
The parents fumed over the poor performance of their child.

Fumes *(n.)* ഫ്യൂംസ്–പുക, ദുർഗന്ധമുള്ള ഗ്യാസ്
The diesel *fumes* made it difficult to breathe.

Fun *(n.)* ഫൺ–തമാശ, രസം
We had a great *fun* at the party.

Function ഫങ്ഷൻ–1. ചടങ്ങ്
(n.) Our school organised a big *function* at the Founder's Day.
2. പ്രവർത്തിക്കുക
(v.) How does this machine *function*?

Fund *(n.)* ഫ് –നിധി, കോശം
We have started a *fund* for the school building.

Fundamental ഫമെന്റൽ–1. മൗലികമായ
(adj.) Right to speech is our *fundamental* right.
2. അടിസ്ഥാന തത്വം
(n.) Understand the *fundamentals* before starting this venture.

Funeral *(n.)* ഫ്യൂണറൽ–ശവദാഹം, സംസ്കരണം
Did you attend the old man's *funeral*?

Funnel *(n.)* ഫണൽ–ചോർപ്പ്, വച്ചൂറ്റി, പുകക്കുഴൽ
Use a *funnel* to fill kerosene in bottle.
We could see the *funnel* of the approaching ship.

Fur *(n.)* ഫർ–രോമക്കുപ്പായം
I bought a *fur* coat during my visit to Kashmir.

Furious *(adj.)* ഫ്യൂറിയസ്–ഉഗ്രകോപം, അമർഷം, ആദ്രം
The manager became *furious* at the blunder of the clerk who sent an important letter at the wrong address.

Furnace *(n.)* ഫർണസ്–ചൂള
During a visit to the steel plant, the students were shown a huge *furnace*.

Furnish *(v.)* ഫർണിഷ്–സമർപ്പിക്കുക, ഉന്നയിക്കുക, അലങ്കരിക്കുക
I would like to *furnish* my flat.

Further *(adj.)* ഫർതർ–1. കൂടുതൽ ദൂരെ
The soldiers were too tired to move *further*.
(adj.) 2. കൂടുതൽ, ഇനിയും, ഇതിലേറെ
I have nothing *further* to say.

Fury *(n.)* ഫ്യൂറി–ഉഗ്രതാണ്ഡവം, പ്രകോപം
Avoid the *fury* of the storm by remaining indoors.

Fuse ഫ്യൂസ്–വിളക്ക്, ഫ്യൂസ്
I want a *fuse* for my electric connection.

Fuss *(n.)* ഫസ്സ്–കോലാഹലം, ബഹളം
Don't make a *fuss* if there is no milk.
Don't be so *fussy* about your clothes.

Futile *(adj.)* ഫ്യൂട്ടൈൽ–വൃഥാ
They made a *futile* attempt to make her join a medical college.

Future ഫ്യൂച്ചർ–ഭാവി, വരുംകാലം
(n.) In *future,* never hesitate to call me when you need help.
If you work hard, your *future* will be bright.
(adj.) What are your *future* plans?

G

Gadget *(n.)* ഗാജിറ്റ്–ചെറിയ ഉപകരണം
He has a good knowledge of the latest *gadgets.*

Gain *(v.)* ഗെയിൻ–1. നേടുക, ആർജ്ജിക്ക
You will *gain* many friends if you have a helpful nature.
(n.) There is no *gain* without pain.
2. ലാഭം, നേട്ടം (ഉാകുക)
Gain and loss are part of any business.

Gait *(n.)* ഗെയ്റ്റ്–നടത്ത
Broken shoe affected her *gait.*

Galaxy *(n.)* ഗാലക്സി–ആകാശഗംഗ
There are numerous stars in the *galaxy.*

Gale *(n.)* ഗെയ്ൽ–കൊടുങ്കാറ്റ്, പിശറ്
Don't go out into the *gale.*

Gallant *(adj.)* ഗാലന്റ്–ധീരൻ, വീരൻ
A *gallant* young man saved the two drowning girls.
(n.) The policeman was rewarded for his *gallantry.*

Gallery *(n.)* ഗാലറി–1. ശില്പശാല
In which *gallery* are you exhibiting your picture?
2. വീഥി, ഗാലറി
The patient's relatives were sitting in the *gallery* in front of the operation theatre.

Gallop *(v.)* ഗാലപ്–1. കുതിച്ചു പായുക
The horses had to *gallop* to keep pace with the motor-car.
(n.) 2. കുളമ്പടി
The *gallop* of Rehman's horse could be heard from a distance.

Gamble ഗാമ്പ്ൾ–1. ചൂത് കളിക്കുക, ചൂതു കളിക്കാരൻ
(n.) David's parents did not know that he had taken to *gambling.*
2. ചൂതാട്ടം
Starting a business is a *gamble.*
(v.) He *gambled* the entire night and lost everything he had.

Game *(n.)* ഗെയിം–1. കളി
What *games* do you play?
2. ഇര
I hear you are big *game* hunter.
3. കളിക്കുള്ള സാധനങ്ങൾ
All kinds of *games* are sold in this shop.

Gang *(n.)* ഗാങ്–സംഘം
The police made intensive efforts to trace the *gang* of car thieves.

Gangway *(n.)* ഗാങ്‌വേ–പാത, ഏണിപ്പടി
I walked down the *gangway* of the theatre to reach my seat in the front row.

Gap *(n.)* ഗാപ്–1. ദ്വാരം, വിടവ്
The thieves made a *gap* in the garden wall to enter the house.
2. ന്യൂനത, പൊരുത്തക്കേട്
The police found many *gaps* in the bank manager's account of the bank robbery.

Garage *(n.)* ഗരാജ്–ഗരാജ്
Our house has a *garage.*

Garbage *(n.)* ഗാർബിജ്–ചപ്പ് ചവറ്
She threw all the useless pieces of furniture in the *garbage.*

Garden *(n.)* ഗാർഡൻ–പൂന്തോട്ടം, ഉദ്യാനം
We have a small *garden* at the back of our house.

Garland ഗാർലൻഡ്–പുഷ്പഹാരം
(n.) We welcomed the chief guest with *garlands.*
(v.) The priest *garlanded* the deity.

Garlic *(n.)* ഗർലിക്–വെളുത്തുള്ളി
Do you use *garlic* in your cooking?

Garment *(n.)* ഗാർമെന്റ്–തുണി, വസ്ത്രം
Some businessmen have made good money in *garment* export.

Garnish *(v.)* ഗാർണിഷ്–അലങ്കരിക്കുക
The cook *garnished* the dish with fresh coriander leaves.

Gas *(n.)* ഗാസ്–വാതകം, പെട്രോൾ
How much does a cylinder of cooking *gas* cost?

Gasp *(v.)* ഗാസ്പ്–1. കിതയ്ക്കുക
Running so fast made Rahul *gasp* for breath.
(n.) 2. ഞെട്ടൽ
Why did you give a *gasp* of surprise when you saw me?

Gate *(n.)* ഗേറ്റ്–വാതിൽ
Our garden wall has an iron *gate.*

Gather *(v.)* ഗാദർ–1. ചേർത്തുവയ്ക്കുക, ഒത്തുചേരുക
Please *gather* you books and put them in young bag.
Many people *gathered* at the meeting.
Really there was a great *gathering.*
2. ശേഖരിക്കുക, തിരഞ്ഞെടുക്കുക
The reporter *gathered* enough information before writing a feature on kidnappings.

Gauge ഗേജ്–അളവ്, അളക്കുക
(n.) If you fix a *gauge* on your cooking gas cylinder you will know the amount of gas inside.
(v.) How do you *gauge* the amount of water in this barrel?

Gay *(adj.)* ഗേ–1. പ്രസന്നമായ, രസകരമായ
Your *gay* laughter cheers me up.
2. തിളക്കമുള്ള, മോടിയായ
Youngsters favour *gay* colours in their clothes.

Gaze *(v.)* ഗേസ്–കണ്ണിമയ്ക്കാതെ നോക്കുക, മിഴി ഉറപ്പിക്കുക, നോട്ടം
I *gazed* at the beautiful painting for a long time.
I stood at the seashore and *gazed* at the sea.
(n.) He fixed his *gaze* at the object moving outside the window.

Gem *(n.)* ജെം–1. രത്നം
Diamond is a precious *gem.*
2. ഉൽകൃഷ്ട വ്യക്തി
She is *gem* of a person.

Gender *(n.)* ജെൻഡർ–ലിംഗം
In the olden times, *gender* was a major cause of bias.

General *(adj.)* ജനറൽ–1. പൊതു, സാർവ്വത്രിക
The *general* elections were marred by many incidents of booth-capturing.
2. സാധാരണ, സാമാന്യ
As a *general* rule, we are at home in the evening.
(n.) 3. സേനാപതി, ജനറൽ
My friend's uncle is a *General* in the army.

Generate *(v.)* ജെനറേറ്റ്–ഉല്പാദിപ്പിക്കുക
News agencies *generate* useful information about the various events.

Generation *(adj.)* ജെനറേഷൻ–തലമുറ
The young *generation* today is more fun-loving than their elders were in their youth.

Generous *(adj.)* ജെനറസ്–ഉദാര, ദാനശീല
May we expect a *generous* donation from you for our charity?
Vagish was always *generous* in sharing his sweets.
(n.) He showed great *generosity.*

Genius *(n.)* ജീനിയസ്–1. ബുദ്ധിശക്തി, പ്രതിഭ
My son has a *genius* for different languages.
2. പ്രതിഭ, ബുദ്ധിശാലി
Kalidas was a *genius,* who wrote "Abhigyan Shakuntalam", one of the greatest plays of the world.

Gentle *(adj.)* ജെന്റിൽ–1. കോമളം, സൗമ്യം
Your manners should always be *gentle.*
2. ഇളം, നേർത്ത
Let us go for a walk and enjoy the *gentle* breeze.

Gentleman *(n.)* ജെന്റിൽമാൻ–മാന്യൻ, കുലീനൻ
A *gentleman* speaks politely and behaves sensibly.

Genuine *(adj.)* ജെന്യുഇൻ–വാസ്തവ, യഥാർത്ഥ
Is your overcoat made of *genuine* fur?

Geography *(n.)* ജിയോഗ്രഫി-ഭൂമിശാസ്ത്രം

Geography was my favourite subject in the school.

Germ *(n.)* ജേം-രോഗാണു, ജീവാണു

Cleanliness is the best protection against *germs.*

Gesture *(n.)* ജെസ്ചർ-ചേഷ്ട, ആംഗ്യം കാട്ടുക

If you want to be a successful public speaker, you must practise effective *gestures.*

Get *(v.)* ഗെറ്റ്-1. നേടുക, ലഭിക്കുക

How many marks did you *get* in Mathematics?

2. സംഭവം നടക്കുക

I hear you *got* married recently.

Getaway *(n.)* ഗെറ്റവേ-വിനോദയാത്ര

Our *getaway* on the weekend was very refreshing.

Get-together *(n.)* ഗെറ്റ്-ടുഗദർ-പാർട്ടി

We had a family *get-together* on the New Year.

Ghost *(n.)* ഗോസ്റ്റ്-ഭൂതം, പ്രേതം

Not all people believe in the existence of *ghosts.*

Gift *(n.)* ഗിഫ്റ്റ്-സമ്മാനം, ഉപഹാരം

Nina received many *gifts* on her birthday.

Gigantic *(adj.)* ജൈജാന്റിക് - അതിവിശാലം, കൂറ്റൻ

While in Mumbai, we went on-board a *gigantic* ship.

Giggle ഗിഗ്ൾ- കുലുങ്ങി ചിരിക്കുക

(v.) The girls *giggled* at his funny outfit.

(n.) The girls were taken by *giggles* at his funny outfit.

Ginger *(n.)* ജിഞ്ചർ-ഇഞ്ചി

I had a cup of *ginger* tea in the morning.

Giraffe *(n.)* ജിറാഫ്-ജിറാഫ്

We saw a tall *giraffe* in the zoo.

Girder *(n.)* ഗിർഡർ-ഉത്തരം, വിട്ടം

Can you count the *girders* of this bridge?

Girl *(n.)* ഗേൾ-പെൺകുട്ടി, ബാലിക

Who is that *girl* in the pink saree?

These *girls* are very talkative.

Gist *(n.)* ഗിസ്റ്റ്-രത്നച്ചുരുക്കം, സാരാംശം

I did not have time to go through the whole book, so I requested him to tell me the *gist* of it.

Give *(v.)* ഗിവ്-നൽകുക, തരിക, എത്തിക്കുക

Please *give* me your pen.

How much milk does this cow *give*?

I have *given up* (stopped) writing.

Glad *(adj.)* ഗ്ലാഡ്-സന്തോഷം, ആഹ്ലാദിക്കുക

Rakhi's parents were *glad* to know about her selection for a good government job.

Glance ഗ്ലാൻസ്-കണ്ണോടിക്കുക, ഒറ്റനോട്ടത്തിൽ

(n.) The doctor could see in a *glance* that the patient was anaemic.

(v.) She has just *glanced* at his letter.

Glare ഗ്ലെയർ-1. തുറിച്ച് നോക്കുക

(v.) Why do you *glare* at me in anger?

(n.) 2. തിളക്കം, കണ്ണഞ്ചുക

We were almost blinded by the *glare* of the car's headlights.

Glass *(n.)* ഗ്ലാസ്-1. കണ്ണാടി, ചില്ല്

Is this bowl made of *glass* or plastic?

2. ഭക്ഷണം, ഗ്ലാസ്

While looking into the *glass,* Sheeba discovered a black spot on her face.

Please give me a *glass* of water.

Glasses *(n.)* ഗ്ലാസസ്-കണ്ണട

I began to wear *glasses* at forty.

Gleam ഗ്ലീം-പ്രഭ, തിളക്കം, തിളങ്ങുക

(n.) A faint *gleam* of sunshine lit up the cloudy afternoon.

(v.) Your necklace *gleams* even in this faint light.

Glee *(n.)* ഗ്ലീ-ഉല്ലാസം, ഹർഷം

Why are you laughing with such *glee*?

Glide *(v.)* ഗ്ലൈഡ്-ഒഴുകുക, വഴുകി പോകുക

The skaters were *gliding* gracefully over the ice.

(adj.) I am a member of the *gliding* club.

Glimmer *(n.)* ഗ്ലിമ്മർ-മങ്ങിയ വെളിച്ചം, അര വെളിച്ചം

In the *glimmer* of the distant candle light, I could not find my shoes.

Glimpse *(n.)* ഗ്ലിംപ്സ്-നോട്ടം, മിന്നൊളി

I caught a *glimpse* of the thief as he ran away.

Glitter ഗ്ലിറ്റർ-തിളക്കം, വെട്ടിത്തിളങ്ങുക

(n.) The *glitter* of the princess's jewellery attracted everybody.

(v.) All that *glitters* in not gold.

Globe *(n.)* ഭൂമണ്ഡലം, ഭൂഗോളം, ഭൂമി

Have you travelled all over the *globe*?

I bought a *globe* to teach my son Geography.

Gloom *(n.)* ഗ്ലൂം-അന്ധകാരം, ഇരുട്ട്, ദുഃഖം, ഉദാസീനത

A lonely man's life is full of *gloom.*

(adj.) Why are you looking so *gloomy*?

Glory *(n.)* ഗ്ലോറി-യശസ്സ്, മഹിമ, പ്രശംസ

Ram's topping the secondary school exam has brought *glory* to his school.

(adj.) Look, what a *glorious* sunset!

Glamour *(n.)* ഗ്ലാമർ-പകിട്ട്, മോഹിപ്പിക്കുന്ന

(n.) She was taken by the *glamour* of the modelling profession.

(adj.) Journalism is a *glamorous* profession and attracts many.

Glossary *(n.)* ഗ്ലോസറി-ശബ്ദാവലി

We must provide a *glossary* of foreign words at the end of this book.

Glove *(n.)* ഗ്ലവ്-കയ്യുറ

Has anybody seen my rubber *glove*?

Glow ഗ്ലോ-ദീപ്തി, തിളക്കം, തിളങ്ങുന്ന, ഉത്സാഹം

(n.) We can see *glow* coming from cinders even after the fire has been extinguished.

(adj.) The photograph of Brindavan Garden was full of *glowing* colours.

(v.) My mother *glowed* with pride when I got the first prize.

Glue *(n.)* ഗ്ലൂ-1. പശ

Do you have some *glue* to seal this envelope?

(v.) 2. ഒട്ടിക്കുക

The carpenter *glued* the two boards together to make a longer shelf.

Glutton *(n.)* ഗ്ലട്ടൻ-വയറൻ, കൊതിയൻ

Don't eat like a *glutton.*

Gnaw *(v.)* നാ-കരളുക, വേദനിപ്പിക്കുക

A rat seems to have *gnawed* a hole in this wooden box.

Go *(v.)* ഗോ-1. പോകുക

When do you *go* to the office?

2. ചെയ്യാനുദ്ദേശിക്കുക

Are you *going* to write him a letter?

3. മുമ്പോട്ട് പോകുക

Go on with your work.

4. അണയുക, അവസാനിപ്പിക്കുക

Have the lights gone *out*?

Goal ഗോൾ-1. ലക്ഷ്യം

(n.) Being a doctor is the ultimate *goal* of my life.

2. ഫുട്ബാൾ, ഹോക്കി ഇവയിലെ ഗോൾ

(n.) We won the match by two *goals.*

Goat *(n.)* ഗോട്ട്-ആട്

Have you ever tasted *goat's* milk?

Gobble *(v.)* ഗോബ്ൾ-വിഴുങ്ങുക

He *gobbled* up the food served to him.

God *(n.)* ഗോഡ്-1. ദൈവം, ഈശ്വരൻ

Trust in *God* and do your duty.

2. ദേവത

Hindus worship many *gods* and *goddess.*

Goggles *(n.)* ഗോഗ്ൾസ്-കൂളിംഗ് ഗ്ലാസ്സ്

I wore *goggles* to protect my eyes from pollution.

Gold *(n.)* ഗോൾഡ്-സ്വർണ്ണം, സമ്പത്ത്

Is your ring made of pure *gold*?

Good *(adj.)* ഗുഡ്-1. നല്ലത്, ഉത്തമം

I and Anil are *good* friends.

2. നല്ല സ്വഭാവമുള്ള

A *good* man is recognised by his behaviour.

3. ഈട് നില്ക്കുന്നത്

Is your car *good* for another two years?

(n.) 4. നന്മ
Always try to do *good* to others.

Goods *(n.)* ഗുഡ്സ്–ചരക്ക്, സാധനം
What *goods* do you transport in your truck?

Goose *(n.)* ഗൂസ്–ഹംസം, വൻവാത്ത്
Do you keep any *goose* in your poultry farm?

Gorge *(v.)* ഗോർജ്–വെട്ടിവിഴുങ്ങുക
The chiid *gorged* himself on the chocolates.

Gorgeous *(adj.)* ഗോർജസ്–ഗംഭീരം, അഴകാർന്നത്, തിളങ്ങുന്നത്
Your saree is indeed *gorgeous.*

Gorilla *(n.)* ഗൊറില–ഗൊറില
Do they have a *gorilla* in the Delhi Zoo?

Gossip *(n. & v.)* ഗോസിപ്–വിടുവാക്ക്, വൃഥാ സല്ലാപം
(n.) Don't waste your time in *gossip.*
(v.) Don't *gossip* about others.

Govern *(v.)* ഗവേൺ–1. ഭരണം നടത്തുക, നിയന്ത്രിക്കുക
Hong Kong is now *governed* by China.
2. നിയന്ത്രിക്കുക
In this delicate matter, I would like to be *governed* by what you say.
(n.) Do you think the *government* would be able to control prices?

Governess *(n.)* ഗവേണസ്–ആയ
She is a governess to our kids.

Gown ഗൗൺ–ഗൗൺ, നെടുങ്കുപ്പായം
What is the price of this *night-gown*?

Grab *(v.)* ഗ്രാബ്–പിടിക്കുക, കവരുക, തട്ടിയെടുക്കുക
Anwar *grabbed* the pickpocket before he could escape.

Grace *(n.)* ഗ്രേസ്–1. കൃപ, ദയ
By the *grace* of God, all the pilgrims were saved when their boat sank in the Ganges.
2. ലാളിത്യം, ചാരുത
There is a *grace* in your gait.
(adj.) It was very *gracious* of the film star to agree to attend the slumdwellers' function.
(v.) Many celebrities *graced* the inauguration of the new departmental store.

Grade *(n.)* ഗ്രേഡ്–1. ശ്രേണി, വർഗ്ഗം, തരം, വകുപ്പ്
How many *grades* of offices do you have in your company?
These are *second-grade* oranges.
(v.) 2. തരംതിരിക്കുക, സ്ഥാനം നൽകുക
The Principal will *grade* the new pupils according to their marks.

Gradual *(adj.)* ഗ്രാജുഅൽ–ക്രമേണ, പടിപടിയായി
The company had a *gradual* and steady progress.

Graduate ഗ്രാജ്എറ്റ്–ബിരുദധാരി
(n.) She is a *graduate* in literature.
(v.) She *graduated* from Princeton College.

Graffiti *(n.)* ഗ്രാഫിറ്റി–പൊതുസ്ഥലത്തെ ചുവരെഴുത്ത്
Graffiti destroys the beauty of monuments.

Grain *(n.)* ഗ്രെയ്ൻ–1. ധാന്യം
Are you a *grain-merchant*?
2. കണിക
There is not a *grain* of truth in your story.

Grammar *(n.)* ഗ്രാമർ–വ്യാകരണം
If you want to master English, you must learn its *grammar* thoroughly.

Grand *(adj.)* ഗ്രാൻഡ്–മഹത്തായ, ബൃഹൽ, ശ്രേഷ്ഠ, വിശിഷ്ട, ശ്രേഷ്ഠ
We visited many *grand* palaces on our trip of Europe.

Grandparent *(n.)* ഗ്രാൻഡ് പേരന്റ് – മുത്തച്ഛൻ, മുത്തശ്ശി, അപ്പൂപ്പൻ, അമ്മൂമ്മ
My *grandparents* live in Rajasthan.

Grant *(n.&v.)* ഗ്രാന്റ്–1. ധനസഹായം
(n.) Does your institution receive a *grant* from the government?
(v.) 2. സമ്മതിക്കുക, അംഗീകരിക്കുക
I *grant* that you may be right, but I am also not wrong.
The employer *granted* the employee's request of drawing some advance against his salary.

Grape *(n.)* ഗ്രേപ്–മുന്തിരിപ്പഴം
Please have some *grapes.*

Grasp അമർത്തിപ്പിടിക്കുക
(v.) Had I not *grasped* the bridge railing, I would have fallen into the river.

2. മനസ്സിലാക്കുക, ഗ്രാഹ്യം
Can you *grasp* what your teacher says?
(n.) The scholar had a good *grasp* on the Vedas.

Grass *(n.)* ഗ്രാസ്-പുല്ല്, തൃണം
Grass grows very rapidly in the rainy season.

Grate *(v.)* ഗ്രേറ്റ്-ഉരയ്ക്കുക, തളിരെ അരിയുക
Mother *grated* the cheese and made balls out of it.

Grateful *(adj.)* ഗ്രേറ്റ്ഫുൾ-നന്ദിയുള്ള, കൃതജ്ഞതയുള്ള
I am *grateful* to you for your help.

Grave *(adj.)* ഗ്രേവ്-1. ഗംഭീര, ഗുരുതര
Why are you looking *grave*?
There was some *grave* news in the letter that mother had written to Ram.
2. പ്രധാന, കടുത്ത
Akbar made a *grave* mistake by not attempting all the questions of his Maths paper.
(n.) 3. കുഴിമാടം, കല്ലറ, ശ്മശാനം
The devotees visited the *grave* of the famous Fakeer.
A *graveyard* near our house has been turned into a park.

Gravel *(n.)* ഗ്രാവ്ൽ-ചല്ലി, ചരൽ
Where can I get some *gravel* for my garden?

Gravy *(n.)* ഗ്രേവി-ചാറ്, കറി
Gravy plays an important role in making a dish delicious.

Graze *(v.)* ഗ്രേസ്-മേയുക, മേയ്ക്കുക, തപ്പുക
The cows were *grazing* in the field.
We might *graze* our arm against the wall if we run too close to it.

Grease ഗ്രീസ്-കൊഴുപ്പ്, ഗ്രീസ്, തൈലം പുരട്ടുക
(v.) It is necessary to *grease* all parts of machine for its smooth functioning.
(n.) Amitabh rubbed some *grease* on his shoes to make the leather softer.

Great *(adj.)* ഗ്രേറ്റ്-1. മഹത്തായ
For inspiration, we should read biographies of *great* men.
2. സുന്ദരമായ
You look *great* in these clothes.
3. വലിയ, വിശാലമായ
Mumbai is the *greatest* city I have ever visited.
4. മികച്ച, ഉറ്റ
Are you and Prakash *great* friends?

Greedy *(adj.)* ഗ്രീഡി-അത്യാഗ്രഹമുള്ള, അതിമോഹ
We all are *greedy* for fortune's favours.
The *greedy* dogs gobbled up their food quickly.
(adv.) Don't swallow your food *greedily*.

Green *(adj.)* ഗ്രീൻ-പച്ച, ഹരിത
The *green* saree in the showcase was very expensive.
2. പച്ചത്തഴപ്പ്, ഹരിതാഭ, മൈതാനം
I like some *green* around my house.

Greet *(v.)* ഗ്രീറ്റ്-1. വന്ദിക്കുക, നമസ്കാരം പറയുക
He *greeted* me very cordially when I called on him.
2. സ്വാഗതം ചെയ്യുക
The principal's speech was *greeted* with a loud applause by the students.

Grey *(adj.)* ഗ്രേ-നരയ്ക്കുക, ചാര നിറമാകുക
Your hair has started turning *grey*.

Grief *(n.)* ഗ്രീഫ്-ദുഃഖം, ശോകം, വ്യഥ
On the death of Anuj's father, his neighbours came to console him in his hour of *grief*.

Grim *(adj.)* ഗ്രിം-1. ഭയാനക, ഭീകര
Why are you looking so *grim*?
2. ദൃഢമായ, ഉറച്ച
If you want to succeed against heavy odds, you must have *grim* determination.

Grin ഗ്രിൻ-ചിരിക്കുക, ചിരി
(n.) He has a happy *grin* on his face.
(v.) She didn't answer me but only *grinned*.

Grind *(v.)* ഗ്രൈൻഡ്-പൊടിക്കുക, അരയ്ക്കുക
The miller *grinds* the corn into flour.
We *grind* a knife to sharpen it.

Grip ഗ്രിപ്-1. പിടി, മനസ്സിൽ തട്ടുന്ന
(n.) The thief could not free himself from the firm *grip* of Ram's hand.
(adj.) The film we saw today had a *gripping* plot.
(v.) 2. മുറുകെ പിടിക്കുക
Grip the bag firmly, lest it should fall.

Groan ഗ്രോൺ-ആർത്തനാദം, ഞരങ്ങൽ
(n.) The sick man's *groans* moved my heart.
(v.) I *groaned* in pain when I fell down the staircase.

Grocer *(n.)* ഗ്രോസർ-പലചരക്കു വ്യാപാരി
Some *grocers* keep their profits to the bare minimum.

Groom *(n.)* ഗ്രൂം-1. വരൻ
You are dressed up like a *groom*.
2. കുതിരക്കാരൻ
Have you engaged a *groom* to look after your horse?
(v.) 3. പഠിപ്പിക്കുക, മെരുക്കുക
It is easy to *groom* an inexperienced worker.

Groove *(n.)* ഗ്രൂവ്-ചാൽ, പാത്തി
The door of my wardrobe slides into a *groove*.

Grope *(v.)* ഗ്രോപ്-തപ്പിതടയുക, തെരയുക
In the darkness, I *groped* around to find a candle.

Gross *(adj.)* ഗ്രോസ്-കടുത്ത, ഭാരിച്ച
The minister's act of giving undue favours was a *gross* misuse of his authority.

Ground *(n.)* ഗ്രൗ-1. നിലം, സ്ഥലം, മൈതാനം
Our school has a large cricket *ground*.
My house stands on a flat *ground*.
2. ആധാരം, അടിസ്ഥാനം, കാരണം
The judge was not convinced by the *grounds* given by the lawyer for his client's bail.
(v.) 3. പൊടിച്ചത് (Grind-ന്റെ ഭൂതകാലം)
She *ground* spices.
(adj.) Fresh *ground* coffee beans smell very pleasant.

Group *(n. & v.)* ഗ്രൂപ്-സംഘം, സമൂഹം, കൂട്ടം ചേരുക, ചേർക്കുക
(n.) A *group* of people was waiting to see the minister.
(v.) The students *grouped* together to move the heavy table.

Grove *(n.)* ഗ്രോവ്-തോപ്പ്, തോട്ടം
Children like to play hide-and-seek in the *grove*.

Grow *(v.)* ഗ്രോ-1. വളരുക, വികസിക്കുക
Your son has *grown* up into a fine young man.
2. വളർത്തുക, വിളയിപ്പിക്കുക
What flowers do you *grow* in your garden?
3. ആയിത്തീരുക
The nights *grow* colder in winter.
(n.) The massive *growth* in Rehman's business has been very surprising.

Growl ഗ്രൗൽ-മുരളുക, അമറുക, മുരൾച്ച
(n.) The *growl* of thunder could be heard at a distance.
(v.) The dog always *growls* at the cat.

Grudge ഗ്രജ്-1. മനസ്സില്ലാ മനസ്സോടെ നൽകുക
(v.) The master *grudged* every rupee that he gave to the lazy servant as wages.
(n.) 2. ദേഷ്യം തോന്നുക, കാലുഷ്യം
I hope you don't hold any *grudge* against me.

Gruff *(adj.)* ഗ്രഫ്-കഠിന, കർക്കശ, പരുഷ
Why has your voice become so *gruff*?

Grumble *(v.)* ഗ്രമ്പ്ൾ-പരാതിപ്പെടുക, മുറുമുറുക്കുക
Some people are always *grumbling*.

Grunt ഗ്ര്-അമറുക, മുരളുക
(v.) Pigs *grunt* as they search for food.
(n.) He only gave a *grunt* of approval when I asked him if he liked my painting.

Guarantee ഗാരന്റി-ഉറപ്പ്, ജാമ്യം നിൽക്കുക
(n.) My car has the *guarantee* for replacement if any fault was found in its functioning.

Guard ഗാർഡ്–1.രക്ഷ, കാവൽ നിൽക്കുക
(v.) You should use sunglasses to *guard* your eyes.
(n.) We put the wire *guard* in front of the fire to keep the children from getting burnt.
2. ഗാർഡ്
As soon as we boarded the train, the *guard* blew his whistle.

Guess ഗസ്–ഊഹിക്കുക, സങ്കല്പിക്കുക
(n.) What is your *guess* about the winner of the India-Pakistan match?
(v.) Can you *guess* how many times I tried to contact you on the phone?

Guest *(n.)* ഗസ്റ്റ്–അതിഥി, വിരുന്നുകാരൻ
We usually have *guests* in winters.

Guide ഗൈഡ്–1. വഴികാട്ടി, ഗൈഡ്, നേതാവ്
(n.) We should engage a *guide* when we go to Ajanta caves.
2. മാർഗ്ഗദർശി ഗ്രന്ഥം, ഗൈഡ്
You should learn from your textbook, not from a *guide*.
(v.) 3. വഴി കാണിക്കുക
Can you *guide* me to the post office?

Guilty *(adj.)* ഗിൽറ്റി–അപരാധി, കുറ്റവാളി
The judge found the accused *guilty* of the crime.
(n.) Your *guilt* is not proved.

Guise *(n.)* ഗൈസ്–വേഷത്തിൽ, ഭാവേന
He was a policeman under the *guise* of a bus passenger.

Gulf *(n.)* ഗൾഫ്–ഉൾക്കടൽ, ഗൾഫ് രാജ്യം
He left India when he got a lucrative job in Persian *Gulf* country.

Gullible *(adj.)* ഗലബ്ൾ–നിഷ്കളങ്ക
Eve was *gullible* enough to believe the words of Satan.

Gulp *(n.)* ഗൾപ്–പെട്ടെന്ന് ഇറക്കുക, മിഴുങ്ങുക
Don't *gulp* down hot tea in a haste.

Gum *(n.)* ഗം–1. പശ
I want to buy a bottle of *gum*.
2. മോണ
Strong teeth require strong *gums*.

Gun *(n. & v.)* ഗൺ–തോക്ക്, വെടിവച്ചിടുക
(n.) Who discovered the *gun-powder*?
The new recruits in the army were taught the use of *guns*.
(v.) The hunter *gunned* down a wolf.

Gurgle *(v.)* ഗർഗ്ൾ–ഗളഗള ശബ്ദമുണ്ടാക്കുക, ഇരമ്പുക
The sea was *gurgling* loudly.

Gust *(n.)* ഗസ്റ്റ്–ശക്തമായ കാറ്റ്
A sudden *gust* of wind blew away my cap.

Gutter *(n.)* ഗട്ടർ–ഓട, ഓവ്
Yesterday's heavy rain caused the *gutters* in our street to overflow.

Gymnasium *(n.)* ജിംനേഷ്യം–വ്യായാമശാല, കളരി
Does your school have a *gymnasium*?
My son is good at *gymnastics*.

Gypsy *(n.)* ജിപ്സി–നാടോടി വർഗ്ഗം
The *gypsy* claimed to foretell the future correctly.

H

Habit *(n.)* ഹാബിറ്റ്–ശീലം, സ്വഭാവം, വഴക്കം
You must leave bad *habits* and cultivate good ones.

Haggard *(adj.)* ഹാഗർഡ്–മെലിഞ്ഞ, കോലം കെട്ട, എല്ലുംതോലുമായ
The *haggard* looking servant was quick in doing tasks efficiently.

Hail *(n.)* ഹെയ്ൽ–1. ആലിപ്പഴം
Last night it rained *hailstones*.
(v.) 2. വിളിക്കുക, സ്വാഗതം ചെയ്യുക
I saw my friend at a distance and *hailed* him.

Hair *(n.)* ഹെയ്ർ–മുടി, കേശം
Some people dye *hair* to hide their premature greying.

Half *(adj.)* ഹാഫ്–പകുതി
The time is *half* past six.

Hall *(adj.)* ഹാൾ–1. വലിയ മുറി, ഹാൾ
The school's annual function was held in a spacious *hall*.
2. സഭാ മന്ദിരം
Did you attend the meeting at the Town *Hall*?

Hallucination *(n.)* ഹാലൂസിനേഷൻ – മതിഭ്രമം
You saw your dead grandfather last night! It must be a *hallucination*.

Halt ഹാൾട്ട്–നിശ്ചലം, തങ്ങൽ, നില്ക്കുക നിർത്തുക
(v.) I did not *halt* till I reached the station.
(n.) A fire accident in our office brought all works to a *halt*.

Hamlet *(n.)* ഹാംലിറ്റ്–ചെറു ഗ്രാമം, ചേരി
My native place is a *hamlet* of a few houses.

Hammer ഹാമർ–ചുറ്റിയൽ, കൊട്ടുവടി (അടിക്കുക)
(n.) Where is you *hammer*?
(v.) Have you *hammered* the nail properly?

Hammock *(n.)* ഹാമക്–ഊഞ്ഞാൽ കിടക്ക
I have fixed a *hammock* in my garden.

Hamper *(v.)* ഹാമ്പർ–1. തടസ്സപ്പെടുത്തുക, വിഘ്നമുാക്കുക
The strikers tried to *hamper* the traffic movement.
2. പെരും കൂട
All the boys had brought *hampers* on the trip.

Hand *(n.)* ഹാൻഡ്–1. കൈ, കരം
Have you hurt your *hand*?
2. സൂചി
The *hands* of my watch are broken.
(v.) 3. നൽകുക, ഏല്പിക്കുക
Please *hand* me over that book.

Handcuffs ഹാൻഡ്കഫ്സ്–വിലങ്ങ്
(n.) The *handcuffs* were dangling from the peg in the police station.
(v.) The police *handcuffed* the thief.

Handicap ഹാൻഡികാപ്–പ്രതിബന്ധം, പ്രതികൂല്യം, അസൗകര്യം
(n.) Not knowing English is a *handicap* on a trip abroad.
(v.) Excess luggage *handicaps* one while travelling.

Handicraft *(n.)* ഹാൻഡിക്രാഫ്റ്റ് – കരകൗശല വിദ്യ, ഹസ്തശില്പം
At the *handicrafts* emporium, one can buy genuine items.

Handkerchief *(n.)* ഹാൻഡ്കെർചീഫ്–തൂവാല, കൈലേസ്
Always carry a *handkerchief* in your pocket.

Handle *(v.)* ഹാൻഡ്ൽ–1. തൊടുക, കൈകാര്യം ചെയ്യുക, നടത്തുക
Can you *handle* this job?
(n.) 2. കൈപ്പിടി
The *handle* of my umbrella is broken.

Hang *(v.)* ഹാങ്–1. തൂങ്ങുക
Hang the picture on the wall.
2. തൂക്കി കൊല്ലുക, വധശിക്ഷ നൽകുക
The murderer was *hanged* to death.

Handsome *(adj.)* ഹാൻഡ്സം–1. സുമുഖൻ
He is a *handsome* young man.
2. വമ്പിച്ച (തുക)
We made a *handsome* profit in our business.

Handy *(adj.)* ഹാൻഡി–ഉപയോഗമുള്ള, സൗകര്യപ്രദമായ
A basket is *handy* when we go for shopping.

Hangar *(n.)* ഹാംഗർ–വിമാനങ്ങൾ നിർത്തുന്ന പുര
The planes were kept in the *hangar*.

Hanger *(n.)* ഹാംഗർ–അലമാരയിൽ ഉടുപ്പ് തൂക്കാനുള്ള ഹാങ്കർ
I *hanged* my shirt in a hanger.

Hanker *(v.)* ഹാങ്കെർ–എന്തിനെയെങ്കിലും അമിതമായി മോഹിക്കുക
He is always *hankering* after money.

Haphazard *(adj.)* ഹാപ്ഹസാർഡ് – സമ്പ്രദായമില്ലാതെ
Your article is written in a *haphazard* way.

Happen *(adj.)* ഹാപ്പൻ–1. സംഭവിക്കുക
Did an accident *happen* here?
2. യദൃശ്ചയാ ഉാകുക
Do you *happen* to know Sudhir?

Happy *(adj.)* ഹാപ്പി–സന്തോഷം, ആനന്ദം, ആഹ്ലാദം
The parents were *happy* to learn about their son's getting a good job.
Many *happy* returns of the day!

Happy-go-lucky *(adj.)* ഹാപ്പി–ഗോ–ലക്കി – ഒന്നും കാര്യമായെടുക്കാത്ത
He is a *happy-go-lucky* person.

Harbour *(n.)* ഹാർബർ-തുറമുഖം
When we went to Mumbai, we saw many ships anchored at the *harbour.*

Hard *(adj.)* ഹാർഡ്-1. കട്ടിയായ, ഉറച്ച
I cannot sleep on a *hard* bed:
2. കഠിനം, വിഷമമേറിയ
Do you find Physics a *hard* subject?
(adv.) If you work *hard,* you can score good marks in the examination.

Hardly *(adv.)* ഹാർഡ്‌ലി-പ്രയാസത്തോടെ
After the night duty, a press worker was so exhausted that he could *hardly* keep his eyes open.

Harass *(v.)* ഹാരസ്-ശല്യപ്പെടുത്തുക
He *harassed* his wife long after their divorce.

Hardship *(n.)* ഹാർഡ്ഷിപ്പ്-ബുദ്ധിമുട്ട്, പ്രയാസം
She has faced a lot of *hardship* in bringing up her children.

Hardware *(n.)* ഹാർഡ്‌വെയർ-കമ്പ്യൂട്ടർ യന്ത്രങ്ങൾ
Buy a new monitor from the computer *hardware* shop.

Hard-working *(adj.)* ഹാർഡ്-വർഥിംഗ്-പ്രയത്നശാലി, അദ്ധ്വാനി
He is one of the most *hard-working* people in his company.

Hare *(n.)* ഹെയർ-മുയൽ
Can you run as fast as a *hare*?

Harm ഹാം-ഹാനി, ദോഷം അല്ലെങ്കിൽ ദ്രോഹം ചെയ്യുക
(n.) The crops suffered great *harm* due to the unseasonal rains.
(v.) The strong should not *harm* the weak.
(adj.) Excessive use of chemicals in agriculture is *harmful.*

Harmony *(n.)* ഹാർമണി-1. സ്വരചേർച്ച
Let us sing in *harmony.*
2. ഒത്തൊരുമ, മൈത്രി
Two neighbouring countries can progress only if they live in *harmony.*

Harness *(v.)* ഹാർണിസ്-1. കുതിരച്ചമയം, കുതിരയെ കെട്ടുക
Harness the horse to the carriage.
(n.) 2. ജോലിക്കിടെ
My friend died in *harness* (on duty).

Harp *(v.)* ഹാർപ്-രാഗാലാപനം, ഒരേ പല്ലവി പാടുക
Why are you *harping* on this topic?

Harsh *(v.)* ഹാർഷ്-കർക്കശം, പരുഷം, നിഷ്ഠൂരം
Do not speak in a *harsh* voice.
(adj.) Do not treat your children *harshly.*

Harvest *(n.)* ഹാർവിസ്റ്റ്-കൊയ്ത്ത്, ഫലം
Farmers are very busy during the time of *harvest* .
(adj.) Have you visited a farm at *harvest* time?

Hassle *(n.)* ഹാസ്ൽ-ബുദ്ധിമുട്ട്
Do you have any *hassle* about coming to my place tomorrow?

Haste *(n.)* ഹേസ്റ്റ്-തിടുക്കം, ധിറുതി
Haste makes waste.
(adj.) I am sorry for my *hasty* decision.

Hat *(n.)* ഹാറ്റ്-തൊപ്പി
You should wear a *hat* when you go out in the sun.

Hatch *(v.)* ഹാച്ച്-1. വിരിയിക്കുക, മുട്ട വിരിയിക്കുക
Don't count the chickens before they are *hatched.*
2. പ്ലാനൊരുക്കുക, പദ്ധതിയിടുക
Rahul's colleagues *hatched* the plan to make an April Fool of him.

Hate *(v.)* ഹേറ്റ്-വെറുക്കുക, നിന്ദിക്കുക
You should not *hate* anyone.
(n.) There should be no feeling of *hatred* in your heart.

Haughty *(adj.)* ഹാട്ടി-ധിക്കാരി
It is useless to argue with him; he is very *haughty.*

Haunt *(v.)* ഹാ് -1. പ്രേതബാധയുള്ള
They entered the bungalow that was believed to be *haunted.*
2. അലട്ടുന്ന, മനസ്സിനെ മഥിക്കുന്ന
What happens to us after death is a question that often *haunts* me.

Have *(v.)* ഹാവ് -1. കൈവശമുാകുക, വയ്ക്കുക
Do you *have* a spare pencil?
2. ഭക്ഷണം/പാനീയം കഴിക്കുക
Will you *have* a cold drink?

(n.) 3. നിർദ്ധനവും ദരിദ്രവും
The nations of the world are divided between the *haves* and the *have-nots.*

Haven *(n.)* ഹേവ്ൻ–1. തുറമുഖം
Despite the storm, our ship safely reached its *haven.*
2. ആശ്രയസ്ഥാനം
My bedroom is my *haven.*

Havoc *(n.)* ഹാവക്–നാശനഷ്ടം, തകർച്ച
The hilly village presented a sad picture of the *havoc* caused by the earthquake.

Hawk *(n.)* ഹാക്ക്–പരുന്ത്
How swiftly can a *hawk* fly?

Hay *(n.)* ഹേ–വയ്ക്കോൽ
Make *hay* while the sun shines.

Haywire *(adj.)* ഹേവഅർ–താറുമാറാകുക
The project started off well, but the problems between the co-workers made the whole thing go *haywire.*

Hazard ഹസാർഡ്–1. അപകടം, അപകടപ്പെടുത്തുക
(n.) The climbers faced many *hazards* on their way to the Everest.
(v.) 2. പന്തയം വയ്ക്കുക, സങ്കല്പിക്കാനാവുക
Can you *hazard* a guess he wants to see you?
(adj.) It was really a *hazardous* journey.

Haze *(n.)* ഹേസ്–1. മങ്ങൽ, മൂടൽ
There was a *haze* over the mountain this morning.
(adj.) Our plane could not take off because of the *hazy* weather.
2. അനിശ്ചിതം, ചിന്താക്കുഴപ്പം
I had *hazy* idea of the weather and surroundings of the hills station before I went there.

Heal *(v.)* ഹീൽ–മുറിവുണങ്ങുക, കരിയുക
Bandage the wound; it will *heal* up quickly.

Head *(n.)* ഹെഡ്–1. തല, ശിരസ്സ്, ബുദ്ധി
My *head* is aching.
2. തലവൻ, അദ്ധ്യക്ഷൻ
Who is the *head* of your company?
3. മുകളറ്റത്ത്, അറ്റത്ത്
When he called on me, I was standing at the *head* of the staircase.
4. തലക്കെട്ട്, ശീർഷകം
What is the *heading* of your article?
(v.) 5. എങ്ങോട്ടെക്കെങ്കിലും തിരിയുക അല്ലെങ്കിൽ നീങ്ങുക
To which direction are you *heading*?

Health *(n.)* ഹെൽത്ത്–ആരോഗ്യം, സ്വാസ്ഥ്യം
Health is wealth.

Heap *(v.&n.)* ഹീപ്–നിറയ്ക്കുക, കുന്നുകൂടുക, കൂന
(v.) Don't *heap* your plate with food.
(n.) Don't jump over that *heap* of stones.

Hear *(v.)* ഹിയർ–1. കേൾക്കുക, ശ്രദ്ധിക്കുക
Can you *hear* me clearly?
2. അറിയുക, കേട്ടല്ലോ
I *hear* you have been promoted.

Hearsay *(n.)* ഹിയർസേ–കേട്ടുകേൾവി
Don't go by *hearsay,* use your own judgement.

Heart *(n.)* ഹാർട്ട്–1. ഹൃദയം
The doctor found nothing wrong with the patient's *heart.*
2. പ്രകൃതി, സ്വഭാവം
You have a warm *heart.*
3. കേന്ദ്രം, മദ്ധ്യഭാഗം
Try to go to the *heart* of the subject.

Hearty *(adj.)* ഹാർട്ടി–മൃഷ്ടാന്നം, വയറ് നിറയെ
We had a *hearty* meal before we set out.

Hearth *(n.)* ഹാർത്ത്–അടുപ്പ്, നെരിപ്പോട്
We sat near the *hearth.*

Heat *(n.)* ഹീറ്റ്–1. ചൂട്, താപം
The *heat* of the burning fire made me sweat.
2. ചൂടാകുക, ആവേശം കൊള്ളുക
Do not speak with such *heat.*

Heave *(v.)* ഹീവ്–1. എടുത്തു പൊക്കുക, ചുമക്കുക
I pitied the labourer when I saw him *heave* a very heavy load on his head.
2. നിറയ്ക്കുക
The parents *heaved* a sigh of relief when their abducted son returned home.

Heaven *(n.)* ഹെവൻ–സ്വർഗ്ഗം, ആകാശം, പരലോകം
God is in the *heaven.*
(adj.) What a *heavenly* sight!

Heavy *(adj.)* ഹെവി–1. ഭാരിച്ച, തൂക്കമുള്ള
Can you lift a *heavy* load?
2. കനത്ത,
We had *heavy* rains last night.
3. വിഷമമുള്ള
I bade him good-bye with a *heavy* heart.

Hedge *(n.)* ഹെജ്–വേലി, ചുറ്റുമതിൽ
You should have a *hedge* around your garden.

Heed ഹീഡ്–1. ഉപദേശം കേൾക്കുക
(v.) They *heeded* the advice of the teacher to recheck the answers before submitting the final sheet.
2. പറഞ്ഞത് കേൾക്കാതിരിക്കുക
(n.) He did not pay any *heed* to his mother's advice to return home early.

Heel *(n.)* ഹീൽ–മടമ്പ്
I do not like shoes with high *heels*.

Hefty *(adj.)* ഹെഫ്ടി–ഭാരിച്ച, വൻ
We spent a *hefty* amount to buy the new car.

Height *(n.)* ഹൈറ്റ്–ഉയരം, പൊക്കം
What is your *height*?

Heir *(n.)* എയ്ർ–അനന്തരാവകാശി
Rahul was the only *heir* to his father's property.

Hell *(n.)* ഹെൽ–നരകം
Do you believe in the existence of heaven and *hell*?

Helm *(n.)* ഹെൽമ്–1. ചുക്കാൻ
How can you guide a boat without a *helm*?
2. നിയന്ത്രണം, തലപ്പത്ത്
Who is at the *helm* of affairs in your firm?

Helmet *(n.)* ഹെൽമെറ്റ്–ശിരോകവചം, ഹെൽമറ്റ്
Don't fail to wear a *helmet* when you ride a scooter.

Help ഹെൽപ്–1. സഹായം ചെയ്യുക
(n.) I got much *help* from my friend.
2. ര ാ മ തും വിളമ്പുക
Would you like a second *helping*?
3. ഒഴിവാക്കുക, അടക്കാൻ കഴിയാതിരിക്കുക
I could not help laughing at the funny joke.

Hen *(n.)* ഹെൻ–പിടക്കോഴി
How many *hens* do you have on your poultry farm?

Hence *(adv.)* ഹെൻസ്–1. അതിനാൽ
I am late, *hence* I must rush.
2. ഇപ്പോൾ മുതൽ
A week *hence* I shall be in Shimla.

Herald *(n.)* ഹെറാൾഡ്–1. അഗ്രദൂതൻ
The death of the king was announced by the *herald.*
(v.) 2. പ്രഖ്യാപിക്കുക
The leader's call to the people *heralded* a new movement against corruption.

Herb *(n.)* ഹെർബ്–പച്ചമരുന്ന്, മൂലിക
I was reading a book on medicinal *herbs.*

Herd *(v.)* ഹെർഡ്–1. മൃഗങ്ങളെ തൊഴുത്തിൽ കെട്ടുക
In the evening, cows were *herded* in the yard.
(n.) 2. പറ്റം, കൂട്ടം
We saw a *herd* of cows grazing in the meadow.

Here *(adv.)* ഹിയർ–ഇവിടെ
Come *here.*

Hereditary *(adj.)* ഹെറിഡിറ്ററി–പരമ്പരാഗതം
Baldness is a *hereditary* disease in their family.

Heritage *(n.)* ഹെറിറ്റിജ്–പൈതൃകം
The national flag and the emblem are the *heritage* of our country.

Hermit *(n.)* ഹെർമിറ്റ്–ഏകാകി, താപസൻ
While passing through the forest, we came across a *hermit.*

Hero *(n.)* ഹീറോ–1. വീരൻ, നായകൻ, ധീരമായ
Rama is the *hero* of the epic *Ramayana.*
(adj.) We should take inspiration from the *heroic* deeds of our freedom fighters.

Hesitate *(v.)* ഹെസിറ്റേറ്റ്–മടിക്കുക, അറച്ച് നില്ക്കുക
Once you take a decision, do not *hesitate* to act upon it.

Heyday *(n.)* ഹേഡേ–സമൃദ്ധികാലം

He had a number of friends in his *heydays.*

Hibernate *(v.)* ഹൈബർണേറ്റ് – ശീതകാലത്ത് നിദ്രകൊള്ളുക

The polar bear *hibernates* in the winters.

Hiccup *(n.)* ഹിക്കപ്പ്–ഇക്കിൾ വരിക

She started having *hiccups* on eating the spicy food.

2. പ്രതിബന്ധം

After the initial *hiccup,* the work proceeded well.

Hide *(v.)* ഹൈഡ്–1. ഒളിക്കുക, ഒളിപ്പിക്കുക

Where have you *hidden* my pen?

(n.) 2. തുകൽ, തൊലി

The shoes made of a superior *hide* last longer.

Hierarchy *(n.)* ഹയറാർക്കി–സിദ്ധശ്രേണി

We have a definite *hierarchy* in our department.

High *(adj.)* ഹൈ–1. ഉയർന്ന, ഉയരമുള്ള

How *high* is the building in which you live?

2. ഉന്നത, പ്രധാന

I have friends in *high* places.

3. പ്രബലമായ, അളവറ്റ

I have nothing but *high* praise for you.

4. ശക്തമായ, ആഞ്ഞുവീശുന്ന

A *high* wind has been blowing since morning.

Highlight ഹൈലൈറ്റ്–1. ഏതിലേക്കെങ്കിലും ശ്രദ്ധ ക്ഷണിക്കുക

(v.) The teacher *highlighted* the need to study well to get good marks in the exams.

2. പ്രധാന ദൃശ്യങ്ങൾ

I watched the *highlights* of the World Cup Finals on TV last night.

Highness *(n.)* ഹൈനസ്–തിരുമനസ്സ്, രാജകീയ പദവി

The minister said, "Welcome to the court, your *Highness!*"

Highway *(n.)* ഹൈവേ–പൊതുനിരത്ത്, ഹൈവേ

Drive carefully on the *highway.*

Hijack *(v.)* ഹൈജാക്ക്–വിമാനം റാഞ്ചുക

The terrorists *hijacked* the plane going to Afghanistan.

Hike *(n. & v.)* ഹൈക്–1. നടത്ത

I like to go on *hikes* in the countyside.

2. വർദ്ധിപ്പിക്കുക

The shopkeepers have *hiked* the prices of everything.

Hilarious *(adj.)* ഹിലേറിയസ്–രസകരമായ, പൊട്ടിച്ചിരിപ്പിക്കുന്ന

That was a *hilarious* joke.

Hill *(n.)* ഹിൽ–കുന്ന്, മല

Lakhs of people visit the shrine of Vaishno Devi in the *hills* every year.

Hind *(adj.)* ഹൈൻഡ്–പിൻഭാഗത്തെ

My hourse fell and injured one of its *hind* legs.

Hinder *(v.)* ഹിൻഡർ–തടയുക, തടസ്സം

The strikers *hindered* the movement of the office-goers by putting roadblocks.

(n.) Don't be a *hindrance* in my work.

Hinge *(n.)* ഹിഞ്ച്–വിജാവരി, കുറ്റി

Oil the *hinges* of the door.

Hint *(n. & v.)* ഹിന്റ്–സൂചന

(n.) The manager gave me a *hint* regarding my increment.

(v.) I *hinted* that I would attend the meeting.

Hip *(n.)* ഹിപ്–നടുവ്, നിതംബം

I fell down and hurt my *hip.*

Hire *(n.&v.)* ഹയർ–വാടക, വാടകയ്ക്കെടുക്കുക

(n.) Let us take taxi on *hire.*

(v.) I *hired* a mechanic to repair my car.

Hiss *(v. & n.)* ഹിസ്–1. ചീറ്റുക, ശീൽക്കാരം

(v.) I became alert when a snake *hissed.*

2. 'സ്' എന്ന് ശബ്ദമുാക്കുക

(n.) The tyre of my cycle gave a *hiss,* so I knew it was punctured.

History *(n.)* ഹിസ്റ്ററി–ചരിത്രം, ഇതിഹാസം

History is an interesting subject.

(adj.) I like to read *historical* novels.

Hit *(v. & n.)* ഹിറ്റ്–1. പ്രഹരം നൽകുക, ഇടിക്കുക
I *hit* the ball straight into the net.
2. ശരിയായ അനുമാനത്തിലെത്തുക, മനസ്സിലാക്കുക
Have you *hit* upon any solution to the Maths problem?
(n.) The boxer's powerful *hit* broke his opponent's jaw.

Hitch *(n.)* ഹിച്–നിസ്സാര തടസ്സം, പ്രശ്നം
I am facing a technical *hitch* while working on my computer.

Hitherto *(adv.)* ഹിദർടു–ഇതേവരെ
Hitherto I thought he was a fool, but now I think he is a rogue.

Hive *(n.)* ഹൈവ്–തേനീച്ച കൂട്
Take care, there is a *hive* on a tree in our garden.

Hoard *(n. & v.)* ഹോർഡ്–ചേർത്തു വയ്ക്കുക, പൂഴ്ത്തിവയ്ക്കുക
(n.) A beehive is a *hoard* of honey.
Hoarders of essential commodities should be punished.
(v.) The miser *hoards* a lot of money.

Hoarding *(n.)* ഹോർഡിംഗ്–നിരത്തുകളിലും മറ്റും വയ്ക്കുന്ന വലിപ്പമേറിയ പരസ്യ ബോർഡുകൾ
I saw a huge *hoarding* on the roadside.

Hoarse *(adj.)* ഹോർസ്–ഒച്ച അടപ്പ്, കർക്കശ. പരുഷ
My voice became *hoarse* due to cold.

Hobby *(n.)* ഹോബി–കമ്പം, അഭിരുചി, ഹോബി
Coin collection is my favourite *hobby*.

Hockey *(n.)* ഹോക്കി–ഹോക്കി
Do you play *hockey* or cricket?

Hoist *(v.)* ഹോയിസ്റ്റ്–പതാക ഉയർത്തുക, പറത്തുക, ഉയർത്തുക
The Prime Minister *hoists* the National Flag at Red Fort on every Independence Day.
My mother *hoisted* the baby upon her shoulder to show it a dancing monkey.

Hold *(v.)* ഹോൾഡ്–1. പിടി, പിടിക്കുക
Hold my *hand*.
2. കൊള്ളുക, സ്ഥാനം പിടിക്ക
How much milk does this bottle *hold*?
3. അർഹത നേടുക, കരസ്ഥമാക്കുക
Does he *hold* a Ph.D?
4. മനസ്സിലാക്കുക
I *hold* that honest men should contest the election.
5. സംഘടിപ്പിക്കുക, നടത്തുക
When are you going to *hold* the club meeting?
6. നിയന്ത്രിക്കുക
Hold your breath and jump into the water.
7. അധികാരം നിലനിർത്തുക, നിയന്ത്രണത്തിലാക്കുക
The army was ordered to *hold* the fort against any attack.

Hole *(n.)* ഹോൾ–ദ്വാരം, തുള
The burglars entered the house by making a *hole* in the rear wall.

Holiday *(n.)* ഹോളിഡേ–ഒഴിവ് ദിവസം, അവധി
Where are you going to spend your *holidays*?

Hollow *(adj.)* ഹോളോ–പൊള്ളയായ, മുഴങ്ങുന്ന
Unlike a cricket ball, a football is *hollow*.
Some pillars, when tapped, make a *hollow* sound.

Holy *(adj.)* ഹോളി–പാവനമായ, പവിത്രമായ
I took my grandmother on a pilgrimage to *holy* places.

Homage *(n.)* ഹോമേജ്–ശ്രദ്ധാഞ്ജലി
The ministers gathered to pay *homage* to the dead Prime Minister.

Home *(n.)* ഹോം–1. വീട്, പാർപ്പിടം, കുടുംബം
Home is the best place to rest after a hard day's work.
2. ആശ്രമം. കേന്ദ്രം
Have you seen the freedom fighters' *home* in Delhi?
(adj.) One who has no home is *homeless*.

Homesick *(adj.)* ഹോംസിക്–ഗൃഹവിരഹവേദന
I always feel *homesick* whenever I go back to the hostel.

Honest *(adj.)* ഓണസ്റ്റ്–സത്യസന്ധൻ, നിഷ്കപടൻ
Our servant is very *honest*.
What is your *honest* opinion on the corruption in our society?
(n.) *Honesty* is the best policy.

Honey *(n.)* ഹണി–തേൻ

Please give me a jar of *honey*.

Honk *(v.)* ഹോങ്ക്–കാറിന്റെ ഹോണടിക്കുക

The car *honked* loudly.

Honorary *(adj.)* ഓണററി–പ്രതിഫലം പറ്റാത്ത

He is the *honorary* president of this organisation.

Honour *(n. & v.)* ഓണർ–1. ബഹുമതി, യശസ്സ്

It was a great *honour* for a boy from the far-off hills to be rewarded for his bravery in Delhi.

Will you give me your word of *honour*?

2. ഉപാധി

My friend's name has figured in this year's Republic Day *Honours* List.

(v.) Honour your word.

Hood *(n.)* ഹുഡ്–1. തൊപ്പി, ശിരോവസ്ത്രം

I want to buy a raincoat with a *hood*.

2. ടോപ്, മൂടി

These days you hardly see a car with a folding *hood*.

Hoof *(n.)* ഹൂഫ്–കുളമ്പ്

As the horseman approached, I could hear its *hoof-beats*.

Hook *(n. & v.)* ഹുക്–കൊളുത്ത്, കുറ്റി, കൊളുത്തിടുക

(v.) The fisherman sat all day on the river bank but *hooked* only three fish.

(n.) Have you fixed a *hook* in the bathroom for hanging a towel?

Hooligan *(n.)* ഹൂളിഗൻ–പോക്കിരി

The boys were behaving like *hooligans* on the Holi festival.

Hoop *(n.)* ഹൂപ്–ലോഹം, പ്ലാസ്റ്റിക് കൊുള്ള പീപ്പിച്ചുറ്റ്, വളയം

Hang the towel in the metal *hoop*.

Hop *(n.&v.)* ഹോപ്–1. ചാടുക, കുതിക്കുക

(n.) The child was curiously watching the sparrows *hopping* from one branch to the other.

(v.) We flew from London to U.S.A. in one *hop*.

Hope *(v.&n.)* ഹോപ്–1. പ്രത്യാശ, ആശിക്കുക

(v.) Hope for the best and be prepared for the worst.

2. പ്രതീക്ഷ പുലർത്തുക, വിശ്വസിക്കുക

I *hope* you will be able to come to my home this evening.

(n.) Hope never dies in human heart.

(adj.) Your handwriting is *hopeless*.

Horde *(n.)* ഹോർഡ്–കൂട്ടം, സംഘം

A *horde* of people arrived at the election booth.

Horizon *(n.)* ഹറൈസൺ–ചക്രവാളം, ദിങ്മണ്ഡലം, കുത്തനെയുള്ള

As we sat on the seashore, we saw a ship on the *horizon*.

(adj.) Draw a *horizontal* (as against vertical) line.

Horn *(n.)* ഹോൺ–1. ഹോൺ

Don't blow your *horn* unnecessarily when you drive.

2. കൊമ്പ്

The farmer painted his bullock's *horns*.

Horoscope *(n.)* ഹൊറാസ്കോപ്–ജാതകം

Their marriage was cancelled as the *horoscopes* did not match.

Horrid *(n.)* ഹോറിഡ്–ഭയങ്കരം, മോശമായി

If you behave in such a *horrid* manner, no one will befriend you.

Horror *(n.)* ഹൊറാർ–ഞടുക്കം, വിഹ്വലത, ബീഭത്സം

I stared in *horror* as the two cars collided.

(adj.) I could not bear to look at the *horrible* accident sight.

Horse *(n.)* ഹാർസ്–കുതിര

Do you know *horse-riding*?

Hose *(n.)* ഹോസ്–കുഴൽ, പൈപ്പ്

I require a long *hose* to water my garden.

Hospital *(n.)* ഹോസ്പിറ്റൽ–ആശുപത്രി

We took the injured man to the *hospital*.

Hospitable *(adj.)* ഹോസ്പിറ്റബ്ൾ – ആതിഥ്യ മര്യാദയുള്ള

She is a *hospitable* lady and treats all her guests very well.

Host *(n.)* ഹോസ്റ്റ്–1. ആതിഥേയ

Our *host* at yesterday's party was very hospitable.

2. കൂട്ടം, പറ്റം
A *host* of fan had besieged the film star.

Hostel *(n.)* ഹോസ്റ്റൽ-പാർപ്പിട മന്ദിരം, സത്രം
My son lives in the college *hostel*.

Hostile *(adj.)* ഹോസ്റ്റൈൽ-വിരോധമുള്ള, പ്രതികൂല
Why are you so *hostile* towards him?

Hot *(adj.)* ഹോട്ട്-1. ചൂട്, ഉഷ്ണം
Give me a *hot* cup of tea.
It is a *hot* day today.
2. എരിവുള്ള, വീര്യമുള്ള
I do not like to eat *hot* things like pepper.

Hotel *(n.)* ഹോട്ടൽ-ഹോട്ടൽ
At which *hotel* do you stay when you visit Mumbai?

Hound *(n.)* ഹൗ് -വേട്ടനായ
Is your dog a *hound*?

Hour *(n.)* ഔർ-മണിക്കൂർ
I shall be back in a couple of *hours*.

House *(n.)* ഹൗസ്-1. വീട്, പാർപ്പിടം
Won't you come to my *house*?
2. സഭ
Our Parliament has two *houses*.
3. സാധനം സൂക്ഷിക്കാനുള്ള സ്ഥലം
Put these bags of grain in your *storehouse*.

Hovel *(n.)* ഹവൽ-കുടിൽ, ചെറ്റപ്പുര
I was shocked to see the stinking *hovel* in which the poor man lived.

Hover *(v.)* ഹവർ-1. വട്ടമിട്ട് പറക്കുക
Excited children looked up as the helicopter *hovered* over our house.
2. പിന്നാലെ കൂടുക
My children *hovered* around me in the expectation that I would tell them a story.

How *(adj.)* ഹൗ-എങ്ങനെ, ഏത് രീതിയിൽ, എന്തുകൊ്
How did you break this dish?
How is your father today?

Howl ഹൗൾ-ഓരിയിടുക, നിലവിളിക്കുക
(v.) The wind *howled,* so I could not hear the knock at the door.
(n.) At night, we heard the *howl* of the jackal.

Hub *(n.)* ഹബ്-1. ചക്രങ്ങൾക്കും കാറിനുമിടയ്ക്കുള്ള ഭാഗം
I have bought decorative *hub-cups* for my car.
2. കേന്ദ്രം
Mumbai is the *hub* of film industry.

Hubbub *(n.)* ഹബബ്-കോലാഹലം
There was a real *hubbub* in the Parliament.

Hue *(n.)* ഹ്യൂ-ഏതെങ്കിലും നിറത്തിന്റെ പ്രത്യേക ഛവി
The sky was painted with bright *hues.*

Hug ഹഗ്-ആലിംഗനം ചെയ്യുക
(n.) The mother gave the child a loving *hug*.
(v.) My grandmother *hugged* me fondly when I called on her.

Huge *(adj.)* ഹ്യൂജ്-വലിയ കൂറ്റൻ
Have you ever seen such a *huge* cake?

Hullabaloo *(n.)* ഹുലാബലൂ-കൂട്ടബഹളം
The teacher shouted to calm the *hullabaloo* in the classroom.

Hum *(v.)* ഹം-1. മൂളിപ്പാട്ട് പാടുക
I *hummed* a tune while taking a bath.
2. മുരൾച്ച
The *hum* of the bees indicated the presence of a hive up in the tree.

Human *(adj.)* ഹ്യൂമൻ-മാനവ, മനുഷ്യൻ, മനുഷ്യത്വം
We are all *human* beings.
Don't behave in such an *inhuman* manner.

Humble *(adj.)* ഹമ്പ്ൾ-1. എളിയ, സാധാരണ
K.R. Narayanan rose from the *humble* beginnings to become the President of India.
2. വിനീതമായി
Rakhi is very *humble,* in spite of being rich.

Humility *(n.)* ഹ്യുമിലിറ്റി-വിനയം
You greatness lies in your *humility*.

Humour *(n.)* ഹ്യുമർ-1. നർമ്മരസം, വിനോദം
You have a good sense of *humour*.
2. മനോനില, ചീത്ത പ്രകൃതി
Why are you in such a bad *humour*?
Ramesh was in good *humour* because he had won a lottery prize.

Hump *(n.)* ഹമ്പ്–മുഴ, കൂന്
The child asked, "How did the camel get that *hump*?"

Hunger ഹങ്കർ–1. ആർത്തി, വിശപ്പ്
(n.) *Hunger* for food can easily be satisfied but not *hunger* for wealth.
(adj.) Are you *hungry* now?
(v.) 2. കൊതിക്കുക
Why do you *hunger* so much for fame?

Hunt *(v.)* ഹ് –1. വേട്ടയാടുക
How many tigers have you *hunted*?
2. തിരയുക, തിരച്ചിൽ
I *hunted* everywhere but could not find my book.
(n.) Everyone joined in the *hunt* for the lost bag.

Hurdle *(n.)* ഹർഡ്ൽ–പ്രതിബന്ധം, വിലങ്ങുതടി
These are just temporary *hurdles*.

Hurl *(v.)* ഹേൾ–എറിയുക, എറിഞ്ഞു വീഴ്ത്തുക, കൊള്ളിക്കുക
Don't *hurl* your books around carelessly.
Don't *hurl* baseless charges at me.

Hurricane *(n.)* ഹരികേൻ–കൊടുങ്കാറ്റ്
The *hurricane* broke many trees in the village.

Hurry ഹറി–വേഗം, തിടുക്കം, ദ്രുതപ്പെടുത്തുക
(n.) You are always in a *hurry*.
(v.) As it was about to rain, the office-goers *hurried* to their homes.

Hurt *(v.)* ഹർട്ട്–1. മുറിവ്, നഷ്ടം (വരുത്തുക)
Ram was mildly *hurt* in the bus accident.
2. ദുഃഖിപ്പിക്കുക, വേദനിപ്പിക്കുക
I felt *hurt* at his unkind remarks.
Please try not to *hurt* anybody.

Husband *(n.)* ഹസ്ബൻഡ്–ഭർത്താവ്, പതി
Now, *husbands* mostly don't feel shy in doing household chores with their wives.

Husk *(n.)* ഹസ്ക്–ഉമി
The grandmother separated *husk* from the rice grains.

Hustle *(v.)* ഹസ്ൽ–ഉന്തുക, പരസ്പരം കൂട്ടിമുട്ടുക
People were *hustling* each other at the railway platform.

Hut *(n.)* ഹട്ട്–കുടിൽ, ചെറ്റപ്പുര
Our servant lives in a *hut* near our house.

Hygiene *(n.)* ഹൈജീൻ–ശുചിത്വം, വൃത്തി
She is very concerned about her personal *hygiene*.

Hymn *(n.)* ഹിം–ഭജന, സ്തോത്രം
Can you recite Sanskrit *hymns* correctly?

Hype ഹൈപ്–പൊക്കികാട്ടുക, അമിത വർണ്ണന
(v.) The media *hyped* the movie greatly.
(n.) Despite the media *hype*, the movie was a big flop.

Hypnotise *(v.)* ഹിപ്നടൈസ്–മോഹനിദ്ര
The magician *hypnotised* the small girl.

Hypocrisy *(n.)* ഹിപോക്രസി–കപടനാട്യം, കൗടില്യം
The politicians emphasise on using Indian goods, while they themselves travel in foreign cars. This is the height of *hypocrisy*!

Hysterical *(adj.)* ഹിസ്റ്റീരികൽ–ഉന്മാദാവസ്ഥ, അപസ്മാരം ബാധിച്ച
She was *hysterical* to know that her long lost son was found.

I

I *(pron.)* ഐ–ഞാൻ
I want to go home.

Ice *(n.)* ഐസ്–മഞ്ഞ്, ഐസ്
Please get me some *ice* from the fridge.

Icon *(n.)* ഐകോൺ – 1. കമ്പ്യൂട്ടർ, സ്ക്രീനിൽ പ്രോഗ്രാമിന്റെ സൂക്ഷ്മചിത്രം
Suddenly the *icons* vanished from my computer.

2. പ്രതീകം
She is the style *icon* of the college.

Idea *(n.)* ഐഡിയാ–ആശയം, ധാരണ, മനോഗതം
What a good *idea*!
How do you like the *idea* of going on a trip to Agra this Sunday?

Ideal *(adj.)* ഐഡിയൽ–ആദർശം, ആദർശ യോഗ്യം
Sohna is an *ideal* place for a picnic.

Identical *(adj.)* ഐഡെന്റികൽ – ഐകരൂപ്യമുള്ള, ഒരേ പോലത്തെ
This problem is *identical* to the one we faced last year.

Identification *(n.)* ഐഡന്റിഫിക്കേഷൻ – തിരിച്ചറിയുക
The bodies of the dead were beyond *identification.*

Identity *(n.)* ഐഡെന്റിറ്റി–വ്യക്തിത്വം, ഏതെങ്കിലും സാധനം അല്ലെങ്കിൽ വ്യക്തിയെ തിരിച്ചറിയുക
This place has lost its artistic *identity.*

Ideology *(n.)* ഐഡിയോളജി–സിദ്ധാന്തം, വിചാരധാര
Hinduism proclaims many *ideologies;* it depends on the followers which one to choose.

Idiom *(n.)* ഇഡിയം–ഭാവാർത്ഥ വാക്യം, വാക്യഭേദം
Can you tell me the meaning of the *idiom* 'apple of the eye'?

Idiot *(n.)* ഇഡിയറ്റ്–മൂഡൻ, വിഡ്ഢി
Don't behave like an *idiot.*

Idle *(adj.)* ഐഡിൽ–അലസ, വ്യർത്ഥ, അലസത
An *idle* minds is devil's workshop.
Why do you waste you time in *idleness*?

Idol *(n.)* ഐഡൽ–വിഗ്രഹം, ബിംബം
Who made the *idol* in this temple?

If *(conj.)* ഇഫ്–1. എങ്കിൽ, എന്നുവരികിൽ
If you ask him politely, he will tell you the truth.
2. ചെയ്തപക്ഷം
Can you tell me the details, *if* you are taking a leave tomorrow?

Ignite *(v.)* ഇഗ്നൈറ്റ്–തീ പിടിക്കുക, കത്തിപ്പിടിക്കുക
Strike a match and *ignite* the fire.
A little spark can *ignite* a stack of dry hay and cause a serious fire.

Ignore *(v.)* ഇഗ്നോർ–അവഗണിക്കുക, നിന്ദിക്കുക
You should not *ignore* your parents.
Why do you *ignore* the poor?
Never *ignore* the signals while driving.

Ignorant *(adj.)* ഇഗ്നറന്റ്–അജ്ഞാനി, അറിവില്ലാത്ത
How can I employ such an *ignorant* person?

Ill *(adj.)* ഇൽ–രോഗം, അസുഖം
She was seriously *ill* last week.

Ill-feelling *(n.)* ഇൽ–ഫീലിംഗ്–നിന്ദാഭാവം
I do hope you have no *ill-feeling* for me.

Ill-treat *(v.)* ഇൽ–ട്രീറ്റ്– മോശമായി പെരുമാറുക
If you *ill-treat* your servant, he will leave you soon.

Illegal *(adj.)* ഇലീഗൽ–നിയമവിരുദ്ധം, അനധികൃതം
It is *illegal* to possess a revolver without a licence.
You will have to face the consequences of your *illegal* actions.

Illegible *(adj.)* ഇലെജബ്ൾ–തെളിയാത്ത, വായിക്കാൻ പ്രയാസമുള്ള
The print on the old newspaper was quite *illegible.*

Illiterate *(adj.)* ഇലിടറേറ്റ് -നിരക്ഷര, നിരക്ഷരത
(adj.) Special classes are held in the nearby school for adult *illiterates.*
(n.) Illiteracy is a major cause of backwardness in the villages.

Illogical *(adj.)* ഇലോജിക്കൽ – യുക്തിരഹിത
Visiting Ladakh in the winters appeared an *illogical* idea to me.

Illuminate *(v.)* ഇലൂമിനേറ്റ്-പ്രകാശം പരത്തുക, പ്രദീപ്തമാക്കുക, മനസ്സിലാക്കുക
The main bazaars and streets are *illuminated* on Diwali.
(n.) Let us go to see the *illuminations* at the Rashtrapati Bhawan.

Illusion *(n.)* ഇല്യൂഷൻ–ഭ്രമം, വഞ്ചന
This line looks longer than the other, but it is an optical *illusion.*
Don't be under the *illusion* that I have not seen through your trick.

Illustrate *(v. & adj.)* ഇലസ്ട്രേറ്റ് – ചിത്രസഹിതം, വ്യക്തമാക്കുക
Books for children should be *illustrated* extensively.

(*adj.*) I want to buy an *illustrated* storybook for my child.

Image (*n.*) ഇമേജ്–1. ചിത്രം, ബിംബം

Have you seen the huge *image* of Kubera at the Reserve Bank entrance?

2. പ്രതിഛായ

One can see one's *image* in the clear water of a lake.

3. പ്രതിരൂപം

You are the very *image* of your father.

4. ധാരണ, ഭാവന

When we go abroad, we should always try to project a good *image* of India.

Imagine (*v.*) ഇമേജിൻ–സങ്കല്പിക്കുക, മനസ്സിലാക്കുക, സമ്മതിക്കുക

She *imagines* that she is a wonderful singer.

Criminals do not want to *imagine* the serious consequences of their action.

(*n.*) If you want to be a poet, you must have a good *imagination*.

(*adj.*) Kalidasa was one of India's most *imaginative* poets.

Imitate (*v.*) ഇമിറ്റേറ്റ്–അനുകരിക്കുക, പകർത്തുക

If you keep *imitating* other people's paintings, you will never become an original painter.

(*n.*) The lady was wearing a necklace of *imitation* pearls.

Immaculate (*adj.*) ഇമാക്യുലേറ്റ്–കുറ്റമറ്റ

His essay was *immaculate*.

Immaterial (*adj.*) ഇമറ്റീരിയൽ – അപ്രധാനം, നിസ്സാരം

When you die, it is *immaterial* what happens to your body.

Immature (*adj.*) ഇമച്യൂർ–പക്വതയില്ലാതെ

His behaviour was too *immature*.

Immediate (*adj.*) ഇമീഡിയറ്റ്–1. ഉടനടി, സത്വരം

Your complaint to the mayor will receive *immediate* attention.

2. അടുത്ത

The police informed the *immediate* relations of the accident victim about his serious condition.

(*adv.*) This payment is to be made *immediately*.

Immense (*adj.*) ഇമെൻസ്–അത്യധികം, വ്യാപകമായ

The famine caused *immense* suffering.

(*adv.*) I liked this book *immensely*.

Immerse (*v.*) ഇമേഴ്സ്–മുക്കുക, നിമജ്ജനം

The kid *immersed* the stick in water.

Immoral (*adj.*) ഇമോറൽ–അസാന്മാർഗ്ഗം, അധർമ്മം

It is *immoral* to trouble your parents.

Immunity (*n.*) ഇമ്യൂണിറ്റി–രോഗത്തിൽ നിന്ന് രക്ഷ

This vaccine offers *immunity* to polio.

Impact (*n.*) ഇംപാക്ട്–പരിണാമം

The direct *impact* of the cartridge controversy was the Revolt of 1857.

Impart (*v.*) ഇംപാർട്ട്–അറിവ് പകരുക

The newspapers *impart* information in detail.

Impartial (*adj.*) ഇംപാർഷ്യൽ– നിക്ഷ്പക്ഷം

The judge was highly *impartial* and announced his decision against the rich and affluent culprits.

Impeccable (*adj.*) ഇംപെകബ്ൾ–കുറ്റമറ്റ, ശ്രേഷ്ഠ

Konkona Sen's performance in Page 3 was *impeccable*.

Imperative (*adj.*) ഇംപെറടീവ് – അനുപേക്ഷണീയം

It is *imperative* that you file your tax returns by the end of this month.

Imperfect (*adj.*) ഇംപെർഫെക്ട–അപൂർണ്ണ, ദോഷമുള്ള

Everything is *imperfect* in the world.

Impertinent (*adj.*) ഇംപർട്ടിനന്റ് – അസംബന്ധ, അനുചിത, ധിക്കാരപരമായ

You must talk to your son about his *impertinent* behaviour.

(*n.*) He must be punished for his *impertinence*.

Impetus (*n.*) ഇംപിറ്റസ്–ഉത്തേജനം, ആവേശം

The tsunami campaign gained *impetus* with the association of celebrities.

Implement ഇംപ്ലിമെന്റ്–1. ഉപകരണം, പണിയായുധം

Do you have some *implement* to open this jammed lock?

(n.) 2. നടപ്പാക്കുക
We *implemented* the plan into action immediately.

Implicate *(v.)* ഇംപ്ലിക്കേറ്റ്-ഉടുക്കുക, ഉൾപ്പെടുത്തുക
She was falsely *implicated* in the controversy.

Implicit *(adj.)* ഇംപ്ലിസിറ്റ്-അന്തർലീനം
The issues that might affect the working of the company in future were *implicit* in his argument.

Imply *(v.)* ഇംപ്ലൈ-എടുത്തുപറയാതെ സൂചിപ്പിക്കുക
He did not say that I was the culprit, but he *implied* that.

Impolite *(adj.)* ഇംപോളൈറ്റ്-മര്യാദകേട്
Do you think it would be *impolite* to ask her to leave us alone for some time?

Import ഇംപോർട്ട്-ഇറക്കുമതി (ചെയ്യുക)
(n.) How are you doing in your *export-import* business?
(v.) Wool is *imported* from Australia.

Important *(adj.)* ഇംപോർട്ടന്റ് - പ്രധാനപ്പെട്ട, സുപ്രധാന
I saw many *important* personalities at the club meeting.
(n.) Don't give any *importance* to his foolish talk.

Impose *(v.)* ഇംപോസ്-അടിച്ചേൽപ്പിക്കുക
Our boss never *imposes* himself on anyone.

Impossible *(adj.)* ഇംപോസിബ്ൾ - അസാദ്ധ്യം
Walking such a long distance is completely *impossible* for me.

Impress *(v.)* ഇംപ്രെസ്-1. മതിപ്പ് തോന്നുക, സ്വാധീനിക്കുക
I was very much *impressed* by the artist's personality.
2. സ്വാധീനം ചെലുത്തുക
He *impressed* on me the value of learning Sanskrit.
(n.) You have created a very good *impression* on the boss.

Imprison *(v.)* ഇംപ്രിസൺ-തടവിലാക്കുക, ജയിലടയ്ക്കുക
I hear the manager of your firm has been *imprisoned* on charges of misappropriation of funds.
(n.) His *imprisonment* lasted for one year.

Impromptu *(adj.)* ഇംപ്രോപ്റ്റ്യൂ-മുൻകൂട്ടി തയ്യാറാക്കാത്ത
She won the first prize in the *impromptu* debate competition.

Improper *(adj.)* ഇംപ്രോപർ - അനുപയുക്ത, അനുചിത
I feel it is *improper* to sign a new project until we complete the previous ones.

Improve *(v.)* ഇംപ്രൂവ്-മെച്ചപ്പെടുത്തുക, പരിഷ്കരിക്കുക
You must *improve* your handwriting.
Is your son's health *improving* now?
(n.) The non-resident Indian was disappointed not to see any *improvement* in the condition of his native village.

Impulse *(n.)* ഇംപൾസ്-ആവേശം, ആവേഗം
On a generous *impulse,* Manoj gave his wrist watch to his friend.
(adv.) If you act *impulsively* now, you may have to regret later.

Impure *(adj.)* ഇംപ്യൂർ-അശുദ്ധ
The water in this region is highly *impure.*

In *(prep.)* ഇൻ-1. അകത്ത്, ഉള്ളിൽ
Please come *in*.
2. ഉ ാ വു ക
Is the boss *in*?
3. ഇൽ
Is your brother *in* the Navy?
4. (അവസ്ഥ)യിൽ
I don't want to go out *in* the dark.
Don't talk *in* such a loud voice.

Inane *(adj.)* ഇനെയ്ൻ-നിരർത്ഥകം
Let's not waste our time in this *inane* discussion.

Inaugurate *(v.)* ഇനോഗ്യുറേറ്റ്-ഉദ്ഘാടനം ചെയ്യുക
My new house will be *inaugurated* next week.

Incarnation *(n.)* അവതാരം
Krishna was an *incarnation* of Lord Vishnu.

Incense *(n.)* ഇൻസെൻസ്-സാമ്പ്രാണി തിരി

I lighted the *incense* sticks to make the room fragrant.

Incentive *(n.)* ഇൻസെൻടീവ്-ഉത്തേജനം

We get separate *incentives* for working late in the office.

Incessant *(adj.)* ഇൻസെസന്റ്-നിരന്തരം

The *incessant* rainstorm made me cancel my trip.

Incident *(n.)* ഇൻസിഡെന്റ്-സംഭവം

The newspapers gave extensive coverage to the child kidnapping *incident*.

Inclined *(adj.)* ഇൻക്ലൈൻഡ്-1. ചായ്‌വ്, ചരിവ്

I am *inclined* to accept your argument.

2. അനുകൂലിക്കുക, യോജിക്കുക

The roof was slightly *inclined* to allow the rain to run off.

(v.) He *inclined* the pot to drain out the water.

Include *(v.)* ഇൻക്ലൂഡ്-ഉൾപ്പെടുത്തുക

The shopkeeper *included* all the purchases of David in a single bill.

Income *(n.)* ഇൻകം-വരവ്, വരുമാനം

What is your monthly *income*?

Increase *(v.)* ഇൻക്രീസ്-വർദ്ധിക്കുക, വർദ്ധിപ്പിക്കുക

I have *increased* my secretary's salary.

Don't *increase* the speed until the road is clear.

(n.) I am expecting an *increase* in my salary.

Incredible *(adj.)* ഇൻക്രെഡിബ്ൾ - അവിശ്വസനീയം

The way he jumped from the multi-storeyed building was *incredible*.

Indebted *(adj.)* ഇൻഡെറ്റഡ്-കൃതജ്ഞത, കടപ്പാട്

I am greatly *indebted* to you for all your help.

Indulge *(v.)* ഇൻഡൽജ്-വിനോദത്തിനായി, എന്തെങ്കിലും ജോലിയിൽ മുഴുകുക

I love to *indulge* myself in shopping on weekends.

Indeed *(adj.)* ഇൻഡീഡ്-തീർച്ചയായും, സത്യമായും

I am *indeed* very glad to see you.

Independent *(adj.)* ഇൻഡിപെൻഡന്റ്-1. സ്വതന്ത്രം, സ്വാധീനം

The property Rahul has inherited has made him *independent*.

2. സ്വാശ്രയത്വം

I like your *independent* attitude.

(n.) Did you attend the *Independence* Day celebrations?

Indicate *(v.)* ഇൻഡിക്കേറ്റ്-കാണിച്ചു കൊടുക്കുക, സൂചിപ്പിക്കുക, പറഞ്ഞു കൊടുക്കുക

Sushil *indicated* his consent to the marriage proposal brought by his auntie.

Indignant *(adj.)* ഇൻഡിഗ്നന്റ്-രോഷം കൊള്ളുക, കോപിക്കുക

Rohit was *indignant* when he was blamed for a mistake made by somebody else.

Individual ഇൻഡിവിഡ്യുഅൽ - വ്യക്തിഗത, വ്യക്തി, ഓരോ

(adj.) The new officer redressed the people's complaints in his *individual* way.

(n.) Isn't Mr. Prasad a pleasant *individual*?

(adv.) Five of us were called into the room *individually* by the principal.

Induce *(v.)* ഇൻഡ്യൂസ്-പ്രേരിപ്പിക്കുക, വശപ്പെടുത്തുക

Ram could not *induce* Anwar to accompany him to the cinema.

(n.) What *inducement* can I offer to make you keep quiet?

Industry *(n.)* ഇൻഡസ്ട്രി-വ്യവസായം, ബിസിനസ്, പരിശ്രമം

After agriculture, *industry* is the second largest employer of the workforce.

(adj.) I have purchased a shed in the *industrial* estate to put up a factory.

Industrious *(adj.)* ഇൻഡസ്ട്രിയസ്-പരിശ്രമി, അദ്ധ്വാനി

To succeed in you career, you should be as *industrious* as an ant.

Infant *(n.)* ഇൻഫന്റ്-നവജാത ശിശു

The *infants* are fed on only milk for a few months.

Infect *(v.)* ഇൻഫെക്ട്-രോഗബാധയുാ വുക, ദുഷിപ്പിക്കുക, വഷളാക്കുക
You were *infected* with typhoid by drinking polluted water.
(n.) The doctor diagnosed Sushila's fever as an *infection*.

Inferior *(adj.)* ഇൻഫീരിയർ-തരംതാണ, മോശമായ
Suresh's performance was in no way *inferior* to Akram's who won the badminton championship.

Inflammable *(adj.)* ഇൻഫ്ളേമബ്ൾ - കത്തിപ്പിടിക്കുന്ന, ജ്വലനസ്വഭാവമുള്ള
He was asked not to smoke at the petrol pump, as petrol is highly *inflammable*.

Inflate *(v.)* ഇൻഫ്ളേറ്റ്-കാറ്റ് നിറച്ച് വീർപ്പിക്കുക
I *inflated* the balloons and decorated the room with them.

Inflict *(v.)* ഇൻഫ്ളിക്റ്റ്-വരുത്തി വയ്ക്കുക, ഏല്പിക്കുക, നൽകുക
Your hasty decision has *inflicted* a big loss on the company.

Influence ഇൻഫ്ളുഅൻസ്-സ്വാധീനം, പ്രഭാവം
(n.) Can you use your *influence* to get me a pass for the fashion show?
(v.) My mother has *influenced* me greatly.
(adj.) Her father is a very *influential* person.

Inform *(v.)* ഇൻഫോം-1. ഗ്രഹിപ്പിക്കുക, അറിയിക്കുക
Why did you not *inform* me that you were not well?
2. പോലീസിന് വിവരം നൽകുക
The thief was caught because someone had *informed* against him.
(n.) What *information* do you have about the flooded localities?

Informal *(adj.)* ഇൻഫോർമൽ-അനൗപ ചാരികം
This will be just an *informal* meeting.

Inherit *(v.)* ഇൻഹെറിറ്റ്-1. അനന്തരാവ കാശമായി ലഭിക്കുക
Do you expect to *inherit* a large amount of money from you rich uncle?
2. പരമ്പരാഗതമായി കിട്ടുക
Reena has *inherited* her mother's good looks and gentle behaviour.

Initial *(adj.)* ഇനീഷ്യൽ-1. പ്രാരംഭ, പ്രഥമ
Once you overcome your *initial* shyness, you can become a good speaker.
(n.) 2. ചുരുക്കി കയ്യൊപ്പിടുക
Put your *initials* on the cheque at the right place.

Initiate *(v.)* ഇനീഷിയേറ്റ്-തുടക്കം കുറിയ്ക്കുക
After remaining silent for a long time, she finally *initiated* the talk.

Injection *(n.)* ഇൻജെക്ഷൻ-കുത്തിവയ്പ്
I'm taking my dog for an *injection.*

Injure *(v.)* ഇൻജർ-1. മുറിവ് അല്ലെങ്കിൽ ദോഷം ഏല്പിക്കുക
I hope you were not seriously *injured* in yesterday's accident.
2. അപമാനിതർ
We felt *injured* at not receiving an invitation for Dinesh's wedding.
(n.) The boy sustained many *injuries* when he fell down from the bicycle.

Ink *(n.)* ഇങ്ക്-മഷി
There is no *ink* in your fountain pen.

Inmate (n.) ഇൻമേറ്റ്-സഹവാസി
When the theft was committed, all the *inmates* of the house were asleep.

Innate *(adj.)* ഇനേറ്റ്-ജന്മസിദ്ധം
She has an *innate* ability to dance.

Innocent *(adj.)* ഇനസന്റ്-നിരപരാധി, നിഷ്കളങ്കത
You have nothing to fear if you are *innocent.*
(n.) Is there any doubt about their child's *innocence*?

Input *(n.)* ഇൻപുട്ട്-നിക്ഷേപം
Let me have your *inputs* to improve my performance further.

Inquiry (Enquiry) *(v.&n.)* ഇൻക്വയറി - അന്വേഷിക്കുക, മനസ്സിലാക്കുക
(v.) Let us *inquire* about the arrival time of the train.
(n.) The police conducted an *inquiry* into the bank robbery.

Insane *(adj.)* ഇൻസെയ്ൻ-മനോനില തെറ്റിയ, ഭ്രാന്തൻ
The *insane* man was taken to the mental hospital.

Insect *(n.)* ഇൻസെക്റ്റ്-കീടം, പ്രാണി
The *insects* filled up the garden after the rain.

Insight *(n.)* ഇൻസൈറ്റ്-ഉൾക്കാഴ്ച, അറിവ്
The movie provides an *insight* into the lives of celebrities.

Insist *(v.)* ഇൻസിസ്റ്റ്-നിർബന്ധിക്കുക
I *insisted* him on going for a drive.

Inspect *(v.)* ഇൻസ്പെക്റ്റ് – പരിശോധിക്കുക
The police *inspected* the house to get some clues.

Inspire *(v.)* ഇൻസ്പയർ-പ്രേരണ, പ്രചോദനം നൽകുക
He claims to be *inspired* by Sachin Tendulkar.

Install *(v.)* ഇൻസ്റ്റാൾ-ഉറപ്പിക്കുക, സ്ഥാപിക്കുക
What will it cost me to *install* an air-conditioner in my bedroom?
(n.) The *installation* of the air-conditioner took the whole day.

Instalment *(n.)* ഇൻസ്റ്റാൾമെന്റ്-തവണ, ഗഡു
Arun bought the new car on *instalments*.

Instance *(n.)* ഇൻസ്റ്റൻസ്-ഉദാഹരണം, മാതൃക
Maharana Pratap was an *instance* for man of great courage and self-respect.

Instant *(n.)* ഇൻസ്റ്റന്റ്-1. തൽക്ഷണം
The *instant* I opened the window, I saw you coming slowly.
(adj.) 2. ഉടനെ, പെട്ടെന്ന്
That tablet gave Sheela *instant* relief from headache.
(adv.) In yesterday's accident, two men died *instantly*.

Instead *(adv.)* ഇൻസ്റ്റെഡ്-പകരമായി, ബദലായി
Why do you take coffee all the time? Have some milk *instead*.

Instinct *(n.)* ഇൻസ്റ്റിങ്ക്റ്റ്-സഹജവാസന, പ്രകൃതി
Just go by your *instinct*, everything will be fine.

Institute *(n.)* ഇൻസ്റ്റിറ്റ്യൂട്ട്-1. സ്ഥാപനം
My son is a student at the Indian *Institute* of Technology.
(v.) 2. ആരംഭിക്കുക, സ്ഥാപിക്കുക
An inquiry was *instituted* to investigate the corruption charges against the minister.

Instruct *(v.)* ഇൻസ്ട്രക്റ്റ്-1. പഠിപ്പിക്കുക, അഭ്യസിപ്പിക്കുക
The handicraft master *instructed* the girls in weaving.
(v.) 2. നിർദ്ദേശം, സൂചന നൽകുക
Please *instruct* Vikas Varma to come to my office at 11 o'clock.
(n.) I gave my servant the necessary *instructions* for the party.
Who is the physical *instructor* at your school?

Instrument *(n.)* ഇൻസ്ട്രുമെന്റ് – ഉപകരണം, യന്ത്രം
Which musical *instruments* do you play?

Insult ഇൻസൽറ്റ്-അപമാനം, അനാദരവ്, അവഹേളിക്കുക
(n.) Unable to bear the *insult* by his master, the servant at last left the job.
(adj.) I felt *insulted* when he did not return my greetings.
(v.) The miser *insulted* his poor, needy friend.

Insurance *(n.)* ഇൻഷൂറൻസ്- ഇൻഷൂറൻസ്
Do you have a medical *insurance*?

Intellect *(n.)* ഇന്റലെക്റ്റ്-ബുദ്ധി, പ്രതിഭ, ബുദ്ധിജീവി
Rabindra Nath Tagore was a person of great *intellect*.
Intellectuals think differently from the ordinary people.
(adj.) I feel happy in the company of *intellectual* people.

Intelligence *(n.)* ഇന്റലിജെൻസ്-1. ബുദ്ധി, കാര്യവിവരം
You are a man of great *intelligence*.
2. വാർത്ത
I run a journal devoted to economic *intelligence*.
3. സൂചന
The police passed on the *intelligence* about the terrorist's movements to the army.

Intense *(adj.)* ഇന്റൻസ്-തീവ്ര, പ്രബല, തീഷ്ണ, ഉൽക്കട
There was *intense* cold in Shimla.
(adv.) Rahul's grandmother dislikes non-veg food *intensely*.

Intention *(n.)* ഇന്റൻഷൻ-ഉദ്ദേശ്യം, അഭിപ്രായം, നിശ്ചയം
I have no *intention* of going to cinema today.

Intern *(n.)* ഇന്റേൺ-ഇന്റേൺ
She worked in the hospital as an *intern* for six months.

Interest *(n.)* ഇന്ററസ്റ്റ്-1. താല്പര്യം, അഭിരുചി
Most Indians take a keen *interest* in the game of cricket.
2. പലിശ
At what *interest* did the bank give you the loan?
(v.) I am not *interested* in gossip.

Interfere *(v.)* ഇന്റർഫിയർ-ഇടപെടുക, തടസ്സമുാക്കുക
I could have finished my homework by now if you had not *interfered*.
(n.) Nobody likes *interference* in personal affairs.

Interior *(adj.)* ഇന്റീരിയർ-ഉൾവശം, ഉള്ളിലായി
I live in the *interior* of the town.

Internal *(adj.)* ഇന്റേണൽ-ആന്തരിക
Have you completed the *internal* audit of your firm?

Interpret *(v.)* ഇന്റർപ്രെറ്റ്-വ്യാഖ്യാനിക്കുക, ദ്വിഭാഷിയായി പ്രവർത്തിക്കുക
Can you *interpret* Russian into Hindi?

Interrupt *(v.)* ഇന്ററപ്റ്റ്-ഇടയ്ക്കു കയറി പറയുക അല്ലെങ്കിൽ തടയുക
Amit's illness *interrupted* his studies.

Interval *(n.)* ഇന്റർവെൽ-ഇടവേള, വിരാമം
We shall have something to eat in the *interval*.

Intervene *(v.)* ഇന്റർവീൻ-ഇടയ്ക്ക് ഇടപെടുക
She *intervened* and suggested an easy solution to the problem.

Interview *(n.)* ഇന്റർവ്യൂ-1. മുഖാമുഖം, ഇന്റർവ്യൂ
Have you received a call for *interview*?
2. സമാഗമം, കൂടിക്കാഴ്ച
(n.) The paper carried a report on the Prime Minister's *interview* given to the BBC.
(v.) The veteran journalist *interviewed* many celebrities during his long career.

Intimate *(adj.)* ഇന്റിമേറ്റ്-1. ഉറ്റ, അടുത്ത
Are you and Sunil *intimate* friends?
(v.) 2. സൂചന നൽകുക, അറിയിക്കുക
Will you *intimate* me the time of your arrival?

Intimidate *(v.)* ഇന്റിമിഡേറ്റ്-ഭീഷണിപ്പെടുത്തുക, ഭയപ്പെടുത്തുക
I was *intimidated* by the unknown person following me.

Intricate *(adj.)* ഇൻട്രിക്കേറ്റ്-സങ്കീർണ്ണമായ
Extracting silk from a silkworm is an *intricate* process.

Intrigue ഇൻട്രീഗ്-ഉത്സാഹം ജനിപ്പിക്കുക, താല്പര്യം വളർത്തുക
(n.) The movie was full of thrill and *intrigue*.
(v.) He was quite *intrigued* by the news.

Introduce *(v.)* ഇൻട്രൊഡ്യൂസ്-പരിചയപ്പെടുത്തുക, ആരംഭിക്കുക, നടത്തുക
Let me *introduce* you to my friend Prakash.
(n.) A brief *introduction* of the author should be included in the book.

Introvert *(n.)* ഇൻട്രോവെർറ്റ്-അന്തർമുഖി
He is an *introvert* and prefers to stay at home on weekends.

Intrude *(v.)* ഇൻട്രൂഡ്-കടന്നു കയറുക
(v.) The media apologised for *intruding* the actor's privacy.
(n.) The *intruders* were sent to the jail immediatoly.
(n.) The Prime Minister said that *intrusion* would not be tolerated.

Intuition *(n.)* ഇൻട്യൂഷൻ-ഉൾവിളി, സഹജബോധം
I'm having a strong *intuition* that we will win this match.

Invade *(v.)* ഇൻവെയ്ഡ്-ആക്രമിക്കുക
The Mughals *invaded* the Rajput kingdoms.

Invalid *(adj.)* ഇൻവാലിഡ്-അസാധു, രോഗി, അശക്തൻ
Without your signature, this cheque is *invalid*.
(n.) His father has been an *invalid* for the last five years.

Invaluable *(adj.)* ഇൻവാല്യുഅബ്ൾ-അമൂല്യമായ
The advice that you gave me was *invaluable*.

Invariably *(adv.)* ഇൻവേരിയബ്ളി - പതിവായി, നിരന്തരം

I *invariably* go for a stroll after dinner.

Invent *(v.)* ഇൻവെന്റ്-ആവിഷ്കരിക്കുക, കുപിടിക്കുക

The gramophone was *invented* by Edison.

Don't *invent* an excuse for your deliberate absence from the Maths class.

(n.) The telephone is a useful *invention.*

Invest *(v.)* ഇൻവെസ്റ്റ്-1. പണം നിക്ഷേപിക്കുക

I *invested* some money in shares.

2. സമയം അല്ലെങ്കിൽ ശക്തി പ്രയോഗിക്കുക

Are you ready to *invest* another year in your struggle?

Investigate *(v.)* ഇൻവെസ്റ്റിഗേറ്റ്-അന്വേഷണം നടത്തുക, ഗവേഷണം നടത്തുക

The police *investigated* the cause of the fire accident.

(n.) The *investigation* into the case is in progress.

Invite *(v.)* ഇൻവൈറ്റ്-ക്ഷണിക്കുക

Have you *invited* Ramesh to the party?

(n.) Thank you for the *invitation*.

Inviting *(adj.)* ഇൻവൈറ്റിംഗ്-ആകർഷകം, മോഹിപ്പിക്കുന്ന

The pool looked so *inviting* that we went for a swim.

Involve *(v.)* ഇൻവോൾവ്-ഉൾപ്പെടുത്തുക, അകപ്പെടുക, പെട്ടുപോകുക

Never get *involved* in a pointless argument.

(n.) Without teacher's *involvement,* the students could not solve the complex Maths problem.

Involved *(adj.)* ഇൻവോൾവ്ഡ് - കുഴയ്ക്കുന്ന, സങ്കീർണ്ണമായ

The message I received was so *involved* that I could not understand it.

Iron *(n.)* അയൺ-1. ഇരുമ്പ്

Is this hammer made of *iron*?

(v.) 2. ഇസ്തിരി ഇടുക

Will you please *iron* my shirt?

Irregular *(adj.)* ഇറെഗുലർ-1. ക്രമം തെറ്റിയ, മുടക്കമുള്ള

I must point out that the procedure you have followed is very *irregular*.

2. പതിവ് തെറ്റിക്കുക

Why is your son so *irregular* in attending school?

Irritate *(v.)* ഇറിറ്റേറ്റ്-ശല്യം ചെയ്യുക, ദേഷ്യം പിടിപ്പിക്കുക

Don't *irritate* the teacher with your funny questions.

2. വേദനയോ നീറ്റലോ ഉാക്കുക

My new shoes *irritate* my toes.

Isolated *(adj.)* ഐസലേറ്റഡ്-പ്രത്യേകം, അകലെയായി

(adj.) The child suffering from chickenpox was kept in an *isolated* room.

(v.) The child suffering from chickenpox was *isolated* from other children.

Issue *(v.)* ഇഷ്യൂ-1. പുറപ്പെടുവിക്കുക, പ്രസിദ്ധീകരിക്കുക, നൽകുക

I have *issued* instructions to the staff about the Annual Day Function.

(n.) 2. സന്താനം

Is she without an *issue*?

3. പ്രശ്നം, വിവാദ വിഷയം

What is the main *issue* in your discussion?

Itch *(n. & v.)* ഇച്ച്-1. ചൊറി, ചിരങ്ങ്, ചൊറിച്ചിൽ

He scratched himself continuously unable to bear the *itch* on his back.

2. അതിയായി മോഹിക്കുക

I am *itching* to go on a hill station.

Item *(n.)* ഐറ്റം-1. സാധനങ്ങൾ, കാര്യം

Please make a list of all the *items* that we have to buy.

2. ഇനം, വിഷയം

What is the next *item* on the agenda?

3. വാർത്ത

Did you read this *item* about a parrot that talks in English?

J

Jab *(v.)* ജാബ്-കുത്തിവയ്ക്കുക
I grimaced in pain when the doctor *jabbed* a needle into my arm.
(n.) I have to go for my cholera *jab* tomorrow.

Jackal *(n.)* ജകൽ-കുറുക്കൻ
The *jackal* in the story fell into a tank of paint.

Jacket *(n.)* ജായ്ക്കിറ്റ്-ജാക്കറ്റ്, കുപ്പായം
Please iron my *jacket.*

Jackfruit *(n.)* ജാക്ക്ഫ്രൂട്ട്-ചക്ക
Mother bought jackfruit from the market.

Jagged *(adj.)* ജാഗിഡ്-1. മൂർച്ചയുള്ള, കൂർത്ത
Be careful; this saw has a *jagged* edge.
2. നിരപ്പില്ലാത്ത
We can see *jagged* rocks on the sea coast.

Jaggery *(n.)* ജാഗറി-ശർക്കര
I love to eat roasted grams with *jaggery.*

Jail *(n.)* ജയിൽ-കാരാഗ്രഹം, തടവറ
How far is the local *jail* from here?
(v.) You can be *jailed* for rash driving.

Jam *(n.)* ജാം-1. ജാം
I want to buy a jar of apple *jam*.
2. തിരക്ക്
Ram somehow managed to reach the station in time despite facing a major *traffic-jam*.

Jar *(n.)* ജാർ-1. ജാർ, കുപ്പി, ഭരണി
Please give me a *jar* of face cream.
(v.) 2. ഉന്തുക
I was badly *jarred* when my bicycle struck the fence.
(adj.) 3. അപശബ്ദമുാക്കുക
You should oil this door to stop its *jarring* sound.

Jaw *(n.)* ജാ-താടിയെല്ല്
I heard you had fallen and dislocated your *jaw*.

Jealous *(adj.)* ജെലസ്-അസൂയാലു
Don't be *jealous* of someone's achivements.

Jeer ജിയർ-കളിയാക്കുക, കുത്തുവാക്ക് പറയുക
(n.) The daughter-in-law started crying as she was unale to tolerate the *jeers* of her mother-in-law.
(v.) If you want to be a good speaker, you must not be afraid of being *jeered* at.

Jelly *(n.)* ജെല്ലി-ജെല്ലി
My wife has set up a small unit for making jams and *jellies.*

Jerk *(n.)* ജെർക്-തപ്പിപിടഞ്ഞ്, ഉന്തു നൽകുക, കുലുക്കുക
When I heard a sound near my bed, I got up with a *jerk*.
(v.) Don't *jerk* the steering wheel.

Jest ജെസ്റ്റ്-പരിഹസിക്കുക, തമാശ
(v.) Don't *jest* on Rakesh's accident as he hurt himself badly.
(n.) Please don't mind what I said in *jest*.

Jewel *(n.)* ജൂവൽ-രത്നം, ആഭരണം
What is this *jewel* in your ring?

Jigsaw *(n.)* ജിഗ്സാ-ചിത്രഖണ്ഡം, പ്രഹേളിക
There were forty pieces in the *jigsaw* puzzle.

Jingle ജിംഗ്ൾ-ഩിലുക്കം, കിലുങ്ങുക, കിലുക്കുക
(n.) We heard the *jingle* of bells.
(adj.) The *jingling* sound in the street made the children run out of their home.
(v.) The young boy *jingled* the coins in his pocket.

Jinx ജിംക്സ്-അശുഭ ലക്ഷണം
(n.) He broke the *jinx* of not starting a new work on Saturday.

(adj.) When the family lost their third child, they thought the house was *jinxed*.

Job *(n.)* ജോബ്–ഉദ്യോഗം, ജോലി, കാര്യം
Did you get the *job* for which you had applied?

Jog ജോഗ്–മെല്ലെ ഓടുക
(n.) I go for a *jog* every morning.
(v.) *Jogging* for half an hour every morning is a healthy exercise.

Join *(v.)* ജോയ്ൻ–1. പങ്കെടുക്കുക, ചേരുക
Would you like to *join* our party?
2. ചെന്നു ചേരുക, കൂടിചേരുക
Does this lane *join* the main road?
3. ചേർക്കുക, കോർക്കുക
Please *join* the two ends of the string.

Joke ജോക്–തമാശ, ഫലിതം (പറയുക)
(n.) If you tell good *jokes*, you will be popular at parties.
(v.) Please stop *joking* and be serious for a while.

Jolly *(adj.)* ജോളി–വിനോദപ്രിയം, പ്രസന്ന
Arun was liked by all because of his *jolly* nature.

Jolt ജോൾട്ട്–തട്ട്, ആഘാതം
Passengers got a severe *jolt* when the bus stopped suddenly.
(v.) The news of my friend's accident *jolted* me badly.

Jot *(v.)* ജോട്ട്–1. ചുരുക്കമായി കുറിയ്ക്കുക
Have you *jotted* down the points of the speech you are going to make?
(n.) 2. തെല്ലും, അല്പം പോലും
We don't care a *jot* for what you say.

Journal *(n.)* ജേർണൽ–പത്രിക, പ്രസിദ്ധീകരണം
Many reputed companies publish their monthly house *journals*.

Journey *(n. & v.)* ജേർണി–യാത്ര, സഞ്ചാരം (ചെയ്യുക)
(n.) How much time will your *journey* to Chennai take?
(v.) The pilgrims *journeyed* on foot from Delhi to Haridwar.

Jovial *(adj.)* ജോവിയൽ–പ്രസന്ന, സരസ
He was in a *jovial* mood yesterday.

Joy *(n.)* ജോയ്–സന്തോഷം, ആഹ്ലാദം, ആനന്ദം
The children while watching the magic show were full of *joy*.
(adj.) Amit returned from the picnic in a *joyful* mood.

Jubilation *(n.)* ജൂബിലിയേഷൻ – ആഘോഷം, കൊട്ടം
Christmas was celebrated with great joy and *jubilation*.

Jubilee *(n.)* ജൂബിലി–ജയന്തി, മഹോത്സവം
They invited all their friends for the silver *jubilee* party of their marriage.

Judge *(n. & v.)* ജജ്–ന്യായാധിപൻ, വിധിയെഴുതുക
My uncle is a *judge* in the High Court.
Never *judge* a man by his clothes.

Judiciary *(n.)* ജൂഡീഷറി–ന്യായ പീഠം
She lost faith in *judiciary* when the court released her son's killer.

Judicious *(adj.)* ജൂഡീഷസ്–വിവേക പൂർണ്ണം
Judicious use of words will make your essay more interesting.

Jug *(n.)* ജഗ്–ജഗ്, കുടം, കുംഭം
Please bring some cold water in a *jug*.

Juggler *(n.)* ജഗ്ലർ–മായാജാലക്കാരൻ
The *juggler* did a trick by tossing five knives together.

Juice *(n.)* ജൂസ്–രസം, പഴച്ചാറ്
Would you like some *orange-juice*?

Jumble ജമ്പ്ൾ–കലക്കുക, കുഴയ്ക്കുക, മിശ്രം
(v.) Ramesh quickly wrote the correct sentence from the *jumbled* up words.
(n.) Human mind is a *jumble* of ideas.

Jump ജമ്പ്–ചാട്ടം, ചാടി കടക്കുക
(n.) I won a prize in high *jump*.
(v.) Don't *jump* to false conclusions.

Junction *(n.)* ജങ്ക്ഷൻ–1. സന്ധി
Be careful while driving through a *junction* of the main road with a lane.
2. ജങ്ക്ഷൻ
Our train halted for half an hour at Mathura *junction*.

Jungle *(n.)* ജംഗ്ൾ–കാട്, വനം
My native place is a village on the edge of the *jungle*.

Juncture *(n.)* ജങ്ക്ചർ–വിശേഷാവസരം, മുഹൂർത്തം
At this *juncture,* our objective should be to build a good rapport with our clients.

Junior *(adj.)* ജൂനിയർ–ഇളയ, ഇളപ്പം
By how many years is your brother *junior* to you?

Jury *(n.)* ജൂറി–നിർണ്ണായക ഗണം
The *jury* was alleged to be partial.

Just ജസ്റ്റ്–1. മാത്രം, ഏകദേശം, ലേശം
(adj.) The poor man had money *just* enough to buy a loaf of bread.
2. നീതിയുക്തം, ഉചിത, നേരായ
The employer's decision to reward the laborious workers was *just*.
(n.) My father is known for his sense of *justice*.
(adj.) 3. ഒന്ന് നോക്കുക
Just look at the rainbow in the sky.
4. ഇപ്പോൾ, ഉടൻ
They are *just* going.

Jut *(v.)* ജട്ട്–പുറത്തേക്ക് തള്ളിനില്ക്കുന്ന
Hammer that nail *jutting* out from the chair.

Jute *(n.)* ജൂട്ട്–ചണം, ജൂട്ട്
He carried the onions in a *jute* bag.

Juvenile *(adj.)* ജൂവനൈൽ–താരുണ്യം, കൗമാരം
You are now too old for such *juvenile* behaviour.

K

Keen *(adj.)* കീൻ–1. ഉത്സുക, ഉത്സാഹി കുശാഗ്രബുദ്ധി
I am very *keen* to spend my vacations in Goa.
2. മൂർച്ചയുള്ള, ഉഗ്ര
Do you have a knife with a *keen* edge?

Keep *(v.)* കീപ്–1. വയ്ക്കുക, സൂക്ഷിക്കുക
You may *keep* this pencil if you need it.
2. ശ്രദ്ധിക്കുക
Keep an eye on the child.
3. നടക്കുക, നടത്തുക
Koop to the left of the road.
4. പൂർത്തിയാക്കുക, നിറവേറ്റുക
Once you make a promise, you must *keep* it up.
5. നോക്കിനടത്തുക
Who *keeps* the house for you?
6. കേടാകാതിരിക്കുക
Can we *keep* these bananas for a couple of days?
7. തുടരുക, നിരന്തരം ചെയ്തു കൊിരിക്കുക
Keep smiling.
(n.) 8. ഭക്ഷണവും താമസസൗകര്യവും
How much do you pay for your *keep*?

Kerb *(n.)* കെർബ്–ഓരം, അരിക്
Don't drive too near the *kerb*.

Kernel *(n.)* കർണൽ–അിപ്പരിപ്പ്
Almond *kernels* are good both for the brain and the eyes.

Kerosene *(n.)* കെറസിൻ–മണ്ണെണ്ണ
Do you cook on a *kerosene* stove?

Ketchup *(n.)* കെച്ചപ്–ടൊമാറ്റോ ചട്നി
Can I have some tomato *ketchup*?

Kettle *(n.)* കെറ്റൽ–കെറ്റിൽ
I use an electic *kettle* for making tea.

Key *(n.)* കീ–താക്കോൽ
Where have you kept the *key* of the safe?

Keyboard *(n.)* കീബോർഡ്–കമ്പ്യൂട്ടറിന്റ അടയാള ചട്ടം
Some of the keys in my *keyboard* are not working.

Keyword *(n.)* കീവേർഡ്-കമ്പ്യൂട്ടറിന്റെ നിർദ്ദേശക പദം
Try some other *keyword* to get the information you are searching for.

Kick കിക്ക്-അടി, തൊഴി (തൊഴിക്കുക, അടിക്കുക)
(v.) Please be careful, this horse *kicks.*
(n.) The goalie dived to his left to clear an angular *kick.*

Kid *(n.)* കിഡ്-1. കുഞ്ഞാട്, കുട്ടി
The young of a goat is called a *kid.*
Tell the *kids* not to play in street.
(v.) 2. തമാശ പറയുക, കളിയാക്കുക
Are you *kidding*?

Kidnap *(v.)* കിഡ്നാപ്-തട്ടികൊണ്ട് പോകുക
The child was *kidnapped* for money.

Kidney *(n.)* കിഡ്നി-വൃക്ക
My doctor is treating me for some *kidney* trouble.

Kill *(v.)* കിൽ-1. കൊല്ലുക, ഹത്യ ചെയ്യുക
Don't you have anything to do except *killing* flies?
2. നാശം ചെയ്യുക, ഇല്ലാതാക്കുക
The cold winter has *killed* the flowers in my garden.

Kind *(n.)* കൈൻഡ്-1. ജാതി, വർഗ്ഗം
I saw all *kinds* of people at the function.
2. തരം, ഇനം
What *kind* of fabric is this?
(adj.) 3. ദയാലു
It was very *kind* of you to help me.

Kindergarten *(n.)* കിന്റർഗാർട്ടൻ-കെ.ജി. സ്കൂൾ
Her daughter is studying in *kindergarten* now.

Kindle *(v.)* കിൻഡ്ൽ-1. കത്തിക്കുക
Kindle the fire; it's so cold.
2. ഭാവന അല്ലെങ്കിൽ അഭിരുചി വളർത്തുക
She *kindled* my interest in photography.

King *(n.)* കിംഗ്-രാജാവ്
The child wished to play the role of the *king.*

Kiosk *(n.)* കിയോസ്ക്-മാടക്കട
Get a newspaper from the nearby *kiosk.*

Kiss കിസ്-ചുംബിക്കുക
(v.) The mother *kissed* her weeping child.
(n.) The mother gave the child a toffee and a *kiss.*

Kit *(n.)* കിറ്റ്-കിറ്റ്, സാധനം, പണിആയുധ പെട്ടി
Has the fisherman taken his *kit* for fishing?

Kitchen *(n.)* കിച്ചൻ-അടുക്കള
Normally I have my meal in the *kitchen.*

Kite *(n.)* കൈറ്റ്-പട്ടം, പരുന്ത്
Do you know how to fly a *kite*?
I saw a *kite* high up in the sky.

Kitten *(n.)* കിറ്റൻ-പൂച്ചക്കുട്ടി
Our cat has given birth to four *kittens.*

Kitty *(n.)* കിറ്റി-ചെപ്പ്
She has some good projects in her *kitty.*

Knack *(n.)* നാക്-പാടവം, മിടുക്ക്
She has a *knack* for writing poetry.

Knead *(v.)* നീഡ്-കുഴയ്ക്കുക, മർദ്ദിച്ച് മയപ്പെടുത്തുക
If you want soft bread, you must *knead* the flour well.

Knee *(n.)* നീ-കാൽമുട്ട്
My left *knee* was injured in a fall.

Kneel *(v.)* നീൽ-മുട്ടുകുത്തുക
Let us *kneel* in prayer.

Knife *(n.)* നൈഫ്-കത്തി, കഠാര
Please sharpen the edge of this *knife.*

Knight (n.) നൈറ്റ്-അശ്വാരൂഢനായ
Every girl has an image of her *knight* in shining armour in her mind.

Knit *(v.)* നിറ്റ്-തയ്ക്കുക
Can you *knit* a sweater?

Knob *(n.)* നോബ്-കുമിള, മുഴ, കൈപ്പിടി
We saw decorative *knobs* on all the doors in the royal palace.

Knock *(v. & n.)* നോക്ക്-കതകിൽ തട്ടുക, ഇടിച്ചിടുക
(v.) Who is *knocking* at the door?
2. അടിക്കുക, ഇടിക്കുക
The champion boxer *knocked* down his opponent very easily.
(n.) My sister opened the door at the first *knock.*

Knot *(n.)* നോട്ട്-1. കെട്ട്, കുടുക്ക്, കെട്ടുക
Please untie this *knot.*

2. സംഘം, കൂട്ടം

Why have these people gathered in *knots*?

3. മരപ്പിരി, ഗ്രന്ഥി

This piece of wood is full of *knots*.

Know *(v.)* നോ-1. അറിയുക

I *know* the way to Surekha's house.

2. വിജ്ഞാനം ഉാവുക

Do you *know* geometry?

3. പരിചയമുാവുക

I *know* Sudhir because he was my classmate.

Knuckle *(n.)* നക്ക്ൾ-വിരൽ, മുട്ട്, കൈപ്പത്തിയിൽ ചേരുന്ന, വിരലിന്റെ ഭാഗം

I knocked at the door with my *knuckles*.

L

Label ലേബ്ൽ-ലേബൽ, ചീട്ട്, നറുക്ക്, ലേബൽ ഒട്ടിക്കുക

(n.) I put a *label* on the bottle to show that it contained a poisonous chemical.

(v.) Have you *labelled* all the packets?

Laboratory *(n.)* ലബോറട്ടറി-പരീക്ഷണശാല

Does your school have a well-equipped science *laboratory*?

Labour ലേബർ-1. പരിശ്രമം, അദ്ധ്വാനം (അദ്ധ്വാനിക്കുക)

(n.) Gandhiji taught us the dignity of *labour*.

(v.) The farmer *labours* in the fields to feed the countrymen.

(n.) 2. തൊഴിലാളി (വർഗ്ഗം), പണിയാൾ

I heard you had some *labour* trouble in your factory.

Lace *(n.)* ലേസ്-1. റേന്തതുണി

She stitched *lace* in her dress.

2. നാട, ചരട്

Tie your *shoelaces*.

3. നാട കെട്ടുക

(v.) *Lace up* your shoes.

Lack ലാക്-കുറവ്, പോരായ്മ (ഉാവുക)

(n.) We always suffer from a *lack* of water in summer.

(v.) The dish *lacked* salt.

Lad *(n.)* ലാഡ്-കുട്ടി, ബാലൻ, യുവാവ്

Your son has grown into a fine young *lad*.

Ladder *(n.)* ലാഡർ-ഏണി

Use the *ladder* to climb up to the roof.

Lady *(n.)* ലേഡി-മഹിള, വനിത

Your daughter has grown into a polished young *lady*.

Lag *(v.)* ലാഗ്-പിന്നിലാവുക, പിന്നോക്കം നില്ക്കുക

Suresh *lagged* behind other athletes in the race because of a pain in his leg.

Lake *(n.)* ലേക്-തടാകം

We went for a swim in the *lake*.

Lamb *(n.)* ലാമ്പ്-ആട്ടിൻ കുട്ടി

My child was delighted to see the frisky young *lamb* jump around.

Lame *(adj.)* ലെയിം-മുടന്തുള്ള

It was so kind of you to help the *lame* man cross the busy street.

Lament ലാമെന്റ്-വിലപിക്കുക, വ്യസനിക്കുക

(v.) We cannot but *lament* the passing away of our dear ones.

(n.) The dead accident victim's relatives' *lament* was heartrending.

Lamp *(n.)* ലാംപ്-വിളക്ക്, ദീപം

As the electricity failed, I lit a *lamp*.

Land *(n.)* ലാൻഡ്-1. ഭൂമി, കര

I have bought a piece of *land* to build a house.

2. ദേശം, പ്രദേശം

I like to read books about faraway *lands*.

(v.) 3. എത്തുക, താഴെ ഇറങ്ങുക
When will your plane *land* in Mumbai?

Landlord *(n.)* ലാൻഡ്ലോർഡ്-വീട്ടുടമ
The *landlord* demanded the rent of three months in advance.

Landmark *(n.)* ലാൻഡ്മാർക്-1. അടയാളം
1. पहचान-चिह्न
Tell me some *landmark* so that I find the way to your place easily.
2. എന്തെങ്കിലും പ്രധാന സംഭവം
The Revolt of 1857 was a *landmark* in Indian history.

Lane *(n.)* ലെയ്ൻ-ഇടവഴി, പാത
Does this *lane* join the main road?

Language *(n.)* ലാംഗ്വേജ്-ഭാഷ
How many *languages* can you speak?

Lantern *(n.)* ലാന്റേൺ-റാന്തൽ, വിളക്ക് കൂട്
Don't go out into the dark of night without a *lantern.*

Lap *(n.)* ലാപ്-1. മടിത്തട്ട്
My cat is fond of sitting in my *lap.*
(v.) 2. മൊത്തി കുടിക്കുക
I put some milk in saucer for my cat to *lap* up.

Lapse ലാപ്സ്-മറവി, തെറ്റ്, പിശക്, കഴിഞ്ഞ് പോകുക, കാലാവധിയാവുക
(n.) I am sorry for this *lapse* on my part.
(v.) How much time has *lapsed* since we met last?

Large *(adj.)* ലാർജ്-വലിയ, വലിപ്പമുള്ള, വിസ്തൃതമായ
I want a *large* tube of tooth-paste.
Some trains are very *large*.

Lash ലാഷ്-1. ചാട്ടകൊടിക്കുക
(v.) The tonga-driver was *lashing* his horse cruelly.
2. കെട്ടുക
People usually *lash* their dogs at their house's entrance.
3. ചുഴറ്റുക
My cat *lashed* its tail in excitement when I threw up the ball.
(v.) The thief was sentenced fifty *lashes* on his back.

4. കൺപീലി
Sheela has long *eye-lashes.*

Lass *(n.)* ലാസ്-പെൺകുട്ടി, കൗമാര പ്രായക്കാരി
She is a very industrious young *lass.*

Last *(adj.)* ലാസ്റ്റ്-1. കഴിഞ്ഞ, പിന്നിട്ട
What were you doing *last* night?
2. അവസാനം, അന്ത്യം, അന്തിമ
You are the *last* to speak.
(v.) 3. നീുനില്ക്കുക
How long will the function *last*?

Latch ലാച്ച്-കൊളുത്ത്, കുറ്റിയിടുക
(v.) Always *latch* the door from inside at night.
(n.) The door could not be closed properly because of the faulty *latch.*

Late *(adj. & adv.)* ലേറ്റ്-1. താമസിച്ച്, വൈകിയ, വിലംബമായ
(adj.) Why are you so *late*?
2. അന്തരിച്ച
Did you know the *late* Mr. Kapur?
(adv.) I came *late* last night.

Lately *(v.)* ലേറ്റ്ലി-ഈയിടെ
Have you seen Mohan *lately*?

Latest *(adj.)* ലേറ്റസ്റ്റ്-ഏറ്റവും പുതിയ
What is the *latest* news in business?

Latrine *(n.)* ലട്രീൻ-മറപ്പുര, കക്കൂസ്
You must clean the *latrine* every day.

Latter *(adj.)* ലാറ്റർ-പിന്നീടുള്ള, ഒടുവിലത്തെ
Between Anil and Sunil, I found the *latter* more intelligent.

Laugh *(v.)* ലാഫ്-ചിരിക്കുക, ചിരി
Laughing is good for health, but we should not *laugh* at others.
(n.) I could hear your *laughter* in the other room.
We all had a good *laugh* when our father told us a story.

Launch *(n.)* ലാഞ്ച്-1. വഞ്ചി, മോട്ടോർ ബോട്ട്
We were taken round the harbour in a *launch.*
(v.) 2. തുടങ്ങി വയ്ക്കുക
Diwali is considered auspicious to *launch* a new business.

Laundry *(n.)* ലാൻഡ്രി–അലക്കുശാല
Send all these dirty clothes to the *laundry*.

Lavatory *(n.)* ലാവറ്ററി–ശൗചാലയം
Where is the *lavatory* in this theatre?

Lavish ലാവിഷ്–ധാരാളിത്തം കാണിക്കുക, ചെലവാളി
(n.) They threw a *lavish* party at their wedding.
(v.) He *lavished* expensive gifts on his wife on her birthday.

Law *(n.)* ലാ–നിയമം, വിധി
You should always abide by the *law*.

Lawn *(n.)* ലാൺ–പുൽത്തകിടി, മൈതാനം
My children like to play in the *lawn* near our house.

Lay *(v.)* ലേ–1. വയ്ക്കുക, വിരിക്കുക, കിടത്തുക
I *laid* my book on this table last night.
2. മുട്ട ഇടുക
Our hen has *laid* an egg.

Layer *(n.)* ലേയർ–പടലം
I saw a thin *layer* of frost on my car.

Layman *(n.)* ലേമാൻ–സാധാരണക്കാരൻ, അവിദഗ്ദ്ധൻ
He is a complete *layman* in the field of computers.

Lazy *(adj.)* ലേസി–അലസൻ– മടിയൻ
It you are *lazy*, you will never succeed in life.

Lead ലീഡ്–ലെഡ്–1. കൊണ്ടുപോകുക, വഴികാട്ടുക
(v.) Where are you *leading* me?
2. നേതൃത്വം നൽകുക
The Geography teacher was to *lead* the students' educational trip to Goa.
3. നയിക്കുക
The old couple *led* a quiet life.
(n.) 4. ഈയം
I require some *lead*-pipes for a water connection.
(adj.) 5. ഈയപെൻസിൽ
Please get me a *lead* pencil.

Leaf *(n.)* ലീഫ്–1. ഇല
In autumn, most trees shed their *leaves*.
2. താള്, പുറം
Don't tear any *leaf* out of your exercise-book.

Leak ലീക്ക്–ചോർച്ച
(v.) Rainwater has *leaked* through the ceiling and spoilt some furniture.
(adj.) We must repair our *leaking* roof before the monsoon starts.
(n.) The *leakage* of toxic waste contaminates the underground water.

Lean *(v.)* ലീൻ–1. കുനിയുക, ചാരുക
I was so tired that I *leaned* against the wall.
2. ആശ്രയിക്കുക
Try to be self-reliant, don't *lean* on others every time a problem arises.
(adj.) 3. മെലിഞ്ഞ, ശോഷിച്ച
You look so *lean*.

Leap *(n.)* ലീപ്–ചാട്ടം, കുതിപ്പ്
He crossed the ditch in one long *leap*.
(v.) How high can you *leap*?

Learn *(v.)* ലേൺ–1. പഠിക്കുക, അഭ്യസിക്കുക
We have to *learn* Chemistry from this year onward.
2. അറിവ് കിട്ടുക
I *learned* that you are going abroad.

Least *(adj.)* ലീസ്റ്റ്–1. ചുരുങ്ങിയത്
The *least* the doctor could do for the dying patient was to inform his relatives about his impending death.
2. ഏറ്റവും കുറഞ്ഞത്
We saw at *least* a hundred people at the meeting.

Leather *(n.)* ലെദർ–തുകൽ
Is your jacket made of *leather*?

Leave *(v.)* ലീവ്–1. പുറപ്പെടുക, യാത്ര തിരിക്കുക
When does this train *leave*?
2. വിടുക, വിട്ടുകളയുക
Please *leave* me alone.
(n.) 3. സമ്മതം, അനുമതി
Who took my book without my *leave*?
4. അവധി, ഒഴിവ്
I have applied for a month's *leave*.

Lecture ലെക്ചർ–വ്യാഖ്യാനം (നൽകുക)
(n.) Did you attend yesterday's *lecture*?
(v.) Every day my father *lectures* me on the merits of yoga and exercise.

Left ലെഫ്റ്റ്–1. ഇടത്,
Always keep to the *left.*
(adj.) 2. ഇടത്തെ
I have learnt to write with my *left* hand.
(adv.) Turn *left* from here.

Leg *(n.)* ലെഗ്–കാൽ, പാദം
You have long *legs.*
2. മേശക്കാൽ
Call a carpenter to repair the *legs* of this table.

Legal ലീഗൽ–1. നിയമ സംബന്ധ
(adj.) I was entangled in *legal* matters.
(adv.) 2. നിയമപരമായി
Ramesh was *legally* entitled to inherit his father's property.

Legend *(n.)* ലെജൻഡ്–ഐതിഹ്യം
(n.) As per the *legend,* Krishna killed many demons when he was just an infant.
(adj.) Lata Mangeshkar is a *legendary* singer.

Legible *(adj.)* ലെജിബ്ൾ–തെളിഞ്ഞ, വായിക്കാവുന്ന
Use a *legible* ink to write your letter.

Legislation *(n.)* ലെജിസ്ലേഷൻ–നിയമ നിർമ്മാണം, നിയമ സഭ, നിയമം
Now that you are a lawyer, you will understand the intricacies of *legislation.*

Legitimate *(adj.)* ലെജിറ്റിമേറ്റ്–ന്യായാനുസൃത, യുക്തമായ
Do you have a *legitimate* reason for taking a leave today?

Leisure *(n.)* ലെഷർ–ഒഴിവ്, വിശ്രമവേള
His job left him little leisure.

Lemon *(n.)* ലെമൺ–നാരങ്ങ
The little girl loves to eat *lemon* pickles.

Lemonade *(n.)* ലെമണേഡ്–നാരാങ്ങാ വെള്ളം
It's so hot; have some *lemonade.*

Lend *(v.)* ലെൻഡ്–കടം കൊടുക്കുക
Would you *lend* me ten rupees?

Length *(n.)* ലെങ്ത്–നീളം
What is the *length* of this river?

Lenient *(adj.)* ലീനിയെന്റ്–അയവുള്ള, പതമുള്ള, സൗമ്യമായ
She is a *lenient* teacher and avoids punishing her students.

Leprosy *(n.)* ലെപ്രസി–കുഷ്ഠരോഗം
This dispensary offers free medical treatment to the *leprosy* patients.

Less *(adj.)* ലെസ്–കുറവ്
You must eat *less* if you want to become slim.

Lesson *(n.)* ലെസൺ–1. പാഠം
Have you revised all the *lessons* for your coming exams?
2. മുന്നറിയിപ്പ്, പാഠം
Let this mistake teach you a *lesson.*

Let *(v.)* ലെറ്റ്–1. അനുമതി നൽകുക
Let me accompany you.
2. വാടകയ്ക്ക് കൊടുക്കുക
I want to *let* a three-room flat.
If this flat is to *let,* please *let* it to me.
3. കഴിയാൻ വിടുക, ഇടപെടാതിരിക്കുക
Let him stay alone.

Letter *(n.)* ലെറ്റർ–1. കത്ത്
Did you receive my *letter*?
2. അക്ഷരം, വർണ്ണം
How many *letters* are there in the English alphabet?

Level ലെവൽ–1. നിരപ്പ്
(n.) How many feet above the sea *level* is Shimla?
2. തലം, നിലവാരം
What is the general *level* of the students in your class?
(adj.) 3. സമതലം, നിരപ്പുള്ളത്
The surface of this table is not quite *level.*
(v.) 4. സമവൃത്തി
He *levelled* his rifle and took aim.

Lever *(n.)* ലിവർ–ഹാൻഡിൽ
Would you please help me pull the *lever*?

Liability *(n.)* ലയബിലിറ്റി–ബാദ്ധ്യത, ഭാരം
After the death of her parents, she was brought up by her uncle as a *liability.*

Liable *(adj.)* ലയബ്ൾ–ഉത്തരവാദിയാകുക, ബാദ്ധ്യസ്ഥമായിരിക്കുക
The defaulters will be *liable* to be punished.

Liberal *(adj.)* ലിബറൽ–ഉദാരമതി, ദാനശീല
The businessman gave a *liberal* donation to the relief fund for earthquake victims.

Liberate *(v.)* ലിബറേറ്റ്–മോചിപ്പിക്കുക, മുക്തമാക്കുക
The domestic appliances have *liberated* the housewife from drudgery.

Liberty *(n.)* ലിബർട്ടി–1. അവകാശം, സ്വാതന്ത്ര്യം
You are now at *liberty* to go home.
2. ധാർഷ്ട്യം
The mischievous students had taken the *liberty* of making April Fool of their teacher.

Library *(n.)* ലൈബ്രറി–ഗ്രന്ഥശാല
I got this book from the *library*.

Licence *(n.)* ലൈസൻസ്–ലൈസൻസ്, അനുമതി
Do you have a *licence* to drive a heavy vehicle?

License *(v.)* ലൈസൻസ്–അംഗീകൃതം
I am a *licensed* electrician.

Lick *(v.)* ലിക്–നക്കുക, നുണയുക
My cat *licks* my legs.

Lid *(n.)* ലീഡ്–അടയ്ക്കുക, മൂടി
Where is the *lid* of the bread-box?

Lie *(n. & v.)* ലൈ–1. കള്ളം (പറയുക)
(n.) Anyone who tells a *lie* is a *liar.*
(v.) Don't *lie* to me.
(v.) 2. കിടക്കുക
Please *lie* on the bed.
3. ചിതറികിടക്കുക
I saw all his books *lying* on the floor.
4. സ്ഥിതിചെയ്യുക
In which continent does India *lie*?

Lieutenant *(n.)* ലെഫ്റ്റനന്റ്–ലെഫ്റ്റനന്റ്
He is promoted to the post of *lieutenant.*

Life *(n.)* ലൈഫ്–1. ജീവിതം
Mother Teresa devoted all her *life* to serving poor.
2. ജീവസ്സുറ്റ
She is full of *life.*
3. ആയുർദൈർഘ്യം
Mishandling reduces the *life* of the machine.

Lift *(v.)* ലിഫ്റ്റ്–1. ഉയർത്തുക
How will you *lift* such a heavy load?
(n.) 2. ലിഫ്റ്റ്
The *lift* in this building is out of order.

Light ലൈറ്റ്–1. വിളക്ക്, ദീപം
(n.) Please switch on the *light.*
2. പ്രകാശം, തെളിച്ചം
In the *light* of the lamp, I read his letter.
(v.) 3. കത്തിക്കുക
Please *light* a candle.
(adj.) 4. മന്ദം, നേർത്ത, നേരിയ
I like fabrics of *light* colours.
5. കനമില്ലാത്ത
I can carry this *light* box.
6. ഹർഷം തോന്നുക
We all felt *light-hearted.*

Lightning *(n.)* ലൈറ്റ്നിംഗ്–മിന്നൽ
There was a sudden flash of *lightning.*

Like ലൈക്–1. ഇഷ്ടപ്പെടുക
(v.) Do you *like* my dress?
(conj.) 2. പോലുള്ള, സാദൃശ്യമുള്ള
I bought a pen *like* yours.

Likely *(adj.)* ലൈക്‌ലി–സാദ്ധ്യതയുള്ള
Are you *likely* to go to Mumbai next week?

Limb *(n.)* ലിമ്പ്–1. അംഗം, അവയവം
I hope none of your *limbs* was injured in the accident.
2. ശാഖ, കൊമ്പ്
I watched the squirrel run up a *limb* of the tree.

Limit ലിമിറ്റ്–1. പരിധി
(n.) There is a *limit* to the powers of the Prime Minister.
(adj.) 2. പരിമിതപ്പെടുത്തുക, നിയന്ത്രിക്കുക
One must try to *limit* one's own expenditure.
(adj.) I have only *limited* interest in classical music.

Limp ലിംപ്–1. മുടന്തുക
(v.) Why are you *limping*?
(adj.) 2. നിർജ്ജീവം, ശിഥിലം
These flowers have become *limp.*

Line *(n.)* ലൈൻ–1. വര, രേഖ
Draw a straight *line.*

2. നിര, വരി
Sit in a *line*, all of you.
3. വഴി, മാർഗ്ഗം
By which *airline* did you travel?
(v.) People *lined* up to cast their vote.

Linen *(n.)* ലിനൻ-ലിനൻ കൊണ്ടാക്കിയ തുണി, വീട്ടുവസ്ത്രങ്ങൾ
Give this dirty *linen* to the washerman.

Linger *(v.)* ലിംഗർ-തങ്ങുക, തങ്ങിനിൽക്കുക
Why are you *lingering* here though the show is over?

Lining *(n.)* ലൈനിംഗ്-വക്ക്, കര
She tore the *lining* of her skirt.

Link *(n. & v.)* ലിങ്ക്-1. കണ്ണി
(n.) Are all the *links* in this chain equally strong?
(v.) 2. ബന്ധം, ബന്ധപ്പെടുക, ചേർക്കുക
Let us *link* hands to dance around the tree.

Lint *(n.)* ലിന്റ്-മുറിവ് വച്ച് കെട്ടാനുള്ള നേർത്ത തുണി
Get some *lint* to dress the wound.

Lip *(n.)* ലിപ്-1. ചുണ്ട്, അധരം
Uma applied vaseline on her cracked *lips*.
2. അറ്റം, വക്ക്, അരിക്
The *lip* of this cup is not clean.

Liquid *(adj.)* ലിക്വിഡ്-ദ്രാവകം, തരളം, ദ്രവം
The doctor has advised me to take only *liquid* food.
(n.) What is the golden-coloured *liquid* in that glass?

Liquor *(n.)* ലിക്വർ-മദ്യം
That is a famous *liquor* shop in this area.

Lisp *(n.)* ലിസ്പ്-വിക്ക്, കൊഞ്ഞ
The child has a *lisp* in his voice.

List *(n.)* ലിസ്റ്റ്-പട്ടിക, സൂചിക
Please prepare a *list* of all the participants in the debate.

Listen *(v.)* ലിസൻ-കേൾക്കുക, ശ്രദ്ധിക്കുക
Students were *listening* attentively to the teacher's talk.
Please *listen* to me.

Literally *(adv.)* ലിറ്ററലി-അക്ഷരാർത്ഥത്തിൽ
They were *literally* on roads after their father's accident.

Literate *(adj.)* ലിറ്ററേറ്റ്-സാക്ഷരത, എഴുത്തും വായനയും അറിയാവുന്ന
My maid-servant is a *literate* and can also read a newspaper.

Literature *(n.)* ലിറ്ററേച്ചർ-സാഹിത്യം
Have you read modern English *literature*?

Litter ലിറ്റർ-ചപ്പും ചവറും
(n.) Dump the *litter* in the dustbin.
(v.) His room was *littered* with old newspapers and magazines.

Little *(adj.)* ലിറ്റ്ൽ-1. ചെറിയ, കൊച്ച്
I saw a *little* boy playing with marbles.
2. ഒരല്പം
I feel a *little* unwell today.
3. അല്പം പോലും, തീരെ
I have *little* time to waste.

Live *(v.)* ലിവ്-1. താമസിക്കുക, പാർക്കുക
Where do you *live*?
2. ജീവിക്കുക, ജീവനുള്ള
Is your grandfather still *living*?
(n.) 3. ഉപജീവനം
How do you earn your *living*?

Liver *(n.)* ലിവർ-കരൾ
My doctor is treating me for *liver* trouble.

Load *(n.)* ലോഡ്-1. ഭാരം, തൂക്കം
Can you carry this heavy *load*?
(v.) 2. കയറ്റുക, ലോഡ് ചെയ്യുക
Have they *loaded* all our household items in the truck?
3. നിറയ്ക്കുക
Have you *loaded* you gun?

Loaf *(n.)* ലോഫ്-1. റൊട്ടി
Go to the bakery and buy a *loaf* of bread.
(v.) 2. വെറുതെ അലഞ്ഞു നടക്കുക
You do nothing but *loaf* in the streets.

Loan *(n.)* ലോൺ-കടം, വായ്പ
Have you repaid the bank *loan*?

Loathe *(v.)* ലോത്ത്-വെറുക്കുക, അനിഷ്ടം കാണിക്കുക
I *loathe* the very sight of him.

Lobby *(n.)* ലോബി-ലോബി, കോലായി
Does this door open into the *lobby*?

Local *(adj.)* ലോകൽ-1. തദ്ദേശ സ്ഥലത്തെ
Where is the *local* bus stop?

2. ചെറിയ സ്ഥലത്ത്

The injury was *local* and was cured in two or three days.

(adv.) Is this electric kettle *locally* made?

Lock ലോക്-പൂട്ട്, താഴ് (പൂട്ടുക)

(v.) Do not forget to *lock* the safe.

(n.) I bought a new *lock* for my cupboard.

Locate *(v.)* ലൊക്കേറ്റ്-സ്ഥിതി ചെയ്യുക, കണ്ടെത്തുക

(v.) Have you been able to *locate* the lost book?

(adj.) Where is your house *located?*

Locomotive *(n.)* ലോകമോട്ടിവ്-തീവണ്ടി എൻജിൻ

Does our country export *locomotives*?

Lodge *(v. & n.)* ലോജ്-1. താമസിക്കുക, പാർക്കുക

I am *lodging* with my aunt these days.

(n.) 2. കുടിൽ, താമസ സ്ഥലം, ചെറുവീട്

When I go for hunting, I stay in a *lodge* in the forest.

Lofty *(adj.)* ലോഫ്റ്റി-1. ഉയർന്ന, ഉയരത്തിലുള്ള

Our old mansion has a *lofty* ceiling.

2. ഉൽകൃഷ്ടമായ, ഉന്നത

I appreciate your *lofty* ideals.

Log *(n.)* ലോഗ്-വിറക് കൊള്ളി

Put a *log* in the fire.

Logic *(n.)* ലോജിക്-യുക്തി

(n.) There was no *logic* in his answer.

(adj.) His answer was completely *logical.*

Logo *(n.)* ലോഗോ-ലോഗോ

We should change the *logo* of our company and make it catchier.

Loiter *(v.)* ലോയിറ്റർ-ചുറ്റിനടക്കുക

He spends all his day *loitering* around the college campus.

Lonely *(adj.)* ലോൺലി-ഏകാകി, ഉദാസീനനായി

I felt so *lonely* after her departure.

Loner *(n.)* ലോണർ-ഏകാന്ത പ്രിയൻ

He is an eccentric *loner* and never meets anyone.

Long *(adj.)* ലോംഗ്-1. നീ

Draw a line four inches *long.*

(adv.) 2. നേരം, കാലം

How *long* will you be away?

3. നീകാലം

I have not seen you for a *long* time.

(v.) ആഗ്രഹിക്കുക, കൊതിക്കുക

I *long* to go on a holiday.

Look ലുക്-1. നോക്കുക

(v.) Look at this picture.

2. അന്വേഷിക്കുക

Are you *looking* for soneone?

3. തോന്നുക

Sushila *looked* charming at the party.

(n.) There was a *look* of surprise on his face.

Loom *(n.)* ലൂം-1. തറി

(n.) Is this *hand-loom* cloth?

(v.) 2. അവ്യക്തമായി, മങ്ങലോടെ

As we sat on the seashore, a ship *loomed* into sight.

Loop *(n.)* ലൂപ്-വളയം, കുടുക്ക്

She made a *loop* in a rope.

Loose *(adj.)* ലൂസ്-1. അയഞ്ഞ, ശിഥിലമായ

This knot is very *loose,* please make it tight.

2. ഇളക്കം തട്ടുക

One of my teeth is getting *loose.*

Loot ലൂട്ട്-കൊള്ളയടിക്കുക

(v.) The robbers *looted* all the money from the house.

(n.) What was the extent of their *loot?*

Lorry *(v.)* ലോറി-ലോറി, ട്രക്ക്

We hired a *lorry* to move our things to the new house.

Lose *(v.)* ലൂസ്-1. നഷ്ടപ്പെടുക

Do not *lose* this pen.

2. തോല്ക്കുക

Did you *lose* the match?

3. കാണാനോ കേൾക്കാനോ, മനസ്സിലാക്കാനോ, പിടിക്കാനോ കഴിയാതെ പോകുക്

If you do not hurry, you will *lose* the train (the picture/lecture/debate etc).

4. വഴിതെറ്റുക

Have you *lost* your way?

Lost *(adj.)* ലോസ്റ്റ്-ഉണർവില്ലാത്ത, ചിന്താമഗ്നനായ

He looks quite *lost* these days.

Lot ലോട്ട്–1. ഒരു കുന്ന് *(n.)*
The whole *lot* of garments was rejected.
(adv.) 2. വളരെയേറെ
She danced a *lot* at the party.
(det.) 3. ധാരാളം
There are a *lot* of mistakes in your drawing.

Lotion *(n.)* ലോഷൻ–ലോഷൻ
Please give me some *lotion* for the boils on my skin.

Lottery *(n.)* ലോട്ടറി–ഭാഗ്യക്കുറി
Buying and selling of *lottery* tickets is banned in Delhi.

Loud *(adj.)* ലൗഡ്–1. ഉച്ചത്തിൽ, തീവ്രമായി
Do not speak in a *loud* voice.
2. കടുത്ത
I do not like *loud* colours.

Lounge *(n.)* ലൗഞ്ച്–വിശ്രമശാല, ലൗഞ്ച്
We sat in the *lounge* of the hotel.

Lousy *(adj.)* ലൗസി–തീരെ മോശമായ
It was a *lousy* dinner.

Love *(v.&n.)* ലൗ–1. പ്രേമിക്കുക, പ്രണയിക്കുക
(v.) I *love* my children.
2. അഭിരുചി തോന്നുക
I *love* music.
3. ആഗ്രഹിക്കുക, നല്ലതായി തോന്നുക
Do you *love* me, master?
(n.) Love is immortal.

Low *(adj.)* ലോ–1. കുറഞ്ഞ
I got this shirt at a very *low* price.
2. താഴന്ന, അടക്കിയ
Please speak in a *low* voice.
3. താഴ്ചയുള്ള, കുനിഞ്ഞ്
Do not build your house on a *low* ground.
(adv.) He bent *low* to speak to the sick old man.

Loyal *(adj.)* ലോയൽ–കൂറുള്ള, വിശ്വസ്തനായ
Our servant is very *loyal*.

Lubricate ലൂബ്രിക്കേറ്റ്–എണ്ണയിടുക, മയപ്പെടുത്തുക
(v.) You must *lubricate* the engine of your car regularly.
(n.) This machine needs *lubrication*.

Lucid *(adj.)* ലൂസിഡ്–ലളിതം, സരളം
The book is written in a *lucid* style.

Luck *(n.)* ലക്–ഭാഗ്യം, സൗഭാഗ്യം
Good *luck* for your exams.
(adj.) You are *lucky* to win such a nice prize.

Lucrative *(adj.)* ലുക്രേറ്റീവ്–ആദായകരമായ
He got a *lucrative* offer from the rival company.

Luggage *(n.)* ലഗേജ് – പെട്ടികിടക്ക, സാധനങ്ങൾ
Keep an eye on the *luggage* during the journey.

Lullaby *(n.)* ലല്ലബി–താരാട്ട്
I sang a *lullaby* to put my child to sleep.

Luminous *(adj.)* ലൂമിനസ്–പ്രകാശ മാനം, തിളങ്ങുന്ന
My wrist-watch has *luminous* hands.

Lump *(n.)* ലംപ്–1. കൂന, പിബം, കൂട്ടം
I put *lumps* of earth into the flower pot.
2. നീര്, മുഴ
What is this *lump* on your arm?

Lunatic *(n. & adj.)* ലുണാറ്റിക്–ഭ്രാന്തൻ, കിറുക്കൻ
(n.) A great loss in busines turned the businessman into a *lunatic*.
(adj.) We have a *lunatic* asylum in this town.

Lunch ലഞ്ച്–ഉച്ചഭക്ഷണം, ലഞ്ച്
(n.) Have you had your *lunch*?
(v.) I'll *lunch* today with my brother-in-law.

Lung *(n.)* ലംഗ്–ശ്വാസകോശം
Too much smoking would damage your *lungs*.

Lush *(adj.)* ലഷ്–പച്ചച്ച, പച്ചത്തഴപ്പുള്ള
The bungalow was surrounded by *lush* green farms.

Luxury *(n.)* ലക്ഷ്വറി–സുഖഭോഗാവസ്ഥ, സുഖപ്രദമായ
I cannot afford to live in *luxury*.
(adj.) Everybody wants to lead a *luxurious* life.

Lyrics *(n.)* ലിറിക്സ്–ഗാനരചന
I liked the *lyrics* of that song.

M

Machine *(n.)* മഷീൻ-യന്ത്രം, മെഷീൻ
Is this a printing *machine*?
Have you insured the *machinery* in your factory?
My brother-in-law is a *mechanic* in Delhi Cloth Mills.

Mad *(adj.)* മാഡ്-1. ഭ്രാന്ത്, ബുദ്ധിഭ്രമം
Has she gone *mad*?
2. ഉന്മത്തം, ക്രോധം
She felt *mad* when her servant burnt her favourite saree while ironing.
3. വിഡ്ഢിത്തം
The idea of leaving your house for ever is really *mad*.

Maestro *(n.)* മായെസ്ട്രോ-സംഗീതാചാര്യൻ
Jagjit Singh is a great ghazal *maestro*.

Magazine *(n.)* മാഗസീൻ-പത്രിക, മാസിക
The new *magazine* has offered many gifts to its subscribers.

Magic *(n.)* മാജിക്-ജാലവിദ്യ
Many people still believe in *magic*.
Yesterday I took my children to a *magic* show.

Magistrate *(n.)* മജിസ്ട്രേറ്റ്-മജിസ്ട്രേറ്റ്, ന്യായാധിപൻ
I was summoned to the *magistrate's* court to give evidence.

Magnet *(n.)* മാഗ്നറ്റ്-1. കാന്തം
(n.) Her eyes are attractive as a *magnet*.
2. വശ്യശക്തി
(adj.) He has a *magnetic* personality.

Magnificent *(adj.)* മാഗ്നിഫിഷ്യന്റ് -അതീവ ശോഭയുള്ള, മനോഹര
You can get a *magnificent* view of the sea from the terrace of our building.

Magnify *(v.)* മാഗ്നിഫൈ-വലുതാക്കി കാണിക്കുക, സ്ഥൂലീകരിക്കുക
This lens *magnifies* the object fifty times.
Look at this small insect through a *magnifying* glass.

Maid *(n.)* മെയ്ഡ്-വേലക്കാരി, ഭൃത്യ, കുമാരി
Our *house-maid* is honest and industrious.

Mail *(n.)* മെയ്ൽ-തപാൽ
Has the postman delivered today's *mail*?

Mailbox *(n.)* മെയ്ൽബോക്സ്-ഈമെയ് ലിലെ മെയ്ൽ ബോക്സ്
My *mailbox* was full of his mails.

Main *(adj.)* മെയ്ൻ-പ്രധാന, മുഖ്യ
The chief guest was the *main* speaker at the school function.
Does this lane join the *main* road?

Maintain *(v.)* മെയ്ൻടെയ്ൻ-1. പുലർത്തുക, പരിപാലിക്കുക
These days it's difficult to *maintain* a big family.
2. വാദിക്കുക
Do you still *maintain* that you were right?
3. (അറ്റകുറ്റ പണി ചെയ്ത്) നേരെയാക്കുക
The old house costs a great deal to *maintain*.

Majestic *(adj.)* മജസ്റ്റിക്-രാജകീയം
(adj.) The Himalayas are regal and *majestic* mountains.
(n.) The *majesty* of Himalayas is unparalleled.

Major *(adj.)* മേജർ-1. പ്രമുഖ, വലിയ
The soldier spent *major* portion of his life in guarding the country's frontiers.
(n.) 2. പ്രായപൂർത്തിയായ
Is your brother a *major* now?

Make മേക്-1. നിർമ്മിക്കുക, ഉണ്ടാക്കുക
(v.) Please *make* me a cup of tea.
My shirt is *made* of cotton.
2. നിർബന്ധിതമാക്കുക
Please don't *make* me go there.

3. നൽകുക

I have to *make* a speech tomorrow.

(n.) At the showroom, television sets of different *makes* were exhibited.

Malaria *(n.)* മലേറിയ–മലമ്പനി

I was down with *malaria* last month.

Male *(n.)* മെയ്ൽ–പുരുഷൻ, ആൺ

A *male* is supposed to support his family.

(adj.) How many *male* children do you have?

Malice *(n.)* മാലിസ്–പക, വൈരം

She intends no *malice* to anyone, but her language is bad.

Mammoth *(adj.)* മാമത്ത്–ബൃഹത്തായ

Yesterday I attended a *mammoth* public meeting.

Man *(n.)* മാൻ–1. മനുഷ്യൻ

All *men* are mortal.

2. പുരുഷൻ. ജോലിക്കാരൻ

Do you know that *man*?

Has the *milkman* not come yet?

Manage *(v.)* മാനേജ്–1. നിർവഹിക്കുക, നോക്കി നടത്തുക

Who *manages* your business?

2. വിജയിക്കുക, സാദ്ധ്യമാകുക

Can you *manage* to come early?

3. വരുതിയിൽ നിർത്തുക

Would you be able to *manage* such naughty children?

Mandatory *(adj.)* മാൻഡേറ്ററി–അനിവാര്യം

The college authorities made it *mandatory* to submit the original documents at the time of admission.

Mane *(n.)* മെയ്ൻ–സട, ജട, കുതിര കുഞ്ചി

The lion's *mane* was shining in the sun.

Manhole *(n.)* മാൻഹോൾ–മാൻഹോൾ

The people called the Municipal Committee to clean the *manhole.*

Mania *(n.)* മാനിയ–ഉന്മാദം

The IPL *mania* came to an end with Rajasthan Royals taking away the trophy.

Manifest *(v.)* മാനിഫെസ്റ്റ്–പ്രകടമാക്കുക, പ്രത്യക്ഷപ്പെടുക

God always *manifests* Himself in human forms.

Manifold *(adj.)* മാനിഫോൾഡ്–പല മടങ്ങ്

The texture paint complementing the décor increased the beauty of the room *manifold.*

Manipulate *(v.)* മാനിപുലേറ്റ് – വശത്താക്കുക

He is a shrewd politician. He can *manipulate* any situation in his favour.

Mankind *(n.)* മാൻകൈൻഡ്–മാനവരാശി

Pollution is harmful to the whole *mankind.*

Manner *(n.)* മാനർ–രീതി, പ്രകൃതി, തരം

Your friendly *manner* of speaking endears you to all.

Manners *(n.)* മാനേർസ്–മര്യാദ

Your polished *manners* ensure a welcome for you everywhere.

Manor *(n.)* മാനർ–പ്രഭുഭവനം

We have a huge *manor* in our native village.

Manpower *(n.)* മാൻപവർ–ആൾശേഷി, ശ്രമശക്തി

The strength of our company is the skilled *manpower.*

Mansion *(n.)* മാൻഷൻ–മാളിക, മന്ദിരം

We live in an old *mansion* built by our grandfather.

Manual മാനുവൽ–1. കൈപ്പണി, ദേഹണ്ഡം *(adj.)*

Manual labour is very expensive abroad.

2. *(n.)* സംഗ്രഹം, ലഘുപുസ്തകം

This *manual* will teach you different recipes of cheese.

Manufacture *(v.)* മാനുറാക്ചർ – ഉല്പാദിപ്പിക്കുക, നിർമ്മിക്കുക

What articles do you *manufacture* in your factory?

Manure *(n.)* മാന്യൂർ–വളം

The farmer added *manure* to the soil to make it more fertile.

Manuscript *(n.)* മാനുസ്ക്രിപ്റ്റ് – കയ്യെഴുത്തു പ്രതി

Have you sent the *manuscript* to the publishers?

Many *(adj.)* മെനി–അനേകം, പല, ധാരാളം

I met *many* old friends at the party.

Map *(n.)* മാപ്–ഭൂപടം, ആലേഖനം

I want to buy a *map* of India.

Marble *(n.)* മാർബിൾ–1. വെള്ളാരം കല്ല്

Are you using *marble* in the construction of your house?

2. ഗോലി, ഗോട്ടി

My son plays *marbles* with his friends every evening.

March മാർച്ച്–അണിയായി പോകുക, മാർച്ച് ചെയ്യുക

(v.) We stood by the side of the road as the soldiers *marched* past.

(n.) The police barricaded the road to stop the agitationist's *march*.

Mare *(n.)* മെയ്ർ–കുതിര

The *mare* was decorated for the wedding.

Margin *(n.)* മാർജിൻ–അരിക്, കര, ഓരം

Always leave a *margin* when you write.

Marine *(adj.)* മറൈൻ–സമുദ്ര

Oil slick is a threat to *marine* animals.

Marital *(adj.)* മാരിറ്റൽ–വിവാഹ സംബന്ധമായ

What is your *marital* status?

Mark *(n.)* മാർക്–1. നമ്പർ, അക്കം

How many *marks* did you get in Mathematics?

2. അടയാളം, ചിഹ്നം, രേഖപ്പെടുത്തുക

We walked straight till we came to a *mark* indicating right turn.

There is a dirty *mark* on your shirt.

(v.) Vikas and Sonia were *marked* absent.

Market *(n.)* മാർക്കറ്റ്–കമ്പോളം, വില്ക്കുക

(n.) I have to go to the *market* to buy some vegetables.

(v.) Our company *markets* electrical appliances.

Marry *(v.)* മാരി–വിവാഹം ചെയ്യുക, നടത്തുക

I hear Rekha *married* a doctor.

Martial *(adj.)* മാർഷ്യൽ–ആയോധന

He is a professional in *martial* arts.

Martyr *(n.)* മാർട്ടർ–രക്തസാക്ഷി

Have you visited the *martyrs'* memorial in Kolkata?

Marvel മാർവ്ൽ–അത്ഭുതം, ആശ്ചര്യപ്പെടുത്തുക

(n.) Your house is full of *marvels* of technology.

(v.) We *marvel* at the way you help your friends.

(adj.) They had a *marvellous* journey through the Himalayas.

Masculine *(adj.)* മാസ്കുലീൻ – പുരുഷോചിതം, പൗരുഷം

You have a deep, *masculine* voice.

Mash *(v.)* മാഷ്–ഉടയ്ക്കുക, കുഴമ്പാക്കുക

Mash the potatoes and add salt to it.

Mask *(n.)* മാസ്ക്–മുഖംമൂടി

The child frightened his friend by wearing a devil *mask*.

Mason *(n.)* മാസൺ–ആശാരി

We shall have to call a *mason* to repair this wall.

Mass *(n.)* മാസ്–കൂട്ടം

Look at the *mass* of dark clouds, it is about to rain.

Masses *(n.)* മാസസ് – ജനസമൂഹം, ആൾക്കൂട്ടം

Your speeches have the power to move the *masses*.

Massacre *(n.)* മാസകർ–കൂട്ടക്കൊല

No Indian would ever forget the Jallianwala *massacre* of 1919.

Massage മസാജ്–തിരുമ്മൽ, ഉഴിച്ചിൽ

(n.) An oil *massage* will relax your tired body.

(v.) *Massage* your hair well.

Massive *(adj.)* മാസീവ്–ബൃഹത്തായ, വിപുലമായ

What is this *massive* machine supposed to do?

Master *(n.)* മാസ്റ്റർ–1. ഉടമ, അധികാരി, അദ്ധ്യാപകൻ

Is your *master* at home?

(v.) 2. സ്വായത്തമാക്കുക

Have you *mastered* this subject?

Masterpiece *(n.)* മാസ്റ്റർപീസ് – അതിശ്രേഷ്ഠമായ സൃഷ്ടി

Taj Mahal is a *masterpiece* of architecture.

Mat *(n.)* മാറ്റ്–പായ്, തടുക്ക്
We should get a new *mat* for our room.

Match *(n.)* മാച്ച്–1. തീപ്പെട്ടി
Where is the *match-box*?
2. മാച്ച്, മത്സരം
Will you accompany me to the cricket *match*?
(adj.) 3. ജോഡി, അനുരൂപമായ, ചേരുന്ന
You are dressed in *matching* colours.
(v.) These colours do not *match*.

Mate *(n.)* മേറ്റ്–1. പങ്കാളി, സഹപാഠി
Anil is my *class-mate.*
2. ഭാര്യാഭർത്താക്കന്മാർ, ജോഡി
We want a *mate* for our parrot.

Material *(n.)* മറ്റീരിയൽ–1. സാധനം, ചരക്ക്
Have you got all the *material* for making a kite?
2. വസ്ത്രം
Will you please show me some good-quality dress *material*?

Maternal *(adj.)* മറ്റേണൽ–തായ്‌വഴി, മാതൃ
She was taken over by *maternal* instincts and refused to send her child to the hostel.

Matrimony *(n.)* മട്രിമണി–ദാമ്പത്യാവസ്ഥ
After facing a lot many problems, they finally entered the *matrimony.*

Matron *(n.)* മേട്രൺ–മേട്രൺ
The *matron* scolded the hostellers who arrived late in the night.

Matter *(n.)* മാറ്റർ–1. വിഷയം
I want to discuss an important *matter* with you.
2. കാര്യം
What is the *matter* with you?
(v.) 3. പ്രാധാന്യം നൽകുക
It *matters* a great deal.

Mattress *(n.)* മാട്രസ്–കിടക്ക, മെത്ത
What is the price of this foam rubber *mattress*?

Mature *(adj.)* മച്യൂർ–പക്വത
She is *mature* enough to solve this problem at her end.

Maverick *(n.)* മാവറിക്–അസാധാരണ വ്യക്തി
Vijay Tendulkar was a *maverick* in the field of Indian theatre.

Maxim *(n.)* മാക്സിം–പ്രമാണം, സൂത്രം
Follow the *maxim* – boss is always right – and you will never be unhappy in your job.

Maximum *(adj.)* മാക്സിമം–പരമാവധി
What is the *maximum* number of people that you invite to your parties?

May *(v.)* മേ–1. ആകാം, (സമ്മതം) ഉാവുക
May I go home now?
I *may* go to Mumbai next month.
You *may* take these clothes to the dry cleaner.
2. ആശിർവാദ രൂപത്തിൽ
May he live long!
3. മേയ് മാസം
(n.) My birthday is on the 1st of *May.*

Mayor *(n.)* മേയർ–മേയർ
He defeated the old *mayor* by just a few votes.

Maze *(n.)* മേസ്–നൂലാമാല
I am caught up in the *maze* of my own problems.

Meagre *(adj.)* മീഗർ–അല്പമാത്രം
Why did you agree to work for such a *meagre* amount?

Meal *(n.)* മീൽ–ഭക്ഷണം
What time do you have your *meal*?

Mean *(v.)* മീൻ–1. അർത്ഥമാക്കുക
Do you really *mean* what you say?
2. അർത്ഥം, അഭിപ്രായം
Tell me what these words *mean* in Sanskrit.
(adj.) 3. മോശമായ, തരംതാണ
Never be *mean-minded.*

Meaning *(n.)* മീനിംഗ്–1. അർത്ഥം
Did you understand the *meaning* of this line?
2. സാർത്ഥകം, അർത്ഥവത്താകുക
Theatre gives *meaning* to my life.

Means *(n.)* മീൻസ്–1. സമ്പത്ത്, വരുമാനം
You are a man of various *means.*

2. ഉപായം, സാധനം
By what *means* did he climb the wall?

Meanwhile *(adj.)* മീൻവൈൽ – ഇതിനിടയ്ക്ക്, അതിനോടകം
You write the letter, *meanwhile* I will get a stamp.

Measles *(n.)* മീസിൽസ്–അഞ്ചാംപനി
The scientists have developed a vaccine for *measles.*

Measure *(v.)* മെഷർ–1. അളക്കുക
Please *measure* the length and breadth of this sheet.
(n.) 2. ഉപായം, നടപടി
New *measures* have been taken to prevent theft and cheating.

Meat *(n.)* മീറ്റ്–മാംസം, ഇറച്ചി
Go to the butcher's shop and buy some *meat.*

Mechanic *(n.)* മെക്കാനിക്–മേസ്തിരി, മെക്കാനിക്
Call a *mechanic* to repair this typewriter.
Manoj is interested in the *mechanism* of television.

Medal *(n.)* മെഡൽ–പതക്കം, മെഡൽ
I hear your son got a gold *medal* for his essay.

Meddle *(n.)* മെഡ്ൽ–തലയിടുക, ഇടപെടുക
We should not *meddle* in other people's affairs.

Medicine *(n.)* മെഡിസിൻ–മരുന്ന്, ഔഷധം
What *medicine* has the doctor prescribed for your fever?
(adj.) There are a number of good *medical* colleges in India.

Mediocre *(adj.)* മിഡീയോകർ–സാമാന്യ നിലവാരമുള്ള, ഇടത്തരം
We don't want *mediocre* performers in our team.

Meditate *(v.)* മെഡിറ്റേറ്റ്–ചിന്തനം ചെയ്യുക
He has been *meditating* upon a workable solution over the past one week.

Medium മീഡിയം–1. ശരാശരി, ഇടത്തരം
I have *medium*-length hair.
(n.) 2. മാദ്ധ്യമം
News channels are a faster *medium* than newspapers.

Medley *(n.)* മെഡ്‌ലി–സമ്മിശ്ര ഗാനം
They danced on the *medley* of Kishore Kumar songs.

Meek *(adj.)* മീക്–വിനീതം, താഴ്മയുള്ള
You cannot forge ahead it you are too *meek.*

Meet മീറ്റ്–1. കൂടിക്കാണുക
Where shall we *meet* tomorrow?
2. സമ്മേളിക്കുക, ഒത്തുചേരുക
Does this lane *meet* the main road?
3. പണമടയ്ക്കുക
Can you not *meet* my bill until next month?
(n.) 4. യോഗം
Will you attend the *meeting*?

Melancholy *(adj.)* മെലങ്കളി–ഉദാസീനത, ദുഃഖം
Why are you in such a *melancholy* mood?

Melody *(n.)* മെലഡി–1. ലയം, രാഗം
I shall now sing you an Indian classical *melody.*
2. സ്വരമാധുരി
We hear the *melody* of singing birds in the morning.
(adj.) You voice is so *melodious.*

Melt *(n.)* മെൽറ്റ്–ഉരുകുക, ഉരുക്കുക, ദ്രവമാകുക
I *melted* the butter to make ghee out of it.
The snow *melted* when the sun came out.
My heart *melted* when I saw the beggar's plight.

Member *(n.)* മെമ്പർ–അംഗം, അംഗത്വം
Will you become a *member* of our club?
Have you renewed your club *membership*?

Memento *(n.)* മമെന്റോ–സ്മരണിക, സ്മൃതിചിഹ്നം
The chief guest was presented a *memento* at the function.

Memo *(n.)* മെമ്മോ–കുറ്റപത്രം
He was issued a *memo* for arriving late in the office every day.

Memory *(n.)* മെമ്മറി–1. ഓർമ്മശക്തി
She has a sharp *memory.*

2. സ്മരണ, ഓർമ്മ
I have happy *memories* of my first visit to America.
(v.) We must *memorise* our parts till the next rehearsal of the play.

Menace *(n.)* മെനസ്-അപകടം, വിപത്ത്, അപകടപ്പെടുത്തുക, ഭീക്ഷണിപ്പെടുത്തുക
(n.) Don't drive in such a way that you become a *menace* to pedestrians.
(v.) It is *menacing* to cross a highway amid speeding trucks.

Mend *(v.)* മെൻഡ്-അറ്റകുറ്റം തീർക്കുക, നേരെയാക്കുക
Cobbler, cobbler, *mend* my shoe!
We will have to *mend* our fence.
Mend your ways if you want to improve your financial condition.

Menial *(adj.)* മീനിയൽ - താഴേക്കിടയിലുള്ള
No one likes to do the *menial* jobs, but some people just don't have a choice.

Mental *(adj.)* മെന്റൽ-1. മാനസിക ചികിത്സാലയം, ഭ്രാന്താശുപത്രി
Is there a *mental*-hospital in your city?
2. മാനസികമായി, മനോവൃത്തി
By *mental* effort, we can remember the details of past happenings.
(adv.) I was *mentally* unprepared for such a situation.
(n.) You have an unusual *mentality* if you do not like any game.

Mention *(n.)* മെൻഷൻ-സൂചന, പരാമർശം
There was *mention* of poor boy's bravery in the article.
(v.) You may *mention* my name to him.

Mentor *(n.)* മെന്റർ-ഉപദേഷ്ടാവ്
He is my *mentor* in singing.

Menu *(n.)* മെനു-വിഭവ പട്ടിക, മെനു
Waiter, please bring the *menu.*

Merchant *(n.)* മെർച്ചന്റ്-വ്യാപാരി, കടക്കാരൻ
My uncle is a wholesale grain *merchant.*

Mercy *(n.)* മെഴ്സി-ദയ, കരുണ
Oh God, have *mercy* on us!

Mere *(adj.)* മിയർ-വെറും, കേവലം
You are still a *mere* kid.

Merely *(adj.)* മിയർലി-കേവലം, മാത്രം, വെറും
I *merely* want to give her a little advice.

Merge *(v.)* മെർജ്-ലയിക്കുക, വിലയം കൊള്ളുക
The large waves in the sea *merged* into each other.

Merit *(n.)* മെരിറ്റ്-യോഗ്യത
The admission in this course will be strictly on *merit* basis.

Mermaid *(n.)* മെർമെയ്ഡ്-ജലകന്യക
The child bought the book The Little *Mermaid.*

Merry *(adj.)* മെറി-1. ആഹ്ലാദ, പ്രസന്ന
Wish you a *merry* Christmas!
2. പ്രസന്നചിത്ത, മതിമറന്ന
The *merry* laughter of children cheers up all.

Mess *(n.)* മെസ്-1. താറുമാറായ
You will have to clear up this *mess* before you leave from here.
2. മെസ്, ഭോജനാലയം
Do you take your food from a *mess*?

Message *(n.)* മെസ്സേജ്-സന്ദേശം
Please give him this *message.*

Messiah *(n.)* മെസയാ-രക്ഷകൻ
He really proved to be a *messiah* for us in the middle of that chaos.

Metal *(n.)* മെറ്റൽ-ലോഹം
Of what *metal* are these articles made?

Method *(n.)* മെഥെഡ്-രീതി, മാർഗ്ഗം, ക്രമം
By what *method* will you solve this sum?

Mew *(v.)* മ്യൂ-മ്യാവൂ (പൂച്ച കരയുക)
I hear a cat *mewing* outside the door.

Microphone *(n.)* മൈക്രോഫോൺ-മൈക്ക്, ഉച്ചഭാഷിണി
We could not hear your speech, as the *microphone* was not working properly.

Microscope *(n.)* മൈക്രോസ്കോപ് - സൂക്ഷ്മദർശിനി
I could inspect the tiny insect only through a *microscope.*

Midday *(n.)* മിഡ്ഡേ-മദ്ധ്യാഹ്നം
I'll finish this work by *midday.*

Middle മിഡിൽ-1. മദ്ധ്യ, ഇടയ്ക്കുള്ള
(n.) Don't disturb me in the *middle* of my work.
There was a pillar in the *middle* of the room.

(adj.) 2. മദ്ധ്യവയസ്കൻ
Who is that *middle-aged* gentleman?

Might *(n.)* മൈറ്റ്–1. ശക്തി, സാമർത്ഥ്യം
I tried with all my *might* to move the heavy load.
2. May യുടെ ഭൂതകാലം
He *might* have returned home.

Migrate *(v.)* മൈഗ്രേറ്റ്–പ്രവാസിയാകുക, നാടു വിടുക
Both his sons have *migrated* to the foreign country in search of better opportunities.

Mild *(adj.)* മൈൽഡ്–1. നേർത്ത, സൗമ്യ, ശാന്ത
You always speak in a *mild* manner.
2. സുഖമുള്ള
The weather is *mild* today.
3. നിസ്സാരമായ
It was the first offence of that woman, so she was given a *mild* sentence.

Mile *(n.)* മൈൽ–നാഴിക, മൈൽ
I walk a couple of *miles* every morning.

Military *(adj.&n.)* മിലിട്ടറി–സൈനിക, സേന, പട്ടാളം
(adj.) Do you get *military* training in your school?
(n.) Strict discipline is followed in the *military*.

Milk *(n.)* മിൽക്ക്–പാൽ
I take a glass of *milk* every morning.

Mill *(n.)* മിൽ–ഫാക്ടറി, പൊടിക്കൽശാല, മിൽ
How many textile *mills* are there in your city?

Millennium *(n.)* മിലേനിയം–സഹസ്രാബ്ദം
Amitabh Bachchan was awarded with the title of the star of the *millennium*.

Million *(adj.)* മില്യൺ–ദശലക്ഷം
The tennis champion earned *millions* of dollars.
I learn your guest is a *millionaire*.

Mince *(v.)* മിൻസ്–കൊത്തി അരിയുക, നുറുക്കുക
I want to buy half a kilogram of *minced* meat.

Mind *(n.)* മൈൻഡ്–1. മനസ്സ്
Is your *mind* in your job?
2. നിശ്ചയം, ഉദ്ദേശം
I thought I would return the same day but now I have changed my *mind*.
(v.) 3. കാര്യമാക്കുക, വിഷമിക്കുക
Don't *mind* what he says. Never *mind*.
4. പരിപാലിക്കുക
Who *minds* your child when you are away?
5. വിഷമം തോന്നുക
Would you *mind* if I smoke?

Mine മൈൻ–1. എന്റെ
(pron.) That book is yours, this one is *mine*.
(n.) 2. ഖനി
During our tour to Bihar, we visited a coal *mine*.

Mingle *(v.)* മിംഗ്ൾ–സമ്മേളിക്കുക, കൂട്ടം ചേരുക
Some policemen in plain clothes *mingled* with the crowd.
I like to *mingle* with all sorts of people.

Miniature *(n.)* മിനിയച്ചർ–ലഘുരൂപം
She made a *miniature* of Hawa Mahal.

Minimum *(adj.)* മിനിമം – ഏറ്റവും കുറഞ്ഞ, ചുരുങ്ങിയ
The trade union demanded an increase in the *minimum* wages.
Who promlses to give tho maximum value at the *minimum* price?

Minister *(n.)* മിനിസ്റ്റർ–മന്ത്രി
A close friend of mine has now become a *minister* in the cabinet.

Minor *(adj.)* മൈനർ–1. ചെറിയ, നിസ്സാര
Don't bother me about such *minor* matters.
(n.) 2. പ്രായപൂർത്തിയാകാത്ത, ചെറിയ പ്രായത്തിലുള്ള
My son can't vote, as he is still a *minor*.

Minus മൈനസ്–1. ന്യൂന
(n.) Arithmetic begins with plus and *minus*.
(prep.) 2. കൂടാതെ, ഇല്ലാതെ
Why have you come *minus* your cap?
As I arrived at my office, I found that I was *minus* my golden chain.

Minute മിനിട്ട്/മൈന്യൂട്ട്–1. മിനിട്ട്, നിമിഷം, ക്ഷണം, മെമ്മോ, നോട്ട്
(n.) I can do this job in ten *minutes*.

(*adj.*) സൂക്ഷ്മം, അതിസൂക്ഷ്മം
I did not notice the *minute* specks of dirt on my specs.
(*adv.*) The advocate studied the case *minutely*.

Miracle (*n.*) മിറാക്ക്ൾ-അത്ഭുതം, ചമത്കാരം
As a *miracle,* most of the passengers were saved when their bus fell into a gorge.
(*adj.*) Yesterday I was involved in an accident but had a *miraculous* escape.

Mirage (*n.*) മിറാജ്-മരീചിക
Don't pursue the dream of making a place in film industry; it's just a *mirage.*

Mirror (*n.*) മിറർ-നിലക്കണ്ണാടി
Who broke the *mirror*?

Mirth (*n.*) മെർത്ത്-ഉല്ലാസം, വിനോദം
There was an atmosphere of *mirth* in the house.

Misapprehension (*n.*) മിസപ്രിഹെൻഷൻ - തെറ്റിദ്ധാരണ
He had this *misapprehension* that the house belonged to Mrs. Reynolds.

Miscellaneous (*adj.*) മിസലേനിയസ് - പലവക, വിവിധ
The box was full of *miscellaneous* sports instruments.

Mischief (*n.*) മിസ്ചീഫ്-1. കുസൃതി, വികൃതി
My youngest son is always up to some *mischief.*
(*adj.*) A *mischievous* boy drew a cartoon on the blackboard.
(*n.*) 2. ദോഷം
You are too late, the *mischief* is done.

Miser (*n.*) മൈസർ-ലുബ്ധൻ, പിശുക്കൻ
Some rich poeple behave like *misers.*
(*adj.*) I do not like people with *miserly* habits.

Misery (*n.*) മിസറി-ദുർദശ, കഷ്ടപ്പാട്, ദുഃഖം
I have seen people live in great *misery* because of poverty.
(*adj.*) Why do you look so *miserable*?

Misfit (*n.*) മിസ്ഫിറ്റ്-അനുയോജ്യമല്ലാത്ത വ്യക്തി
Being the youngest one, she often felt she was a *misfit* in the organisation.

Mishap (*n.*) മിസഹാപ്-നിസ്സാരമായ അപകടം
She passed off falling from stairs as a small *mishap.*

Mislead (*v.*) മിസ്ലീഡ്-വഴിതെറ്റിക്കുക, തെറ്റിധരിപ്പിക്കുക
(*v.*) The advertisements of fairness creams *mislead* the masses.
(*adj.*) The advertisements of fairness creams are *misleading.*

Misprint (*n.*) മിസ്പ്രിന്റ്-അച്ചടിപിശക്
The document was full of *misprints.*

Miss (*v.*) മിസ്-1, കൈവിട്ടു പോകുക, കിട്ടാതിരിക്കുക
If you do not hurry, you will *miss* the train.
2. അസാന്നിദ്ധ്യം അനുഭവപ്പെടുക
We shall all *miss* you when you go away.
3. കാണാനോ കേൾക്കാനോ ചെയ്യാനോ കഴിയാതിരിക്കുക
I learnt she was at the party but I *missed* her.
4. കാണാതാവുക
One of my books is *missing.*
(*n.*) 5. കുമാരി
What is your name, *miss*?

Missile (*n.*) മിസൈൽ-മിസൈൽ
The nuclear *missile* destroyed the whole city.

Mission (*n.*) മിഷൻ-1. സ്ഥാനപതി കാര്യാലയം
Are you working with the poor Indian *mission* in the USA?
2. ദൗത്യം
I was sent on a *mission* to Sri Lanka.
3. ജീവിത ലക്ഷ്യം
Spreading education among the poor is the *mission* of my life.

Missionary (*n.*) മിഷിനറി-മതപ്രചാരകൻ
The school was established by some Christian *missionaries.*

Mist (*n.*) മിസ്റ്റ്-മൂടൽമഞ്ഞ്
I did not go for my morning walk because of the *mist.*

Mistake മിസ്റ്റേക്-1. തെറ്റ്, അബദ്ധം (ചെയ്യുക)

(n.) You have made a *mistake* in this sentence.

I took your book by *mistake.*

(v.) 2. തെറ്റിദ്ധരിക്കുക

I *mistook* you for your younger brother.

Misunderstand *(v.)* മിസ് അർസ്റ്റാൻഡ് - തെറ്റായി മനസ്സിലാക്കുക

I completely *misunderstood* what he said.

Misuse മിസ്യൂസ്-ദുരുപയോഗം ചെയ്യുക

(n.) It was a clear case of *misuse* of power.

(v.) He was accused of *misusing* the funds of the company.

Mite *(n.)* മൈറ്റ്-പാറ്റ, പുഴു

She sprayed the insecticide to kill the *mites.*

Mitigate *(v.)* മിറ്റിഗേറ്റ്-ദോഷം, കുറയ്ക്കുക, ഇല്ലാതാക്കുക

Plantation of trees *mitigated* the effects of soil erosion.

Mix *(v.)* മിക്സ്-1. കലർത്തുക ചേർക്കുക

Sita *mixed* some water in orange squash to make a cold drink.

2. ഇടപഴകുക

You are good at *mixing* with people.

(adj.) 3. ചിന്താകുഴപ്പത്തിലാകുക

You are all *mixed* up.

(n.) Water is a *mixture* of hydrogen and oxygen.

Moan മോൺ-ഞരങ്ങുക

(v.) Are you in pain? You were *moaning* in your sleep.

(n.) The wounded man's *moans* could be heard all night.

Mob *(n.)* മോബ്-1. ഇളകിയ ജനക്കൂട്ടം, പൊതുജനം

From my window, I saw the police firing in the air to disperse the riotous *mob.*

(v.) 2. വളയുക, ശല്യപ്പെടുത്തുക

As we stood outside the theatre, we saw the popular film star being *mobbed* by his fans.

Mobile *(adj.)* മൊബൈൽ-ചലിക്കുന്ന, സഞ്ചരിക്കുന്ന

We have a *mobile* post office in our city.

Mock *(v.)* മോക്-1. അപഹസിക്കുക, കളിയാക്കുക

If I fail, my friends would *mock* at me.

(adj.) 2. കൃത്രിമ, അനുകരണാത്മക

Have you ever participated in a *mock* Parliament?

Model *(adj.)* മോഡൽ-1. മാതൃക

I bought a *model* aeroplane for my son.

Please show me the *model* of the proposed hospital building.

2. ആദർശ

Your son is a *model* student.

(n.) 3. മോഡൽ

I learn your daughter is working as a *model.*

(v.) 4. അനുകരിക്കുക

She is *modelling* herself on her aunt.

Moderate *(v.)* മോഡറേറ്റ്-1. അടക്കമുള്ള, ശാന്തമായ, ആഗ്രഹങ്ങൾ ഒതുക്കിയ

If you *moderate* your demands a little, the firm may be able to concede them.

2. ശമിക്കുക

Now the storm is *moderating.*

(adj.) 3. മിതമായ

I like the *moderate* weather of your town.

Modern *(adj.)* മോഡേർൺ-ആധുനിക, നവീന

You should always have a *modern* outlook in life.

Modest *(adj.)* മോഡസ്റ്റ്-1. വിനീത, വിനയ ശീലമുള്ള

The *modest* behaviour of Sushila impressed everyone at the party.

2. മിതമായ, നിസ്സാര

I paid a *modest* price for this embroidered table-cloth.

Moist *(adj.)* മോയിസ്റ്റ്-നനഞ്ഞ, കുതിർന്ന

Dry your *moist* hands with this towel.

Moment *(n.)* മോമെന്റ് -നിമിഷം, ക്ഷണം

Getting the Nobel Prize is the happiest *moment* of any scientist.

Our friend should be here any *moment.*

(adj.) It will be just *momentary* pain.

Monastery *(n.)* മൊണാസ്ട്രി-മഠം
The monks were resting in the *monastery*.

Money *(n.)* മണി-രൂപ, പണം
Can you lend me some *money*?

Monitor *(n.)* മോണിട്ടർ-വിദ്യാർത്ഥി നായകൻ, മോണിട്ടർ
My son has been made the *monitor* of his class.

Monk *(n.)* മോങ്ക്-സന്യാസി
The *monks* helped the wounded man they found.

Monopoly *(n.)* മൊണോപളി-കുത്തക
The company has a *monopoly* in garment making.

Monotony *(n.)* മൊണോട്ടണി-വിരസത, മുഷിവ്
(n.) The atmosphere in a call centre is shrouded with *monotony*.
(adj.) Working in call centres often tends to become *monotonous*.

Monsoon *(n.)* മൺസൂൺ-കാലവർഷം
Now that the *monsoon* is near, we must repair our leaking roof.

Monster *(n.)* മോൺസ്റ്റർ-ചെകുത്താൻ
These kids are little *monsters*.

Month *(n.)* മൻത്-മാസം
I have not come to you for a *month*.
(adj.) Is this a *monthly* magazine?

Monument *(n.)* മോണുമെന്റ്-സ്മാരകം, കീർത്തി സ്തംഭം
Have you seen all the old *monuments* in Delhi?

Mood *(n.)* മൂഡ്-മനോനില, മനസ്ഥിതി
The boss seems to be in a happy *mood* today.
I want to speak to him when he is in a better *mood*.

Moon *(n.)* മൂൺ-ചന്ദ്രൻ
Look at the full *moon*!

Mop *(n.)* മോപ്-ചൂല്, തുടയ്ക്കുന്ന തുണി
Ask the maid-servant to clean the floor with a *mop*.
(v.) a

Moral *(adj.)* മോറൽ-1. ധാർമ്മിക, സാന്മാർഗ്ഗിക, സദാചാര
We should try to lead a *moral* life.
(n.) 2. ശിക്ഷ, ഗുണപാഠം
What is the *moral* of this story?

More മോർ-കൂടുതൽ, അധികം
(adj.) Put *more* milk in this cup.
I have *more* pencils than pens.
(adv.) You must walk *more* briskly.

Morning *(n.)* മോണിംഗ്-പ്രഭാതം, രാവിലെ
At what time do you get up in the *morning*?

Morsel *(n.)* മോർസൽ-ഒരുപിടി
I pitied the beggar entreating everyone for a *morsel* of food.

Mortal മോർട്ടൽ-മനുഷ്യൻ, മർത്യൻ
(adj.) All men are *mortal*.
No *mortal* can expect to live longer than a hundred years.

Mortgage *(n.)* മോർട്ട്ഗേജ്-പണയപ്പെടുത്തുക
They *mortgaged* their house to send their son abroad.

Mosque *(n.)* മോസ്ക്-മുസ്ലീം പള്ളി
The *mosque* was beautifully decorated on Eid.

Mosquito *(n.)* മസ്കിറ്റോ-കൊതുക്
Mosquitoes breed in the stagnant water.

Moss *(n.)* മോസ്-പായൽ
Don't swim in that lake, it is full of *moss*.

Most *(adj. & adv.)* മോസ്റ്റ്-1. ഏറ്റവുമധികം, അത്യധികം
(adv.) Whick book do you find the *most* interesting?
(adj.) മിക്ക, ഏറെക്കുറെ എല്ലാ
Most of my friends are science students.

Moth *(n.)* മോത്ത്-തുണി തിന്നുന്ന പുഴു
These naphthalene balls will protect your clothes from *moths*.

Mother *(n.)* മദർ-അമ്മ, മാതാവ്
The *mother* picked up the child in her arms.

Mother-tongue *(n.)* മദർടംഗ്-മാതൃഭാഷ
What is your *mother-tongue*?

Motif *(n.)* മോട്ടിഫ്-ഏതെങ്കിലും പ്രത്യേക ചിത്രം
Each chapter in the book started with a *motif* related to Lord Krishna.

Motion *(n.)* മോഷൻ–1. ഗതി. ചലനം
You must not open the door of the compartment while the train is in *motion.*
2. പ്രമേയം, നിർദ്ദേശം
Was your *motion* carried in the meeting?

Motive *(n.)* മോട്ടീവ്–ലക്ഷ്യം, പ്രയോജനം
What was your *motive* in telling me a lie?

Motto *(n.)* മോട്ടോ–ആപ്തവാക്യം
The *motto* of my life is — Never despair!

Mould മോൾഡ്–1. കുഴയ്ക്കുക, മൂശയിടുക
(v.) If you want to become a sculptor, you must first learn how to *mould* clay.
(n.) 2. മൂശ, അച്ച്
Get me the star-shaped *mould*; I'll prepare cookies.
3. പൂപ്പൽ
Don't eat that bread, it is full of *mould.*

Mound *(v.)* മൗ്–കുന്ന്, കയറ്റം
My children like to climb a *mound* near our house.

Mount *(v.)* മൗ്–1. കയറുക, സവാരി ചെയ്യുക
Can you *mount* a horse?
2. ഫ്രെയിമിടുക
Please *mount* my photographs with silver frames.
3. വർദ്ധിക്കുക, പെരുകുക
Don't you think that your debts are *mounting* up?

Mountain *(n.)* മൗിൻ–പർവ്വതം, മല
Next summer, I shall go trekking in the *mountains.*
(adj.) Nepal is a *mountainous* country.

Mourn *(v.)* മോൺ–അനുശോചിക്കുക, ദുഃഖമാചരിക്കുക
We all *mourned* the death of our kind neighbour.

Mouse *(n.)* മൗസ്–എലി
I want to buy a *mouse*-trap.

Moustache *(n.)* മുസ്റ്റാഷ്–മീശ
He had long and bushy *moustache* like that of Veerappan.

Mouth *(n.)* മൗത്ത്–1. വായ, മുഖം
Always keep your *mouth* clean.
2. നദീമുഖം
We went on a trip in a launch up to the *mouth* of the river.

Move *(v.)* മൂവ്–1. നീക്കം ചെയ്യുക, മാറ്റുക
Who has *moved* my cot?
2. വന്നുപോകുക, നടക്കുക
From my seat, I watched the guests *moving* about the hall.
3. വീടോ സ്ഥലമോ മാറുക
We *moved* from Mumbai to Delhi many years ago.
4. വികാരധീനരാകുക, പ്രേരിതരാകുക
We were *moved* to tears by his sad story.

Movie *(n.)* മൂവി–ചലച്ചിത്രം, സിനിമ
Let's go out for a *movie.*

Moving *(adj.)* മൂവിംഗ്–ഹൃദയസ്പർശി
The scene of the mother rushing to the hospitals with her ill child was very *moving.*

Mow *(v.)* മോ–വെട്ടുക, ചെത്തി നിരപ്പാക്കുക
Has the gardener *mowed* the lawn?

Much *(pron.)* മച്ച്–വളരെ, ഏറെ
How *much* did you pay for this pen?
(adj.) Is there *much* water in the jug?
(adv.) Thank you very *much.*

Mud *(n.)* മഡ്–ചെളി
Take care Rakesh, lest you would fall in the *mud.*
Don't bring your *muddy* shoes into the room.

Muddle മഡ്ൽ–സർവ്വത്ര കുഴപ്പം, താറുമാറ്
(n.) Everything in the house was in a *muddle.*
(v.) If your mind is *muddled,* you cannot think clearly.

Mug *(n.)* മഗ്–കോപ്പ
I like to drink coffee from a *mug.*

Multiply *(v.)* മൾട്ടിപ്ലൈ–1. ഗുണിക്കുക
If we *multiply* 4 by 6, the result is 24.
2. വർദ്ധിപ്പിക്കുക, ഇരട്ടിക്കുക
Flies *multiply* fast.
(n.) Have you learnt *multiplication*?

Multitude *(n.)* മൾട്ടിട്യൂഡ്-കൂട്ടം, പൊതുജനം

I was impressed by the *multitude* of people at yesterday's public meeting.

Mumble *(v.)* മംബ്ൾ-പിറുപിറുക്കുക, പുലമ്പുക

The child was *mumbling* in the sleep.

Munch *(v.)* മഞ്ച്-ഒച്ചയോടെ കഴിക്കുക

We watched the movie *munching* on popcorn.

Mundane *(adj.)* മന്റേൻ-നിസ്സാര

Stop musing over these *mundane* issues.

Municipal *(adj.)* മുൻസിപ്പൽ-നഗര സഭ, മുൻസിപ്പൽ

Are you a candidate for the coming *municipal* elections?

Murder മർഡർ-കൊലപാതകം, കൊല ചെയ്യുക

(v.) The young girl was *murdered* at midnight.

(n.) Has the police caught the *murderer*?

Who was accused of the *murder*?

Murmur മർമ്മർ-മുറുമുറുക്കുക, അടക്കം പറയുക

(n.) When I entered the room, the *murmur* of conversation stopped.

(v.) She *murmured* but no one heard what she said.

Muscle *(n.)* മസൽ-മാംസപേശി

We should work manually to strengthen our *muscles*.

(adj.) I have *muscular* pain in the left arm.

Museum *(n.)* മ്യൂസിയം-കാഴ്ചബംഗ്ലാവ്, മ്യൂസിയം

Have you seen the Salar Jang *museum* of Hyderabad?

Music *(n.)* മ്യൂസിക്-സംഗീതം

I love *music* very much but I am not skilled in it.

(adj.) Which *musical* instrument do you play?

Muslin *(n.)* മസ്ലിൻ-മൽമൽ

Is your frock made of *muslin*?

Must മസ്റ്റ്-തീർച്ചയായും, അവശ്യവസ്തു

(v.) It is very late, I *must* go home now.

(n.) This book is a *must* for every student of history.

Mute *(adj.)* മ്യൂട്ട്-മൂകൻ, നിശ്ശബ്ദ

(adj.) He is *mute* by birth.

(adj.) She replied with a nasty smile; it was a *muted* reaction.

Mutiny *(n.)* മ്യൂട്ടണി-കലാപം

The Revolt of 1857 was dismissed by the British as a sepoy *mutiny*.

Mutter *(v.)* മട്ടർ-കുശുകുശുക്കുക, പിറുപിറുക്കുക

What are you *muttering* under you breath?

Mutton *(n.)* മട്ടൺ-ആട്ടിറച്ചി

I went to the butcher's shop to buy some *mutton*.

Mutual *(adj.)* മ്യൂച്ചൽ-പരസ്പരം

Mutual understanding is necessary to keep a relationship alive.

Muzzle *(v.)* മസ്ൽ-വായ് മൂടിക്കെട്ടുക

You should *muzzle* your ferocious dog.

2. അടക്കുക, നിയന്ത്രിക്കുക

How can democracy survive when the Press is *muzzled*?

3. തോക്കിന്റെ ദ്വാരം

Be careful while cleaning the *muzzle* of the gun.

Mystery *(n.)* മിസ്റ്ററി-രഹസ്യം, ഗൂഢത

The detective novel ended with the solving of the murder *mystery*.

Mystical *(adj.)* മിസ്റ്റികൽ-ഗഹനമായ

She has a pair of *mystical* eyes.

Myth മിത്ത്-1. കല്പിത കഥ

(n.) Some consider the story of Lord Rama a *myth*, while some find it genuine.

(adj.) Bakasura was a *mythical* demon with a crane's body.

2. പുരാണ കഥ

(n.) The Hindu *mythology* talks about numerous gods and goddesses.

(adj.) She loves to hear *mythological* stories from her grandmother.

N

Nag *(v.)* നാഗ്-പിന്നാലെ കൂടി ശല്യം ചെയ്യുക, തല പറിക്കുക

Don't *nag* your servant so much.

Nail നെയ്ൽ-1. ആണി, ആണി തറയ്ക്കുക

(v.) *Nail* a new board on the wall.

(n.) Hang this picture on that *nail.*

2. നഖം

Always keep your *nails* clean.

Never bite your *nails.*

Naive *(adj.)* നായ്‌വ്-നിഷ്കപട, ശുദ്ധഗതി

(adj.) Don't be so *naive* to work for free.

(n.) They laughed at her for her *naivety.*

Naked *(adj.)* നേക്കഡ്-1. നഗ്ന

I pitied the *naked* child in the arms of the beggar.

2. തുറന്ന, അനാവൃത

Was fire caused by the *naked* electric wireɔ?

Name നെയിം-1. പേര്, പേരിടുക

(v.) Whatever you want, just *name* it.

2. പ്രശസ്തി, പേരെടുക്കുക

(n.) What is your *name*?

I am sure your son will make a *name* for himself.

Nap *(n.)* നാപ്-കുട്ടിയുറക്കം, മയക്കം

Do you take a *nap* after lunch?

Naphthalene *(n.)* നാഫ്തലീൻ-പാറ്റ ഗുളിക

I put some *naphthalene* balls in the woollens to protect them from insects.

Napkin *(n.)* നാപ്കിൻ-നാപ്കിൻ, കൈതൂവാല

Please keep some *napkins* on the dinner table.

Narrate *(v.)* നറേറ്റ്-കഥാവർണ്ണനം ചെയ്യുക

Please *narrate* the whole incident to me.

Narrow *(adj.)* നാരോ-ഇടുങ്ങിയ, കുടുസ്സായ

Can our car pass through a *narrow* lane?

Nasal *(adj.)* നേസൽ-മൂക്കിന്റെ

I have a cold, please give me some *nasal* drops.

Nasty *(adj.)* നാസ്റ്റി-1. ചീത്ത, വല്ലാത്ത

This chemical has a *nasty* smell.

(adv.) Don't behave so *nastily.*

2. അപകടകാരി

There is a *nasty* bend in the road.

Nation *(n.)* നേഷൻ-1. രാഷ്ട്രം, പ്രജാസമുച്ചയം

For the progress of mankind, friendly ties between all *nations* are essential.

2. ദേശീയത

What is your *nationality*?

(adj.) I think you are acting in an anti-*national* manner.

Native *(n.)* നേറ്റീവ്-സ്വദേശി

I am a *native* of India.

(adj.) Hindi is the *native* language of northern India.

Nature *(n.)* നേച്ചർ--1. പ്രകൃതി, സ്വഭാവം, നിസർഗം

Have you seen the beauty of *nature* in the hills?

Natural *(adj.)* നാചറൽ-നൈസർഗ്ഗിക, സ്വാഭാവിക

It is *natural* for the parents to feel concerned when their child is ill.

Naughty *(adj.)* നാട്ടി-വികൃതി, കുസൃതി

My younger son is very *naughty.*

Near *(adj.)* നിയർ-സമീപം, അടുത്ത്

Who was the man sitting *near* you at the party?

My school is *near* Birla Mandir.

Nearly *(adv.)* നിയർലി-ഏറെക്കുറെ, മിക്കവാറും

My job is *nearly* finished.

Neat *(adv.)* നീറ്റ്-വൃത്തിയായി, ചിട്ടയായി

You are very *neatly* dressed.

(adj.) His room is very *neat.*

Necessary *(adj.)* നെസസറി-ആവശ്യമായ, തീർച്ചയായും വേ

If you want to score good marks, it is *necessary* for you to study hard.

Neck *(n.)* നെക്-കഴുത്ത്
She has a beautiful long *neck*.

Necklace നെക്‌ലസ്-മാല
This *necklace* will look more beautiful on a long neck.

Nectar *(n.)* നെക്ടാർ-പൂമ്പൊടി, പരാഗം
The honeybees collect *nectar* from flowers.

Need നീഡ്-ആവശ്യം, അനിവാര്യത
(n.) There was a great *need* of field workers in the new political party.
(v.) I *need* somebody's help in this matter.
Need I go to the market immediately?
(adj.) The *needy* should apply for help.

Needle *(n.)* നീഡിൽ-സൂചി
Bring a *needle* and thread to stitch this button.
The *needle* of this meter is not working.

Negative *(adj.)* നെഗറ്റീവ്-1. നിഷേധാത്മക
I have received a *negative* reply to my proposal.
(n.) 2. നെഗറ്റീവ്, ചിത്രമൂലം
Can you develop this *negative*?

Neglect *(v.)* നിഗ്ളെക്ട്-അവഗണിക്കുക, ശ്രദ്ധിക്കാതിരിക്കുക
You must not *neglect* your homework.
(n.) You will be dismissed for your *negligence*.

Negotiable *(adj.)* നെഗോഷിയബ്ൾ - വിലപേശാവുന്നത്, കൂടിയാലോചന നടത്തുക
(adj.) The prices of all the items in the shop are *negotiable*.
(v.) She *negotiated* the price of the jewellery.
(n.) The demands of the workers are still under *negotiation*.

Neighbour *(n.)* നേബർ-അയൽവാസി
Our *neighbour* is a very friendly person.

Neither *(adv.)* നീദർ-1. രണ്ടുമല്ല, അതുമല്ല, ഇതുമല്ല
I *neither* saw nor heard you coming.
2. ഇല്ല
You do not play hockey and *neither* do I.

Nephew *(n.)* നെഫ്യൂ-അനന്തരവൻ
I have one *nephew* and two nieces.

Nerve *(n.)* നെർവ്-നാഡി, ധൈര്യം
You are a man of strong *nerves*.

Nervous *(adj.)* നെർവസ്-1. വെപ്രാളപ്പെടുക, പരിഭ്രമിക്കുക
Don't be so *nervous*, father will not punish you.
2. നാഡീസംബന്ധമായ
The patient was suffering from a *nervous* breakdown.

Nest നെസ്റ്റ്-കിളിക്കൂട്
(v.) Don't disturb the sparrows when they are *nesting*.
(n.) The tree in our garden is full of *nests*.

Net *(n.)* നെറ്റ്-വല
Do you use a *hair-net*?

Network *(n.)* നെറ്റ്‌വർക്-ശൃംഖല
India has the largest *network* of railways.

Neutral *(adj.)* ന്യൂട്രൽ-നിക്ഷ്പക്ഷ
I always remain *neutral* when two people quarrel.

Never *(adv.)* നെവർ-ഒരിക്കലുമില്ല
I have *never* seen such a strange animal before.

New *(adv.)* ന്യൂ-പുതിയ, നൂതന, നവീന
When did you buy this *new* car?
I am not *new* to this city.
(adv.) My sister is *newly* married.

News *(n.)* ന്യൂസ്-വാർത്ത, വൃത്താന്തം
You can read the *news* in the daily papers.
Where is today's *newspaper*?

Next *(adj.)* നെക്സ്റ്റ്-അടുത്ത, വരുന്ന
Next week I am going on a holiday.

Nibble *(v.)* നിബ്ൾ-കരളുക
A mouse has *nibbled* my notebook.

Nice *(adj.)* നൈസ്-സുന്ദര, മനോഹര
You look *nice* in this dress.
This restaurant serves *nice* food.

Niche *(n.)* നീഷ്-പ്രത്യേക സ്ഥാനം
By doing selected roles, Konkona Sen has carved a *niche* for herself in the film industry.

Nickname *(n.)* നിക്നെയിം–അപരനാമം
My son Vikram's *nickname* is Bittu.

Niece *(n.)* നീസ്–അനന്തരവൾ
My *niece* came to stay with us during her holidays.

Night *(n.)* നൈറ്റ്–രാത്രി
What were you doing last *night*?

Nimble *(adj.)* നിംബ്ൾ–ചൊറുചൊറുക്കുള്ള
A *nimble* boy like you should easily win the race.

Nip *(v.)* നിപ്–കടിച്ച് തിന്നുക
The child *nipped* on the biscuit.

No നോ–ഇല്ല, പറ്റില്ല
(adj.) Have you *no* money to lend me?
(adv.) When he asked me if I could accompany him, my answer was *'no'*.

Nobody *(n.)* നോബഡി–ആരുമല്ല
Nobody came here.

Noble *(adj.)* നോബ്ൾ–ഉൽകൃഷ്ട, ഉദാത്ത
It was really a *noble* service.
You have indeed done a *noble* deed.
I appreciate your *noble* sentiments.

Nod നോഡ്–1. സമ്മതം മൂളുക
(n.) Give me a *nod* when you need a glass of water.
(v.) If you agree with me, just *nod* your head.
2. ആയുക
The old lady was *nodding* in her chair.

Noise *(n.)* നോയ്സ്–ബഹളം, ശബ്ദം
No *noise,* please!

Nomad *(n.)* നോമാഡ്–നാടോടി
The *nomads* were looking for a suitable place to spend the night.

Nominate *(v.)* നോമിനേറ്റ്–നാമനിർദ്ദേശം ചെയ്യുക
A local leader was *nominated* by his party to contest the municipal elections.

None *(prep.)* നൺ–ആരും (തന്നെ) ഇല്ല
None of my friends stays in Mumbai.

Nonsense *(n.)* നോൺസെൻസ്–അബദ്ധം, വിഡ്ഢിത്തം
Don't talk *nonsense*!

Noon *(n.)* നൂൺ–ഉച്ച, പകൽ പന്ത്രണ്ടു മണി സമയം
I shall return by *noon*.

Norm *(n.)* നോം–മാനദണ്ഡം
India has her own cultural and political *norms.*

Normal *(adj.)* നോർമൽ–സാധാരണ, സാമാന്യ
The *normal* weather in December is chilly and cold.
Today my temperature has come down to *normal.*
(adv.) When do you *normally* go to bed?

Nose *(n.)* നോസ്–മൂക്ക്
You have a very sharp *nose.*

Notable *(adj.)* നോട്ടബ്ൾ–ശ്രദ്ധേയമായ, അസാധാരണ
Congratulations on your *notable* success in the examination.

Note *(n.)* നോട്ട്–1. നോട്ട്, കുറിപ്പ്
Please give him this *note* when he comes.
2. രൂപാ നോട്ട്
Do you have a ten-rupee *note*?
3. സ്വരം
Can you play all the *notes* on this musical instrument?
(v.) 4. ശ്രദ്ധിക്കുക, കുറിയ്ക്കുക
Please *note* the contents of this letter carefully.

Noted *(adj.)* നോട്ടെഡ്–പ്രശസ്ത, പേർകേട്ട
My brother is *noted* scientist.

Nothing *(n.)* നത്തിംഗ്–ഒന്നുമില്ല
I have *nothing* to give you.

Notice *(n.)* നോട്ടീസ്–1. അറിയിപ്പ്, നോട്ടീസ്
Did you not read the *notice* saying that parking is not allowed here?
2. ശ്രദ്ധിക്കുക
I smiled at Hari but he took no *notice.*
(v.) 3. കാണുക
I *noticed* that you had left the door open.
(adj.) The error was not *noticeable.*

Notion *(n.)* നോഷൻ–ധാരണ, അഭിപ്രായം, പക്ഷം
You seem to have no *notion* about how to tackle this job.

Notorious *(adj.)* നൊട്ടോറിയസ് – കുപ്രസിദ്ധ
Veerappan was *notorious* for smuggling sandalwood.

Nourish *(n.)* നറിഷ്–പോഷിപ്പിക്കുക
We need more fertiliser and water to *nourish* the plant.
(adj.) I like a simple but *nourishing* meal.

Novel *(n.)* നോവൽ–1. ആഖ്യായിക
Do you like to read *novels*?
(adj.) 2. പുതുമയുള്ള
Your idea is indeed *novel*.
(n.) 3. നവീന/കൗതുക വസ്തു
Is there a shop of *novelties* near your house?

Now *(adv.)* നൗ–ഇപ്പോൾ, ഈ സമയത്ത്, ഉടൻ
Can you come *now* or in the evening?
Boys, *now* listen to me carefully.

Nowhere *(adv.)* നോവെയർ–ഒരിടത്തും (തന്നെ) ഇല്ല
I looked for you but could find you *nowhere*.
The book was *nowhere* to be found.

Nucleus *(n.)* ന്യൂക്ലിയസ്–കേന്ദ്രം
Could the doctor locate the *nucleus* of the pain?

Nudge *(v.)* നജ്–തോുക, മുട്ടുകൊ് തട്ടുക
I shall *nudge* you when you nod.

Nuisance *(n.)* ന്യൂയിസൻസ്–ശല്യം, കഷ്ടം
It's such a *nuisance* waiting for someone all alone.

Numb *(adj.)* നമ്പ്–മരവിപ്പ്
My foot has gone *numb*.

Number *(n.)* നമ്പർ–1. അക്കം, എണ്ണം, നമ്പർ
Write down some *numbers* on this sheet of paper.
2. സംഘം, ഒട്ടേറെ
I met a *number* of old friends at the meeting.
(v.) Gita *numbers* Rita among her best friends.
3. എണ്ണുക, എണ്ണമെടുക്കുക
Have you *numbered* the pages of your manuscript?

Nurse നഴ്സ്–നഴ്സ്, ശുശ്രൂഷ ചെയ്യുന്നയാൾ
(n.) I learn your daughter has qualified as a *nurse*.
(v.) *Nurse* your young child and he will grow strong.
(adj.) I was admitted to a *nursing* home.

Nurture *(v.)* നർചർ–1. നോക്കിവളർത്തുക
She *nurtures* her plants as someone *nurtures* his children.
2. വികസിപ്പിക്കുക
It is important to *nurture* a good work environment.

Nut *(n.)* നട്ട്–1. കുരു, അി
Can you break this *nut* with your teeth?
2. നട്ട്
Bring some *nuts* and screws for repairing this door.

Nutrition *(n.)* ന്യൂട്രിഷൻ–പോഷകാഹാരം
(n.) You should take care of your *nutrition* well.
(adj.) Milk has high *nutritional* value,
(adj.) We should have *nutritious* food.

Nylon *(n.)* നൈലോൺ–നൈലോൺ
Socks made of *nylon* last longer.

O

Oar *(n.)* ഓർ–തുഴ
I rowed the boat with a pair of *oars*.

Oath *(v.)* ഓത്ത്–1. ശപഥം, സത്യപ്രതിജ്ഞ
The President is administered the *oath* of office by the Chief Justice of India.

Obese *(adj.)* ഒബീസ്–സ്ഥൂലിച്ച
She was an obese child.

Obey *(v.)* അനുസരിക്കുക
My children *obey* my instructions.
(adj.) They are *obedient* children.

(n.) We shall act in *obedience* to our manager's orders.

Object *(n.)* ഓബ്ജെക്ട്–1. ഉദ്ദേശ്യം, ലക്ഷ്യം
What is the *object* of your foreign tour?
2. വസ്തു, സാധനം
What is that *object* floating in the lake?
(v.) 3. എതിർപ്പ്, എതിർക്കുന്നു
I *object* to your rude remarks.
(n.) I have an *objection* to them.
(adj.) Your habit of coming late to every important meeting is *objectionable*.

Oblige *(v.)* ഓബ്ലൈജ്–1. കടപ്പാടുള്ള, ഉപകാരം ചെയ്യുക
Dinesh *obliged* his friends with dinner party.
2. ബാദ്ധ്യപ്പെടുത്തുക, കടപ്പാടുള്ളവനാക്കുക
Do not *oblige* me to accompay you.
My duties *oblige* me to work late.

Oblivious *(adj.)* ഓബ്ളിവയസ്–ഓർമ്മയില്ലാതെ, അറിയാതെ
He was sleeping on his desk *oblivious* of the people around him.

Obnoxious *(adj.)* ഒമ്പനോക്ഷസ്–വെറുപ്പോടെ
The worms inside the garden were *obnoxious*.

Obscene *(adj.)* ഓബ്സീൻ–അശ്ലീല
The scenes that the director claimed to be aesthetic were considered *obscene* by the censor board.

Obscure *(v.)* ഓബ്സ്ക്യൂർ–1. മൂടിവയ്ക്കുക, കാണാനാവാത്ത
Everything was *obscured* by the mist.
(adj.) 2. അവ്യക്തം, ദുരുദ്ദേശം
Your motive in writing such a letter is *obscure* to me.
3. അജ്ഞാത
This poem was composed by an *obscure* poet.

Observe *(v.)* ഒബ്സെർവ്–1. കാണുക, അവലോകനം ചെയ്യുക
Observe how a pair of sparrows makes its nest.
2. നിയമവും നിർദ്ദേശവും പാലിക്കുക
All good players *observe* rules of fair play.
3. അഭിപ്രായം പറയുക
My friend *observed* that I should not attend the club meeting.
(n.) The rising level of river water was under *observation* of the flood control department.

Obsess *(v.)* ഓബ്സെസ്–ഏതെങ്കിലും കാര്യം ദൃഢമായി മനസ്സിലുറപ്പിയ്ക്കുക
She seems to be *obsessed* with cleanliness.

Obsolete *(adj.)* ഓബ്സലീറ്റ്–പഴഞ്ചൻ
Making students learn the text has become an *obsolete* teaching technique now.

Obstacle *(n.)* ഓബ്സ്റ്റക്ക്ൾ–തടസ്സം, പ്രതിബന്ധം
Is there any *obstacle* in your taking a holiday tomorrow?

Obstinate *(adj.)* ഓബ്സ്റ്റിനെയ്റ്റ്–പിടിവാശി, ദുരാഗ്രഹി
Raju is an *obstinate* child.
(n.) Sometimes he shows great *obstinacy*.

Obstruct *(v.)* ഓബ്സ്ട്രക്റ്റ്–തടസ്സപ്പെടുത്തുക
The path was *obstructed* by the farmer's cart.
(n.) Illiteracy is a great *obstruction* in the path of progress.

Obtain *(v.)* ഒബ്ടെയ്ൻ–നേടുക, കരസ്ഥമാക്കുക
Have you *obtained* visa for your proposed visit to America?

Obvious *(adj.)* ഓബ്വിയസ്–സ്പഷ്ടം, വ്യക്തം, പ്രത്യക്ഷം
It is *obvious* that you are preparing for a journey.
Uma's angry looks made it *obvious* that she was displeased with Rekha.

Occasion *(n.)* ഒക്കേഷൻ–അവസരം, സംഭവം, ചടങ്ങ്
We gave a party on the *occasion* of our son's first birthday.
That party was a happy *occasion*.

Occupation *(n.)* ഒകുപേഷൻ–ജോലി, തൊഴിൽ
What is your father's *occupation*?

Occupy *(v.)* ഓകുപൈ–1. പാർക്കുക, താമസിക്കുക
Which room are you *occupying* in this hotel?
2. കയ്യടക്കുക
The landlord was fighting a case in the

court against the tenants who had *occupied* his house.

3. വ്യാപൃതമാകുക

How do you *occupy* yourself during the holidays?

Occur *(v.)* ഒകർ–1. സംഭവിക്കുക

A serious accident *occurred* near our house last evening.

The total solar eclipse is a rare *occurrence*.

2. മനസ്സിൽ തോന്നുക

Has it *occurred* to you that you are taking a risk?

Ocean *(n.)* ഓഷ്യൻ–സമുദ്രം

The *ocean* was gurgling with life.

Odd *(adj.)* ഓഡ്–1. അവലക്ഷണം, അസാധാരണം

How *odd* that you should find me at home in the morning!

It is really *odd* that you should be here at this hour.

2. ഒറ്റ സംഖ്യ (1, 3, 5 ഇത്യാദി)

I asked the students to write down some *odd* numbers.

3. താല്ക്കാലിക, ഇടയ്ക്കിടെയുള്ള, ചില്ലറ

They need a person to do *odd* jobs in the factory.

Odour *(n.)* ഓഡർ–ഗന്ധം, നാറ്റം

The *odour* of frying garlics is very strong.

Many chemicals have a bad *odour*.

Offend *(v.)* ഒഫെൻഡ്–പിണക്കുക, അപമാനിക്കുക

I hope I have not *offended* you by my plain speaking.

(n.) Is it not an *offence* in America to drive on the left hand side of the road?

Offer *(n.)* ഓഫർ–1. നിർദ്ദേശം

I regret to inform you that your *offer* is not acceptable to me.

(v.) 2. നിർദ്ദേശിക്കുക, നൽകാൻ തയാറാകുക

I *offer* to pay your railway fare if you want to visit Agra.

Office *(n.)* ഓഫീസ്–1. കാര്യാലയം

I have my *office* tomorrow.

2. അധികാര പദവി

He is holding the *office* of foreign affairs.

Often *(adv.)* ഓഫൺ–പലപ്പോഴും, അടിക്കടി

I *often* play chess with my neighbour.

Ointment *(n.)* ഓയിന്റ്മെന്റ്–ലേപനം, മരുന്ന്

Can you give me some *ointment* for boils?

Old *(adj.)* ഓൾഡ്–1. പ്രായം

How *old* is your father?

2. പ്രായം ചെന്ന, വൃദ്ധ

My father is a very *old* man.

3. ഏറെക്കാലമായി

Anil and I are *old* friends.

4. പഴയ, പൊട്ടാൻ പോകുന്ന

My shoes are getting *old*.

Omen *(n.)* ഒമെൻ–ശകുനം

Throbbing of the right arm of men is considered a good *omen*.

Ominous *(adj.)* ഓമിനസ്–അപശകുനം

The black cat is considered *ominous* by many.

Omit *(v.)* ഒമിറ്റ്–വിട്ടുകളയുക, ചെയ്യാതിരിക്കുക

Do not *omit* Amitabh's name from the list of invitees.

We read the play *omitting* the last two scenes.

Once *(adv.)* വൺസ്–ഒരിക്കൽ

I have visited America only *once*.

2. എന്നോ ഒരിക്കൽ

Once upon a time, there lived a great king.

Only വൺലി–1. മാത്രം, കേവലം

(adv.) She *only* did it for a joke.

I came to the party *only* because you were coming.

(adj.) 2. ഒറ്റയ്ക്ക്, ഏകമാത്ര

Sunil is the *only* boy who can solve this problem.

This bus is for ladies *only*.

Onset *(n.)* ഓൺസെറ്റ്–ഏതെങ്കിലും ചീത്തകാര്യത്തിന്റെ തുടക്കം

This seems to be the *onset* of typhoid.

Onto *(prep.)* ഓൺടു–എന്തിന്റെയെങ്കിലും മേൽ

Stick this paper *onto* the cardboard.

Onwards *(adv.)* ഓൺവർഡ്സ്–മുതൽക്ക്

I'll go on a leave from next month onwards.

Open *(v.)* ഓപ്പൺ–1. തുറക്കുക, പ്രത്യക്ഷമാകുക

Please *open* the door.

2. തുറക്കുക (പുസ്കം, ടിൻ, വായ തുടങ്ങിയവ)

Please *open* the book (the tin/the mouth, etc.)

(adj.) 3. പൊതു

It was an *open* mango eating competition in which we contested.

4. തുറന്ന, മുക്തമായ

You should take a walk in the *open* air.

5. തുറന്ന, ഉദാര

Have an *open* mind when you argue with others.

Operation *(n.)* ഓപ്പറേഷൻ–1. ശസ്ത്രക്രിയ, ഓപ്പറേഷൻ

The surgeon took two hours to perform the *operation.*

2. പ്രവർത്തനം, പ്രക്രിയ, വ്യാപാരം

The boys watched with interest the *operation* of the huge machine.

Opinion *(n.)* ഒപിനിയൻ–അഭിപ്രായം, നിർദ്ദേശം

What are your political *opinions*?

Ask an expert to give his *opinion* on the feasibility of your plan.

Opponent *(n.)* ഓപ്പോണന്റ്–എതിരാളി, പ്രതിയോഗി, വിരോധി

We defeated our *opponents* in the cricket match.

Opportunity *(n.)* ഓപ്പർട്യൂണിറ്റി–അവസരം

I would like to have an *opportunity* to visit Kashmir.

Oppose *(v.)* ഒപ്പോസ്–എതിർക്കുക, നേരിടുക

I *oppose* your proposal as I think it is unwise.

(n.) He went abroad in *opposition* to his parent's wishes.

Opposite *(adv.)* ഓപ്പസിറ്റ്–1. എതിരെ

I live *opposite* the post office.

(adj.) 2. വിപരീതം, നേരെ എതിരായ

You are an *opposite* of your brother in temperament.

Oppressive *(adj.)* ഒപ്രസീവ്–കിരാത

The Indians opposed the *oppressive* British policies.

Opt *(v.)* ഓപ്ട്–തിരഞ്ഞെടുക്കുക

Which subject will you *opt* for?

Optician *(n.)* ഒപ്ടീഷ്യൻ–നേത്ര പരിശോധകൻ

I'll go to an *optician* to get my eyes tested.

Optimist *(n.)* ഓപ്ടിമിസ്റ്റ്–ശുഭാപ്തി വിശ്വാസി

I am an *optimist* and always hope that things will change for the better.

Option *(n.)* ഓപ്ഷൻ–വികല്പം

I had no *option* but to stay back.

Oral *(adj.)* ഓറൽ–വാക്കാലുള്ള

How did you fare in your *oral* examination?

Orator *(n.)* ഓറേറ്റർ–പ്രഭാഷകൻ, പ്രാസംഗികൻ

A political leader has to be a good *orator.*

Orbit ഓർബിറ്റ്–ഉപഗ്രഹ ഭ്രമണ പഥം

(n.) The planets revolve around the sun in their fixed *orbits.*

(v.) The planets *orbit* the sun.

Orchard *(n.)* ഓർചർഡ്–പഴത്തോട്ടം

I have brought some apples for you from my *orchard.*

Orchestra *(n.)* ഓർക്കിസ്ട്രാ–വാദ്യവൃന്ദ സംഘം

The *orchestra* was playing Italian music.

Ordeal *(n.)* ഓർഡിൽ–അഗ്നിപരീക്ഷ

Working in shifts is really an *ordeal.*

Order ഓർഡർ–1. ആജ്ഞ/ഉത്തരവ് (നൽകുക)

(v.) The commander *ordered* the souldiers to fire.

2. ആവശ്യപ്പെടുക, ഓർഡർ ചെയ്യുക

My father has *ordered* a new sofa set from the furniture shop.

(n.) 3. ക്രമം, അനുക്രമം

Arrange these words in an alphabetical *order.*

4. പ്രവർത്തന രീതി

Your wrist-watch does not seem to be in working *order.*

5. ക്രമസമാധാനം

It is the duty of the police to maintain the law and *order.*

Ordinary *(adj.)* ഓർഡിനറി–സാധാരണ, സാമാന്യ, നിസ്സാര

I bought an *ordinary* time-piece, but it works well.

(adv.) Ordinarily, we spend our evenings in Connaught Place.

Organise *(v.)* ഓർഗനൈസ് – സംഘടിപ്പിക്കുക, സംഘടന

Our school is going to *organise* a fete this winter.

(n.) May I become a member of your *organisation*?

Oriented *(adj.)* ഓറിയന്റഡ്–ഉന്മുഖ

Her approach is always result-*oriented.*

Origin *(n.)* ഒറിജിൻ–ഉത്ഭവം, ആരംഭം

Has the doctor found out the *origin* of your illness?

Original *(adj.)* ഒറിജിനൽ–1. മൂല

Is this picture *original* or is it a copy?

2. പഴയകാല, ആദ്യ

The *original* way of travelling was on foot, now we travel by train.

Ornament *(n.)* ഓർണമെന്റ്–ആഭരണം

It is in the nature of women to like *ornaments*.

Orphan *(n.)* ഓർഫൻ–അനാഥ

This little boy is an *orphan,* he lost his parents in an accident.

Orthodox *(adj.)* ഓർതഡോക്സ്–മാമൂൽ പ്രിയർ

She belongs to an *orthodox* family.

Other *(adj.&n.)* അദർ–1. അന്യ, ഇതര, മറ്റേ

This room is my office, the *other* one is the library.

2. അന്യ, വ്യത്യസ്ത

Some people like milk, *others* do not.

3. അടുത്ത സമയത്ത്

I met Prakash the *other* day.

Out *(adv.)* ഔട്ട്–1. പുറത്ത്

Do not go out in the rain.

2. പൊലിയുക, അവസാനിക്കുക, വേറെയാവുക

The lights suddenly went *out.*

3. പുറത്താവുക

The results of the election are *out* at last.

Outcome *(n.)* ഔട്ട്കം–ഫലം

Growth in sales is the *outcome* of the hard work we put in.

Outdated *(adj.)* ഔട്ട്ഡേറ്റഡ്–കാലഹരണപ്പെട്ട

This machine has become *outdated.*

Outing *(n.)* ഔട്ടിംഗ്–കറക്കം, ചുറ്റിക്കറങ്ങൽ

Let's go for an *outing.*

Ovation *(n.)* ഒവേഷൻ–അഭിനന്ദനം

She received a standing *ovation* for her performance.

Oven *(n.)* അവ്ൻ–അടുപ്പ്, തന്തൂർ

My wife has bought an electric *oven.*

Over ഓവർ–1. മുകളിൽ, അപ്പുറം

(prep.) The boys climbed *over* the fence.

2. മേലേ, അധികാരി

I always sleep with the blanket *over* my face.

Who is *over* in your department?

(adj.) 3. അവസാനിച്ചു, കഴിഞ്ഞു

When will the show be *over*?

4. വീണ്ടും

Please go through the sum *over* and *over* again.

5. ഏറെ, പരം

Over five hundred people attended the function.

Overwhelming *(adj.)* ഓവർവെൽമിംഗ്–തീവ്രമായ

I felt an *overwhelming* need for solitude.

Owe *(v.)* ഓ–1. തരാനുള്ള, കിട്ടാനുള്ള

When can you repay the money you *owe* me?

2. കടപ്പാടുള്ള

I *owe* my present position in life to the guidance of my father.

Own ഓൺ–1. ഉടമ, നാഥൻ (ആവുക)

(v.) My father *owns* this house.

(adj.) 2. സ്വന്തം, സ്വകാര്യ

I make my *own* breakfast.

Ox *(n.)* ഓക്സ്–കാള

The farmer ploughed the land with the help of an *ox.*

P

Pace പേസ്–ചുവട്, നടത്ത, ഒപ്പമെത്തുക
(n.) Please walk quickly and try to keep *pace* with me.
(v.) I *paced* up and down the room.

Pacify *(v.)* പാസിഫൈ–ശാന്തമാക്കുക, പിണക്കം മാറ്റുക
The little girl was *pacified* only when we offered her a bar of chocolate.

Pack *(v.)* പാക്ക്–1. കെട്ടുക, പാക്ക് ചെയ്യുക
Have you *packed* all your things?
(n.) 2. പെട്ടി, കൂട്, ടിൻ
How much tea does this *pack* contain?

Pad *(n.)* പാഡ്–എഴുതാൻ ഒരേപോലെ മുറിച്ച, കടലാസ് സഞ്ചയം
I want to buy a letter *pad.*

Paddy *(n.)* പാഡി–നെല്ല്
Our train travelled through *paddy* fields.

Page *(n.)* പേജ്–താള്
How many *pages* of this book have you read?

Pail *(n.)* പെയ്ൽ–തൊട്ടി, ബക്കറ്റ്
I filled the *pail* with water from the tap.

Pain *(n.)* പെയ്ൻ–വേദന, ബുദ്ധിമുട്ട്, വ്യഥ, വേദനിപ്പിക്കുക
The doctor gave me a tablet to relieve the *pain* in my stomach.
(v.) You misbehaviour *pained* me greatly.

Paint *(v.)* പെയിന്റ്–1. ചിത്രം വരയ്ക്കുക, ചായമടിക്കുക
Do you know how to *paint*?
(n.) 2. ചായം
What *paint* would you like for the walls of your room?

Pair *(n.)* പെയ്ർ–ജോഡി
I want to buy a new *pair* of shoes.

Palace *(n.)* പാലസ്–കൊട്ടാരം, രാജമന്ദിരം, മാളിക
The Queen of England lives in Buckingham *Palace.*

Pale *(adj.)* പെയ്ൽ–വിളറിയ, വിവർണ്ണ, തേജസ്സറ്റ
Your face looks so *pale.*

Palm *(n.)* പാം–1. ഉള്ളംകൈ, കൈപ്പടം
Can you read a *palm*?
2. പന, തെങ്ങ്
Kerala is a land of *palm* trees.

Palpitate *(v.)* പാൽപിറ്റേറ്റ്–ശക്തമായ നെഞ്ചിടിപ്പ്
My heart was *palpitating* with fear.

Paltry *(adj.)* പാൾട്രി–തുച്ഛമായ
I was offered a *paltry* amount of money to do that work.

Pamper *(v.)* പാമ്പർ–അതിയായി ലാളിക്കുക
If you *pamper* the child, you will spoil it.

Pamphlet *(n.)* പാംഫ്ലിറ്റ്–ലഘുലേഖ, പത്രിക
Our party has brought out a *pamphlet* on its aims and objectives.

Pan *(n.)* പാൻ–തട്ട്, പാത്രം
Make an omelette in the *pan.*

Pane *(n.)* പെയ്ൻ–കണ്ണാടിച്ചില്ല്
Who broke this window *pane*?

Panel *(n.)* പാനൽ–1. ജനാലയിലെ കണ്ണാടി
The child broke the glass *panel.*
2. സമിതി
The *panel* of judges declared them the clear winners.

Pang *(n.)* പാങ്–കടുത്ത, ഉഗ്രമായ
On seeing her winning the race, she was taken over by a sudden *pang* of jealousy.

Panic പാനിക്–ഭീതി, പരിഭ്രമം, സംഭ്രമം
(n.) Panic spread in the crowd when it saw a man waving a pistol.
(v.) Please don't *panic.*

Pant *(v.)* പാന്റ്–കിതയ്ക്കുക
Sunil ran so fast that he began to *pant.*

Pants *(n.)* പാന്റ്സ്–പാന്റ്
I bought a new pair of *pants* yesterday.

Paper *(n.)* പേപ്പർ–1. കടലാസ്
Give me a piece of *paper*.
2. പത്രം
Where is today's *paper*?
3. ചോദ്യപേപ്പർ
Yesterday's question *paper* was very difficult to answer.
4. പ്രബന്ധം
The professor read out a *paper* on atomic energy.
5. പ്രമാണം, രേഖ
This building is mine, I have the *papers* to prove it.

Par *(n.)* പാർ–ഗുണനിലവാരം
She is a writer *par* excellence.

Parable *(n.)* പാരബ്ൾ–ദൃഷ്ടാന്ത കഥ
The *parables* of Panchatantra are still as fresh as they were ages ago.

Parachute *(n.)* പാരഷൂട്ട്–പാരഷൂട്ട്
The man jumped from the helicopter with a *parachute*.

Parade പരേഡ്–കവാത്ത്, പരേഡ് ചെയ്യുക
(n.) The *parade* will take place on the *parade* ground.
Thousands of people watch the Republic Day *Parade*.
(v.) The army will *parade* at dawn.

Paradise *(n.)* പാരഡൈസ്–പറുദീസ, സ്വർഗ്ഗം
Kashmir is called the *paradise* on earth.

Paradox *(n.)* പാരഡോക്സ്–വിരോധാഭാസം
It is really a *paradox* that despite being an introvert, he likes to chat with strangers.

Paragraph *(n.)* പാരഗ്രാഫ്–പാര, ഖണ്ഡിക
Write an essay of three *paragraphs* on Diwali.

Parallel പാരലൽ–1. സമാന്തരമായി
This lane runs *parallel* to the main road.
(n.) 2. സാദൃശ്യം
His quality of work is without *parallel*.

Paralyse *(v.)* പാരലൈസ്–പക്ഷപാതം പിടിപ്പിക്കുക, സ്തംഭിപ്പിക്ക, ചലനശക്തി ഇല്ലാതാകുക
I was *paralysed* with fear to see two armed men in the house.

Parameter *(n.)* പാരാമീറ്റർ–മാനദണ്ഡം
Flawless language cannot be the only *parameter* to a good story.

Paranoid *(adj.)* പാരനോയിഡ്– എന്തെങ്കിലും അശുഭമുാകുമെന്ന അകാരണമായ സംശയഗ്രസ്തം
Stop being a *paranoid* about going out in the evening.

Parboil *(v.)* പാർബോയ്ൽ–അരവേവ്
Mother *parboiled* the rice.

Parcel *(n.)* പാർസൽ–പാർസൽ, പൊതി കെട്ടുക
Please wrap up this *parcel* for me.

Pardon പാർഡൻ–ക്ഷമായാചനം, മാപ്പ് ചോദിക്കുക
(n.) I beg your *pardon*.
The thief asked the judge for *pardon*.
(v.) Many prisoners were *pardoned* on the eve of the king's birthday.

Parents *(n.)* പേരന്റ്സ്–അച്ഛനമ്മമാർ
Where are your *parents*, little boy?
Karam Singh has a royal *parentage*.

Park *(n.)* പാർക്–1. ഉദ്യാനം, പൂന്തോട്ടം
We go to the *park* every evening.
2. പാർക്ക് ചെയ്യുക, നിർത്തിയിടുക
Parking is not allowed here.
(v.) May I *park* my motor cycle here while I visit the market?

Parliament *(n.)* പാർലമെന്റ്–പാർലമെന്റ്, ജനസഭ
There was a chaos in the *Parliament*.

Part *(n.)* പാർട്ട്–1, ഭാഗം, ഖണ്ഡം
This book is divided into three *parts*.
2. പങ്ക്
I have a major *part* in the play to be put up by our club.
(v.) 3. പിരിയുക, വേർപെടുത്തുക
The two friends were sad when they *parted* to go in different directions.
4. പക്ഷം, വശം
We thank you for taking our *part*.

Partial *(adj.)* പാർഷ്യൽ–1. ഭാഗികം, അപൂർണ്ണം
I am only in *partial* agreement with what you say.
2. പക്ഷപാതപരം
Parents are naturally *partial* to their children.

Participate *(v.)* പാർട്ടിസിപ്പേറ്റ്– പങ്കെടുക്കുക
Will you *participate* in the dance competition?

Particle *(n.)* പാർട്ടിക്ൾ–കണം
Some *particles* of dust are sticking to your shirt.

Particular *(adj.)* പർട്ടിക്യുലർ–1. പ്രത്യേക, ശ്രേഷ്ഠം, വിശേഷ
There are many pictures in this art gallery, but I want to look at this *particular* one.
(adv.) We should be *particularly* careful on dark nights.
2. നിർബന്ധമായ
Ramesh is very *particular* about his food.
3. വിവരണം
Please give *particulars* of all your achievements.

Partition പാർട്ടിഷൻ–വിഭജനം, ഭാഗം വയ്ക്കുക, പങ്കുവയ്ക്കുക
(n.) We divided our sitting room into two parts with a *partition.*
(v.) The two brothers *partitioned* their house.

Partner *(n.)* പാർട്ട്ണർ–പങ്കാളി, ജീവിത പങ്കാളി
Would you like to become my *partner* in setting up a business?

Party *(n.)* പാർട്ടി–1. കക്ഷി, പാർട്ടി
Which political *party* do you belong to?
2. സല്ക്കാരം, വിരുന്ന്
Yesterday I was invited to a tea *party.*
3. കക്ഷിചേർന്നയാൾ
My brother was never a *party* to the fraud.

Pass *(v.)* പാസ്–1. വിജയിക്കുക
Has your son *passed* his final examination?
2. കടന്നുപോവുക
The days are *passing* very quickly.
3. തീർപ്പു കല്പിക്കുക
The judge *passed* sentence.
4. കൈമാറുക
Please *pass* the salt.
5. കടന്നുപോവുക
Will you *pass* a bookshop on your way to office?
(n.) 6. പ്രവേശന പത്രം
Please show your entry *pass* before you go in.

Passage *(n.)* പാസേജ്–1. ഇടനാഴി
My room is at the end of the *passage.*
2. ഉദ്ധരണി, ഭാഗം
Please read out to me any *passage* from your article.

Passenger *(n.)* പാസഞ്ചർ–യാത്രക്കാരൻ, വഴിപോക്കൻ
Passengers are requested not to lean out of the windows.

Passion *(n.)* പാഷൻ–വികാരം, മനോഗതി, അനുരാഗം
This short story is full of *passion.*

Passive *(adj.)* പാസീവ്–നിഷ്ക്രിയ
In the olden times, women played a *passive* role in the worldly affairs.

Passport *(n.)* പാസ്പോർട്ട്–പാസ്പോർട്ട്, വിദേശ യാത്രാനുമതി രേഖ
Have you obtained your *passport* for your proposed foreign tour?

Past പാസ്റ്റ്–1. ഭൂതകാലം
Our *past* mistakes proved to be a learning experience.
(prep.) 2. മണികഴിഞ്ഞ് (സമയ സൂചകം)
I'll see you at half *past* ten.
(adv.) 3. കടന്നുപോവുക
She walked *past* me without even looking at me.
(n.) 4. പിൽക്കാലം
We often try to forget our *past,* but it haunts us always.

Paste *(n.)* പേസ്റ്റ്–1. പേസ്റ്റ്
I want to buy a tube of tooth-*paste.*
(v.) 2. പതിക്കുക
A notice was *pasted* on the wall.

Pastime *(n.)* പാസ്റ്റ്ടൈം–വിനോദം, നേരമ്പോക്ക്
My favourite *pastime* is reading.

Pasture *(n.)* പാസ്ചർ–പുൽത്തകിടി
We strolled around the green *pastures.*

Pat *(v.)* പാറ്റ്–തട്ടുക, അഭിനന്ദിക്കുക
I *patted* the boy on the back.
(n.) My teacher's *pat* on my back encouraged me to do better.

Patch *(n.)* പാച്ച്–1. തു്, ഖണ്ഡം
I repaired the puncture in my bicycle with a *patch* of rubber.
2. പാട്, വടു
What are these *patches* on your arm?

Path *(n.)* പാത്ത്–പഥം, വഴി
I walked by the *path* across the lawn.

Pathetic *(adj.)* പാത്തറ്റിക്–മനസ്സലിയിക്കുന്ന, കരുണാജനകം
This story has a *pathetic* ending.

Patient *(n.)* പേഷ്യന്റ്–1. രോഗി
The doctor's waiting room was full of *patients.*
(adj.) 2. ക്ഷമയോടെ
Be *patient,* you will also be served food.
(adv.) My dog waited *patiently* for me to return.

Patriot *(n.)* പേട്രിയറ്റ്–രാജ്യസ്നേഹി, ദേശഭക്തൻ
Subhash Chandra Bose was a great *patriot.*

Patron *(n.)* പേട്രൺ–രക്ഷാധികാരി
Shah Jahan was a *patron* of art and architecture.

Patter *(n.)* പാറ്റർ–ചറുപിറെ
The rain fell on the roof with a *patter.*

Pattern *(n.)* പാറ്റേൺ–1. രൂപം, പാറ്റേൺ
Meena used a paper *pattern* to make her new dress.
2. മാതൃക
Your behaviour should be a *pattern* for others.
(v.) 3. രൂപപ്പെടുത്തുക
Children often *pattern* their personality after that of their parents.

Pauper *(n.)* പാപ്പർ–പാപ്പർ, ദരിദ്രൻ
A rich man all his life, he died a *pauper.*

Pause *(v.)* പാസ്–വിരാമം, ഇടസമയം
The speaker *paused* for a minute and took a sip of water.
(n.) After a brief *pause,* he spoke again.

Pavement *(n.)* പേവ്മെന്റ്–നടപ്പാത
Pedestrians should always walk on the *pavement.*

Pavilion *(n.)* പവലിയൻ–മണ്ഡപം, പവലിയൻ
After being caught by Ricky Ponting, Sehwag went back to the *pavilion.*

Paw *(n.)* പാ–പാദം, കൈപ്പത്തി
I gently removed the thorn from my dog's *paw.*

Pawn പാൺ–കരു, ഈട്, ജാമ്യം
(n.) The servant was used as a *pawn* by the rich industrialist in the murder case.
(v.) The servant was *pawned* by the rich industrialist in the murder case.

Pay *(n.)* പേ–1. ശമ്പളം, വേതനം
Have you received this month's *pay*?
(v.) 2. വില നൽകുക, അടയ്ക്കുക
What did you *pay* for this pen?
3. കാണാൻ പോവുക
I hope to *pay* you a visit this week.

Pea *(n.)* പീ–പയർ
Pea is my favourite vegetable.

Peace *(n.)* പീസ്–സമാധാനം, ശാന്തി
Please don't quarrel, let us have *peace.*
(adj.) I liked to do my writing in the *peaceful* atmosphere of a secluded place.

Peacock *(n.)* പീകോക്–മയിൽ
He is as proud as a *peacock.*

Peak *(n.)* പീക്–കൊടുമുടി, ശിഖരം
The mountaineering team reached the *peak* after a hard struggle.
(adj.) One of my friends always wears a *peaked* cap.

Peal *(n.)* പീൽ–1. മണിനാദം
As we approached the temple, we could hear the *peal* of the temple bells.
2. ഗർജ്ജനം, ചടപട ശബ്ദം
There was a *peal* of thunder and then the rain started.

Peanut *(n.)* പീനട്ട്–1. നിലക്കടല
We enjoyed roasted *peanuts* while basking in the sun.
2. വളരെ ചെറിയ തുക
Why are you working for *peanuts* when you have so much of talent?

Pear *(n.)* പേയർ–സബർജൻ പഴം
The mother sliced the *pears* for the child.

Pearl *(n.)* പേൾ–മുത്ത്
I bought a necklace of *pearls* as a present for my wife.

Peasant *(n.)* പെസന്റ്–കൃഷിക്കാരൻ

As our trains passed through the countryside, we saw *peasants* working in the fields.

Pebble *(n.)* പെബ്ൾ–ചരൽ, കല്ല്

Children are fond of collecting coloured *pebbles.*

Peck *(v.)* പെക്–കൊത്തിതിന്നുക

The sparrows *pecked* at the grains on the floor.

Peculiar *(adj.)* പിക്യുലിയർ–വിചിത്രമായി, പ്രത്യേക രീതിയിൽ

Why are you behaving in such a *peculiar* fashion today?

Pedal *(n.)* പെഡൽ–പെഡൽ

One of the *pedals* of my bicycle is broken.

Pedestrian *(n.)* പെഡസ്ട്രിയൻ – കാൽനടക്കാരൻ

Pedestrians should watch out while crossing busy streets.

Pedlar *(n.)* പെഡ്ലർ–പെട്ടിക്കടക്കാരൻ

I bought this brush from a *pedlar* at the door.

Peek *(v.)* പീക്–ഒളിഞ്ഞു നോക്കുക

The beggar child *peeked* at the children celebrating Diwali.

Peel *(v. & n.)* പീൽ–തൊലിക്കുക, അടർത്തുക

(v.) I like to help my mother to *peel* potatoes.

(n.) Throw the *peels* in the dustbin.

Peep *(v.)* പീപ്–എത്തിനോക്കുക

I *peeped* into the room to see if there was anyone inside.

Peer *(v.)* പീർ–ഉറ്റുനോക്കുക

The old man *peered* at me through his thick spectacles.

Peevish *(adj.)* പീവിഷ്–ചിണുങ്ങുക, രൂക്ഷമായി

She gave him *peevish* glances when he came late.

Peg *(n.)* പെഗ്–കൊളുത്ത്, ആണി

I took off my coat and hung it on a *peg.*

Pen *(n.)* പെൻ–പേന

I bought a *pen* for my son as a birthday gift.

Penalty *(n.)* പെനാൽറ്റി–പിഴ, ശിക്ഷ

In this library, you have to pay a *penalty* for returning the book late.

Penance *(n.)* പെനൻസ്–തപസ്സ്

Ravana performed *penance* for several years and pleased Lord Shiva.

Pencil *(n.)* പെൻസിൽ–പെൻസിൽ

Have you sharpened your *pencil*?

Pending *(adj.)* പെൻഡിംഗ്–ശേഷിക്കുന്ന

If you have leisure time, finish your *pending* work.

Penetrate *(v.)* പെനിട്രേറ്റ്–തുളച്ചുകയറുക

The surgeon's knife *penetrated* deep into the patient's body.

Penknife *(n.)* പെൻനൈഫ്–പേനാകത്തി

I sharpened my pencil with a *penknife*.

Pension *(n.)* പെൻഷൻ–പെൻഷൻ, അടുത്തൂൺ

How much *pension* does your father get?

People *(n.)* പീപ്ൾ–1. ജനം

The railway platform was full of *people.*

2. ആൾക്കാർ

People say that we shall have a cold winter this year.

Peon *(n.)* പിയോൺ–ശിപായി

The officer asked the *peon* to get a glass of water.

Pepper *(n.)* പെപ്പർ–കുരുമുളക്

The dish became tastier with a tinge of *pepper.*

Perception *(n.)* പെർസെപ്ഷൻ–പ്രേക്ഷണം, തിരിച്ചറിയൽ, ഗ്രഹിക്കുക

(n.) The circumstances were same, but their *perception* differed.

(v.) How do you *perceive* this problem?

I could *perceive* from his appearance that he was a foreigner.

Perch *(v. & n.)* പേർച്ച്–ചേക്കയിരിക്കുക

(v.) The cuckoo *perched* on a branch high in the tree and sang melodiously.

(n.) The bird sang sweetly from its *perch* on the tree.

Perfect *(adj.)* പെർഫെക്ട്-തികവൊത്ത, ശരിയായ

Can you make a *perfect* copy of this design?

Perform *(v.)* പെർഫോം-പാലിക്കുക, പൂർത്തിയാക്കുക, അഭിനയിക്കുക

I always *perform* my duties sincerely.
All the actors *performed* their roles remarkably in the play.
(n.) My son was appreciated for his good *performance* in the school play.

Perfume *(n.&v.)* പെർഫ്യൂം-സുഗന്ധ/പരിമള തൈലം

(n.) She wears a very pleasing *perfume.*
(v.) She *perfumed* her hanky before putting it in the purse.

Perhaps *(adv.)* പെർഹാപ്സ്-ഒരു പക്ഷേ, ചിലപ്പോൾ

Perhaps I will be in Mumbai next week.

Peril *(n.)* പെരിൽ-നാശം, അപകടം

Our journey through the forest was full of *peril.*

Period *(n.)* പീരിയഡ്-1. കാലാവധി, കാലഘട്ടം

We lived for a short *period* in Agra before shifting to Delhi.
2. യുഗം, കാലം
The *period* of Chandra Gupta Maurya was the golden age of Indian history.
3. പീരിയഡ്
My son has seven *periods* in school.

Perish *(v.)* പെരിഷ്-നശിക്കുക, മരിക്കുക

More than a hundred people *perished* in the cyclone.

Permanent *(adj.)* പെർമനെന്റ്-സ്ഥിരം

Have you been made *permanent* in your job?
Is this temporary arrangement or a *permanent* one?

Permit *(v.)* പെർമിറ്റ്-അനുമതി നൽകുക

Please *permit* me to go home early today.
(n.) Do I have *permission* to use your pen?

Perpetual *(adj.)* പെർപചൽ-നിരന്തര, സന്തത

There was a *perpetual* smile on her lips.

Perplexed *(adj.)* പെർപ്ലെക്സ്ഡ് - അന്ധാളിക്കുക

He was *perplexed* when fired from his job.

Per se *(adv.)* പെർ സെ-എങ്കിലും

The theme of the novel was interesting *per se,* but the language was bad.

Persecute *(v.)* പെർസിക്യൂട്ട്-പീഡിപ്പിക്കുക, അതിക്രമം കാട്ടുക

Hitler *persecuted* Jews mercilessly during the Second World War.
(n.) Religious *persecution* was common all over the world in the past.

Persevere *(v.)* പർസിവിയർ-ഉറച്ചു നിൽക്കുക, സ്ഥിരോത്സാഹം

The brave always *persevere* in the face of struggle.
(n.) The mountaineers could conquerthe high peak only through *perseverance.*

Persist *(v.)* പെർസിസ്റ്റ്-ഒരേ പിടിയായി നില്ക്കുക, ചെയ്തുകൊിരിക്കുക

Why do you *persist* in your unfriendly behaviour towards him?

Person *(n.)* പേർസൺ-വ്യക്തി

When I reached the office, two *persons* were waiting for me.
I came in *person* to attend to this important matter.
(adj.) I keep my *personal* letters in a separate file.

Personality *(n.)* പെർസണാലിറ്റി-

1. വ്യക്തിത്വം
The man in black at the party had a pleasing *personality.*
2. പ്രശസ്ത വ്യക്തി
Tagore was an unmatched *personality.*

Personnel *(n.)* പർസണൽ-ജീവനക്കാരൻ, സ്റ്റാഫ്

We need some more technical *personnel* in the department.

Perspective *(n.)* പർസ്പെക്ടീവ്-കാഴ്ചപ്പാട്, ദർശനം, വീക്ഷണം

When you cannot change the situation, it is better you change your *perspective.*

Perspiration *(n.)* പർസ്പിരേഷൻ-വിയർപ്പ്

Beads of *perspiration* rolled down the labourer's face.

Persuade *(v.)* പർസ്വേഡ്–സമ്മതിപ്പിക്കുക, ബോദ്ധ്യപ്പെടുത്തുക

My friend wanted to leave, but I *persuaded* him to stay on.

Pertinent *(adj.)* പർട്ടിനന്റ് –പ്രസക്തമായ

She had raised a *pertinent* question in her article.

Perturb *(v.)* പർട്ടർബ്–വിഷമിക്കുക, പരിഭ്രമിക്കുക

We were *perturbed* with the non-arrival of the maid-servant.

Peruse *(v.)* പെറൂസ്–അവലോകനം ചെയ്യുക

Peruse the story well to detect the errors.

Pervade *(v.)* പെർവെയ്ഡ്–വ്യാപിച്ചിരിക്കുക

God *pervades* everywhere.

Pessimist *(n.)* പെസിമിസ്റ്റ്–നിരാശാവാദി

Never be a *pessimist,* always be an optimist.

Pest *(n.)* പെസ്റ്റ്–1. കീടം, പ്രാണി

The farmer sprayed the pesticides to kill the *pests.*

2. ദേഷ്യം പിടിപ്പിക്കുന്ന, ചൊടിപ്പി ക്കുന്നയാൾ

Her son is quite a *pest.*

Pester *(v.)* പെസ്റ്റർ–ശല്യപ്പെടുത്തുക

My child *pestered* me with questions.

Pet *(n.)* പെറ്റ്–വളർത്തുമൃഗം

We have two *pets,* a dog and a cat.

Petal *(n.)* പെറ്റൽ–ഇതള്, പുഷ്പദലം

In the flower show, I saw roses with big *petals.*

Petition *(n.)* പെറ്റിഷൻ–അപേക്ഷ, നിവേദനം

The people of the locality sent a *petition* to the mayor asking for adequate supply of drinking water.

Petrified *(adj.)* പെർട്ടിഫൈഡ്–അതിയായ ഭയഭീതി

We were *petrified* to encounter armed men in the house.

Petrol *(n.)* പെട്രോൾ–പെട്രോൾ

Do you have enough *petrol* in your car for a long trip?

Petty *(adj.)* പെറ്റി–നിസ്സാര, തുഛ

Why are you quarrelling over such a *petty* thing?

Phantom *(n.)* ഫാന്റം–സാങ്കല്പിക ഭൂതപ്രേതാദികൾ

I don't believe in the existence of *phantoms.*

Phase *(n.)* ഫേസ്–ഘട്ടം

Their relationship was going through a bad *phase.*

Phenomenal *(adj.)* ഫിനോമിനൽ –ശ്രദ്ധേയമായ

She played a *phenomenal* role in taking the company to new heights.

Phenomenon *(n.)* ഫിനോമിനൻ –സ്വാഭാവിക സംഭവം

The arrival of monsoons is a natural *phenomenon.*

Philosophy *(n.)* ഫിലോസഫി–തത്വജ്ഞാനം, ദർശനം (ശാസ്ത്രം)

I was a student of *philosophy* in college.

Dr. Radhakrishanan was a noted *philosopher.*

Phobia *(n.)* ഫോബിയ–എന്തിനെയെങ്കിലും കുറിച്ച് അത്യധിക ഭയം

She has a *phobia* for heights.

Phone *(n.)* ഫോൺ–ഫോൺ

Can I use your *phone*?

Photograph *(n.)* ഫോട്ടോഗ്രാഫ്–ഫോട്ടോ

I took many *photographs* during my trip to Kashmir.

Phrase *(n.)* ഫ്രേസ്–പദപ്രയോഗം

He is fond of using idiomatic *phrases* in his speeches.

Physical *(adj.)* ഫിസിക്കൽ–ശാരീരിക

A *physical* fitness certificate was required for the job.

Physician *(n.)* ഫിസിഷ്യൻ–ഭിഷഗ്വരൻ, ഡോക്ടർ

Is there a *physician* nearby?

Pick *(v.)* പിക്–1. എടുക്കുക

Please *pick* up those pieces of paper.

2. തിരഞ്ഞെടുക്കുക

Please *pick* a good book for me.

Pickle *(n.)* പിക്ക്ൾ–അച്ചാർ

Indian *pickles* have become popular abroad.

Picnic *(n.)* പിക്നിക്–ഉല്ലാസയാത്ര

Our class went on a *picnic* last Sunday.

Picture *(n.)* പിക്ചർ–ചിത്രം, പടം

His drawing room is decorated with beautiful *pictures.*

Picturesque *(adj.)* പിക്ചറെസ്ക് – ആകർഷകം, മനോഹരം

Kashmir had *picturesque* mountains.

Piece *(n.)* പീസ്–തു്, ഭാഗം

I tore the letter into small *pieces.*

Pierce *(n.)* പിയേർസ്–തുളയ്ക്കുക, കുത്തുക

These days many girls have their noses *pierced* so that they may wear nose-rings.

Piggy bank *(n.)* പിഗ്ഗി ബാങ്ക്–കുട്ടികളുടെ ചെപ്പ്, കുടുക്ക

The child dropped the one-rupee coin in the *piggy bank.*

Pigheaded *(adj.)* പിഗ്ഹൈഡഡ്–ദുശ്ശാഠ്യം

The child was *pigheaded* enough not to acknowledge his mistake.

Pile *(n. & v.)* പൈൽ–അട്ടി, കൂട്ടം

(n.) Please give this *pile* of dirty clothes to the washerman.

(v.) She *piled* up all her clothes on the bed before packing them.

Pilgrim *(n.)* പിൽഗ്രിം–തീർത്ഥ യാത്രികർ

During my trip to Amarnath, I saw many *pilgrims* making the journey to the holy cave barefoot.

Pill *(n.)* പിൽ–ഗുളിക

Nowadays there is a *pill* for almost every ailment.

Pillar *(n.)* പില്ലർ–തൂണ്, സ്തംഭം

The *pillars* of the old palace were painted in gold.

Pillow *(n.)* പില്ലോ–തലയണ

I cannot sleep without a *pillow.*

Pilot *(n. & v.)* പൈലറ്റ്–വൈമാനികൻ, പൈലറ്റ്

(n.) My son is a *pilot* in the Indian Airlines.

(v.) He *piloted* the ship very carefully through the storm.

Pimple *(n.)* പിമ്പ്ൾ–മുഖക്കുരു

She fumed over the *pimple* she got on her face.

PIN *(n.)* പിൻ– പിൻ നമ്പർ

Specify the *PIN* code on the letter.

Pin *(n. & v.)* പിൻ–മൊട്ടുസൂചി (കുത്തുക)

(v.) Please *pin* these sheets of paper together.

(n.) I need a safety *pin.*

Pinch *(v.)* പിഞ്ച്–1. നുള്ളുക

I cried out in pain when he *pinched* my arm.

(n.) 2. നുള്ള്

Please put a *pinch* of salt in this curry.

Pine *(v.)* പൈൻ–കൊതിക്കുക, ആധി പിടിപ്പിക്കുക

She *pined* for the return of her missing son.

Pink *(adj.)* പിങ്ക്–പാടലവർണ്ണം, പിങ്ക്, ഇളം റോസ്

Jaipur is called the *Pink* City.

Pinpoint *(v.)* പിൻപോയിന്റ് –ഏതെങ്കിലും കാര്യം കൃത്യമായി വിവരിക്കുക

Can you *pinpoint* the main reason behind the argument?

Pioneer *(n.)* പയനിയർ–അഗ്രഗാമി

The Americans have been *pioneers* in space travel.

Pious *(adj.)* പയസ്–ദൈവഭക്തിയുള്ള

My grandmother is a very *pious* lady.

Pipe *(n.)* പൈപ്പ്–1. കുഴൽ, പൈപ്പ്

Even in olden days, water was carried through underground *pipes.*

2. പൈപ്പ്

Do you smoke a *pipe?*

Piracy *(n.)* പൈറസി–പുസ്തകം, വീഡിയോ ടേപ് ഇവയുടെ അനധികൃതമായി പകർത്തൽ, കടൽകൊള്ള

Video *piracy* is a glaring problem these days.

Pit *(n.)* പിറ്റ്–കുഴി, കു്

I fell into a *pit* on a dark night and injured my leg.

Pitch *(n.)* പിച്ച്–1. കളിസ്ഥലം

The rains dampened the cricket *pitch.*

2. ഉച്ചസ്വരം

The children were shouting at a high *pitch.*

Pitcher *(n.)* പിച്ചർ–മൊന്ത, കുടം

Do you have some water in that *pitcher?*

Pity *(n.)* പിറ്റി–കരുണ ദയ

My wife felt *pity* for the beggar.

Placard *(n.)* പ്ലകാർഡ്–പരസ്യപത്രം, പ്ലകാർഡ്

"We want justice" read the *placard* in the woman's hand.

Place *(v.)* പ്ലേസ്–1. വയ്ക്കുക

Place the box in this corner.

(n.) 2. സ്ഥലം, സ്ഥാനം

Is there any quiet *place* where we can talk?

Plagiarism *(n.)* പ്ലേഗറിസം–സാഹിത്യ മോഷണം

The author was alleged of *plagiarism.*

Plague *(n.)* പ്ലേഗ്–രോഗം

Many people in Surat died of *plague.*

Plain *(n.)* പ്ലെയ്ൻ–1. മൈതാനം

A fierce battle was fought on this *plain* once upon a time.

(adj.) 2. സ്പഷ്ടം, വ്യക്തം

My instructions to you were quite *plain.*

3. സാധാരണ

My wife likes to wear a *plain* white dress.

4. വിരൂപ, സുന്ദരിയല്ലാത്ത

Our neighbour's wife is rather *plain-looking.*

Plait *(n.)* പ്ലെയ്റ്റ്–മുടി പിന്നൽ, മടിച്ചിൽ

She always ties her hair in two *plaits.*

Plan *(n.)* പ്ലാൻ–1. പദ്ധതി

What are your *plans* for the summer holidays?

2. രൂപരേഖ

Have you submitted the *plan* of your proposed house to the municipality?

(v.) 3. പദ്ധതിയിടുക, തീരുമാനിച്ചുറപ്പിക്കുക

When are you *planning* to get married?

Plane *(n.)* പ്ലെയ്ൻ–1. വിമാനം

I went to Mumbai by *plane.*

2. ചിന്തേരി

A carpenter cannot work without a *plane.*

Planet പ്ലാനിറ്റ്–ഗ്രഹം

The earth is one of the *planets* in the solar system.

Plank *(n.)* പ്ലാങ്ക്–പലക, പാളി

The villager built his house with wooden *planks.*

Plant *(v. & n.)* പ്ലാന്റ്–1. ചെടി, (നടുക), സസ്യം

(v.) Which flower trees have you *planted* in your garden?

(n.) 2. This is an evergreen *plant.*

3. During our trip to Darjeeling, we visited a tea *plantation.*

Plaster പ്ലാസ്റ്റർ–1. പ്ലാസ്റ്റർ, പൂശ്

The *plaster* of the wall was chipped.

(v.) 2. പൊട്ടിയ എല്ലിന് പ്ലാസ്റ്ററിടുക

The doctor *plastered* his broken leg.

Plastic *(n.)* പ്ലാസ്റ്റിക്–പ്ലാസ്റ്റിക്

Many household articles are made of *plastic.*

Plate *(n.)* പ്ലേറ്റ്–തട്ടം, പ്ലേറ്റ്

He brought some sweets in a *plate.*

(v.) 2. പൂശുക

My wrist-watch is *gold-plated.*

Platform *(n.)* പ്ലാറ്റ്ഫോം–പ്ലാറ്റ്ഫോറം

Please give me a *platform* ticket.

Play *(v. & n.)* പ്ലേ–1. കളി (കളിക്കുക)

(v.) What games do you like to *play*?

2. വായിക്കുക

Can you *play* the piano?

(n.) 3. നാടകം, തമാശ

I have acted in many *plays.*

Plea *(n.)* പ്ലീ–അപേക്ഷ, അഭ്യർത്ഥന

I urged him not to be so thoughtless but he ignored my *pleas.*

Please പ്ലീസ്–1. ദയവായി

Please take a seat.

(v.) 2. സന്തോഷിക്കുക

I shall be *pleased* to help you.

The new servant's hardworking nature *pleased* the master.

(adj.) 3. പ്രസന്ന

She has *pleasing* features.

Pledge *(n. & v.)* പ്ലെജ്–പ്രതിജ്ഞ (എടുക്കുക), വാക്ക് (നൽകുക)

(n.) It's my *pledge* to help you whenever you need me.

(v.) Our government has *pledged* to eradicate poverty from the country.

Plenty *(n.)* പ്ലന്റി–1. യഥേഷ്ടം

We have *plenty* of time to catch the train.

(adj.) 2. വളരെയേറെ, അധികം

Apples are *plentiful* in Kashmir.

Pliers *(n.)* പ്ലൈയേഴ്സ്-കൊടിൽ, പ്ലാസ്

The electrician pulled the cables by *pliers.*

Plight *(n.)* പ്ലൈറ്റ്-ദുർദശ, ദുരവസ്ഥ

The chief minister was moved by the *plight* of the blast victims.

Plot *(n.)* പ്ലോട്ട്-1. പുരയിടം

I have recently bought a *plot* of land.

2. കഥാതന്തു

This story has an interesting *plot.*

(v.) 3. ഗൂഢാലോചന നടത്തുക

The army general *plotted* to overthrow the government.

Plough *(n. & v.)* പ്ലൗ-കലപ്പ (ഓട്ടുക), നിലമുഴുക

(n.) Our farmers should use mechanised *ploughs*.

(v.) The farmer *ploughed* his field before sowing the seeds.

Pluck *(v.)* പ്ലക്ക്-1. പറിക്കുക, പൊടിക്കുക

Do not *pluck* flowers.

(n.) 2. ധൈര്യം, തന്റേടം

The little boy was full of *pluck.*

Plug പ്ലഗ്-1. വൈദ്യുത പ്ലഗ്

Get a new *plug* for the television cable.

(v.) 2. ദ്വാരമടയ്ക്കുക

She *plugged* her ears on listening to the minister's speech.

Plum *(n.)* പ്ലം-പ്ലം പഴം

The child liked to eat fresh *plums.*

Plumage *(n.)* പ്ലൂമിജ്-പക്ഷിയുടെ പൂട

The pigeon had a thick *plumage.*

Plumber *(n.)* പ്ലമ്പർ-നീർക്കുഴൽ മേസ്തിരി, പ്ലമ്പർ

I called the *plumber* to repair our wash-basin.

Plume *(adj.)* പ്ലൂം-പീലി, തൂവൽകൂട്ടം

The peacock has beautiful *plumes.*

Plump *(adj.)* പ്ലംപ്-സ്ഥൂലിച്ച

She is rather *plump,* isn't she?

Plunder *(v. & n.)* പ്ലർ-കൊള്ളയടിക്കുക, കൊള്ള

(v.) The dacoits *plundered* the rich man's mansion.

(n.) They loaded the *plunder* in a truck and drove away.

Plunge *(n. & v.)* പ്ലഞ്ച്-വെള്ളത്തിലേക്ക് ചാടുക, മുങ്ങുക

(v.) I *plunged* into the water to save the drowning child.

(n.) A careless *plunge* into the water can be harmful.

Ply *(v.)* പ്ലൈ-കൂലിയ്ക്ക് വി ഓടിക്കുക

The man was *plying* rickshaw on the road.

Pneumonia *(n.)* ന്യൂമോണിയ-ന്യൂമോണിയ, ശ്വാസകോശ രോഗം

The child was suffering from *pneumonia.*

Poach *(v.)* പോച്-ഒളിവേട്ട (ചെയ്യുക)

Poaching is banned by the governments of most of the countries.

Pocket *(n. & v.)* പോക്കറ്റ്-കീശ, കീശയിലാക്കുക

(n.) My *pockets* are always full of odds and ends.

(v.) He *pocketed* the note after reading it.

Poetry പൊയട്രി-കവിത

She has been writing *poetry* since she was a child.

Poignant *(adj.)* പോഇന്യന്റ്-തുളയ്ക്കുന്ന, മൂർച്ചയുള്ള

It was a *poignant* tale of an orphaned girl.

Point *(n.)* പോയിന്റ് -1. ചൂിക്കാണിക്കുക

Can you *point* out the man who spoke to you?

(n.) 2. മുന

He pricked me with the *point* of his pencil.

3. വിഷയം

There are several *points* in your article which I wish to discuss with you.

Poise *(n.)* പോയിസ്-ആത്മവിശ്വാസ രീതി

She delivered her speech with *poise* and confidence.

Poison *(n.)* പോയിസൺ-വിഷം

Potassium cyanide is a deadly *poison.*

(adj.) Not all snakes are *poisonous.*

(v.) വിഷം കൊടുക്കുക

Socrates was *poisoned* to death.

Poke *(v.)* പോക്-കുത്തികയറ്റുക

The little girl *poked* a stick into the hole in the garden.

Pole *(n.)* പോൾ-1. മുള, വടി

There is a telephone *pole* just opposite our house.

2. ധ്രുവം

The explorers went up to the North *Pole.*

Police *(n.)* പോലീസ്-പോലീസ്

Where is the nearest *police* station?

Policy *(n.)* പോളിസി-നയം

It is my *policy* to pay all my bills without delay.

Polish *(n. & v.)* പോളിഷ്-1. പോളിഷ് (ചെയ്യുക)

(n.) I want some *polish* for my car.

(v.) He *polished* his shoes before wearing them.

(adj.) 2. പരിഷ്കൃത

He is a *polished* gentleman.

Polite *(adj.)* പൊളൈറ്റ്-മര്യാദ, യോഗ്യ

He is always *polite* in his behaviour.

(n.) Politeness costs nothing.

Political *(adj.)* പൊളിറ്റിക്കൽ-രാഷ്ട്രീയ

I have participated in *political* activities since my school days.

Poll *(n.)* പോൾ-വോട്ടെടുപ്പ്

We might have a mid-term *poll* very soon.

Pomegranate *(n.)* പോമിഗ്രനേറ്റ്-മാതളങ്ങ

There was a *pomegranate* tree in the village.

Pomp *(n.)* പോംപ്-മോടി, ആഡംബരം

The festival was celebrated with *pomp* and enthusiasm.

Pond *(n.)* പോ് -കുളം

There is a small *pond* outside our village where we go for a swim.

Ponder *(v.)* പോർ-ചിന്തിക്കുക

Please *ponder* on all aspects of the situation before taking a decision.

Pool *(n.)* പൂൾ-കുളം

I go to the swimming *pool* every evening.

Poor *(adj.)* പൂർ-1. ദരിദ്ര, നിർദ്ധന

India is a *poor* country.

2. പാവം, ഭാഗ്യംകെട്ട

The *poor* dog had injured its paw.

3. തരംതാണ, മോശമായ

This cloth is of *poor* quality.

Popular *(adj.)* പോപ്പുലർ-ജനപ്രിയ

My son is *popular* among his school-mates.

Population *(n.)* പോപ്പുലേഷൻ-ജനസംഖ്യ

What is the *population* of your city?

Porch *(n.)* പോർച്ച്-പൂമുഖം

I halted the car in the *porch* of the house.

Pore *(n.)* പോർ-രന്ധ്രം

Regular bathing keeps the *pores* of our skin clean.

Porridge *(n.)* പോറിജ്-റവ, പോറിജ്

I had some *porridge* in breakfast.

Port *(n.)* പോർട്ട്-തുറമുഖം

Cochin is one of the finest *ports* in India.

Porter *(n.)* പോർട്ടർ-ചുമട്ടുകൂലി, പോർട്ടർ

The *porter* put my luggage in the train.

Portfolio *(n.)* പോർട്ട്ഫോളിയോ - ഛായാചിത്രം, വിതരണം, യോഗ്യതാ രേഖ ഇവയുടെ സംഗ്രഹം

She had an impressive *portfolio.*

Portion *(n.)* പോർഷൻ-ഭാഗം, ഖണ്ഡം

We have so far completed only a small *portion* of our course.

Portrait *(n.)* പോർട്രിറ്റ്-ചിത്രം, ഛായാപടം

He asked a well-known artist to paint a *portrait* of his father.

Pose പോസ്-1. വൈഷമ്യം ഉാക്കുക

Pollution *poses* a major threat to the environment.

(n.) 2. ഫോട്ടോ എടുക്കാൻ നില്ക്കുന്ന ഭാവം

She got her photograph clicked in Madhubala *pose.*

Posh *(adj.)* പോഷ്-കേമമായ

They live in a *posh* colony.

Position *(n.)* പൊസിഷൻ-1. സ്ഥാനം

Who has moved my writing table from its original *position*?

2. പദവി

My brother has got a *position* as a lecturer.

3. അവസ്ഥ

You should stand in an upright *position.*

4. പരിതസ്ഥിതി

In my present *position,* I cannot help you.

Positive *(adj.)* പോസിറ്റീവ്-തീർച്ചയുാവുക

Are you *positive* that she loves you?

Possess *(v.)* പൊസസ്-സ്വന്തമായുാക

Do you *possess* a TV set?

(n.) I put all my *possessions* in the room.

Possible *(adj.)* പോസിബ്ൾ-സാദ്ധ്യമായ

Is it *possible* to leave for Mumbai immediately?

If *possible,* come back before the nightfall.

(adj.) I may *possibly* meet you in Kolkata.

Post *(n. & v.)* പോസ്റ്റ്-1. തപാൽ (മാർഗ്ഗം അയക്കുക)

(n.) Send this letter by *post.*

(v.) Please *post* this letter.

(n.) 2. പദവി, ഉദ്യോഗം

I am trying for a *post* in this office.

3. തൂണ്

The fence was made of wooden *posts.*

Poster *(n.)* പോസ്റ്റർ-പോസ്റ്റർ, ചുവരെഴുത്ത്

During election time, *posters* appear everywhere.

Posterity *(n.)* പോസ്റ്ററിറ്റി-ഭാവിതലമുറ

We must make some investments for the good of our *posterity.*

Posthumous *(adj.)* പോസ്റ്റ്യൂമസ് - മരണാനന്തരം

The general received the *posthumous* medal for bravery.

Postpone *(v.)* പോസ്റ്റ്പോൺ-മാറ്റിവയ്ക്കുക

Our examinations have been *postponed.*

Posture *(n.)* പോസ്ചർ-ഇരുപ്പും നിൽപും നടപ്പും, ദേഹാഭ്യാസ നില

Always maintaining a good *posture* ensures good health.

Pot *(n.)* പോട്ട്-പാത്രം

My wife uses stainless steel *pots* for cooking.

Potential പൊട്ടെൻഷ്യൽ-1. സംഭാവ്യ

A good salesman must know tricks of attracting the *potential* buyers.

(n.) 2. സിദ്ധി, സാദ്ധ്യത

She has a great *potential* as a dancer.

Pouch *(n.)* പൗച്-സഞ്ചി

A baby kangaroo remains in its mother's *pouch* for some time.

Pounce *(v.)* പൗൺസ്-ചാടിവീഴുക

The cat *pounced* on the pigeon.

Poultry *(n.)* പൗൾട്രി-കോഴി

I get fresh eggs every day from my friend's *poultry* farm.

Pound *(v.)* പൗ്-നെഞ്ചിടിപ്പ്

My heart was *pounding* with fear.

Pour *(v.)* പോർ-ഒഴിക്കുക

Please *pour* some hot water in this glass.

Poverty *(n.)* പോവർട്ടി-ദാരിദ്ര്യം, നിർദ്ധനത

Many people live in *poverty.*

Powder *(n.)* പൗഡർ-പൊടി, പൗഡർ

Please give me a pack of face *powder.*

Power *(n.)* പവർ-1. പ്രബലം, അധികാരം

The police have the *power* to arrest people.

2. ശക്തി

I shall do everything in my *power* to help you.

(adj.) My uncle is a *powerful* man.

Practice *(n.)* പ്രാക്ടീസ്-ശീലം, വഴക്കം

It is a dangerous *practice* to get off a moving bus.

Practise *(v.)* പ്രാക്ടിസ്-ശീലം, വളർത്തുക, അഭ്യസിക്കുക

I have to *practise* my part in the play.

Praise *(n. & v.)* പ്രെയ്സ്-പ്രശംസ(ിക്കുക)

(n.) He is unaffected by *praise* or blame.

(v.) My son's teacher *praised* him for his good marks.

Pray *(v.)* പ്രേ–പ്രാർത്ഥിക്കുക
We *pray* to God to help us.
(n.) People from all communities used to attend Gandhiji's samadhi for *prayer* meetings on October 2.

Preach *(v.)* പ്രീച്–പ്രവചിക്കുക, ഉപദേശിക്കുക
Gandhiji *preached* truthfulness and continence.

Precaution *(n.)* പ്രികാഷൻ–മുൻകരുതൽ
I took the *precaution* of locking my house before going out.

Precede *(v.)* പ്രിസീഡ്–ആദ്യം വരുന്ന, ആദ്യം സംഭവിക്കുന്ന
Please follow me, I shall *precede* you.

Precious *(adj.)* പ്രഷ്യസ്–വിലപിടിച്ച, അമൂല്യ
A very *precious* painting has been stolen from the museum.

Precise *(adj.)* പ്രിസൈസ്–കൃത്യമായ, ശരിയായ
If you follow my *precise* directions, you can easily find my house.

Predecessor *(n.)* പ്രിഡിസെസർ–മുൻഗാമി
We did not like our present manager's *predecessor* very much.

Preen *(v.)* പ്രീൻ–അലങ്കരിക്കുക, ഒരുങ്ങുക
She spent an hour *preening* herself in front of the mirror.

Predicament *(n.)* പ്രിഡികമെന്റ്–ദുരവസ്ഥ, ദുർഗതി
The *predicament* of the parents at the loss of their son was unimaginable.

Predict *(v.)* പ്രെഡിക്റ്റ്–പ്രവചിക്കുക
An astrologer has *predicted* that I shall settle abroad.

Preface *(n.)* പ്രെഫിസ്–ആമുഖം, മുഖവുര
I requested the minister to write a *preface* for my book.

Prefer *(v.)* പ്രിഫർ–ഇഷ്ടപ്പെടുക
Do you *prefer* tea a coffee?

Prejudice *(n.)* പ്രെജുഡിസ്–വിരോധം
He seems to have a *prejudice* against me.
(v.) മുൻകൂട്ടിയുള്ള സ്പർദ്ധ
The newspaper gossip *prejudiced* her against him.

Preliminary *(adj.)* പ്രിലിമിനറി–പ്രാഥമിക
The finalists will be selected after the *preliminary* round.

Premier *(adj.)* പ്രീമിയർ–സർവ്വോത്തമ
It is a *premier* hotel in the city.

Premiere *(n.)* പ്രിമിയർ–നാടകത്തിന്റേയോ സിനിമയുടേയോ ആദ്യ പൊതുദർശനം
The actress was hounded by media at the *premiere.*

Premises *(n.)* പ്രിമിസിസ്–ഭവനം, പരിസരം
No one is allowed on these *premises* after 7 P.M.

Prepare *(v.)* പ്രിപെയർ–1. ഉാക്കുക
What sweet dish have you *prepared* today?
2. തയ്യാറാക്കുക
He is not *prepared* to help me.
(n.) Have you made the *preparations* for the journey?

Prescribe *(v.)* പ്രിസ്ക്രൈബ്–കുറിപ്പടി എഴുതുക
The doctor *prescribed* an effective medicine.
(n.) കുറിപ്പടി
I have lost the *prescription* somewhere.

Prestige *(n.)* പ്രെസ്റ്റീജ്–അന്തസ്സ്, സൽപ്പേര്
(n.) The school has maintained its *prestige* over the years.
(adj.) This is the most *prestigious* school in the city.

Present *(v.)* പ്രെസന്റ്–1. സമ്മാനിക്കുക
The guest of honour *presented* a trophy to the school.
(n.) 2. ഉപഹാരം, സമ്മാനം
I received many *presents* on my birthday.
(adj.) 3. ഹാജരാകുക
Were you *present* when the fire broke out?
4. നിലവിലുള്ള, ഇപ്പോഴത്തെ
Our *present* teacher is very good.

Preserve *(v.)* പ്രിസെർവ്–1. രക്ഷിക്കുക, കാത്തുസൂക്ഷിക്കുക
Preserve this document carefully.
(n.) പരിരക്ഷണം
Food *preservation* is a growing industry.

Preside *(v.)* പ്രിസൈഡ്–അദ്ധ്യക്ഷപദം അലങ്കരിക്കുക
Who is going to *preside* over our meeting?

Press *(n.)* പ്രസ്സ്–1 അച്ചടിശാല, മുദ്രണാലയം
In what *press* was this book printed?
2. വർത്തമാന പത്രം, പത്രം
I often write letters to the *press*.
(v.) 3. സമ്മർദ്ദം ചെലുത്തുക
Please do not *press* me to eat more.
4. അമർത്തുക
I *pressed* the button of the door bell.

Presume *(v.)* പ്രിസ്യൂം–സങ്കല്പിക്കുക
Don't *presume* his consent to work with us.

Pretext *(n.)* പ്രിടെക്സ്റ്റ്–ഒഴിവുകഴിവ്
She left the job on the *pretext* of getting married.

Pretend *(v.)* പ്രിടെൻഡ്–ഭാവിക്കുക
He likes to *pretend* that he is a rich man.

Priest *(n.)* പ്രീസ്റ്റ്–പുരോഹിതൻ, പാതിരി.
The temple *priest* bathed deities in the morning.

Pretty *(adj.)* പ്രിറ്റി–മനോഹരി, സുന്ദരി
She is a *pretty* girl.

Prevail *(v.)* പ്രിവെയ്ൽ–1. വിജയിക്കുക
After a hard struggle, we *prevailed* over the opposite team.
2. സമ്മതിപ്പിക്കുക
Can I *prevail* on you to have dinner with us?

Prevent *(v.)* പ്രിവെന്റ്–തടയുക
I tried to *prevent* the boys from quarrelling.
(n.) Prevention is better than cure.

Previous *(adj.)* പ്രിവിയസ്–മുമ്പത്തെ
Have you read the *previous* page?

Prey *(v.)* പ്രേ–1. പതിയിരുന്നാക്രമിക്കുക, കവർച്ച
Leopards *prey* on deer.
(n.) 2. ഇര
This forest is full of birds of *prey*.

Price *(n.)* പ്രൈസ്–1. വില
What is the *price* of this TV set?
2. മൂല്യം
This ancient work of art is *priceless*.

Prick *(v.)* പ്രിക്–കുത്തുക, തറയ്ക്കുക
A thorn *pricked* my foot.

Pride *(n.)* പ്രൈഡ്–അഭിമാനം, ഗർവ്വം
I take *pride* in my son's academic record.

Prince *(n.)* പ്രിൻസ്–രാജകുമാരൻ
The *prince* punished the culprit.

Primary *(adj.)* പ്രൈമറി–1. പ്രാഥമിക
I have admitted my son to a *primary* school.
2. മൗലിക, അടിസ്ഥാന
My *primary* intention in coming here was to meet you.

Principal *(n.)* പ്രിൻസിപ്പൽ–1. കലാലയാദ്ധ്യക്ഷൻ, പിൻസിപ്പൽ
Who is the *principal* of your college?
(adj.) 2. പ്രധാന, മുഖ്യ
The *principal* item we sell is cosmetics.

Principle *(n.)* പ്രിൻസിപ്പിൾ–1. സിദ്ധാന്തം, തത്വം
He is a man of noble *principles*.
2. അടിസ്ഥാന തത്വം
Have you understood the *principle* of this law of Physics?

Print *(n. & v.)* പ്രിന്റ്–അച്ചടിക്കുക, അച്ചടി, മുദ്രണം
(n.) My book is at present under *print*.
(v.) We *print* books of high standard.

Prior *(adj.)* പ്രയർ–മുമ്പ്
We met him *prior* to his trip aboard.

Prison *(n.)* പ്രിസൺ–ജയിൽ
The thief was sent to the *prison*.

Private *(adj.)* പ്രൈവറ്റ്–1. സ്വകാര്യ
I work in a *private* concern.
(adv.) 2. ഒറ്റയ്ക്ക്, തനിയെ
May I speak to you *privately*?

Privilege *(n.)* പ്രിവിലിജ്–പ്രത്യേകാനുകൂല്യം, വിശേഷാധികാരം
It would be a *privilege* for us to have you with us for dinner.

Prize *(n.)* പ്രൈസ്–സമ്മാനം, പുരസ്കാരം
Who won the first *prize* in the music contest?

Probable *(adj.)* പ്രോബബ്ൾ–സാദ്ധ്യതയുള്ള
It is *probable* that most of these boys will pass.

Probation *(n.)* പ്രൊബേഷൻ–താല്കാലിക, പരീക്ഷണ കാലം
He is on *probation* for six months.

Probe *(v.)* പ്രോബ്–രഹസ്യവിവരങ്ങളറിയാനുള്ള ചോദ്യം ചെയ്യൽ
The press was *probing* into the personal life of the actor.

Problem *(n.)* പ്രോബ്ലം–പ്രശ്നം
We must learn to live with our *problems.*

Proceed *(v.)* പ്രൊസീഡ്–1. മുമ്പോട്ട് പോകുക
After a short rest, we *proceeded* on our way.
2. ചെയ്യാൻ തുടങ്ങുക
After taking a cup of tea, mother *proceeded* to cook the dinner.
(n.) 3. നടപടി
Have you read the account of the court *proceedings* in the murder case?

Process പ്രൊസസ്–1. ക്രിയകളുടെ ശൃംഖല
Though a failure, the project proved to be a learning *process* for us.
(adj.) 2. സംസ്കരിച്ച സാധനങ്ങൾ
It is better to avoid *processed* food to stay healthy.

Procession *(n.)* പ്രൊസെഷൻ–ഘോഷയാത്ര
All trafffic was blocked by the Durga Puja *procession.*

Proclaim *(v.)* പ്രൊക്ലെയിം–പ്രഖ്യാപിക്കുക
A man went round the market *proclaiming* the news.

Procure *(v.)* പ്രൊക്യൂർ–നേടുക
Can you *procure* a pen and a paper?

Produce *(v.)* പ്രൊഡ്യൂസ്–1. ഉല്പാദിപ്പിക്കുക, സൃഷ്ടിക്കുക
The magician *produced* a rabbit from his hat.
2. രചിക്കുക, നിർമ്മിക്കുക
Where is this car *produced*?
(n.) 3. ഉല്പന്നം, വിളവ്
The farmers brought their *produce* to the market.

Profess *(v.)* പ്രഫസ്–മനോഭാവം പ്രകടിപ്പിക്കുക
She *professed* her resentment for the new budget scheme.

Profession *(n.)* പ്രഫഷൻ – വൃത്തി, തൊഴിൽ
I am a lawyer by *prefession.*
2. പ്രഖ്യാപനം
It is foolish to believe his *professions.*

Proficient *(adj.)* പ്രഫിഷന്റ്–സമർത്ഥ(ൻ)
He is *proficient* in both English and Hindi.

Profit *(n. & v.)* പ്രോഫിറ്റ് – ലാഭം (സമ്പാദിക്കുക), ആദായം (ഉാകുക)
(n.) He sold his goods at a big *profit.*
(v.) He *profited* by the sale of his car.

Programme *(n.)* പ്രോഗ്രാം–പരിപാടി
Have you chalked out your *programme* for the vacation?

Progress *(n.)* പ്രോഗ്രസ്–1. പുരോഗതി, ഉന്നതി
My teacher was pleased with my *progress.*
(v.) 2. മുന്നേറുക
How far have you *progressed* with the book you are writing?

Prohibit *(v.)* പ്രൊഹിബിറ്റ്–നിരോധിക്കുക
Smoking is *prohibited* in the cinema hall.

Project *(n.)* പ്രൊജെക്റ്റ്–1. പദ്ധതി
Have you prepared a *project* report for the industry you want to set up?
(v.) 2. പ്രകടമാക്കുക, കാഴ്ചവയ്ക്കുക
Thio company is trying to *project* a new image in the market.

Prolific *(adj.)* പ്രോലിഫിക്–സമൃദ്ധ, ബഹുല
Gulzar is a *prolific* writer.

Prolong *(v.)* പ്രോലോംഗ്–ദീർഘിപ്പിക്കുക, വിപുലമാക്കുക
I would not like to *prolong* my stay in Kolkata.

Prominent *(adj.)* പ്രോമിനന്റ്–പ്രമുഖ, പ്രധാന
I saw many *prominent* people at the glittering function.

Promisc *(n.)* പ്രോമിസ്–1. വാഗ്ദാനം (ചെയ്യുക)
You should always keep your *promise.*
2. വാക് (നൽകുക)
She shows *promise* as a singer.
(v.) My mother *promised* to buy me a watch on my birthday.

Promote *(v.)* പ്രമോട്ട്–1. കയറ്റം (കിട്ടുക)
My son has been *promoted* to the higher class.

(n.) 2. സ്ഥാനക്കയറ്റം

My brother has been given a *promotion* to the rank of captain.

Prompt *(adj.)* പ്രോംപ്റ്റ്–സത്വര

You must take *prompt* action to remedy this situation.

Prone *(adj.)* പ്രോൺ–ഏതെങ്കിലും രോഗം അല്ലെങ്കിൽ സ്ഥിതി ബാധിക്കാനുള്ള സാദ്ധ്യത

Diabetic patients are *prone* to many other diseases.

Pronounce *(v.)* പ്രനൗൺസ്–1. ഉച്ചരിക്കുക, കേൾപ്പിക്കുക

Some words are very difficult to *pronounce.*

(n.) 2. ഉച്ചാരണ ശുദ്ധി

You must improve your *pronunciation.*

Proof *(n.)* പ്രൂഫ്–തെളിവ്

(n.) What is the *proof* that he committed the theft?

(v.) Can you *prove* that he committed the theft?

Propaganda *(n.)* പ്രൊപഗാൻഡ–പ്രചാരണം

Despite the whole *propaganda,* the movie was a big flop.

Proper *(adj.)* പ്രോപർ–1. ശരിയായ

Put all these books in the *proper* place.

(adv.) 2. ഉചിത

You are not dressed *properly.*

Property *(n.)* പ്രോപർട്ടി–വസ്തുവക, ഭൂസ്വത്ത്

He owns residential *property* in Goa.

Proportion *(n.)* പ്രപോർഷൻ–അനുപാതം

What is the *proportion* of boys and girls in you class?

Propose *(v.)* പ്രപോസ്–1. ഉദ്ദേശിക്കുന്ന

I *propose* to go abroad in the near future.

2. വിവാഹാഭ്യർത്ഥന നടത്തുക

I hear Madhav has *proposed* to Meena.

Proprietor *(n.)* പ്രൊപ്രൈറ്റർ–ഉടമ

The *proprietor* of the hotel received me at the door.

Prospect *(n.)* പ്രോസ്പെക്റ്റ്––1. സാദ്ധ്യത

Do you have good *prospects* in this concern?

2. പ്രത്യാശ

I look forward to the *prospect* of seeing you.

Prosper *(v.)* പ്രോസ്പർ–സമ്പന്നമാകുക

His business has *prospered* fast.

Now he is *prosperous.*

Protect *(v.)* പ്രൊട്ടെക്റ്റ്–സംരക്ഷിക്കുക, രക്ഷിക്കുക

I wear a hat to *protect* myself from the sun.

Protest പ്രൊട്ടെസ്റ്റ്–പ്രതിഷേധിക്കുക

(n.) The union organised a *protest* against low wages.

(v.) The employees *protested* against the policy of the management.

Protrude *(v.)* തള്ളിനില്ക്കുക

The branches of the tree were *protruding* from the old wall of the cave.

Proud *(adj.)* പ്രൗഡ്–1. അഭിമാനി, ഗർവ്വിഷ്ഠ

Every mother is *proud* of her children.

2. അഭിമാന പൂരിതമായ

Abhinav Bindra's winning of Olympic gold medal was a *proud* moment for the whole nation.

Prove *(v.)* പ്രൂവ്–തെളിയിക്കുക

Can you *prove* your charge of theft against this man?

(n.) തെളിവ്

Do you have any *proof*?

Provide *(v.)* പ്രൊവൈഡ്–1. നൽകുക, ലഭ്യമാക്കുക

We *provided* the poor family with a shelter.

2. കരുതിവയ്ക്കുക

Wise people *provide* for their old age.

(n.) 3. ഭക്ഷ്യ–പാനീയങ്ങൾ

Go to the market and buy some *provisions.*

Provoke *(v.)* പ്രവോക്–പ്രകോപിപ്പിക്കുക

Do not *provoke* me with nasty remarks.

Prudent *(adj.)* പ്രൂഡന്റ്–വിവേകപൂർണ്ണ

Prudent use of electricity would contribute in conservation of power.

Psychology *(n.)* സൈക്കോളജി–മാനസിക നില

She understands the *psychology* of children very well.

Pub *(n.)* പബ്-മദ്യശാല

I met him at the *pub* last week.

Public *(adj.)* പബ്ലിക്-1. സാധാരണ

Is this a *public* thoroughfare?

2. പൊതു

A restaurant is a *public* place.

(n.) 3. പരസ്യമായി

There are certain things that I cannot say in *public*.

4. ജനത, പൊതുജനം

The truth was made known to the general *public*.

Publish *(v.)* പബ്ലിഷ്-പ്രസിദ്ധീകരിക്കുക

Has your book been *published*?

Puddle *(n.)* പഡിൽ-വെള്ളം നിറഞ്ഞ, ചളി കു

Our lane becomes full of *puddles* in the rainy season.

Pull *(v.)* പുൾ-വലിക്കുക

Please *pull* down the curtain.

Pulp *(n.)* പൾപ്-ദശ, സത്ത്, കുഴ്

She made a thick *pulp* of tomatoes.

Pulse *(n.)* പൾസ്-നാഡി

The doctor felt my *pulse*.

Pump *(v.)* പമ്പ്-1. പമ്പ് ചെയ്യുക, കാറ്റ് നിറയ്ക്കുക

I *pumped* air into the tube.

(n.) 2. പമ്പ്

I have purchased a new water *pump*.

Puppet *(n.)* പപ്പിറ്റ്-1. പാവ കളി

We enjoyed watching the *puppet* show.

2. താളത്തിനൊത്തു തുള്ളുന്ന

Stop being a *puppet* in his hands.

Punctual *(adj.)* പംക്ചൽ-സമയനിഷ്ഠയുള്ള

You should always be *punctual*.

Punish *(v.)* പണിഷ്-ശിക്ഷിക്കുക

You should be *punished* for your misbehaviour.

Pupil *(n.)* പ്യൂപ്ൾ-1. ശിക്ഷ്യൻ, വിദ്യാർത്ഥി

He has been my *pupil* since he was a child.

2. കൃഷ്ണമണി

A cat's *pupils* are dilated in the dark.

Puppy *(n.)* പപ്പി-നായ്ക്കുട്ടി

The little girl pampered the *puppy*.

Purchase *(v.)* പർചേസ്-1. വാങ്ങുക

For how much did you *purchase* this tape recorder?

(n.) 2. വാങ്ങിയ വസ്തുക്കൾ

She put all her *purchases* in a bag.

Pure *(adj.)* പ്യൂർ-1. ശുദ്ധ

We should always drink *pure* water.

2. തികച്ചും

This is *purely* my personal opinion.

Purpose *(n.)* പർപസ്-1. ഉദ്ദേശ്യം

What was the *purpose* of your trip?

(adj.) 2. കരുതികൂട്ടി

I did not strike you *purposely*, it was an accident.

Purse *(n.)* പേഴ്സ്-മടിശ്ശീല, പേഴ്സ്

I *bought* a *purse* as a present for my wife.

Pursue *(v.)* പെർസ്യൂ-പിന്തുടരുക

The policeman *pursued* the thief and caught him.

Push *(v.)* പുഷ്-1. തള്ളുക

I *pushed* the door open.

(n.) 2. തള്ള്

We gave the heavy box a good *push* to move it.

Put *(v.)* പുട്ട്-1. വയ്ക്കുക

Where have you *put* my spectacles?

2. *Put on* ധരിക്കുക

Put on your clothes quickly.

3. *Put off* വേണ്ടെന്ന് വയ്ക്കുക

I cannot *put off* my visit to Mumbai.

4. *Put out* അണയ്ക്കുക

Please *put out* the light.

Puzzle *(v.)* പസ്ൽ-1. അന്ധാളിക്കുക

Your actions *puzzle* me.

(n.) 2. പ്രശ്നം, കടങ്കഥ

Can you solve this crossword *puzzle*?

Pyre *(n.)* പൈർ-ചിത

The body was burnt on the *pyre*.

Q

Quack *(n.)* ക്വാക്-അരവൈദ്യൻ

Do not ever visit that doctor. He is a *quack* and does not hold a medical degree.

(v.) 2. ക്വാക്-ക്വാക് ശബ്ദമുാക്കുക

The ducks *quacked* until they were fed.

Quadruped *(n.)* ക്വാഡ്രുപെഡ്-നാൽക്കാലി

A cow is a *quadruped.*

Quail *(v.)* ക്വെയ്ൽ-നടുങ്ങുക

The convict *quailed* when he was sentenced.

Quaint *(adj.)* ക്വെയ്ന്റ്-വിചിത്ര, വിലക്ഷണ

The old man's house was old and *quaint.*

I saw a *quaint* old lady.

Quake *(v.)* ക്വേക്-വിറയ്ക്കുക, കുലുങ്ങുക

You are *quaking* with cold.

Qualify *(v.)* ക്വാളിഫൈ-1. യോഗ്യത നേടുക

You do not *qualify* for this post.

(adj.) 2. അംഗീകാരം നേടുക

Are you *qualified* as a doctor?

3. യോഗ്യത

What are your *qualifications*?

Quality *(n.)* ക്വാളിറ്റി-1. ഇനം, തരം

This tea is not of good *quality.*

2. മേന്മ, ഗുണം

Honesty is one of the *qualities* of an ideal businessman.

Qualm *(n.)* ക്വാം-ബുദ്ധിമുട്ടുക, പ്രയാസം

I have no *qualms* about going to his place again and again.

Quantity *(n.)* ക്വാിറ്റി-1. അളവ്, മാത്ര

Pearls are found in large *quantities* in this part of the sea.

Just add a small *quantity* of water to the medicine.

Quarantine *(n.)* ക്വാരൻടീൻ-ഒപ്പം ഇരിക്കാനോ കഴിക്കാനോ വിസമ്മതിക്കുക, സാംക്രമിക രോഗികളെ മാറ്റി പാർപ്പിക്കുക

We may not see Umesh because he is in *quarantine.*

Quarrel ക്വാറൽ-വഴക്ക്(കൂടുക), കലഹ(ം, ിക്കുക)

(v.) The children are *quarrelling* about who should have the red pen.

(n.) We don't know the cause of their *quarrel.*

Quarry-1. മട, കല്ലുവെട്ടാം കുഴി

(v.) Large quantities of slate are *quarried* in Wales.

(n.) 2. ഇര

The hunter followed his *quarry* for several hours.

Quart *(n.)* ക്വാർട്ട്-1.14 ലിറ്റർ

There are two pints in a *quart.*

Do you need three *quarts* of milk?

Quarter *(n.)* ക്വാർട്ടർ-1. നാലിലൊന്ന് ഭാഗം

It is *quarter* to four.

Would you like to have a *quarter* of bread?

2. ദിശ

We went to all the *quarters* of Rohtak district.

(adv.) You may pay your instalments *quarterly.*

Quartz *(n.)* ക്വാർട്ട്സ്-വെങ്കല്ല് കെട്ട്

Sometimes gold is found in *quartz.*

Queen *(n.)* ക്വീൻ-1. രാജപത്നി, റാണി

King Dashratha had three *queens.*

2. രാജ്ഞി, രാജകീയ

Queen Elizabeth was a very successful ruler.

(adj.) She has *queenly* manners.

Queer *(adj.)* ക്വീർ–1. വിചിത്ര, വിശേഷപ്പെട്ട

Ahmad is a *queer* man. He talks to nobody.

2. അസ്വസ്ഥത

Rishi felt a little *queer* after taking rice.

3. സംശയാലു

We should not trust the *queer* characters.

Quell *(v.)* ക്വെൽ–തടയുക, അമർത്തുക

The fighting was *quelled* by the police.

Quench *(v.)* ക്വെൻച്–തീയണയ്ക്കുക

The flames were *quenched* with gallons of water.

Query ക്വറി–1. ചോദ്യം, സംശയം

(n.) Please solve my *queries* marked in this book.

(v.) 2. അന്വേഷിക്കുക

I would like to *query* these facts.

Quest *(n.)* ക്വെസ്റ്റ്–തേടുക

The herd of elephants wandered in the jungle in *quest* of water.

Question *(n.)* ക്വെസ്ചൻ–1. ചോദ്യം

I request you to answer my *questions.*

2. ആലോചിക്കേ കാര്യം

The *question* is, how to beat the competitors.

3. സംശയം, സന്ദേഹം

Please accept my proposal without any *question.*

(v.) 4. ചോദ്യം ചെയ്യുക

I would like to *question* you.

Queue *(n.)* ക്യൂ–നിര, ലൈൻ

Please stand in a *queue.*

Please take your place in the *queue.*

(v.) 2. ലൈനായി നില്ക്കുക

People *queue* at the bus-stop.

Quick *(adj.)* ക്വിക്–വേഗം, സത്വര, പെട്ടെന്ന്

We should take *quick* decisions.

Rishi Raj has a very *quick* mind.

Be *quick* please. We don't have much time.

"Quick march", said the drill-master.

(adv.) Please don't walk *quickly.*

Quiet ക്വയറ്റ്–നിശ്ശബ്ദം, മൗനം, ശാന്തം

(adj.) Be *quiet*, please.

Some people like a *quiet* life.

(n.) I love the sweet *quiet* of the countryside.

(v.) Try to *quieten* the child.

(adv.) Please move *quietly.*

Quill *(n.)* ക്വിൽ–തൂവൽ

In olden times, people used to write with *quill.*

Quit *(v.)* ക്വിറ്റ്–വിടുക

"*Quit* the hall at once", ordered the teacher.

Quite *(adv.)* ക്വയിറ്റ്–തികച്ചും, പൂർണ്ണമായും, തീർച്ചയായും

The orange was *quite* nice in taste.

Are you *quite* certain that you will pass?

Quiver *(v.)* ക്വിവർ–വിറയ്ക്കുക, ഇളകുക

The leaves of the tree *quivered* in the wind.

(adj.) Minakshi sang the song in a *quivering* voice.

Quiz *(n.)* ക്വിസ്–ചോദ്യോത്തര പ്രശ്നം

Let us try to answer this poetry *quiz.*

Quota *(n.)* ക്വോട്ട–ക്വോട്ട

The mail messages in my inbox exceeded the *quota.*

Quote *(v.)* ക്വോട്ട്–1. ഉദ്ധരിക്കുക

The people ofter *quote* Shakespeare.

2. വില ഇടുക

Ask Mr. Gopal to *quote* a price for his TV set.

R

Rabbit *(n.)* റാബിറ്റ്–മുയൽ

The *rabbit* is a small and furry animal that digs holes in the earth to live in.

Race *(n.)* റേസ്–1. ജാതി, വംശം

We all belong to the human *race.*

2. ഓട്ടം

Suresh came first in the 3 kilometre *race.*

(v.) 3. ഓടുക

Let us *race* to the next door.

Hamid *races* his pigeons every day.

Rack *(n.)* റാക്–1. സാധനം സൂക്ഷിക്കുന്ന തട്ട്

Put these books in the *rack.*

(v.) 2. കഴയ്ക്കുക, വേദനിക്കുക

After working in the field the whole day, his body *racked* with pain.

3. പ്രയോഗിക്കുക

Try to *rack* your brain to solve the problem.

Racket *(n.)* റാകിറ്റ്–1. കോലാഹലം, ബഹളം, കലകലശബ്ദം

What a *racket* the children are making!

2. റാകിറ്റ്

We use a *racket* while playing badminton.

Radar *(n.)* റഡാർ–യാത്രയിൽ ദിശ മനസ്സിലാക്കാൻ സഹായിക്കുന്ന റേഡിയോ യന്ത്രം

Aeroplanes use *radar* to find their direction.

Radiant *(adj.)* 1. പ്രസന്ന ഭാവമുള്ള, തേജസ്സുറ്റ

Asha was *radiant* when she learnt that she had stood first in the class.

2. തിളങ്ങുക

The morning sun was *radiant.* It made everything look bright.

Radiate *(v.)* റേഡിയേറ്റ്–1. പ്രസരിപ്പിക്കുക, രശ്മികളോ താപമോ പുറത്തേക്ക് വിടുക

The electric heater *radiates* heat to all parts of the room.

(n.) പ്രസാരക യന്ത്രം

The room is heated by electric *radiators.*

Radio *(n.)* റേഡിയോ–1. ആകാശവാണി കേന്ദ്രം

My father works in All India *Radio,* New Delhi.

2. റേഡിയോ സെറ്റ്

We bought a new *radio* set.

(v.) 3. കമ്പിയില്ലാ കമ്പി ഉപകരണത്തിലൂടെ വിവരം നൽകുക

Ships in danger *radio* for help.

Radish റാഡിഷ്–മുള്ളങ്കി

We can buy a bunch of *radishes* at the green-grocer's.

Radium *(n.)* റേഡിയം–1. വിലപിടിച്ച ധാതു

Radium is used in the treatment of many diseases.

Radius *(n.)* റേഡിയസ്–1. വ്യാസാർദ്ധം

The teacher asked the students to draw a circle with a *radius* of 5 centimetres.

2. വലയം

This job is not within the *radius* of our expertise.

Rag *(n.)* റാഗ്–പഴന്തുണി, കീറതുണി

The beggar's clothes were in *rags.*

(v.) 2. കഷ്ടപ്പെടുത്തുക, ശല്യം ചെയ്യുക, റാഗിംഗ്

The senior students of the medical college *ragged* the first year students.

Rage റേജ്–ക്രോധം, രോഷം, കോപിച്ച് തുള്ളുക

(n.) Sultana could not control her *rage* when Rashid broke her toy.

(v.) His father *raged* about the room as if he were mad.

A storm was *raging* all night long.

Raid റെയ്ഡ്–തിരച്ചിൽ (നടത്തുക)

(v.) The police *raided* an illicit liquor distillery.

(*n.*) Many areas were destroyed in the air *raids.*
The enemy *raiders* attacked the radio station.

Rail (*n.*) റെയ്ൽ–1. കൈപ്പിടി, അഴി, കമ്പി
When you come down the stairs, keep your hand on the *rail.*
2. റെയ്ൽവേ
These parcels should be sent by *rail.*
My cousin works in the *railways.*

Rain റെയ്ൻ–മഴ (പെയ്യുക), പേമാരി, വർഷപാതം
(*n.*) Don't go out in the *rain.*
Rajasthan has had a low *rainfall* this year.
(*v.*) It is *raining.* You should put on your *raincoat.*
(*adj.*) Lay by something for a *rainy* day.

Raise (*v.*) റെയ്സ്–1. ഉയർത്തുക, നിർത്തുക, ഉത്തേജിപ്പിക്കുക
She *raised* her arms above her head.
2. വർദ്ധിപ്പിക്കുക, ശമ്പള വർദ്ധന (നൽകുക)
The manager agreed to *raise* her wages from the next month.
3. സമാഹരിക്കുക, ശേഖരിക്കുക
We should *raise* enough funds to buy a new TV set for our school.
4. ഉച്ചത്തിൽ സംസാരിക്കുക
Please *raise* your voice so that we may be able to hear you.

Raisin (*n.*) റെയ്സ്ൻ–ഉണക്ക മുന്തിരിങ്ങ, ദ്രാക്ഷം, കിസ്മിസ്
Raisins are put in cakes and puddings.

Rake റേക്–1. വാരി കൂട്ടുക
(*v.*) The farmers were *raking* up the hay.
(*n.*) I need a *rako* to gather the hay.
2. തിരയുക, തപ്പിനോക്കുക
We *raked* among the heap but could not find the bracelet.

Rally (*n.*) റാലി–1. റാലി
The leader addressed a youth *rally.*
(*v.*) 2. ആജ്ഞാനുവർത്തികളായി ഒത്തുചേരുക
The young students *rallied* around their leader.

Ram (*n.*) റാം–1. കൊറ്റനാട്
A male sheep is called *ram.*
2. കുത്തിനിറയ്ക്ക
I hastily *rammed* my papers into my bag.
3. കൂട്ടിമുട്ടുക
The steamer *rammed* our boat in the dark night.

Random റാൻഡം–നിരുദ്ദേശപരം, മനപൂർവ്വമല്ലാതെ
(*n.*) The enemy fired at *random.*
(*adj.*) You should not mind his *random* remarks.

Range (*n.*) റെയ്ഞ്ച്–1. അടുപ്പ്
Dinner was cooked on the kitchen *range.*
2. വ്യാപ്തി, പരപ്പ്
This gun has a *range* of twenty-five miles.
(*v.*) 3. വിഹരിക്കുക
Elephants *range* in the thick forest.

Rank (*n.*) റാങ്ക്–1. വരി
The boys stood in a *rank.*
(*v.*) 2. കണക്കാക്കുക
Do you not *rank* me among your intimate friends?
(*n.*) 3. തലം, ശ്രേണി
Is he an artist of a high *rank*?
(*v.*) 4. പദവി, സ്ഥാനം
An admiral *ranks* higher than a captain.

Ransack (*v.*) റാൻസാക്–കൊള്ളയിടുക
The burglars *ransacked* the house and took away some valuables.
2. പരിശോധിക്കുക, തിരയുക
My wife *ransacked* the suitcase but she could not find her wrist watch.

Ransom (*v.*) റാൻസം–1. ആവശ്യപ്പെട്ട മൂല്യം അടയ്ക്കുക
The ruler was *ransomed* by the capitalists.
(*n.*) മോചന ദ്രവ്യം
The kidnappers demanded a large *ransom* for the child they had kidnapped.

Rap റാപ്–കതകിൽ തട്ടുക
(*n.*) Give a *rap* on the door.
(*v.*) I *rapped* on the door but nobody opened it.

Rapid *(adj.)* റാപിഡ്-ശീഘ്ര ഗതി, പെട്ടെന്ന്
We should make a *rapid* journey by Frontier Mail.

Rapport *(n.)* റാപോ-സൗഹാർദ്ദം
I share a good *rapport* with most of my colleagues.

Rapture *(n.)* റാപ്ചർ-ഹർഷോന്മാദം
She was into *raptures* to stand first in the whole university.

Rare *(adj.)* റെയ്ർ-ദുർലഭ, അപൂർവ്വ
I have got some *rare* stamps in my collection.
2. ചിലപ്പോഴൊക്കെ
Ganesh lives far away from his parents, so he pays *rare* visits to them.
(adj.) We *rarely* see a chariot these days. They are out of fashion.

Raring *(adj.)* റെയറിംഗ്-അതിയായ താല്പര്യം
They were *raring* to bid for the new project.

Rascal *(n.)* റാസ്കൽ-1. ആഭാസൻ, നീചൻ
He is a *rascal,* don't trust him.
2. കുസൃതി കുടുക്ക
The little *rascal* has finished the whole packet of biscuits.

Rash *(adj.)* റാഷ്-1. മുൻപിൻ നോക്കാതെ
Don't be *rash* in taking a decision.
(n.) 2. ചുവന്ന കുരു
When we saw the *rash,* we came to know that the young boy had chicken-pox.

Raspberry *(n.)* റാസ്ബെറി-റാസ്ബെറി പഴം
I like *raspberries* very much.

Rat *(n.)* റാറ്റ്-എലി
The cat caught a *rat.*

Rate റേറ്റ്-1. നിരക്ക്
(n.) Please tell us your *rates.*
2. അനുപാതം, തരം
This is a first-*rate* TV set.
(v.) 3. കരുതുക, വിലയിരുത്തുക
Don't *rate* your chances of success highly.
4. ആദരിക്കുക, സ്ഥാനം നൽകുക
Indians *rate* Kalidasa as one of the greatest poets of the world.
(n.) 5. ഗതി
The cycle was moving at the *rate* of ten miles an hour.
6. നിരക്ക്
The *rate* of interest for home loans has risen.

Rather *(adv.)* റാദർ-1. അല്പം
My mother is feeling *rather* ill today.
2. മറിച്ച് (അഥവാ ശരിക്ക് പറഞ്ഞാൽ)
The rising sun is golden, *rather* red.
3. ഒരു പരിധിവരെ
Your brother's behaviour is *rather* foolish.

Ratio *(n.)* റേഷിയോ-അനുപാതം
The sex *ratio* of men to women is falling in our country.

Ration റേഷൻ-ദൗർലഭ്യമുള്ളപ്പോൾ സാധനങ്ങൾ കുറച്ച് മാത്രം നൽകുക
(n.) There was shortage of grain in the country, so each family received a *ration* every week.
(v.) Grain was *rationed.*

Rational *(adj.)* റാഷണൽ-യുക്തി സഹം
Her argument was *rational* and logical.

Rationale *(n.)* റേഷനേൽ-യുക്തി
The sales representative explained the *rationale* behind the new product.

Rattle *(v.)* റാറ്റ്ൽ-1. കിടുങ്ങുക
The storm makes windows and doors *rattle* noisily.
2. കിലുക്കുക
The child *rattled* the coins in the tin box.

Rave *(v.)* റേവ്-1. പിച്ചും പേയും പറയുക
She *raved* in her sleep when she had a nightmare.
2. അബദ്ധം പറയുക
The young lady *raved* about the film stars.

Raw *(adj.)* റാ-1. അസംസ്കൃത
All the *raw* materials for building the house have been acquired.
2. വേകാത്ത
We prefer *raw* vegetables.

Ray *(n.)* റേ-കിരണം

We should expose ourselves to the direct *rays* of the sun early in the morning.

Razor *(n.)* റേസർ-ക്ഷൗരകത്തി

The barber uses the *razor* to shave.

Re *(pre.)* റീ-വീും

1. Reappear (പരീക്ഷയ്ക്ക്) വീും ഇരിക്കുക

His brother *reappeared* in the B.A. examination.

2. Recall *(v.)*-ഓർമ്മിക്കുക, അനുസ്മരിക്കുക

We can *recall* the days when we were children.

3. Recount *(v.)* വീും എണ്ണുക, വർണ്ണിക്കുക

He *recounted* how he had shot the lion.

(n.) The defeated candidate requested a *recount* of votes in the election.

4. Reconstruct *(v.)*-വീും നിർമ്മിക്കുക

The shop destroyed in the fire has been *reconstructed.*

5. Reopen *(v.)* വീും തുറക്കുക

Our school closes on Saturday evening and *reopens* on Monday morning.

6. Rewrite *(v.)* വീും എഴുതുക

Your story is badly written. Please *rewrite* it.

Reach *(v.)* റീച്ച്-1. എത്തുക

We hope to *reach* Delhi tomorrow morning.

2. എത്തിക്കുക

Will you *reach* me that bag please?

3. (വരെ) നിർമ്മിക്കുക

The labourers are making a new road but it hasn't *reached* Shahdara yet.

(n.) 4. ശേഷി, കഴിവ്

Dry fruits are out of *reach* of a common man.

(v.) 5. ആകുമ്പോൾ, പ്രായത്തിലെത്തുമ്പോൾ

When I *reach* the age of sixty, I shall reduce my working hours.

React *(v.)* റിയാക്റ്റ്-പ്രതികരിക്കുക, പ്രതികരണം

The accused *reacted* fiercely to the charge.

(n.) What was the *reaction* of your father?

Read *(v.)* റീഡ്-1. വായിക്കുക

We should not *read* lying down on the bed.

2. വായിച്ചു കേൾപ്പിക്കുക

Now please *read* me the story of Rama.

The boy will *read* this letter to his grandmother.

3. ആശയം മനസ്സിലാക്കുക

You cannot *read* my thoughts.

(adj.) 4. The Delhi Public Library has a big *reading* room.

(n.) 5. Hundreds of *readers* come there every day.

Ready *(adj.)* റെഡി-1. തയ്യാർ

Please come soon. Breakfast is *ready.*

Be *ready* to do anything for your country.

2. തക്ക മറുപടി

Amitabh always has a *ready* answer.

(adv.) 3. അപ്പോൾ തന്നെ

Come to me any time. I will *readily* help you.

Real *(adj.)* റിയൽ-യഥാർത്ഥ

(adj.) Are these pearls *real*?

Yes, these are *real* pearls.

(adv.) Have you *really* lost your book?

(n.) In *reality,* no man is as powerful as he appears to be.

Realise *(v.)* റിയലൈസ്-ബോദ്ധ്യമാവുക

It was only after the failure that we *realised* our mistake.

Realm *(v.)* റിലം-രാജ്യം, ലോകം

Ghosts exist only in the *realms* of fantasy.

Reap *(v.)* റീപ്-വിള കൊയ്യുക

As you sow so shall you *reap.*

Rear *(n.)* റിയർ-1. പിൻ ഭാഗത്തെ

We want to sit in the *rear* of the bus.

There was a garden at the *rear* of the palace.

(v.) 2. പിൻ കാലിൽ നില്ക്കുക

When horses take fright, they *rear.*

3. മൃഗങ്ങളെ വളർത്തുക

The farmer *rears* milch animals.

Reason *(n.)* റീസൺ–1. കിരണം

Do you know the *reason* of her absence?

2. യുക്തി

He was foolish for he refused to listen to *reason.*

(v.) 3. ബോദ്ധ്യം വരുത്തുക

When the teacher *reasoned* with the naughty pupii, he begged his pardon.

Rebel റെബൽ–കലാപം, കലാപകാരി

(v.) Students *rebel* against the rules of their school.

(adj.) All the *rebel* candidates in the election fray were expelled by their parties.

(n.) The district is swarming with *rebels.*

Rebuke *(v.)* റിബ്യൂക്–ശാസിക്കുക, വിലക്കുക

Our father often *rebuked* us for not speaking the truth.

(n.) The *rebuke* chastened us.

Receive *(v.)* റിസീവ്–1. ലഭിക്കുക

We hope to *receive* a letter from our father.

2. സ്വീകരിക്കുക, സല്ക്കരിക്കുക

The lady *received* her guests.

Recent *(adj.)* റീസന്റ്–അടുത്തിടെ, ഈയിടെ

Have you fully recovered from your *recent* illness?

(adv.) I came to know *recently* that she went to Shimla last month.

Reception *(n.)* റിസപ്ഷൻ–1. സ്വീകരണ മുറി

The manager is busy, please sit at the *reception*.

2. ആദരവ്, സല്ക്കാരം, സ്വാഗതം

My aunt gave a warm *reception* when I went to see her.

3. സ്വീകരണ സമ്മേളനം

Most of the guests have been personally invited to the wedding *reception.*

Recess *(n.)* റിസെസ്–ഇടവേള

Can we go out to play during the twenty-minute *recess* at school?

Recipe *(n.)* റെസിപി–പാചകവിധി

Mother gave us the *recipe* for making a masala dosa.

Reciprocate *(v.)* റെസിപ്രൊകേറ്റ് – അന്യോന്യം ചെയ്യുക

She *reciprocated* his smile with a frown.

Recite *(v.)* റിസൈറ്റ്–ഉച്ചത്തിൽ ചൊല്ലുക

The leader *recited* the poem 'Vande Mataram' from the beginning till the end.

Reckless *(adj.)* റെക്‌ലെസ്–മുൻപിൻ നോക്കാതെ, അലക്ഷ്യമായ

Motorists are being fined for *reckless* driving.

Reckon *(v.)* റെകൺ–1. കണക്കാക്കുക, എണ്ണുക, കരുതുക

The price was *reckoned* high.

I *reckon* Premchand among our best writers.

2. വിശ്വസിക്കുക, ആശ്രയിക്കുക

Can you *reckon* on her help?

Recognise *(v.)* റികഗ്നൈസ്–1. തിരിച്ചറിയുക

We can easily *recognise* our neighbour in this picture.

2. അംഗീകരിക്കുക, ആദരവ് നൽകുക

Gita *recognises* that Rama is a better singer than she (Gita) is.

(n.) Bangladesh got *recognition* from India in the very beginning.

Recoil *(v.)* റികോയ്ൽ–പിന്മാറുക

She *recoiled* in disgust on seeing an open dustbin.

Recollect *(v.)* റെകളക്റ്റ്–പഴയ കാര്യം ഓർമ്മിക്കുക

She cannot *recollect* when Raja came to see her last summer.

(n.) Recollection of my past fills me with many sweet memories.

Recommend *(v.)* റെകമൻഡ്–1. ഉപദേശിക്കുക

This motor-cycle is defective. I would *recommend* purchasing another.

2. ശുപാർശ ചെയ്യുക

Can you *recommend* her to a good watchmaker?

3. അംഗീകൃതമായ

This book has been *recommended* for the tenth class by the Central Board of Secondary Education.

Reconcile *(v.)* റെക്കൺസൈൽ–1. വഴക്ക് തീർക്കുക, പൊരുത്തപ്പെടുക

Amitabh was glad to be *reconciled* to his cousin after they quarrelled.

After both the parties had apologised, the two became *reconciled.*

(adj.) I have learnt to *reconcile* with my fate.

Record *(n.)* റെക്കോർഡ്, വിവരണം, രേഖ

Has she a good *record*?

2. കളിയിലെ റിക്കോർഡ്

Salim has broken the *record* for the high jump.

It is on *record* that I have done this work and not she, though she may claim credit for it.

(v.) 3. രേഖപ്പെടുത്തുക

Father's voice has been *recorded* on the tape.

Recover *(v.)* റികവർ–1. നഷ്ടപ്പെട്ട സാധനം വീടെുക്കുക

I *recovered* my bag which I had lost in the market.

2. സുഖപ്പെടുക

Has she *recovered* from her illness?

(n.) We are delighted to learn about her *recovery* from pneumonia.

Recreation *(n.)*റിക്രയേഷൻ–വിനോദം, ഉല്ലാസ വിധി

My favourite *recreation* is playing cards.

Gardening is a good *recreation*.

Recruit *(n.)* റിക്രൂട്ട്–1. നിയമിക്കുക

Many *recruits* will join the police force.

(v.) 2. ചേർക്കുക

The object is to *recruit* 500 policemen a month.

Rectify *(v.)* റെക്റ്റിഫൈ–തെറ്റ് തിരുത്തുക

How long will you take to *rectify* this mistake?

Recur *(v.)* റികർ–ആവർത്തിക്കുക

The imagery of fire *recurs* throughout the novel.

Recycle *(v.)* റീസൈക്കിൾ–പുനഃസംസ്കരിക്കുക

Use paper bags; they are easy to *recycle.*

Redden *(v.)* റെഡെൻ–കരുവാളിക്കുക

The young girl *reddened* when the principal shouted at her.

2. ചുവപ്പിക്കുക, പഴുപ്പിക്കുക

The sun *reddens* the plums.

Reddish *(adj.)* റെഡിഷ്–അല്പം ചുവന്ന

Her hair was painted in *reddish* colour.

Redeem *(v.)* റിഡീം–വഷളാകാതെ നോക്കുക

She *redeemed* the blunder by apologising and rectifying the mistake.

Reduce *(v.)* റിഡ്യൂസ്–1. കുറയുക, ഇടിയുക

Has the price of wheat been *reduced*?

(n.) Yes, there has been a small *reduction* in the price.

2. കുറയ്ക്കുക

How can I reduce my weight?

Reel *(n.)* റീൽ–1. ക്യാമറയുടെ റീൽ

Have you got a *reel* of film for your camera?

2. രംഗം പ്രത്യക്ഷപ്പെടുക

The scene *reeled* before my eyes.

Refer *(v.)* റിഫർ – 1. (അടുത്തേക്ക്) അയക്കുക, സമർപ്പിക്കുക

The matter was *referred* to the Headmaster for settlement.

2. അറിവു നേടാൻ മറിച്ച് നോക്കുക

I have to *refer* to this book of general knowledge.

3. പരാമർശിക്കുക

When I talk about corruption, I am not *referring* to anyone here.

Referee *(n.)* റെഫറി-അമ്പയർ
Rajiv was appointed *referee* at the football match.

Refine *(v.)* റിഫൈൻ-വൃത്തിയാക്കുക, പരിഷ്കൃത, വിശിഷ്ട
Sudha is quite *refined* in her behaviour.
(n.) I work in a sugar *refinery.*

Reflect *(v.)* റിഫ്ളെക്റ്റ്-1. ആലോചിക്കുക
Reflect before you make a decision.
2. പ്രതിഫലിക്കുക, പ്രതിബിംബം
A mirror *reflects* light.
(n.) You can see your *reflection* in the mirror.

Reform *(v.)* റിഫോം-പരിഷ്കരിക്കുക
The new principal has greatly *reformed* the administration of the school.
(n.) People are pleased with the new manager's *reforms* of the bonus rules.

Refrain *(v.)* റിഫ്റെയ്ൻ-1. ചെയ്യാതിരിക്കുക
We must *refrain* from spitting on the floor.
People must *refrain* from talking in the cinema hall.
(n.) 2. ഗാനത്തിലെ ആവർത്തിക്കുന്ന വരി
All the students should join in singing the *refrain* of this song.

Refresh *(v.)* റിഫ്രെഷ്-ഉന്മേഷം വരിക/ വരുത്തുക, പുതിയ ശക്തി കൈവരിക
Sleep *refreshes* us when we feel tired.
(n.) Refreshments were provided after the meeting.
(adj.) When you are tired, a cup of tea is very *refreshing.*

Refrigerator *(n.)* റിഫ്റിജെയ്റ്റർ - സാധനങ്ങൾ തണുപ്പിക്കുന്ന യന്ത്രം, ഫ്രിജ്
The housewife took a bottle of Coca Cola out of the *refrigerator.*

Refuge *(n.)* റിഫ്യൂജ്-രക്ഷ നേടുക
During the rain, we took *refuge* under a shade.

Refugee *(n.)* റെഫ്യൂജി-അഭയാർത്ഥി
Delhi was crowded with *refugees* following the partition of India.

Refuse *(v.)* റിഫ്യൂസ്-1. വിസമ്മതിക്കുക
I asked her for help, but she *refused.*
(n.) Her *refusal* disappointed me.
2. അവശിഷ്ടങ്ങൾ
The industrial *refuse* should be disposed off properly.

Regal *(adj.)* റീഗൽ-രാജകീയ
He was not a king, but his robes were *regal.*

Regard *(v.)* റിഗാർഡ്-1. ആദരിക്കുക, ബഹുമാനിക്കുക
(v.) I *regard* Pratibha as my best friend.
(n.) I have great *regard* for Pratibha.
2. ശുഭാശംസകൾ
Please give my best *regards* to your mother.
(v.) 3. ശ്രദ്ധിക്കുക
Why don't you *regard* your parent's advice?
4. -യുടെ കാര്യത്തിൽ, സംബന്ധിച്ച്
As *regards* Sudha, I will write to you at once.

Regiment *(n.)* റെജിമെന്റ് -1. സേനാദലം
There were many *regiments* in I.N.A.
(v.) 2. അച്ചടക്കം പാലിക്കുക
The tourists *regimented* into large parties for sightseeing.

Region *(n.)* റീജൻ-ഭാഗം, പ്രദേശം
In India, there are many *regions,* so there are many *regional* languages.

Register റെജിസ്റ്റർ - 1. റെജിസ്റ്റർ, രേഖപ്പെടുത്തുക
(n.) The teacher checked the attendance *register* thoroughly.
(v.) You have to *register* your case with the police.
(adj.) 2. രജിസ്റ്റേർഡ് പോസ്റ്റ്
I sent you certificates by *registered* post.

Regressive *(adj.)* റിഗ്രെസീവ്-പ്രതിഗമനം
The theme of the movie seemed to be *regressive.*

Regret റിഗ്രെറ്റ്-1. ഖേദിക്കുക
(v.) I *regret* being so late for the meeting.
We *regret* for breaking the agreement.

2. ദുഃഖവിവരം പറയുക

(v.) I *regret* to tell you my mother-in-law is ill.

(n.) There was great *regret* in the town at the minister's death.

Yes, I failed but I have no *regrets.*

Regular (adj.) റെഗുലർ-പതിവ്, മുടങ്ങാതെ

Our *regular* hours of work at the office are from 10 to 5:30.

Try to be *regular* in your office.

(adv.) These days trains run *regularly.*

(n.) *Regularity* is the key to success.

Regulate (v.)റെഗുലേറ്റ്

This valve *regulates* the flow of water.

Regulation (n.) നിയന്ത്രിക്കുക

The new rules and *regulations* of the company were made clear to all.

Rehabilitate (v.) റിഹാബിലിറ്റേറ്റ്-പുനരധിവാസം ചെയ്യുക

The government was taking measures to *rehabilitate* the earthquake victims.

Rehearse (v.) റിഹഴ്സ്-പൂർവ്വാഭ്യാസം ചെയ്യുക

This is the second time we are going to *rehearse* the play.

(n.) It will be the final *rehearsal.*

Reign (v.) റെയ്ൻ-ഭരിക്കുക, ഭരണം നടത്തുക

The English rulers *reined* over India for about one hundred and fifty years.

(n.) The queen introduced many reforms during her *reign* of forty-five years.

Rein (n.) റെയ്ൻ-കടിഞ്ഞാൺ

When the *reins* were pulled tightly, the horse reared.

Relent (v.) റിലെന്റ്-അയയുക

After denying for long, she *relented* and agreed to come for the excursion.

Reinforce (v.) റീഇൻഫോഴ്സ്-ബലപ്പെടുത്തുക, ശക്തമാക്കുക

When China attacked our country, our army was *reinforced.*

The army would be *reinforced* to meet enemy attacks.

Reject (v.) റിജെക്റ്റ്-നിരാകരിക്കുക, റദ്ദാക്കുക

I was foolish to *reject* Indra's offer of help.

The lady *rejected* a cup in the crockery shop because it was cracked.

Rejoice (v.) റിജോയ്സ്-സന്തോഷിക്കുക, ആഹ്ലാദിക്കുക

The family *rejoiced* when the son returned home from a foreign trip.

(n.) There was great *rejoicing* among the cricketers when they won the match.

Relate (v.) കഥ പറയുക, വിവരിക്കുക

The hunter *related* some of his adventures in the Himalaya's jungles.

Relation (n.) റിലേഷൻ-1. ബന്ധു, സ്വന്തക്കാർ

I have many uncles, cousins, nieces and other *relations* in Delhi.

2. ബന്ധം

Relations between teachers and students in our school are very good.

Relax (v.) റിലാക്സ്-1. വിശ്രമിക്കുക

After the test, we *relaxed.*

2. അയവാക്കുക

Relax your grip on my arm, you are hurting me.

Release (v.) റിലീസ്-വിടുക, മോചിപ്പിക്കുക

The judge ordered the police to *release* the innocent boy.

Relish റെലിഷ്-1. ഉത്സാഹത്തോടെ ഉറ്റുനോക്കുക

She *relished* the idea of going abroad.

(n.) 2. ആസ്വദിച്ച്

The child ate the chocolate with great *relish.*

Relief (n.) റിലീഫ്-1. ആശ്വാസം (തോന്നുക), ശമനം (ഉാവുക)

Father got *relief* from headache after I rubbed some balm on his forehead.

2. സഹായം

The timely *relief* sent for the refugees saved their lives.

(v.) When he took one tablet of Aspro, his headache was immediately *relieved.*

Religion *(n.)* റിലിജൻ-മതം, ധർമ്മം
We should not discriminate on the basis of religion.
(adj.) Arvind Ghosh was a *religious* man.

Reluctant *(adj.)* റിലക്റ്റന്റ്-മടിയുള്ള
Vivek is usually *reluctant* to take sweets.
(n.) I show *reluctance* to share my room with anybody.
(adv.) The beggar accepted the old clothes *reluctantly*.

Rely *(v.)* റിലൈ-വിശ്വസിക്കുക, ആശ്രയിക്കുക
We should always *rely* on our own efforts.
(adj.) Are you a *reliable* person?

Remain *(v.)* റിമെയ്ൻ-നിലകൊള്ളുക, തുടരുക
The weather *remained* very hot on Monday.
The shop will *remain* closed on Sunday.
(n.) After dining, the *remains* should be collected for the birds.
Take 4 from 13, and what is the *remainder*?

Remark റിമാർക്-അഭിപ്രായം (പറയുക) ടിപ്പണി നൽകുക
(v.) The chief guest *remarked* favourably about the arrangements made by us.
(adj.) There were many *remarkable* books in the book exhibition.
(n.) I wish to make a few *remarks* about the elections.

Remedy *(n.)* റെമഡി-1. മരുന്ന്
The physician suggested the patient a *remedy* for his fever.
2. പരിഹാരം
No *remedy* is left to correct this situation.

Remember *(v.)* റിമെംബർ-ഓർത്തുവയ്ക്കുക, മനപാഠമാക്കുക
You should *remember* your lesson every day.

Remind *(v.)* റിമൈൻഡ്-ഓർമ്മിപ്പിക്കുക
Please *remind* me about it when you come again.
(n.) The company sent the *reminders* to all its members.

Reminisce *(v.)* റെമിനിസ്-കഴിഞ്ഞ കാര്യങ്ങൾ ഓർമ്മിപ്പിക്കുക
(v.) She was *reminiscing* her days at school.
(n.) The book is a collection of *reminiscences* of her days at school.

Remit *(v.)* റിമിറ്റ്-ഇളച്ച് കൊടുക്കുക
The child requested to *remit* the fine charged by the teacher.

Remnant *(n.)* റെമ്നന്റ്-ശേഷിക്കുന്ന ഭാഗം
The *remnants* of the dinner will be fed to the dogs.

Remorse *(n.)* റിമോഴ്സ്-പശ്ചാത്താപം
The criminal expressed his *remorse* for his crimes.

Remote *(adj.)* റിമോട്ട്-വളരെ മുമ്പ്
Many Buddhist monuments were built in the *remote* past.

Remove *(v.)* റിമ്യൂവ്-1. അഴിക്കുക, ഊരിവയ്ക്കുക
Please *remove* your shoes when you enter the temple.
2. നീക്കം ചെയ്യുക
Will you *remove* the stain from my shirt?

Render *(v.)* റെൻഡർ-നൽകുക, സമർപ്പിക്കുക
Doctors *rendered* their services free of charge at the charitable health check-up camp.
We hope to *render* certain services to your company.

Renew *(v.)* റിന്യൂ-പുതുക്കുക
We should *renew* our library membership for one more year.
We must *renew* the decorations of our shop.
(n.) The *renewal* of their contract gave them much satisfaction.

Renounce *(v.)* റിനൗൺസ്-ത്യജിക്കുക
We *renounced* our plan to go on a vacation.

Renovate *(v.)* റിനവേറ്റ്-നവീകരിക്കുക, പുതുക്കി പണിയുക
I am getting my house *renovated.*

Renown *(n.)* റിനൗൺ-1. പ്രശസ്ത
He is a doctor of *renown.*
(adj.) 2. Renowned-സുപ്രസിദ്ധ
Ashoka was a *renowned* king if India.

Rent *(n.)* റെന്റ് -1. വാടക
How much *rent* do you pay for your shop?
(v.) 2. വാടകയ്ക്ക് കൊടുക്കുക
Will you *rent* this house?
3. വാടകയ്ക്കെടുക്കുക
I *rented* this house two years ago.

Repair റിപയർ-1. അറ്റകുറ്റ പണി (ചെയ്യുക)
(n.) The house is under *repair.*
Your watch is beyond *repairs,* you must buy a new one.
(v.) 2. നന്നാക്കുക, കേട് മാറ്റുക
The cobbler will *repair* our shoes.
Has your TV been *repaired*?

Repay *(v.)* റിപേ-വിടുക, തിരിച്ച് അയക്കുക
Have you enough money to *repay* your debts?
We can never *repay* our mother for her kindness and affection.

Repeat *(v.)* റിപീറ്റ് -1. വീും പറയുക
Her mother was almost deaf so I had to *repeat* my question.
2. ആവർത്തിക്കുക
Can you *repeat* what you said?
(adj.) I made *repeated* attempts to see you.
(adv.) I have told you *repeatedly* not to be talkative.

Repel *(v.)* റിപെൽ-1. തുരത്തുക, ചെറുത്തു തോല്പിക്കുക
The enemy's attack was *repelled.*
2. അറപ്പ് തോന്നിപ്പിക്കുക
The way he ate with dirty hands and licked his finger *repelled* everybody.

Repent *(v.)* റിപെന്റ് -പശ്ചാത്തപിക്കുക
If we *repent,* father will forgive us.
(n.) Is your *repentance* sincere?

Replace *(v.)* റിപ്ലേസ്-1. മാറ്റുക, മാറ്റിനൽകുക
These cells are defective, kindly *replace* them.
2. തിരിച്ചുവയ്ക്കുക, (മുൻ സ്ഥാനത്ത് വയ്ക്കുക)
We can take the magazine down from the shelf, but after reading we must *replace* it.
3. (സ്ഥാനത്ത്) വയ്ക്കുക
Hamid is unwell, so he has been *replaced* with Majid in the team.

Replenish *(v.)* റിപ്ലെനിഷ്-നികത്തുക
The only way to *replenish* the shortage of greenery is by plantation of trees.

Replete *(adj.)* റിപ്ലീറ്റ്-സമ്പൂർണ്ണം
The book is *replete* with pictures.

Replica *(n.)* റെപ്ലിക്ക-തനിപ്പകർപ്പ്
This book seems to be a *replica* of a famous novel.

Reply റിപ്ലൈ-വാക്കാലോ എഴുതിയോ മറുപടി നൽകുക
(v.) The judge asked repeatedly, but the thief did not *reply.*
(n.) I received no *reply* from my parents.

Report റിപോർട്ട്-1. വിവരണം (നൽകുക)
(v.) The occurence was *reported* in the Hindustan Times.
(n.) Have you got the *report* of the meeting?
(v.) 2. പരാതി കൊടുക്കുക, എതിരായി വിവരം നൽകുക
He was *reported* to the police for trespassing.
3. ജോലിക്ക് ഹാജരാകുക
I have been ordered to *report* for duty.

Repose *(n.)* റിപോസ്-വിശ്രമം, ഉറക്കം
After a day's *repose,* I shall try to join my night duty.

Represent *(v.)* റെപ്രിസെന്റ് -പ്രതിനിധാനം ചെയ്യുക
Leander Paes *represented* India in Atlanta Olympics and won a bronze medal in tennis.

Repress *(v.)* റിപ്രെസ്-അടക്കുക, അമർച്ച ചെയ്യുക
(v.) She somehow *repressed* her desire to go on a holiday.
(adj.) Her anger *repressed* for several days suddenly burst out at a minor mistake.
(adj.) The British had formed a *repressive* government in India.

Reprimand *(v.)* റെപ്രിമാൻഡ്–കുറ്റപ്പെടുത്തുക, ശാസിക്കുക
The police *reprimanded* the people for spreading false rumours.

Reproduce *(v.)* റിപ്രൊഡ്യൂസ്–ചിത്രണം ചെയ്യുക, പകർത്തുക
The artist *reproduced* the scene in an oil painting.
(n.) It was really a good *reproduction*.

Reptile *(n.)* റെപ്റ്റൈൽ–ഇഴജന്തു
A snake is a *reptile*.

Reputation *(n.)* റെപ്യുട്ടേഷൻ–സൽപേര്, കീർത്തി, യശസ്
Your father lived up to his *reputation*.
Netaji Subhash was a man of blameless *reputation*.
If you do anything wrong, your *reputation* will suffer.

Request *(v.)* റിക്വെസ്റ്റ്–അപേക്ഷിക്കുക
You are *requested* not to talk loudly.
(n.) The candidate made a *request* to the voters to vote for him.
Luckily, the *request* was granted.

Require *(v.)* റിക്വയർ–ആവശ്യമുക്കുക
The hungry man *requires* food.
I *require* you to be here now.
(n.) Can you meet all my *requirements*?

Rescue റെസ്ക്യൂ–രക്ഷ (ചെയ്യുക)
(n.) My friend always comes to my *rescue* when I need him.
(v.) The youngman dived into the river to *rescue* the drowning boy.

Research *(n.)* റിസർച്ച്–ഗവേഷണം
The scientists conducted many *researches*.
(adj.) She has been deputed as *research* adviser.

Resemble *(v.)* റിസെമ്പ്ൾ–ഛായയ്ക്ക് സാമ്യം തോന്നുക, സാദൃശ്യം ഉാവുക
You *resemble* your father closely.
(n.) There was a family *resemblance* between all the sisters.

Resent *(v.)* റിസെന്റ്–നീരസം തോന്നുക, ദേഷ്യം തോന്നുക
She *resented* his rude remarks about her character.
Though her brother treated her badly, Pramila didn't feel any *resentment*.

Reserve *(v.)* റിസർവ്–കരുതി വയ്ക്കുക
I always *reserve* some money for the weekend.
(n.) You should spend some money and keep the rest in *reserve*.
(v.) The best fruits are *reserved* for the loving child.

Reside *(v.)* റിസൈഡ്–താമസിക്കുക, പാർക്കുക
We *reside* in New Delhi.
(n.) They are *residents* of Rohtak.
Where is your *residence*?

Residual *(adj.)* റെസിഡ്യൂഅൽ– അവശിഷ്ടം
(adj.) The *residual* waste products were disposed off immediately.
(n.) The *residue* left after the distillation of the petroleum is used to make paraffin wax.

Resign *(v.)* റിസൈൻ–രാജി സമർപ്പിക്കുക
The Prime Minister asked the minister facing corruption charges to *resign* from the cabinet.
(n.) The minister's *resignation* was forwarded to the President for acceptance.

Resist *(v.)* റെസിസ്റ്റ്–ചെറുക്കുക, നേരിടുക
The Indian army is able to *resist* all aggressions by the enemy.
(n.) Despite the thief's *resistance*, the police arrested him.

Resolute *(adj.)* റെസല്യൂട്ട്–ദൃഢനിശ്ചയമുള്ള, സ്ഥിരചിത്തത
Explorers have to be *resolute* in the face of difficulties.

Resolve *(v.)* റിസോൾവ്–1. പ്രതിജ്ഞ ചെയ്ക
We should *resolve* not to tell a lie.
2. നിർദ്ദേശം പാസാക്കുക
It is *resolved* to re-elect the president.
(n.) It's my *resolve* not to tell a lie.

Resort റിസോർട്ട്–ആശ്രയം (എടുക്കുക)
(n.) As a last *resort*, I'll have to borrow some money.
(v.) He *resorted* to smuggling because he was not satisfied with his honest earnings.

Resource *(n.)* റിസോഴ്സ്-വിഭവം, ഉപായം
I used all my *resources* to set up this new business.
(adj.) He is very *resourceful* person, and can make good use of everything he has.

Respect റെസ്പെക്റ്റ്-1. ബഹുമാന(ം, ിക്കുക)
(v.) We should *respect* our elders and never be rude to them.
(n.) We show *respect* to our uncle whenever he pays a visit to us.
2. ഒരു പരിധിവരെ
I may agree with her in some *respects,* but on the whole I think she is not right.

Respond *(v.)* റെസ്പോ് -ഉത്തരം നൽകുക, പ്രതികരിക്കുക
The enquiry-clerk *responded* quickly to my questions.
(n.) The patient's *response* to the medicine is quite good.

Responsible *(adj.)* റെസ്പോൺസിബ്ൾ- ഉത്തരവാദി
We are not *responsible* for the losses you suffer.
Who is *responsible* for breaking the looking glass?

Rest റെസ്റ്റ്-വിശ്രമം (എടുക്കുക)
(n.) Please take*rest* for a while.
(v.) They *rested* under a big tree.

Restaurant *(n.)* റെസ്റ്ററാന്റ് -ഭക്ഷണശാല
Let us go to a good *restaurant* for lunch.

Restore *(v.)* റെസ്റ്റോർ-1. തിരിച്ച് നൽകുക
The police *restored* all the stolen articles to its owner.
2. പുതുക്കുക
The old picture was cleaned and *restored.*
3. സൂക്ഷിച്ച് വയ്ക്കുക
We must *restore* the books to the shelf after reading them.

Restrain *(v.)* റെസ്ട്രേയ്ൻ-തടയുക, നിയന്ത്രിക്കുക
Restrain your dog from attacking people.
(n.) Saints keep their passions under *restraint.*

Restrict *(v.)* റെസ്ട്രിക്റ്റ്-ചുരുക്കുക, പരിമിതപ്പെടുത്തുക
Restrict yourself to two cups of tea a day.
(n.) There are no *restrictions* on walking here.

Result *(n.)* റിസൽറ്റ്-ഫലം
The *result* of the hockey match was a draw.
(v.) The accident *resulted* in a fracture in Abdulla's leg.

Resume *(v.)* റിസ്യൂം-ആരംഭിക്കുക, വീും തുടങ്ങുക
After some rest, we must *resume* work.

Retail *(n.)* റീടെയ്ൽ-ചില്ലറ
Usually the shopkeepers buy goods in large quantities and sell in *retail* to make profit.

Retain *(v.)* റീടെയ്ൻ-കൈവശം വയ്ക്കുക
You must *retain* this pen until you know who owns it.

Retire *(v.)* റിട്ടയർ-1. ഉറങ്ങുക
You must *retire* early tonight.
2. സേവനത്തിൽ നിന്ന് വിരമിക്കുക
My father *retired* at the age of sixty-two.
(n.) He is now living in *retircmont.*

Retort *(v.)* റിട്ടോർട്ട്-(ദേഷ്യത്തോടെ) മറുപടി പറയുക
The clerk *retorted* with anger when he was questioned by the manager.

Retreat *(v.)* റിട്രീറ്റ്-പിൻവാങ്ങുക
The general commanded his troops to *retreat.*
(n.) Their *retreat* was carried out very quietly.

Retrospect *(n.)* റെട്രോസ്പെക്റ്റ്-അയവിറക്കുക, പഴയ കാര്യങ്ങൾ പറയുക
In *retrospect,* I laugh at how foolish I had been.

Retrieve *(v.)* റിട്രീവ്-വീടുക്കുക
How can we *retrieve* the lost data from the computer?

Return *(v.)* റിട്ടേൺ 1. മടക്കുക
You must *return* the pen she lent you.
2. മടങ്ങിവരിക, തിരിച്ച് നൽകുക
We *returned* to Mumbai by the Frontier Mail.

3. ലോക് സഭയിലേക്കും മറ്റും വീും തിരഞ്ഞെടുക്കപ്പെടുക
Mr. A.B. Vajpayee was *returned* by a good majority to the parliament.

Reveal *(v.)* റിവീൽ-വെളിപ്പെടുത്തുക
I promised Amitabh that I would never *reveal* his secrets.
The truth was *revealed* at last.

Revenge *(n.)* റിവെഞ്ച്-പ്രതികാരം, പ്രതിരോധം
He swore to take a *revenge* on his enemies.
Revenge is not a remedy to establish peace on earth.

Reunion *(n.)* റീയൂണിയൻ-പുനഃസംഗമം, പാർട്ടി
All the old students were invited for the college *reunion*.

Revenue *(n.)* റെവന്യൂ-വരുമാനം
Income tax is one of the major sources of *revenue* for the government.

Reverberate *(v.)* റിവർബറേറ്റ്-മാറ്റൊലി
After the performance, the auditorium *reverberated* with the sound of claps.

Revere *(v.)* റിവീർ-ആദരിക്കുക
Gulzar is *revered* as one of the greatest lyricists in the industry.

Reverse റിവേഴ്സ്-നേരെ തിരിച്ചായി
(n.) What is there at the *reverse* of the painting?
(v.) Writing is *reversed* in the mirror.
(adj.) The new policy had the *reverse* effect of what was expected.

Revert *(v.)* റിവർട്ട്-തിരിച്ച് വരിക
We *reverted* back to the old rules.

Review റിവ്യൂ-1. നിരൂപണം
(n.) The movie got good *reviews* in newspapers.
(v.) The movie was favourably *reviewed* in the newspapers.
2. അവലോകനം
(n.) The company decided to hold an annual *review* of the progress.
(v.) The company *reviewed* the progress over the past one year.

Revise *(v.)* റിവൈസ്-വീും പഠിക്കുക, ഹൃദിസ്ഥമാക്കുക
We can improve our composition if we *revise* it.
Your essay needs *revision*.

Revive *(v.)* റിവൈവ്-1. പുനർ ജീവിക്കുക
The plant *revived* after I watered it.

Revolt റിവോൾട്ട്-കലാപം നടത്തുക
(v.) The peasants *revolted* against their landlords.
(n.) The peasants' *revolt* was badly crushed.

Revolve *(v.)* റിവോൾവ്-കറങ്ങുക, നാല് ചുറ്റും വലയം വയ്ക്കുക
The moon *revolves* round the earth, and earth *revolves* round the sun.

Reward റിവാർഡ്-സമ്മാനം (നൽകുക), പുരസ്കാരം (നൽകുക)
(n.) The conductor of the D.T.C. bus, who found the gentleman's purse, was given a *reward* for returning it.
(v.) The boy who saved the little girls was *rewarded* for his bravery.

Rhyme *(n.)* റൈം-കവിത, പദ്യം
The children recited nursery *rhymes*.

Rhythm *(n.)* റിഥം-ലയം, താളം, ചേർച്ചയോടെ
The audience started to clap in *rhythm* with the music.

Rib *(n.)* റിബ്-വാരിയെല്ല്
Eve was said to be born from Adam's *rib*.

Ribbon *(n.)* റിബൺ-പട്ടുനാട, റിബൻ
The hair of the girl was tied with a *ribbon*.

Rice *(n.)* റൈസ്-അരി
In Bengal, people mostly take *rice*.

Rich *(adj.)* റിച്-1. സമ്പന്ന, ധനിക
Hard work made him a *rich* man.
2. കൊഴുപ്പുള്ള
I cannot digest *rich* food. It makes me feel ill.

Rid *(v.)* റിഡ്-ഒഴിവാക്കുക, കളയുക
Get *rid* of this old cycle.

Riddle *(n.)* കടങ്കഥ
Can you guess the answer to this *riddle*?

Ride *(v.)* റൈഡ്-സവാരി ചെയ്യുക, ഓടിക്കുക
Can you *ride* a motorcycle?

(n.) We had a pleasant *ride*.
Both the donkey and the *rider* fell into the stream.

Ridiculous (adj.) റിഡികുലസ്- അപഹാസ്യമായ
You look *ridiculous* in this long gown.
Your fringed hair makes you look *ridiculous*.

Rifle റൈഫ്ൾ-1. തോക്ക്
(n.) I went out armed with a *rifle*.
(v.) 2. കൊള്ളയടിക്കുക
The whole house has been *rifled*.

Rift (n.) റിഫ്റ്റ്-വിടവ്
The difference of opinion created a *rift* between them.

Right (adj.) റൈറ്റ്-1. ശരിയായ
It was not *right* of you to help my opponent.
2. വലത് (കൈ അല്ലെങ്കിൽ രീതി)
We write with our *right* hand. Is it not the *right* way to write?
3. കൃത്യം
Is your watch *right*?
(n.) 4. അവകാശം
You have no *right* to shout at me.
(adv.) 5. ശരിയായി തന്നെ
Somebody has *rightly* remarked that truth always wins.

Rigid (adj.) റിജിഡ്-കടുത്ത, അയവില്ലാത്ത
He is a *rigid* old man, and does not welcome changes.

Rigorous (adj.) റിഗറസ്-സൂക്ഷ്മമായ, കർക്കശമായ
The performance did not meet the *rigorous* standards.

Rim (n.) റിം-വൃത്താകൃതിയിലുള്ള സാധനത്തിന്റെ അരിക്
The *rim* of her spectacles was golden in colour.

Ring (n.) റിംഗ്-1. മോതിരം
The bride wears three *rings* on her fingers.
(v.) 2. മുഴക്കുക
The peon will *ring* the bell.

Rinse (v.) റിൻസ്-വെടിപ്പാകുക, അലക്കുക
Mother *rinses* woollen sweaters in warm water.

Riot റയട്ട്-കലഹം, കലാപം, കോലാഹലം
(n.) The rebels who took part in the *riot* broke many articles in the shop.
(v.) They *rioted* the streets also.

Rip റിപ്-കീറുക
(v.) I *ripped* my dress.
(n.) There was a big *rip* in my dress.

Ripe (adj.) റൈപ്-1. പഴുത്ത, പാകമായ
We should eat fruit when it is *ripe*.
2. പക്വതയാർന്ന
I have reached the *ripe* age of seventy-two.

Ripple (n.) റിപ്ൾ-കുഞ്ഞല
The air was creating small *ripples* in the pond.

Rise (v.) റൈസ്-1. എഴുന്നേല്ക്കുക, ഉദിക്കുക
The sun *rises* in the morning and sets in the evening.
We can see the sun *rising* in the morning.
2. എതിർക്കുക, വിരുദ്ധമായി അണിനിരക്കുക
Some day, the exploited peole will *rise* against the cruel ruler.
(n.) 3. വർദ്ധന, വൃദ്ധി
There has been a *rise* in the prices of some essential commodities.

Risk റിസ്ക്-അപകടം (ഏറ്റെടുക്കുക), ഭാഗ്യപരീക്ഷണം നടത്തുക
(n.) You are taking a *risk* of displeasing your boss if you just stay away from work.
(v.) Vinayak *risked* his life to save a child from drowning.

Ritual (n.) റിചൽ-ക്രിയാവിധി
His last *rituals* were performed in Haridwar.

Rival (n.) റൈവൽ-എതിരാളി, പ്രതിയോഗി
Rita and Gita were *rival* candidates for the post of receptionist.
There has been a long *rivalry* between the two companies.

River (n.) റിവർ-നദി, പുഴ, ആറ്
Ganga and Yamuna are holy *rivers*.
We can see boats sailing on the *river*.

Road (n.) റോഡ്-നിരത്ത്, വഴി
Rama is driving a car along the *road*.
Many people like to go by *road*.
Is this the *road* to India Gate?

Roam *(v.)* റോം–ചുറ്റുക, കറങ്ങുക
Let us *roam* about in the woods and enjoy the beauty of Nature.

Roar *(n.)* റോർ–1. ഗർജ്ജനം, അലർച്ച
The tiger sprang up towards me with a *roar*.
(v.) 2. പൊട്ടിച്ചിരിക്കുക, ഉച്ചത്തിൽ ശബ്ദമുണ്ടാക്കുക
The listener *roared* with laughter at my story.

Roast *(v.)* റോസ്റ്റ്–വറക്കുക
The cook *roasted* the chicken.

Rob *(v.)* റോബ്–കൊള്ളയടിക്കുക
The pickpockets *robbed* the passengers and disappeared quickly.
(n.) Three armed *robbers* were arrested by the police immediately after the *robbery*.

Robe *(n.)* റോബ്–മേൽകുപ്പായം
The girl was dressed in an attractive *robe*.

Robot *(n.)* റാബോ(ട്ട്)–യന്ത്രമനുഷ്യൻ
It seems in future, all the work would be done by the *robots*.

Robust *(adj.)* റോബസ്റ്റ്–തടിമിടുക്കുള്ള, കരുത്തായ
Despite being old, he is quite *robust* and healthy.

Rock *(n.)* റോക്–1. പാറ
There are many big *rocks* in the sea.
(v.) 2. ആട്ടുക, ഊഞ്ഞാലാട്ടുക
She *rocked* her baby and sang a lullaby to put him to sleep.

Rocket *(n.)* റോക്കറ്റ്–റോക്കറ്റ്
Rockets are also used as signals of distress.

Rod *(n.)* റാഡ്–ചൂ
Carry the fishing *rod* with you.

Rogue *(n.)* റോഗ്–ഗു, ദുഷ്ടൻ
Beware of him, he is a *rogue*.

Role *(n.)* റോൾ–1. പങ്ക്
What will be my *role* in this campaign?
2. നാടകം അല്ലെങ്കിൽ സിനിമയിലെ വേഷം
She played the *role* of a widowed mother in the play.

Roll *(v.)* റോൾ–1. ഉരുളുക
The baby is about to *roll* down the bed.
(n.) പേര് വിവര പട്ടിക
I will call the *roll* now.
3. ഇടി മുഴക്കം
Suddenly, the sky became dark and they heard a *roll* of thunder.

Romance *(n.)* റൊമാൻസ്–സാഹസിക/പ്രേമ കഥകൾ
Modern young girls mostly read nothing but books of *romance*.

Roof *(n.)* റൂഫ്–മേൽക്കൂര, മച്ച്
The *roof* was made of stones and bricks.

Room *(n.)* റൂം–1. സ്ഥലം, സ്ഥാനം
Is there *room* for me in the compartment?
2. മുറി
There is enough space in the *room*.
3. അവസരം
There is *room* for improvement in this situation.

Root *(n.)* റൂട്ട്–1. വേര്
The *roots* keep the plant steady, and help it to grow.
2. മൂല കാരണം
The family doctor is trying to get to the *root* of my mother's illness.

Rope *(n.)* റോപ്–1. കയറ്, വടം
The cows were tied with strong *ropes*.
(v.) 2. കയറിട്ട് കെട്ടുക
The traveller *roped* his horse to the tree and lay down to take rest.

Rosary *(n.)* റോസറി–ജപമാല
The old woman was carrying a string of *rosary* beads in her hands.

Rose *(n.)* റോസ്–1. റോജാ, പനിനീർ, ചുവന്ന
My garden is full of a large variety of *roses*.
(adj.) The young girl had *rosy* cheeks.

Rotate *(v.)* റൊട്ടേറ്റ്–അച്ചുതിൽ കറങ്ങുക
Apart from revolving around the sun, the planets also *rotate* on their own axis.

Rotten *(adj.)* റോട്ടൻ–അളിഞ്ഞ, അഴുകിയ
The basket is full of *rotten* mangoes.

Most of the walnuts in the box were *rotten.*

Rough *(adj.)* റഫ്-1. വിലകുറഞ്ഞ, പരിക്കൻ

I need some *rough* cloth.

2. കർക്കശ, കടുത്ത

Don't be *rough* with women and babies.

Father was angry and spoke in a *rough* voice.

3. പെട്ടെന്ന് വരച്ച

This is a *rough* drawing.

(adv.) 4. ഏറെക്കുറെ

There were *roughly* thirty persons in the gathering.

5. നിർദ്ദയമായി

The policeman *roughly* pushed the prisoner into the cell.

Round *(n.)* റൗ്-1. (പുതിയ) വട്ടം

The company is considering a fresh *round* of interviews from next week.

2. സന്ദർശനം

The director is on his daily *round.*

3. മത്സരത്തിന്റെ ഒരു വട്ടം

Australia has qualified for the next *round.*

4. പ്രശംസാപ്രക്രിയ

He was welcomed with a huge *round* of applause.

5. ഉപസംഹരിക്കുക

(v.) He *rounded* his speech with a quotation.

6. ചുറ്റിയടിക്കുക

(v.) His car was *rounding* the whole city.

7. വൃത്താകാരം

(adj.) The table was *round* in shape.

8. നാല് ചുറ്റും

(adv.) The dog went *round* and round the car.

Route *(n.)* റൂട്ട്-മാർഗ്ഗം, വഴി

We must take the shortest *route* from here to Ambala.

Routine *(n.)* റുട്ടീൻ-ദിനചര്യ

Whenever visitors call on me all of a sudden, it affects my daily *routine.*

Rove *(v.)* റോവ്-അലയുക, കറങ്ങുക

You spent all day *roving* through the jungle.

Row *(n.)* റോ-1. നിര, വരി

The people were standing in a *row* near the ration shop.

(v.) 2. തുഴയുക

The boatmen *row* their boats. They make the boats travel through the water.

Rowdy *(adj.)* റൗഡി-പോക്കിരി, വഴക്കാളി

They are a group of *rowdy* teenagers.

Royal *(adj.)* റോയൽ-രാജകീയ

He belongs to the *royal* family of Rajasthan.

Royalty *(n.)* റോയൽറ്റി-പകർപ്പവകാശം, റോയൽറ്റി

The author was offered a *royalty* for his work.

Rub *(v.)* റബ്-തേയ്ക്കുക, പുരട്ടുക

Don't *rub* harder, your shoes are already shining.

(n.) Please give me a rubber to *rub* pencil-marks.

Rubbish *(n.)* റബിഷ്-1. ചപ്പ് ചവറ്

We must thrown our *rubbish* in the dustbin.

2. അബദ്ധം, അസംബന്ധം

She is talking *rubbish.* Really she knows nothing about it.

Rude റൂഡ്-ധിക്കാരം, ധാർഷ്ട്യം

Amita is a polite girl. She is not *rude.*

It is *rude* to speak with your mouth full.

Such *rudeness* can't be excused.

Ruffian *(n.)* റഫിയൻ-ഗു, അക്രമി

The landlord was attacked by a gang of *ruffians.*

Rug *(n.)* റഗ്-കമ്പളി, വിരി, ചവിട്ടുമെത്ത

Our cat likes to sit on the *rug.*

We have a *rug* in the car.

The lady purchased a fine *rug.*

Ruin റൂയിൻ-നാശം (വരുത്തുക), അവശിഷ്ടം

(n.) We visited the *ruin* of an old palace.

(v.) A severe earthquake totally *ruined* the big city.

Rule *(n.)* റൂൾ–1. ചട്ടം
You will be disqualified for disobeying the *rules* of the club.
(v.) 2. ഭരിക്കുക
Aurangzeb, the mighty Mughal emperor, *ruled* India for many years.

Rumour *(n.)* റൂമർ–കിംവദന്തി
People started stocking foodrains following *rumours* of food shortage.

Run *(v.)* റൺ–1. ഓടുക
The policeman is *running* after the thief.
2. ഒഴുകുക
He is *running* for parliament.
3. നടത്തുക
The Ganges *runs* through a thick valley.
4. മേൽനോട്ടം വഹിക്കുക
Who is *running* the business?

Rural *(adj.)* റൂറൽ–ഗ്രാമീണ
Most of our relatives live in the *rural* areas.

Rush *(v.)* റഷ്–1. ഓടുക, രക്ഷപ്പെടുക
The building caught fire and the people *rushed* out of it.
2. വേഗം ചെയ്യുക
You are very late. You should *rush* to the office.
After the accident, the injured were *rushed* to the hospital.
(n.) 3. ആൾത്തിരക്ക്
There was a great *rush* at the main gate of the cinema hall.

Rust റസ്റ്റ്–തുരുമ്പ്
(n.) There were patches of *rust* on the motorbike.
(v.) The motorbike had *rusted.*

Rustic *(adj.)* റസ്റ്റിക്–നാടൻ, നിഷ്കളങ്ക
There is a *rustic* charm in his mannerisms.

Ruthless *(adj.)* റൂഥ്ലെസ്–നിർദ്ദയനായ
Aurangzeb was a *ruthless* king.

S

Sachet *(n.)* സാഷേ–ചെറിയ പായ്ക്കറ്റ്
Get a *sachet* of coffee from the nearby shop.

Sack സാക്–1. ചാക്ക്
She filled up the *sack* with potatoes.
(v.) 2. ജോലിയിൽ നിന്ന് പിരിച്ചുവിടുക
He was *sacked* from the job because of bad behaviour.

Sacred *(adj.)* സേക്രിഡ്–പവിത്ര, പാവന, മതപര
Gita is a *sacred* book of Hindus.

Sacrifice *(v.)* സാക്രിഫൈസ്–ത്യാഗം ചെയ്യുക, കഷ്ടപ്പെടുക
Those who *sacrifice* their personal interests for a great cause never fail.
(n.) His *sacrifices* for the country will always be remembered.

Sad *(adj.)* സാഡ്–വിഷമിച്ചിരിക്കുക
Why are you so *sad* today?
(n.) ദുഃഖം
I cannot understand the reason of your *sadness.*

Saddle *(n. & v.)* സാഡ്ൽ–ജീനി, കോപ്പ്
(n.) The rider put the *saddle* on his horse's back.
(v.) We *saddled* our horses and got ready to march.

Safe സേഫ്–1. സുരക്ഷിതം
Is it *safe* driving in this area?
(n.) 2. അലമാരി, സേഫ്
Keep the money in the *safe.*

Safeguard *(v.)* സേഫ്ഗാർഡ്–സംരക്ഷണം നൽകുക
He promised to *safeguard* our interests in the deal.

Saffron *(adj.)* സാഫ്റൺ-കുങ്കുമം
She was wearing a *saffron*-coloured saree.

Sag *(v.)* സാഗ്-ഞാന്നു കിടക്കുക, ഉലച്ചിൽ തട്ടിയ
The skin on her arms was *sagging.*

Sage *(n.)* സേജ്-ജ്ഞാനി, സിദ്ധൻ
(n.) A true *sage* is he who has the deepest love for mankind.
(adj.) His *sage* advice saved my life.

Sail *(n. & v.)* സെയ്ൽ-കപ്പൽപായ്, ജലയാത്ര (ചെയ്യുക)
(n.) Jack put up the *sail* of the ship.
(v.) He will not *sail* until all dangers are over.

Saint *(n.)* സെയിന്റ്-പുണ്യവാളൻ, മഹാത്മാവ്
Many people claim to be saints, but very few of them are true.

Sake *(n.)* സേക്-കാരണം, ഹേതു
She will help for our mother's *sake.*
You should go for a walk for the *sake* of your health.
Please do come home for the *sake* of your dear mother.

Salad *(n.)* സലഡ്-സാലഡ്
She preferred to have *salad* over a heavy meal.

Salary *(n.)* സാലറി-ശമ്പളം
I receive a good *salary* as a manager in the firm.

Sale *(n.)* സെയ്ൽ-1. വില്പന, വിക്രയം
He made a good profit on the *sale* of his car.
2. ലേലം വിളി
Furniture is put up for *sale* at this shop every Sunday.
3. വില കുറച്ച് വില്ക്കുക
I purchased my shoes at a reduction *sale.*

Salient *(adj.)* സേലിയന്റ്-പ്രമുഖ
What are the *salient* features of this book?

Salon *(n.)* സലോൺ-സലൂൺ
She went to a beauty *salon* to get her hair cut.

Salt *(n.)* സാൾട്ട്-ഉപ്പ്
We add *salt* to make our food tasty.
There is *salt* in the sea water.
(adj.) The sea water is *salty.*

Salute *(v. & n.)* സല്യൂട്ട്-അഭിവാദ്യം (നൽകുക)
(v.) An English man *salutes* a lady by raising his hat.
(n.) Soldiers must greet their officers with a *salute.*

Salvation *(n.)* സാൽവേഷൻ-മുക്തി, മോക്ഷം
Buddha showed the path of *salvation* to man.

Same *(adj.)* സെയിം-1. ഒരേ, അതേ
Luv and Kush were born on the *same* day.
2. തുല്യം (ഒരേ പോലെ)
Her twin daughters look the *same* in height and appearance.
Whether you come to me or I come to you, is all the *same* to me.

Sample *(n.)* സാമ്പ്ൾ-1. മാതൃക, സാമ്പിൾ
By a small *sample* we may judge the whole piece.
(v.) 2. രുചി നോക്കുക
Mother allowed us to *sample* the Diwali sweets while she was making them.

Sanction *(v.)* സാങ്ക്ഷൻ-അനുമതി നൽകുക
The officer refused to *sanction* my leave.

Sanctuary *(n.)* സാങ്ക്ചറി-സങ്കേതം, അഭയകേന്ദ്രം
There is a bird *sanctuary* in Bharatpur.

Sand *(n.)* സാൻഡ്-1. മണൽ
They took the children to play on the *sands.*
2. (അർത്ഥം) ഇളക്കം തട്ടുന്ന അടിത്തറ
You cannot build up a house on *sand.*

Sandal *(n.)* സാൻഡൽ-വള്ളിച്ചെരിപ്പ്
The child put on his *sandals* before going to market.

Sandalwood *(n.)* സാൻഡൽവുഡ്-ചന്ദനം
The perfume had the fragrance of *sandalwood.*

Sandcastle *(n.)* സാൻഡ് കാസ്ൽ-മണൽ കൊട്ടാരം
The kids made a *sandcastle* at the beach.

Sandstorm *(n.)* സാൻഡ്സ്റ്റോം–പൊടിക്കാറ്റ്
The *sandstorm* blinded our vision.

Sandwich *(n.)* സാൻഡ്‌വിജ്–ര് റൊട്ടി കഷണങ്ങൾക്കിടയ്ക്ക് വെണ്ണയോ ജാമോ വയ്ക്കുക
Do you like jam *sandwiches*?

Sane *(adj.)* സെയ്ൻ–കാര്യവിവരമുള്ള, സുബുദ്ധിയുള്ള
You should take a decision in a *sane* state of mind.
(adj.) We must behave *sanely* in times of stress and strain.

Sapphire *(n.)* സഫൈർ–ഇന്ദ്രനീലം
The astrologer advised her to wear a *sapphire.*

Sarcasm *(n.)* സർകാസം–പരിഹാസ ചുവ
(n.) Sarcasm was dissolved in his words.
(adj.) He made a *sarcastic* comment on her looks.
(adv.) She laughed *sarcastically* at her.

Sash *(n.)* സാഷ്–അരക്കച്ച, പട്ടുകച്ച
Village-girls put on coloured and decorated *sashes.*

Satellite *(n.)* സാറ്റ്ലൈറ്റ്–ഉപഗ്രഹം
The moon is a *satellite* of the earth.

Satire *(n.)* സാറ്റയർ–വ്യംഗ്യരചന
That author is good at writing *satire.*

Satisfy *(v.)* സാറ്റിസ്ഫൈ – തൃപ്തിപ്പെടുത്തുക, സംതൃപ്തി നൽകുക
It is difficult to *satisfy* a greedy person.
(n.) Good shopkeepers aim at the *satisfaction* of their customers.
(adj.) Your work is not *satisfactory.*

Sauce *(n.)* സാസ്–ചട്നി, സാസ്
Tomato *sauce* is eaten with bread pakoras.

Saucer *(n.)* സാസർ–(കപ്പിനൊപ്പമുള്ള) പ്ലേറ്റ്, തട്ടം
He put the cup on the *saucer.*

Savage *(n.)* സാവേജ്–കാട്ടത്തം, കിരാത
Is man not still a *savage*?
(adj.) Everybody hates his *savage* behaviour.

Save *(n.)* സേവ്–1. ഭക്ഷിക്കുക, സൂക്ഷിച്ച് വയ്ക്കുക
Save something for tomorrow.
2. സുരക്ഷിതമാക്കുക, അപകടത്തിൽ നിന്ന് രക്ഷിക്കുക
She was *saved* from drowning by a life-guard.
3. നഷ്ടപ്പെടാതെ ലാഭിക്കുക
You must *save* time by cycling to work.

Saw *(n.)* സാ–ഈർച്ച വാൾ
The carpenter cuts the wood with his *saw.*
(v.) ഈർച്ച വാൾ കൊ് മുറിക്കുക
He is *sawing* the wood.

Say *(v.)* സേ–പറയുക
Listen to what others *say* and do what you ought to do.
(n.) Saying and doing are two different things.

Scald *(v.)* സ്കാൽഡ്–തിളച്ച വെള്ളത്തിൽ വീണ് പൊള്ളുക
Don't *scald* your tongue in other people's broth.
A cat who is *scalded* once fears even cold water.

Scale *(v.)* സ്കെയ്ൽ–1. ചിതമ്പൽ
Scrape the *scales* off the fish before cooking it.
2. അളവ്, മാത്ര
At present, we grow vegetables and fruits on a small *scale* only.
3. തുലാസ്, അളവ് യന്ത്രം
Have you a *scale* for measurements?
(v.) 4. കേറി ചാടുക
You cannot *scale* the wall unless someone lifts you.

Scalp *(n.)* സ്കാൽപ്–തലയോട്ടി
She massaged her *scalp* with oil.

Scam *(n.)* സ്കാം–കുംഭകോണം, വിവാദം
The minister was badly caught in the *scam.*

Scamper *(v.)* സ്കാമ്പർ–ഓടികളിക്കുക
The children *scampered* round the playground.

Scan *(v.)* സ്കാൻ–ശ്രദ്ധിച്ച് നോക്കുക, സൂക്ഷ്മമായി പരിശോധിക്കുക
You should *scan* this page to see if there are any spelling mistakes.

Scanty *(adj.)* സ്കാന്റി–ദുർലഭമായ, അല്പമായ
We received *scanty* rainfall this year.

Scandal *(n.)* സ്കാൻഡൽ–അപവാദം, കളങ്കം, നിന്ദ

A lie has no legs, but a *scandal* has wings.

Never listen to *scandals.*

(adj.) There has never been a *scandalous* tale without some foundation.

Scar *(n.)* സ്കാർ–പാട്, കറ, കളങ്കം

God will not look you over for medals, but for *scars*!

Scarce *(adj.)* സ്കാർസ്–ദുർലഭം, അപര്യാപ്തം, വളരെ കുറച്ച്

Some animals are becoming *scarce* in India.

Strawberries are *scarce* this year.

(adv.) I had *scarcely* sat down when the bell rang.

Scare സ്കെയർ–ഭയം, പേടി, ഭീതി, പേടിപ്പിക്കുക, വിരട്ടി ഓടിക്കുക

(n.) A good *scare* is worth more to a man than good advice.

The crows got a *scare* when they saw a *scare*-crow.

(v.) The *scare*-crow *scares* away the crows.

Scarf *(n.)* സ്കാർഫ്–സ്കാർഫ്

She wore a *scarf* to protect herself from cold.

Scarlet *(adj.)* സ്കാർലെറ്റ്–സിന്ദൂര വർണ്ണം

Her dress was *scarlet* in colour.

Scatter *(v.)* സ്കാറ്റർ–ചിതറുക

The string broke and all the pearls *scattered* on the floor.

Scenario *(n.)* സിനാറിയോ–ദൃശ്യസൂചി

The worst *scenario* would be backing out from the competition.

Scene *(n.)* സീൻ–നാടക രംഗം, കൺമുന്നിലെ ദൃശ്യം

The curtain was lowered at the end of each *scene.*

They were charmed by the beautiful *scene.*

The *scenery* was very beautiful.

Scent *(n.)* സെന്റ്–സുഗന്ധം

I like the *scent* of roses.

The sweet *scent* of lavender filled the garden.

(v.) The air was *scented* with honeysuckle.

Schedule ഷെഡ്യൂൾ–പരിപാടി, പദ്ധതി (ഇടുക)

(n.) This *schedule* allows you one week to finish the work.

(v.) The bus is *scheduled* to arrive at 8.15 A.M.

Scheme *(n.)* സ്കീം–1. പദ്ധതി

His *scheme* to fake certificates got him into trouble.

(v.) 2. കരുനീക്കം നടത്തുക, ഗൂഢതന്ത്രം പ്രയോഗിക്കുക

The prime minister *schemed* to dethrone the king.

Scholar *(n.)* സ്കോളർ–പണ്ഡിതൻ

He is really a *scholar* and knows a lot about different things.

School *(n.)* സ്കൂൾ–വിദ്യാലയം, സ്കൂൾ

We learn different lessons in the *school.*

Science *(n.)* സയൻസ്–ശാസ്ത്രം

Science increases our power of observation.

Science without religion is lame.

(adj.) The laboratory is full of *scientific* instruments.

Scissors *(n.)* സിസർസ്–കത്രിക

Ila cut out the picture with a pair of *scissors.*

These *scissors* are very sharp.

Scold സ്കോൾഡ്–ശാസിക്കുക, വഴക്കുപറയുക, ശകാരം

(v.) I was *scolded* for coming home very late.

(n.) You'll get a *scolding* from mother for breaking the dish.

Scope *(n.)* സ്കോപ്–1. സാദ്ധ്യത

There is lot of *scope* in a career in journalism.

2. പ്രവർത്തന സൗകര്യം

What is the *scope* of work in this project?

Scooter *(n.)* സ്കൂട്ടർ–സ്കൂട്ടർ

Do you own a *scooter*?

Scorch *(v.)* സ്കോർച്ച്–കരിയ്ക്കുക

The iron was very hot. It *scorched* the cloth.

(adj.) The farmer worked under the *scorching* sun.

Score സ്കോർ-(കളിയിൽ) എണ്ണം (എടുക്കുക)

(v.) The captain *scored* two goals for his team.

Has Vishwa Nath *scored* yet?

(n.) The *score* at the end of the game was two hundred for five.

Scorn *(n.)* സ്കോൺ-അവജ്ഞ, പുച്ഛം, തിരസ്കാരം

Silence is the most perfect expression of *scorn.*

(adj.) Of all griefs, the most bitter is a *scornful* jest.

Scoundrel *(n.)* സ്കൗൺഡ്രൽ-അക്രമി, കള്ളൻ

This *scoundrel* stole my pen.

Scout *(n.)* സ്കൗട്-സ്കൗട്

A *scout* is supposed to do a good deed every day.

Scowl *(v.)* സ്കൗൾ-മുഖം ചുളിക്കുക, തുറിച്ച് നോക്കുക

The old man *scowled* at her when she abused him.

Scramble *(v.)* സ്ക്രാമ്പ്ൾ-പൊത്തിപ്പിടിച്ച് കയറുക

The monkey *scrambled* up the trees.

Scrap *(v.)* സ്ക്രാപ്-തു്

Throw away these *scraps* of paper.

Scrape *(n.)* സ്ക്രേപ്-വിഷമസന്ധി, കഷ്ടപ്പാട്

You are so mischievous that you often get into a *scrape.*

Scratch *(v.)* സ്ക്രാച്ച്-ചുരുക, പോറലേല്ക്കുക

Who *scratched* the paint off this almirah?

My legs were *scratched* by thorns.

(n.) Her hands were covered with *scratches* from the thorns.

Scream സ്ക്രീം-നിലവിളി(ക്കുക)

(n.) The girl let out a sudden *scream* when she was frightened.

(v.) The child *screamed* loudly when she saw a dog.

Screen *(n.)* സ്ക്രീൻ-1. സിനിമാ, തിരശ്ശീല

My father writes stories for the *screen.*

(v.) 2. പ്രദർശിപ്പിക്കുക

All the feature films are *screened* only after they are certified by the Censor Board.

Screw *(v.)* സ്ക്രൂ-പിരിയാണി (മുറുക്കുക)

(v.) The carpenter *screwed* down the lid of the box.

(n.) I need some nails and *screws* to repair this table.

Scribble *(v.)* കുത്തികുറിയ്ക്കുക

If you *scribble* your homework, the teacher will make you rewrite it properly.

Script *(n.)* സ്ക്രിപ്റ്റ്-1. ലിപി, എഴുത്ത്

Your *script* is altogether illegible.

2. തിരക്കഥ

Have you reviewed the *script* of Shekhar's play?

Scripture *(n.)* സ്ക്രിപ്ചർ-ദിവ്യഗ്രന്ഥം, വിശുദ്ധ പുസ്തകം

The Hindu *scriptures* teach various ways to reach the God.

Scrub *(v.)* സ്ക്രബ്-വെള്ളവും ബ്രഷും ഉപയോഗിച്ച് വൃത്തിയാക്കുക

Please *scrub* the kitchen floor.

Scrutiny *(n.)* സ്ക്രൂട്ടിനി – സൂക്ഷ്മ പരിശോധന

(n.) Her work was under close *scrutiny.*

(v.) Her work was closely *scrutinised.*

Sculpture *(n.)* സ്കൾപ്ചർ-ശില്പ കല

I intend to take a course in *sculpture* at the arts college.

The exhibition was filled with fine pieces of *sculpture.*

Scuttle *(v.)* സ്കട്ൽ-1. ഓടുക

A frightened rabbit *scuttled* into the hole as I passed by the field.

2. മുക്കി കളയുക

The enemy was trying to capture the ship, but the captain *scuttled* it.

Sea *(n.)* സീ-1. സമുദ്രം

Oil has been found under the *sea.*

2. സമുദ്ര സ്ഥിതി, തിരയിളക്കം

There was a stormy *sea* running that day.

Seal *(n.)* സീൽ-മുദ്ര, അച്ചടയാളം

Put the office *seal* on this letter.

2. സീൽ മത്സ്യം

Seals live in the sea.

(v.) മുദ്രവച്ച് അടയ്ക്കുക

The police *sealed* the room so that it could be examined later.

Seam സീം-ഏപ്പ്, ര് തുണി ചേർത്ത് തുന്നുക

(n.) The tailor sewed the *seam* carefully.

(v.) She carefully *seamed* the two pieces of the old cloth together.

Search സെർച്ച്–പരിശോധന (നടത്തുക) അന്വേഷണം (നടത്തുക) തിരച്ചിൽ (നടത്തുക)

(v.) *Search* others for their virtues, and yourself for your vices.

(n.) You can make a *search* for your lost book.

All day long the *search* went on.

Season (n.) സീസ്ൺ–ഋതു, കാലം

There are six *seasons* in a year in India.

(adj.) This work is *seasonal*, not permanent.

Seasoned (adj.) സീസൺഡ്–പരിചയ സമ്പന്നൻ

He is a *seasoned* writer and has written a number of books.

Seat സീറ്റ്–കസേര(യിൽ ഇരിക്കുക)

(n.) Let me bring you a *seat*.

(v.) This cinema hall *seats* about a thousand people.

Please be *seated*. He is just coming.

Secluded (adj.) സെക്ലൂഡിഡ്–ഒഴിഞ്ഞ, വിജനമായ

We enjoyed a few quiet moments at a secluded beach.

Second (n.) സെക്കന്റ്–മിനിട്ടിന്റെ അറുപതിലൊരു ഭാഗം, സെക്കന്റ്

How many *seconds* are there in a minute?

(adj.) രണ്ടാമത്തെ

Monday is the *second* day of the week.

I shall buy a *second-hand* typewriter.

After the primary school, students go to the *secondary* school.

Secret (n.) സീക്രിറ്റ്–1. രഹസ്യം

He who confides his *secrets* in a servant makes him his master.

(adv.) രഹസ്യ, ഗൂഢ

The robbers made a *secret* plan to rob the bank.

(n.) This is a matter of utmost *secrecy*.

(adj.) Why should we be so *secretive* about our plans?

Secretary (n.) സെക്രിട്ടറി–സെക്രട്ടറി

We can telephone his *secretary* if we need to see him earlier.

Section (n.) സെക്ഷൻ–1. ഖണ്ഡം, ഭാഗം

How many *sections* are there in this catalogue?

2. വിഭാഗം

My brother is a *section-officer* in the Law Ministry.

Sector (n.) സെക്ടർ–മണ്ഡലം, മേഖല

The new budget provided some relief to the service *sector*.

Secular (adj.) സെക്യുലർ–മതേതര

India is a *secular* country.

Secure (adj.) സിക്യൂർ–1. സുരക്ഷിതം

Baby is *secure* in her pram.

2. നിശ്ചിതം

Your victory is *secure*.

(v.) 3. കരസ്ഥമാക്കുക

My son *secured* sixty-six percent marks.

See (v.) സീ–കാണുക

We *see* the moon.

A wise man *sees* as much as he ought to, not as much as he can.

Seed (n.) സീഡ്–വിത്ത്

Most plants grow from a *seed*.

We put *seeds* in the ground.

Seek (v.) സീക്–തിരയുക

Seek and you shall find.

Seem (v.) സീം–തോന്നുക

You *seem* to be sick. What's the matter?

See-saw (n.) സീ–സാ– മേലോട്ടും കീഴോട്ടുമുള്ള ചലനത്തിനുള്ള ഊഞ്ഞാൽ തട്ട്

Kamla and Vimla are on a *see-saw*.

The *see-saw* moves up and down.

Seize (v.) സീസ്–വളഞ്ഞ് പിടികൂടുക

The smuggled goods were *seized* by the customs officers.

Seldom (adv.) സെൽഡം–വല്ലപ്പോഴും, വിരളമായി

Barking dogs *seldom* bite.

Select (v.) സെലക്റ്റ്–തിരഞ്ഞെടുക്കുക

I *selected* one banana out of three.

(n.) Were not you a member of the *selection* board?

The *selectors* of the party-candidates will meet tomorrow morning.

Self *(n.)* സെൽഫ്–ആത്മ, സ്വയം

The best victory is to conquer one's own *self*.

(adj.) *Self* help is the best help.

Self control is the best form of discipline.

Selfish *(adj.)* സെൽഫിഷ്–സ്വാർത്ഥത

Don't be too *selfish*.

(n.) *Selfishness* is the root of all evils.

Sell *(v.)* സെൽ–വിൽക്കുക

What does the baker *sell*?

(n.) *Sale* of liquor is prohibited in Haryana.

Semester *(n.)* സെമിസ്റ്റർ–അദ്ധ്യായന ഘട്ടം

The course is divided into four *semesters*.

Semi *(pre.)* സെമി–പകുതി, അർദ്ധ

My brother is employed in a *semi-government* concern.

Seminar *(n.)* സെമിനാർ–ചർച്ചായോഗം

I will leave for the *seminar* tomorrow.

Send *(v.)* സെൻഡ്–അയക്കുക

He wants to *send* a parcel to his son.

My mother is ill. She must be *sent* for the doctor.

Mr. Agarwal *sends* us his good wishes.

(n.) Who is the *sender* of this letter?

Senior സീനിയർ–മുതിർന്ന, മുതിർന്ന (ഉദ്യോഗസ്ഥൻ)

(adj.) Vagish is the *senior* of the two brothers.

(n.) We must consult our *seniors*.

Sensation *(n.)* സെൻസേഷൻ–കോളിളക്കം

(n.) The news created a lot of *sensation* among the masses.

(adj.) The news channels feature only *sensational* stories these days.

Sense *(n.)* സെൻസ്–ഇന്ദ്രിയം, ബോധം

We have five *senses*, a *sense* of smell, a *sense* of touch, a *sense* of hearing, a *sense* of seeing and a *sense* of taste.

No man in his *senses* behaves in a silly manner.

Sensible *(adj.)* സെൻസിബ്ൾ–വിവേകമുള്ള, കാര്യവിവരമുള്ള

No *sensible* person would disagree with you.

Sentence *(n.)* സെന്റൻസ്–1. വാചകം

The best *sentence* is the shortest one.

(v.) ശിക്ഷ (നൽകുക)

The thief was *sentenced* to one month's imprisonment.

(n.) The murderer was given the death *sentence*.

Sentiment *(n.)* സെന്റിമെന്റ്–മനോവികാരം, മനോഭാവം

What were her *sentiments* about you?

(adj.) His approach towards this problem is *sentimental*.

Separate സെപ്പറേറ്റ്–1. വെവ്വേറെ

(adj.) They came into the room *separately*.

(v.) വേർതിരിക്കുക

Separate the good mangoes from the bad ones.

(adj.) വ്യത്യസ്ത

I cut the apple into two *separate* parts.

(n.) *Separation* is not always bad.

Septic *(adj.)* സെപ്ടിക്–വിഷയുക്തം

The wound turned *septic*.

Sequel *(n.)* സീക്വൽ–തുടർച്ച

The director is planning to make a *sequel* to the movie.

Sequence *(n.)* സ്വീക്വൻസ്–ക്രമം

The editor ensures that the scenes of the movie are in correct *sequence*.

Sergeant *(n.)* സാർജെന്റ്–സാർജെന്റ്

My uncle was *sergeant* in the army.

Serial *(adj.)* സീരിയൽ–ക്രമസംഖ്യ

What is your *serial* number?

Series *(n.)* സീരീസ്–ശൃംഖല

My favourite publisher is coming up with a new *series* of romantic novels.

Serious *(adj.)* സീരിയസ്–1. ഗൗരവം

One must be *serious* about one's career.

(adv.) My father is *seriously* ill.

2. പ്രധാനപ്പെട്ട

This is a *serious* issue and requires immediate action.

Sermon *(n.)* സെർമൺ–സൂക്തം, ഉപദേശം
A religious *sermon* changed his life completely.

Serve *(v.)* സെർവ്–1. സേവിക്കുക, സഹായിക്കുക
We should *serve* our nation selflessly.
My uncle *served* the country as a soldier for fifteen years.
2. വിളമ്പുക
The dinner was *served* to each and every member of the family.
(n.) He is our faithful *servant.*

Session *(n.)* സെഷൻ–യോഗം, സഭ, സത്രം
The court is in *session.*
In the next *session,* we shall do an advance course.

Set *(n.)* സെറ്റ്–1. (റേഡിയോ)സെറ്റ് മുതലായവ
Have you purchased a radio *set*?
(v.) 2. അസ്തമിക്കുക
The sun has *set.*
3. നിയോഗിക്കുക
The manager *set* the clerks to work and went to see the owner.

Settle *(v.)* സെറ്റൽ–1. തീർപ്പാക്കുക
The two parties *settled* the dispute.
2. വാസം ഉറപ്പിക്കുക
Our forefathers had *settled* in West Punjab.
(n.) We came to a *settlement* with one another.
Our forefathers were among the first *settlers* in Fiji.

Seven *(adj.)* സെവൻ–ഏഴ്
There are *seven* days in a week.

Several *(adj.)* സെവറൽ–ചിലത്, നിരവധി, അനേകം
I requested you *several* times but you did not care.
The workers had put forth *several* demands but none of them was fulfilled.

Severe *(adj.)* സിവിയർ–കടുത്ത, ഗുരുതരമായ, തീവ്ര, ഉഗ്ര
The burn caused me *severe* pain.
My father is just recovering from a *severe* illness.

Sew *(v.)* സോ–തുന്നുക
Mother can *sew* expertly.
She *sews* bottuns on Gita's coat.
Rajni is *sewing* a dress for her doll.

Sex *(n.)* സെക്സ്–ലൈംഗിക
Every citizen of India enjoys equal rights irrespective of his/her *sex.*
Modern movies are full of *sex* and violence.

Shabby *(adj.)* ഷാബി–1. മുഷിഞ്ഞ, കീറിപ്പറിഞ്ഞ
My skirt is *shabby.* I want to buy a new one.
2. ദുഷ്പെരുമാറ്റം
Vivek's treatment of his friends is very *shabby.*

Shade *(n.)* ഷെയ്ഡ്–1. തണൽ
The cow is lying in the *shade* of a tree.
2. അല്പം വ്യത്യാസം, വർണ്ണഭേദം
There were many *shades* of opinion among the friends.
Give me a lighter *shade* of blue.

Shadow *(n.)* ഷാഡോ–1. നിഴൽ
Shadows grow longer towards evening.
(v.) 2. പിന്തുടരുക
The fugitives were *shadowed* by the police.

Shake *(v.)* ഷേക്–കുലുക്കുക, ഇളക്കുക
If you don't wake up, I shall *shake* you up.
The earthquake has *shaken* the foundations of the houses.

Shallow *(adj.)* ഷാലോ–ആഴമില്ലാത്ത
This pond is too *shallow* to swim in.
We can't swim in *shallow* water.

Sham *(n.)* ഷാം–അടവ്, അസത്യം
His illness is merely a *sham,* he is quite well.
(v.) She was not hurt, she was only *shamming.*

Shame *(n.)* ഷെയിം–നാണക്കേട്, മാനമില്ലായ്മ
Shame is worse than death.

Shampoo ഷാമ്പൂ–ഷാമ്പു ചെയ്യുക, (മുടി) വൃത്തിയാക്കുക
(v.) You must *shampoo* your hair, it is very dirty.
(n.) I shall buy a *shampoo.*

Shape ഷേപ്–രൂപം, ആകൃതി, രൂപം നൽകുക
(n.) What is the *shape* of his radio set?
(v.) I am *shaping* clay into a ball.

Share ഷെയർ–പങ്കുവയ്ക്കുക, വീതിക്കുക
(*v.*) Let us *share* the cake among us.
(*n.*) Where is my *share* of the sweets?

Shark (*n.*) ഷാർക്–സ്രാവ്
Have you ever seen a *shark*?

Sharp (*adj.*) ഷാർപ്–1. മൂർച്ചയുള്ള
Is your knife *sharp*?
I heard a *sharp* cry of pain.
2. തീവ്ര(ഗതിയിൽ), ബുദ്ധിസാമർത്ഥ്യം
His memory is very *sharp*.
(*v.*) *Sharpen* your pencil with a *sharpener.*

Shatter (*v.*) ഷാറ്റർ–തകർന്ന് തരിപ്പണമാകുക
The looking glass fell to the ground and was *shattered.*

Shave (*v.*) ഷേവ്–ക്ഷൗരം ചെയ്യുക, മുഖം വടിക്കുക, ഷേവ് ചെയ്യുക
I *shave* myself every morning.

Shawl (*n.*) ഷാൾ–അംഗവസ്ത്രം, കമ്പളി ഷാൾ
Put on your *shawl* before you go out.

She ഷി–അവൾ (സ്ത്രീലിംഗം)
(*pron.*) *She* is a lovely woman.
(*adj.*) I have two he-goats and four *she*-goats.

Sheaf (*n.*) ഷീഫ്–കെട്ട്, കുല
What does this *sheaf* contain?

Shear (*v.*) ഷിയർ–കത്രിക്കുക
Sheep are *sheared* once a year.

Sheath (*n.*) ഷീഥ്–ഉറ, ആവരണി
He put his sword in its *sheath.*

Shed (*v.*) ഷെഡ്–പൊഴിക്കുക
In autumn, the trees *shed* their leaves.
The young girl *shed* tears when her mother went out.

Sheen (*n.*) ഷീൻ–തിളക്കം
In summers, the skin loses its *sheen.*

Sheep (*n.*) ഷീപ്–ചെമ്മരി ആട്
A *sheep* is an animal that has a coat of wool.
A man who looks after *sheep* is called a shepherd.

Sheepish (*adj.*) ഷീപിഷ്–നാണിച്ച് തല കുനിക്കുക, സങ്കോചം തോന്നുക
She looked *sheepish* when caught copying in exams.

Sheer (*adj.*) ഷീർ–കുത്തനെയുള്ള, കിഴുക്കാം തൂക്കായ
Over the edge of the cliff was a *sheer* drop.

Sheet (*n.*) ഷീറ്റ്–താള്, പുറം
How many *sheets* of paper do you need?

Shelf (*n.*) ഷെൽഫ്–അലമാര, തട്ട്
The baby's toys are on the *shelf.*
Our *shelves* are full of books.

Shell (*n.*) ഷെൽ–1. ആവരണം, തോട്, ഉപരിതലം
A *shell* is the outside of anything. The outside of a nut is the *shell.*

Shelter ഷെൽറ്റർ–അഭയം (തേടുക), ആശ്രയം
(*v.*) The children *sheltered* under a tree until it stopped raining.
(*n.*) We took *shelter* in a house until the storm was over.

Shepherd (*n.*) ഷെപേർഡ്–ആട്ടിടയൻ
The *shepherd* secured his sheep from the wolf.

Shield ഷീൽഡ്–1. രക്ഷിക്കുക
How can I tell a lie to *shield* you from punishment?
(*n.*) 2. കവചം, പരിച
The soldier came out armed with a sword and a *shield.*

Shift ഷിഫ്റ്റ്–1. ഷിഫ്റ്റ്
One week he works the day *shift* and the next week the night *shift.*
(*v.*) 2. എടുത്ത് മാറ്റുക, നീക്കം ചെയ്യുക
Who has *shifted* my chair?
Shiftless (*adj.*) 3. ഉത്സാഹ രഹിതൻ, അലസൻ
My servant is a *shifless* person. He does not work willingly.
Shifty (*adj.*) 4. സൂത്രക്കാരൻ
Beware of him. He is a *shifty* fellow. He can't be trusted.

Shimmer (*v.*) ഷിമർ–മിന്നിതിളങ്ങുക
The waves in the river were *shimmering* in sunlight.

Shine (*v.*) ഷൈൻ–1. തിളങ്ങുക
Make hay while the sun *shines.*
2. മിനുക്കുക
Have you *shined* your shoes today?

Ship *(n.)* ഷിപ്-കപ്പൽ, നൗക
A *ship* is a large vessel for carriage of passengers and goods by sea.
Battle-*ships* are used in war.

Shirk *(v.)* ഷെർക്-ഒഴിഞ്ഞുമാറുക
Lazy men *shirk* work.
My brother does not *shirk* any job.

Shirt *(n.)* ഷർട്ട്-ഉടുപ്പ്, കുപ്പായം
I bought three readymade *shirts.*

Shiver ഷിവർ-(തണുപ്പ്, ഭയം അല്ലെങ്കിൽ ദേഷ്യം കൊ്) വിറയ്ക്കുക, ഞടുങ്ങുക
(v.) He is *shivering* with cold.
(n.) A *shiver* ran through him when someone touched him in the dark.

Shock *(n.)* ഷോക്-ഞടുക്കം, ഞെട്ടൽ
The news of my friend's death was a great *shock* for me.
(v.) I was *shocked* when my best friend cheated me.

Shoe *(n.)* ഷൂ-ചെരിപ്പ്
I want to buy a new pair of *shoes.*

Shoot ഷൂട്ട്-1. വെടി (വയ്ക്കുക)
(v.) The farmer *shoots* the fox that kills his chickens.
(n.) How many *shots* did you hear?
2. മൊട്ട്, മുളപൊട്ടുക
We saw a lot of new *shoots* on the plant.

Shop *(n.)* ഷോപ്-കട, സ്റ്റോർ
Shops were closed on Sunday.

Shore *(n.)* ഷോർ-കര, തീരം
We can find many shells on the sea-*shore.*
The children walked along the *shore* picking up pebbles.

Short *(adj.)* ഷോർട്ട്-ചെറിയ, കുറിയ, അല്പം
Short prayers reach heaven.
(v.) Wherever you can *shorten* a sentence, do so.

Shortlist *(v.)* ഷോർട്ട്ലിസ്റ്റ്-സംക്ഷിപ്ത പട്ടികയിൽ പേര് ചേർക്കുക
Five candidates were *shortlisted* for the interview.

Shoulder *(n.)* ഷോൾഡർ-തോൾ, ചുമൽ
The labourer carried the luggage on his *shoulders.*
(v.) I can happily *shoulder* all the responsibilities.

Shout *(n.)* ഷൗട്-അപഹസിക്കുക
Am I deaf? Why are you *shouting* at me?
Your *shouts* could be heard from outside.

Show *(v.)* ഷോ-1. കാണിക്കുക
Show me the man who did this.
2. പറയുക, ധരിപ്പിക്കുക
Please *show* me how to do this job.
Would you *show* me the way to the bus-stop?
3. പ്രകടമാക്കുക
Her face *showed* how happy she was.
(n.) 4. പ്രദർശനം
Are you going to the film-*show*?

Showdown *(n.)* ഷോഡൗൺ-വഴക്ക്
There was a huge *showdown* in the Parliament.

Shower *(n.)* ഷവർ-മഴ, പേമാരി
Rakhi and Rina have been caught in a *shower* in rain.

Shred *(n.)* ഷ്രെഡ്-1. തുംതുമാവുക
In the scuffle, his shirt was torn to *shreds.*
2. ലേശം പോലും
There was not a *shred* of truth in his report.

Shrewd *(adj.)* ഷ്രൂഡ്-കുശാഗ്രബുദ്ധി
A *shrewd* businessman would never say such a thing.

Shriek *(v.)* ഷ്രീക്-നിലവിളിക്കുക
The kids *shrieked* with joy.

Shrill *(adj.)* ഷ്രിൽ-കർക്കശ, തുളച്ചു കയറുന്ന
She has a *shrill* voice.

Shrine *(n.)* ഷ്രൈൻ-സമാധി
Many foreigners visit the *shrine* of Swami Vivekananda.

Shrink *(v.)* ഷ്രിങ്ക്-ചുരുങ്ങുക, സങ്കോചം തോന്നുക
Your sweater may *shrink* if you wash it.
Some persons *shrink* from meeting a stranger.

Shroud ഷ്രൗഡ്–ശവത്തുണി, ആവരണം ചെയ്യുക

(n.) The dead body was wrapped in a *shroud.*

(v.) Silence was *shrouding* the atmosphere.

Shrub *(n.)* ഷ്രബ്–കുറ്റിച്ചെടി

The rose *shrub* in the garden looks beautiful.

Shrug ഷ്രഗ്–തോൾ ചുരുക്കുക

(v.) The shopkeeper simply *shrugged* when I told him that his prices were very high.

(n.) Mother answered with a *shrug.*

Shudder *(v.)* ഷഡർ–നടുങ്ങുക, വിറയ്ക്കുക

The terrible thought made her *shudder.*

(n.) A *shudder* passed through me when I looked at the dead body.

Shuffle *(v.)* ഷഫ്ൾ–ചീട്ട് കശക്കുക

She *shuffled* the cards well.

Shun *(v.)* ഷൺ–ഒഴിഞ്ഞു നില്ക്കുക, അകന്നു കഴിയുക

We should *shun* cheats.

Shunt *(v.)* ഷൺട്–പാളത്തിൽ നിന്ന് മാറ്റിയിടുക

Our carriage was *shunted* aside until the Toofan Express had passed.

Shut *(v.)* ഷട്–അടയ്ക്കുക, മൂടുക, അടച്ചിടുക

Shut all the doors and windows.

Shut your eyes.

Shut up! Keep quiet.

The concern was *shut* down because it was running in loss.

If you come to the hotel late, you will be *shut* out.

Shy *(adj.)* ഷൈ–1. സങ്കോചപ്പെടുക, നാണിക്കുക

Don't feel *shy* before the interview-board.

(adv.) Why do you answer *shyly* when you are asked a question?

(v.) 2. ഒഴിഞ്ഞുമാറുക

He always *shies* away from work.

Sibling *(n.)* സിബ്ലിങ്–കൂടപ്പിറപ്പ്

How many *siblings* do you have?

Sick *(adj.)* സിക്–രോഗിയായ, അസുഖമുള്ള

It is very difficult for a *sick* man to move briskly.

Side *(n.)* സൈഡ്–1. അരിക്

Sonia was riding by the *side* of the road.

2. വശം

When you prepare a manuscript, don't write on both *sides* of the paper.

3. കൂടെ

You must stand by my *side.*

4. ദിശ

People gathered from all *sides* of the area.

5. പക്ഷം

Is she on your *side* or Amitabh's?

Sieve *(n.)* സീവ്–ഇളക്കിമറിക്കുക, അരിക്കുക

These seeds will grow better if the soil is *sieved* before they are sown.

Sift *(v.)* സിഫ്റ്റ്–അരിക്കുക, അരിച്ചെടുക്കുക

We must *sift* the flour before baking.

The magistrate tried to *sift* the truth from the murderer's story.

Sigh *(v.)* സൈ–നെടുവീർപ്പിടുക, ദീർഘ ശ്വാസമെടുക്കുക

It is better not to *sigh* for days that are gone.

She heaved a *sigh* of relief when the loan was paid back.

Sight *(n.)* സൈറ്റ്–കാഴ്ച, ദൃഷ്ടി, കാഴ്ചപ്പാട്, കാഴ്ചകാണൽ

Her uncle lost his *sight* in an accident.

We went for *sight*-seeing.

Sign *(v.)* സൈൻ–1. കയ്യൊപ്പിടുക

Never forget to *sign* a letter before you post it.

(n.) 2. ചിഹ്നം

There was no *sign* of life in the patient.

Signal സിഗ്നൽ–സൂചന (നൽകുക), സിഗ്നൽ (നൽകുക)

(n.) A red *signal* is a *signal* of danger.

The bell gives the *signal* for a new period.

(v.) The referee *signalled* the players to begin.

The driver of the bus *signals* when he wants to stop it.

Signature *(n.)* സിഗ്നേചർ-കയ്യൊപ്പ്

Please put your *signature* on the cheque.

Is this your usual *signature*?

Signify *(v.)* സിഗ്നിഫൈ-സൂചന നൽകുക, അഭിപ്രായം പറയുക

We put up our hands to *signify* that we agreed with the speaker.

(n.) We must understand the *significance* of the Prime Minister's speech.

Silence *(n.)* സൈലൻസ്-മൗനം, നിശ്ശബ്ദം

Silence is wisdom, when speech is folly.

Silence is a friend that will never betray.

(adj.) *Silent* men are deep and dangerous.

Silk *(n.)* സിൽക്-പട്ട്

My shirt is made of *silk.*

(adj.) I usually wear *silken* clothes.

Silly *(adj.)* സിലി-ബാലിശം, നിരർത്ഥകം

We must not say *silly* things.

The clown does *silly* things to make us laugh.

Silver *(n.)* സിൽവർ-വെള്ളി, രജത

Some coins are made of *silver.*

His wife has a *silver* ring.

Similar *(adj.)* സിമിലർ-സമാനം, ഒരേ പോലെ തന്നെ

My pen is *similar* to yours.

(n.) There is a great *similarity* between you and me.

Simmer *(v.)* സിമർ-ചെറിയ തീയിൽ വേവിക്കുക

Let the gravy *simmer* for a while.

Simple *(adj.)* സിമ്പിൾ-ലളിതമായ, സാധാരണ

A *simple* life has its own reward.

The greatest truths are the *simplest,* and so are the greatest men.

Simultaneous *(adj.)* സിമൾറ്റെയ്ന്യസ്-ഒരേ സമയത്ത്

Several *simultaneous* blasts took place in the city.

Sin *(n.)* സിൻ-പാപം

The recognition of *sin* is the beginning of happiness.

Since *(adv.)* സിൻസ്-ഇതുവരെ

She came to Delhi two years ago and ever *since* she has been living here.

Sincere *(adj.)* സിൻസിയർ-സത്യസന്ധൻ

Ramesh is a *sincere* man.

Sing *(v.)* സിംഗ്-പാടുക

I shall *sing* you a song.

(n.) We gave the poor *singer* somemoney.

Singe *(v.)* സിഞ്ച്-ചെറുതായി കരിയുക

I *singed* my eyebrows while bending over the flame.

Single *(adj.)* സിംഗിൾ-1. അവിവാഹിത

Are you still *single*?

2. ഏകമാത്ര

The bush has a *single* flower.

(adv.) Do you sell these packets *singly*?

Singular *(n.)* സിംഗുലർ-ഏകവചന

Do you know the *singular* of 'children'?

(adj.) Rita's rescuing of the young child from drowning was a deed of *singular* bravery.

Sinister *(adj.)* സിനിസ്റ്റർ-കപട, അമംഗള

He looks *sinister* to me.

Sink *(v.)* സിങ്ക്-1. മുങ്ങുക

The ship *sank* in the storm.

A stone cannot float on the water. It *sinks.*

2. മുക്കുക

Our warship *sank* one of the enemy's ships.

3. (ശബ്ദം) അമർന്നുപോകുക

Your voice *sank* amidst the loud noise and we could hardly hear you.

Sip സിപ്-അല്പാല്പമായി കുടിക്കുക, ചെറിയ ഇറുക്ക്

(n.) You must take small *sips.*

(v.) I *sipped* my coffee slowly because it was very hot.

Sir *(n.)* സർ-1. സ്ഥാനപ്പേര്

Sir Francis Drake was a great English seaman.

2. ശ്രീമാൻ

Follow me, *sir.*

Siren *(n.)* സൈറൻ–മുന്നറിയിപ്പായി, അപകടസൂചന
The ship's *siren* sounded when the fog came down.

Sister *(n.)* സിസ്റ്റർ–1. സഹോദരി
My *sister* works in Ahmedabad.
2. ആശുപത്രിയിലെ നഴ്സ്
This *sister* nursed the patient in the hospital.

Sit *(v.)* സിറ്റ്–1. ഇരിക്കുക
Please *sit* down for a while.
2. പൊരുന്നയിരിക്കുക
The hen has been *sitting* for five days.

Site *(n.)* സൈറ്റ്–സ്ഥാനം
This is a good *site* for the shop.

Situation *(n.)* സിറ്റ്യുവേഷൻ–1. സ്ഥിതി, അവസ്ഥ
The *situation* is now under control.
2. ജോലി, ഉദ്യോഗം
Uncle obtained a *situation* as a clerk.

Size *(n.)* സൈസ്–വലിപ്പം, അളവ്
What is the *size* of your shirt?

Sizzle *(v.)* സിസ്ൽ–ശബ്ദത്തോടെ പൊരിക്കുക
Sausages were *sizzling* in the frying pan.

Skate *(n.)* സ്കേറ്റ്–മഞ്ഞിലൂടെ വഴുതി പോകാൻ സഹായകമായ പാദുകം
Have you got a new pair of *skates*?
Skating is a good fun.
Have you ever gone for *skating*?

Skeleton *(n.)* സ്കെലിടൺ–1. അസ്ഥികൂടം
Have you ever seen the *skeleton* of an animal in the museum?
2. അടിസ്ഥാന രൂപരേഖ
I'll prepare a *skeleton* for the next year's programmes.

Sketch *(n.)* സ്കെച്ച്–ഏകദേശ ചിത്രം
The artist drew a pencil *sketch.*

Ski *(v.)* സ്കി–മഞ്ഞിൽ തെന്നുന്നതിനുള്ള തടിപലക
Is the snow firm enough for us to *ski*?
One who *skies* is a *skier.*

Skid *(v.)* സ്കിഡ്–വഴുതി നിയന്ത്രണം നഷ്ടപ്പെടുക
The motorcycle *skidded* on the wet road.

Skill *(n.)* സ്കിൽ–വൈദഗ്ദ്ധ്യ, സാമർത്ഥ്യം പാടവം
The mechanic maintained his *skill* in repairing sewing machines.
(adj.) He was a *skilled* workman.

Skim *(v.)* സ്കിം–1. പത അല്ലെങ്കിൽ അഴുക്ക് മാറ്റുക
Mother *skimmed* the milk before drinking it.
2. മുകൾപരപ്പിൽ മെല്ലെ നീന്തുക
Seagulls *skim* the water in search of fish.

Skin *(n.)* സ്കിൻ–തൊലി, ചർമ്മം
Our body is covered with *skin.*
Peel off the *skin* before you eat the orange.

Skip *(v.)* സ്കിപ്–ഇടയ്ക്ക് വിട്ടുകളയുക, മറിക്കുക
These two pages are too difficult.
You can *skip* them.

Skirmish *(n.)* സ്കിർമിഷ്–ഏറ്റുമുട്ടൽ
One of our soldiers was lost in a *skirmish* with the enemy.

Skirt *(n.)* സ്കർട്ട്–പാവാട, സ്ത്രീകളുടെ വസ്ത്രം
The poor woman's *skirt* was covered with dust.

Skull *(n.)* സ്കൾ–തലയോട്ടി
The motor-cyclist fractured his *skull* in the accident.

Sky *(n.)* സ്കൈ–ആകാശം
Birds fly in the *sky* and chirp cheerfully.

Slack *(adv.)* സ്ലാക്–മാന്ദ്യം, അയഞ്ഞ
Business is *slack* this month.

Slam *(v.)* സ്ലാം–(കതകും മറ്റും) ശക്തിയായി അടയ്ക്കുക, ശക്തിയായി അടിക്കുക
Don't *slam* the door as you go out, or the noise will awaken the baby.

Slang *(n.)* സ്ലാംഗ്–സംസാര ഭാഷ
'Shut up' is the *slang* for 'be quiet'.

Slap *(v.)* സ്ലാപ്–തല്ലുക, അടികൊടുക്കുക
Was it not wrong of you to *slap* the baby?

Slash സ്ലാഷ്–കീറൽ, മുറിവ്
(n.) The razor left a *slash* on his cheek.
(v.) He *slashed* his cheek while shaving.

Slate സ്ലേറ്റ്–എഴുതാനുള്ള കൽപ്പലക, സ്ലേറ്റ്

(n.) Children used to do their sums on the *slates.*

(v.) The roof of the old house has just been *slated.*

Slaughter സ്ലാടർ–കൊല (ചെയ്യുക)

(n.) There was a great *slaughter* in the battle.

(v.) Animals are *slaughtered* for food.

Slave *(n.)* സ്ലേവ്–അടിമ

In the 19th century, there were *slaves* in America.

Abraham Lincoln considered *slavery* illegal.

Slay *(v.)* സ്ലേ–വെട്ടികൊല്ലുക, അറക്കുക

Hunters *slay* many animals while hunting.

Has the butcher *slain* two cocks?

Sleek *(adj.)* സ്ലീക്–തിളങ്ങുന്ന, മനോഹരമായ

The ipod was very *sleek.*

Sleep സ്ലീപ്–ഉറക്കം, നിദ്ര

(n.) Seven to eight hours *sleep* is essential for human beings.

(v.) The baby is *sleeping* in cradle.

Sleeper *(n.)* സ്ലീപർ–1. ഉറങ്ങുന്നവർ

Some people are light *sleepers,* others are heavy *sleepers.*

2. ട്രെയിനിൽ ഉറങ്ങാനുള്ള ബർത്ത്

I reserved a *sleeper* on the train to Mumbai.

Sleeve *(n.)* സ്ലീവ്–കുപ്പായത്തിന്റെ കൈ

I tore the *sleevc* of my shirt.

Slender *(adj.)* സ്ലെൻഡർ–നീ നേർത്ത

Sony has beautiful hands with long *slender* fingers.

Slice സ്ലൈസ്–കഷണം (ആക്കുക)

(n.) Can I have a *slice* of bread?

(v.) She *sliced* the apple.

Slide *(v.)* സ്ലൈഡ്–അനായാസം ചലിക്കുക

The window *slides* up and down very easily.

The children love to *slide* on ice.

(n.) 2. കണ്ണാടിപ്പലക

Children prepared *slides* for their experiments in the science class.

Slight *(adj.)* സ്ലൈറ്റ്–അല്പം, ചെറുതായി

I am not in the *slightest* hurry.

(adv.) Are you not *slightly* better today than yesterday?

Slim സ്ലിം–1. മെലിയുക

(v.) Some people *slim* down by avoiding heavy meals.

2. ക്ഷീണം

She has *slim* hopes of getting what she wants.

Slime *(n.)* സ്ലൈം–ചെളി

(n.) *Slime* deposited on the walls in the rainy season.

(adj.) The pond was very *slimy.*

Sling *(n.)* സ്ലിങ്ഗ്–1. ഒടിഞ്ഞ കൈയ്ക്ക് താങ്ങ് നൽകാനുള്ള ബാൻഡേജ്

His fractured arm was put in a *sling.*

2. എറിയുക

Tell the children not to *sling* stones at the puppy.

Slip *(n.)* സ്ലിപ്–1. തെറ്റ്

You have made a *slip* in the bill.

(v.) 2. വീഴുക (വഴുതി)

The looking-glass *slipped* through my fingers and was broken.

(adj.) The heavy rain has made the ground *slippery.*

Slipper *(n.)* സ്ലിപർ–വള്ളി ചെരിപ്പ്

Mother will buy a pair of *slippers* for me today.

Slit സ്ലിറ്റ്–കീറുക, വിടവ്

(v.) I received an envelope and *slit* it open with a knife.

(n.) The boys watched the football match through a *slit* in the fence.

Slogan *(n.)* സ്ലോഗൻ–മുദ്രാവാക്യം

She won the first prize in the *slogan* writing contest.

Slope *(n.)* സ്ലോപ്പ്-ചരിവ്, കയറ്റം

It is very difficult to walk up the *slope* of the hill.

Slow *(adj.)* സ്ലോ-1. മന്ദഗതി

The clock is *slow*. It is showing incorrect time.

My work is making *slow* progress.

2. മാന്ദ്യമുള്ള

She is very *slow* to understand anything.

(v.) 3. മെല്ലെ പോവുക

Slow down before reaching the stop signal.

(adv.) He walked *slowly*.

Slum *(n.)* സ്ലം-ചേരി

There are *slums* close to that colony.

Slumber *(n.)* സ്ലംമ്പർ-നീ ഉറക്കം, ഗാഢ നിദ്ര

The family was in a deep *slumber* when the thieves came.

Sly *(adj.)* സ്ലൈ-കപട, സൂത്രക്കാരൻ, അവിശ്വസനീയ

The shopkeeper is *sly*. He speaks politely but sells inferior things.

Small *(adj.)* സ്മാൾ-1. ചെറിയ, കുറച്ച്, അല്പ, ലഘു

Small courtesies matter a lot in life.

2. നിസ്സാര

Don't worry. It is a *small* quarrel, it will be over soon.

Smart *(adj.)* സ്മാർട്-1. ചുറുചുറുക്കുള്ള, സമർത്ഥനായ, ബുദ്ധിമാനായ

Do you want a *smart* worker for your office?

Really you are very *smart.*

2. കാണാൻ ശേലായ

The soldiers were praised for their *smart* appearance.

(v.) 3. കലങ്ങുക, വേദന

The thick smoke from the bonfire made my eyes *smart.*

Smash *(v.)* സ്മാഷ്-തകർന്ന് തരിപ്പണമാകുക

The furniture *smashed* into pieces.

Smear *(v.)* സ്മിയർ-അഴുക്ക് പുരട്ടുക, വൃത്തികേടാക്കുക

Please don't *smear* the page with your dirty hands.

Smell *(v.)* സ്മെൽ-മണക്കുക, ഗന്ധം നൽകുക

We *smell* with our nose.

Roses *smell* sweet.

(n.) All are attracted by the sweet *smell* of flowers.

Smile *(n. & v.)* സ്മൈൽ-പുഞ്ചിരി, പുഞ്ചിരിക്കുക

(n.) Smile is the language of love.

(v.) A face that does not carry a *smile* is never pretty.

Smith *(n.)* സ്മിഥ്-ലോഹപണിക്കാരൻ, കൊല്ലൻ

In our villages, there are many artisans such as *blacksmith, tinsmith, goldsmith etc.*

The *blacksmith* works with iron, he makes horse shoes.

Smoke *(n. & v.)* സ്മോക്-പുക, പുകവലിക്കുക

(n.) Where there is *smoke,* there is fire.

(v.) Smoking is prohibited. Please don't *smoke* here.

Smooth *(adj.)* സ്മൂഥ്-കോമളം, മൃദുവായ

Smooth words make *smooth* ways.

Smother *(n.)* സ്മോദർ-വാരിപൂശി, കുളിച്ച്

The player returned home from the playground *smothered* in mud.

Smoulder *(v.)* സ്മോൽഡർ-നീറി കത്തുക

The fire has not gone out. It is *smouldering.*

Smudge *(v.)* സ്മജ്-പടരുക

Water *smudged* the kohl of her eyes.

Smuggle *(v.)* സ്മഗ്ൾ-കള്ളകടത്ത് (നടത്തുക)

In olden days, *smugglers* brought wines.

Nowadays some people *smuggle* watches and jewellery.

Snack *(n.)* സ്നാക്-അല്പാഹാരം

We ordered tea and *snacks*.

Snake *(n.)* സ്നേക്-പാമ്പ്, സർപ്പം

All *snakes* are not poisonous.

Snakes are worshipped in India on Nagpanchami.

Snap *(v.)* സ്നാപ്-1. കടിക്കുക

Do not tease the dog. It may *snap* at your hand.

2. ഫോട്ടോ എടുക്കുക
He *snapped* you as you were coming round the corner.

Snarl *(v.)* സ്നാൾ–1. പല്ലിറുമ്മി മുരളുക
Her dog *snarls* at the visitors.
2. പരുഷമായി പറയുക
The angry mother *snarled*, "Why didn't you straight come home from your school?"

Snatch *(v.)* സ്നാച്–1. തട്ടിയെടുക്കുക, കവരുക
The thief *snatched* the girl's chain and ran away.
2. മിഴുങ്ങുക, പെട്ടെന്ന് കഴിക്കുക
I want only five minutes to *snatch* some food.

Sneak *(v.)* സ്നീക്–കണ്ണുവെട്ടിച്ച് കടക്കുക
I saw the thief *sneak* down the stairs and out of the shop.

Sneer *(v.)* സ്നീർ–നിന്ദിക്ക, കളിയാക്കുക
He is only a beginner at tennis, so we should not *sneer* at him for missing easy shots.

Sneeze *(v.)* സ്നീസ്–തുമ്മുക
You are catching a cold. You have *sneezed* many times today.
(n.) Mostly *sneezing* is a sign of cold.

Snide *(adj.)* സ്നൈഡ്–വ്യംഗാർത്ഥകം
He made a *snide* remark on her performance.

Sniff *(v. & n.)* സ്നിഫ്–മണം പിടിക്കുക, ചീറ്റുക
Please don't *sniff*, use your handkerchief.

Snob *(n.)* സ്നോബ്–പൊങ്ങച്ചക്കാരി
She is a big *snob*.

Snooze സ്നൂസ്–ഉച്ചയുറക്കം, മയക്കം
(n.) The labourers had a *snooze* after lunch.
(v.) The labourers *snoozed* after lunch.

Snore *(v.&n.)* സ്നോർ–കൂർക്കം (വലിക്കുക)
(n.) I was distrubed the whole night by my brother's *snores*.
(v.) Your *snoring* was intolerable.

Snow *(n. & v.)* സ്നോ–മഞ്ഞ്, ഹിമം
(n.) The *snow* was falling from the sky.
(v.) It started *snowing* in the hills.

Snub *(v.)* സ്നബ്–രോഷത്തോടെ പറയുക
She *snubbed* him badly for entering the room without asking for permission.

Soak *(v.)* സോക്–1. നനയുക
You have been out in the rain and are *soaked*.
2. വെള്ളത്തിൽ മുക്കിവെയ്ക്കുക
Soak the raisins in water for two hours.

Soap സോപ്–സോപ്പ് (ഇടുക)
(n.) Which *soap* do you use?
(v.) He *soaped* himself well to clean the dirt.

Soar *(v.)* സോർ–ഉയർന്നു പോകുക, വളരുക
Don't *soar* too high to fall, but stoop to rise.
Last year, the prices of foodgrains *soared* up very high.

Sob *(v. & n.)* സോബ്–ഏങ്ങികരയുക, ഏങ്ങലടി
(v.) The baby was *sobbing*.
(n.) Her *sobs* could be heard clearly from outside.

Sober *(adj.)* സോബർ–1. യുക്തിസഹമായ, കാര്യമായ
Pay heed to your teacher's *sober* advice.
2. ലഹരി വിട്ട
He is now *sober*.

Society *(n.)* സൊസൈറ്റി–1. സമൂഹം, സൊസൈറ്റി
Society doesn't love its critics.
2. മറ്റുള്ളവരോട് സൗഹൃദം
We like the *society* of interesting people.

Sock *(n.)* സോക്–കാലുറ, സോക്സ്
I bought a pair of *socks*.
I need a clean pair of *socks* today.

Soda *(n. & adj.)* സോഡാ–ക്ഷാരംശമുള്ള വെള്ളം, സോഡ
Soda bicarbonate is used in baking.
In small towns, people enjoy *soda-water*.

Sofa *(n.)* സോഫ–സോഫ, ഇരിപ്പിടം
Father bought a new *sofa*-set from the market.

Soft *(adj.)* സോഫ്ട്–മൃദുത്വമാർന്ന, മൃദുവായ, മൃദുലം
Wool is *soft* to touch.
You mother is *soft-hearted*.

Soggy *(adj.)* വളരെ നനഞ്ഞ് കുതിർന്ന
The sandwiches became *soggy* when left in open.

Soil *(v. & n.)* സോയ്ൽ–1. അഴുക്കാക്കുക, ചപ്പ് ചവറ്
(v.) She will *soil* her dress if she sits on the muddy grass.
(n.) 2. മണ്ണ്
This *soil* is very fertile.

Solace *(n.)* സോളിസ്–സാന്ത്വനം, ആശ്വാസം
After travelling to so many places, I found *solace* in my own home.

Solar *(adj.)* സോളർ–സൗര, സൂര്യനെ സംബന്ധിച്ച
The earth is a part of the *solar* system. It revolves round the sun.

Soldier *(n.)* സോൾജർ–സൈനികൻ
Soldiers fight and kings become heroes.
There are many *soldiers* in an army.

Sole *(adj.)* സോൾ–1. ഏക, ഒരേഒരു
She was the *sole* child of her parents.
(n.) 2. ചെരുപ്പിന്റെ അടിവശം
Please show me a shoe with a rubber *sole*.

Solemn *(adj.)* സോളം–ഗൗരവമേറിയ, ഗംഭീര
The manager had a *solemn* manner when he addressed the staff.

Solid *(adj.)* സോളിഡ്–കട്ടി, വര
The patient cannot take *solid* food. He can only take tea or milk.

Solidarity *(n.)* സോളിഡാരിറ്റി–ഐക്യം, യോജിപ്പ്
They expressed their *solidarity* with her opinion.

Solitary *(adj.)* സോളിറ്ററി–ഏകാന്ത, വിജന
Few people like to live in *solitary* places.

Solution *(n.)* സൊല്യൂഷൻ–1. പരിഹാരം
Provide me a *solution* to this problem.
2. പ്രശ്നത്തിന്റെ പ്രതിവിധി
The *solution* of these two chemicals can be explosive.

Solve *(v.)* സോൾവ്–പരിഹരിക്കുക, തീർപ്പുാക്കുക
Let me help you *solve* that crossword puzzle.
Solve your problems yourself.

Sombre *(adj.)* സോംബർ–മങ്ങിയ, ഇരു, ഉത്കണ്ഠാജനക
The graveyard was shrouded with a *sombre* darkness.

Some *(pron. & adj.)* സം–ചില (ആളുകൾ അല്ലെങ്കിൽ സാധനം)
Some are born great, *some* achieve greatness.
Some men are wise and *some* are otherwise.
Sometimes a half is better than the whole.
Do you want *something* to drink?

Son *(n.)* സൺ–മകൻ, പുത്രൻ
We all are the *sons* and daughters of Mother India.

Song *(n.)* സോംഗ്–ഗാനം
Which is your favourite *song* in the album?

Soon *(adv.)* സൂൺ–അടുത്തുതന്നെ, വേഗം, പെട്ടെന്ന്
Don't worry, we shall *soon* be back.
Sooner or later, the strong need the help of the weak.

Soot *(n.)* സൂട്ട്–അഴുക്ക്, കരി
Clouds of *soot* rose from the chimney.

Soothe *(v.)* സൂഥ്–സാന്ത്വനപ്പെടുത്തുക, ആശ്വസിപ്പിക്കുക
The boy was very excited but his sister *soothed* him and made him calm.

Sophisticated *(adj.)* സോഫിസ്റ്റികേറ്റഡ് – അനുഭവസമ്പന്നയും ബുദ്ധിമതിയും
She is a smart and *sophisticated* lady.

Sore *(adj.)* സോർ–1. കഴപ്പുള്ള, നോവുന്ന
My eyes are *sore* from reading too much.
(n.) 2. മുറിവ്, പരിക്ക്
My *sores* have healed.

Sorrow *(n.)* സോറോ–ദുഃഖം, വ്യഥ
Sorrow will pay no debts.
Sorrows are our best educators.

Sorry *(adj.)* സോറി–1. വ്യസനിക്കുന്നു
I am *sorry* I shall not be able to come.
2. ഏതെങ്കിലും കാര്യത്തെ കുറിച്ച് അറിഞ്ഞ് ദുഃഖം പ്രകടിപ്പിക്കുക
I am *sorry* to know that your mother is ill.

Sort *(n.)* സോർട്ട്–1. തരം, ഇനം
What *sort* of sweets do you like most?

(v.) 2. വേർതിരിക്കുക, തരം തിരിക്കുക
Sort out these letters quickly.

Soul *(n.)* സോൾ-1. ആത്മാവ്
I must put my heart and *soul* into my studies.
2. ഏതെങ്കിലും (വ്യക്തി), ആരുംതന്നെ
There is not even a single *soul* in the house.

Sound *(n.)* സൗ് - 1. ശബ്ദം, ധ്വനി
Listen! What *sounds* can you hear?
Did you hear the *sound* of a shot?
(v.) 2. ശബ്ദം പുറപ്പെടുവിക്കുക, കേൾക്കുക
How does it *sound*?
(adj.) 3. സുഖമായി
She has reached safe and *sound.*
A *sound* body has a *sound* mind.

Soup *(n.)* സൂപ്-രസം, സൂപ്പ്
You must start your lunch with a bowl of chicken *soup.*

Sour *(adj.)* സൗർ-പുളിക്കുന്ന, അമ്ലമായ, കാറലുള്ള
Lemons taste *sour.* Grapes are sweet.
(adv.) The manager replied very *sourly* because he was unhappy.

Source *(n.)* സോർസ്-1. സ്രോതസ്സ്, ഉത്പത്തി
The *source* of the Ganges is a spring in the Himalayas.
2. ആധാരം, മൂല കാരണം
His friendship is a *source* of great pleasure to us.

South *(n.)* സൗഥ്-തെക്ക്, ദക്ഷിണ ദിശ
The *south* is on our right at sunrise.
(adj.) Chennai is in the *southern* part of India.

Sovereign *(adj.)* സോവ്റിൻ-പരമാധികാര
A *sovereign* nation is a nation which has freedom and power to rule itself.
India which was once ruled by British is now a *sovereign* state.

Sow *(v.)* സോ-വിതയ്ക്കുക, നടുക, പാകുക
Sow good work and you will reap satisfaction.
The farmers *sowed* the seeds after they had ploughed the fields.

Spa *(n.)* സ്പാ-ആരോഗ്യ ജല ഉറവ
I will go to a health *spa* this weekend.

Space *(n.)* സ്പെയ്സ്-അകലം, അന്തരം, ബഹിരാകാശം, ആകാശം
Leave proper *space* between words.
Man can travel into *Space* in a *spaceship.*

Spacious *(adj.)* സ്പേഷ്യസ്-വിശാലമായ, വിസ്തൃത
Our library hall is quite *spacious.*

Span *(n.)* സ്പാൻ-വീതി
The railway bridge across the canal has a *span* of fifty yards.

Spank *(v.)* സ്പാങ്ക്-1. ചുട്ട അടി, തല്ല് (കൊടുക്കുക)
The boy who teases cats and puppies deserves a good *spanking.*
2. നിരത്തി അടിക്കുക
The teacher *spanked* the students who had disobeyed him.

Spanner *(n.)* സ്പാനർ-നട്ട് മുറുക്കാനുള്ള ഉപകരണം, കട്ട മുറുക്കി
The electrician tightened the nuts with a *spanner.*

Spare *(v.)* സ്പെയർ-1. നൽകാനാവും
I can *spare* a little money, if you want.
(adj.) 2. അധികമുള്ള, എക്സ്ട്രാ
Come and stay with us, we have a *spare* room.

Spark *(n.)* സ്പാർക്-തീപ്പൊരി, സ്ഫുലിംഗ്
Sparks flew from the fire.

Sparkle *(v.)* സ്പാർക്ക്ൾ-തിളങ്ങുക, മിനുങ്ങുക
Diamonds *sparkle,* and so do stars in the sky.

Sparrow *(n.)* സ്പാരോ-കുരുവി
A *sparrow* built a nest in the tree.

Sparse *(adj.)* സ്പാർസ്-വിരളം
The population in Ladakh is quite *sparse.*

Speak *(v.)* സ്പീക്-സംസാരിക്കുക, പറയുക
Speak well of your friend, of your enemy say nothing.
(n.) His *speech* was impressive.
The *speaker* remained undisturbed even when the audience started hooting.

Spear *(n.)* സ്പിയർ-കുന്തം
Caveman used *spear* to hunt.

Special *(adj.)* സ്പെഷൽ-വിശേഷ, വിശിഷ്ട
This is my father's *special* pen. No one else may write with it.

Specific *(adj.)* സ്പെസിഫിക്-പ്രത്യേക

What was the *specific* reason behind the fight?

Specimen *(n.)* സ്പെസിമൻ-മാതൃക, ദൃഷ്ടാന്തം

Please give us some *specimens* of your new publications.

Speck *(n.)* സ്പെക്-പൊട്ട്, പുള്ളി

Now the ship was a mere *speck* on the horizon.

Spectacle(s) *(n.)* സ്പെക്ടക്ൾ(സ്)-1. ഗംഭീര കാഴ്ച

Our annual procession was a very fine *spectacle.*

2. കണ്ണട

Please lend me your *spectacles.*

Spectator *(n.)* സ്പെക്റ്റേറ്റർ-കാണികൾ, പ്രേക്ഷകൻ

Many *spectators* stood round the field to watch the hockey match.

Speculate *(v.)* സ്പെകുലേറ്റ്-അനുമാനിക്കുക

Scientists *speculated* about the possibility of life on Mars.

Speech *(n.)* സ്പീച്-സംസാരശേഷി, പ്രസംഗം, ഭാഷ

Speech is the gift of all, but thought of few.

Speech is silver, silence is golden.

Speed സ്പീഡ്-വേഗം പോകുക, ഗതി, നടത്ത

(v.) If we *speed* up our work, we shall be able to finish it before Sunday.

(n.) Your *speed* of working is not satisfactory.

Spell *(v.)* സ്പെൽ-1. ഉച്ചരിക്കുക

Can you *spell* my name?

(n.) 2. മായാജാലം

The fairy cast a *spell* on the little boy and turned him into a young ox.

Spelling *(n.)* സ്പെല്ലിംഗ്-അക്ഷരശുദ്ധി

He is very bad at *spellings.*

Spend *(v.)* സ്പെൻഡ്-1. ചെലവഴിക്കുക, കഴിച്ചുകൂട്ടുക

I have *spent* the whole week in my research.

2. ചെലവു ചെയ്യുക

How much money did you *spend* on your new TV set?

My brother is a *spendthrift.* He spent all the money he had.

Sphere *(n.)* സ്പിയർ-പ്രവർത്തന മേഖല

(n.) This work is beyond my *sphere* of specialisation.

2. ഗോളാകൃതി

(adj.) Most of the celestial bodies are *spherical* in shape.

Spice *(n.)* സ്പൈസ്-1. മസാല

Addition of *spices* made the food tastier.

2. രസകരം, എരിവും പുളിയും

Media added *spice* to the whole incident.

Spider *(n.)* സ്പൈഡർ-ചിലന്തി, എട്ടുകാലി

Spiders spin webs in which they catch insects.

Spill *(v.)* സ്പിൽ-തൂകുക

You will *spill* the milk if you do not hold the jug straight.

The milk was *spilt* due to my carelessness.

Spin സ്പിൻ-നൂൽ നൂൽക്കുക, കറക്കം, ചുറ്റൽ

(v.) In the village, the old lady was *spinning* wool.

(n.) I have been in a *spin* since I came to this place.

Spinach *(n.)* സ്പിനിച്-ചീര

Spinach is very good for health.

Spine *(n.)* സ്പൈൻ-നട്ടെല്ല്

She has some defect in her *spine.*

Spire *(n.)* സ്പൈർ-ഗോപുരം സ്തൂപം

The *spire* of Salisbury Cathedral is one of the highest in the world.

Spirit *(n.)* സ്പിരിറ്റ്-1. ഉത്സാഹം

Roma was a girl of *spirit.* She knew what she wanted to do and no one could stop her from doing that.

2. ആത്മാവ്

Some people believe that the *spirits* of the dead exist in this world.

Spit *(v.)* സ്പിറ്റ്-1. തുപ്പുക

Don't *spit* on the floor. *Spitting* is prohibited here.

(n.) 2. മാംസം വേവിക്കാനുള്ള കമ്പി
The chicken was roasted on the *spit.*

Spite *(n.)* സ്പൈറ്റ്–വൈരാഗ്യം, പക
Don't tear his exercise-book out of *spite.*
(adj.) No one likes *spiteful* people.
(v.) Never *spite* others.

Splash *(v.)* സ്പ്ലാഷ്–തളിക്കുക, കുടയുക
She *splashed* some water on her face.

Splatter *(v.)* സ്പ്ലാറ്റർ–ഒഴിക്കുക
She *splattered* water all over the room.

Splendid *(adj.)* സ്പ്ലെൻഡിഡ്–ഗംഭീര, പകിട്ടോടെ, ഉൽകൃഷ്ടമായി, പ്രൗഢി
The prince lived in a *splendid* palace.
(adv.) Lila sang *splendidly* at the concert.
(n.) The rich man lived in great *splendour* in his newly built palace.

Splinter സ്പ്ലിന്റർ–ചെറിയ ചീള്, തുുതുാകുക
(n.) The soldier was severely wounded by a shell *splinter.*
(v.) The wooden cup crashed to the floor and *splintered.*

Split *(v.)* സ്പ്ലിറ്റ്–വീതിക്കുക, പിളരുക
The friends *split* the bill and paid Rs. 50 each.
Differences of opinion *split* the association.

Spoil *(v.)* സ്പോയ്ൽ–കളയുക, വഷളായ
Don't *spoil* my time with your foolish talk.
(adj.) A *spoilt* child never cares for his parents.

Spoke *(n.)* സ്പോക്–ചക്രത്തിൽ നിന്ന് റിമ്മിലേക്കുള്ള കമ്പി
The hub of a wheel is connected with *spokes* to the rim.

Sponge *(n.)* സ്പോഞ്ച്–സ്പോഞ്ച്
Have you a *sponge* to clean the slate?
Wash the scooter with a *sponge* and clean water.

Spontaneous *(adj.)* സ്പൊൺടെയ്ന്യസ്–സ്വമനസ്സാലെ, പ്രകൃത്യാ
His comic acts evoke a *spontaneous* laughter.

Spooky *(adj.)* സ്പൂകി–ഭയാനക, പേടിപ്പെടുത്തുക
Going inside the deserted bungalow was a *spooky* experience.

Spoon *(n.)* സ്പൂൺ–കരി
Stir the gravy with a wooden *spoon.*

Sport *(n.)* സ്പോർട്ട്–വിനോദം, സ്പോർട്ട്സ്
Wrestling in one of the international *sports.*

Spot *(n.)* സ്പോട്ട്–സ്ഥാനം, സ്ഥലം, പാട്, കറ
Please find a quiet *spot* where we can discuss the matter.
My clothes are *spotless.*

Spout *(n.)* സ്പൗട്ട്–1. കിവാൽ
Our teapot lost its *spout.*
(v.) 2. ചേർപ്പിലൂടെ ചോർത്തുക
Tea *spouted* from the broken teapot.

Sprain സ്പ്രെയ്ൻ–ഉളുക്ക്
(n.) It was a bad *sprain.*
(v.) She fell and *sprained* her toe.

Spray സ്പ്രേ–തളിക്കുക, ചീറ്റുക, തൂവാനം
(v.) He *sprayed* fresh paint on his motorcycle.

Spread സ്പ്രെഡ്–വിരിക്കുക, വിടർത്തുക പകർച്ച
(v.) Please *spread* a cloth on the table.
The parrot *spread* its wings and flew away.
(n.) Doctors try to prevent the *spread* of contagious diseases.

Spring സ്പ്രിംഗ്–1. വസന്തം
In *spring,* flowers begin to grow.
2. സ്പ്രിംഗ് ഭാഗം
The *spring* of your watch is broken, so it stopped.
(v.) 3. തുള്ളിച്ചാടുക
The little lambs *spring* about in the field.

Sprinkle *(v.)* സ്പ്രിംഗ്ൾ–അല്പാല്പം തളിക്കുക, തൂവുക
Please *sprinkle* some salt on the salad.

Sprint സ്പ്രിന്റ്–അല്പദൂരത്തേക്ക് ഓട്ട പന്തയം
(n.) We cheered when our friend won the *sprint.*
(v.) *Sprint* along the road and catch the train.

Sprout മുളപ്പിച്ച ധാന്യം
(n.) I had *sprouts* in the breakfast.
(v.) The seeds *sprouted* at the appropriate time.

Spur സ്പർ-പ്രേരണ, പ്രചോദനം നൽകുക, ആ ക്ഷണത്തിൽ
(n.) The performer thought of a wonderful trick at the *spur* of the moment.
(v.) Hunger *spurred* the poor man to seek work.

Spurt *(v.)* സ്പർട്ട്-പുറത്ത് ചാടുക
Water *spurted* out of the broken pipe.

Spy *(n.)* സ്പൈ-ചാരൻ
Isn't it a dangerous thing to be a *spy*?

Squabble സ്ക്വാബ്ൾ-കശപിശ കൂടുക, കലഹിക്കുക
(n.) We never like *squabble* about petty things.
(v.) Never *squabble* with your relations.

Squadron *(n.)* സ്ക്വാഡ്രൻ-സൈനിക വ്യൂഹം
The commander ordered his *squadron* to attack.

Squall *(v. & n.)* സ്ക്വാൾ-നിലവിളിക്കുക, കാറ്റും പിശറും
(v.) Don't *squall*, I shall not hurt you.
(n.) The boat was overturned in a *squall*.

Squander *(v.)* സ്ക്വാൻഡർ-ധൂർത്തടിക്കുക
She *squandered* a lot of money on shopping.

Square *(n.)* സ്ക്വെയർ-1. സമചതുരം
A *square* has four equal sides.
(adj.) 2. നല്ല
We give every customer a *square* deal.
3. മൃഷ്ടാന്നം, സന്തോഷജനകം
I could not have a *square* meal for a week.
(v.) 4. ചതുഷ് കോണമുാക്കുക
Square the corners of this wood.

Squash *(v.)* സ്ക്വാഷ്-ഉടച്ച് കുഴമ്പാക്കുക
She *squashed* the boiled tomatoes to make the soup.

Squat *(v.)* സ്ക്വാറ്റ്-കുത്തിയിരിക്കുക
Monkeys were *squatting* on the tree.

Squeak *(n.)* സ്ക്വീക്-കിരുകിരു ശബ്ദമുാക്കുക
I heard a faint *squeak* from the bedroom.
(v.) The old stool *squeaked* as Ram climbed on it.

Squeal *(v.)* സ്ക്വീൽ-ആർത്ത് വിളിക്കുക
The children *squealed* with joy when the dancing monkey entered the stage.
(n.) The children's *squeals* could be heard from a long distance.

Squeeze *(v.)* സ്ക്വീസ്-1. പിഴിയുക
Squeeze two lemons together in the glass.
2. അമർത്തുക
Don't *squeeze* my hand.

Squint സ്ക്വിന്റ്-കോങ്കണ്ണ്, കണ്ണ് ചിമ്മുക
(n.) He has a *squint* in her eye.
(v.) We *squinted* in the bright sunlight.

Squirrel *(n.)* സ്ക്വിറൽ-അണ്ണാൻ
A *squirrel* lives in a tree. It has a long bushy tail.

Stab *(v. & n.)* സ്റ്റാബ്-കുത്തുക, കുത്തി കയറ്റുക
(v.) A robber *stabbed* him in the neck.
(n.) There were two *stab* wounds on the body.

Stable *(n. v. & adj.)* സ്റ്റേബ്ൾ-1. പശുതൊഴുത്ത്
(n.) Jesus was born in a *stable*.
2. തൊഴുത്തിൽ/ലായത്തിൽ കെട്ടുക
(v.) Can we *stable* our horses in this shed?
3. അചഞ്ചലം, സ്ഥിരം, ഈടുക
(adj.) Was the provincial government not *stable*?

Stack സ്റ്റാക്-കൂട്ടം, അട്ടി
(n.) Get the red book from the *stack*.
(v.) *Stack* the books well on the shelf.

Stadium *(n.)* സ്റ്റേഡിയം-മൈതാനം, സ്റ്റേഡിയം
We saw the hockey match in the National *Stadium*.

Staff *(n. & v.)* സ്റ്റാഫ്-1. ജീവനക്കാർ, ഉദ്യോഗസ്ഥ വൃന്ദം
(n.) Have you not recently joined the *staff* of this office?
(v.) Our office is *staffed* by seven employees.
2. വടി
The old man walked with the help of a long wooden *staff*.

Stag *(n.)* സ്റ്റഗ്–കലമാൻ
The *stag* was caught by its horns in a thorny bush.

Stage *(n.)* സ്റ്റേജ്–1. വേദി, ലക്ഷ്യം, ഘട്ടം
Would you like to go on the *stage*?
Her cancer is on the final *stage*.
(v.) 2. അരങ്ങേറുക
The play had been *staged.*

Stagger *(v.)* സ്റ്റാഗർ–പ്രാഞ്ചി പോകുക, അടിതെറ്റുക
I *staggered* to know that he had died in the accident.
He *staggered* as he got up suddenly.

Stagnant *(adj.)* സ്റ്റാഗ്നെന്റ് –കെട്ടികിടക്കുന്ന വെള്ളം
(adj.) Stagnant water is a cause of various diseases.
(v.) Water *stagnated* on the road in the rainy season.

Stain *(n. & v.)* സ്റ്റെയ്ൻ–1. പാട് അല്ലെങ്കിൽ അടയാളം (ഇടുക)
(n.) The ink fell and left a *stain* on the table.
2. നിറം പറ്റുക, കറ വീഴുക
Her fingers were *slainod* with blue ink.

Stair *(n.)* സ്റ്റെയ്ർ–പടി, ഏണിപ്പടി, സോപാനം
Is there a toilet at the top of the *stairs*?
All the *stairs* together are called a *stair-case.*

Stake സ്റ്റേക്–പണയം
(n.) If we lose this contract, we will lose our credibility. *Stakes* are very high.
(v.) Why are you *staking* your future by getting involved in this issue?

Stale *(adj.)* സ്റ്റെയ്ൽ–1. പഴകിയ
The meal is *stale.* It is not fit to be eaten.
We can throw our *stale* bread to the birds.
2. പഴഞ്ചൻ
This joke is *stale.* There is nothing new or fresh about it.

Stalk *(n.)* സ്റ്റാക് – 1. ത്
This rose has a long *stalk*.
(v.) 2. പിന്നാലെ പതുങ്ങി പോവുക
Our party *stalked* the tiger in the jungle.

Stall *(n.)* സ്റ്റാൾ–1. ചെറിയ കട, സ്റ്റാൾ
Delhi station has many *bookstalls.*
(v.) 2. പൊടുന്നനേ നില്ക്കുക
The engine of my car *stalled,* so I had to push the car to the side of the road.

Stamina *(n.)* സ്റ്റാമിന–കരുത്ത്
He can play cricket all day. He has a lot of *stamina.*

Stammer *(v.)* സ്റ്റാമർ–വിക്കി പറയുക, വിക്കോടെ
When a man *stammers,* the listeners laugh.
(n.) He speaks with a slight *stammer.*

Stamp *(n.)* സ്റ്റാമ്പ്–1. തപാൽ മുദ്ര
Some children like to collect postage *stamps.*
2. സ്റ്റാമ്പ്
Have you brought a rubber-*stamp* and an ink pad?
(v.) 3. സ്ഥാപിക്കുക
This action *stamps* him as *rogue.*

Stand *(v. & n.)* സ്റ്റാൻഡ്–1. നില്ക്കുക
1. ബസ്സും മറ്റും നിർത്തിയിട്ടിരിക്കുന്ന സ്ഥലം
Can you *stand* on your head?
(v.) Everyone *stood* up when the President came in.
(n.) Where is the cycle-*stand?* I want to *stand* my bike.
(v.) 3. സഹിക്കുക
I cannot *stand* all this noise.

Standard *(n.)* സ്റ്റാൻഡർഡ്–നിലവാരം, മാനദണ്ഡം
His work does not reach the required *standard*.

Standstill *(n.)* സ്റ്റാൻഡ്സ്റ്റിൽ–നിശ്ചലം
The economy of the country came to a *standstill* after the war.

Stanza *(n.)* സ്റ്റാൻസാ–പദ്യം, ഭാഗം
Do you remember the second *stanza* of the song?

Star *(n.)* സ്റ്റാർ–നക്ഷത്രം, താരം
Stars twinkle at night.
(adj.) The sky was *starry,* and there was no moon.

Starch സ്റ്റാർച്–അന്നജം, കഞ്ഞിപ്പശ മുക്കുക
(n.) Starch is an important part of our diet.
(v.) Starch the collar of this shirt. That will keep its shape better.

Stare *(v.)* സ്റ്റെയ്ർ-തുറിച്ച് നോക്കുക, നോട്ടം

I *stared* with surprise at the strange snake.

Don't *stare* at the girl or she will think you are rude.

(n.) It was difficult to face his angry *stare*.

Stark *(adj.)* സ്റ്റാർക് – കഠിനവും അനിവാര്യവും

The book explores the *stark* realities of life.

Start സ്റ്റാർട്ട്-ആരംഭം (കുറിയ്ക്കുക)

(v.) We must *start* our work today.

(n.) Remember to take your medicine before making a *start* in the morning.

Startle *(v.)* സ്റ്റാർട്ട്ൽ-അത്ഭുതസ്തബ്ധരാകുക

We were *startled* when a thief ran out of the door.

Starve *(v.)* സ്റ്റാർവ്-പട്ടിണി കിടക്കുക, പട്ടിണി കൊ് മരിക്കുക

It is a sin to waste food when a large number of people are *starving* in our country.

(n.) Many died of *starvation* during the floods last year.

State *(n.)* സ്റ്റേറ്റ്-1. സംസ്ഥാനം, സർക്കാർ

India is divided into many *states*.

(v.) 2. പ്രസ്താവിക്കുക

It is *stated* that all people involved in the accident are safe.

(n.) The prisoner's *statement* was found to be a false one.

(n.) 3. സ്ഥിതി, അവസ്ഥ

The house was in a poor *state*.

Station *(n.)* സ്റ്റേഷൻ-1. കാര്യാലയം, നിലയം, സ്ഥാനം, താവളം

All workers should remain at their *stations* for the next twenty-four hours.

(v.) 2. പാർപ്പിക്കുക

The soldiers were *stationed* to Solan.

Stationary *(adj.)* സ്റ്റേഷണറി-സ്ഥിരമായ, അചഞ്ചലമായ

The sun is *stationary*.

Stationery *(n.)* സ്റ്റേഷണറി-എഴുത്ത് സാമഗ്രികൾ

Our address must be printed on all our *stationery*.

Stationer *(n.)* സ്റ്റേഷണർ-എഴുത്ത് സാമഗ്രി വ്യാപാരി

My uncle is a well-known *stationer*.

Statuary *(n.)* സ്റ്റാച്ചുഅറി-ശിലാമൂർത്തി, സഞ്ചയം

The *statuary* in this museum is remarkable.

Statue *(n.)* സ്റ്റാറ്റ്യൂ-പ്രതിമ

The *statue* of Mahatma Gandhi, the Father of Nation, stands in the middle of the municipal park.

Stature *(n.)* സ്റ്റാച്ചർ-ഉയരം, നീളം

Men are generally of larger *stature* than women.

Status *(n.)* സ്റ്റാറ്റസ്-1. നില, അവസ്ഥ

Please mention your marital *status* here.

2. പദവി

The job offered him good *status* apart from a good salary.

Staunch (adj.) സ്റ്റാഞ്ച്-ഇളക്കം തട്ടാത്ത

He is a *staunch* follower of Buddhism.

Stay സ്റ്റേ-തങ്ങുക, നില്ക്കുക, താമസം

(v.) The train does not *stay* for long at the station.

(n.) I had a pleasant *stay* in Ooty last summer.

Steady *(adj.)* സ്റ്റെഡി-നിരന്തരം, ഒരേപോലെ

Slow and *steady* wins the race.

(adv.) I work *steadily* all day.

Steal *(v.)* സ്റ്റീൽ-മോഷ്ടിക്കുക

Our maid-servant *stole* some money from my mother's purse.

Steam *(n.)* സ്റ്റീം-ആവി, ബാഷ്പം

Some engines are driven by *steam*.

(v.) I like to watch the trains *steam* out of the station.

Steel *(n.)* സ്റ്റീൽ-മറ്റു ധാതുക്കൾ ചേർത്ത് സുദൃഢമാക്കിയ ധാതു

The cap of my fountain pen is made of the best *steel*.

Steep സ്റ്റീപ്-1. കുത്തനെ (ചരിവ്, കയറ്റം)

The hill is very *steep*. It is almost straight up.

(v.) 2. കുതിർത്തുവയ്ക്കുക
My wife lets the clothes *steep* all night before she washes them.

Steer *(v.)* സ്റ്റീർ–ഓടിക്കുക, നീങ്ങുക
The seamen *steered* east in the hope of finding land.
(adj.) Please tighten the *steering*-wheel of the car.

Stem *(n.)* സ്റ്റെം–1. തടി
This tree has a very big *stem.*
(v.) 2. തടയുക
We should try to *stem* the flood by putting down sandbags.

Step *(n.)* സ്റ്റെപ്–1. ചുവട്
The baby moved towards the mother with small *steps.*
The discovery of radium was a great *step* forward in the science of healing.
(v.) 2. ഇറങ്ങുക
We should *step* out together.
(adj.) 3. ര ാ ന മ്മ
Lila is Renu's *step*-mother. Renu is a *step*-daughter of Lila.

Stereo *(n.)* സ്റ്റീരിനോ–സ്റ്റീരിയോ സിസ്റ്റം
The *stereo* in my car is not working properly.

Stereotype സ്റ്റീരിയോടൈപ്–ഒരേ രീതിയിലുള്ള, തനിപകർപ്പായ
(n.) The women have broken the *stereotype* of being the housewives.
(v.) Serials *stereotype* the relationship between a mother-in-law and a daughter-in-law.

Stern *(adj.)* സ്റ്റേൺ–കർശനമായ, കർക്കശമായ, അച്ചടക്കത്തോടെ
The Principal of our college was very *stern.*
Soldiers follow *stern* discipline.
The captain *sternly* ordered the soldiers to fight the enemy.

Stew *(v.)* സ്റ്റ്യൂ–1. കുക്കർ പോലുള്ള അടച്ച പാത്രത്തിൽ പാകപ്പെടുത്തുക
I'll *stew* some vegetables for dinner.
(n.) 2. വേവിച്ച മാംസം
I have some *stew* for dinner.

Steward *(n.)* സ്റ്റുവാർഡ്–മേലന്വേഷകൻ, കാര്യസ്ഥൻ
After the death of her father, Alka made her uncle the *steward* of her property.

Stick *(v.)* സ്റ്റിക്–1. പതിക്കുക
Did you *stick* the stamp to the envelope?
(n.) 2. വടി
My old grandfather uses a *walking-stick.*

Stiff *(adj.)* സ്റ്റിഫ്–കടുത്ത, ദുർഘട, വിഷമകരമായ
You have a *stiff* manner. You are not a good friend.
It was very *stiff* to climb to the top of the hill.

Stifle *(v.)* സ്റ്റൈഫ്ൾ–ശ്വാസം മുട്ടുക
I was almost *stifled* by the stale air in the room.

Stigma *(n.)* സ്റ്റിഗ്മ–കളങ്കം
There is still a social *stigma* attached to single women.

Stile *(n.)* സ്റ്റൈൽ–പടി, ഏണിപ്പടി
Help the old man over the *stile.*

Still *(adv.)* സ്റ്റിൽ–1. ഇപ്പോഴും
Vagish is *still* sitting. He has not moved up till now.
(adj.) 2. സ്ഥിരമായ, നിശ്ചല
Still waters run deep.

Stimulate *(v.)* സ്റ്റിമുലേറ്റ്–പ്രേരിപ്പിക്കുക, ഉത്തേജനം നൽകുക
Jai Prakash Narayan's kind words *stimulated* the dacoits and smugglers to give up their bad ways of living.

Sting *(n.&v.)* സ്റ്റിംഗ്–കുത്ത് (ഏല്പിക്കുക)
(n.) A wasp can hurt us with its *sting.*
(v.) A bee *stung* me in my face.

Stink *(v.)* സ്റ്റിംക്–നാറ്റം പരത്തുക
His clothes were *stinking.*

Stipend *(n.)* സ്റ്റൈപൻഡ്–ബത്ത
He was getting a *stipend* of Rs 2000 while working as an intern.

Stir *(v.)* സ്റ്റിർ–അനങ്ങുക, ഇളക്കുക
Nobody *stirred* when a dacoit came into the house.
Stir the solution.

Stitch *(n. & v.)* സ്റ്റിച്–തുന്നുക, തയ്ക്കുക
(n.) A *stitch* in time saves nine.
(v.) The tailor *stitches* the shirt.

Stock സ്റ്റോക്–ശേഖരം, സ്റ്റോക്ക്
(n.) We are sorry we have no grain in our *stock.*

(*v.*) Do you *stock* toothpaste and toothbrushes?

Stocking (*n.*) സ്റ്റോക്കിംഗ്–സോക്സ്

The policeman wears a pair of black *stockings.*

In winter, the children usually wear colourful *stockings.*

Stomach (*n.*) സ്റ്റൊമക്–ആമാശയം, വയറ്, ഉദരം, ദഹനക്കേട്

If we eat food so quickly, we shall get *stomach-ache.*

The patient had a weak *stomach* and could not digest solid food.

Stone (*v. & n.*) സ്റ്റോൺ–കല്ല് (എറിയുക)

(*v.*) The rioters *stoned* the speaker in the public meeting.

(*n.*) There was a heap of *stones* on the ground.

Stool (*n.*) സ്റ്റൂൾ–1. ചായാൻ തട്ടില്ലാത്ത കസേര, സ്റ്റൂൾ

She sat on the four-legged *stool.*

2. ശൗചം

The doctor examined the report of the urine and *stool* of the patient.

Stop (*v.*) സ്റ്റോപ്–1. എന്തെങ്കിലും കാര്യം, വി ഇവ നിർത്തുക

We *stopped* the car at the signal.

Usually we *stop* our work at 5.30 P.M.

Please *stop* talking now.

(*n.*) 2. വികൾ നിർത്തുന്ന സ്ഥലം

Where is the *bus-stop*?

Store (*n.*) സ്റ്റോർ–1. ശേഖരം, സഞ്ചയം, സംഗ്രഹം

We have a lot of goods in *store* for the bad weather.

Have you a good *store* of hay for your cow?

2. സാധനങ്ങൾ വയ്ക്കുന്ന സ്ഥലം

We put our broken pieces of furniture in our *store.*

(*v.*) 3. ശേഖരിച്ച് വയ്ക്കുക

Never *store* more than you need.

Storey (*n.*) സ്റ്റോറി–നില, പലനില

We lived in a three-*storeyed* house.

In large cities, some buildings have more than twenty *storeys.*

Stork (*n.*) സ്റ്റോർക്–കൊക്ക്

A *stork* is a large bird that usually lives near pools.

Storm (*n.*) സ്റ്റോം–1. കൊടുങ്കാറ്റ്

The *storm* raged all day.

(*v.*) 2. ആക്രമിക്കുക

The army was ordered to *storm* the town at midnight.

Story (*n.*) സ്റ്റോറി–കഥ, ചരിതം

The old man told us the *story* of his journeys.

Would you tell me the *story* of your life?

Stout (*adj.*) സ്റ്റൗട്ട്–പുഷ്ടിയുള്ള ശരീരം, പക്ഷെ പൊണ്ണത്തടിയില്ല

Vivek looks *stout* but he lacks stamina.

Hanuman has a *stout* body.

Straight (*adv.*) സ്ട്രെയിറ്റ്–1. നേരെ

This road goes *straight* to Rohtak.

(*v.*) 2. നിവർക്കുക, നേരെയാക്കുക

Straighten this bent wire and then use it.

(*adj.*) 3. നേരായ, സരളമായ

I want a *straight* answer from you.

Tell us the story in a *straight*-forward way.

Strain സ്ട്രെയ്ൻ–സർവ്വശക്തിയും പ്രയോഗിക്കുക, പിരിമുറുക്കം, സമ്മർദ്ദം

(*v.*) They *strained* their ears to hear what the speaker was saying.

(*n.*) In the fast life of metropolitan cities, people work under great *strain.*

Straits (*n.*) സ്ട്രെയ്റ്റ്സ്–വിഷമാവസ്ഥ, കഷ്ടപ്പാട്, ദുർഗതി

We were in dire *straits* when we lost all our money.

Strange (*adj.*) സ്ട്രെയ്ഞ്ച്–1. അത്ഭുതകരം

It is *strange* that he is not here. He always comes at this time.

2. അപരിചിത

The new boy is still *strange* to the school.

This handwriting is *strange* to me. I don't know who has written this.

Strangle (*v.*) സ്ട്രാൻഗ്ൾ–കഴുത്തു ഞെരിച്ചു കൊല്ലുക

The victim was *strangled* to death.

Strap (*v.*) സ്ട്രാപ്–ചേർത്ത് കെട്ടുക

Strap the two packets together. I want to carry them in one hand.

Strategy *(n.)* സ്ട്രാറ്റജി-തന്ത്രം
What will be our new marketing *strategy*?

Straw *(n.)* സ്ട്രാ-1. പുല്ല്, വയ്ക്കോൽ
Straw is used for making mats.
2. തണുത്ത പാനീയം കുടിക്കാനുള്ള കുഴൽ
Bring me a *straw* to drink Coca Cola.

Strawberry *(n.)* സ്ട്രാബെറി-സ്ട്രാബെറി
Do you like *strawberries*?

Stray *(adj.)* സ്ട്രേ-1. അലഞ്ഞുനടക്കുന്ന, വഴി തെറ്റിയ
Stray animals are causing serious traffic problems these days.
(v.) 2. വ്യതിചലിക്കുക
We *strayed* from the road and lost our way.

Streak *(n.)* സ്ട്രീക്ക്-1. കിരണം
A *streak* of lightning flashed in the dark sky.
(v.) 2. വേഗത്തിൽ പായുക
The racing cars were *streaking* on the track.

Stream *(n.)* സ്ട്രീം-1. കൂട്ടം
I saw a *stream* of people coming out of the cinema house.
2. ഒഴുകുക
Tears *streamed* down his cheeks.
3. അരുവി
Hundreds of *streams* flow down the Himalayas.

Street *(n.)* സ്ട്രീറ്റ്-തെരുവ്
Take care when you cross the *street.*

Strength *(n.)* സ്ട്രെങ്ത്-1. ശക്തി, കരുത്ത്
I have no *strength* to lift this heavy load.
2. അംഗസംഖ്യ, സൈനിക ശക്തി
We equalled the enemy in *strength.*
(v.) Strengthen your roof, otherwise it will fall in.

Strenuous *(adj.)* സ്ട്രെന്യുവസ്-ശ്രമകരമായ
Preparing the database of all the customers was a *strenuous* job.

Stress സ്ട്രെസ്-സമ്മർദ്ദം, പിരിമുറുക്കം, ഭാരം, ബലം (നൽകുക)
(n.) Can you bear the *stress* of working late?
In prayer, we lay *stress* on making a relation with the God.
(v.) Father *stressed* the need for special care.

Stretch *(n.)* സ്ട്രെച്-1. തുടർച്ചയായി
Can you work for six hours at a *stretch*?
(v.) 2. നീട്ടുക
Stretch your arms full length.

Stretcher *(n.)* രോഗിയെ കിടത്തി കൊണ്ടുപോകാനുള്ള തട്ട്, സ്ട്രെച്ചർ
The patient was carried on a *stretcher.*

Strict *(adj.)* സ്ട്രിക്റ്റ്-അച്ചടക്ക പ്രിയൻ, കർക്കശമായ
Father is very *strict.*

Stride *(v.)* സ്ട്രൈഡ്-1. നീട്ടി നടക്കുക
He *strode* out of the room.
(n.) 2. നീ ചുവട്
Vamana took three long *strides* and measured the underworld, the earth and the sky.

Strife *(n.)* സ്ട്രൈഫ്-തർക്കം, വടംവലി
The *strife* between the two parties ended after the election.

Strike *(v.)* സ്ട്രൈക്ക്-1. (മണി) അടിക്കുക
When the clock *struck* five, the office was closed.
2. തട്ടുക
The ship *struck* a large rock.
3. തല്ലുക
The naughty boy *struck* the donkey with a stick.
(n.) 4. പണിമുടക്ക്
The mill workers are on *strike* these days.

String *(n.)* സ്ട്രിങ്-1. ചരട്, നൂല്
I need a *string* to make a garland of flowers.
2. ആളുകളുടെ അല്ലെങ്കിൽ സാധനങ്ങളുടെ നിര
A *string* of people waited in front of the ration shop.

Strip *(v.)* സ്ട്രിപ്-1. കൊള്ളയടിക്കുക
The bungalow was *stripped* of everything of value by the robbers.
2. വസ്ത്രം അഴിക്കുക, നഗ്നമാകുക
The men *stripped* of their clothes and dived into the river.

Strive *(v.)* സ്ട്രൈവ്– പരിശ്രമിക്കുക

I *strove* hard to reach the peak of the mountain.

Stroke *(n.)* സ്ട്രോക്ക്–1. അടി, ഷോട്ട് (ക്രിക്കറ്റ് അല്ലെങ്കിൽ ഗോൾഫിൽ)

The cat killed a number of mice in a single *stroke.*

The batsman made a good *stroke* at the ball.

(v.) 2. തട്ടിതടവുക

She *stroked* her pet dog affectionately as it sat in her lap.

Stroll *(v.&n.)* സ്ട്രോൾ–നടക്കുക, കാൽനട

(v.) We were *strolling* in the garden when you saw us.

(n.) We went out for a *stroll* in the garden.

Strong *(adj.)* സ്ട്രോങ്–1. ബലിഷ്ഠമായ, പ്രബലമായ

The king sent a *strong* army to fight against the enemy.

Rakesh is very *strong.* He can carry a heavy load.

2. കാറും കോളും നിറഞ്ഞ

On stormy days, *strong* winds blow.

3. ഉറപ്പുള്ള

This fence is *strong* enough to keep out the animals.

4. കടുപ്പമുള്ള

Don't you like *strong* tea?

(n.) He has the *strength* of a bull.

Structure *(n.)* സ്ട്രെക്ചർ–1. കെട്ടിടം, നിർമ്മാണ ജോലി

This *structure* cost me five lakhs nine thousand rupees.

2. കെട്ടുറപ്പ്

This cinema has a weak *structure.*

Struggle *(v. & n.)* സ്ട്രഗ്ൾ–പാടുപെടുക, ഏറ്റുമുട്ടൽ

(v.) The people *struggled* to get out of the burning house.

(n.) You will be able to beat off your attackers after a hand-to-hand *struggle.*

Stubble *(n.)* സ്റ്റബ്ൾ–ചെറുതായി മുറിച്ച താടി

He looks good with a one-day *stubble.*

Stubborn *(adj.)* സ്റ്റബൺ–പിടിവാശിയുള്ള, വിട്ടുകൊടുത്ത

I see that you are too *stubborn* to change you mind.

(adv.) He refused to move from that place *stubbornly.*

Study *(v.&n.)* സ്റ്റഡി–1. പഠനം (നടത്തുക)

(v.) We *studied* the case very carefully and made a report.

(n.) Your *study* of fish has enabled you to know much about their habits.

2. വായനമുറി

Late Prime Minister Nehru's *study* had bookcases on every wall.

Stuff *(n.)* സ്റ്റഫ്–ദ്രവ അല്ലെങ്കിൽ ഖര സാധനം, വിവിധ സാധനങ്ങൾ, പാഴ്‌വസ്തുക്കൾ

You have a lot of *stuff* in your house that must be thrown away.

What sort of *stuff* do you put in the cushions?

(v.) 2. പാഴ്‌വസ്തുക്കൾ നിറയ്ക്കുക

She *stuffed* her doll with rags.

(adj.) In museum, we can see *stuffed* animals which almost look alive.

Stumble *(v.)* സ്റ്റമ്പ്ൾ–1. കാലിടറുക

The old beggar *stumbled* while crossing the road.

2. യദൃശ്ചയാ മനസ്സിലാകുക

At last, we *stumbled* on the explanation.

Stump *(n.)* സ്റ്റമ്പ്–1. മരക്കൊമ്പ്

We sat on a tree-*stump* to rest.

2.ഏതെങ്കിലും സാധനത്തിന്റെ തു്

I took the *stump* of pencil and wrote down her address.

Stun *(v.)* സ്റ്റൺ–1. സ്തബ്ധനാകുക

The old man was *stunned* when he learnt that his only son had died.

Stunt *(n.)* സ്റ്റ ് – 1. അപകടകരമായ അടവുകൾ

The actor performs all his *stunts* himself.

2. വേലത്തരം

The whole affair was merely a publicity *stunt.*

3. മുരടിപ്പിക്കുക

(v.) Irregular rains *stunted* the growth of plants.

Stupid *(adj.)* സ്റ്റുപിഡ്–ബുദ്ധി ശൂന്യമായ, മൂഢ

Only a *stupid* person walks in the middle of a road.

(n.) I am ashamed of my *stupidity*.

(adv.) The servant behaved very *stupidly* in front of the guests.

Sturdy *(adj.)* സ്റ്റർഡി-കരുത്തുള്ള, ഉറപ്പുള്ള

Don't worry, you are quite *sturdy* and will soon recover from measles.

Style *(n.)* സ്റ്റൈൽ-ശൈലി, ശേല്, സ്റ്റൈൽ

I did not like your *style* of dress.

(adj.) Vagish has bought a *stylish* pair of shoes.

Suave *(adj.)* സ്വാവ്-സൗമ്യ, സഭ്യ, മനോജ്ഞ

Her performance was *suave* as always.

Subdue *(v.)* സബ്ഡ്യൂ-1. തോൽപ്പിക്കുക, വിജയിക്കുക

We shall fight our enemies until we *subdue* them.

2. ശമിക്കുക

The baby's cries gradually *subdued*.

Subject *(n.)* സബ്ജെക്റ്റ്-വിഷയം

We have to learn eleven *subjects* simultaneously.

2. പ്രജ

The king must be kind to his *subjects*.

(v.) 3. ഇരയാവുക

The poor girl is *subjected* to her step-mother.

Sublime *(adj.)* സബ്ലൈം-ഉന്നത, ഉയർന്ന, ഉദാത്ത, വിശ്രുത

Wordsworth felt the *sublime* presence of God in Nature.

The bravery of the Rani of Jhansi was *sublime*.

Submarine *(n.)* സബ്മറീൻ-1. അന്തർവാഹിനി, കപ്പൽ, സമുദ്ര ജീവി

The *submarine* surfaced after an hour.

Sea-anemones are *submarine* creatures.

Submerge *(v.)* സബ്മെർജ്-മുങ്ങുക

The submarine *submerged* after it left the port.

Submit *(v.)* സബ്മിറ്റ്-1. സമർപ്പിക്കുക

The general agreed to *submit* to the enemy.

2. അവതരിപ്പിക്കുക

I shall *submit* my plan for a new hospital to the council.

Subordinate സബോഓർഡിനെയ്റ്റ്-1. രാം തരം, താഴ്ത്തി കെട്ടുക

(adj.) In many places in India, women are still considered *subordinate* to men.

(v.) The quality was *subordinated* to quantity.

2. കീഴുദ്യോഗസ്ഥൻ

(n.) You should treat your *subordinates* well to gain respect from them.

Subscribe *(v.)* സബ്സ്ക്രൈബ്-1. സംഭാവന നൽകുക

Did you *subscribe* to the Lions Club?

(n.) Have you paid your half-yearly *subscription*?

(v.) 2. യോജിക്കുക

I don't *subscribe* to your view.

Subsequent *(adj.)* സബ്സീക്വന്റ്-തുടർന്നുള്ള പിന്നീടുള്ള

His first and all the *subsequent* visits were kept secret.

(adv.) Subsequently, all the Indians settled in Ghana came back to India.

Substance സബ്സ്റ്റൻസ്-പദാർത്ഥം, വസ്തു, ദ്രവ്യം

Is not chalk a white *substance*?

Wood is a *substance,* and so is sand and so is sugar.

Substitute സബ്സ്റ്റിറ്റ്യൂട്ട് - പകരം, തൽസ്ഥാനത്ത്

(n.) Soniya cannot play the violin today, so Sony will be her *substitute*.

(v.) Sony has been *substituted* for Soniya.

(n.) This *substitution* will serve the purpose.

Suburb *(adj.&n.)* സബർബ്-പ്രാന്ത പ്രദേശം

(adj.) Every day I go to my shop by the *suburban* railway.

(n.) We live in the *suburbs* of Delhi.

Subway *(n.)* സബ്വേ-ഭൂഗർഭ നടപ്പാത

Let us go by the *subway;* there is a lot of traffic on the road.

Succeed *(v.)* സക്സീഡ്-1. വിജയിക്കുക
If we do not *succeed* in the first attempt, we must try again.
(n.) We wished him *success* in his new profession.
I passed my examination with great *success*.
(v.) 2. പിൻഗാമി
Mr. Prakash was *succeeded* as director by Mr. Mahajan.
The prince *succeeded* his father to the throne.
(n.) He was his father's *successor*.
(adj.) His son has become a *successful* doctor.

Succumb *(v.)* സക്കം-കീഴടങ്ങുക, മരിക്കുക
He *succumbed* to a heart failure.

Such *(adj.)* സച്-ഇത്തരം, ഇങ്ങനത്തെ
Such behaviour will be disliked by everybody.
Beware of flatterers, *such* men are dangerous.
I had never seen *such* a large monkey.
We were in *such* a hurry that we forgot our suitcase.

Suck *(v.)* സക്-1. കുടിക്കുക
The children were *sucking* the cold drinks through straws.
2. ഉറുഞ്ചുക
Don't *suck* your thumb.

Sudden *(adj.)* സഡ്ൻ-ആകസ്മികം, പെടുന്നനേ
We heard a *sudden* cry but could not see anything in the dark.
(adv.) The train stopped *suddenly* and a young woman fell forward.

Sue *(v.)* സ്യൂ-വ്യവഹാരം നടത്തുക, കേസ് കൊടുക്കുക
The actress *sued* the journalists for libel.

Suffer *(v.)* സഫർ-വേദനിപ്പിക്കുക, കഷ്ടപ്പെടുക
My father often *suffered* toothaches.
(n.) The kind man was moved by the *suffering* of the poor old woman.

Suffice *(v.)* സഫൈസ്-മതിയാവുക, ധാരാളമാവുക
One week *sufficed* for him to recover from his illness.
(adj.) Don't worry, I have *sufficient* money for shopping.

Suffocate *(v.)* സഫക്കെയ്റ്റ്-ശ്വാസം മുട്ടുക
I felt *suffocated* working in that organisation.

Sugar *(n.)* ഷുഗർ-പഞ്ചസാര, ശർക്കര
Sugar is made from a plant called *sugar*-cane.

Suggest *(v.)* സജെസ്റ്റ്-നിർദ്ദേശം നൽകുക, അഭിപ്രായം പറയുക
The doctor *suggested* that she should take rest for one week.
(n.) He made this *suggestion* after a complete check-up.

Suicide *(n.)* സ്യൂയ്സൈഡ്-ആത്മഹത്യ
Why did the old lady commit *suicide*?

Suit *(n.)* സൂട്ട്-1- വസ്ത്രം, സൂട്ട്
The tailor made a nice *suit* for me.
(v.) 2. യോജിക്കുക
Tea does not *suit* me. I take milk.
Will it *suit* you if we start at 7 o'clock?
(adj.) I think it will be *suitable*.
(adv.) We must come to office *suitably* dressed.

Sulk *(v.)* സൾക്-വിഷണ്ണ, വാശിയുള്ള
Never sit and *sulk* in a corner.

Sullen *(adj.)* സളൻ-ഉദാസീനമായ, ഉത്സാഹ രഹിത
The atmosphere was *sullen* in the evening.

Sum *(n.)* സം-1. ഗണിത ശാസ്ത്രത്തിലെ ചോദ്യം അല്ലെങ്കിൽ ഉത്തരം
Yesterday she got all the three *sums* correct.
(v.) 2. ആകത്തുക, സാരം
We can *sum* up all we have discussed.

Summary *(n.)* സമ്മറി-രത്നച്ചുരുക്കം, സാരാംശം
I don't have time to read the whole novel; just tell me its *summary*.

Summer *(n.)* സമ്മർ-വേനൽക്കാലം, ഗ്രീഷ്മ
We enjoyed the *summer* vacation very much.

Summit *(n.)* സമിറ്റ്-1. കൊടുമുടി, തുഞ്ചം
It is very hard to climb the *summit* of Mount Everest.
2. ഉച്ചകോടി
At the *summit* meeting, the world leaders discussed ways to control nuclear arms.

Summons *(n.)* സമൺസ്–1. കോടതിയിൽ ഹാജരാകാനുള്ള ചീട്ട്

Have you received *summons* to attend the court day after tomorrow?

(v.) 2. വിളിപ്പിക്കുക

The General *summoned* his officers to discuss plans for the battle.

Sun *(n.)* സൺ–സൂര്യൻ

The *sun* shines during the day. The moon shines at night.

In summer, people do not sit in the *sun.*

Oh, it is a very beautiful *sun-lit* room!

(adv.) We started on a *sunny* day.

2. പ്രസന്ന ഭാവം

His *sunny* nature warms every heart.

Sunday *(n.)* സൺഡേ–ഞായറാഴ്ച

Sunday is the first day in a week.

Sunday is the weekly holiday in many countries.

Superfluous *(adj.)* സൂപർഫ്ളുവസ് – ഉപരിപ്ലവം, ആവശ്യമില്ലാത്തത്

Delete the *superfluous* words from your article.

Superintendent *(n.)* സൂപരിന്റൻടെന്റ്–സൂപ്രൈ

The *superintendent* of police in our zone is a very intelligent person.

Superior സുപീരിയർ–മുതിർന്ന, സീനിയറായ

(adj.) An editor is *superior* to a proofreader in the press.

Uncle has got a *superior* position in his office.

(n.) Be respectful to your *superiors.*

Supernatural *(adj.)* സൂപർനാചറൽ–അലൗകികമായ, അനിതര സ്വാഭാവികമായ

Stories about ghosts describe *supernatural* events.

Superstition *(n.)* സൂപർസ്റ്റിഷൻ–അന്ധവിശ്വാസം

There is a *superstition* which makes some people afraid of walking under a ladder.

Supervise *(v.)* സൂപർവൈസ്–മേൽനോട്ടം വഹിക്കുക, നിരീക്ഷിക്കുക

Our mother *supervises* her domestic work every day.

The Principal asked the teacher to *supervise* the examinees.

(n.) All the teachers are busy in *supervision* during the exams.

Supper *(n.)* സപ്പർ–അത്താഴം

Supper is the last meal of a day.

Have you had your *supper* or not?

Supply *(v.&n.)* സപ്ലൈ–വിതരണം ചെയ്യുക, എത്തിക്കുക, സപ്ലൈ ചെയ്യുക

(v.) The milkman *supplies* us milk.

Some shopkeepers *supply* all we want.

(n.) We have enough *supply* of provisions for this month.

Support സപോർട്ട്–1. പിന്തുണയ്ക്കുക, സഹായിക്കുക

(v.) The kind rich man *supported* many poor students.

2. പിന്തുണ നൽകുക

Without the *support* of all its partners, the coalition government cannot function.

(n.) I couldn't have been successful without your *support.*

Suppose *(v.)* സപോസ്–ഉദ്ദേശിക്കുക, മനസ്സിലാക്കുക, വിചാരിക്കുക, സങ്കല്പിക്കുക

She is *supposed* to be at home by 8 o'clock in the evening.

I do not *suppose* we shall see each other again.

The work was over earlier than we had *supposed.*

(conj.) Supposing it rains, what shall we do?

Suppress *(v.)* സപ്രസ്–അമുക്കുക, അമർത്തുക, തടയുക

The soldier *suppressed* his fear and went on fighting.

(n.) The people rose against the *suppression* of the tyrant ruler.

Supreme *(adj.)* സുപ്രീം–പരമോന്നത

King Mahendra was the *supreme* ruler of Nepal.

Have you ever seen the *Supreme* Court of India?

The army remained *supreme* in the country after the war.

Sure *(adj.)* തീർച്ചയായും, ഉറപ്പായും, നിശ്ചയമായും

I am *sure* we have enough money for shopping.

Are you *sure* of coming tomorrow?
She is *sure* that she will be successful in the test.

Surface *(v. & n.)* സർഫിസ്-ഉപരിതലം
(v.) The submarine *surfaced* after an hour.
(n.) The *surface* of the teapot has been scratched.

Surgeon *(n.)* സർജൻ-ശസ്ത്രക്രിയാ വിദഗ്ദ്ധൻ, സർജൻ
The *surgeon* performed the difficult operation skilfully.

Surname *(n.)* സർനെയിം-ഉപനാമം
My name is Jaigopal Pipasu. Pipasu is my *surname.*

Surpass *(v.)* സർപാസ്-മുമ്പിലാകുക, പിന്നിലാക്കുക
Asha has *surpassed* Usha in English, but Usha is better in Sanskrit.
Your performance in the drama *surpassed* everybody else's.
Rakesh was intelligent, but my brother soon *surpassed* him.

Surplus *(n.)* സർപ്ലസ്-മിച്ചം, അധികം വരുന്ന
The farmers use as much grain as they need and sell the *surplus* to other villagers.
India grows more tea than she needs for herself, so she sells this *surplus* to foreign countries.

Surprise സർപ്രൈസ്-ആശ്ചര്യപ്പെടുക, അമ്പരക്കുക
(v.) She will be *surprised* to see me.
(n.) It was a great *surprise* to him when he was declared first in the university.

Surrender സറർ-കീഴടങ്ങുക
(n.) Has the general accepted the *surrender* of the enemy?
(v.) The enemy was so powerful that they made us *surrender* the fort.

Surround *(v.)* സറൗ്-1. വലയം ചെയ്യുക, ചുറ്റപ്പെടുക
The bungalow is *surrounded* by gardens.
(n.) 2. അന്തരീക്ഷം
The *surroundings* of the bungalow are very beautiful.

Survey സർവേ-അളന്ന് തിട്ടപ്പെടുത്തുക, സർവേ ചെയ്യുക
(v.) Before we buy a plot, we ask a *surveyor to survey* the land.
(n.) The Principal gave us a *survey* of the year's work.

Survive *(v.)* സർവൈവ്-1. അതിജീവിക്കുക, മരണത്തിൽ നിന്ന് രക്ഷപ്പെടുക
Only one hundred people in the village *survived* the epidemic.
The father is *survived* by two daughters and a son.
(n.) 2. രക്ഷപ്പെട്ട വ്യക്തി
This woman was one of the *survivors* of the disaster.

Suspect *(v.)* സസ്പെക്റ്റ്-സംശയിക്കുക, അവിശ്വസിക്കുക
She *suspects* her husband to be a spy.
(n.) She has *suspicion* that he will kill her.
(adj.) She is very *suspicious* about him.
(adv.) She is acting *suspiciously*.

Suspend *(v.)* സസ്പെൻഡ്-1. നിർത്തിവയ്ക്കുക
The chairman suddenly fell ill during the meeting and we had to *suspend* it until the next week.
2. തൂക്കിയിടുക
Can you *suspend* the electric lamp from the middle of the ceilling?
3. സസ്പെൻഡ് ചെയ്യുക
After the inquiry, the general manager was *suspended*.

Sustain *(v.)* സസ്ടെയ്ൻ-നിലനില്ക്കുക, ഉപജീവനം കഴിക്കുക, ജീവിച്ച് പോവുക
During the famine, many people did not have enough food to *sustain* themselves.
During their long march, the men were *sustained* by tinned food.

Swallow *(n.)* സ്വാളോ-1. മേവൽ പക്ഷി
Many *swallows* gather and twitter in the sky at sunset.
(v.) 2. മിഴുങ്ങുക
You must chew your food thoroughly before you *swallow* it.

Swamp *(v.)* സ്വാംപ്–1. വെള്ളം നിറയ്ക്കുക, മുക്കികളയുക

They were afraid that the huge waves would *swamp* their boat.

(n.) 2. ചതുപ്പുനിലം

There are many large *swamps* in Myanmar.

Swan *(n.)* സ്വാൻ–അരയന്നം

Swan is a very beautiful water bird.

Swarm സ്വാം–കൂട്ടം, പറ്റം

(v.) After the show, the spectators *swarmed* on to the road.

(n.) A *swarm* of honeybees attacked him when he disturbed the honeycomb.

Sway *(v.)* സ്വേ–1. ആടുക, ആടികളിക്കുക

The branches of the trees *sway* in the wind.

2. ഭരണം

(n.) India was under the *sway* of British for over a hundred years.

Swear *(v.)* സ്വെയ്ർ–1. ശപഥം ചെയ്യുക, പ്രതിജ്ഞയെടുക്കുക

We *swear* we shall serve our nation.

You must *swear* that you will speak only the truth.

2. ദേഷ്യത്തിൽ ശപിക്കുക

The thief *swore* when he bumped his head against a pole in the dark.

Sweat സ്വെറ്റ്–വിയർക്കുക

(v.) You are *sweating.* You must change your shirt.

(n.) His brow is wet with honest *sweat.*

Sweep *(v.)* സ്വീപ്–1. തൂത്തുവാരുക, വൃത്തിയാക്കുക

The servant *sweeps* the room clean.

(adj.) He uses a *sweeping* brush.

2. ഒഴുക്കെടുത്ത് പോവുക

The flood *swept* away the whole colonies on the banks of the river.

Sweet *(adj.)* സ്വീറ്റ്–1. മധുരിക്കുന്ന, സുരഭിയായ

Rose has a *sweet* smell.

Her voice was very *sweet.*

(n.) 2. മധുരപലഹാരം

Eating too many *sweets* in not good for health.

Swell *(v.)* സ്വെൽ–1. നീര് കെട്ടുക, വീർക്കുക

A bee has stung her hand. It is *swelling* up.

If we soak rice in water for half an hour, it *swells.*

(n.) 2. നീര്

You had a *swelling* in you neck.

Swelter *(v.)* സ്വെൽടർ–വിയർത്ത് കുളിക്കുക

With no shelter from the sun, we lay *sweltering* on the sand.

Swerve *(v.)* സ്വെർവ്–തിരിയുക

The ball *swerved* just as the batsman prepared to hit it.

Swift *(adj.)* സ്വിഫ്റ്റ്–അതിവേഗം പായുന്ന, ചുറുചുറുക്കുള്ള

Are you a very *swift* runner?

(adv.) Seeing the policemen, the thief *swiftly* ran round the corner.

Swim *(v.)* സ്വിം–നീന്തുക, നീന്തി പോവുക

Can you *swim*?

(n.) I want to go for a *swim.*

I am a good *swimmer.* I used to go to the *swimming*-pool regularly.

Swine *(n.)* സ്വൈൻ–പന്നി

Swine ate dirty things.

Swing സ്വിംഗ്–1. ഊഞ്ഞാൽ (ആടുക)

(n.) Let the children play on the *swing.*

(v.) The strong wind made the washing on the line *swing* about.

2. ആട്ടുക

We *swing* our arms when we walk.

Swirl *(v.)* സ്വേൾ–ചുഴറ്റിയാടുക

The leaves *swirled* in the wind.

Switch *(v.&n.)* സ്വിച്ച്–ബട്ടൺ (അമർത്തുക) വിഷയം മാറ്റുക, മാറിപ്പോവുക

(v.) *Switch* on the light for it is getting dark.

I *switched* the conversation to another less painful subject.

(n.) Where is the *switch*-board in your house?

Swoop *(v.)* സ്വൂപ്–റാഞ്ചുക

We saw an owl *swoop* on a mouse and kill it.

Sword *(n.)* സ്വോർഡ്–വാൾ
The soldier drew his *sword* and rushed to the enemy.
Swords are not used in battle these days.

Symbol *(n.)* സിമ്പൽ–പ്രതീകം, ചിഹ്നം
Re. is the *symbol* for rupee.
A white flag is the *symbol* of surrender.

Sympathy *(n.)* സിമ്പതി–സഹതാപം, അനുകമ്പ
I have no *sympathy* with students who waste their time.
(v.) We must *sympathise* with the poor and the needy.
(adj.) We must feel *sympathetic* towards invalids.

Symptom *(n.)* സിംപ്ടം–രോഗലക്ഷണം
A gumboil is a *symptom* of decaying teeth.

Syndicate *(n.)* സിൻഡികേറ്റ്–തൊഴിൽ സംഘടന
Are you a member of New Era Writers' *syndicate*?

Synonym *(n.)* സിനനിം–പര്യായം
Can you suggest a few *synonyms* for the word 'promise'?

Synopsis *(n.)* സിനോപ്സിസ്–കഥാസാരം
Send me a *synopsis* of the novel before sending the whole manuscript.

Syrup *(n.)* സിറപ്–സർബത്ത്, പാവ്
Would you prepare some sugar *syrup*?

System *(n.)* സിസ്റ്റം–1. സമ്പ്രദായം, പദ്ധതി
It is difficult to do a job well unless you have some *system*.
2. വ്യൂഹം, യൂഥം
Have you got any knowledge about the solar *system*?

T

Table *(n.)* ടേബ്ൾ–1. മേശ
Put the teapot on the *table*.
2. അനുക്രമണിക
Before we buy a book, we always look at the *table* of contents.

Tablet *(n.)* ടാബ്ലെറ്റ്–ഗുളിക, മരുന്ന്
The doctor told me to take the *tablet* every four hours.

Taboo *(n.)* ടാബൂ–നിഷേധം, വിലക്ക്
Divorce is still considered a *taboo* in many Indian societies.

Tack *(v.)* ടാക്–1. തൂക്കി ഇടുക
If you *tack* the dress, I shall be able to try it on.
2. കാറ്റിനെതിരെ കപ്പലോടിക്കുക
We had to *tack* to reach the harbour.
3. മുള്ളാണി അടിക്കുക
I *tack* the picture to the frame.

Tackle *(v.)* റ്റാക്ൾ–1. കൈകാര്യം ചെയ്യുക, മുഴുകുക
Aunt says she must *tackle* a lot of sewing today.
2. *(n.)* മത്സ്യം പിടിക്കാനുള്ള ഉപകരണം
You can buy a fishing *tackle* at this shop.
3. ഫുട്ബാൾ മത്സരത്തിൽ എതിരാളിയെ തടഞ്ഞു നിർത്തുക
That was a fine *tackle*!

Tact *(n.)* റ്റാക്ട്–വിദ്യ, അടവ്, വശം
You have the *tact* of persuading the men to go back to work.

Tadpole *(n.)* റ്റാഡ്പോൾ–തവളക്കുഞ്ഞ്
We caught a *tadpole* in the garden.

Tag *(n.)* റ്റാഗ്–ഞാത്ത്, ലേബൽ
Every article in the shop should bear a *tag* showing its price.

Tail *(n.)* റ്റെയ്ൽ–1. വാൽ
Most animals and birds have *tails*.
The monkey uses its *tail* when climbing trees.

2. തുഞ്ചം
I fastened a *tail* to my kite.

Tailor *(n.)* റ്റെയ്‌ലർ-തയ്യൽകാരൻ, തുണി തുന്നുന്നയാൾ
Is your cousin not a *tailor*?
My *tailor* is expert in stitching woollen suits.

Take *(v.)* റ്റേക്-1. കൊ് പോകുക
Father is going to *take* Hamid and Majid to the sea for fishing.
2. പിടിക്കുക
My father *takes* the 9 a.m. bus to go to his office.
3. തോന്നുക
It will *take* half an hour to reach there.
4. കൊു പോവുക
Please *take* this bag to your mother.
5. വാടകയ്ക്കെടുക്കുക
We have *taken* this room for a month.
6. വിജയം നേടുക
After heavy fighting, the army *took* control of the city.
7. എടുക്കുക
Do you *take* any interest in drawing?
Balwant Singh will *take* off his turban.

Tale *(n.)* റ്റെയ്‌ൽ-1. കഥ, ചരിതം
The mother told the child a fairy *tale* before making her sleep.
2. വിവരണം, വൃത്താന്തം
The reporters told different *tales* about the accident.

Talent *(n.)* റ്റാലെന്റ്-പ്രതിഭ, യോഗ്യത, പാടവം
She showed her *talent* for painting at a very early age.
(adj.) Raja is a very *talented* boy.

Talk റ്റോക്-സംസാരിക്കുക, പറയുക, സംഭാഷണം നടത്തുക
(v.) The baby cannot *talk* yet; as she grows up, she will learn to *talk*.
Vagish often *talks* to his parents about his college.
Please stop *talking* and listen to me.
(n.) We had a long *talk* about going to Mumbai.

Tall *(adj.)* റ്റോൾ-ഉയരമുള്ള, പൊക്കമുള്ള
Sony is a *tall* girl.
Rita is *taller* than Sony.
She is the *tallest* in our family.
There are some very *tall* buildings in Mumbai.
How *tall* are you?

Tame റ്റെയിം-ഇണക്കമുള്ള, വളർത്ത്
(adj.) A cat is a *tame* animal. It is not wild.
There are *tame* elephants in the zoo on whose backs children can have rides.
(v.) Coaches *tame* animals in circus.

Tamper *(v.)* റ്റാംപർ-മാറ്റം വരുത്തുക, കൃത്രിമം കാണിക്കുക
Why are you *tampering* with the report I prepared?

Tan റ്റാൻ-അധികനേരം വെയിലത്തിരുന്നാലുാകുന്ന നിറംമാറ്റം
(n.) Prolonged exposure to sun gave her skin a dusky *tan*.
(v.) Prolonged exposure to sun *tanned* her skin.

Tangible *(adj.)* റ്റാൻജിബ്‌ൾ-സ്പഷ്ടമായ
The tension between them was quite *tangible*.

Tangle ടാൻഗ്ൾ-ചുറ്റിപ്പിണഞ്ഞ, കുഴഞ്ഞ
(n.) Her hair is in a *tangle*.
(v.) The kitten played with knitting wool and *tangled* it up.

Tank *(n.)* ടാങ്ക്-കുളം, ടാങ്ക്
We have a *tank* for rainwater at our backdoor.
2. മിലിട്ടറി ട്രക്
Tanks are used in war. They are able to cross rough land.
3. എണ്ണകപ്പൽ
A ship specially made to carry oil is called a *tanker*.

Tantrum *(n.)* ടാൻട്രം-വികൃതി, കന്നത്തരം
Tantrums that this child throws are difficult to handle.

Tap *(n.)* ടാപ്-പൈപ്പിന്റെ ടാപ്
See that all the *water-taps* are turned off before you leave the house.
Who left the *tap* running?
2. ചെറുതായി തട്ടുക
She felt a *tap* on her shoulder.

Tape *(n.)* ടേപ്-അളവ് നാട

The dress-maker uses a *tape* when he measures a man for a new dress.

2. ശബ്ദം റിക്കാർഡ് ചെയ്യുക, റിക്കോർഡ് ചെയ്ത ശബ്ദം

(v.) Did you *tape* Lata's new song?

(n.) Have you heard Lata's latest *tape*?

Tar *(n.)* ടാർ-ടാർകോൾ, കീൽ

Tar was applied to the roof of the house to make it waterproof.

Tardy *(adj.)* ടാർഡി-താമസിപ്പിക്കുക, മന്ദഗതിയായ

I was *tardy* in replying to her letter.

Target *(n.)* ടാർഗിറ്റ്-ലക്ഷ്യം

Their *target* was to collect five thousand rupees for the poor.

Tariff *(n.)* ടാരിഫ്-താരിപ്പ്, വിലവിവരപ്പട്ടിക

The *tariff* at our hotel was hundred rupees for lunch and dinner.

Tarnish *(v.)* ടാർണിഷ്-മങ്ങലേല്ക്കുക, കരിപുരളുക

Your silver glasses will be *tarnished* unless you polish them often.

Your bad behaviour will *tarnish* your name.

Tarpaulin *(n.)* ടാർപ്പാളിൻ-താർപ്പടം

The luggage was packed on a lorry and covered with a large *tarpaulin*.

Tart *(adj.)* ടാർട്ട്-ചവർപ്പുള്ള, പുളിക്കുന്ന

Some fruits are very *tart*.

This mango is very *tart*. It can't be eaten.

Task *(n.)* ടാസ്ക്-1. ജോലി, കർത്തവ്യം

One of my *tasks* is to teach my niece.

(v.) 2. അധിക പ്രവർത്തന ഭാരം (ചുമക്കുക)

Never *task* your strength by carrying heavy loads.

Taste ടേസ്റ്റ്-1. രുചി, സ്വാദ്, ആസ്വദിക്കുക, രുചിക്കുക

(n.) Lemons have a sour *taste*.

(v.) The brave never *taste* defeat.

(adj.) Water is *tasteless*.

(adj.) Aunt made a *tasty* cake for us.

2. ഗുണദോഷങ്ങളറിയുക, അഭിരുചി

My sister has a good *taste* in makeup.

Tattered *(adj.)* റ്റാറ്റേർഡ്-കീറിപ്പറിഞ്ഞ

The beggar covered himself with a *tattered* blanket on the cold winter night.

Tattoo ടാറ്റൂ-പച്ചകുത്ത്

(n.) I got a *tattoo* painted on my ankle.

(v.) I got my ankle *tattooed*.

Taunt ടാ്-അധിക്ഷേപം

(n.) As a child, I often had to endure *taunts* on being fat.

(v.) As a child, I was *taunted* for being fat.

Taut *(adj.)* ടാട്ട്-മുറുകിയ

In youth, the skin is *taut*. But in the old age, it begins to sag.

Tax *(v. & n.)* ടാക്സ്-നികുതി (ചുമത്തുക)

(v.) The new law did not *tax* the people heavily.

(n.) Have you paid the income *tax*?

Taxes are levied on property, income, profits and many other items.

Taxi *(n.)* ടാക്സി-വാടക വി

Taxis go about the streets for people to hire them. They are driven by *taxi*-drivers.

Bring me a *taxi* for New Delhi railway-station.

Tea *(n.)* ടീ-ചായ

Mother makes *tea*. She pours boiling water on *tea*-leaves, and mixes milk and sugar. Thus *tea* becomes *ready*.

The Darjeeling *tea* is famous world over.

Teach *(v.)* ടീച്-പഠിപ്പിക്കുക, വിദ്യാഭ്യാസം നൽകുക

The teachers *teach* us very efficiently.

We must *teach* the baby to talk properly.

Team *(n.)* ടീം-കൂട്ടുചേർന്നു പ്രവർത്തിക്കുന്ന സംഘം

Ravi is a member of the cricket *team* in his school.

(adj.) We should do our work with a *team* spirit.

Tear ടിയർ-1. കീറുക, പൊട്ടിക്കുക, മുറിക്കുക

(v.) Rama has *torn* her frock.

(n.) Her mother will mend the *tear*.

2. കണ്ണുനീർ
When we cry, *tears* drop from our eyes.
She was in *tears* to see her new doll broken.

Tease *(v.)* ടീസ്-ശല്യപ്പെടുത്തുക, കളിയാക്കുക
Don't *tease* animals.
Don't take my words seriously, I was only *teasing* you.

Technical *(adj.)* ടെക്നിക്കൽ-സാങ്കേതിക
Have you got a *technical* training to handle this kind to machinery?
It is a *technical* error. Ordinary man can't judge it.

Tedious *(adj.)* ടീഡിയസ്-മുഷിപ്പിക്കുന്ന, ക്ഷീണിപ്പിക്കുന്ന
The speaker's speech became *tedious* after he had been talking for twenty minutes.

Teem *(v.)* ടീം-നിറഞ്ഞിരിക്കുക
The road was *teeming* with various big and small vehicles.

Teenage *(adj.)* ടീനേജ്-കൗമാരപ്രായം
(adj.) She is a mother of two *teenage* children.
(n.) *Teenagers* often find the advice of their parents rubbish.

Teetotaller *(n.)* ടീടോട്ടലർ-മദ്യപാനം ചെയ്യാത്തയാൾ
When offered a drink, he politely refused and said that he was a *teetotaller.*

Telecommunications *(n.)* ടെലികമ്യൂണിക്കേഷൻസ്-വാർത്താവിനിമയ
The government will invest more money in the industry of *telecommunications.*

Telegraph *(n.)* ടെലിഗ്രാഫ്-കമ്പി, കമ്പിയടിക്കുക
Telegraph was one of the initial steps towards telecommunications.

Telepathy *(n.)* ടെലിപ്പതി-അതീന്ദ്രീയ ബോധം
I was feeling that you would come today and you came. Was it a case of *telepathy*?

Telephone ടെലിഫോൺ-ടെലിഫോൺ
(v.) Mother *telephoned* father.
You can *telephone* from here.
(n.) Never talk senselessly on *telephone.*

Telescope *(n.)* ടെലിസ്കോപ്പ്-ദൂരദർശിനി
Telescopes are also used at sea.
The scientists use *telescopes* to study the stars.

Television *(n.)* ടെലിവിഷൻ-ടെലിവിഷൻ
Television has now become a necessity.

Tell *(v.)* ടെൽ-1. പറയുക, പ്രകടമാക്കുക
Tell me what you want.
Kindly *tell* the principal that I want to see him.
2. സങ്കല്പിക്കുക
It is difficult to *tell* the end of this struggle.
3. ആജ്ഞ നൽകുക
I have *told* you many times that you must obey the rules of the institution.

Temper *(n.)* ടെമ്പർ-മനോനില, പ്രകൃതി
My father is in a bad *temper* today because he is very angry with me.

Temperament *(n.)* ടെമ്പരമെന്റ്-പ്രകൃതി, സ്വഭാവം
Rupa has a sad *temperament,* she is often unhappy.

Temperate *(adj.)* ടെമ്പറേറ്റ്-സന്തുലിത, സംയമിത
Bangalore has a *temperate* climate.
You are a very *temperate* man, for you neither eat nor drink more than what is good for you.

Temperature *(n.)* ടെമ്പറേച്ചർ-കാലാവസ്ഥ
The girl had a high *temperature* yesterday, but now she is normal.
What was the maximum *temperature* yesterday?

Tempest *(n.)* ടെമ്പസ്റ്റ്-കൊടുങ്കാറ്റ്, കാറ്റുപിശറും
The *tempest* destroyed the ships on the seashore.
(adj.) Our ship rolled heavily in the *tempestuous* sea.

Template *(n.)* ടെംപ്ലേറ്റ്-മാതൃക
I have prepared the *template* for you.
Now prepare all the documents in the same style.

Temple *(n.)* ടെമ്പ്ൾ–ക്ഷേത്രം

I visit the *temple* every morning.

Tempo *(n.)* ടെമ്പോ–1. സംഗീത രചനയുടെ ഗതി

The *tempo* in this song keeps on changing from slow to fast.

2. സാധനം കൊ് പോകാനുള്ള ത്രിചക്ര വാഹനം

Load the material in a *tempo.*

Temporary *(adj.)* ടെമ്പററി–താല്കാലിക, അസ്ഥായിയായി

The church hall will be used as a *temporary* school until the new school is built.

This post is quite *temporary.*

I want to get a *temporary* job because I am waiting for my appointment in the university.

(adv.) I have managed a room *temporarily.*

Tempt *(v.)* ടെംപ്റ്റ്–പ്രലോഭിപ്പിക്കുക, വശീകരിക്കുക, പ്രേരിപ്പിക്കുക

Do not *tempt* the little boy to eat too many sweets.

Can I *tempt* you to have some more of this cake?

(n.) I can't resist the *temptation* of buying clothes.

(adj.) The cake is very *tempting,* but I cannot eat any more.

Tenant *(n.)* ടെനന്റ്–വാടകക്കാരൻ

Every month the landlord collects the rent from his *tenants.*

Our *tenant* is a very gentle fellow.

Tend *(v.)* ടെന്റ്–1. പരിചരിക്കുക, ശ്രദ്ധിക്കാൻ പ്രേരിപ്പിക്കുക

Nurses *tend* sick people. They serve mankind.

Ranjana's accident will *tend* to make her more careful while crossing roads.

2. ആയിത്തീരുക, ചായ്‌വുാകുക

Father *tends* to get tired in the evening.

Tender *(adj.)* ടെൻഡർ–1. കോമലമായ, സഹൃദയത്വമുള്ള

You have such *tender* skin that you get rashes after a short exposure to sun.

Mother is *tender* with her baby.

2. ഇളം പ്രായം

This solid food is not suitable for the child at *tender* age.

(n.) 3. ടെൻഡർ, ദർഘാസ്

The council has invited *tenders* for the building of a hall.

(n.) 4. സമർപ്പിക്കുക

Have you *tendered* your resignation from the post of editor?

Tenement *(n.)* ടെനമന്റ് – ചെറിയ പാർപ്പിടങ്ങൾ

Two large houses have been divided into *tenements.*

Tennis *(n.)* ടെന്നീസ്– ടെന്നീസ് കളി

Two players played on a *tennis* court.

Tennis is very popular in European countries.

Tense *(adj.)* ടെൻസ്–1. പിരിമുറുക്കുമുള്ള

The whole audience was *tense* with excitement about the result of the music competition.

(n.) 2. കാലം

There are three *tenses* in grammar-past *tense,* present *tense* and future *tense.*

Tent *(n.)* ടെന്റ്–കൂടാരം, ടെന്റ്

A *tent* is made of canvas. It is held in place by *tent*-pegs.

Tentative *(adj.)* ടെന്റേടീവ്–അനിശ്ചിതം

I have decided the name of my book, though it is still *tentative.*

Tenure *(n.)* ടെന്യൂർ–കാലാവധി

She wrote many fiery articles during her *tenure* as a journalist in the newspaper.

Term *(n.)* കാലാവധി, കാലയളവ്

I was absent from college for the whole of the summer *term.*

Terms *(n.)* ടേംസ്–ഉപാധികൾ, ധാരണ

Find out the *terms* on which we can get a room for the holidays.

If you are willing to sell your house, we can settle the *terms.*

Terminate *(v.)* ടെർമിനേറ്റ്–അവസാനിപ്പിക്കുക, തീരുക
The manager *terminated* the services of the clerk because he had disobeyed him.

Terminal *(adj.)* ടെർമിനൽ–ത്രൈമാസിക, അവസാന
Have you had your *terminal* examinations?

Terminus *(n.)* ടെർമിനസ്–റെയിൽ അല്ലെങ്കിൽ ബസിന്റെ അവസാന സ്റ്റേഷൻ
Wait for them at the bus *terminus.*
All passengers must leave the lorry at the *terminus.*

Terrace *(n.)* ടെറസ്–മട്ടുപ്പാവ്
Rachna and Minakshi had tea on the *terrace.*

Terrible *(adj.)* ടെറിബ്ൾ–ഭയാനകമായ, തീവ്രമായ, വളരെ മോശമായ
There was a *terrible* storm in which many ships were wrecked.
I can't bear this *terrible* cold.

Terrify *(v.)* ടെറിഫൈ–ഭയപ്പെടുത്തുക, വിരട്ടുക, ഭീതി തോന്നുക
Our dog *terrified* the ducks when it jumped into the pond.
I am *terrified* of walking home at night.

Territory *(n.)* ടെറിറ്ററി–പ്രദേശം, മേഖല
There is a great deal of forest *territory* in India.

Terror *(n.)* ടെറർ–ഭയം, ഭീതി
Animals have a great *terror* of fire.
She has a particular *terror* of floods.

Test ടെസ്റ്റ്–പരീക്ഷണം (നടത്തുക), പരിശോധന (നടത്തുക)
(n.) Her teacher gave her a *test* in spelling.
(v.) Before we buy an equipment we should always *test* it.

Testament *(n.)* ടെസ്റ്റമെന്റ്–സംഹിത
The Old and New *Testaments* are the two parts that make up the Bible.

Testify *(v.)* ടെസ്റ്റിഫൈ–സാക്ഷി, മൊഴി നൽകുക, വാദിക്കുക
When we speak to the judge, we *testify* before him.
(n.) What we say is our *testimony.*

Tether *(v.)* ടെദർ–കെട്ടുക
Tether your horse to this post while you go for shopping.

Text *(n.)* ടെക്സ്റ്റ്–പാഠം, മൂലവിഷയം
The *text* of a book does not include the picture.
We have a separate *textbook* for each subject in college.

Textile *(n.)* ടെക്സ്റ്റൈൽ–തുണി, വസ്ത്ര വ്യവസായം
My friend works in a *textile* mill.

Than *(conj.)* ദാൻ–നെകാൾ, –നെ അപേക്ഷിച്ച്
A motorcycle can go faster *than* a bicycle.

Thank താങ്ക്–നന്ദി (പറയുക), കൃതജ്ഞത (പ്രകടിപ്പിക്കുക)
(v.) You must *thank* your lucky stars that you were not in the house when the robbers attacked it.
(n.) Please convey my *thanks* to your mother for the nice sweets she sent for me.
(adj.) I am *thankful* to you for your timely help.

That *(pron.)* ദാറ്റ്–അത്, അതായത് എന്നുവച്ചാൽ, ആ
This is the dog *that* bit the thief. This is the cat *that* killed a rat.
I told Ramesh I hated him, and *that* he should leave the room immediately.
He is a cutler, *that* is to say, a man who sells knives and sharp tools.
This is the girl *that* lives in Lajpat Nagar.

Thatch *(v.)* താച്–ഓല മേയുക
(adj.) The cottage had been newly *thatched.*
The farmer lived in a *thatched* hut.

Thaw താ–ദ്രവണം, ഉരുകുക
(n.) After the *thaw,* the streams flow fast.
(v.) The ice on the pond will *thaw* when the weather gets warmer.

The *(adj.)* ദ, ദി–അത്, അതേ (അത്ര)
The moon is very cool. *The* sun is very hot.
The man you met steals money.
The shopkeeper you know is a dishonest man.
I saw *the* fellow you had wanted.

The sooner you go from this sad atmosphere, *the* better you will feel.
I saw a cow on *the* road. *The* cow was grazing *the* grass.

Theatre *(n.)* തിയേറ്റർ-നാടകവേദി, നാട്യശാല
Had you gone to the *theatre* last night?
2. ആശുപത്രിയിൽ ശസ്ത്രക്രിയ നടത്തുന്ന മുറി
The patient was moved to the operation *theatre.*

Theft *(n.)* തെഫ്റ്റ്-കളവ്
The police arrested a man for the *theft* of my bicycle.
Theft is a crime.

Theme *(n.)* തീം-കഥാസാരം, വിഷയം
Please tell me the *theme* before narrating the whole story.

Then *(adv.)* ദെൻ-ആ സമയത്ത്, അന്ന്
Come, let us go to him at about 9 P.M., he will be at home by *then.*
We know it is wrong, *then* what is the alternative for it?

Thence *(adv.)* ദെൻസ്-അവിടെ നിന്ന്, അതിന് ശേഷം
We went to Delhi and *thence* to Amritsar.

Theory *(n.)* തിയറി-സിദ്ധാന്തം, വിശ്വാസം
If anybody wants to study art properly, he should also learn the *theory* of it.
Old stories had been based on the false *theory* that the sun is revolving and the earth is stationary.

Therapy *(n.)* തെറാപി-ഔഷധമില്ലാത്ത ചികിത്സ
(n.) Aroma *therapy* is said to relieve tension and stress.
(adj.) Visiting that quiet and calm place was a *therapeutic* experience in itself.

There *(adv.)* ദെയർ-1. അവിടെ (ആ സ്ഥലത്ത് അല്ലെങ്കിൽ സ്ഥിതിയിൽ)
Please do not go *there,* be seated.
2. ഉ്, ഉായിരിക്കുക
There are fifteen students in the class.
There is no money in my purse.

Therefore *(adv.)* ദെയർഫോർ-അതുകൊ്, അക്കാരണത്താൽ, അതിനാൽ
We are going to the cinema in the evening, *therefore* we will be home late.

Thermometer *(n.)* തെർമോമീറ്റർ-താപമാപിനി, തെർമോമീറ്റർ
A *thermometer* measures temperature.
Do you know how to read a *thermometer*?

Thesaurus *(n.)* തിസാറസ്-പര്യായകോശം
Consult a *thesaurus* and tell me a better word for 'big'.

Thesis *(n.)* തീസിസ്-ഗവേഷണ പ്രബന്ധം
I did my *thesis* on modern Indian literature.

They *(pron.)* ദെ-അവർ, അവ
There are your notebooks. *They* are on the table.

Thick *(adj.)* തിക്-1. കട്ടിയുള്ള, കനത്ത, കൊഴുത്ത
It is hard to walk through the *thick* forest.
This board is *thicker* than that.
(n.) 2. കഠിന സമയം
I shall be with you through *thick* and thin.
3. നടുവിൽ
Don't disturb me, I am in the *thick* of a job.
What is the *thickness* of it?

Thicket *(n.)* തികിറ്റ്-കുറ്റിക്കാട്
The robbers were hiding in the *thicket.*

Thief *(n.)* തീഫ്-1. മോഷ്ടാവ്, കള്ളൻ
People who steal things are called *thieves.* They are put into prison.
Did anybody see the *thief* leaving the house?
(v.) 2. മോഷ്ടിക്കുക
Someone has been *thieving* the sweets I think.

Thigh *(n.)* തൈ-തുട
Her *thighs* were swollen, the doctor prescribed an ointment.

Thin *(adj.)* തിൻ-നേർത്ത, മെലിഞ്ഞ, ക്ഷീണിച്ച
If you do not eat your dinner well, you will grow *thin.*

You are a *thin* girl but she is a fat.

This needle is too *thin.* Please get me a thicker one.

Thing *(n.)* തിങ്-വസ്തു, സാധനം

Please give me *something* to eat.

A *thing* of beauty is a joy for ever.

Think *(v.)* തിങ്ക്-1. ആലോചിക്കുക

Look before you leap. *Think* before you speak.

2. മനസ്സിലാക്കുക

Father *thinks* that Rajan is a nice man.

We should never *think* of taking what belongs to others.

I *think* you should see the doctor.

(n.) All philosophers are *thinkers.*

Thirst *(n.)* തേഴ്സ്റ്റ്-ദാഹം, മോഹം, കൊതി

The traveller quenched his *thirst* at the well.

My son has a great *thirst* for knowledge.

This *(pron. & adj.)* ദിസ്-ഈ, ഇത്

What is *this*?

Would you rather have *this* pen or that one?

Please look at *these* mangoes.

Did you find *this* purse on the road?

I intend to go to Kolkata *this* month.

Thither *(adv.)* തിദർ-ഇവിടെയും അവിടെയും

He was running hither and *thither.*

Thorn *(n.)* തോൺ-മുള്ള്

Baby's balloon settled on a rose bush and was punctured by its *thorns.*

Life is full of *thorns.*

Thorough *(adj.)* തറോ-സമഗ്ര, സമ്പൂർണ്ണ

You need a *thorough* check-up.

(adv.) Check the luggage *thoroughly.*

Thoroughfare *(n.)* തറോഫെയർ-പൊതുവഴി

This is not a *thoroughfare.*

We can pass this way, it is a *thoroughfare.*

Though *(conj.)* ദോ-എങ്കിലും, ഒരുപക്ഷേ

The medicine will do you good, *though* you may not like the taste of it.

She walks as *though* her feet hurt her.

Thousand *(adj.)* തൗസൻഡ്-ആയിരം

Ten hundreds make a *thousand.*

A family man has to face a *thousand* and one worries in life.

Thrash *(v.)* ത്രാഷ്-അടിക്കുക, തല്ലുക

The mother will *thrash* the child if she catches him stealing the coins.

Thread ത്രെഡ്-നൂല് (കോർക്കുക)

(v.) I will *thread* the needle.

(n.) Have you a reel of black *thread*?

Threat ത്രെറ്റ്-ഭീഷണി (പെടുത്തുക)

(v.) The teacher *threatened* to punish the whole class if there was any more noise.

(n.) The gardener's *threat* to thrash the boys who steal the mangoes has frightened them away.

Three *(adj.)* ത്രീ-മൂന്ന്

Three little pigs had a race. The black pig came *third.*

Three is an odd figure.

Thresh *(v.)* ത്രെഷ്-മെതിക്കുക

After harvesting, the crops were *threshed* to get the grains.

Threshold *(n.)* ത്രെഷോൾഡ്-നടപ്പുര

As soon as we crossed the *threshold* of uncle's house, his dog barked loudly.

Thrift *(n.)* ത്രിഫ്റ്റ്-മിതവ്യയം, ചെലവ് കുറയ്ക്കൽ

By continuous *thrift,* Vagish saved enough money to buy a bike.

(adj.) Mother taught us all to be *thrifty.*

Thrill ത്രിൽ-രോമാഞ്ചം, ഹരം

(n.) I can't forget the *thrill* of winning my first prize.

(adj.) It was a *thrilling* moment when the mother found her lost baby.

(v.) The news that she had won a prize *thrilled* her parents.

Thrive *(v.)* ത്രൈവ്-വളരുക, വികസിക്കുക

We *thrive* on fresh air and wholesome food.

Throat *(n.)* ത്രോട്ട്-തൊ, കണ്ഠം

The *throat* is the front part of the neck.

Wear a scarf lest you should get a sore *throat.*

Throb *(v.)* ത്രോബ്–തുടിക്കുക

If you run very fast, you heart will *throb* loudly.

Throne *(n.)* ത്രോൺ–രാജസിംഹാസനം

The English are loyal to the *throne.*

(v.) The young queen was *dethroned* by rioters.

Throng *(v.)* ത്രോങ്–തടിച്ച് കൂടുക, കൂട്ടം ചേരുക

People *thronged* the roads.

Throttle *(v.)* ത്രോട്ട്ൽ – കഴുത്ത് ഞെരിക്കുക, കഴുത്ത് ഞെക്കുക

The tight collar of my overcoat is *throttling* me.

Through *(prep.)* ത്രൂ–അതിലൂടെ, കാരണം

The sun shines *through* the day and moon shines *through* the night.

The accident happened *through* my own carelessness.

Throw *(v.)* ത്രോ–എറിയുക, വീഴ്ത്തുക

The horse *threw* its rider off.

Throw me the ball, I will kick it.

This information may *throw* light upon the mystery of the rich man's death.

Thrust *(v.)* ത്രസ്റ്റ്–കടത്തുക, ഇടുക

Hari *thrust* his hand into his pocket to find out how many coins were there.

Thumb *(n.)* തമ്പ്–തള്ളവിരൽ

We have two *thumbs.* The *thumb* is the thickest of our fingers.

Illiterate persons put their *thumb* impressions as signature.

Thump *(v.)* തമ്പ്–ശക്തിയായി മിടിക്കുക

My heart was *thumping* with fear.

Thunder *(n.)* തർ–1. ഇടിമുഴക്കം

The lightning flashed and the *thunder* roared.

(v.) 2. പാഞ്ഞുവരിക

This engine came *thundering* along the rails.

3. ക്രോധം പൂ് അലറുക, അട്ടഹസിക്കുക

The manager *thundered* - "Get out of here at once."

Thursday *(n.)* തേഴ്സ്ഡേ–വ്യാഴാഴ്ച

Thursday comes after Wednesday.

Thus *(adv.)* ദസ്–അങ്ങനെ, അതുകൊ്

We knew that he was dishonest, *thus* we did not believe him.

Thwart *(v.)* ത്വാർട്ട്–കാര്യം നടക്കാതിരിക്കുക

The work pressure at office *thwarted* my vacation plans.

Tick *(v.)* ടിക്–ശരി അടയാളം ഇടുക

The manager *ticked* the names of the employees who had been late in the morning.

Ticket *(v.)* ടിക്കറ്റ്–ടിക്കറ്റ്

Always buy a *ticket* when you travel by bus or train.

Tickle *(n.)* ടിക്ക്ൾ–ഇക്കിളിയിടുക

Baby laughs when mother *tickles* his toes.

Tide *(n.)* ടൈഡ്–വേലിയേറ്റം

At low *tide,* the sea falls and goes far out.

Time and *tide* wait for none.

Tidy ടൈഡി–വെടിപ്പായ, സുസജ്ജമായ

(adj.) Asha always keeps her room *tidy.*

(v.) She is *tidying* her room.

Tie *(v.)* ടൈ–1. കെട്ടുക

Mother, please *tie* my shoelaces.

Do you know how to *tie* a knot?

(n.) 2. കഴുത്തിൽ കെട്ടുന്ന ടൈ

Father wears a *tie* round his neck.

Tiger *(n.)* ടൈഗർ–കടുവ, വ്യാഘ്രം

Tiger is a wild animal.

Tight *(adj.)* ടൈറ്റ്–ഇറുക്കം, മുറുക്കം, വായു, വെള്ളം കടക്കാത്ത

My new shoes are too *tight.*

Food should be kept in *air-tight* tins.

(v.) Tighten your belt and wear your coat.

Tile ടൈൽ–ഓട്, ടൈൽ (ഇടുക)

(n.) The bathroom *tiles* are of golden colour.

(v.) The masons were *tiling* the kitchen.

Till *(prep.)* ടിൽ–1. വരെ

The farmer works from morning *till* evening.

Do not put off *till* tomorrow what you can do today.

(*v.*) 2. നിലം ഉഴുതുക

The cultivators *till* the soil.

(*n.*) 3. പണം സൂക്ഷിക്കുന്ന അറ

While the cashier was out, someone robbed the *till*.

Timber (*n.*) ടിമ്പർ-തടി

A huge forest of *timber* has been destroyed by fire.

Time (*n.*) ടൈം-1. സമയം

What is the *time* now?

We want to reach the office in *time*.

2. കാലം

Time seemed to stand still.

3. തവണ, പ്രാവശ്യം, കുറി

It is useless to repeat, I heard you the first *time* itself.

Cowards die many *times* before their death.

Timid (*adj.*) ടിമിഡ്-ഭീരു, പേടിതൊൻ, സംശയാലു

The child is still a little *timid* when he meets the puppy.

Squirrels are *timid* creatures.

Tin (*n.*) ടിൻ-ടബ്ബ, ടിൻ, പാട്ട

We need two *tins* of vegetable oils.

Tinge (*v.* & *n.*) ടിൻജ്-നിറം ചാർത്തുക, ഛവി

(*v.*) The rays of the setting sun *tinge* the clouds pink.

(*n.*) There is no *tinge* of regret in his voice.

Tingle (*v.*) ടിങ്ങ്ൾ-വിറക്കുക, പുളകിപ്പിക്കുക

Cold air makes my ears *tingle*.

A cold bath will make you *tingle* all over.

Tinkle (*v.*) ടിങ്ക്ൾ-കിലുങ്ങുക

The bells on the pony's harness *tinkle* as it trots along.

Tint ടിന്റ്-നേർത്ത ചായം, നിറം, ഛവി

(*v.*) You can *tint* the sky in your picture with some light blue paint.

(*n.*) There were *tints* of yellow and gold in the morning sky.

Tiny (*adj.*) ടൈനി-വളരെ ചെറിയ, പിഞ്ച്

A *tiny* lamp was burning near the shrine.

The *tiny* boy won the race.

The midge is a *tiny* insect.

A fly is very small. It is *tiny*.

Tip (*v.*) ടിപ്-1. തട്ടിയിടുക

I *tipped* my glass over by mistake.

2. അറ്റം, തുമ്പ്

She touched the cat with the *tip* of her cane.

Tiptoe (*n.*) ടിപ്ടോ-മെല്ലെ, വിരലിലൂന്നി നടക്കുക

The thief entered the room on *tiptoes* and stole the money.

Tire (*v.*)-ക്ഷീണിക്കുക, ക്ഷീണിപ്പിക്കുക

The long journey by bus has *tired* me.

Climbing up that steep hill will *tire* you.

Tissue (*n.*) ടിഷ്യൂ-1. ദേഹകരണം

The body is held together by muscular *tissues*.

2. ഒരുപിടി, ഒട്ടേറെ

You answered with a *tissue* of lies.

Titbits (*n.*) ടിറ്റ്ബിറ്റ്സ്-സരസഭാഷണം

We always find him ready with jokes and funny *titbits*.

Title (*n.*) ടൈറ്റിൽ-1. പുസ്തകത്തിന്റെ പേര്

What is the *title* of your novel?

2. പദവി, പട്ടം

Some Indians were honoured with the *title* 'Sir' for their services to the British during the latter's rule in India.

Titter (*v.*) ടിറ്റർ-അമർത്തി ചിരിക്കുക, വെറുതെ ചിരിക്കുക

Why are you *tittering* without any reason?

To (*prep.*) ടു-1. ലേക്ക്, വരെ

The old lady is going *to* the market.

It is five minutes *to* four.

2. വേ1, എന്ന്

The old man is going *to* buy meat.

Do you want *to* finish your job today?

Toast ടോസ്റ്റ്-1. മൊരിച്ച റൊട്ടി

(*v.*) Mother *toasts* bread for the family's breakfast.

(*n.*) Would you like *toast* and coffee for breakfast?

(v.) 2. കുശലപാനം ചെയ്യുക

Let us *toast* the newly weds.

Tobacco *(n.)* ടബാക്കോ–പുകയില

Chewing or smoking *tobacco* is injurious to health.

Today ടുഡേ–ഇന്ന്, ഇപ്പോഴത്തെ

(n.) *Today* is this day. Yesterday was the day before *today.*

Today is a holiday.

(adv.) He is leaving *today.*

Toddle *(v.)* ടോഡ്ൽ–പിച്ചവയ്ക്കുക

The baby can't walk properly yet, but he can *toddle.*

Toe *(n.)* ടോ–കാൽവിരൽ

We have five *toes* on each foot.

Toffee ടോഫി–മുട്ടായി, ടോഫി

The children like *toffee* very much.

Together *(adv.)* ടുഗദർ–1. ഒന്നിച്ച്, ഒപ്പം

My brother and I had gone for a walk *together.*

2. എല്ലാ (സാധനങ്ങളും) ആയി

We gathered *together* our belongings and left.

Toil *(v.)* ടോയ്ൽ–കഠിന പരിശ്രമം ചെയ്യുക

The farm-workers *toil* until late in the evening.

Toilet *(n.)* ടോയ്‌ലിറ്റ്–കുളിപ്പുര, ഉടുപ്പണിയാനും മുടി ചീകാനുമുള്ള സ്ഥലം, ശൗചാലയം

Every day Shanta spends minimum twenty minutes in her *toilet.*

Token *(n.)* ടോക്കൺ–ചിഹ്നം, അടയാളം, സങ്കേതം

The enemy waved a white flag as a *token* of surrender.

Tolerate *(v.)* ടോലറെയ്റ്റ്–സഹിക്കുക, ധാരണ ഉാക്കുക, മറ്റുള്ളവരുടെ ചീത്ത ശീലങ്ങൾ സഹിക്കുക

We have to *tolerate* in others what we permit in ourselves!

We *tolerated* each other for thirty years.

Toll *(v.)* ടോൾ–1. മണിഅടിക്കുക

The bell ringers will *toll* the bell during the funeral service.

(n.) 2. നിരത്ത്കരം, ചുങ്കം

In some countries, people pay a *toll* to use the motorways.

Tomato *(n.)* ടൊമാറ്റോ–ടൊമാറ്റോ

Can you tell what colour a *tomato* is?

Tomato is a vegetable.

Tomb *(n.)* ടോംബ്–ശവകല്ലറ, സമാധി, കബറ്

Muslims bury a dead body in the ground and build a *tomb* over it.

Tomorrow *(n.)* ടുമാറോ–നാളെ

Tomorrow is the day after today.If this is Monday, *tomorrow* will be Tuesday.

Do not put off till *tomorrow* what you can do today.

Tone *(n.)* ടോൺ–സ്വരം, ശബ്ദം, ധ്വനി

The piano has an excellent *tone.*

I knew by the angry *tone* of Vatsya's voice that he was annoyed.

Tongue *(n.)* ടങ്–1. നാക്ക്, മൊഴി

We taste with our *tongue.* We also speak with it.

Nature has given us two ears and one *tongue,* remember this.

To speak kindly does not hurt the *tongue.*

Be slow of *tongue* and quick of eye.

2. ഭാഷ

What is your mother-*tongue*?

Tonic *(n.)* ടോണിക്–ആരോഗ്യ സംവർദ്ധകമായ പദാർത്ഥം

Mother's milk is a *tonic* for infants.

Tonight *(n.)* ടുനൈറ്റ്–ഇന്ന് രാത്രി

Tonight is the night of today.

Tonsil *(n.)* ടോൺസിൽ–കുറിനാക്ക്, കണ്ഠപിണ്ഡം

If we open our mouth wide in front of a mirror, we shall be able to see our *tonsils.*

Too *(adv.)* ടൂ–അതും, വളരെയധികം, കൂടുതൽ, ആവശ്യത്തിലേറെ

You can see a star. Can you see a fairy *too*?

The patient is *too* weak to walk.

Never be *too* clever.

Your shoes are *too* big for you.

Tool *(n.)* ടൂൾ–ഉപകരണം, ആയുധം
Hammer is a *tool.* Plumbers and carpenters have *tools.*

Tooth *(n.)* ടൂത്ത്–പല്ല്, ദന്തം
Go to the dentist if you have a *tooth-ache.*
We chew with our *teeth.*
My comb has lost three of its *teeth.*

Top *(n.)* ടോപ്–1. പമ്പരം
Can you spin the *top* round and round?
(adj.) 2. പരമോന്നതം
Please give *top* priority to this work.
(n.) The staff was corrupt from *top* to bottom.

Topic *(n.)* ടോപിക്–വിഷയം, ചർച്ചാ വിഷയം
Fashion, films and politics are the *topics* on which people generally talk.
What are the *topics* of today's discussion?

Topple *(v.)* ടോപ്ൾ–മറിഞ്ഞു വീഴുക, മറിച്ചിടുക
The big pile of books *toppled* over.
The pile of bricks came *toppling* down.

Torch *(n.)* ടോർച്ച്–ഞെക്ക്വിളക്ക്, ടോർച്ച്
My friend gave me a *torch* to see my way in the night.

Torment ടോർമെന്റ്–കഷ്ടപ്പെടുത്തുക, വിഷമം നൽകുക
(v.) Sudha was *tormented* by a toothache.
(n.) The prisoner could not bear the *torment* in the cell and died.

Tornado *(n.)* ടൊർണാഡോ–ചുഴലിക്കാറ്റ്
The *tornado* in Orissa uprooted a number of trees.

Torpedo *(v.)* ടോർപിഡോ–നാശകയന്ത്രം, പടകപ്പൽ
The ship sank within a few minutes of being *torpedoed.*

Torrent *(n.)* ടോറന്റ്–കുത്തൊഴുക്കുള്ള നദി, പേമാരി
After the heavy rain, the stream became a *torrent.*
It rained in *torrents.*

Tortoise *(n.)* ടോർറ്റസ്–ആമ, കൂർമ്മം
Some *tortoises* live on land and the others in sea.

Torture *(v. & n.)* ടോർചർ–പീഡനം ഏല്പിക്കുക, യാതന ഏല്പിക്കുക
The police *tortured* the thief to make him tell about the things stolen by him.
(n.) Political prisoners were put to *torture.*

Toss ടോസ്–നാണയം അല്ലെങ്കിൽ പന്ത് മേലേക്ക് എറിയുക, ഉയരത്തേക്ക് എറിയുന്ന പ്രക്രിയ
(v.) *Toss* the ball over the wall.
The ball was *tossed* from one player to another.
(n.) In cricket much depends on which team wins the *toss.*

Total *(adj.)* ടോട്ടൽ–പൂർണ്ണം, ആകെ, മൊത്തം, എല്ലാം
The ship struck the rock and became a *total* wreck.
(v.) കൂട്ടുക
Now you *total* up the bills and I shall check them.

Totter *(v.)* ടോറ്റർ–തപ്പിതടയുക, വേച്ച് പോവുക
Young children *totter* about when they first try to walk.
The old man *tottered* along and nearly fell once or twice.

Touch ടച്ച്–1. സ്പർശിക്കുക, തൊടുക
(n.) The nurse had a gentle *touch.*
(v.) I can barely *touch* the ceiling.
2. അലിവ് തോന്നുക, മനസ്സിൽ തട്ടിക്കുക
We were *touched* by her kindness.
3. സമ്പർക്കത്തിൽ വരിക
Are you in *touch* with Mr. Sanjay Pandit?

Tough *(adj.)* ടഫ്–1. കടുത്ത, ദൃഢ
Meat that is *tough,* is difficult to cut and cat.
2. കഠിന
To succeed both in education and sports is really a *tough* job.

Tour *(n.)* ടൂർ–യാത്ര, പര്യടനം
We made a *tour* of the city.
Many *tourists* visit the Taj Mahal every day.
(v.) We are *touring* the Himalayas this summer.

Tournament *(n.)* ടൂർണമെന്റ്-കളിയുടെ മത്സരം

What was the result of India-Australia cricket *tournament*?

Tout *(v.)* ടൗട്ട്-ശക്തമായി പ്രചരിപ്പിക്കുക

The product was *touted* as the best among its rivals.

Tow *(v.)* ടോ-വലിക്കുക, കെട്ടിവലിക്കുക

The lorry *towed* the battered car to the garage.

The damaged ship was *towed* back to the port.

Towards *(prep.)* ടുവാർഡ്സ്-നേർക്ക്, വേി, അതിലേക്ക്

Vagish walked *towards* the car.

The millionaire behaves generously *towards* all poor people.

Towel *(n.)* ടവ്വൽ-തോർത്ത്, ടവ്വൽ

We wipe our wet hands on the *towel*.

Have you a bath-*towel* in your bathroom?

Tower *(v. & n.)* ടവർ-ഗോപുരം, മണിമേട

The tall fir trees *tower* over the small house.

We can hear the bells ringing in the clock-*tower*.

Town *(n.)* ടൗൺ-പട്ടണം, ചെറിയ നഗരം

A *town* is a small city.

There are streets and shops in a *town*.

She would rather live in a village than in a *town*.

Toxic *(adj.)* ടോക്സിക്-വിഷലിപ്തം

Vehicles release *toxic* gases in the air.

Toy *(n.)* ടോയ്-1. കളിപ്പാട്ടം

Children play with their *toys*.

(v.) 2. കളിക്കുക, പെരുമാറുക

All the time she talked, she was *toying* with her purse.

Trace *(v.)* ട്രേസ് - 1. കത്തുക, പുറത്തെടുക്കുക

The police are trying to *trace* the man who stole the van.

2. പകർത്തുക

You can *trace* a map from your atlas.

(n.) 3. അല്പമാത്ര, ചെറിയ അളവിൽ

The soup has a *trace* of onion in it.

Track *(v.)* ട്രാക്-1. അന്വേഷിക്കുക, പിന്തുടരുക

Hunters *track* elephants by their footprints.

2. പരിക്കൻ പാത, ഊട് വഴി

There was only a rough *track* across the ground.

Tractor *(v.)* ട്രാക്ടർ-യന്ത്രകലപ്പ, ട്രാക്ടർ

Tractors are used by farmers for pulling the plough.

Trade *(n.)* ട്രേഡ്-1. വ്യാപാരം, കൈമാറ്റം

Speculation is the romance of *trade*.

(v.) 2. വ്യാപാരം ചെയ്യുക

We *trade* in second-hand cars.

Tradition *(n.)* ട്രഡിഷൻ-പാരമ്പര്യം

Everywhere the basis of principles is *tradition*.

Traffic *(n.)* ട്രാഫിക്-ഗതാഗതം, പോക്കുവരവ്

A big city like Delhi faces many *traffic* problems.

Tragedy *(n.)* ട്രാജഡി-ദുരന്തം, ദാരുണ സംഭവം

Life is a *tragedy* - we are its spectators.

You cannot forget your personal *tragedy*.

Trail *(n.)* ട്രെയ്ൽ-പിന്നാലെ നീളുക

The aeroplane left a long *trail* of white smoke behind it.

Train *(n.)* ട്രെയ്ൻ-1. തീവി, റെയിൽ വ ി

Some *trains* carry people. They are called passenger-*trains*. Some *trains* carry goods.They are called goods-*trains*.

(v.) 2. പരിശീലിപ്പിക്കുക

The mother *trained* Nina well in household work.

(adj.) Is she a *trained* teacher?

(n.) I am under *training*.

Traitor *(n.)* ട്രെയ്റ്റർ-രാജ്യദ്രോഹി, വിശ്വാസ വഞ്ചകൻ

The rogue was condemned to death as a *traitor*.

Tram *(n.)* ട്രാം-വൈദ്യുതി കൊ് പാളത്തിലൂടെ ഓടുന്ന വി

Trams in Delhi have been replaced by buses.

Tramp *(n.)* ട്രാംപ്-1. പദയാത്ര, ഊര് തെ ി

We went for a *tramp* across the woods.

No one will trust a *tramp* like you.

(v.) 2. ചവിട്ടി മെതിക്കുക

Don't *tramp* about the garden.

Trample *(v.)* ട്രാംപ്ൾ-ചവിട്ടി അരയ്ക്കുക, പുഛിക്ക

The kids *trampled* the grass.

Trance *(n.)* ട്രാൻസ്-സമാധി, മയക്കം

She was walking on the road in a state of *trance.*

Tranquil *(adj.)* ട്രാൻക്വിൽ-ശാന്തം

My mind was *tranquil* and at peace.

Transact *(v.)* ട്രാൻസാക്റ്റ്-പൂർത്തിയാക്കുക

When my father *transacted* all his business, he left Bhagalpur.

(n.) He made many *transactions.*

Transfer *(v.)* ട്രാൻസ്ഫർ-സ്ഥലം മാറ്റുക, വേറെ സ്ഥലത്ത് കൊ് പോകുക

The luggage was *transferred* from the station to the ship.

She *transferred* the almirah from one room to another.

Transform *(v.)* ട്രാൻസ്ഫോം-രൂപാന്തരം വരുത്തുക

The witch *transformed* the goat into a princess.

Transfusion *(n.)* ട്രാൻസ്ഫ്യൂഷൻ-രോഗം കാരണം ദുഷിച്ച രക്തം മാറ്റി പുതിയ രക്തം കടത്തുക

Many patients have been saved because of blood *transfusion.*

Transgress *(v.)* ട്രാൻസ്ഗ്രെസ്-ലംഘിക്കുക, അതിക്രമിച്ച് കടക്കുക

We must remember the promise not to *transgress* again.

Translate *(v.)* ട്രാൻസ്ലേറ്റ്-പരിഭാഷപ്പെടുത്തുക, വിവർത്തനം ചെയ്യുക

The New Testament was *translated* from Greek into English.

What has been *translated* is a *translation*.

(n.) The art of *translation* requires a good knowledge of many l anguages.

Transmit *(v.)* ട്രാൻസ്മിറ്റ്-അയക്കുക, പ്രസാരണം ചെയ്യുക

That message was *transmitted* by telephone.

Usually messages are *transmitted* by radio.

Transparent *(adj.)* ട്രാൻസ്പെരന്റ് - സുതാര്യം

Clear water is *transparent.*

Glass is *transparent.*

Transport ട്രാൻസ്പോർട്ട്-ഒരു സ്ഥലത്ത് നിന്ന് മറ്റൊരിടത്തേക്ക് കൊു പോകുക, ചരക്ക് നീക്കം

(v.) Many ships are required to *transport* food across the oceans.

(n.) The ships are used for *transport.*

Trap *(n.)* ട്രാപ്-1. എലിപത്തായം

Have you set a *trap* to catch the mice?

2. കെണി

The army fell into a *trap,* as they found themselves between the sea and the enemy.

Trauma *(n.)* ട്രാമാ-ക്ഷതം, ദുഃഖകഥ

Manto's story Toba Tek Singh deals with the *trauma* of partition.

Travel ട്രാവൽ-യാത്ര (ചെയ്യുക) സഞ്ചരിക്കുക

(v.) We have been *travelling* for over a month now.

(n.) Air *travel* is quick but expensive.

Traverse *(n.)* ട്രാവേഴ്സ്-കടക്കുക, തരണം ചെയ്യുക

It took us ten days to *traverse* the desert.

Tray *(n.)* ട്രേ-ട്രേ, തട്ടം

The mother brought tea in a *tray.*

Treachrous *(adj.)* ട്രെചറസ്-വിശ്വാസ വഞ്ചകൻ, ചതിയൻ

The *treacherous* scientist sold some of his country's secrets to the enemy.

(n.) We didn't think you could be guilty of such *treachery.*

Tread *(v.)* ട്രെഡ്-കാലുകുത്തുക, ചവിട്ടി മെതിക്കുക

Don't *tread* on the carpet with your muddy boots.

Don't *tread* on the cat's tail.

The mob passing through these fields have *trodden* down the plants.

Treadle *(n.)* ട്രെഡ്ൽ-ചവിട്ട് മെഷീൻ

Have you bought a *treadle* sewing machine from the agency?

Treason *(n.)* ട്രീസൺ-രാജ്യദ്രോഹം

Treason is one of the most serious crimes.

Treasure *(v.)* ട്രഷർ-നിധിപോലെ സൂക്ഷിക്കുക, നിധി

I *treasure* my gold watch.

(n.) Many *treasures* of gold and silver have been found in old castles.

Treat ട്രീറ്റ്-1. ചികിത്സ നടത്തുക

(v.) Doctors *treat* their patients.

(n.) 2. ഇമ്പം പകരുന്ന അനുഭവം

It was a *treat* to hear such good singing.

(v.) 3. കൈകാര്യം

Old age needs to be *treated* gently in words as well as in deeds.

Tree *(n.)* ട്രീ-മരം, വൃക്ഷം

There are many *trees* in the wood.

A saw can fell a *tree* that took a hundred years to grow.

Trek ട്രെക്-മലകയറ്റം

(n.) They finally reached the top after a three-day *trek* across the mountains.

(v.) Let's go *trekking* this summer.

Tremble *(v.)* ട്രെമ്പ്ൾ-വിറയ്ക്കുക

We *tremble* when we are excited or full of fear.

Tremendous *(adj.)* ട്രെമൻഡസ്-ഭയങ്കര, ഭയാനക

There was a *tremendous* explosion, and the house crumbled to the ground.

Tremor *(n.)* ട്രെമർ-കുലുക്കം, ഭൂകമ്പം

Cold weather made a *tremor* run through her limbs.

Trench *(n.)* ട്രെഞ്ച്-കിടങ്ങ്, ഓട

Trenches have been dug across the town to drain off the water.

Trend *(n.)* ട്രെൻഡ്-പുതിയ ഫാഷൻ

(n.) It is usually the movie stars who set the *trends* in fashion.

(adj.) She loves to wear *trendy* clothes.

Trespass *(v.)* ട്രെസ്പാസ്-അതിക്രമിച്ച് കടക്കുക, അനുവാദമില്ലാതെ പ്രവേശിക്കുക

They were caught *trespassing* on government property.

Trial *(n.)* ട്രയൽ-പരീക്ഷണം, പരിശോധന

The latest car model is having its *trial* this week.

Truth fears no *trial*.

Triangle *(n.)* ട്രയാങ്ക്ൾ-ത്രികോണം

Can you draw a *triangle*?

Tribe *(n.)* ട്രൈബ്-ഗോത്രവർഗ്ഗം

There are many *tribes* in India.

Tribunal *(n.)* ട്രൈബൂണൽ-പ്രത്യേക കോടതി, നീതി പീഠം

The Supreme Court is the highest *tribunal* in India.

Tributary *(n.)* ട്രിബ്യൂറ്ററി-പോഷക നദി, കൈവഴി

Yamuna is a *tributary* of Ganga.

Tribute *(n.)* ട്രിബ്യൂട്ട്-പ്രശംസ, ആദരാജ്ഞലി

The newly elected member of Parliament paid *tribute* to the voters who had voted for him in theelections.

Trick ട്രിക്-യുക്തി, കബളിപ്പിക്കുക

(n.) Every profession has its *tricks*.

(v.) We are bitter against those who *trick* us.

Trickle *(v.)* ട്രിക്ക്ൾ-തുള്ളിതുള്ളിയായി വീഴുക

A tear *trickled* down her cheeks.

Tricycle *(n.)* ട്രൈസിക്കിൾ-മൂന്ന് ചക്രമുള്ള സൈക്കിൾ

A *tricycle* runs on three wheels.

Trifle *(n.)* ട്രൈഫ്ൾ-നിസ്സാര കാര്യം, തുച്ഛമായ

Mother told Raju not to cry over *trifles*.

Those who apply themselves too much to *trifles* usually become incapable of achieving great things.

Trifles make perfection and perfection is not *trifle*.

Trigger *(n.)* ട്രിഗർ-കാഞ്ചി

The gunners pressed the *triggers* and the guns went off.

Trim *(v.)* ട്രിം-വെട്ടി നിരപ്പാക്കുക, വെടിപ്പാക്കുക

I must *trim* the hedge because it looks so untidy.

Trinket *(n.)* ട്രിങ്കിറ്റ്-വിലകുറഞ്ഞ ആഭരണം

I shopped for *trinkets* in the Tibetan market.

Trio *(adj.)* ട്രിയോ-മൂവർ സംഘം

These comedians are a comical *trio.*

Trip ട്രിപ്-1. യാത്ര, കറക്കം

(n.) Uncle and aunt have gone for a *trip* to the sea.

2. മറിഞ്ഞു വീഴുക

(v.) Tommy *tripped* over a loose stone.

Tripod *(n.)* ട്രിപോഡ്-മുക്കാലി, മൂന്ന് കാലുള്ള സ്റ്റാൻഡ് (ക്യാമറ സെറ്റ് ചെയ്യുന്നതിന്)

The photographer set up a *tripod* for taking some snapshots.

Triumph *(n.)* ട്രയംഫ്-വിജയം, നേട്ടം, സാഫല്യം

We were given a day's holiday to celebrate our *triumph* in the football cup.

Trivial *(adj.)* ട്രിവിയൽ-നിസ്സാര, തുച്ഛ, ചെറിയ

I made only a *trivial* motoring offence.

Trolley *(n.)* ട്രോളി-കൈവി

In the hospital, tea is served from a *trolley.*

Troop *(n.)* ട്രൂപ്-1. സംഘം, കൂട്ടം

A *troop* of school children marched along the pavement.

2. സേനാ, സേനാദലം

The *troop* galloped into battle.

Trophy *(n.)* ട്രോഫി-വിജയ സ്മാരകം, വിജയവേളയിൽ സമ്മാനിക്കുന്ന വസ്തു

Vagish won a *trophy* in swimming.

Trot ട്രോട്ട്-കുതിക്കുക, ചുവട്വച്ച് നടക്കുക

(n.) This horse always keeps up a steady *trot.*

(v.) The child *trotted* along besides his father.

Trouble *(v.)* ട്രബ്ൾ-1. ഉപദ്രവിക്കുക, ശല്യപ്പെടുത്തുക

Don't *trouble* your teacher by asking silly questions.

I am sorry to *trouble* you.

2. വൈഷമ്യം

The *trouble* with opportunity is that it always comes in the disguise of hard work.

Trough *(n.)* ട്രോഫ്-ചാല്, മൃഗങ്ങൾക്ക് തീറ്റയിട്ടുകൊടുക്കുന്ന പാത്തി

The farmer poured the horses' food into the *trough.*

Trousers *(n.)* ട്രൗസർസ്-ട്രൗസേർസ്, പൈജാമ

Do you want to make a new pair of *trousers*?

Trout *(n.)* ട്രൗട്ട്-പുഴമീൻ, ആറ്റ് മീൻ

Have you ever seen a *trout* in the river?

Truant *(adj.&n.)* ട്രുഅന്റ്-കുഴിമടിയൻ, വേലകള്ളൻ

They are a bunch of *truant* schoolboys.

(n.) Don't be a *truant.*

Truck *(n.)* ട്രക്ക്-1. ലോറി, ട്രക്

Our transport company owned about fifty *trucks.*

2. കൈവി

The railway porter piled our luggage on his *truck.*

Trudge *(v.)* ട്രജ്-ക്ഷീണിച്ച് വലഞ്ഞ് നടക്കുക

We had to *trudge* more than 9 kilometres through a dust-storm.

True *(adj.)* ട്രൂ-സത്യം, യഥാർത്ഥ, നേരുള്ള

Say what is *true.*

(n.) If you tell the *truth,* you don't have to remember anything.

Truth wins in the end.

Trumpet *(n.)* ട്രമ്പിറ്റ്-1. കൊമ്പ് വാദ്യം, കാഹളം

My uncle plays the *trumpet* in a military band.

(v.) 2. ഉദ്ഘോഷിക്കുക, പ്രചരിപ്പിക്കുക

Netaji Subhash's praise was *trumpeted* throughout India.

Trunk *(n.)* ട്രങ്ക്–1. തുമ്പിക്കൈ

An elephant has a *trunk.* It is his long nose.

2. മരത്തിന്റെ കൊമ്പ്

The stem of a tree is called a *tree trunk.*

3. ഇരുമ്പ് പെട്ടി

We put our clothes in a *trunk.*

Trust ട്രസ്റ്റ്–വിശ്വസിക്കുക, വിശ്വാസം അർപ്പിക്കുക

(v.) Love all but *trust* a few.

A wise man does not *trust* anything blindly.

(n.) Have *trust* in God.

Try *(v.)* ട്രൈ–1. പരിശ്രമിക്കുക, പ്രയത്നിക്കുക

Time is short, but I shall *try* to catch the bus.

2. വസ്ത്രം ധരിച്ച് അളവ് ശരിയാണോ എന്ന് നോക്കുക

You had better *try* on the coat before you buy it.

(n.) 3. പ്രയത്നം, ശ്രമം, ഉദ്യമം

Come on, it is worth a *try.*

Tub *(n.)* ടബ്–വെള്ളം പിടിച്ച് വയ്ക്കുന്ന തൊട്ടി, ടബ്ബ്

Mother stored water in a *tub.*

Father bought a bath *tub* for daily use.

Tube *(n.)* ട്യൂബ്–കുഴൽ, ട്യൂബ്

The inner part of a bicycle tyre contains a rubber *tube.*

The water runs along a *tube* into the boiler.

Tuberculosis *(n.)* ട്യൂബർകുലോസിസ് – ക്ഷയരോഗം

Tuberculosis is a very dangerous disease.

Tuck *(n.)* ടക്–1. മടക്ക്, ചുരുള്, ഞൊറി

I shall put a *tuck* in you dress as it is too long for you.

(v.) 2. തെറുത്തുവയ്ക്കുക

I *tucked* the napkin under my chin.

Tuesday *(n.)* ട്യൂസ്ഡേ–ചൊവ്വാഴ്ച

If this is Sunday, the day after tomorrow will be *Tuesday.*

Tuft *(n.)* ടഫ്റ്റ്–കുഞ്ചം, കൊ, കൊത്ത്

There was sand and few *tufts* of coarse grass.

Tug*(n. & v.)* ടഗ്–കെട്ടിവലിക്കുക

(n.) A *tug* is a little ship. It helps to pull a big ship into dock.

(v.) We shall *tug* the boat out of the water on to the river bank.

Tuition *(n.)* ട്യൂഷൻ–ട്യൂഷൻ

He takes private *tuitions* at home.

Tulip *(n.)* ട്യൂലിപ് – കപ്പിന്റെ ആകൃതിയിലുള്ള ബഹുവർണ്ണ പുഷ്പം

A *tulip* is a spring flower. We can grow *tulips* in many different colours.

Tumble *(v.)* ടമ്പ്ൾ–വീണുപോകുക, മറിഞ്ഞുവീഴുക

Ila fell down and broke her leg and Uma came *tumbling* after.

Tumbler *(n.)* ടംബ്ലർ–കണ്ണാടി ഗ്ലാസ്

The child broke the glass *tumbler.*

Tumult *(n.)* ട്യൂമൾട്ട്–സമരം, കോലാഹലം, ബഹളം

I tried to make my voice heard above the *tumult,* but in vain.

Tune ട്യൂൺ–രാഗം, ഈണം, സ്വരം പുറപ്പെടുവിക്കുക, ശ്രുതി ചേർക്കുക

(n.) Can you play a *tune* on the piano?

(v.) I *tune* my violin before playing it.

Tunnel *(n.)* ടണൽ–തുരങ്കം

Trains sometimes run through the *tunnels.*

Turban *(n.)* ടർബൻ–തലപ്പാവ്

In India, some people wear *turbans* on their heads.

Turbulent *(adj.)* ടർബ്യൂലന്റ്–അക്രമാസക്ത, ഇളകിയ, പ്രബുദ്ധ

Nothing could control the *turbulent* mob.

Turkey *(n.)* ടർകി–തുർകി കോഴി

A *turkey* is a big bird. The Americans like to eat it.

Turmoil *(n.)* ടർമോയിൽ–കോളിളക്കം, കലങ്ങി മറിഞ്ഞ

The state was in *turmoil* after the sudden death of the Chief Minister.

Turn *(n.)* ടേൺ–1. തവണ, ഊഴം

Gopal is having a ride on a horse. It will be my *turn* after him.

It is my *turn* to bat.

Ram's *turn* was next.

(v.) 2. തിരിയുക, മറിയുക

The horse will *turn* around when it comes to the fence.

3. മറിച്ച് നോക്കുക

Shyama likes *turning* over the pages in her storybook.

(v.) 4. നന്മയ്ക്കു പകരം നന്മ

One good *turn* deserves another.

Turnip *(n.)* ടർണിപ്–മധുരമുള്ളങ്കി

A *turnip* is a vegetable. Mother cooks *turnips* for dinner.

Tusk *(n.)* ടസ്ക്–ആനകൊമ്പ്

Ivory is obtained from the *tusks* of elephants.

Tussle *(n.)* ടസ്ൽ–അടിപിടി

The child got into a *tussle* with his sister for a chocolate.

Tutor *(n.)* ട്യൂട്ടർ–അദ്ധ്യാപകൻ

Rabindra Nath was not willing to go to school, so he had to have a private *tutor.*

Tweed *(n.)* ട്വീഡ്–കട്ടിയുള്ള കമ്പിളി തുണി, ട്വീഡ്

Do you like to wear a *tweed* jacket?

Twelve *(adj.)* ട്വെൽവ്–പന്ത്രണ്ട്

The child can count up to *twelve.*

Three is one *twelfth* of thirty-six.

The school education is over after *twelfth* standard.

Twenty *(adv.)* ട്വെന്റി–ഇരുപത്

Two tens make *twenty.*

Twice *(adv.)* ട്വൈസ്–ര് പ്രാവശ്യം

Brush your *teeth* twice a day.

Twig *(n.)* ട്വിഗ്–ചുള്ളികമ്പ്, കൊമ്പ്

The birds were sitting on the *twigs* while singing.

Twilight *(n.)* ട്വൈലൈറ്റ്–സന്ധ്യവെളിച്ചം, അസ്തമയത്തിന് തൊട്ടുമുമ്പ്

We must go for a walk in the *twilight.*

Twin *(adj.)* ട്വിൻ–ഇരട്ട (കുഞ്ഞുങ്ങൾ)

Lava and Kusha were *twins.*

Twinkle *(v.)* ട്വിങ്ക്ൾ–മിന്നുക

The stars *twinkle* in the sky.

In the dark, we could see the stars *twinkling.*

Your eyes *twinkled* with mischief.

Twirl *(v.)* ട്വേൾ–തിരിക്കുക, വിരൽ കൊ് കറക്കുക

He *twirled* the pen in his hand.

Twist *(v.)* ട്വിസ്റ്റ്–പിരിയുക, ശക്തി നൽകുക, തിരിക്കുക, ഉരുളുക

Rope is made by *twisting* lengths of cord together.

Mary *twisted* her ankle when she fell.

Twist those strings together to make a strong rope.

Twitter *(v.)* ട്വിറ്റർ–ചിലയ്ക്കുക

The birds *twitter* cheerfully in the trees.

Two *(adj.)* ടു–ര്

One plus one make *two.*

There are *two* words for everything.

We select either according to the *relevance.*

Tycoon *(n.)* ടൈകൂൺ–വ്യവസായ പ്രമുഖൻ

He is a powerful business *tycoon.*

Type ടൈപ്–തരം, ഇനം, രീതി, അച്ചടി അക്ഷരം

(n.) We find several *types* of vegetables.

Different kinds of *types* are often used for one printed page.

(v.) Please ask the *typist* to *type* carefully.

Typhoid *(n.)* ടൈഫോയിഡ്–സന്നിപാത ജ്വരം

Typhoid is often caused by eating and drinking impure food or drink.

Tyrant *(n.)* ടൈറന്റ്–സ്വേച്ഛാധികാരി, കിരാത ഭരണം

The Roman Emperor Nero was a *tyrant.*

The Romans suffered under his *tyranny.*

Tyre *(n.)* ടയർ–റബ്ബറിന്റെ ടയർ

My car has four *tyres.*

Tyres are usually made of rubber.

U

Ugly *(adj.)* അഗ്ലി-വിരൂപ

Cinderella had two *ugly* sisters. They were unkind to her.

Ulterior *(adj.)* അൾടീരിയർ-രഹസ്യമായി സൂക്ഷിച്ച, നിഗൂഢ

The servant agreed to work for us at a very low price. There must be some *ulterior* motive behind it.

Ultimate അൾട്ടിമേറ്റ്-ആത്യന്തിക, സർവ്വോത്തമ

(adj.) Serving our clients with honesty is the *ultimate* aim of this organisation.

(n.) The movie was the *ultimate* in cinematography.

(adv.) An unbalanced diet will *ultimately* lead to poor health.

Ultimatum *(n.)* അൾടിമേറ്റം-അന്ത്യശാസനം

She issued an *ultimatum* — either he finds a job or they will get divorced.

Umbrella *(n.)* അംബ്രല-കുട

An *umbrella* protects us from the rain or the sun.

Umpire *(n.)* അമ്പയർ-വിധികർത്താവ്, റെഫറി, അമ്പയർ

The *umpire* declared that the batsman had been run out.

Umpteen *(adj.)* അംപ്ടീൻ-എണ്ണമറ്റ, ധാരാളം

I can watch that movie *umpteen* number of times.

Un *(pre.)* അൺ-രഹിത, അല്ലാത്ത

Unable *(adj.)* അണേബ്ൾ-അയോഗ്യ, കഴിയാത്ത

I shall be *unable* to attend the meeting tomorrow.

Unaffected *(adj.)* അൺഅഫെക്റ്റഡ്-ബാധിക്കപ്പെടാത്തത്, കൂസലില്ലാത്തത്

He was totally *unaffected* by the loss.

Unanimous *(adj.)* യുനാനിമസ്-എതിരില്ലാത്ത, ഏകകണ്ഠമായി

The farmers were *unanimous* in their opposition to selling their fields to the industrialist.

Uncle *(n.)* അങ്ക്ൾ-മാമൻ, ചിറ്റപ്പൻ, വല്യച്ഛൻ

Father's brother is *Uncle* Gopal.

Mother's brother is *Uncle* Lal. Minakshi is fond of both her *uncles*.

Under *(prep.)* അർ-താഴെ, കീഴിൽ, കുറവായി

The dog jumps over the fence. The pig crawls *under* it.

I was sitting *under* a tree.

I am working *under* the supervisor.

(adj.) Are you *under*-age?

Undergo *(v.)* അർഗോ-സഹിക്കുക, അനുഭവിക്കുക

The doctor says Asha will have to *undergo* an operation.

Underground *(adj.)* അർഗ്രൗണ്ട്-ഭൂഗർഭ

We found an *underground* passage leading from the temple to the palace.

Undermine *(v.)* അർമൈൻ-അപകടപ്പെടുത്തുക, ദോഷം വരുത്തുക

By smoking too much, he has *undermined* his health.

Don't *undermine* your health by getting up very late every day.

Undersigned *(n.)* അർസൈൻഡ്-താഴെ ഒപ്പിട്ടയാൾ

The *undersigned* is directed to inform you that your services are no longer required for the trust.

Understand *(v.)* അർസ്റ്റാൻഡ്-അർസ്റ്റാൻഡ്, മനസ്സിലാക്കുക, അറിയുക

Mother seems to *understand* every word the baby says.

I *understand* how radio and television work.

അർടേക്-ഏറ്റെടുക്കുക, ചുമതലയേല്ക്കുക

Prof. Raman has *undertaken* to deliver a lecture once a week.

Underwear *(n.)* അർവെയർ-അടിവസ്ത്രം

Have you washed your *underwear*?

Undesirable *(adj.)* അൺഡിസൈറബ്ൾ- അനഭലഷണീയ, അനാവശ്യമായ

Your presence is *undesirable* here.

Rogues are *undesirable* persons, people do not want to be friendly with them.

Undo *(v.)* അൺഡു-1. ഇല്ലാതാക്കുക, ഉപേക്ഷിക്കുക

When the new manager is appointed, he usually *undoes* most of the work done previously.

2. തുറക്കുക (കൊളുത്തോ ബട്ടണോ)

We must *undo* all our buttons before taking off our shirt.

Undoubtedly *(adv.)* അൺഡൗടഡ്‌ലി, നിസ്സംശയം, തീർച്ചയായും

We shall *undoubtedly* reach Mumbai by next week.

Undue *(adj.)* അൺഡ്യൂ-അനുചിതമായ

You should not take *undue* advantage of your friends.

Uneasy *(adj.)* അൺഈസി-അസ്വസ്ഥ മാകുക

Uneasy lies the head that wears a crown.

Mother becomes *uneasy* if you come late.

Uneducated *(n.)* അൺഎഡ്യുക്കേറ്റഡ്- നിരക്ഷര, വിദ്യാവിഹീന

I spend my spare time in teaching the *uneducated.*

Unemployed *(adj.)* അൺഎംപ്ലോയ്ഡ്- തൊഴിൽ രഹിത

Are you still *unemployed*?

(n.) Unemployment is a great curse.

Unequal *(adj.)* അൺഈക്വൽ-1. അയോഗ്യ

The manager is *unequal* to his task.

അസമാനം, ചിലപ്പോൾ നല്ലത്, ചിലപ്പോൾ ചീത്ത

Your quality of work is very *unequal,* sometimes it is fair, sometimes not.

Unexpected *(adj.)* അണെക്സ്പെക്റ്റഡ് - അപ്രതീക്ഷിതം, മുൻകൂട്ടി കാണാത്ത

Amar's visit to us was quite *unexpected,* as we thought he was still out of station.

Unfair *(adj.)* അൺഫെയർ-അന്യായമായ

It was so *unfair* to demote him from a senior post.

Unfit അൺഫിറ്റ്-അയോഗ്യ, അസ്വസ്ഥം

You were *unfit* to play hockey because you had hurt your knees.

Unfold *(v.)* അൺഫോൾഡ്-തുറക്കുക, പ്രത്യക്ഷമാകുക

Unfold the letters and read it.

A wonderful view of nature *unfolded* before us.

Uniform *(adj.)* യൂണിഫോം-1. ഒരേ പോലത്തെ, സമാനമായ

All the benches in our school are *uniform.*

The legs of a chair are of *uniform* length.

(n.) യൂണിഫോറം

Soldiers, policemen and firemen always wear their *uniforms.*

Union *(n.)* യൂണിയൻ-സംഘടന, ഐകമത്യം

Union is strength.

A trade *union* is a group of workers in the same trade who join together to get fair wages and good conditions of work.

Unique *(adj.)* യുനീക്-ഏകമാത്രം, നിസ്തുലം, അനുപമ

Qutub Minar is a *unique* monument.

Unit *(n.)* യൂണിറ്റ്-1. സംഘം

We work as a *unit* in the office.

(adj.) ഭാഗം

The book is divided into five *units.*

ഘടകം

Hectare is a *unit* of area.

Universe *(n.)* യൂനിവേഴ്സ്-പ്രപഞ്ചം, വിശ്വം

The earth is only a part of the *universe.*

University *(n.)* യൂണിവേഴ്സിറ്റി- സർവ്വകലാശാല

A *University* should be a place of light, of liberty, and of learning.

Unknown *(adj.)* അൺനോൺ-അജ്ഞാതം, അറിയപ്പെടാത്തത്

Take delight in being *unknown* and unregarded.

He who can live *unknown* is really a gentleman.

Unless *(conj.)* അൺലെസ്-ഇല്ലെങ്കിൽ, അത് വരെ

You must not go out *unless* you have your shoes on.

He cannot go home *unless* I pay him fare.

Unlike *(adj.)* അൺലൈക്-ഒരേപോലെ അല്ലാത്തത്, സമാനമല്ലാത്തത്

Your appearance is quite *unlike* your brother's.

അൺലൈക്‌ലി-സാദ്ധ്യതയില്ലാത്ത, അസംഭവ്യ

It is *unlikely* that I would be present there on Monday.

അൺമിസ്റ്റേകബ്ൾ- സ്പഷ്ടമായ, തെറ്റാത്തത്

The voice I hear was *unmistakable,* because it could not be anyone else's but Rajendra's.

അൺറീസണബ്ൾ- അനുചിതമായ

In our shop, you will not find *unreasonable* rates.

Untidy *(adj.)* അൺടൈഡി-താറുമാറായ, കോലംകെട്ട

Never leave your room *untidy.*

(adv.) The woman is *untidily* dressed.

Until *(prep.)* അൺടിൽ-വരെ

Asha will not go to bed *until* 9.30 P.M.

Wait here *until* I come to fetch you.

Unwell *(adj.)* അൺവെൽ-അസ്വസ്ഥം, രോഗഗ്രസ്തം

I am feeling *unwell* now. Kindly allow me to leave early.

Up *(adv.)* അപ്-1. മുകളിൽ

Kamla and Vimla went *up* the hill.

It is the time to wake *up.*

Get *up* early in the morning.

Stand *up* when an elderly person comes to you.

Climb *up* the tree for plucking mangoes.

2. പൂർണ്ണമായി

I ate *up* all the bananas.

3. അതിലും ഉയരെ

Please speak *up,* I cannot hear you well.

Uphold *(v.)* അപ്ഹോൾഡ്-ഉയർത്തി പിടിക്കുക, സമർത്ഥിക്കുക

No sensible person would *uphold* the idea that the dowry system is a good thing.

Upon *(prep.)* അപോൺ-മേലെ

Once *upon* a time, there was a king.

The birds are sitting *upon* the turret.

Upper *(adj.)* അപ്പർ-(മറ്റൊന്നിനെക്കാൾ) ഉയരെ, മേൽ

I live in the *upper* storey.

Parliament has two houses — the *upper* house and the lower house.

Upright *(adj.)* അപ്റൈറ്റ്-1. നേരെ, നിവർന്ന്

Please stand *upright* while I measure your height.

2. സത്യസന്ധ

We can trust Ravi, for he has always been *upright* in his dealings with us.

അപ്റോർ-മുറവിളി, കോലാഹലം, ബഹളം

The girls made such an *uproar* that the head-mistress had to come to quieten them.

Upset അപ്സെറ്റ്-ഖിന്ന, വിഷമമുള്ള, തകിടം മറിക്കുക

(adj.) Shanta was very much *upset* when she heard about her husband's accident.

(v.) Never *upset* other people's programmes.

Urge *(n.)* അർജ്-മോഹം, കൊതി, അതിയായ ഇച്ഛ

Anupam had an *urge* to eat ice-cream.

Subhash Chandra Bose had felt a great *urge* to achieve the freedom of our country from the British.

Urgent *(adj.)* അർജന്റ്-അടിയന്തിര, അത്യാവശ്യ

I got an *urgent* message from my aunt and went to see her at once.

(n.) The *urgency* of the message frightened my mother.

Use *(n. & v.)* യൂസ്-ഉപയോഗിക്കുക

(n.) It is a great misfortune to be of no *use* to anybody.

What is the *use* of being a cross? It doesn't do any good.

(v.) We *use* our cycles to ride.

(adj.) A pin is a very *useful* thing.

A fountain pen is *useless* unless it has ink in it.

Usual *(adj.)* യൂഷ്വൽ-സാധാരണ, പതിവ്, മുമ്പത്തെപോലെ

Uncle has gone out for his *usual* morning walk.

Always go to school at the *usual* time.

(adv.) When do you get up *usually*?

Utensil *(n.)* യുടെൻസിൽ–പാത്രം

A pan is a cooking *utensil.*

Utilise *(v.)* യൂട്ടിലൈസ്–പ്രയോജനപ്പെടുത്തുക

We should *utilise* natural resources.

Utmost *(adj.)* അറ്റ്മോസ്റ്റ്–പരമാവധി

Don't worry, I will go to the doctor with the *utmost* speed.

Utter അട്ടർ–1. അല്പം മൊഴിയുക

She *uttered* a few words in foreign language.

2. *(adj.)* തനി

He is an *utter* coward.

V

Vacant *(adj.)* വേക്കന്റ്–ഒഴിവ്, കാലി

The shop will be *vacant* on Monday and we can then move in.

(n.) There is no *vacancy* in the office.

Vacation *(n.)* വകേഷൻ–നീ ഒഴിവ്

We have two months' *vacation* each year.

വാക്സിനേറ്റ്–കുത്തി വയ്ക്കുക

The children are being *vaccinated.*

(n.) Vaccination against contagious diseases is essential.

The *vaccinators* should take care of cleanliness.

Vacuum *(n.)* വാക്വം–ശൂന്യത, വായു പുറത്തു കളഞ്ഞ

Tinned food is mostly *vaccum* packed. It is put into a tin and all the air is forced out of the tin-pot before it is sealed.

Vagabond *(n.)* വാഗബോ് –നാടോടി, അലഞ്ഞുതിരിയുന്ന

We don't know about his whereabouts; he is a *vagabond.*

Vague *(adj.)* വേഗ്–അവ്യക്തം, അവിടെയും ഇവിടെയും തൊടാതെ

When I asked my son where he had been, he gave me *vague* answer.

Vain *(adj.)* വെയ്ൻ–വ്യർത്ഥം, നിഷ്ഫല

Hari made a *vain* search for his pen. He couldn't find it anywhere.

(adv.) He shouted in *vain* for help.

Valiant *(adj.)* വാലിയന്റ്–വീര, ശൂര, സാഹസി

Abhimanyu was a *valiant* warrior.

(adv.) The soldiers fought for their country *valiantly.*

Valid *(adj.)* വാലിഡ്–സാധുവായ, ഈടുള്ള

Give me a *valid* reason for coming late every day.

Valley *(n.)* വാലി–താഴ്‌വര

A *valley* is a place between two hills.

Value *(n.&v.)* വാല്യു–മൂല്യം (നിർണ്ണയിക്കുക) വില (വയ്ക്കുക)

(n.) The chief *value* of my motorcycle is that it lets me get about so quickly.

Physical exercises are of great *value* for strengthening your muscles.

(v.) The automobile dealer had *valued* my old scooter at five thousand rupees.

I *value* the advice my elders give me.

(adj.) I find his advice *valuable* in many ways.

Valve *(n.)* വാൽവ്–വാൽവ്

A *valve* prevents the air from leaking out of tyre.

Van *(n.)* വാൻ–വി, അടച്ച് മൂടിയ അറയുള്ള വാഹനം

A *van* is a car that is used for carrying load.

We put trunks in the luggage *van.*

Vanish *(v.)* വാനിഷ്–മറയുക, അപ്രത്യക്ഷമാകുക

When the sun rose, the mist *vanished.*

Vapour *(n.)* വേപർ-ബാഷ്പം, നീരാവി
Vapour rises from boiling water.

Varnish വാർണിഷ് - വാർണിഷ്, മിനുക്കെണ്ണ, മിനുക്കുക
(n.) The windows have been given a new coat of *varnish.*
(v.) He painted the door and then *varnished* it.

Vary *(v.)* വേരി-മാറ്റുക, മാറുക, രൂപാന്തരപ്പെടുത്തുക
The weather *varies* from day to day.
The size of the books *varied.* Some were large, others were small.
(adj.) The police tried *various* ways to make the thief confess.

Vase *(n.)* വേസ്-ഫ്ളവർവേസ്
We put flowers in a *vase.* It is called a *flower-vase.*

Vast *(adj.)* വാസ്റ്റ്-വിസ്തൃതമായ, വിശാലമായ, വലിയ
This printing machine has cost a *vast* sum of money.

Vault *(n.)* വാൾട്ട്-സുരക്ഷിത സ്ഥാനം, ഖജനാവ്
Valuables are stored in a *vault* at the bank.

Vegetable *(n.)* വെജിറ്റബ്ൾ-പച്ചക്കറി, സസ്യജാലങ്ങൾ
Potatoes, pumpkins, carrots, onions, turnips and beans are all *vegetables.*
A farmer grow *vegetables* in the field.

Vehicle *(n.)* വെഹിക്ക്ൾ-വി, വാഹനം
Motor cars, buses, trucks and carts are all *vehicles.*
Language is a good *vehicle* for expressing our feelings.

Veil *(v. & n.)* വെയ്ൽ-മൂട്പടം, മുഖംമറയ്ക്കുക
(v.) Muslim women are always *veiled* when they go out of their homes.
Could you *veil* your disgust at his conduct?
(n.) The bride wore a colourful *veil.*

Vein *(n.)* വെയ്ൻ-നാഡി, ഞരമ്പ്
He is so skinny that one can clearly see his *veins* on his hands.

Velvet *(n.)* വെൽവെറ്റ്-സൂര്യപടം, വെൽവെറ്റ്
Velvet is a soft cloth. It is smooth to touch.

Vengeance *(n.)* വെൻജൻസ്-പ്രതികാരം
Nothing is more poisonous than *vengeance.*
In fact, *vengeance* has no foresight.

Venom *(n.)* വെനം-വിഷം
The *venom* of a cobra is highly powerful and causes death quickly.
(adj.) The word *venomous* is often used to mean very unkind or spiteful.

Ventilation *(n.)* വെന്റിലേഷൻ-കാറ്റോട്ടം, വായുസഞ്ചാരം
The room needed *ventilation* after remaining closed for two days.
(v.) Father opened the window to *ventilate* the room.

Venture *(v. & n.)* വെൻചർ-സാഹസം ചെയ്യുക
(v.) Do not *venture* into the woods on such a dark night.
(n.) It is a risky *venture* to start a college in the village.

Venue *(n.)* വെന്യൂ-പരിപാടി നടക്കുന്ന സ്ഥലം
I will reach the *venue* in an hour.

Veranda *(n.)* വരാൻഡാ - ഇറയം, കോലായി, വരാന്ത
I like to sit in *veranda* in the evening and talk to the neighbours.

Verb *(v.)* വെർബ്-ക്രിയ
there are two kinds of *verbs* - transitive and intransitive.

Verbatim *(adv.)* വെർബാറ്റിം-പദാനുപദം
She copied the article for Internet *verbatim.*

Verdict *(n.)* വെർഡിക്റ്റ്-1. തീർപ്പ്, വിധി
Honour the*verdict* of the jury.
ആലോചിച്ചുറപ്പിച്ച നിർണ്ണയം
What is your *verdict* on the quality of this cloth?

Verge *(n.)* വെർജ്-അരിക്, ഓരം, വശം
There is a *verge* of bricks on each side of the road.

Verify *(v.)* വെരിഫൈ-സത്യാവസ്ഥ അന്വേഷിച്ചറിയുക
Your statement must be *verified* by a witness.

Vermin *(n.)* വെർമിൻ-കീടം, കൃമി, പുഴു, ചെള്ള്
Lice and fleas are considered to be *vermin.*
(adj.) Don't neglect the dog, otherwise it will be *verminous.*

Vernacular *(n)* വെർണകുലർ-പ്രാദേശിക ഭാഷ
In India, we have several *vernaculars.*

Verse *(n.)* വേർസ്-കവിത, പദ്യം
A *verse* is a short piece of poetry.
Can you recite a *verse* from Milton's poetry?

Version *(n.)* വേർഷൻ-വിവരണം, പതിപ്പ്, വർണ്ണന
We both saw the same accident, but Amit's *version* of it was different from that of mine.

Versus *(prep.)* വേഴ്സസ്-എതിർ, വിരുദ്ധ, തമ്മിൽ
Today's international match is Pakistan *versus* India.

Vertical *(adj.)* വെർട്ടിക്കൽ-കുത്തനെ, ലംബമാനം
He rode the bike in an almost *vertical* position.

Very വെരി-1 വളരെ, അത്യന്തം
(adv.) I am *very* fond of ice-cream.
Thank you for telling me a *very* interesting tale.
(adj.) അളവ്, മാത്ര
The *very* idea of it makes me sad.
3. അതുതന്നെ, മറ്റാരുമല്ല
He is the *very* person I sought to see.

Vessel *(n.)* വെസൽ-പാത്രം
Empty *vessels* make much noise.
2. രക്ത ധമനികൾ
Our veins are blood-*vessels.* They carry blood throughout the body.

Vest *(n.)* വെസ്റ്റ്-1. ബനിയൻ, അടിവസ്ത്രം
It is essential to wear a *vest* in winters.
(V.) നിക്ഷിപ്തമാകുക
In India, power is *vested* usually in the Prime Minister and the cabinet.

Vested Interest *(adv.)* വെസ്റ്റഡ് ഇന്ററസ്റ്റ്-സ്വാർത്ഥ, സ്ഥാപിത താല്പര്യം
He has a *vested interest* in whatever he is doing for you.

Veteran *(n.)* വെറ്ററൻ-അനുഭവസമ്പന്നൻ
Our manager is a *veteran* at management.

Veterinary *(n.)* വെറ്റനറി-മൃഗ ചികിത്സ, മൃഗ ഡോക്ടർ
Our cow was ill, so we took it to the *veterinary* surgeon.

Vex *(v.)* വെക്സ്-ശല്യപ്പെടുത്തുക, വലയ്ക്കുക
We will *vex* our teacher if we keep asking him silly questions.
We should avoid *vexing* our mother.

Via *(prep.)* വയാ-ആ വഴി, അതിലൂടെ, മാർഗ്ഗം
One of the ways from Delhi to Kolkata is *via* Varanasi.

Viable *(adj.)* വയബ്ൾ-പ്രായോഗികം
Do you think this project is commercially *viable*?

Vibrate *(v.)* വൈബ്രേറ്റ്-വിറയ്ക്കുക, പ്രകമ്പനം
Father's voice *vibrated* with anger.
(n.) The *vibration* of the engine shook us.

Vicar *(n.)* വികാർ-വികാരി, പാതിരി
The *vicar* lives in a church.

Vice *(n.)* വൈസ്-ദുർഗ്ഗുണം, ദോഷം
Gambling is a *vice* that leads to great unhappiness.

Vice *(prefix.)* വൈസ്-ഉപ
Since you are the *Vice*-Captain, you will take the Captain's place when he is ill.
The Principal could not come, so the *Vice*-Principal presided over the meeting.

Vicinity *(n.)* വിസിനിറ്റി-പരിസരം, ചുറ്റുപാട്
There are beautiful gardens in the *vicinity* of this village.

Victim *(n.)* വിക്റ്റിം-ഇര, പീഡിതർ
There are many *victims* of this road accident.
Food is being collected for the *victims* of the floods.

Victory *(n.)* വിക്ടറി-വിജയം, സഫലത
Our army won a great *victory* over Pakistan in the battle on the North-Western border.
Everyone hankers after a *victory.*

Abha was the *victor* in the last race in the sports.

(adj.) She was *victorious.*

View വ്യൂ-ദൃശ്യം, നോക്കുക, നിരീക്ഷിക്കുക

(n.) We had a clear *view* from the top of the hill. Really it was a lovely *view.*

(v.) We can *view* the inside of the castle.

Viewpoint *(n.)* വ്യൂപോയിന്റ്-വാദഗതി, കാഴ്ചപ്പാട്

Consider this issue from my *viewpoint.*

Vigil *(n.)* വിജിൽ-ജാഗ്രത, കാവൽ

(n.) The watchman kept *vigil* all night.

(v.) The police was *vigilant* all the time and caught the thief in a few days.

Vigour *(n.)* വിഗർ-ഓജസ്സ്, കരുത്ത്, ഉത്സാഹം

We will not win many games unless we put more *vigour* into our play.

The *vigour* with which you work is amazing.

Vile *(adj.)* വൈൽ-ദുഷ്ട, നീച, ചീത്ത

Do you think me capable of such *vile* conduct?

Villa *(n.)* വില്ല-ഗ്രാമ മന്ദിരം

My father has a beautiful *villa* in a small town.

Village *(n.)* വില്ലേജ്-ഗ്രാമം

Is there a high school in your *village*?

Many *villagers* go to big cities for better livelihood.

Villain *(n.)* വില്ലൻ-ദുഷ്ടൻ, പ്രതിനായകൻ, അക്രമി

In many plays, the *villain* meets bad end.

(adj.) Rama killed Ravan for his *villainous* acts.

Vine *(n.)* വൈൻ-മുന്തിരിവള്ളി

Vine is a creeping plant. Grapes grow on the grape *vine.*

Vinegar *(n.)* വിനിഗർ-വിന്നാഗിരി, വിനിഗർ

Vinegar is used in many kinds of pickles.

Violent *(adj.)* വയലന്റ്-രൂക്ഷമായ, ശക്തിയായ, അക്രമാസക്തം

The *violent* storm blew down the huts.

(adj.) Why are you knocking *violently* on the window?

Violet *(adj.)* വയലറ്റ്-ഒരു പുഷ്പം, പാടല വർണ്ണം, കത്തിരിക്കാ നിറം

Violet is a flower. It is pale purple in colour.

Violet is also a colour. It is like the colour of the flower of the same name.

Violin *(n.)* വയലിൻ-വയലിൻ

You are learning to play the *violin.*

Can you play some tunes on it?

Viper *(n.)* വൈപർ-അണലി, വിഷപ്പാമ്പ്

Have you ever seen a *viper*?

Virgin *(n.)* വെർജിൻ - കുമാരി, അവിവാഹിത, കന്നി

Rima was married last year. Her sister Kusum still remains a *virgin.*

(adj.) *Virgin* soil of this forest is very fertile.

Virtue *(n.)* വെർച്യൂ-സദ്ഗുണം, സവിശേഷത

No *virtue* is small.

The *virtues* of society are vices of the saint.

Vision *(n.)* വിഷൻ-1. കാഴ്ച, ദർശനം

He has to wear eye-glasses as his *vision* is weak.

Writing needs men of *vision.*

(adj.) 2. ദൃശ്യമായ

The India Gate is *visible* from the Qutub Minar.

The students have some *visual* aids such as maps and charts in their lessons.

Visionary വിഷനറി-ദിവ്യദർശി

(n.) Gautam Buddha was really a *visionary.*

(adj.) Gautam Buddha was a *visionary* preacher.

Visit വിസിറ്റ്-സന്ദർശനം, കൂടിക്കാഴ്ച

(v.) My mother has gone to *visit* my grandmother.

(n.) An old friend paid a *visit* to my father.

Vital *(adj.)* വൈറ്റൽ–1. അനിവാര്യം (ജീവന്)

Air is *vital* to us, for without it we would soon die.

2. ഓജസ്സുറ്റ, ജീവത്തായ

He has a *vital* personality.

3. നിർണ്ണായകം

Getting good marks in the examination is *vital* to you.

Vitamin *(n.)* വൈറ്റമിൻ–വിറ്റാമിൻ, ജീവകം

Always take a balanced food enriched with multi-*vitamins.*

Vivacious *(adj.)* വിവേഷ്യസ്–ഉത്സാഹ ശീലം, ചുറുചുറുക്കുള്ള

She is known for her *vivacious* nature.

Vivid *(adj.)* വിവിഡ്–ഉജ്ജ്വല, മിന്നുക, ശക്തിയായ

A *vivid* lightning flash lit the sky.

Vocabulary *(n.)* വൊകാബുലറി–പദാവലി

We can improve our *vocabulary* by learning some new words everyday.

Your dictionary has a *vocabulary* of six thousand words.

Vocal *(adj.)* വോകൽ–1. വായ്പാട്ട്

She excels in *vocal* music.

2. തുറന്നു സംസാരിക്കുക

You should be *vocal* about your grievances.

Vocation *(n.)* വൊകേഷൻ–തൊഴിൽ

Finally, he has got into the *vocation* he likes.

Voice *(n.)* വോയ്സ്––1. ശബ്ദം, ധ്വനി, നാദം

The poor have no *voice* in this world.

Lata has such a pleasant *voice* that everybody enjoys listening to her songs.

2. ക്രിയാവാച്യം

A verb has two *voices* — active *voice* and passive *voice.*

Void *(n.)* വോയ്സ്–ശൂന്യത, വ്യർത്ഥത

I often feel a *void* in my life.

Volatile *(adj.)* വോളറ്റൈൽ–1. ബാഷ്പീകരിക്കുന്ന

Perfume is a *volatile* liquid.

2. അസ്ഥിര

She has a *volatile* nature.

Volcano *(n.)* വൊൾകാനോ–അഗ്നിപർവ്വതം

In Kangra, there is a *volcano* which disgorges fire.

Volley വോളി–കൂട്ടവെടി, ശരവർഷം

(n.) A *volley* of missiles was fired to push the enemy back.

(v.) In tennis, the players *volley* the ball. They keep *volleying* before it has touched the ground.

Volume *(n.)* വോള്യും–1. പുസ്തകം, ഗ്രന്ഥം

This *volume* contains all of Sharat Chandra's writings.

2. അളവ്

The *volume* of sound coming from your transistor is too low.

Voluntary *(adj.)* വോളന്ററി–സന്നദ്ധ, സ്വയമേവ

To members of Arya Samaj render many *voluntary* services.

This library has been running on *voluntary* contributions.

(v.) The brave women *volunteered* themselves to go into the burning house.

Vomit *(v.)* വൊമിറ്റ്–ശർദ്ദിക്കുക, വിസർജ്ജിക്കുക

She was seriously ill and began to *vomit.*

The chimney of the mill *vomits* black smoke.

Voracious *(adj.)* വൊറേഷസ് – അത്യാർത്തിയോടെ

He is a *voracious* reader and always carries a book with himself.

Vote വോട്ട്–സമ്മതിദാനം, തിരഞ്ഞെടുക്കുക

(n.) *Vote* is the most important instrument of democracy.

(v.) The panchayat member did not *vote* for the corrupt president.

Voucher *(n.)* വൗചർ-രസീത്, ചീട്ട്

Have you signed your salary *voucher*?

Am I not entitled to a gift *voucher*?

Vow *(n.)* വൗ-വ്രതം, ശപഥം, പ്രതിജ്ഞ

A newly married man and woman take *vows* to love and cherish each other.

Vowel *(n.)* വൗഅൽ-സ്വരം

The English language has five *vowels* - a, e, i, o, u.

Voyage *(n.)* വോയേജ്-യാത്ര (ചെയ്യുക)

We were seasick on the *voyage* around the world.

(v.) I have an ambition to *voyage* around the world.

Vulgar *(adj.)* വൾഗർ-അശ്ലീലം, അസഭ്യം

Don't indulge in *vulgar* talk.

Vulture *(n.)* വൾചർ-കഴുകൻ, അത്യാഗ്രഹി

Vultures feed on the dead bodies of animals.

W

Wacky *(adj.)* വാകി-വിചിത്ര, കോമാളി

She is full of such *wacky* ideas.

Waddle *(v.)* വാഡ്ൽ-താറാവിന്റെ നടത്ത

Very fat people often *waddle* as they walk along.

Ducks *waddle*.

Wade *(v.)* വേയ്ഡ്-വെള്ളത്തിൽ നടക്കുക, നദി നടന്നു കടക്കുക

I like to *wade* in the river. You are not *wading* but having a swim.

Wafer *(n.)* വേഫർ-നേർത്ത ബിസ്ക്കറ്റ്

Usually we take a *wafer* with an ice cream.

Wag വാഗ്-1. വായാടി, തമാസക്കാരൻ, സരസൻ

Uncle Arora is quite a *wag*.

(v.) 2. ആട്ടുക

The puppy *wags* its tail when it is happy.

Wage *(n.)* വേജ്-വേതനം, കൂലി

Harish's *wages* as a mason is 90 rupees a day.

Give the labourer his *wage* before his perspiration be dry.

Waggon, Wagon *(n.)* വാഗൺ-മാട്ടുവണ്ടി

Usually every farmer has a *wagon* on his farms. He carries hay in the *wagon*.

Waif *(n.)* വെയ്ഫ്-അനാഥൻ, ആരോരുമില്ലാത്തവൻ

No one knows the sufferings of a *waif*.

He was sad because he was a *waif*.

Wail വെയ്ൽ-വിലപിക്കുക, നിലവിളി

(v.) Don't *wail* over your lost money, for I am sure you will soon find it.

(n.) The *wails* of the aircrash victims' relatives could be heard in the hospital.

Waist *(n.)* വെയ്സ്റ്റ്-അരക്കെട്ട്

Do you wear a belt round your *waist*?

I like to wear a *waist* band.

Wait വെയ്റ്റ്-കാത്തിരിക്കുക, കാത്തിരിപ്പ്

(v.) *Wait* here until I come back.

(n.) I had a long *wait* for the train.

True *waiting* means *waiting* with eagerness.

Wake *(n.)* വേക്-ഉണരുക, ഉണർത്തുക

Please *wake* me up whenever you want.

I usually *wake* up at six o'clock in the morning.

(adj.) Were you *awake* the whole night?

Walk വാക്-1. നടത്ത, നടക്കുക

(v.) I *walk* to the office every day.

(n.) Let us go for a morning *walk*.

2. വഴി
We use the *walk* along the top of the cliff to get to our village.

Wall *(n.)* വാൾ-ഭിത്തി, മതിൽ
We raised the *walls* of our house.
Wall-paper is used for decorating the *walls*.

Wallet *(n.)* വോലിറ്റ്-പഴ്സ്
Always keep your all-route bus pass in your *wallet*.

Walnut *(n.)* വാൾനട്ട്-അക്രോട്ടി
The wood of the *walnut* tree is used for making fine furniture.

Walrus *(n.)* വോൾറസ്-കടൽകുതിര
A *walrus* is a large sea animal which looks like a seal.

Waltz വാൾസ്-നൃത്തം, നൃത്തം ചെയ്യുക, ഈ നൃത്തത്തിന് വായിക്കുന്ന സംഗീതം
(n.) Two persons played an old-time *waltz*.
(v.) He *waltzed* you round and round.

Wan *(adj.)* വാൻ-മഞ്ഞളിപ്പ്, വിവർണ്ണത, അവശത
He was ill for many days so his face was pale and *wan*.

Wand *(n.)* വാൻഡ്-മാന്ത്രിക വടി
In a fairy tale, the fairy always waves her magic *wand* to make dreams come true.

Wander *(v.)* വാ ർ-അ ലയു ക
He was *wandering* around the whole city.

Wane വെയ്ൻ-ക്ഷയിക്കുക, നശിക്കുക
(v.) As time passed, my hopes of getting money *waned*.
(n.) From today, the moon will be on the *wane*.

Want *(n. & v.)* വാ്-ആവശ്യം, അഭാവം ഉാവുക, ആഗ്രഹിക്കുക
(n.) Poor people are in *want* of food.
(v.) Father's shoes *want* mending.
Do you *want* more money?

War *(n.)* വാർ-യുദ്ധം, പോര്, ശത്രുത
Soldiers win *wars* and generals get the credit.

Ward വാർഡ്-ആശ്രിതൻ, വാർഡ്, രോഗികളുടെ മുറി, രക്ഷിക്കുക
(n.) Since his parents died he has been the *ward* of his grandfather.
She was in the children's *ward*.
(v.) A warden *wards* his area and looks after his patients.

Wards *(suffix.)* വാർഡ്സ്-താഴേക്ക്
Is the Chinese language written *downwards*?

Warden *(n.)* വാർഡൻ-അദ്ധ്യക്ഷൻ, മേൽനോട്ടാധികാരി
The *warden* in our boarding school was very kind.
Were you not a traffic *warden* at the time of your retirement?

Warder *(n.)* വാർഡർ-ജയിലർ, വാർഡൻ, ജയിലിലെ ഇൻചാർജ്
The *warder* of our jail was a very cruel man.

Wardrobe *(n.)* വാർഡ്റോബ്-അലമാരി, വസ്ത്രം വയ്ക്കുന്ന സ്ഥലം
Is your *wardrobe* not out of fashion?
Bring my suit from the *wardrobe*.

Ware *(n.)* വെയ്ർ-ചരക്ക്, വില്പന സാധനം
Wares of all kinds are stored in warehouses.

Warm വാം-ഇളം ചൂട്, ചൂടാക്കുക
(adj.) It is a *warm* day.
In western countries, people use *warm* water for bathing.
(v.) Please *warm* some water for me.
Warm your palms on the heater.

Warn *(v.)* വാൺ-മുന്നറിയിപ്പ് നൽകുക, ഉപദേശിക്കുക
The manager *warned* the clerk about his repeated negligence.
I *warned* him not to skate on thin ice.
(n.) Your failure in the monthly tests is a kind of *warning* to you.

Warrant *(n.)* വാറന്റ്-അറസ്റ്റ് വാറന്റ്
A policeman will not search your house unless he has a *warrant* from a magistrate.
Can you pay my bill until you get a *warrant* from the treasurer?

Wary *(adj.)* വേരി-സൂക്ഷിക്കുക, കരുതലോടെ ഇരിക്കുക
Be *wary* of the dog, for it is very fierce.
(adj.) Please walk *warily* lest you should fall.

Wash വാഷ്–അലക്കുക, കുളിക്കുക, കുളി

(n.) Daily *wash* is essential for good health.

(v.) We should *wash* ourselves regularly to remain clean.

Wasp *(n.)* വാസ്പ്–കടന്തൽ

A *wasp* can sting. It has black and yellow stripes on its body.

Waste *(n.)* വേസ്റ്റ്–പാഴാകുക

(v.) We must not *waste* food.

Don't *waste* your money in buying things you don't need.

(n.) Haste makes *waste.*

Watch *(n.)* വാച്ച്–1. പോക്കറ്റിലേയോ, കയ്യിലെയോ വാച്ച്

Father had a pocket *watch.*

Mother wore a *watch* round her wrist.

(v.) 2. നോക്കുക, കാവൽക്കാരൻ

We *watched* for our friend coming home at night.

A *watchman* is a man who *watches* the building during the night.

Water വാട്ടർ–വെള്ളം (നൽകുക) തളിക്കുക

(n.) We drink *water* when we are thirsty.

The pond is full of muddy *water.* The sea is full of salty *water.*

(v.) You should *water* the lawn every day in dry weather.

Every morning, I *water* my potted plants.

Watt *(n.)* വാട്ട്–വാട്ട്

This is a 100-*watt* bulb.

Wave വേവ്–1. വീശുക, ആട്ടുക

(v.) *Wave* your hand to us as you leave.

When the guard *waved* his green flag, the train steamed off.

(n.) 2. തിര, അലമാല, തരംഗം

A *wave* turned their boat over.

How long is this cold *wave* going to last?

Wavelength *(n.)* വേവ്ലങ്ത്–പൊതു താല്പര്യം

We enjoy working together because we are on the same *wavelength.*

Waver *(v.)* വേവർ–തീരുമാനത്തിലെത്താതിരിക്കുക, അസ്ഥിരമാകുക

Don't *waver* too long about buying the almirah, otherwise someone else may buy it.

Wax *(v. & n.)* വാക്സ്–വലുതാകുക, മെഴുക്

(v.) The new moon will *wax* until it is full.

(n.) *Wax* is used for making candles.

Way *(n.)* വേ–1. വഴി, മാർഗ്ഗം, നിരത്ത്

(v.) The little child lost his *way.* He could not find his *way* back home.

Which is the *way* to the interstate bus stand?

2. ദിശ, വശം

Always look at both the *ways* before crossing the road.

3. വിധി, രീതി, ഉപായം

This book tells you the *way* to use words in sentences.

4. ദൂരം

Will you meet me half *way*?

We *(pron.)* വീ–ഞങ്ങൾ, നമ്മൾ

We reside in a big bungalow.

Weak വീക്–ദുർബലം, ക്ഷീണിച്ച, അവശ (വ്യക്തി)

(adj.) She is feeling *weak* after her illness.

(n.) Have the *weak* no right to live?

We all have *weaknesses.*

Wealth *(n.)* വെൽത്ത്–സമ്പത്ത്, സ്വത്ത്

The rich man gave away all his *wealth* to build a hospital for the poor people.

Wealth is not his who has it, but his who enjoys it.

Weapon *(n.)* വെപൺ–ആയുധം

Swords, shields, spears and guns are *weapons.*

Swords and shields are old types of *weapons.*

Wear വെയ്ർ–1. ധരിക്കുക, അണിയുക

(v.) The poor lady is *wearing* an old dress.

She always *wears* the same dress.

That beautiful girl always *wears* a happy smile.

(n.) In readymade clothes shop, you can find children's *wear* also.

2. തേയ്മാനം

This table is showing signs of *wear* and tear.

Weary വിയറി–ക്ഷീണിത, തളർന്ന, തളർച്ച, മുഷിപ്പിക്കുക

(adj.) Are you not *weary* after the day's work?

(v.) Please don't *weary* me with your silly talk.

(adv.) We walked the last two kilometres *wearily.*

Weather *(n.)* വെദർ–കാലാവസ്ഥ

A change in the *weather* is enough to renew the world and ourselves.

When two Englishmen meet, their talk usually begins with a discussion on *weather.*

Weave വീവ്–നെയ്യുക, ഇഴ

(n.) Do you prefer a loose *weave* for your sweater?

(v.) The *weaver wove* some fine cloth.

Web *(n.)* വെബ്–വല

Flies were caught in the spider's *web.*

(adj.) A duck has *webbed* feet.

Wedding *(n.)* വെഡിംഗ്–വിവാഹം, കല്യാണം

Have you got Ramesh's *wedding* card?

How many guests have you invited to the *wedding*?

Wedge *(v.&n.)* വെജ്–ആപ്പ്, കീലം

(v.) Please *wedge* the door open.

The cutter *wedged* the log.

(n.) Take out the *wedge* from the log.

Wednesday *(n.)* വെൻസ്ഡേ–ബുധനാഴ്ച

Wednesday is the day between Tuesday and Thursday.

Weed വീഡ്–കള

(n.) A *weed* is a wild plant.

(v.) The gardener is *weeding* the field.

Week *(n.)* വീക്–1. ആഴ്ച, വാരം

There are seven days in a *week* and fifty-two *weeks* in a year.

2. പ്രവൃത്തി ദിവസം

Every day of the *week* is *week*-day except Saturday and Sunday.

Weep *(v.)* വീപ്–കേഴുക, കരയുക

She *wept* bitterly when her father died.

Weigh *(v.)* വേ–തൂക്കമെളക്കുക

How much do you *weigh*?

(n.) Do you know your exact *weight*?

Weird *(adj.)* വിയഡ്–വിചിത്രം, അലൗകികം, അസാമാന്യം

In childhood, I used to hear *weird* sounds from the pond.

Welcome *(n. & v.)* വെൽകം–സ്വാഗതം, വരവേല്ക്കുക

(n.) They gave us a warm *welcome.*

(v.) Aunt *welcomed* us warmly.

Welcome everybody.

Weld *(v.)* വെൽഡ്–ലോഹം കൂട്ടിച്ചേർക്കുക, വെൽഡ് ചെയ്യുക

A welder *welds* pieces of metal by heat and pressure.

Standing by each other in the times of need has *welded* our friendship.

Welfare *(n.)* വെൽഫെയ്ർ–ക്ഷേമം, സുസ്ഥിതി

Mother looks after the *welfare* of the family.

Well *(n.)* വെൽ–1. കിണർ

The *well* is full of water.

(adj.) 2. നല്ല, സുഖമുള്ള

I am not *well.*

(adv.) 3. നല്ല രീതിയിൽ, ഗംഭീരമായി

He is doing very *well* in business.

I know him very *well.*

4. സബാഷ്

Well done!

(adj.) 5. സന്തോഷ ജനകം

All is *well* that ends *well.*

6. ഭാഗ്യമായി, നന്നായി

It was *well* for us that we were not inside the auditorium when a fire broke out there.

(adv.) 7. പ്രശസ്തർ

Indian cine artistes are quite *well* known in Russia.

West *(n.)* വെസ്റ്റ്–പടിഞ്ഞാറ്, പശ്ചിമ

Can the east and the *west* meet?

(adv.) The *west* wind always brings us rain.

Do you like to visit the *western* part of the country?

(adj.) This building faces *west.*

Wet വെറ്റ്–1. നനഞ്ഞ, ഈറനായ

(adj.) It is raining. It is a *wet* day.

(v.) 2. നനയ്ക്കുക

Please *wet* the towel and wash the table-glass.

Whale *(n.)* വെയ്ൽ–തിമിംഗലം

Whale is the biggest creature in the sea.

Wharf *(n. & v.)* വാർഫ്–തുറമുഖം, ജട്ടി, നങ്കുരമടിക്കുക

A ship was unloaded at the *wharf.*

The captain ordered his men to *wharf* the ship.

What *(pron.)* വാട്ട്–1. എത്ര, എന്ത്

What is the time by your watch?

What is the use of a saw?

What will be your excuse for reaching home late?

2. ബാക്കി ഉായിരുന്ന

I have finished replies to *what* letters were left.

3. വിസ്മയദ്യോതകം

What nonsense!

Wheat *(n.)* വീറ്റ്–ഗോതമ്പ്

Wheat is the major harvest of northern India.

Wheel വീൽ–ചക്രം, വീൽ, കറക്കുക, കറങ്ങുക

(n.) A car has four *wheels.* My uncle has a two-*wheeler.* A rickshaw has three *wheels.*

Wheeze *(v.)* വീസ്–കഷ്ടപ്പെട്ട് ശ്വാസ മെടുക്കുക, വലിവ് ഉാവുക

She started *wheezing* while climbing the stairs.

When വെൻ–1. എപ്പോൾ?

When did the train leave?

When are you going to Mumbai?

2. എന്ന്, അന്ന്, അപ്പോൾ, ഇപ്പോൾ

How can I tell *when* he will be able to come?

You will see me next Sunday *when* I shall attend a meeting of the welfare association.

Speak *whenever* you like.

Where *(adv.)* വെയർ–1. എവിടെ, അവിടെ

Where does the king live? The king lives in a palace. That is *where* he lives.

Masoodpur is the village *where* I live.

My friends follow me *wherever* I go.

Whereabouts *(n.)* വെയർഎബൗട്ട്സ്–ഉള്ള സ്ഥലം, വിവരം

Can you give me an idea about his *whereabouts*?

Whet *(v.)* വെറ്റ്–മെച്ചമാക്കുക, പരിഷ് കരിക്കുക

Whet the language of this article and make it more readable.

Whether *(conj.)* വെദർ–1. വേണോ വേയോ, ഏതാണ്

I have not yet decided *whether* to go out or to stay in.

2. ഉോ ഇല്ലയോ

The child asked the mother *whether* there was any more milk left.

Which വിച്–1. ഏത്, അത്, ആര്, ആരോ

(adj.) Try to find out *which* man stole my sewing machine.

Mother asked Harish *which* pen he had selected.

The book *which* I bought is on the shelf.

This is the bookshop *which* also sells magazines.

(pron.) 2. ഏതെങ്കിലും ഇതിലേത്

Which of these lanes shall we prefer?

I'll solve *whichever* question you say.

Whiff *(n.)* വിഫ്–ഗന്ധം, നേർത്ത നാറ്റം

Did you not notice a *whiff* of cigar smoke as you entered the room?

While *(n.)* വൈൽ–1. സമയം, നിമിഷം

Father will worry if you do not get home in a short *while.*

I shall telephone you in a little *while.*

(conj.) 2. ആ സമയത്ത്, അതിനിടെ

Amit brought the milk, *while* Minakshi prepared the breakfast.

Whim *(n.)* വിം–ഭ്രമം, ചാപല്യം

He lives in a world of his own *whims* and fancies.

Whimper *(v.)* വിംപർ–ചിണുങ്ങി കരയുക

The baby *whimpered* for milk.

Whine *(n.)* വൈൻ–കേഴുക, വിലപിക്കുക

Never whine about your worries, but try to be more careful.

Whip വിപ്–ചാട്ടവാറ് കൊടിക്കുക, ചമ്മട്ടി (പ്രയോഗിക്കുക)

(v.) The cartman is in a hurry and *whips* his bull.

(n.) The tongawala has a long *whip.*

Whirl *(v.)* വേർൾ–1. ശക്തിയായി ചുഴറ്റുക, കറക്കുക

The strong wind *whirled* the dead leaves round and round in the garden.

(n.) 2. പരിഭ്രാന്തി, കറക്കം

Your mind is now in a *whirl.* Please think about your problem coolly later on.

Whisk വിസ്ക്–ആട്ടിയകറ്റുക, വീശുക

(v.) The cow *whisks* flies with its long tail.

(n.) While the husband ate, the wife kept the flies away with *whisk.*

Whisker *(n.)* വിസ്കർ–താടിരോമം, പൂച്ച മീശ

Cat's *whiskers* were long and white in colour.

Whisky *(n.)* വിസ്കി, മദ്യം

Whisky is an alcoholic drink made from grains.

Whisper വിസ്പർ–അടക്കം പറയുക, മന്ത്രിക്കുക, കാതിലോതുക

(v.) Whisper to mother so that no one else can hear.

(n.) In the presence of teacher, students spoke in *whispers.*

Whistle *(adj.)* വിസ്ൽ–ശീട്ടി (അടിക്കുക), ചൂളം (അടിക്കുക)

(n.) The guard blows a *whistle.*

(v.) The policeman *whistled.*

White *(adj.)* വൈറ്റ്–വെള്ളനിറം, വെളുത്ത, നരച്ച

The old lady's hair was completely *white.*

My house is being *white*-washed.

(v.) The new toothpowder has *whitened* my teeth.

Whither *(adv.)* വിദർ–എവിടെയെങ്കിലും

We may go *whither* we wish.

Who *(pron.)* ഹു–1. ആ

Minakshi is the girl *who* sang the song.

The policeman enquired about the person *whose* purse was stolen.

2. ആര്

Who informed Nisha we were there?

Who was the lady wearing the blue saree?

Whole *(adj. & n.)* ഹോൾ–അപ്പാടെ, മുഴുവൻ, മൊത്തം, പൂർണ്ണമായി

(adj.) The *whole* city was filled with rats.

I have spent the *whole* night coughing.

I will spend the *whole* rainy season in Mumbai.

(n.) We must sell our plot as a *whole.*

Had your father not kept the *whole* of his money in the bank?

(adj.) We must not *wholly* believe what others say.

(adj.) We are selling these shoes at *wholesale* prices.

Why *(adv.)* വൈ–1. എന്തിന്, എന്തുകൊ്

Why do you think that I have no money?

Why have you come to meet me?

2. അത് കാരണം, അതിനായി

This is *why* I informed you about the matter very early.

Wick *(n.)* വിക്–തിരി

Before lighting the kerosene lamp, you must see that the *wick* is clean.

Wicked *(adj.)* വികിഡ്–ദുഷ്ട, പാപി, ചീത്ത, ദുസ്വഭാവി

Man is not born *wicked,* he becomes so, as he becomes sick.

(n.) To see and listen to the *wicked* is the beginning of *wickedness.*

Wicker വികർ–പെരമ്പ്, വള്ളിമെടഞ്ഞ കൂട

Warn the child not to sit on a *wicker.*

Do you not want to buy a *wicker* basket?

Wicket വിക്കിറ്റ്–വിക്കറ്റ്, ചെറുവാതിൽ, ചീർപ്പ്

A *wicket* is one of the two sets of three sticks which are used in cricket.

(*adj.*) As the main gate was closed, we entered the building through the *wicket* door.

Wide (*adj.*) വൈഡ്–വീതിയുള്ള, വിശാല
The door of the cow shed is *wide* open.
(*n.*) The *width* of the door is five feet.
For years, I have wandered far and *wide* in the deserts of life.

Widow (*n.*) വിഡോ–വിധവ
A rich *widow's* tears dry soon.
Being the *widow* of a traitor is dreadful.

Widower (*n.*) വിഡോവർ–വിഭാര്യൻ
A *widower* cannot forget his first wife even when he gets married again.
വീൽഡ്–കയ്യാളുക, നിർവഹിക്കുക, നിയന്ത്രിക്കുക
The manager *wielded* his power very carefully.

Wife (*n.*) വൈഫ്–പത്നി, ഭാര്യ
Ascend a step to choose a friend, descend a step to choose a *wife*.

Wig (*n.*) വിഗ്–മുടിയുടെ ടോപ് (അസ്സൽ അല്ലെങ്കിൽ കൃത്രിമ മുടികൊണ്ട് ഉണ്ടാക്കിയത്)
In olden days, people used to wear *wigs* on their heads.

Wiggle (*n.*) വിഗ്ൾ–വേഗത്തിലാടുക, ചലിപ്പിക്കുക
The dog *wiggled* its tail on seeing its master.

Wild (*adj.*) വൈൽഡ്–1. ഹിംസ്ര, വന്യ, കാട്ടു
Lions are *wild* animals.
2. കാറും കോളും നിറഞ്ഞ, ഭയാനക
It was a *wild* night, with wind and heavy rain.
3. മതിമറക്കുക, അത്യന്തം ആഹ്ലാദിക്കുക
I was *wild* with joy when I won the first-prize.
(*n.*) 4. വനം, വിജന സ്ഥലം
I saw a hunter hunting in the *wild*.

Will, Would (*v.*) വിൽ–1. ഭാവി സൂചകം
വുഡ്–വിൽ–ന്റെ ഭൂതകാല രൂപം
You *will* send me a letter, won't you?
She *will* not attend the marriage, *will* she?
I shall ask you the question you *would* not want to answer.
My friend told me that he *would* not reach in time.
(*n.*) 2. ഇച്ഛാശക്തി, അഭിപ്രായം
You have no *will* of your own.
Great men have the *will* to succeed.
3. നിശ്ചയ ദാർഢ്യം സൂചിപ്പിക്കുന്ന പ്രയോഗം
Don't worry, I *will* reach there whatever happens.
(*v.*) 4. വിൽപത്രം
Shanker had *willed* all his property to his only daughter.
(*n.*) Character is a perfectly educated *will*.

Willow (*n.*) വിലോ–ക്രിക്കറ്റ് ബാറ്റുണ്ടാക്കാൻ ഉപയോഗിക്കുന്ന തടിയുള്ള വൃക്ഷം
Willow is mostly used for making cricket bats.

Wilt (*v.*) വിൽറ്റ്–വാടികരിയുക, ഉണങ്ങുക
The scorching sun made the flowers in our garden *wilt*.

Wily (*adj.*) കൗശലമുള്ള, ധൂർത്ത
Beware of her, she is cunning and *wily*.
He is a *wily* fellow, never trust him.
വിൻ–വിജയം (നേടുക), ജയം, ജയിക്കുക
(*v.*) Who will *win* the race?
(*n.*) Our team has had three *wins* and two losses in this year's cricket tournaments.

Wince (*v.*) വിൻസ്–വേദനകൊണ്ട് പുളയുക
I *winced* in pain when he held my hand tightly.

Wind (*v.*) വിൻഡ്–1. വളഞ്ഞു പുളഞ്ഞു പോകുക
The streams *wind* their way through the wood.
I saw a *winding* track. It *wound* through the wood.
2. ചുറ്റുക
Wind the wire round this stick.

Wind (*n.*) വിൻഡ്–കാറ്റ്
There was a strong *wind* yesterday and the leaves were blown off the trees.
(*adj.*) It was a *windy* night. We could not sleep well.

Window *(n.)* വിൻഡോ-ജനാല

The *windows* were open when it rained. The *window*-panes were smashed by the storm.

Wine *(n.)* വൈൻ-വീഞ്ഞ്, മുന്തിരിമദ്യം

French *wines* are supposed to be very good.

Wing *(n.)* വിംഗ്-1. ചിറക്

A bird has two *wings.* It flies with its *wings.*

An aeroplane has *wings.*

2. വിഭാഗം

Students from the primary *wing* will be taken for a picnic.

(v.) 3. പറക്കുക

The summer was over and the swallows were *winging* their ways away.

Wink വിങ്ക്-കണ്ണുചിമ്മുക, കണ്ണടിക്കുക, വളരെ കുറച്ച് സമയം

(v.) There is a time to *wink* as well as to see.

(n.) You have not slept a *wink* all day.

Winter *(n.)* വിന്റർ-ശീതകാലം, തണുപ്പുകാലം

Winter is a cold season. It is the coldest season in the western countries.

Wipe *(v.)* വൈപ്-തുടയ്ക്കുക

Wipe the crockery with the tea cloth.

The table is wet, please *wipe* its top.

Wire *(n. & v.)* വൈർ-കമ്പി, കമ്പി അടിക്കുക

Please don't forget to send me a *wire.*

Wire me to inform about the time of your arrival.

Wise *(adj.)* വൈസ് - ബുദ്ധിമാൻ, വിവേകമതി

We must listen to her advice, for she is a *wise* lady.

It was *wise* of the mother to keep her child indoors while he had a cold.

Wish *(adj.)* വിഷ്-ഇച്ഛ, ആഗ്രഹിക്കുക, മോഹിക്കുക

(v.) I *wish* I were a king!

(n.) If a man could have half his *wishes,* he would double his troubles.

If *wishes* were horses, beggars might ride.

Wistful *(adj.)* വിസ്റ്റ്ഫുൾ-നിരാശയോടെ

The writer gave a *wistful* sigh on getting the rejection letter.

Wit *(n.)* വിറ്റ്-സരസനായ, ബുദ്ധി

Wit without employment is a disease.

(adj.) My uncle is a very *witty* person.

Witch *(n.)* വിച് - മായാജാലക്കാരി, അഭിചാരകാരിണി

In fairy tales, *witches* have very important roles.

With *(prep.)* വിത്-കൂടെ, അടുത്ത്, ഒപ്പം, സഹിതം

Bring your brother *with* you.

With the arrival of the President, the Republic Day function started.

We saw a policeman *with* a rod in his hand.

Never find faults *with* others.

Withdraw *(v.)* പിൻവലിക്കുക, പൈസ ബാങ്കിൽ നിന്നെടുക്കുക

Withdraw a sum of Rs 5000 from the bank next week.

Wither *(v.)* വിദർ-ഇല കൊഴിയുക

The leaves *withered* away in autumn.

Within വിതിൻ-1. കാലാവധിക്കുള്ളിൽ

He was back *within* an hour.

2. *(adv.)* വ്യക്തി അല്ലെങ്കിൽ വസ്തുവിന്റെ ഉള്ളിൽ നിന്ന്

All the blessings were coming from deep *within* her.

Without *(n.)* വിതൗട്ട്-കൂടാതെ, ഇല്ലാതെ

Had you not gone out *without* your shoes?

Witness വിറ്റ്നസ്-സാക്ഷി, മൊഴി നൽകുക, ദൃക്സാക്ഷി

(n.) She is the only *witness* who has seen the accident.

(v.) I have really *witnessed* many odd things in my life.

Wizard *(n.)* വിസാർഡ്-മായാവി, മാന്ത്രികൻ, പ്രതിഭാശാലി, വിദഗ്ദ്ധൻ

Do you still believe in witches and wizards?

I have a great regard for Kalidasa, he was a *wizard* indeed.

Woe *(n.)* വോ-കദന, ശോക, വിഷാദ
The villagers told many tales of *woe* that befell them when the river flooded their houses.

Wolf വുൾഫ്-ചെന്നായ്, കൊതിയോടെ ഭക്ഷിക്കുക
(n.) One day, a *wolf* attacked me in the wood.
Ravi behaves like a friend but he is really a *wolf* in sheep's clothing.
(v.) The hungry beggar greedily *wolfed* down the food.

Woman *(n.)* വുമൺ-സ്ത്രീ, മഹിള, നാരി
Baby is little girl. When she grows up she, will be a *woman.*

Wonder വർ - അത്ഭുതപ്പെടുക, അമ്പരക്കുക, വിസ്മയം
(v.) I *wonder* where Sarla has gone.
How I *wonder* what you are!
(n.) As knowledge increases, *wonder* deepens.

Wood *(n.)* വുഡ്-1. കാട്, വനം
There are many trees in the *wood.*
2. തടി, വിറക്
We get *wood* from trees. This table is made of *wood.*
(adj.) *Wooden* furniture is long lasting.

Wool *(n.)* വൂൾ-കമ്പിളി
My mother bought some *wool* to knit a sweater for me.
Bring a ball of *wool* from the almirah.
(adj.) Have you got a *woollen* jersey?

Word *(n.)* വേർഡ്-1. വാഗ്ദാനം, വാക്ക് നൽകുക, ആശ്വാസ വചനം
Give me your *word* that you will pay me a visit next Sunday.
2. സന്ദേശം, വിവരമറിയിക്കുക
Send me a *word* when you hear from Rachna.
3. വാക്ക്, പദം
He who does not know the force of *words* can't know a man.
This is the *word for word* message he gave me.
(v.) 4. വാക്കുകളാക്കുക
How shall I *word* this story?

Work വർക്-ജോലി (ചെയ്യുക)
(v.) Everybody is *working.* Daddy *works* in the office. Mother *works* in the kitchen. Brother *works* in the garden.
(n.) I have some urgent *work* to do in the office.
An ounce of *work* is worth many pounds of words.
Work is worship.

World *(n.)* വേൾഡ്-ലോകം, വിശ്വം, ജഗത്
The *world* is the place we live in.
The *world* is nothing but an endless seesaw.
The *world* is a net; the more we stir in it, the more we are entangled.

Worm *(n.)* വേം-കീടം, പുഴു, വിര
A *worm* is a small creature that lives in the ground. It creeps like a snake.
Don't be a book-*worm.*

Worry വറി-വിഷമിക്കുക, വിഷമം, ചിന്ത
(v.) Mother *worries* about Raju's cought.
(n.) It is a *worry* for her.
My life is full of *worries.*

Worship വർഷിപ്പ്-പൂജ (ചെയ്യുക), ആരാധിക്കുക
(n.) Do your duty and act according to the rules of reason, this is true *worship.*
(v.) For your happiness *worship* God.

Worth *(ad).& n)*-വർത്-വിലയുള്ള, യോഗ്യം, അർഹം
(adj.) This book is *worth* five hundred rupees.
Your work is *worthy* of reward.
(n.) The *worth* of this gem is unknown.

Wound വൂ-പരിക്ക് (പറ്റുക), മുറിവ് (ഏൽക്കുക)
(v.) Uncle Sharma was *wounded* in the war.
(n.) His *wounds* were not serious.

Wrapper *(n.)* റാപർ-പൊതിയാനുള്ള കടലാസ്
The child ate the candy and threw away the *wrapper.*

Wrap *(n.)* റാപ്-പൊതിയുക, പുതയ്ക്കുക, ധരിക്കുക
(v.) Please *wrap* this book by paper.
(n.) Don't take the book out of its *wrapper.*

Wrath *(n.)* റാത്-ക്രോധം
I could not control my *wrath* at his foolish action.

Wreath *(n.)* റീത്–പുഷ്പചക്രം

The people showed respect to their dead leader with the *wreaths* of flowers.

Wreck റെക്–1. നാശം, തകർച്ച, നാശനഷ്ടം

(n.) Nothing could be saved from the *wreck*.

(n.) 2. തകർന്നു പോകുക, നശിച്ചു പോകുക

The bogey ran off the rail-track and was *wrecked*.

Wrench റെഞ്ച്–ദുഃഖം, മാനസിക പീഡ, അമർത്തുക, മുറുക്കുന്നതിനുള്ള യന്ത്രം

(n.) I felt a *wrench* when my younger brother left home.

Use your *wrench* and tighten the screws of my bike.

(v.) *Wrench* the screw of your pressure cooker with this small instrument.

Wrestle *(v.)* റെസ്ൽ–ഗുസ്തി (പിടിക്കുക), മല്ലയുദ്ധം (ചെയ്യുക)

The physical training instructor taught his pupils how to box and *wrestle*.

(n.) *Wrestling* is very popular in Japan.

Wretch *(adj.)* റെച്–പാവം, കഷ്ടപ്പെടുന്നയാൾ, നീചൻ, ഹീനൻ

Tho poor *wretch* looked so distressed that I felt sorry for him.

The man who stole the money from the poor widow was a wicked *wretch*.

Wriggle *(v.)* റിഗ്ൾ–ഇഴയുക, തെളിയുക

I watched the worn *wriggling* across the path.

Wring *(v.)* റിംഗ്–1. പിഴിയുക, ഞെക്കുക

Wring the wet shirt to get the water out of it.

2. ഭേദ്യം ചെയ്യുക

At last, the policemen *wrung* the truth from the thief.

Wrinkle റിങ്ക്ൾ–ചുളിവ് (വീഴുക)

(n.) The old man was worn and wearied. His face was full of *wrinkles*.

The baby *wrinkled* its face and began to cry.

Wrist *(n.)* റിസ്റ്റ്–കണങ്കൈ, മണിബന്ധം

My *wrist* is itching; please, rub some balm.

Have you got your *wrist*-watch back?

Write *(v.)* റൈറ്റ്–എഴുതുക, എഴുത്തുകുത്ത് (നടത്തുക)

I can read the words you *write*.

I haven't *written* a letter since long.

(n.) കയ്യെഴുത്ത്, എഴുത്തുകാരൻ

Your *writing* is not clear.

R.K. Narayan is a famous *writer*.

Wrong റോംഗ്–തെറ്റ്, അനുചിതം, ചീത്ത

(adj.) It is *wrong* to tell a lie.

What is *wrong* with this radio-set?

It is *wrong* to steal.

(n.) The remedy for *wrongs* is to forget them.

(adv.) My message was *wrongly* interpreted.

X

Xmas *(n.)* ക്രിസ്മസ്–ക്രിസ്തുവിന്റെ ജന്മദിനം, ഡിസംബർ 25

Sometimes we spell Christmas as *Xmas*.

Xmas is an important festival of Christians.

Xerox സിറോക്സ്–പകർപ്പ്

(n.) This is a xerox of the original document.

(v.) Get this document *xeroxed*.

X-ray *(n.)* എക്സ്റേ–എക്സ്റേ

X-ray was a very important discovery in the field of medicine.

{*X* is a letter in English. We don't use if often at the beginning of a word. We use *X* in words like ox, axe, fox, example etc.}

Y

Yacht *(n.)* യാട്ട്-ചെറിയ നൗക, കളിവള്ളം

We cruised around the river in a small *yatch.*

Yam *(n.)* യാം-ചേന, കാച്ചിൽ

Yam is used in spicy preparation of vegetables.

Yam is a favourite vegetable of African people.

Yard *(n.)* യാർഡ്-1. ഗജം

Three feet make one *yard.*

2. മുറ്റം, കളം

There is a fence round the *yard.*

Yardstick *(n.)* യാർഡ് സ്റ്റിക്-മാനദണ്ഡം, അളവ്കോൽ

What would be the *yardstick* to judge the performance by?

Yarn *(n.)* യാൺ-1. നൂൽ

There was a shortage of *yarn,* so the weavers had to face unemployment.

2. കഥ

The old sailor told his children an interesting *yarn.*

Yawn യാൺ-കോട്ടുവാ (ഇടുക)

(v.) She *yawned* and put down the book she was reading.

(n.) "I'm feeling sleepy," she said with a *yawn.*

Year *(n.)* ഇയർ-1. വർഷം, കൊല്ലം

A *year* has twelve months and fifty-two weeks.

2. പ്രായം, വയസ്സ്

You look young for your *years.*

A leap *year* comes once in four *years.*

(adv.) Companies give bonus to their employees from *yearly* profits.

Yearn *(v.)* യേൺ-കൊതിക്കുക, അതിയായി മോഹിക്കുക

Abha is *yearning* for a bicycle.

The mother *yearns* to see her lost son.

Yeast *(n.)* യീസ്റ്റ്-പുളിക്കാനുള്ള പൊടി, യീസ്റ്റ്

Yeast is added to flour and water to make bread.

Yell യെൽ-നിലവിളിക്കുക, അട്ടഹസിക്കുക, മുറവിളി

(n.) The speaker was greeted with *yells* of challenge.

(v.) I saw the dog *yelling* with pain.

Yellow *(adj.)* യെലോ-മഞ്ഞ

A fully ripe banana is *yellow.*

Children mostly like *yellow* colour.

Yes *(inter.)* യെസ്-അതെ, തീർച്ചയായും, ശരിക്കും

If you can do something, you must say — *Yes,* I can.

I want a straignt *yes* or no from you.

Yesterday *(n. & adv.)* യെസ്റ്റർഡേ-ഇന്നലെ

Yesterday is the day before today.

Have you got *yesterday's* newspaper?

Yet യെറ്റ്-1. ഇതേ വരെ

(adv.) Has the manager not come *yet*? Sorry, he is not here *yet.*

(conj.) 2. എന്നിട്ടും

The work is very hard, *yet* it is worth trying.

She wasn't well, *yet* she managed to appear for the examination.

Yield *(v.)* യീൽഡ്-1. ഉല്പാദിപ്പിക്കുക, വിളവ് എടുക്കുക

Your efforts will definitely *yield* success.

2. പരാജയം സമ്മതിക്കുക, മുട്ടുകുത്തുക

Though the warrior was defeated, he refused to *yield* the post.

(n.) 3. വിള

We have an excellent *yield* of mangoes this year.

Yoke *(n.)* യോക്-നുകം, പരാധീനത, നുകത്തിൽ കെട്ടുക

They worked under the *yoke* of a cruel master.

(v.) Yoke your bulls to the carts.

Yolk *(n.)* യോക്-മഞ്ഞക്കരു

The *yolk* of an egg is a very useful part of it.

You *(pron.)* യൂ-നിങ്ങൾ

You should go home now.

(poss. pron.) Is this bag *yours*?

(poss. adj.) Is this *your* book?

Young *(adj.)* യങ്-1. ചെറിയ, ഇളയ, പ്രായം കുറഞ്ഞ

A *young* child is called a baby. A *young* tiger is called a cub. A *young* sheep is called a lamb. A *young* goat is called a kid.

(n.) 2. കുട്ടികൾ, യുവജനങ്ങൾ, യുവാവ്, യുവതി

The old know what they want, the *young* are bewildered.

Youngster *(n.)* യങ്സ്റ്റർ-കൗമാരപ്രായക്കാർ

This movie will appeal more to the *youngsters.*

Youth *(n.)* യൂത്ത്-യുവത്വം, കൗമാര ദശ

In *youth,* they suffer less from their own mistakes than from older people's wisdom.

In *youth,* we run into difficulties; in old age, difficulties run into us.

Yummy *(adj.)* യമി-ആസ്വാദ്യം

The food at the party was *yummy.*

Z

Zeal *(n.)* സീൽ-ഉത്സാഹം, ആവേശം

He has a great *zeal* for work.

Zeal without knowledge is like an expendition in the dark.

Zebra *(n.)* സീബ്ര-വരയൻ കുതിര, ആഫ്രിക്കൻ മൃഗം

A *zebra* has white and black stripes on its body.

സീബ്രാക്രോസിംഗ്-കാൽനടക്കാർക്ക് റോഡ് മുറിച്ച് കടക്കാൻ കറുപ്പും വെള്ളയും വരയിട്ട ഭാഗം

Vehicles must stop at the *zebra crossing* to allow the pedestrians to cross the road safely.

Zest *(n.)* സെസ്റ്റ്-അഭിരുചി, ഉത്സാഹശീലം

He has a *zest* for knowledge.

Zero *(n.)* സീറോ-പൂജ്യം

In winter, in most western countries, the temperature falls below *zero* and the ponds freeze.

He got *zero* marks in Mathematics.

Zigzag സിഗ്സാഗ്-വളഞ്ഞുപുളഞ്ഞ് (മുമ്പോട്ട് നീങ്ങുക)

(adj.) Draw a *zigzag* line to represent rivers.

(v.) The boat had to *zigzag* to avoid being struck by big rocks.

Zinc *(n.)* സിങ്ക്-നാകം

Zinc is a hard white metal.

Zip സിപ്-സിപ്

(n.) Undo the *zip* of the bag.

(v.) Zip the bag properly.

Zodiac *(n.)* സോഡിയാക്-രാശി ചിഹ്നം

My *zodiac* sign is Cancer.

Zone *(n.)* സോൺ-മേഖല, മണ്ഡലം

During the floods, people were evacuated from the danger *zone.*

Zoo *(n.)* സൂ-മൃഗശാല, കാഴ്ചബംഗ്ലാവ്

Many wild animals and birds are kept in the *zoo.*

What did you like best at the Delhi *zoo*?

Zoom *(v.)* സൂം-1. കുതിച്ച് പായുക അടുത്തുള്ള ചിത്രം കാണിക്കുക

The aeroplane *zoomed* into the air.

2. അടുത്തുള്ള ചിത്രം കാണിക്കുക

Zoom in the picture; I can't see it.